Handbook Utility Management

Andreas Bausch • Burkhard Schwenker

Editors

Handbook Utility Management

 Springer

Prof. Dr. Andreas Bausch
Professor of Business Administration
and International Management
School of Economics and
Business Administration
Friedrich Schiller University Jena
Carl-Zeiss-Straße 3
07743 Jena
Germany

and

Adjunct Professor of Strategic
Management and Controlling
Academic Director Executive MBA
in European Utility Management
School of Humanities and Social Sciences
Jacobs University Bremen
Campus Ring 1
28759 Bremen
Germany
andreas.bausch@wiwi.uni-jena.de
a.bausch@jacobs-university.de

Prof. Dr. Burkhard Schwenker
Chief Executive Officer
Roland Berger Strategy Consultants
Am Sandtorkai 41
20457 Hamburg
Germany
burkhard_schwenker@de.rolandberger.com

ISBN 978-3-540-79348-9   e-ISBN 978-3-540-79349-6
DOI 10.1007/978-3-540-79349-6
Springer Dordrecht Heidelberg London New York

Library of Congress Control Number: 2009929713

Cover design: WMXDesign GmbH, Heidelberg, Germany

Printed on acid-free paper

Springer is part of Springer Science+Business Media (www.springer.com)

Preface

Traditionally, the supply of electricity and gas has been in the hands of vertically integrated monopolistic businesses, either state owned or under mixed private and state ownership. This began to change in the early 1980s, first in America and later in Europe. With the deregulation and liberalization of the European electricity and gas market this vertically integrated value chain broke down and separate market segments began to form, moving in the direction of greater competition.

During the 1990s, many European countries began to restructure their electric power sectors with the aim of introducing competition, achieving greater performance, and thus providing long-term benefits to consumers. The restructuring process was finally triggered by the European Commission's 1996 directive 'Concerning Common Rules for the Internal Market in Electricity', the intention of which was the creation of a common European electricty market. In June 1998, the first natural gas directive was passed by the European Parliament and the Council. It created the foundation for a harmonized European gas market by defining 'Common Rules for the Internal Market for Natural Gas'. In order to push the member states into faster implementation of EU guidelines, the so-called 'Directives of Acceleration' came into force in August 2003.

Ever since, the directions have been implemented in rather varied ways in the EU's different member states. From a utility company's perspective, the deregulation progressing towards an integrated market environment has resulted in new challenges and a substantial need for strategic reorientation. Practically the entire set of strategic variables now needs to be reconsidered, from product portfolio and value chain specialization through anorganic growth and internationalization to organizational design and controlling systems, to name but a few.

In the context of these developments, we have aimed at compiling a Handbook of Utility Management in which many of the tremendous challenges energy supply companies face today are addressed, so as to provide readers with a broader picture of the state of the art in this exciting field. In recent years many books have been published on deregulation of the electricty and gas industry, but in most of them the emphasis has been on policy, technological and economic issues. In contrast, the focus of the Handbook is on managerial issues. After a number of basic introductory chapters on such general management topics as innovation, value-based management, entrepreneurial orientation, and corporate growth (Part I), fundamentals of utility management associated with changing market structures and industry dynamics are elaborated (Part II). The further chapters are organized along the different value chain activities and markets of the industry: power generation (Part III), energy trading and wholesale (Part IV), transmission and distribution (Part V), and retail (Part VI). Region-specific features of the utility markets (Part VII) and special issues such as cooperations among utilities, climate protection and energy efficiency (Part VIII) bring the Handbook to a close.

Looking back, we can truthfully say that we have spared no effort in assembling a multi-author work that reflects the current character of the field of 'Utility Management' in terms of both scientific inquiry and practical application. Needless to say, whether and to what extent we have reached our goal can only be judged by you, our colleagues, clients, and students. We sincerely invite your input. Please feel free to e-mail us and let us know what you like about the book and what features need improvement.

Our sincere appreciation goes to the authors of the chapters included in this Handbook for their valuable contributions. Although time pressure and busy schedules are typical for today's work environments, you have sacrificed your time for this cooperative endeavor. We owe very special thanks to Michael Hunoldt and Dr. Thomas Fritz, whose editorial contributions have been most helpful and who have provided us with practical adminstrative assistance. We also thank Prof. Dr. Wolfgang Pfaffenberger and Veit Schwinkendorf for their intellectual support. We would also like to thank Torsten Oltmanns, who assisted us in launching the book project. Finally, we are also indebted to Dr. Werner A. Mueller of Springer for his continuous encouragement.

Andreas Bausch

Burkhard Schwenker

Jena, Bremen, and Hamburg, June 2009

Overview

Part I: Introduction to Management

Part II: Fundamentals in Utility Management

Part III: Power Generation

Part IV: Energy Trading and Wholesale

Part V: Transmission and Distribution

Part VI: Retail

Part VII: Regional Peculiarities in the Utility Markets

Part VIII: Special Issues in Utility Management

Contents

Part IV: Energy Trading and Wholesale

List of Contributors

Luis Atienza Serna
> Executive President and Chief Executive Officer of Red Eléctrica de España, Spain

Dr. Hans Auer
> Senior Research Assistant at Energy Economics Group at the Vienna University of Technology, Austria

Prof. Dr. Andreas Bausch
> Professor of International Management at the Friedrich Schiller University of Jena, and Adjunct Professor of Strategic Management and Controlling and Academic Director of the Executive MBA in European Utility Management at Jacobs University Bremen, Germany

Dr. Janice A. Beecher
> Director of the Institute of Public Utilities at the Michigan State University, United States of America

Dirk Beeuwsaert
> Chief Executive Officer at GDF SUEZ Energy International, Belgium

Dr. Wulf H. Bernotat
> CEO and Chairman of the Board of Management of E.ON AG, Germany

Dr. Michiel Boersma
> Chairman of the Executive Board of Essent N.V., The Netherlands

Dr. Werner Brinker
> Chief Executive Officer and Chief Officer Sales and Marketing of EWE AG, Germany

Prof. Dr. Gert Brunekreeft
> Professor of Energy Economics at Jacobs University Bremen and Director of the Bremer Energie Institut, Germany

Anatoly Chubais
> Chief Executive Officer at RAO UES of Russia, Russia

Denis Depoux
> Senior Partner and Head of Utilities Competence Center of Roland Berger Strategy Consultants, France

Prof. Dr. Rik W. De Doncker
> Professor and Director of the E.ON Energy Research Center at RWTH Aachen University, heading both the Institute for Power Electronics and Electrical Drives (ISEA) and the Institute for Power Generation and Storage (PGS), Faculty of Electrical Engineering and Information Technology at the RWTH Aachen University, Germany

Prof. Dr. Ulrich Ehricke
> Director of the Institute for European Law at the University of Cologne and the Institute for Energy Law at the University of Cologne, and Judge at the Court of Appeals (OLG) Düsseldorf, Germany

Prof. Dr. Wolf Fichtner
> Professor of Energy Economics at Universität Karlsruhe (TH), Germany

Dr. Wolfgang Fink
> Managing Director German Advisory of Goldman Sachs, Germany

Prof. Dr. Michael Frese
> Professor of Work and Organizational Psychology at the Justus Liebig University Giessen, Germany, and the London Business School, United Kingdom

Gonzalo Garcia
> Managing Director European Utilities and Infrastructure of Goldman Sachs, United Kingdom

Clark W. Gellings
> Vice President of Technology at the Electric Power Research Institute in Palo Alto, United States of America

Prof. Dr. Reinhard Haas
> Associate Professor at the Energy Economics Group at Vienna University of Technology, Austria

Daniel Hackländer
> Associate at the Institute for Energy Law at the University of Cologne, Germany

Dr. Jürgen Hambrecht
> Chairman of the Board of Executive Directors of BASF SE, Germany

Dr. Christoph Helle
    Managing Director of MVV Energie AG, Germany

Christian Hewicker
    Managing Consultant and Head of Markets and Regulation at KEMA
    Consulting GmbH, Germany

Anouk Honoré
    Research Fellow at the Oxford Institute for Energy Studies, United
    Kingdom

Dr. Ronald Huisman
    Associate Professor at the Erasmus School of Economics, Applied
    Economics, Erasmus University Rotterdam, The Netherlands

Michael Hunoldt
    Research Associate of International Management at the Friedrich Schiller
    University of Jena, Germany

Dr. Ulrich Jobs
    Chief Operating Officer of RWE AG, Germany

Prof. Dr. Henning Kagermann
    Co-Chief Executive Officer of SAP AG, Germany

Prof. Dr. Claudia Kemfert
    Director of the Energy, Transportation, and Environment Department at the
    German Institute of Economic Research, and Professor of Environmental
    and Energy Economics at the Humboldt University Berlin, Germany

Dr. Stefanie Kesting
    Senior Consultant at KEMA Consulting GmbH, Germany

Prof. Dr. Rolf W. Künneke
    Associate Professor at the Faculty of Technology, Policy, and
    Management, Section Economics of Infrastructures, Delft University of
    Technology, The Netherlands

Matthias Kurth
    President of the Federal Network Agency for Electricity, Gas,
    Telecommunications, Post and Railway, Germany

Prof. Dr. Reinhard Madlener
> Professor of Energy Economics and Management and Director of the
> Institute for Future Energy Consumer Needs and Behavior (FCN), Faculty
> of Business Administration and Economics / E.ON Energy Research
> Center at the RWTH Aachen University, Germany

Dr. Werner Marnette
> Former Minister for Economic Affairs in Schleswig-Holstein, and former
> Chief Executive Officer of Norddeutsche Affinerie AG, Germany

Lars Matysiak
> Research Associate of International Management at the Friedrich Schiller
> University of Jena, Germany

Prof. Dr. Kenneth B. Medlock III
> Fellow in Energy Studies at the James A. Baker III Institute for Public
> Policy, and Adjunct Professor at the Department of Economics at the Rice
> University, United States of America

Rafael Miranda Robredo
> Chief Executive Officer of ENDESA, Spain

Dr. Michal C. Moore
> Senior Fellow at the Institute for Sustainable Energy, Environment and
> Economy at the University of Calgary in Alberta, Canada, and former
> Regulatory Commissioner for the State of California, United States of
> America

Prof. Dr. Günter Müller-Stewens
> Professor of Management and Organization at the University of St. Gallen,
> Switzerland

Prof. Dr. Wolfgang Pfaffenberger
> Professor of Economics at the Jacobs University Bremen, Germany

Anke Radloff
> Gas Market Analyst within Strategic Planning at the Wintershall Holding
> AG, Germany

Dr. Andreas Radmacher
> Member of the Executive Board of RWE Energy AG, Portfolio
> Management & Sales Management, Germany

Prof. Dr. Andreas Rauch
> Professor of Entrepreneurship and New Business Venturing at Rotterdam School of Management, Erasmus University, The Netherlands

Christian Redl
> Research Assistant at the Energy Economics Group at the Vienna University of Technology, Austria

Dr. Christoph Riechmann
> Director in the Energy Practice at Frontier Economics Ltd., Germany

Dan Roberts
> Associate Director at Frontier Economics Ltd., United Kingdom

Hilde A. K. Rosenblad
> Senior Adviser at Nord Pool Spot AS, Norway

Dr. Peter Rosin
> Partner, Head of the German Energy Group and Co-head of the Global Energy & Utilities Industry Group at Clifford Chance, Germany

Dr. Oliver Runte
> Executive Director of citiworks AG, Germany

Markus Schimmer
> Research Associate of Management and Organization at the University of St. Gallen, Switzerland

Prof. Dr. Burkhard Schwenker
> Chief Executive Officer of Roland Berger Strategy Consultants, Germany

Veit Schwinkendorf
> Partner and Head of the Energy & Chemicals Competence Center of Roland Berger Strategy Consultants, Germany

Dr. Fereidoon P. Sioshansi
> President of Menlo Energy Economics, United States of America

Prof. Dr. Yong-Hua Song
> Professor of Electrical Engineering at the University of Liverpool, United Kingdom

Francesco Starace
> Head and Managing Director of the Renewable Energies Division of Enel S.p.A., Italy

Prof. Dr. Jonathan Stern
> Director of Natural Gas Research at the Oxford Institute for Energy Studies, United Kingdom

Jing Sun
> Lecturer at the Beihang University, China

Prof. Dr. Fritz Vahrenholt
> Chief Executive Officer of RWE Innogy GmbH, Germany

Maaike Vos – van Gool
> Marketing Manager at Essent N.V., The Netherlands

Matthias Warnig
> Managing Director of Nord Stream AG, Switzerland

Reinier Zwitserloot
> Chairman of the Board of Executive Directors of the Wintershall Holding AG, Germany

Part I:
Introduction to Management

1 Managing in an International Environment

Henning Kagermann[1]

Abstract

As companies face increasing competition and margin pressures in home regions, strategies for globalization have become attractive vehicles for continuing top-line growth and moving beyond domestic markets. To be competitive in a global economy, companies must attract, develop, and retain the best people to strengthen all areas of the value chain. In addition, companies must adopt new models of collaboration, not only among employees, but also with partner networks, to gain traction in foreign markets. This chapter looks at the challenge and opportunity of globalization and shares business principles, practices, and models observed in organizations that have successfully navigated changing landscapes.

Keywords: globalization, talent development, business network

---

[1] Prof. Dr. Henning Kagermann is Co-Chief Executive Officer of SAP AG, Germany.

A. Bausch and B. Schwenker (eds.), *Handbook Utility Management,*
DOI: 10.1007/978-3-540-79349-6_1, © Springer-Verlag Berlin Heidelberg 2009

1.1   Introduction

As companies face increasing competition and margin pressures at home, strategies for globalization and market diversification have become attractive vehicles for continuing top-line growth and extending brands and offerings beyond domestic markets.

To be competitive and up to date in a global economy, companies must attract, develop, and retain the best people to strengthen all areas of the value chain, from research and development to sales and consulting, and help them to embrace new practices as they increasingly engage across geographic borders. In addition, companies must adopt new models of collaboration, not only among their internal network of employees, but also across business boundaries, in order to successfully gain traction in new and foreign markets.

In the face of global growth opportunities, business leaders may be asking:

- What are the challenges and opportunities of globalization?
- How can an organization build a global talent network to support its efforts?
- How can an organization overcome cultural differences to maximize collaboration and productivity?
- What core principles or practices can be used to encourage a global workforce to act in concert under common objectives?
- What factors contribute to an optimal climate for coordinated research and development?
- How can external areas of the business – such as partner networks – be engaged to support globalization efforts?

In this chapter, we will look at the challenge and opportunity of globalization and share business principles, practices, and models observed in organizations that have successfully navigated changing landscapes. We will also identify core business areas to address, including talent development, research and development, and the creation of partner ecosystems, as fundamental to successful globalization.

In addition, the chapter introduces the principle of business network transformation, which facilitates collaboration and coordination among external networks to heighten innovation, facilitate the development of new markets, and deliver superior aggregate value to customers around the world.

1.2   Building a Global Talent Network

The talents of people in an organization are key to its growth and success. Each employee contributes to the results of the organization, and in this way the strength of the employee base determines the level of results that can be achieved.

Until recently, most companies with a foothold in emerging markets could count on an abundant supply of labor to support growth. Today, however, the pool of skilled workers is limited, and we anticipate that competition for talented employees will intensify.

In the developed world, the skills crisis is exacerbated by declining birth rates and the retirement of the Baby Boomer generation, who are taking with them valuable experience and intellectual capital and leaving knowledge gaps in the global workforce.

Faced with this situation, business leaders in every industry are taking steps to build a global network of talent to maintain operations and win the increasingly difficult recruitment and retention battle ahead.

Some of the strategies business leaders are employing include:

- *Obtaining a concise and accurate picture of the workforce:* Business leaders are capitalizing on technology, such as business analytics, to keep abreast of talented people. The resulting workforce demographic data can help identify trends in headcount development, turnover rates, and workforce composition. For example, business leaders are using analyses of workforce composition to assemble and mobilize new teams in response to emerging opportunities.
- *Institutionalizing knowledge:* To minimize business disruption when replacing workers and re-organizing teams across geographic borders, companies are identifying workers with crucial skills who are moving into new positions or retirement and capturing their knowledge and business contacts, among other assets.
- *Planning for succession:* Business leaders are identifying and preparing top talent and potential successors for key positions to ensure business continuity as leaders and key contributors retire or leave.
- *Actively recruiting top talent at entry level:* To identify and attract talented employees early in their careers, companies are establishing programs to engage high-performing students around the world. For example, the SAP University Alliances program has a network of nearly 900 colleges and universities in 30 countries and currently engages over 150,000 students worldwide, equipping graduates with the information technology (IT) and business process management skills needed to successfully enter and compete in today's job market.
- *Taking advantage of an ecosystem:* As in other business areas, companies are collaborating with their partners to develop joint talent-sourcing efforts. For example, SAP has engaged its ecosystem to attract and train qualified consultants whose skills are in line with market demands. The program includes a combination of co-branded communications and talent demand generation programs.

1.2.1 Globalization of Talent Management and Development

While it is important to have strong pools of talent in global offices, the next step is to give employees new perspectives and practices to work across geographic borders and to embrace and contribute to the process of globalization across the whole company, including all subsidiaries.

In 1999, a small team of SAP employees from Denmark, Germany, The Netherlands, Singapore, Switzerland, and the United States worked together and proposed something that had never happened at SAP: a global leadership development program. Previously, all management and leadership development efforts had happened at the local or regional level.

This team felt that there was a need to launch a global leadership development program for SAP executives to increase global understanding, cultural diversity, teamwork, communication, networking, learning, and synergies among top management. In addition, SAP was looking to strengthen the global talent pool for internal promotions, increase employee satisfaction with the SAP management style and work environment, and promote retention of valuable talent in the management team, among other aims.

The SAP executive board accepted the team's recommendations and agreed to play a key role in the design and delivery of the program. Their first task was to nominate candidates – 32 senior executives who were to report directly to the board. After receiving proposals from a dozen business schools and meeting with people from six of them, SAP chose to work with INSEAD, and the design team charged the SAP executive board to identify four strategic topics that would be assigned to groups of participants. The program had a strong 'action learning' component, in which participants were each assigned to one of four project teams, each of which tackled a strategic topic assigned by the board. Each team had a board member as a sponsor/coach, who guided the team as it addressed 'its' topic.

1.2.2   Global Leadership Development

The first Global Leadership Development Program at SAP was delivered in 2000, and such a program now runs once a year. To date, about 250 of SAP's top executives have taken part in the learning program. The program has helped board members get acquainted with top talent outside their own functional area, and the recommendations from the teams have made substantial contributions to strategic challenges and opportunities for SAP. As intended, the leadership concepts have helped build a common leadership language at the top of the company.

1.2.3   Global Performance Management

Like leadership development, performance management also operated in a decentralized fashion at SAP, with individual countries creating forms and processes to document employee performance and development. When leaders suggested making the execution of employee reviews a global process, managers in several countries rebuffed the idea, saying that they preferred to stay with the processes they had become accustomed to.

However, as managers increasingly had global teams with direct reports based in several countries, they began to express frustration that they had to fill out substantially different performance planning and appraisal forms for different employees and became more receptive to a globally unified and orchestrated process, which was developed and continues to contribute to SAP's successful global management today.

1.2.4   How Can an Organization Overcome Cultural Differences to Maximize Collaboration and Productivity?

As global teams increasingly engage across countries and regions, some will find the process of adjusting to cultural differences more intuitive than others. Most teams, we have found, need to be trained.

One study report (Orleman, 1992) on cross-cultural differences that we have learned from cites many contrasting work styles, cultures, and beliefs that must be understood and overcome for global teams to collaborate productively. For example, the report observes that Americans, who value open communication, work with their office doors open unless they are conducting a private 'closed door' meeting. In France, on the other hand, people knock on a door to announce they are entering and then enter. In the United States, this is often interpreted as 'rude', though in fact it is only a difference of culture and habit.

These types of misinterpretations happen thousands of times a day in global organizations across the corporate landscape, when they could be averted or used as an opportunity for an open-minded examination and greater understanding of other cultures. The impact of judgment of differences in culture and habit includes deterioration in relationships, decreased collaboration, and reduced productivity, among other effects. These costs are too high, given that the adoption of a few simple practices can encourage teams to work in global concert despite differences in work styles, culture, and beliefs.

Some of the guidelines that became instrumental in building a global workforce at SAP include:

(1) During the selection process, identify candidates who have the knowledge, style, skills, sensitivity, and intuitive flexibility to understand a different culture, adjust their behavior, and communicate about their own paradigms and objectives in a way that can be understood.

(2) Next, provide training to the employee. Any employee who will be managed by, manage, or be on a team with people from different cultures should be trained in the implications of working across cultures. Training should clarify the role culture plays in shaping thoughts, perceptions, and behavior and examine cultural stereotypes and the values behind these stereotypes; discuss the impact of culture on business, meetings, information, hierarchy, and leadership; and identify skills and traits required for cross-cultural interaction.

(3) Remind employees to assume difference until similarity is proven among their colleagues. By assuming that a colleague from another culture is different, employees may more naturally inquire into the nature of the colleague's behavior with an open mind, rather than rushing into misinterpretation.

(4) Encourage managers who manage people from other cultures to understand that the individual being managed may operate within a different paradigm. For example, giving constructive or negative feedback, a skill which American managers are taught and expected to apply, is rare in France. A French manager stated that "The French get offended by positive or negative feedback. If you question my job, you are questioning my honor, my value, and my very being".

(5) Remind employees that understanding leads to trust, which is required in any productive relationship or organization. By taking the time to understand one another, employees of global corporations can transcend their differences and work together to accomplish the organization's goals and objectives.

1.2.5 What Core Principles or Practices Can Be Used to Encourage a Global Workforce to Act in Concert Toward Common Objectives?

To be competitive in a global environment, companies must support employees not only in efforts to overcome cultural differences, but also in working closely together toward a common goal, regardless of physical location. Only in concert can companies and their employees assume or retain the position of market leader. In this way, globalization can continue to help, not hinder, a company's growth and business success.

At SAP, we faced this challenge at the end of 2003, a time at which, right after the Internet bubble, we decided we needed to adapt our strategy to achieve double-figure growth rates again. This led us in 2005 to announce quite ambitious goals for 2010, including the goal of doubling our addressable market and tripling our customer base from 32,000 to 100,000. Our strategy was to aggressively target small and medium-sized enterprises, expand to address a new segment of the workforce within medium-sized and large enterprises, and shift to a platform architecture that would enable companies to better align IT with their business requirements.

Our new targets immediately brought to light global implementation challenges and issues of culture and identity within the organization. SAP's success was (and still is) definitely based on its 'German DNA', but it was clear that the same DNA could not simply be expected to build a global culture. The challenge was how to preserve the company's strengths while evolving globally.

This caused us to inquire how we could take advantage of a global footprint without a negative impact on the productivity of an established workforce that might be influenced by the tremors of change in the organization. And also, how we could achieve compatible standards and non-silo attitudes, so that individuals in geographically dispersed units could perform and deliver in global concert.

As a start, we examined our entire value chain, consisting of upstream activities centered on research, design, and development, and downstream activities focused on marketing, sales, localization, and support. By the end of 2005, most downstream functions at SAP were operating in a coordinated but geographically distributed and decentralized manner. Prime among these were sales, marketing, and consulting. Customer support was organized in a regional and linguistically decentralized way, but with one global P&L. This decentralized but coordinated format was working well.

Compared with downstream functions, SAP's upstream functions of research, design, and development were regarded as headquarters functions and thus German-centric. Change was under way, but we needed to accelerate this change, in part because of the opportunities presented in the US market, including its innovation-friendly environment, a workforce of software developers who had strengths in simplifying and improving user interfaces, and a huge number of potential partners who could contribute to the co-innovation of new products.

In addition, India had become an economically attractive center for software development. As a major player in the software industry, SAP could not afford to neglect this opportunity. We faced two options: develop new work in India that was not being done elsewhere or begin to share existing work done elsewhere with developers in India. The latter approach made most sense: it was a less risky option for the company, given that headquarters would have more oversight.

The India ramp-up idea met with mixed reactions from the development teams in Germany. Concerns focused on productivity, quality, and deadline issues, in part due to rumors of high turnover rates in India.

We considered the issues and concluded that not only would development in India not be a threat to our German development teams, but that its capacity could be critical to averting potential staffing bottlenecks in Europe and the United States.

In addition to targeting India, SAP recruited development resources in other foreign markets for localization and special customer development programs. This activity, which later became SAP Labs, was originally organized in a hub-and-spoke model, with Germany in the center and other countries as the outlying 'spokes'. The first foreign spoke was the West Coast Palo Alto unit in the United States in 1996. In 1998, SAP established a SAP Lab in Bangalore, India. That same year, the company inaugurated labs in Canada, France, and Japan, to be followed in 2001 by Israel. Today, SAP's global research and development (R&D)-workforce is distributed across 21 locations around the world.

1.3   What Factors Contribute to an Optimal Climate for Coordinated Research and Development?

By the end of 2005, SAP found that its research and development model was under strain, since it placed an ever-increasing load of management responsibility for project leads on Walldorf as the number of labs and related personnel grew.

Recognizing the problem, we opted to streamline the model and began to transition it from a hub-and-spoke design to a peer-to-peer network that was more conducive to true collaboration and shifted project leadership among the global locations.

SAP then took several steps to make the peer-to-peer network model a success. Among the key steps were:

(1) Identifying the unique strengths each lab could offer in order to realize a model of 'distributed capabilities' within which each lab could be assigned worldwide responsibility and co-located resources for a specific project or aspect of development.
(2) Developing consistent standards and practices in order to synchronize across labs. Since SAP produces 'mission critical' enterprise software, the company needed to ensure the development of robust, high-quality software.
(3) Reinforcing a global innovation culture within SAP and encouraging common IT practices across the labs. In order to do this, SAP's Palo Alto lab hosted an SAP developer's challenge. This week-long get-together assembled 40 employees from labs around the world to exchange information on their local labs, discuss their development practices, and debate ways to improve cross-lab coordination.

1.4   How Can External Areas of the Business – such as Partner Networks – Be Engaged to Support Globalization Efforts?

Building a coordinated, global team of talent is critical to, but not the only factor in, the process of successful globalization. Organizations must also look beyond the four walls of their own business and build partner ecosystems that can offer support and innovation in the area of site selection, assortment optimization, consumer insights, inventory financing, marketing, and competitive expertise, and also help tackle any issues relating to a specific culture or infrastructure, such as language, currency, taxation, and/or regulatory mandates.

1.4.1   The Ecosystem Approach: Managing Business Networks in a Global Economy

Over the past three decades, sector after sector of the global economy has migrated away from the vertically integrated enterprise toward an increasingly disaggregated model of specialized enterprises interoperating to create end-to-end deliverables (see Table 1.1). Recently, SAP conducted research together with Geoffrey Moore to investigate the new driving forces behind today's business networks and the transformation realized by these networks.

In recent years, business networks have come to the fore, enabling companies to deliver faster innovation to customers at lower cost by sharing investments, assets, and ideas. New market opportunities are being unlocked by combining the products and services of the business network participants in creative ways and leveraging each other's market access and infrastructure on a global basis.

Table 1.1: Business network transformation

Issue	'Built to last' global companies	'Built to adapt' business networks
Competitive advantage	Efficiency, stability and reach	Differentiation, adaptability and speed
Mode of operation	Command and control	Connect and collaborate
Source of innovation	Internal R&D	Co-innovation
Focus of attention	Supply	Demand
Organizing paradigm	Value chain	Alliance

At the same time, these business networks require organizations to collaborate across business boundaries and corporate cultures – not just across global offices within the organization – bringing new challenges to the process of 'managing in an international environment'. To navigate this transition effectively and to engage external networks productively, business leaders must be able to employ the right model for their business and the market they intend to penetrate.

1.4.2   Different Models for Different Markets

Business networks arise at two stages in the evolution of a market or a product (see Table 1.2). In the 'emerging stage', 'collaborative business networks' enable companies to explore and develop an emerging opportunity. The collaborative business network is a new breed of business network, one that focuses on value maximization rather than on cost minimization. Such a network is typically highly complex and largely undefined, so that the emphasis for the network partners is on communication, interaction, iteration, fast failure, and faster recovery, all tending toward delivering a complete solution to an end-customer. In these networks, there is typically a ringleader who has a vision for what is possible and domain expertise that rallies the other parties to pursue it. We call such entities the 'orchestrators' because they must lead through influence rather than enforce their will through power.

As the market is established, it progresses from emerging to 'scaling'. In order for any process or offer to scale, it must be transformed from custom creation to repeatable production. Now the network must operate under a new social contract, one which puts a high value on efficiency.

We call these efficiency-focused networks 'coordinated business networks', and they are driven not by personal relationships of trust but rather by transactions specified by contract. As these networks ramp to maturity, their operations become increasingly driven by a 'concentrator', a member of the network who has gained greater bargaining power than the others and who drives the performance of the whole network to its own greater benefit.

As product and service categories pass through their life cycles, the relative role of the business network oscillates between collaboration and coordination, the former focused on enabling new and emerging markets, the latter on scaling mature ones.

Table 1.2: Collaborative and coordinated business networks

Issue	Collaborative business networks	Coordinated business networks
Phase of maturity	Emerging	Scaling and mature
Best fit	Complex systems	Volume operations
Focus	Relationships	Transactions
Performance	Adaptability	Efficiency
Engagement model	Alliance	Contract

Note that the values of coordinated business networks are essentially identical to those of a traditional vertically integrated enterprise operating in a mature market. In today's outsourcing-oriented economy, however, the lowest transaction costs are very often found 'outside' the firm. The goal of participating in a coordinated network is to avail oneself of these economies while meeting or exceeding the reliability of a single end-to-end provider. We are taking a familiar model and simply disaggregating it, letting each company leave behind non-core, or context, tasks to focus on its own core, the goal being for all to generate greater differentiation and therefore higher returns on invested capital.

By contrast, collaborative business networks are driven by a different imperative. They seek to bring about something never before accomplished: either the completion of a program or project that transcends the capabilities of established offerings, or the incubation of a market that requires the involvement of many different participants. In both cases, the goal is to tap into sources of funds that are not available to coordinated networks. The prize is the attainment of gross margins that are much higher, since there are no efficient alternatives in the market. Over time, however, if the need is sufficiently broad and perennial, the transactional model will find its way into the market and the balance of power will shift back to the coordinated network.

1.5   The Business Network Life Cycle

Companies typically follow a specific life cycle when it comes to their use of either the collaborative or the coordinated network model. Some companies may be pulled into the cycle by outside forces; however, those that actively transform their network can gain a strong competitive advantage.

One strategy for proactively transforming the network is for business leaders to map out their network and the players in it, identify their 'stronger hand' – the type of network supporting their core franchise – and strengthen their abilities in the 'opposite' network type. Most organizations will find that new business value almost always comes from mining the capabilities of the network type that is foreign to the core business model.

1.6   How Technology Can Support Business Network Transformation and Globalization

As companies become global and establish multinational operations, Chief Information Officers (CIOs) will be increasingly challenged to support network-based business models that leverage the strengths and abilities of many organizations to deliver the highest value of product or service to customers at the lowest cost for all parties. Complete transparency of all aspects of the product life cycle and the ability to respond to this insight and information will give companies a competitive advantage in the global market.

IT's role in this market shift is to help companies maintain brand integrity through the process of outsourcing and interacting with a large network of partners and suppliers. To do this effectively, companies must build a global supply chain in which partners can work to a defined set of priorities and quality levels. The burden on IT is not only to meet compliance mandates, but also to find partners that can integrate successfully into the network model and operate to meet high standards.

One technology that supports this mandate is known as web services. Web services enable business processes to communicate across companies, ensuring that a command such as 'cancel order' issued by one company's IT systems is correctly understood and executed by the company's suppliers' systems, irrespective of whether the companies use the same underlying software. This means that employment of an integrated platform that supports web services is critical. Seeing this business trend emerging, SAP decided years ago to transform its own solution architecture. The service-oriented architecture (SOA) is a reality in the market today and acts as an enabler for business network transformation.

1.7   The Challenge for Management in the Era of Business Network Transformation

The ability to operate effectively in a global environment requires awareness of business models and practices at many levels, including talent sourcing and development programs, research and development coordination, and the ability to engage effectively with partner networks to facilitate entry into new and attractive markets. The transformation is possible, but requires a shift in thinking from a command-and-control paradigm to a more decentralized and collaborative structure that engages the strengths not only of various offices and regions within a company, but also beyond the walls of the business to partners and even customers, who are increasingly interested in engaging in the process of value creation.

Thus the increasing importance of business networks for growth through faster differentiation and stronger competitive advantage takes the challenge of managing in an international environment to another level. The better the network adapts to new market conditions, the faster a company has to demonstrate its own strategic agility.

What facilitates this agility is having in place underlying IT and communications structures that can allow different software systems to communicate effectively, manage the exchange of information across the network for a coordinated approach to satisfying customer demand, and enable people to make better decisions by virtue of real-time insight based on a single source of truth. In the years ahead, businesses will continue to move to new, network-based models of engagement, since existing models of cost minimization are becoming increasingly irrelevant given widespread commoditization. Managed well, the new types of collaborative networks offer huge potential for value creation, so long as Chief Executive Officers (CEOs) contend successfully with a number of issues and challenges in successfully generating and sustaining that value.

References

Kagermann, H., Lay, P. & Moore, G. 2008. Business network transformation: rethinking relationships in a global economy. San Bruno: TCG Advisors.

Rangan, S. 2006. SAP in 2006: aiming for global concert. Fountainebleau: INSEAD.

Orleman, P. A. 1992. The global corporation: managing across cultures. Unpublished MSc dissertation University of Pennsylvania.

Orleman, P. & Borner, H. 2008. The talent supply chain: leveraging the global talent market. In D. Pantaleo & N. Pal (Eds.), From Strategy to Execution. Turning Accelerated Global Change into Opportunity: 187-214. Berlin/Heidelberg: Springer.

2 Superior Performance Through Value-based Management

Andreas Bausch[1]

Michael Hunoldt[2]

Lars Matysiak[3]

Abstract

Value-based management provides managers with tools and techniques supporting the development and implementation of value-creating strategies. It further offers incentives which encourage managers to realize only those strategies which create value. In this chapter we present a brief overview of four important concepts of value-based management and of their popularity among the DAX-23 companies. Because of its extreme importance we then portray the EVA/MVA concept of Stern/Stewart in more detail. Moreover, we outline selected applications and techniques of value-based management with reference to strategy development, mergers & acquisitions, and performance management. We substantiate our theoretical discussion with an empirical analysis of the value creation of the DAX-23 companies. Lastly, we evaluate German utility companies' EVAs and compare them to EVAs of Austrian and Swiss utilities.

Keywords: value-based management, superior performance, EVA

[1] Prof. Dr. Andreas Bausch is Professor of International Management at the Friedrich Schiller University of Jena, and Adjunct Professor of Strategic Management and Controlling and Academic Director of the Executive MBA in European Utility Management at Jacobs University Bremen, Germany.

[2] Michael Hunoldt is Research Associate in International Management at the Friedrich Schiller University of Jena, Germany.

[3] Lars Matysiak is Research Associate in International Management at the Friedrich Schiller University of Jena, Germany.

A. Bausch and B. Schwenker (eds.), *Handbook Utility Management,*
DOI: 10.1007/978-3-540-79349-6_2, © Springer-Verlag Berlin Heidelberg 2009

2.1   Introduction

Within the last two decades, increasing competition on the global capital markets in general and a growing influence of institutional investors in particular have triggered the growing popularity of value-based management concepts. They have also intensified the pressure on corporations to focus on value orientation. Creating value requires investments on which returns exceed the capital cost of investment. This implies, first of all, that managers must be able to identify and implement value-creating strategies. But since property rights theory (e.g., Alchian & Demsetz, 1972) and agency theory (e.g., Jensen & Meckling, 1976) argue that managers' and shareholders' interests may differ, this ability is insufficient. Managers must, secondly, be offered incentives that are in alignment with value-creating strategies. Such incentives must align managers' interests with those of shareholders. Otherwise, managerial behavior dictated by self-interest may destroy value. Value-based management is a solution for both challenges mentioned. Not only does value-based management provide managers with metrics and analytical techniques for identifying value-creating strategies; it also aligns managers' and shareholders' interests by linking managers' compensation and promotions directly to value creation (Ryan & Trahan, 2007; Martin & Petty, 2000). Value-based management can be defined as an "approach to management that aligns a company's overall aspirations, analytical techniques and management processes to focus management decision making on the key drivers of value" (Koller, 1994). Consequently, implementing a comprehensive value-based management system helps a company to attain the goal of value maximization.

The idea of value-based management can be traced back to the end of the 19th century (e.g., Marshall, 1890). However, this concept did not become widely recognized and popular until Alfred Rappaport published his seminal book "Creating Shareholder Value" in 1986. Since then, numerous consulting firms have developed different value-based measures to enable corporations to make strategic and operational decisions in line with the goal of value creation. The most important metrics are the economic value added (EVA), which was popularized and trademarked by Stern Stewart & Co., the cash flow return on investment (CFROI), conceptualized by HOLT Planning Associates/Boston Consulting Group, and the return on invested capital (ROIC), developed by McKinsey & Co. All these measures concentrate on value creation and are mathematically linked to a series of value drivers. Another essential advantage of value-based metrics is that they capture real value creation by taking account of the risk notion, the impact of inflation, and partly opportunity costs, which is not the case for traditional accounting-based performance measures. Copeland et al. (2000) even state that value is the only performance measure that uses complete information.

The fact that creating sustainable intrinsic value ought to be a firm's ultimate goal can be illustrated by its connection to superior economic performance in the long run. In fact, creating value and attaining a competitive advantage are two sides of the same coin. In strategic management literature, superior economic performance is seen as the result of a sustained competitive advantage. Within an industry, a superior strategy leads to a competitive advantage.[4] The consistent implementation of one of Porter's (1980) generic strategies (cost leadership, differentiation, or focus) together with a strategic group membership is thus considered to be the source of a competitive advantage. A firm that has gained a sustained competitive advantage is then able to create more economic value than rival firms, with economic value defined as the difference between the total perceived customer benefits and the full economic costs of a firm's products or services (Barney & Hesterly, 2006). In terms of the EVA concept, a competitive advantage leads to a return on capital employed (ROCE) above the industry average of the weighted average cost of capital (WACC). Consequently, focusing on value creation is equivalent to concentrating on attaining a competitive advantage, which entails superior economic performance.

2.2   Concepts of Value-based Management

2.2.1   Overview of Different Concepts

The four above-mentioned works on shareholder value and value-based management stand out from all other concepts in this stream of research because of their scientific and practical acceptance. They share the idea that increasing the fundamental company value should be the ultimate target of corporate management. Pursuing this objective is beneficial not only to shareholders, but also to all stakeholders, because without shareholders' risky investments none of the stakeholders' claims could be satisfied (Rappaport, 1986). In this section, we outline the key aspects of the four concepts, after which Table 2.1 at the end of this section offers a brief synopsis.

Concept of Rappaport

Alfred Rappaport (1986) contends that accounting-based performance measures such as net profit, return on investment (ROI), and return on equity (ROE) are inadequate measures to assess the achievement of the proclaimed goal of value creation for shareholders. Instead, Rappaport advocates the use of the shareholder value (SV) as a key performance indicator. SV is the difference between the company value and the market value of debt. Company value can be calculated as the net present value of cash flows from operations plus a residual value and the market value of tradable securities. Three main items have to be determined for this calculation: the free cash flows available to compensate debtholders and shareholders, the residual value after the planning horizon, and the cost of capital. The cost of capital is calculated as the WACC, using the aspired (market value-based) capital structure to weigh the after-tax cost of debt and the cost of equity. The lat-

---

[4] In contrast, traditional industrial organization research explains superior economic performance by industry effects and ignores firm behavior variables.

ter is determined in accordance with the capital asset pricing model (CAPM). In addition to SV, Rappaport (1999) introduces the shareholder value added (SVA). It is a measure for residual firm performance within one period and reflects a change in shareholder value.

Concept of Copeland/Koller/Murrin

Tom Copeland, Tim Koller, and Jack Murrin (2002) distinguish between two ways of calculating SV: the 'entity model' and the 'economic profit model'. The entity model follows the aforementioned approach of Rappaport (1986) with only minor adaptations. In the economic profit model, the sum of the currently invested capital and the present value of all future economic profits constitute company value. The authors define economic profit as the residual rent of the invested capital, i.e., the difference between ROIC and WACC. To discount future economic profits, the WACC is applied.

Concept of Lewis

Thomas G. Lewis (1995) suggests total shareholder return (TSR) on the basis of stock price changes and dividend payments as a key performance indicator. Lewis identifies three drivers that increase future free cash flows (FCF) and thus TSR: increasing returns, growth in activities whose returns exceed their cost of capital, and dividend payments whenever an investment in activities whose returns are above their cost of capital is impossible. To measure the return on an activity, Lewis propagates the CFROI, because to his mind traditional accounting-based performance measures are not sufficiently correlated with company value. The CFROI is a ratio of the cash flow a company has generated to the cash invested in the company's assets in a given period. It represents an internal rate of return. The cash value added (CVA) as a residual profit measure of an investment for a specific period depends on the difference between the investment's CFROI and its cost of capital. The latter is calculated on the basis of a broad portfolio of companies listed in the most important national economies. This implies a standardized cost of capital without firm-specific adjustments. Lewis explicitly rejects the WACC with the cost of equity according to the CAPM, as empirical substantiation for it is lacking.

Concept of Stern/Stewart

The concept of Joel M. Stern and G. Bennett Stewart builds on the EVA. Its starting point is a firm's net operating profit after taxes (NOPAT). From the NOPAT a charge for the capital employed (CE), which is used to generate the NOPAT, is subtracted to yield the EVA. The capital charge is calculated by applying the standard WACC to the CE. The EVA is a measure of residual profits from an entity perspective for one period. The analog multi-periodical measure is the market value added (MVA). It is a cumulative measure of firm performance, which illustrates the assessment of the NPV of all current and planned investment projects of a company.

Table 2.1: Comparison of valuation methods of value-based management concepts (following Hahn & Hintze, 2006)

	Cost of capital	Performance measure per period		Present value over life cycle
		Residual	Return	
Rappaport	WACC, cost of equity according to CAPM	SVA	Return on sales	SV
Copeland et al.	WACC, cost of equity according to CAPM	Economic profit	ROIC	Equity value
Lewis	Empirically determined average cost of capital	CVA	CFROI	Market value of equity
Stern/Stewart	WACC, cost of equity according to CAPM	EVA	ROCE	MVA

From an external point of view, MVA is the difference between the market value of a company and its book value. From an internal perspective, MVA is equal to the net present value of all future EVAs. The EVAs are discounted with the WACC. Maximizing MVA should be one a firm's top priorities, and EVA should be used to measure periodical performance (Stern et al., 1996; Stewart, 1999).

2.2.2 Overview of Performance Measures Utilized by the DAX-23 Companies

As already pointed out, the concepts of value-based management portrayed all have their origins in Anglo-American science and consulting practice. How appropriate they are for Europe in general and for Germany in particular has been a topic of discussion for quite a while. Anyway, the importance of value-based management concepts in Germany has increased sharply in recent years. Today, almost all management systems of the DAX-23 companies are directly or indirectly value-based. About 70% of the DAX-23 companies utilize the EVA as their key performance indicator (see Figure 2.1), including roughly 9% that employ a revised EVA (R-EVA). The R-EVA differs from the EVA in that it uses market values – instead of book values – to determine the cost of capital (Bacidore et al., 1997). Because of the enormous practical relevance of the Stern/Stewart concept, we offer a detailed description of the EVA and MVA and all underlying calculations in the following section.

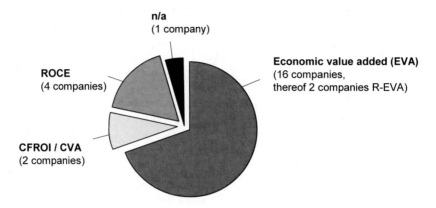

Figure 2.1: Value-based management applied by the DAX-23 companies (without banking/finance/insurance; status as of 1st quarter 2007)

2.2.3   Calculation and Interpretation of EVA and MVA

Stern et al. (1996) underline that they conceived a consistent integrated financial management system that is based on one key figure: the EVA. Some of the major advantages of their approach are its simplicity and its straightforwardness. Because of the power of this concept, it is essential to fully understand all variables that affect the EVA, all necessary steps of the EVA calculation, and all underlying assumptions. The constitutive formula for the EVA as defined in Section 2.2.1 is

$$EVA = NOPAT - WACC * CE \quad (1)$$

The NOPAT is derived by subtracting (fictitious) taxes according to the corporate tax rate from the earnings before interest and taxes (EBIT). Applying the corporate tax rate on the EBIT implicitly assumes a completely equity-financed investment. A number of adjustments are recommended to transform the accrual-based EBIT into NOPAT. Among them are the capitalization and amortization of costs associated with strategic investments such as research and development costs or marketing costs. In practice, however, very few adjustments are usually made, as they increase the complexity of the EVA approach dramatically while only marginally improving its explanatory power (Stewart, 1994).

The CE is defined as all operating capital necessary to generate the NOPAT. This is commonly the sum of the net working capital (the difference between current assets and current liabilities) and the net fixed assets (all long-term assets less accumulated depreciation).

The capital charge for the CE is calculated with the WACC, which uses the aspired market value-based equity-to-capital ratio and debt-to-capital ratio to weigh the cost of equity (CoE) and the after-tax cost of debt ($CoD_{a.t.}$).

$$WACC = \frac{Equity}{Equity + Debt} * CoE + \frac{Debt}{Equity + Debt} * CoD_{a.t.} \qquad (2)$$

Both CoE and $CoD_{a.t.}$ are the sum of a risk-free rate and company-specific risk premiums. CoE is derived from the CAPM as follows:

$$CoE = E(r_i) = r_f + \beta * [E(r_m) - r_f] \qquad (3)$$

The dependent variable $E(r_i)$ denotes the expected return on an individual security. The variable r_f is the rate of return for a risk-free investment, usually a long-term government bond rate. The beta factor, β, represents a firm's systematic risk. It is a sensitivity factor, indicating how a share's return reacts to a market or index movement. The independent variable $E(r_m)$ reflects the expected return of the market or index. Consequently, the difference $[E(r_m)-r_f]$ is the risk premium expected for an investment in the market rather than an investment in the risk-free alternative.

The after-tax cost of debt is calculated as follows, where s is the marginal tax rate:

$$CoD_{a.t.} = CoD_{b.t.} * (1 - s) \qquad (4)$$

It is important to take account of the tax shield of debt financing at this point of the calculation, because the EVA would be underestimated otherwise. This is because the NOPAT was derived with tax expenditures and on the assumption of complete equity financing. The cost of debt before taxes may either be calculated from expected interest payments according to long-term debt contracts or by adding the rate of return on a risk-free investment and a risk premium derived from credit spreads and credit ratings.

As the capital charge includes both the cost of debt and the cost of equity, it can be interpreted as the amount necessary to compensate debtholders and shareholders for the risk they bear with their investments. Furthermore, this calculation of the capital charge implicates that the EVA accounts for differences in capital structures.

Restating formula (1), which is frequently labeled the capital charge formula for the EVA, offers some additional information regarding the circumstances in which value is created. To this end, NOPAT as an absolute accounting-based performance measure from an entity perspective is divided by CE to result in the ROCE as a relative measure.

$$ROCE = \frac{NOPAT}{CE} \qquad (5)$$

Combining formula (1) and formula (5) leads to the value spread formula of the EVA.

$$EVA = (ROCE - WACC) * CE \qquad (6)$$

Obviously, the difference between ROCE and WACC determines whether value is created or not. Firms only create value by employing capital in the case of a positive difference. If ROCE equals WACC, the firm's profit is just sufficient to compensate both debtholders and shareholders for the risk they bear. No value is created beyond this compensation. Finally, a negative difference implies that the CE is not able to earn sufficient profits to pay the cost of capital.

Formula (6) illustrates the existing ways to increase EVA over an investment's life cycle:

(a) Increase the ROCE, which implies increasing the NOPAT that is generated by the current CE.
(b) Increase the amount of CE as long as the ROCE exceeds the WACC.
(c) Divest if the ROCE is lower than the WACC.
(d) Adapt financial management methods that lower the WACC (e.g., by a change of capital structure).

The EVA concept may be extended with the MVA, as defined in Section 2.2.1. With regard to the MVA, it is noteworthy that from an external perspective it is usually calculated as the difference between the market value of equity and the book value of equity, where market value of equity is the product of the number of outstanding shares and the share price. This simplification assumes that market and book value of debt do not differ. Furthermore, this calculation is only correct if efficient capital markets are assumed. The internally calculated MVA as discounted future EVAs is equal to the externally calculated MVA only if expectations on the stock market are the same as expectations within the firm. With respect to interpretation of the MVA it has to be noted that a positive MVA is a signal of overall value creation and a negative MVA is a signal of overall value destruction, through business activity. While a negative EVA of a single year may be overcompensated by other years' positive EVAs, a negative MVA gives an indication that circumstances exist in which restructuring, spin-out, or liquidation might make sense. All in all, in the long run, maximizing the MVA is the ultimate financial goal of shareholder-centered management. In accordance with the interdependence of MVA and EVA, this entails maximizing EVAs (Stewart, 1994).

2.3   Applications and Techniques of Value-based Management

2.3.1   Overview

Integrated value-based management systems influence the strategy, structure, processes, analytical techniques, and performance measures of a firm (Arnold, 1998). The most prominent areas of application include strategy development, mergers & acquisitions (M&A), and performance measurement. We explain techniques of value-based management selected from those used in these areas in this section. Depending on the area of application, the unit of investigation varies from a company over specific business units and subsidiaries to investment projects (see Figure 2.2).

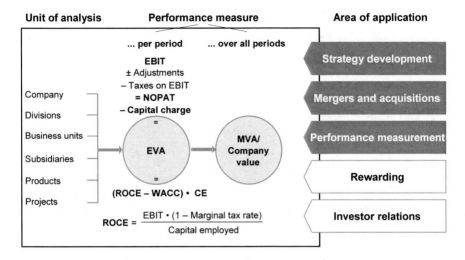

Figure 2.2: Areas of application of value-based management

2.3.2   Strategy Development

Strategy development can be regarded as one of the most important areas in which to apply value-based management tools, as strategy has a very substantial and long-lasting effect on the value-creating potential of a company (Morin & Jarrell, 2001). While value-based management cannot be understood as a creative tool that could be used to develop strategy alternatives, its metrics are extremely useful in assessment of the sustainability and desirability of potential strategies. One of its unique strengths is that it links strategy formulation to financial management while centering on value creation. Distinguishing between the two levels of corporate strategy and business unit strategy, a firm's strategy development process is aimed at either creating a parenting advantage or at gaining and sustaining a competitive advantage (Johnson et al., 2006).

On the level of corporate strategy, choosing to do business in attractive industries is crucial. Industry attractiveness greatly depends on growth potential. This implies that establishing business units in fast-growing industries or creating growth through internationalization or with new, innovative products and services is desirable. The potential for value creation that results from corporate strategic decisions must be fully tapped by consistent business unit strategies (see Figure 2.3). Their focus should be on improving the relative profit margin, e.g., by technology-based differentiation or cost optimization, which is reflected in a favorable competitive position.

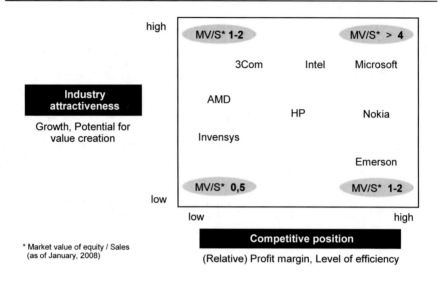

Figure 2.3: Drivers of company value

Management decisions on industries and business units in which to remain and in which to invest and on acquisitions or divestments to be made should be derived from value considerations (Malmi & Ikäheimo, 2003). Regarding corporate strategy, value-based management can be utilized as a portfolio management technique. In this case the business units of a firm are the units of investigation. Figure 2.4 links each unit's current EVA (EVA$_c$) as a single-period performance indicator to the net present value (NPV) of all of its estimated future free cash flows.

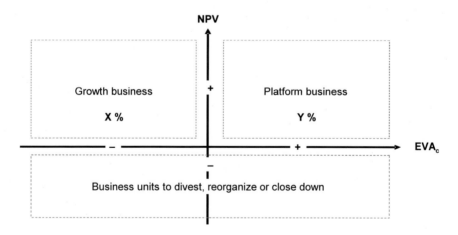

Figure 2.4: Portfolio balance

Only business units with a positive NPV create value in the long run. Therefore, business units with a negative NPV should be either divested, reorganized, or closed down – irrespective of whether or not they earn a positive EVA. Among the business units with a positive NPV there may be some with negative EVAs for the current and upcoming business years. This is acceptable, because the positive NPV indicates that any negative EVA is overcompensated by the discounted future cash flows. The desired proportion of business units with currently negative EVA, i.e., 'growth businesses', and business units with currently positive EVA, i.e., 'platform businesses', depends on corporate strategy. In this context it should be a company's goal to realize a portfolio balanced between overall value creation and current earnings. This is essential because 'platform businesses' offer the funding necessary to invest further in 'growth businesses' and thus to convert these to 'platform businesses' in the future. Based on the profitability index a company can also identify the business units with the highest value added, which should be given priority when scarce firm resources are to be allocated.

Value-based management cannot only be used for corporate strategy purposes but also to formulate and assess strategies at business unit level. To realize a sustained competitive advantage at business unit level, the consistent implementation of one of Porter's (1980) generic strategies is inevitable. A thorough analysis of a business unit's value drivers assists with keeping a consistent strategy focus and determining management priorities. To this end, first of all an overview of all value drivers of a business has to be generated. In a second step, a sensitivity analysis reveals the strength of the influence of a value driver on business unit value. This sensitivity of the value driver is then compared with the degree to which management is able to influence the value driver. Value drivers with little impact on company value may be integrated into an early warning system if management can control them. Otherwise, they have a low priority. In the case of value drivers with a strong link to company value, managers may choose risk-reducing strategies if their influence on the value driver is limited. If their influence is high, however, the value driver should be a key performance indicator with strong priority.

2.3.3   Mergers & Acquisitions

Two of the most significant value-based management techniques that are regularly employed during acquisition processes are company valuation and dilution analysis. We explain their main features in the next two sections.

2.3.3.1 Company Valuation

If company shares are traded on the stock market, multiplication of the number of shares outstanding by the current share price yields the market value of equity at any point in time. For companies without publicly traded shares, it is more comlicated to determine their equity value or, from an entity perspective, their company value. One way to approximate the company value is offered by the multiples approach. Its goal is a conclusion by analogy. First, reference companies are identified. It is imperative that they closely resemble the target company. Furthermore, the value of the reference companies has to be known. This is the case when either the reference company itself is listed or the reference company was a previous transaction target for which the purchase price was published. The first case is termed 'trading comparables' and the latter case, 'transaction comparables'. Common multiples include the sales multiple, the EBIT multiple, and the EBITDA multiple. They are the result of dividing the known value of the reference company by its sales, its EBIT, or its EBITDA, respectively. To obtain an approximation for the value of the target company, the multiple is then multiplied by the sales, the EBIT, or the EBITDA of the target company (Penman, 2007). Because of its simplistic nature, the multiples approach is employed at an early stage of the acquisition process, aimed at gaining a first assessment of a company's value.

Especially in later stages of the acquisition process, information is evident that cannot be accounted for by the multiples approach. In this case, the DCF method is often preferable (Damodaran, 2002). It usually consists of a phase of 5 years for which explicit planning of FCF is meaningful and a phase beyond this planning horizon (see Figure 2.5).

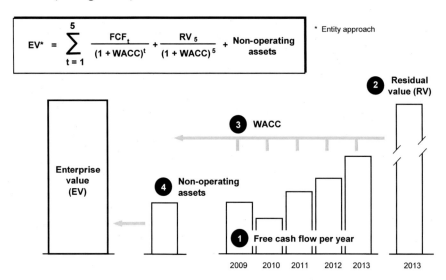

$$EV^* = \sum_{t=1}^{5} \frac{FCF_t}{(1 + WACC)^t} + \frac{RV_5}{(1 + WACC)^5} + \text{Non-operating assets}$$

* Entity approach

Figure 2.5: DCF approach with two phases

For the first phase, each year's FCF is estimated and discounted with the WACC. For the second phase, a residual value at the end of period five is calculated. When an exit is assumed, this residual value may be obtained via the multiples approach. With assumption of a going concern, the perpetuity model may be utilized. This means that a linear (positive, negative, or zero) growth of the last estimated FCF, possibly adjusted, is assumed in perpetuity. Company value is then reflected in the sum of the discounted FCFs of the first phase, the discounted residual value of the second phase, and the company's non-operating assets (Higgins, 2007).

2.3.3.2 Earnings Dilution

Earnings dilution describes the situation when the earnings per share (EPS) of an acquirer may be higher before a transaction than they are after it. On the one hand, a transaction entails performance effects that affect the numerator of the EPS. These may include the earnings of the target firm, synergies, transaction costs, restructuring costs, integration costs, goodwill depreciation, and financing costs. On the other hand, the number of issued shares may be changed by a transaction, which will have an impact on the denominator of the EPS. Diminished EPS in the first periods following a transaction are quite normal and not necessarily a sign of a wrong strategy. Since desired synergies of M&As may not be realized until a few years after the transaction, short-term EPS reductions should be tolerated if they are overcompensated by long-term EPS increases. Unfortunately, investors in the capital market frequently determine the fair price of a company's stock by multiplying its EPS by the price-to-earnings ratio (P/E ratio) of its industry. In this case, the earnings dilution leads directly to a stock price decline with all its negative consequences, including higher financing costs (Bausch, 2003).

2.3.4   Performance Measurement

Performance measurement is of decisive importance in a company's high-level strategic and financial control processes, which include target setting, performance monitoring, and responding to differences between expected and actual results (McTaggert et al., 1994). Performance measurement is therefore a key element when management focuses on value creation. Firm performance can be measured on different levels (see Figure 2.6). From an entity perspective, the operating performance of the company as a whole is relevant. The entity perspective reflects the management's point of view. Taking an equity perspective implies assessing corporate performance from the shareholders' viewpoint, which includes all operating and non-operating elements. Lastly, the residual perspective, which is emphasized by value-based management approaches, examines the value created after both debtholders and shareholders have received adequate compensation for their investment in the company (Bloxham, 2003). Within each of these three categories, absolute performance measures can be distinguished from relative performance measures.

Entity perspective's absolute performance can be measured by means of either EBIT or NOPAT, the only difference being that NOPAT includes tax effects. Thus, NOPAT can be understood as the earnings available to pay interest to debtholders and dividends to shareholders. In relative terms, the ROCE reflects the rent earned by the capital employed. Only if the ROCE is at least equal to the WACC, risk-adequate compensations of shareholders and debtholders are assured. Especially NOPAT and ROCE may serve to assess the performance of the management of strategic business units (SBUs) of a company, because they reflect operating business only and do not include financial income or expenses. In addition, use of the ROCE is appropriate to compare management performance between different SBUs within a firm or even between different companies, as it corrects for firm size.

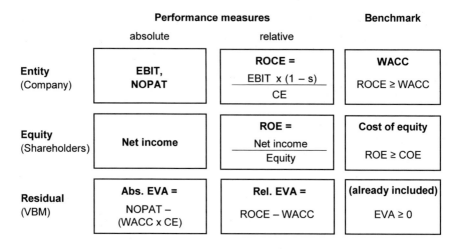

Figure 2.6: Different perspectives on performance measurement

The adequate absolute performance measure from a shareholder's point of view is net income. This includes the operating income, financial income, and taxes. Since all other claims have been settled, net income as the bottom line of the income statement reflects the amount of money that could be completely paid out to shareholders. Presumably, it does not matter to shareholders whether income has been generated via operations or via financing activities. The corresponding relative performance measure is the ROE, defined as the ratio of net income to equity. Only if the ROE at least reaches the cost of equity, the company's earnings are adequate to compensate shareholders for their risky investment (Higgins, 2001).

The absolute performance measure from a residual perspective is the EVA, while the relative one is the spread, or relative EVA. Because the risk-adequate returns for both shareholders and debtholders are already included in the calculation of the EVA, there is no benchmark that has to be met. The EVA is an excellent measure, as it points out how much value has been created (or destroyed) during a business year, all of which can be allocated to shareholders (Ehrbar, 1998). To assess managers' performance, EVA is only meaningful if managers are also accountable for financing. Comparing EVAs for different SBUs within a firm reveals where value is created and where value is destroyed. The explanatory power of EVAs is restricted, however, when there are significant age differences and differences in growth strategies. Older companies tend to have more hidden assets and thus less depreciation than younger ones. Companies relying on M&A for growth have higher goodwill and thus higher goodwill depreciation than companies relying on internal growth. Depreciation differences result in NOPAT differ-ences, which could be misinterpreted as differences in management capabilities.

Successful performance management and measurement depends heavily on a sound understanding of the variables actually affecting the value of the business. A progressive disaggregation of performance measures and their linkages with forward-looking value drivers provide important insights into the sources of value creation (Young & O'Byrne, 2001). Therefore, the chosen performance measure, e.g., the ROCE, has to be broken down into its determinants. These can then be linked to operational value drivers that can be controlled by management (see Fig-ure 2.7).

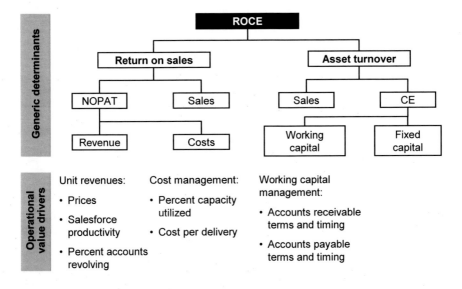

Figure 2.7: ROCE determinants and operational value drivers (following Koller, 1994)

2.4   Value Creation by Large German Firms

Having depicted the power of selected techniques of value-based management in the previous section, in this section we analyze the value creation of large German companies. To address the issue of value creation we evaluated the EVA of the DAX-listed companies[5] (not including companies from the banking and insurance sector) during 2000-2007. In total, the 23 companies destroyed a value of about € 200 billion during the period under review.[6] This sum consists of a cumulated value creation of about € 29 billion, as against € 229 billion of value destruction.

---

[5] Companies in the DAX as of June 1, 2007.

[6] The average WACC for all companies and all years was 6.5%.

Four companies account for two thirds of the total value created. Of the total value destroyed about three fourths is allotted to only 4 companies.

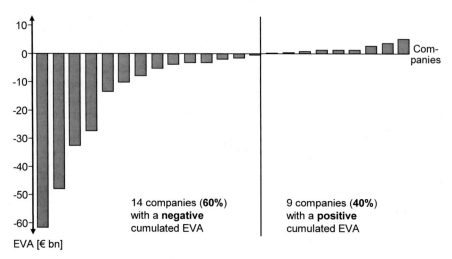

Figure 2.8: Cumulated EVA (in billions of euros) of DAX-23 companies from 2000-2007

Out of the 23 companies, only 9 exhibit a positive cumulated EVA during the 2000-2007 period (see Figure 2.8). Moreover, only 2 companies consistently created value in the period under review, whereas 7 companies show constantly negative EVAs.

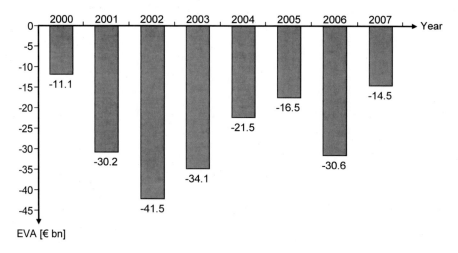

Figure 2.9: Annual EVAs (in billion of euros) of DAX-23 companies from 2000 to 2007

For each of the 8 years the DAX-23 companies' activities resulted in a negative EVA (see Figure 2.9). The year 2002 saw the highest negative value of € 42.2 billion, while the lowest negative value of € 11.8 billion was recorded in 2000.

However, two periods with different developments can be identified. During the first period (2000-2002) the sum of the EVAs of the DAX-23 companies decreased significantly from minus € 11.1 billion to minus € 41.5 billion. In 2002 only 4 out of the 23 companies had a positive EVA. The second period (2002-2007) was characterized by an opposite trend. Although the sum of the EVAs was still negative in every year, the value destruction decreased steadily (except in 2006, which was characterized by abnormal strategic investment expenses). During this second period the value destruction was reduced by nearly 66%, to minus € 14.5 billion.[7]

The drivers of value creation and destruction may be derived from an investigation of the ROCE (as described in Section 2.3.4). First of all, it is obvious from Figure 2.10 that the DAX-23 companies' average ROCE reached its minimum in 2001. The highest value destruction took place in 2002, however. This implies a rise in the WACC from 2001 to 2002 which could not be offset by the higher ROCE.

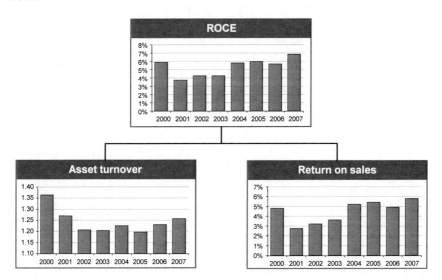

Figure 2.10: Annual average ROCE of DAX-23 companies and its drivers

For the subsequent years, the overall positive trend of the ROCE goes along with the development of the cumulated EVA. Dividing the ROCE into asset turnover and return on sales (ROS) reveals the causes of the ROCE development. As-

---

[7] It should be kept in mind that the DAX-23 companies' EVAs in the period investigated do not offer any information about the companies' MVA.

set turnover decreased until the year 2002. It then stagnated until it started to rise again from 2005 to 2007. ROS, on the other hand, dropped significantly from 2000 to 2001. In the years after 2001 it showed a more or less stable upward trend.

One potential explanation for our findings is that the strongly negative EVAs in the time period researched may be due to a phase of comparatively high investment activities in growth business units by the DAX-23 companies. In accordance with the explanations in Section 2.3.2, we would expect the negative EVAs to be offset by positive EVAs in the future. The positive trend starting in the year 2002 supports this view. Nonetheless, we cannot exclude the possibility that our negative findings are the result of a systematic bias in the evaluation of WACC components, especially too-high costs of equity.

2.5   Value Creation by Large and Medium-sized German Utilities

In the previous section, the inter-industry investigation of the DAX-23 companies revealed enormous value destruction for the years from 2000 to 2007. In addition, two periods with differing trends in development of the EVAs were discernible. In this section we shift our focus to 94 companies operating within the German utility industry. Three of these firms are considered large, with sales exceeding € 10 billion. The other 91 firms have annual sales ranging from € 50 million to € 10 billion and are considered medium sized. We were able to gather data for this sample for the period from 1999 to 2005.

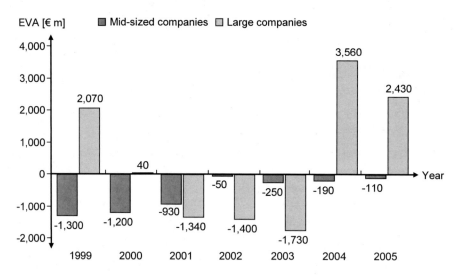

Figure 2.11: Comparison of annual value creation by large and medium-sized German utility companies

As in the case of the DAX-23 companies, the cumulated EVA over all periods and all firms was negative, with a value of minus € 394 million. This cumulated figure consists of a total value creation of € 12.9 billion and a value destruction of € 13.3 billion. The top four companies account for about 86% of the created value, while the bottom four companies account for about 59% of the value destruction. Of the 94 firms in the sample, 34 exhibit a positive cumulated EVA over the total period. Only 7 companies, however, constantly earned positive EVAs in each year. Of the 60 firms with a negative cumulated EVA, 22 destroyed value in each year of the period under investigation.

As Figure 2.11 reveals, large and medium-sized utilities differ in EVA genera-tion. The 91 medium-sized companies in our sample continuously improved their performance. From a cumulated value destruction of € 1.3 billion in 1999 they arrived at a cumulated value destruction of only € 107 million in 2005. The large utility firms, on the other hand, started with a cumulated EVA of € 2.1 billion in 1999, which steadily declined until it reached its minimum of minus € 1.7 billion in 2003. In 2004 the cumulated value creation jumped to an apex of € 3.6 billion, followed by another decline to € 2.4 billion in 2005. It is furthermore noteworthy that the three large utility firms cumulatively created a value of € 3.6 billion, whereas the 91 medium-sized firms destroyed € 4.0 billion in value.

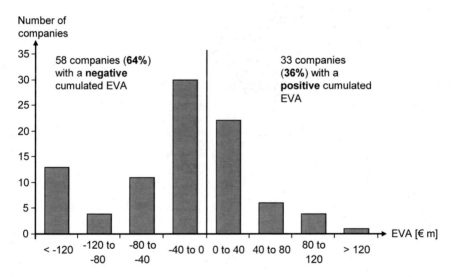

Figure 2.12: Distribution of medium-sized German utility companies by cumula-tive value creation from 1999 to 2005

Figure 2.12 depicts how many of the 91 medium-sized utility companies generated or destroyed how much value. All in all, the number of firms that destroyed value exceeds the number of firms that generated value. Moreover, it is obvious that the vast majority of firms are neither generating nor destroying a lot of value: 22 firms generated up to € 40 million, while 30 firms destroyed up to

€ 40 million. While there were only two firms that created more than
€ 120 million during the period investigated, 13 firms destroyed more than
€ 120 million. In this last group, the companies' value destruction ranges between
€ 120 million and € 569 million.

Another interesting aspect is highlighted by our comparison of the annual
average EVA of 91 medium-sized German utilities with 11 Austrian and 12 Swiss
medium-sized utilities (see Figure 2.13). The German utilities reveal a positive
trend from 1999 to 2005. The average value destruction decreased from about
€ 14 million in 1999 to only about € 1 million in 2005. Austrian firms exhibit their
highest value destruction in 2001 with an average of € 45 million. There is a
positive trend until the year 2005, in which the lowest value destruction of only
€ 4 million took place. The Swiss utility companies show the strongest turn-
around. From a low of € 52 million of value destruction in 1999 the continuously
improved to a high of about € 20 million value creation in the years 2004 and
2005. Country specific regulatory regimes and competitive intensities account for
a major part of the observed variance between German, Austrian, and Swiss utility
companies' average EVAs.

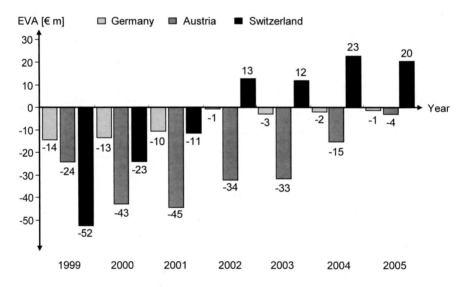

Figure 2.13: Comparison of annual average value creation by German and Austrian & Swiss medium-sized utility companies

One reason for the overall positive trend in the three countries is the
improvement of the ROCE from 7.6% in 1999 to over 10% since 2002. Detailed
analyses show that up to 2002 improvements in both the asset turnover and the
ROS were possible. From 2003 onward the ROS decreased. The constantly high
ROCE could only be sustained because of a continued increase in asset turnover.
This increase in asset turnover does not have its roots in sales growth but in a
decrease of the asset base. Two main reasons for this are improved asset

management and postponements of investment in replacements and expansions (Bausch et al., 2006).

Altogether, the differences in value creation between different companies, between different years, and between different countries indicate that within the utility industry there was value destruction and value creation at the same time. In any year, there were always companies with positive EVAs, regardless of the total value destruction or creation of the whole sample. This implies that, regardless of the circumstances, the opportunity to generate positive EVAs always existed in the years from 1999 to 2005. Further analysis of the data reveals that the gap between the 10 companies with the highest value creation and the 10 with the greatest value destruction has widened in recent years. Deregulation in the utility industry has increased firms' strategic options. Consequently, employing the previously described techniques of value-based management may help any utility firm to take the right actions that will allow to create value and to be among the leading firms in its industry.

References

Alchian, A. A. & Demsetz, H. 1972. Production, information costs and economic organization. The American Economic Review, 62: 777-795.

Arnold, G. 1998. Corporate financial management. London: Pitman Publishing.

Bacidore, J. M., Boquist, J. A., Milbourn, T. T. & Thakor, A. V. 1997. The search for the best financial performance measure. Financial Analysts Journal, 53: 11-20.

Barney, J. B. & Hesterly, W. S. 2006. Strategic management and competitive advantage: concepts and cases. Upper Saddle River: Pearson/Prentice Hall.

Bausch, A. 2000. Die Multiplikator-Methode – Ein betriebswirtschaftlich sinnvolles Instrument zur Unternehmenswert- und Kaufpreisfindung in Akquisitionsprozessen? Finanz Betrieb, 2: 448-459.

Bausch, A. 2003. Earnings Dilution in Unternehmensakquisitionen – Bedeutung und Gestaltungsmöglichkeiten (Parts I and II). M&A Review, 14: 260-265, 304-309.

Bausch, A., Fritz, T., Holst, A., Schiegg, T. & Schumacher, T. 2007. Value Creator III – Eine empirische Untersuchung von Energieversorgungsunternehmen in Deutschland, Österreich und der Schweiz. Bremen/Kronberg.

Bloxham, E. 2003. Economic value management – applications and techniques. Hoboken: John Wiley & Sons.

Copeland, T., Koller, T. & Murrin, J. 2002. Unternehmenswert – Methoden und Strategien für eine wertorientierte Unternehmensführung (3rd ed.). Frankfurt/New York: Campus.

Damodaran, A. 2002. Investment valuation – tools and techniques for determining the value of any asset (2nd ed.). New York: John Wiley & Sons.

Ehrbar, A. 1998. EVA – The real key to creating wealth. New York: John Wiley & Sons.

Hahn, D. & Hintze, M. 2006. Konzepte wertorientierter Unternehmensführung. In D. Hahn & B. Taylor (Eds.), Strategische Unternehmensplanung – Strategische Unternehmensführung (9th ed.): 83-114. Berlin, Heidelberg: Springer.

Higgins, R. C. 2007. Analysis for financial management (8th ed.). New York: McGraw-Hill.

Jensen, M. C. & Meckling, W. H. 1976. Theory of the firm: managerial behavior, agency costs, and ownership structure. Journal of Financial Economics, 3: 305-360.

Johnson, G., Scholes, K. & Whittington, R. 2008. Exploring corporate strategy (8th ed.). Harlow: FT Prentice Hall.

Koller, T. 1994. What is value-based management? The McKinsey Quarterly, 3: 87-101.

Lewis, T. G. 1995. Steigerung des Unternehmenswertes – Total Value Management. Landsberg/Lech: verlag moderne industrie.

Malmi, T. & Ikäheimo, S. 2003. Value based management practices – some evidence from the field. Management Accounting Research, 14: 235-254.

Marshall, A. 1890. Principles of economics: an introductory volume. London: Macmillan.

Martin, J. D. & Petty, J. W. 2000. Value based management: the corporate response to the shareholder revolution. Boston: Harvard Business School Press.

McTaggart, J. M., Kontes, P. W. & Mankins, M. C. 1994. The value imperative – managing for superior shareholder returns. New York: The Free Press.

Morin, R. A. & Jarrell, S. L. 2001. Driving shareholder value – value-building techniques for creating shareholder wealth. New York: McGraw-Hill.

Penman, S. H. 2007. Financial statement analysis and security valuation (3rd ed.). Boston: McGraw-Hill.

Porter, M. E. 1980. Competitive strategy: techniques for analyzing industries and competitors. New York: The Free Press.

Rappaport, A. 1986. Creating shareholder value – the new standard for business performance. New York: The Free Press.

Rappaport, A. 1999. Shareholder Value – Ein Handbuch für Manager und Investoren. Stuttgart: Schäffer-Poeschel.

Ryan, H. E. & Trahan, E. A. 2007. Corporate financial control mechanism and firm performance: the case of value-based management systems. Journal of Business Finance & Accounting, 34: 111-138.

Stern, J. M., Stewart, G. B. & Chew, D. H. 1996. EVA: an integrated financial management system. European Financial Management, 2: 223-245.

Stewart, G. B. 1991. The quest for value – the EVA management guide. New York: HarperBusiness.

Stewart, G. B. 1994. EVA: fact and fantasy. Journal of Applied Corporate Finance, 7: 71-84.

Young, S. D. & O'Byrne, S. F. 2001. EVA and value-based management – a practical guide to implementation. New York: McGraw-Hill.

3 Ways to Corporate Growth

Burkhard Schwenker[1]

Abstract

Growth is at the core of every corporate strategy. Only growth creates the momentum that is needed to drive an above-average increase in earnings and create jobs. From a global perspective, however, few industries match the sheer variety of conditions for growth that the utility industry must meet. Decentralized organizations are best able to cope with the demands that growth places on companies' agility and their ability to transform themselves. Essentially, companies can grow in one of two ways. Either they tread the path of organic expansion and ramp up their own business activities, or they team up with other market players. Both alternatives present specific advantages, whose significance varies very considerably depending on the precise competitive situation. In saturated markets, external growth takes precedence. Whatever path a company chooses, growth places heavy demands – professionally, but also on a very basic human level – on the management.

Keywords: growth, decentralization, cooperation

---

[1] Prof. Dr. Burkhard Schwenker is Chief Executive Officer of Roland Berger Strategy Consultants, Germany.

A. Bausch and B. Schwenker (eds.), *Handbook Utility Management,*
DOI: 10.1007/978-3-540-79349-6_3, © Springer-Verlag Berlin Heidelberg 2009

3.1   Growth Is a Strategic Necessity

3.1.1   Five Reasons for a Growth Strategy

Growth is a strategic necessity in the corporate sector. This principle is valid for all enterprises that intend to stay around for the long haul, including those in the energy sector. Basically, there are five reasons why there is no alternative to a growth strategy.

First, shareholders have a right to see the value of the company in which they have invested their money increase continually. Adding value is the whole purpose of every investment. Unlike many other industries, the energy sector has not nearly done all it can to improve efficiency in the production and distribution of electric power. This, however, can only be one aspect of any strategy to raise profits. Why? Because every time efficiency is improved, this leaves less room for further efficiency gains. This effect can be offset only by growth across the whole enterprise.

Second, it is important to tap economies of scale through growth. To maximize the utility of the learning curve, quick exploitation of new opportunities – i.e., rapid conquests of new markets – is vital. Moreover, a certain critical mass must be reached before economies of scale take effect. Both objectives therefore necessarily demand growth into new dimensions of size.

Third, moves to deregulate markets are intensifying competition and thereby increasing the pressure on margins. When one company gains a competitive advantage, others close the gap faster than ever. Regulatory bodies also stoke the fires of competition. Growth, however, can make up for both of these negative effects.

Fourth, only growing companies give employees and investors the future outlook that both these groups demand. Companies can only hold on to top performers if they offer attractive career development prospects. And such prospects open up automatically when a firm is growing fast. For their part, investors have wide range of opportunities in which they could invest their money. Current returns are one key issue, of course, but so too are the potential profits that can be expected in light of corporate strategy. Growth alone helps companies to generate compelling momentum.

Fifth, competition is heating up not only because of the liberalization of regular markets, but also because of globalization. Globalization is forcing companies to become larger. New corporate groups are emerging around the world. Up to now, the incumbent power utilities in the major industrialized countries have enjoyed an enviable lead. Even this lead can be eroded very quickly if market players do not resolutely pursue growth strategies, however. Whereas Europe and North America were easily the center of mergers and acquisitions (M&A) activity as late as the mid-1990s, 60% of all mergers now take place in Asia. Incumbents must therefore move swiftly to prepare for growing competition in the energy sector too.

3.1.2   The End of the V-Curve

There is, then, no alternative to growth. It must nevertheless be stressed that growth must always be accompanied by constant efforts to improve the efficiency of corporate structures. Past strategies commonly experienced what is known as the V-curve. Structures were first slimmed down to a healthy size before companies dared to venture out in the direction of growth. Today, no-one can afford the luxury of such a strategy. It is simply too slow. Moreover, advanced management systems have done away with the need for such an approach. The modern growth formula presents itself as a cycle that continually generates fresh funds for further growth. Excellent operational performance lays the foundation for superior cashflow, out of which further investment in growth can then be funded. The resultant economies of scale allow cashflow to increase still further, thereby freeing up resources for ongoing improvements in performance and/or another round of investment in expansion (see Figure 3.1).

Figure 3.1: Formula for growth

3.1.3   How Declining Transaction Costs Open up New Dimensions

A sharp drop in transaction costs has made growth perceptibly easier. A telephone call from Germany to the USA that would have cost the equivalent of 75 eurocents in 1997 today costs just 1 cent.

The development of new technologies has also made shipping and transportation faster and more flexible. Relative to 1990, global container transshipment volumes will probably have increased ninefold by 2015. Data processing has also become easier. Indeed, until now some kinds of data simply could not be handled in a reasonable length of time. Meanwhile, the cost of storing data has plummeted by a factor of 5 million since the end of the 1970s. When transaction costs are in decline, the optimal size of a company – the optimal ratio of sales to average costs – increases (see Figure 3.2). This is not an option, however: it is a requirement. Lower transaction costs automatically give a more important role to production costs and, hence, to economies of scale. These factors must be exploited if a company is to defend (or improve) its cost position in an increasingly fiercely contested marketplace.

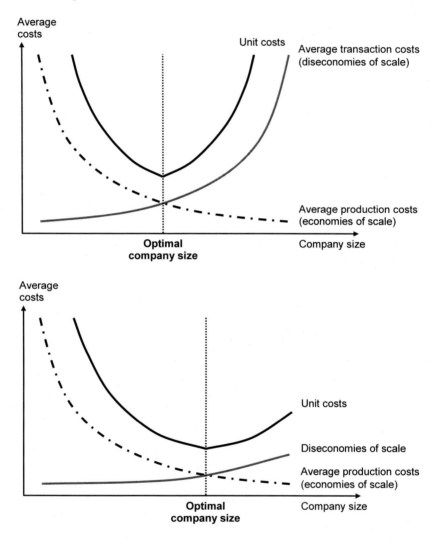

Figure 3.2: Growth into new dimensions (Schwenker & Bötzel, 2006)

3.1.4   Special Challenges to the Energy Sector

For utilities, growth strategies must accommodate a number of industry-specific challenges. The capital market places very high expectations in companies that are regarded as conservative, predictable, and noncyclical investments. In Germany, energy companies must deliver a long-term shareholder return of around 9% in the form of share price gains and dividend payouts. The same figure is customary in the other European markets, whereas expectations are slightly higher in the USA. Since every company must seek to surprise the market in a positive manner, double-digit profit growth is the order of the day.

The problem is that growth in incumbents' regular markets is substantially lower. In Western Europe, it is predicted that the electricity market will grow by just 2.1% per annum between now and 2015. The prediction for gas is not much better, at 2.6%. More attractive figures are emanating from the corresponding markets in the former Soviet Union, which are expected to grow by 4.1% and 5.6%, respectively, per annum. China's electricity market too is expanding by 6.5% per annum and its gas market, by 11% per annum. The message is clear: Utilities that want to grow vigorously have no choice but to penetrate these new markets.

At the same time, investment in replacement is desperately needed in established markets. Many power plants have been in service for decades and will soon need to be replaced. Germany's withdrawal from nuclear energy and the EU's goal of ramping up the use of renewable energies only add to the pressure to invest. Both the generation and the distribution of power are affected. In Germany alone, it is estimated that around 500 kilometers of new extra-high-voltage cables are needed to handle the electricity generated by offshore wind parks.

Regulation comes from two sides and determines the framework for all strategies. On the one hand, markets are being liberalized step by step; in Germany, for example, the law explicitly encourages new players to enter the market. On the other hand, regulators are subjecting companies to ever stricter rules and controls. Integrating these rules into a growth strategy is then made difficult by national policies that differ considerably. In addition, the prices that utilities are allowed to charge third parties for the use of their power grids are being squeezed relentlessly.

3.2   Ways to Growth

3.2.1   The Basic Building Blocks of a Growth Strategy for Utilities

Long-term growth in the energy sector rests on three pillars (see Figure 3.3): vertical integration, size and a leading market position, and business expansion through the integration of electricity and gas activities.

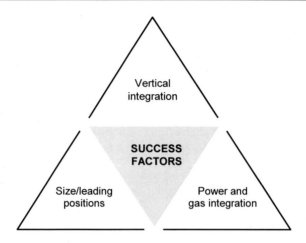

Figure 3.3: Success factors for growth in the utility sector

Vertical integration is what happens when a company plays an active role in every link in the value chain, from power generation to direct delivery to customers. This strategy significantly reduces a utility's dependence on the very volatile energy-trading exchanges. The purchase price for energy can thus be calculated more reliably – a singularly important factor if companies are to work profitably in a mass market. Moreover, established players can reinforce their market position relative to newcomers, who must first set up their own structures. The fundamental rule should be to generate at least 40% of the electricity sold in house, or at least to obtain fixed sourcing rights. As the discussion of climate change continues and prices for coal and gas rise, companies would do well to maintain a fair balance between renewable and fossil fuels. Besides the need to reduce positions of dependence, it is also crucial to strike the right balance between upstream and downstream activities. When market conditions change, companies can then step up their activities in those segments in which money can currently be made.

Size and market position are important, for three reasons. One is that economies of scale should be realized. This begins with the cost of invoicing and covers everything up to power plant capacity utilization and the benefits of greater clout in negotiations with upstream suppliers. (In segments with few suppliers, such as power plant construction, or for certain energy sources, such clout will be limited at best, however.) The second reason is that power plant parks become more flexible with increasing size. Outages can be absorbed more readily. Similarly, a broader portfolio of power plants that use different energy sources enables divergent price trends for the different sources to be balanced out. Also, the bigger the business, the easier it is to finance replacement investment. Finally, growing in size leads to higher revenues, which in turn pave the way to further growth in future.

The third pillar is the addition of gas to a utility's energy business. Almost all of Europe's major players have made inroads into this market. Gas now accounts for a sizable chunk of their sales. Contrary to past diversification strategies, the relevant business activities themselves exhibit both great similarities and overlapping customer bases in this case. The electricity and gas businesses complement each other, thereby laying a solid foundation for growth. Synergies can be tapped at every link in the value chain.

3.2.2   Growth Must Add Value

A lot is expected of growth if it is to rank as 'good growth', however. Size alone is not necessarily an asset. Bubbles should be avoided: Growth must be worthwhile. Lasting growth must be based on a successful blend of quantity and quality. The capital market shows no mercy – and rightly so – to takeover bids that only present strategic arguments and are not backed up by hard economic data.

3.2.2.1 A Three-step Analysis

The value of growth can be broken down and analyzed in three steps. First, extra sales must also deliver extra profit. In other words, either add-on business must penetrate profitable new markets, or the economies of scale mentioned above must be realized in relation to the larger volume. Second, growth must create value. However, this happens only if generated returns are higher than the cost of capital and thereby sustainably strengthen the company's financial position. Third, the additional free cashflow can be used to fund further investment and thus generate even greater economies of scale. If all three steps are followed, growth becomes self-perpetuating and fuels further growth.

3.2.2.2 Growth that Strengthens the Substance of a Company

Companies that set out to grow give themselves more substance than other firms. Roland Berger Strategy Consultants recently investigated the 1,700 largest companies in North America, Europe, and Japan from 1991 through 2005 (see Figure 3.4). A comparison of those companies that experienced profitable growth with the others in the group revealed that the outperformers increased their productivity significantly faster. They also did the same with both free cashflow and shareholder value growth, as well as creating many more jobs than most companies.

Everyone therefore stands to benefit when a company makes it into the league of outperformers. Our study also found that many companies are not successful, however. Barely 27% of the firms examined had experienced above-average growth. By contrast, nearly a third had seen sales and profits shrink. For close to one fifth of the companies, even higher sales had evaporated with no impact on profitability. Clearly, growing profitably is a stiff challenge.

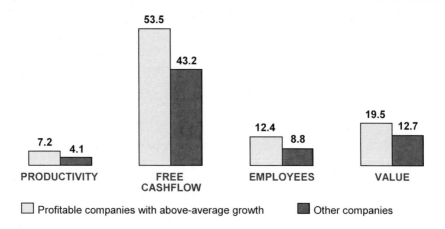

Figure 3.4: Growth is more than revenues (Avg. growth rates of the 1,700 largest companies in the triad (North America, Europe and Japan) 1991-2005 [%] p.a.)

3.2.2.3 *Patterns of Success in the Energy Sector*

Growth and size have a similarly important role in the energy sector. A Roland Berger study of electricity companies worldwide produced unequivocal findings: Large companies are by far the most profitable (see Figure 3.5). Also, they increase their profits over time much more strongly than smaller companies do. In 2006, corporate groups with sales in excess of $ 25 billion delivered a return on capital employed of over 18%. This impressive performance compares with a median return on capital employed (ROCE) figure of just 11.2% for electricity firms.

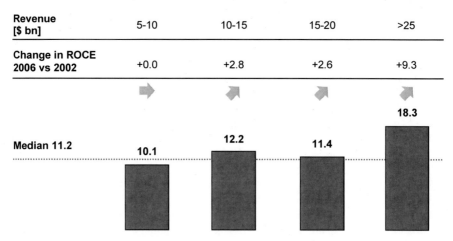

Basis: Median of performance-rated companies

Figure 3.5: Profitability and company size (profitability of electricity companies by company size, 2006 ROCE [%])

Growth, coupled with rising energy prices around the globe, drove tangible improvements between 2002 and 2006. Among the very top performers in the global electric power industry, ROCE rose from 12.9% to a good 19%, in line with the findings of our study. At the other end of the scale, the worst performers merely managed to improve from 6.7% to 7.6%. To put it another way, the top performers fared only 1.9 times better than the low performers in 2002, but had increased this differential to a factor of 2.5 by 2006. Growth pays dividends.

3.3   Finding the Right Blend of External and Organic Growth

As we have already seen, companies must see growth as a multidimensional task. Neither cost-cutting, nor organic or external growth nor mergers, acquisitions, and collaborative ventures alone will get the job done. In isolation, none of these actions can drive profit growth on the scale that is needed. As the following simplified calculation (see Figure 3.6) shows, the important thing is to find the right blend of all these actions.

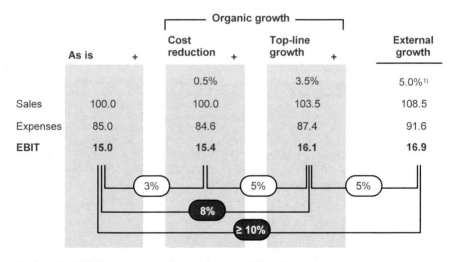

1) Growth of 5% through acquisitions compared to "As is"

Figure 3.6: Contributions to growth

If a company reduces its cost base by 0.5% while at the same time boosting revenue from its existing business base by 3.5%, the result is merely an 8% increase in earnings before interest and taxes (EBIT). Though that may sound ambitious in the light of prevailing conditions, it is not enough to satisfy the expectations that the capital market places on this industry. External growth must be added to achieve double-digit growth of at least 10%. This long-term growth target derives from an average total shareholder return of about 9% measured in Germany over many years. A composite of share price gains and dividend payouts, this figure must be exceeded if companies are to outperform expectations and pleasantly surprise the market.

3.3.1 Organic Growth

In terms of EBIT, organic growth can be achieved simply by capping costs. Over a three- to five-year period, the most recent wave of efficiency-enhancing programs yielded improvements of around 0.5% per annum relative to the initial cost base. Further organic growth can be realized by increasing sales. Given constant improvements in the cost base, additional sales revenues will then have a direct and positive impact on profits. Revenue growth can be achieved not only by boosting the volume of electricity sold, but also by raising prices (provided the market accepts such moves). The need for fresh investment in new power plants is acute. In addition, substantial capacity is due to go off line in the years ahead. Overcapacity is therefore likely to be extremely rare for a long time to come. As a result, it is reasonable to assume that prices will at least remain stable despite tighter regulation. On the other hand, scarcely any room is left for the large electricity groups in particular to realize further physical growth on their home markets. Regulators are consciously creating conditions that are heavily biased in favor of new market players.

3.3.2 External Growth

In light of regulatory restrictions, external growth – mostly outside their domestic markets – is the only way for top utilities to generate and indeed sell more electricity. Two paths lead to this goal. One is to collaborate and thereby enter into temporary and loose affiliations with other companies. The other is to take over competitors or agree to a merger of equals.

3.3.2.1 Mergers and Acquisitions

M&As are the fastest way to grow. Established customer relationships and sales structures can be purchased in this way. Expertise in markets that exhibit different structures from the buyer's home market are bought in automatically. All these benefits make M&As a popular tool. Since 2003, the lull that ensued when the New Economy bubble burst has given way to brisk M&A activity in the energy sector. Back then, the total transaction volume did not exceed $ 158 billion. By 2007, however, this figure had soared to $ 600 billion. More than 40% of the deals signed in 2007 were cross-border transactions. The energy sector is internationalizing rapidly as electricity groups try to close the gap on the oil and gas multinationals.

M&As open up new markets. This creates new, fast-growing business activities while allowing companies to side-step the restrictions imposed on their domestic markets. Bearing in mind the billions they have to invest over a period of decades (e.g., in new power plants or new sources of raw materials), energy companies need the kind of security that can be provided only by mergers or acquisitions.

At the same time, M&As are fraught with considerable risks. Depending on the dynamics of market growth, companies often let themselves be talked into paying steep – sometimes too-steep – acquisition premiums. These costs must be recouped as quickly as possible. Synergies must be exploited fast. A direct correlation exists between the window of time in which companies can leverage synergies and the amount paid for the acquisition premium (see Figure 3.7). One rule of thumb puts this window at only two years, even in the case of an average premium. If synergies are not tapped in this period, the merger will ultimately destroy value.

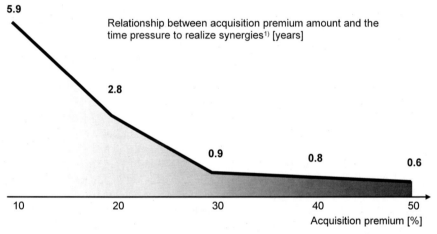

1) Example assumes an additional 5% return on equity (ROE)

Figure 3.7: The price of acquisitions (Schwenker, 2001)

Such enormous pressure and the compulsion to act swiftly can breed a certain recklessness in attempts to marry the two corporate cultures together. When this happens, the one new company may remain permanently divided into two camps. This risk is greater still in the context of cross-border M&As. In such cases, the clash of corporate philosophies is often exacerbated by political struggles between the governments in the countries concerned. The latter prefer to see the emergence of national champions, who themselves go on spending sprees beyond their home borders. And energy is usually seen as an industry that is essential to national security issues.

Competition law must likewise be regarded as a limiting factor. It is not always clear whether antitrust authorities will approve a business combination – or how drastic the conditions they impose will be. Watchdog organizations have become increasingly suspicious as energy prices have continued to rise. The result is a heavy burden for the utility industry. It is no longer enough for companies simply to track market developments. In addition, general conditions and constraints, the public mood, and political pressures must all be factored into their strategies as early as possible.

3.3.2.2 Cooperation

Cooperation is one alternative to a merger or an acquisition, albeit a limited one. On their home markets, large utilities can seek to collaborate with regional peers to shore up their strategic position and complement their existing business. Regulators will always make very certain that such moves do not excessively hinder competition, however. In the international arena, cooperative ventures are a useful way to gain a foothold in new, politically difficult markets. Incumbent players in the target markets can likewise benefit by enriching their skills and competencies.

Since the mid-1990s, collaboration in the economy in general has followed a clear trend. Although joint ventures were preferred to begin with, they are now very few and far between. Where enterprises do engage in collaboration, they now tend to favor strategic alliances. At the same time, companies around the globe obviously think more carefully about where cooperation is genuinely worthwhile and have focused their efforts much more sharply. As a result, cooperation these days concentrates on marketing, production, and research and development (R&D) activities. The importance of marketing and R&D in particular has risen significantly. Since 2000, their shares of collaborative ventures have both doubled, to 20% and 11%, respectively.

Today, one third of the sales revenues generated worldwide are generated in the context of collaboration. Where a company does decide to cooperate with others, this does not mean tying the knot for ever. Such a partnership can, however, be a preamble to acquisition: 78% of all collaborative ventures come to an end because one of the partners is acquired by the other; 17% are dissolved at some point; and only 5% end because one partner is acquired by a third party (see Figure 3.8).

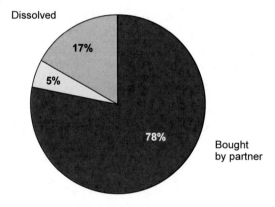

Figure 3.8: Why cooperative ventures end (end of cooperative ventures [%])

One thing should nevertheless be clear to everyone who wants to grow with the aid of others: There is no guarantee of success. Only roughly every second acquisition actually yields the success that the partners involved had hoped for. Similarly, partners who cooperate rate only 42% of collaborative ventures as successful or very successful. All too often – as in the case of M&As – the risks are talked down while the benefits are talked up. Sober, realistic assessment is imperative.

3.4   The Right Way to Organize Growth

Just doing the right thing is not the same as doing it right. Companies that opt for growth strategies must also foster a culture that is beneficial to such strategies.

3.4.1   Decentralization Keeps Companies Agile

Decentralized or distributed organizational structures are the best way to create the optimal conditions for growth. This principle holds true irrespective of the specific steps that are taken to achieve growth. The important thing – as evidenced by a study conducted by Roland Berger in collaboration with the Confederation of German Industry (BDI) and other partners – is to strike the right balance between centralization and decentralization. Key system head functions – links in the value chain that give a company a crucial competitive advantage over its competitors – require special attention and should, where appropriate, remain under central control. On the other hand, structures that are decentralized to the greatest extent possible are best able to respond to the changing demands of the environment in which they operate. On this score, difficult challenges await utility companies in the next few years. They are compelled to take investment decisions that they will not be able to change for decades. This industry in particular is at the core of efforts to combat global climate change and reduce emissions that are harmful to the climate. At the same time, it is becoming ever harder to predict market developments with any degree of certainty. Globalization has made heavyweight industrial customers much more mobile.

Decentralization affords many benefits. It eases the burden on top management. That is especially important because growth requires a coherent strategy. Pivotal strategic decisions must be taken by the Chief Executive Officer (CEO) and other board members. Distributed structures take the burden of conducting business off the hands of corporate management, however. The latter is then better able to focus on strategic issues. In organizations with centralized management structures, day-to-day business often chokes off any strategic initiatives and stifles growth – and that at a time when, as we have seen, far-reaching strategic decisions lie ahead of the utility industry.

3.4.1.1 Close Proximity to the Market

Distributed companies stay closer to the markets they serve, regardless of whether their top echelons are organized by region, by product group or by customer segment. As companies become ever more international in their outlook, this issue will become increasingly important. Growth strategies can be tailored to the specific needs of each individual market. Decentralization makes this easier by shortening decision paths. Decision-making processes take less time and are less complex. Once made, decisions can also be implemented faster, primarily because the conditions for communication are vastly superior in smaller units. The number of communication partners is more manageable, and direct communication is easier.

3.4.1.2 Encouraging Innovation

Decentralized structures create the ideal setting in which to nurture the self-motivation of executives and employees alike. The reason is simple: Decentralized units are generally responsible for specific processes and are thus able to identify much more strongly with what they do. In addition, more open channels for direct interaction within small, homogenous units make it easier to get employees to buy into shared goals. In the relative anonymity of a large organization, that alone is a far more difficult challenge. Thus, the conditions for innovation are put in place. Freedom, and even a certain degree of creative chaos, must nevertheless be counterbalanced by hard and fast schedules, priorities, and budgets.

3.4.1.3 Transparency and Responsibility for Profits

Where responsibility for decisions is delegated, the managers of distributed units can act largely independently. They serve as 'in-company entrepreneurs', shouldering responsibility for the outcomes of their decisions – both metaphorically and literally, in the form of profit and loss. Decentralized structures are fundamental to the principle of responsibility for profits, as well as being an essential factor in transparency both inside the company and toward the outside world. Success or failure can only be attributed unequivocally if the cause and effect of decisions is anchored in individual units – and if people do not have the option of hiding behind each other.

3.4.1.4 Integrating Other Companies

The adaptability of corporate structures is crucial to the whole issue of growth. When an entire organization has to be realigned, decentralized companies have the edge in terms of flexibility. Distributed units tend to handle self-contained processes and are therefore relatively easy to regroup, for example. In the event of an acquisition, merger, or collaborative venture, it is again easier to integrate individual modules – or to dispose of them if the portfolio needs to be adjusted. This issue in particular is of interest to utilities, who are increasingly committing to forms of cross-border collaboration that lead to overlaps in individual markets and attract the attention of the antitrust authorities. In this context, it is important to maintain flexible corporate structures so that any necessary revectoring can be done quickly and efficiently.

3.4.2   The Human Factor

Being able to grow is not enough to ensure that a company's plans will succeed, however. The organization must also be willing to grow. No one company owns the rights to growth potential in various markets. Any management team can get a slice of the cake if it acts decisively and is convinced of what it is doing. Blaming a generally adverse business climate for one's own poor performance is too easy. The crucial issue is to seize opportunities as they arise. This is the yardstick by which the quality of management can be measured. Every industry, every region, has companies that overcome downturns and outperform the average even in turbulent times. In recent years too, those utilities that did not hesitate but channeled all their energies into growing their core business have – despite setbacks – fared better than their rivals. As international integration intensifies in future, managers will be expected to be even more inventive and imaginative. The easy pickings have already been carved up.

The ability to grow is a matter of strategic, organizational, and structural considerations. It is the right attitude, however – the willingness to grow – that transforms ability into real growth. Many companies lack the flexibility they need. "Forbes" magazine recently compared its current list of the 100 largest US companies with the first "Forbes 100" list published in 1917. Of the companies on the initial list, 61 no longer exist today, and only 18 of the remaining 39 still rank among the biggest and best.

Three issues are critical to the right attitude to growth. One is a company's culture of trust and performance. The second is a deep conviction of its own strengths. The third is sufficient optimism to believe that its plans will indeed come to fruition. A Roland Berger Strategy Consultants survey of the growth orientation among top managers in Germany and Austria revealed one absolutely vital guiding principle: People are a more important driver of growth than processes or systems (see Figure 3.9).

According to a survey among top managers, 42% feel that corporate leadership is the relevant force that drives growth. This includes not only the ideas of the CEO and the board, but also those of the supervisory board and advisory council. Specific skills and competencies (30%) in production or logistics, say, complement the human factor, as do enterprise-specific factors (with a weighting of 28%), such as business systems and brand management.

One element underpins every vision of growth, however: trust. Unless you get your people to buy into growth, you will inevitably run out of steam and run the risk of missing opportunities. Good management should always be aware that change – especially for the people who make up the company – means a significant loss of security and predictability. The advantage of ratios, earnings forecasts, quantified strategies, communicated objectives, and flowcharts, on the other hand, is that they convey a sense of security. Five-year sales targets let employees know where they are headed. Flowcharts let them know where they stand.

Drivers	Relevance[1]	Examples
People	— 42% →	• CEO, board member, managing director • Supervisory/advisory board member
Competencies	— 30% →	• Process competency (manufacturing, logistics, sales) • Relationship management • Innovation
Business systems and specifics	— 28% →	• Business system • Brand management • System (e.g., ERP, HR)

1) Weighted survey findings

Figure 3.9: What matters most in facilitating growth

Yet the world is changing – and ever faster. Companies can no longer quantify everything for the long haul. Objectives have to be adjusted more quickly. It is not always possible to say with conviction that a flowchart will remain unchanged for the next few years. All of this erodes people's sense of security. The only form of security companies can still offer to their employees is people: the management, the leaders. That is precisely why values are becoming so important to today's firms. Corporate ethics is naturally an issue in the battle to regain trust. In the context of management, of leadership, however, we are talking more about personal values – values such as integrity and reliability. Good managers always set a good example. If you want your people to work hard to realize new strategies, you must do the same and show them that you are doing it.

If you fail to set this good example, your company is more in danger than ever before of disappearing from the map. When the Standard & Poor's 500 share index was launched in the USA at the start of the twentieth century, a listed company could expect to stay in the index for 65 years or so. Today, firms stay on the list for an average of just 10 years. Managers must respond to the ever faster pace of change with intellectual flexibility too. The half-life of successful models is dwindling all the time. The demands on managers have never been as challenging as they are today.

References

Roland Berger Strategy Consultants et al. 2008. Systemkopf Deutschland Plus –
   Die Zukunft der Wertschöpfung am Standort Deutschland. Management
   Summary. Berlin: BDI-Drucksache Nr. 405.
Schwenker, B. 2001. Synergie-Effekte nutzen – oder: Wie man richtiges Synergie-
   Management aufsetzt. Hamburg: Roland Berger Strategy Consultants.
Schwenker, B. & Bötzel, S. 2006. Auf Wachstumskurs – Erfolg durch Expansion
   und Effizienzsteigerung. Berlin, Heidelberg, New York: Springer.
Schwenker, B. & Spremann, K. 2008. Unternehmerisches Denken zwischen Stra-
   tegie und Finanzen – Die vier Jahreszeiten der Unternehmung. Berlin, Heidel-
   berg: Springer.

4 Diversification and the Achievement of Scope Economies

Markus Schimmer[1]

Günter Müller-Stewens[2]

Abstract

The utility industry is undergoing major regulatory changes, freeing up a competition between alternative business models. Diversification marks one of the main themes in this struggle for success. The question of how companies can add value by engaging in multiple businesses inevitably relates to the concept of economies of scope. This chapter introduces the concept as a rationale for diversification, highlights its practical limitations, and discusses whether it explains the exhibited diversification trends within the utility industry. The chapter concludes by supporting the relevance of the concept for explaining diversification in general and the trends within the utility industry in particular.

Keywords: diversification, economies of scope, utility industry

[1] Markus Schimmer is a Research Associate at the University of St. Gallen, Switzerland.

[2] Prof. Dr. Günter Müller-Stewens is Professor of Management and Organization at the University of St. Gallen, Switzerland.

A. Bausch and B. Schwenker (eds.), *Handbook Utility Management,*
DOI: 10.1007/978-3-540-79349-6_4, © Springer-Verlag Berlin Heidelberg 2009

4.1   Introduction

The deregulation of the electricity sector in the European Union has formulated new market rules for an industry that has long been dominated by regulated, state-owned monopolies. Hence, the introduction of a free-enterprise system is translating into a spate of strategic options that allows firms to redefine their strategic postures (Bausch et al., 2007). Some industry trends have emerged from these new opportunities and challenges. Faced with an enlarged international group of competitors, utility firms started to consider internationalization as the imperative to defend their national market positions, thereby initiating a process of concentration within the European market. Furthermore, a trend to unbundling and diversification arose (Bozem, 2004). Many electricity companies have started to enter into related network-based services, such as gas, giving rise to the so-called multi-utility business model. Both of these trends to scale and redefine the business models accounted and are still accounting for an increase in mergers and acquisitions (M&A) activity within the industry. Catalyzed by the rich amounts of funds accumulated in the past and the availability of capital for such a profitable industry, utility companies peaked their deal volume in 2007 (PWC, 2007).

From today's perspective, the regulatory shift and the succeeding rise of new firm strategies with their performance implications allow to investigate the relevance of some basic economic principles within this industry. In particular, the concept of economies of scope seems to offer a promising explanation for the diversification strategies exhibited within the utility industry. To explore this explanation, this chapter pursues two objectives. On a general level, it wants to illustrate the concept of economies of scope and its role within diversification strategies. Grounded on these thoughts, it then strives to identify the factors underlying the rationales for multi-utility business models.

The chapter is organized in three parts. First, it conveys the theoretical background relating to strategic management of diversification. In doing so, it focuses on three questions: How has the perception of diversification changed over time? What types of diversification exist? What are the implications of diversification for firm performance? Second, it elaborates on the concept of economies of scope, one of the main motivators for diversification. This is also carried out by focusing on three central questions: What are economies of scope according to economic theory? How does the concept have to be adjusted for it to yield valid arguments for diversification? What are potential sources of economies of scope? Having revisited these central ideas from strategic management and economics, we then pass on to an analysis of potential economies of scope in the utility industry.

4.2   Corporate Strategy and Diversification

The focus of strategy is on the search for competitive advantages as sources for superior firm performance. These advantages are assumed to originate from companies' distinct corporate- and business-level strategies (Porter, 1987). Andrews

(1971) defines corporate-level strategy as the discipline of identifying the businesses in which a firm should compete, whereas the business-level strategy formulates how this competition is to be structured. Thus, corporate strategy aims at ensuring that the company adds up to more than the sum of its business units. To justify the distinct accumulation of businesses and prevent a valuation discount, however, corporate strategy needs to do more. It needs to convince the company's shareholders that the business portfolio is worth more under the corporation's management than under any other ownership (Goold et al., 1994). Otherwise, companies run the risk of losing the mandates to operate their businesses to other, more capable parent companies. The means of adding value and counteracting the threat of a potential break-up are in the hands of the corporate headquarters and at the heart of its activities. However, the same applies to various kinds of costs. In consequence of this coexistence of upside and downside potentials, firms face the challenging question of the optimal size, composition, and management of their corporate portfolios.

The question of the size and composition of corporate portfolios is closely related to the concept of diversification. In his seminal work, Ansoff (1957) laid down four generic product-market strategies that also constitute capital allocation options and choices for strategic change. Out of these, diversification marks the process of entering new business markets with new products or services. In contrast to the strategies of product- or market-development, which focus solely on one dimension of change, diversification addresses both the market and the product dimension, thus constituting the most radical choice within the set of product market strategies. A company's choice from this set of alternatives is ideally driven by changing business opportunities and the company's assessment of these.

4.2.1   Historical Patterns of Firm Diversification

In previous decades, however, firms' diversification behavior was mainly governed by trends stemming from changing market beliefs about the optimal degree of diversification. During the 1950s and 1960s, "faith in general management skills seemed to justify a kind of virtuous circle of corporate growth and diversification" (Goold & Luchs, 1993). Yet, by the late 1960s, conglomerates were encountering profitability problems that resulted in large conglomerate discounts on the stock markets. The 1970s became the era of portfolio management tools which since then have directed portfolio decision making. Performance results improved as underperforming businesses were systematically divested and the corporate portfolios were kept balanced with growth- and cash-generating businesses. However, the technocratic approach was short sighted, as it neglected questions concerning both the fit between the businesses and the need for business-specific management approaches (Ghoshal & Nohria, 1989; Hamermesh & Roderick, 1984). Performance again declined. To relieve the issue of information asymmetry between the corporate center and the firm divisions, value-based planning techniques became the guiding principles for capital allocation choices across a corporation's units. But also these tools did not help in defining the content of corporate strategies (Goold et al., 1993). Addressing this important gap, in 1982 Peters and Waterman gave the initial but nonetheless abstract advice "to stick to the knitting" (Peters & Waterman, 1982). As their advice left plenty of room for elaboration, subsequent years brought up further content-related concepts and theories, which were welcomed by practice and led to refocusing. In particular, the notions of synergy and core competences put forward by Prahalad and Hamel (1990) offered additional guidance in assessment of the fit and quality of diversification plans. In recent years, strategy research stepped beyond the content dimension and started identifying factors relevant to the crafting of better processes of strategic decision making. Innovative ideas such as that of a dominant logic restricting the perception of a company (Prahalad & Bettis, 1986) began to offer some help in reflecting the cognitive and behavioral routines that restrict companies trying to achieve their optimal strategies, including those concerning diversification.

4.2.2   Diversification Types and Their Implications for Corporate Management

So far, the concept of diversification has been introduced, but not further specified. Yet, diversification strategies can take various forms, which may pose different challenges to the corporation's management. As a framework for these, four dimensions can be identified by which diversification strategies can be distinguished: (1) the degree of concentration (Jacquemin & Berry, 1979); (2) the relatedness of the businesses to be combined (Barney & Hesterley, 2006); (3) the direction of diversification (Hitt et al., 2003); and (4) the mechanisms to implement the diversification (Müller-Stewens & Lechner, 2005). The degree of concentration is defined by the number of businesses a company is engaged in and shows how its turnover is composed of the divisions' individual turnovers. The degree of relatedness indicates how similar the businesses are in the corporate portfolio. At this, similarity needs to be operationalized by a set of criteria that is deemed to be relevant for the aimed analysis. The criteria may vary and include indicators for the material relatedness of the products from the different divisions (such as distribution channels) or intangibles (such as required management know-how). The direction of diversification can be divided into three types: vertical diversification, product diversification, and geographic diversification. Vertical diversification refers to the question of the stages of the industry's value chain at which a company wants to be active. Product diversification relates to the span of products and services a company decides to offer. In this, it is not necessary that the products stretch across different industries; even within an industry diversification is possible. For example, within banking a company could offer products in classic retail banking, asset management, and investment banking. The geographic diversification addresses the question of the geographic extent over which firms should engage themselves. The means of implementing the diversification plans are internal development or external sourcing in the form of acquisitions, mergers, joint ventures, or licensing agreements. Considering the dynamism of change and the time-consuming path dependence in investment chains, the alternative of internal development is less frequently chosen than the one available in external sources, which provide a rich menu of ready-prepared diversification options (Müller-Stewens & Lechner, 2005).

Table 4.1: Diversification levels and management complexity (Müller-Stewens & Brauer, 2009)

Level of complexity	Type of diversification	Description
1	Nondiversified company	The company focuses on a section of a value chain within one industry only.
2	Vertically diversified company	The company generates more than 90% of its turnover with one core business that stretches over the whole value chain of one industry segment.
3	Horizontally diversified within one industry	The company generates more than 90% of its turnover with one core business that stretches across several industry segments (such as cars and trucks in the automotive industry) that show different success factors and competitors. It is vertically focused.
4	Horizontally and vertically diversified within one industry	The company generates more than 90% of its turnover with one core business that covers several industry segments. Within the different segments, the company is widely integrated.
5	Diversified into unrelated businesses from various industries	The sales are distributed between businesses from different industries in such a way that no business contributes more than 70% to the corporation's turnover. The businesses are strategically and operationally independent.
6	Diversified into strategically related businesses from various industries	The sales are distributed between businesses from different industries in such a way that no business contributes more than 70% to the corporation's turnover. The businesses draw strategically on common intangible resources.
7	Diversified into strategically and operationally related businesses from various industries	The sales are distributed between businesses from different industries in such a way that no business contributes more than 70% to the corporation's turnover. The businesses are widely interlinked in terms of both strategy and operations.

The aforementioned characteristics of diversification strategies help to identify types that may pose greater challenges to management than others. It is proposed that the level of management complexity, and with it the chances of justifying such a company set-up to the shareholders, is in direct proportion to the criteria developed above. Table 4.1 displays the assumed relationship, which finds support in both theory and practice.

4.2.3   The Performance Implications of Diversification

The relationship between diversification and performance has been intensively investigated in recent decades. Management, finance, and industrial economics scholars have tried to answer two basic questions: First, how does the performance of diversified multi-business firms differ from the performance of specialized nondiversified companies? And second, what type of diversification yields the highest returns? Despite a variety of empirical studies, these questions have been left unanswered. It has not proved possible to establish either the relationship between diversification and performance or the performance implications of different diversification types in a consistent manner.

As far as the question of how diversification affects performance is concerned, no single generally valid relationship seems to exist (Lubatkin & Chatterjee, 1994; Markides & Williamson, 1996; Montgomery & Wernerfelt, 1988). However, the hypotheses proposed and tested in the various attempts to reveal such causalities have provided several elements that are relevant in many diversification–performance relationships. Yet, it is necessary to assume varying degrees of relevance for the cause–effect relationships identified, depending on the individual context and the specifics of each diversification strategy. Assessing the role of the individual up- and downside potentials for specific strategies requires an overview of these elements. In terms of aspects revealing positive performance implications, the literature provides the following: Diversification establishes a wider set of resources that offers a larger degree of flexibility in the face of market dynamics; companies may be capable of adapting faster to changes as they can draw on a wider base of experience and become more skilled in handling and reconfiguring diverse resources (Helfat & Eisenhardt, 2004); furthermore, there might be various types of synergies for a specific set of businesses, which would render a merged unit more profitable (Chatterjee, 1986; Leland, 2007). Negative performance implications can be expected from the increasing level of management complexity and its constituents, such as increasing market distance and bureaucratic inefficiencies (Markides, 1995; Prahalad & Bettis, 1995).

When we come to the question of which type of diversification is superior, research also does not provide a straight answer. Researchers initially focused on the intuitive idea that related businesses most probably offer the highest potential for synergies (Collis & Montgomery, 1998; Rumelt, 1974; Wrigley, 1970). Though the first empirical studies supported the suggested relationship (Rumelt, 1974; Wrigley, 1970), later ones refuted this idea and have even claimed the opposite (Michel & Shaked, 1984). Reasons for this dismal record can be sought in various areas. First, 'relatedness', as a concept commonly focusing on products, might be ill-defined and distract from the real sources of upside potential, such as intangible management resources (Miller, 2006). Yet, chances of finding a universally valid operationalization that yields unequivocal empirical findings for all possible samples seem to be small. Second, some researchers consider relatedness research is flawed as it is based on a level of analysis too abstract to provide reliable antecedents of performance outcomes (King et al., 2004; Ramanujam & Varadarajan, 1989). Even if related mergers tend to imply a larger synergy potential, why should performance gains result from this potential in an unconfined and cost-free way? Again, it seems more probable that management needs to work hard to realize the synergies (Chatterjee, 2007). This might create direct and indirect costs that could exceed the expected benefits and thus turn the ultimate balance into a negative one (Kanter, 1998; St. John & Harrison, 1999).

Table 4.2: Diversification patterns of European energy giants (Müller-Stewens & Brauer, 2009)

Company	Number of divisions	Divisions (turnover 2005 in € bn)	Direction of diversification	Part of largest division
Royal Dutch Shell (NL)	5	Oil products (200.3), Chemicals (26.2), Exploration & Production (20.2), Gas and Power (11.6), Others (0.8)	Vertical diversification	77 %
BP (GB)	4	Refining & Marketing (170.6), Gas, Power & Renewable (19.0), Exploration & Production (12.3), Others (11.0)	Vertical diversification	81%
Total (F)	3	Downstream (99.9), Chemicals (22.3), Upstream (20.9)	Vertical diversification	70%
E.ON (G)	5	E.ON Energie (24.1), E.ON Ruhrgas (16.8), E.ON UK (10.1), E.ON Nordic (3.5), E.ON US (2.1)	Market diversification	43%

Though some see these contradictory findings as proof enough to claim that research which assumes "that the degree of diversity and profitability are cross-sectionally related [...] fail[s] to provide generalizable conclusions" (Datta et al., 1991; King et al., 2004), another interpretation is possible. The mechanisms which the conflicting articles yield in combination with the fact that multiproduct firms are the rule rather than the exception in today's economy allows some valuable, albeit general, statements on diversification: Large companies tend to engage in several businesses that benefit from each other in various and very different ways. What rationale gives reason for a distinct grouping of businesses depends largely on the context and the specific capabilities of the company under investigation. Hence, diversification patterns vary, even within industries. There are no unconfined rules for success. Research can yield lists of potential up- and downsides, of pitfalls within the realization processes and of valuable capabilities that catalyze success in a range of contexts. Value creation, however, largely remains the result of the firm specific diversification process that needs to be in line with the corporation's strategy and various context factors.

Yet, industry factors matter, as they define an important part of a company's context and therewith ultimately strategic decision making within an industry (Bain, 1968). Table 4.2 illustrates how some of the largest European companies in the energy sector have settled in their quest for performance. The small sample indicates that the firms rely on similar strategies for facing the above-mentioned questions and challenges.

4.3   Economies of Scope as an Imperative for Diversification

Ignoring such industry patterns for a long time, economic theory viewed the distribution of economic activities among firms as given (Nelson, 1972). Enterprises were regarded as black boxes. It was not until Williamson (1975) published his transaction cost theory that economics reached out to explain the varying configuration patterns of enterprises within different industries. In 1979, Williamson noted that firms and markets "evolve in active juxtaposition with one another" in an effort "to reach a complementary configuration that economizes on [production and] transaction costs" (Williamson, 1979b). The scope of business activities of modern companies moved into researchers' focus. It turned out that the theoretical framework used by Williamson to explain vertical integration (Williamson, 1975) could be extended to explain multiproduct diversification. While the analysis of vertical integration rests on questions about the internalization of the supply of inputs (such as raw materials) to a single production process, diversification "represent[s] a mechanism for capturing integration economies with the simultaneous supply of inputs common to a number of production processes geared to distinct final product markets" (Teece, 1980). As a production process that capitalizes on these economies is more efficient than separate production processes, it becomes clear why the presence of such economies gives rise to multiproduct firms (Panzar & Willig, 1975).

4.3.1   Production Economics and the Relationship Between Economies of Scale and Scope

The essential simplicity of this idea becomes clear when the concept of economies of scope is revisited from a production economics perspective. This will also formally clarify the link with the concept of economies of scale and thus demonstrate that both notions draw on a common idea, namely that of subadditivity. Production economics generally distinguishes three types of productions: Parallel production, combined production, and joint production. The first type, parallel production, refers to production processes that are independent from each other and offer no economies. The second type, combined production, characterizes production processes that necessarily yield different products. A common example of such a production is the distillation process of oil yielding various kinds of fuels, ranging from heavy oil to petrol. The third type, joint production, is central to this chapter and refers to all cases of production for which the costs of producing two products are lower than the combined costs of producing each product separately. The formal expression of the cost function for a superior joint production of two products is (Panzar & Willig, 1981):

$$C(Y_1, Y_2) < C(Y_1, 0) + C(0, Y_2)$$

where C = costs of production, Y_1 = output of product 1, and Y_2 = output of product 2.

The left side of the inequation expresses the costs of the joint production within one company, whereas the right side adds up the costs for the same output coming from two distinct productions, probably occupied by two companies. The inequation shows a special case of a more general concept, that of subadditivity. Subadditivity extends the argument above to nonspecialized productions and is the condition in place for natural monopolies (Faulhaber, 1975). The following inequation with the firm index in the superscript states the proposed relationship between the productions.

$$C(Y_1, Y_2) < C(Y_1^1, Y_2^1) + C(Y_1^2, Y_2^2) \ \ \forall \ \ Y_1 = Y_1^1 + Y_1^2 \ ; \ Y_2 = Y_2^1 + Y_2^2$$

The concept of subadditivity has the appeal that it is the origin of two important concepts frequently applied in strategic management. If the inequation refers to the production of homogeneous goods, then it presents the idea of scale effects, whereas with its polar case of the exclusive production of heterogeneous goods it represents the idea of economies of scope (Baumol et al., 1982; Faulhaber, 1975). Hence, both types of economies are based on the idea of a cost reduction induced by a change in the production output, whether this change is merely quantitative or also qualitative. Although both economies are formally specified as cost advantages stemming from a more efficient use of input factors, both economies can also be interpreted from a demand-side perspective relating to outputs rather than costs (Helfat & Eisenhardt, 2004). For example, if a firm uses excess resources to diversify, it generates greater revenues per unit of input. This is logically equivalent to the inequation for economies of scope, in which the firm achieves lower costs per unit of output by allocating the costs of a set of inputs to a greater number of output units. Hence, economies of scope can describe both demand-side revenue enhancements from greater output and cost reductions from shared inputs (Helfat & Eisenhardt, 2004).

4.3.2   Economies of Scope in Management Research

Economies of scope form the core element in a theory of multiproduct firms authored by Baumol et al. in 1982. This theory sets assumptions that also underlie the conclusions which follow directly from the production functions in the previous section. It is important to revisit these assumptions, as they stem from a neoclassical school of thought and cloud some factors that need to be taken into account when arguments are to be based on economies of scope. First, the concept assumes that no mobility barriers exist. Firms are assumed to be able to freely enter and exit industries, their decisions on whether to do so being solely made on price information. Second, there are no transaction costs for changing the scope. The integration of resources comes without any friction. In sum, these assumptions constitute a perfectly contestable market (Baumol et al., 1982). Though necessary for crafting a model that yields such fundamental insights, these conditions do not hold in reality.

Relaxing them will complement the notion of economies of scope with some restrictions that render it more valid for its practical application. Entry barriers in the form of direct costs created by the internalization of productions increase the amount of economies required to justify internalization. Furthermore, market alternatives may exist that also allow capture of the economies of scope (Helfat & Eisenhardt, 2004; Teece, 1980). A market-based alternative referred to by Williamson (1979a) as 'relational contracting' is a form of bilateral governance in which the autonomy of the parties is maintained. With these two relaxations of the initial assumptions at hand, i.e., the one of costs for the internalization and that of market alternatives for realization of the economies by means of cooperation, Teece (1980) concludes that economies of scope from joint production do not necessarily call for a joint production within one company. Rather, internalization within one company only proves efficient if the transaction costs for realization of the economies under separate ownership, such as costs from contracting and opportunism, are higher than the costs for the integration (Helfat & Eisenhardt, 2004). Hence, this economic justification of diversification depends on the costs associated with the different alternatives to exploit the economies of scope. From this perspective, strategic alliances or other forms of cooperation become substitutes for diversification. The question of by which of these means (i.e., diversification or cooperation) the economies of scope are to be captured translates into the question of which alternative promises the largest amount of economies of scope after costs.

To assess the costs associated with the distinct alternatives, some initial thoughts on potential sources of costs are necessary. As concerns the internalization of a new product–market combination the potential downsides depend on the vehicle of the diversification strategy. As discussed, firms can either develop the product–market combination internally or enter it directly by means of M&A. The former induces a longer time-to-market than does the acquisition of an existing market participant, and costs can arise in the sense of missed market opportunities during this lead-time. M&A transactions, however, may reduce the potential net amount of economies by involving other costs, such as overpayment and unrealized potentials during the post-merger integration phase (Sirower, 1997; Varaiya & Ferris, 1987). As far as the market-based alternative, relational contracting, is concerned, transaction costs move into focus. These relate back to transaction cost economics, which names the dimensions of transactions that constitute the costs of them. Hence, transaction frequency, uncertainty, and asset specificity (Williamson, 1975 & 1979a) come into play in decisions on whether market contracting can be the superior means of capturing economies of scope.

4.3.3   Potential Sources of Economies of Scope

In the sections above, the idea of economies of scope was introduced as an efficiency-measure from production economics in order to help to explain the existence of multibusiness firms and also such forms of cooperation as alliances. In addition, factors were identified that determine the costs of capturing these economies in dependence on whether the production is internalized or the economies are realized by means of cooperation. What have not been discussed so far are the actual sources of economies of scope. What reasons does economic theory state for the existence of scope economies? What practical counterparts does management research offer?

The existence of economies of scope is theoretically based on input factors that have the characteristic of not becoming entirely consumed in a distinct production process, so that they can be simultaneously deployed in several such processes (Panzar & Willig, 1975; Willig, 1979). Regarding the possibilities for such a simultaneous use, Baumol et al. (1982) differentiate two types of factors that display the required characteristic: public and quasi-public factors of production. Public factors have the characteristic that, once acquired, they can be freely deployed for the production of other outputs (Baumol et al., 1982). Hence, the production processes can still be executed individually. Quasi-public factors, in contrast, are factors that share the trait of indivisibility. This means they are physically not available in smaller units. In consequence, their acquisition often results in overcapacities that can be exploited for further purposes, such as the production of another product (Baumol et al., 1982; Willig, 1979).

Management scholars have come up with classifications and groupings of factors that build upon the two abstract categories mentioned above. Teece (1980) translates public factors into 'know-how'. More specifically, he refers to technological know-how, management know-how, organizational know-how and goodwill, for example that stemming from brand-induced customer loyalty. All these knowledge assets can be leveraged across multiple production processes without being consumed. However, this statement only holds true as long as the deployment of the know-how does not draw on other resources than information. As soon as managers or other resources become involved, their capacity constraints become relevant and the public factor know-how is turned into a scarce resource. With respect to quasi-public factors, Teece (1980) refers to "two types of indivisibilities", which he finds prevalent in some physical assets and distinct types of information. He counts machines and other long-term assets such as plants and equipment as some of these physical assets. With regard to the indivisibility associated with information, the constraint already mentioned applies: Know-how is generally attached to people, whose time is restricted, and forms the indivisible capacity, rendering many forms of know-how to quasi-public factors. Bailey and Friedlaender (1982) compiled an even more concrete list of reasons for which economies of scope could arise. These include: (1) The presence of a fixed factor of production (e.g., a distribution channel) that is not fully occupied by the production of one product; (2) economies of networking in industries where capacity slacks can be taken up by linking network parts via hubs (e.g., the airline industry); (3) reuse of inputs in more than one product (e.g., abstracts of articles can be reused in various outlets); and (4) sharing of intangible assets (e.g. research or other forms of business know-how).

4.4   Diversification and the Achievement of Economies of Scope in the Utility Industry

An industry in which diversification strategies have gained more and more importance within recent years is the utility industry, which is the main theme of this book. As the thoughts presented above offer the tools needed to investigate whether economies of scope account for the diversification trend within the utility industry, the general sections give way to an analysis of the industry. First, the directions for diversification are derived from the industry structure of energy utilities with reference to the opportunities provided by other related utility sectors. Concrete potentials for economies of scope are then identified, yielding valuable insights into the observable diversification patterns of the industry.

4.4.1   The Utility Industry and Potential Directions of Diversification

Utility industries are typically characterized by vertical production processes producing intermediate products at upstream stages, which are then transferred downstream, often based on a network infrastructure. Downstream, these intermediate products are then used with other input factors to generate a final output. The output frequently consists of one or more services to the final customer. For electricity markets, the vertical structure exhibits a four-tier structure. At the upper end of the production stream the generation of electricity takes place, which is then transmitted via high-voltage networks at the second level of value creation. The third level, further downstream, covers the distribution of electricity to the end-consumer. The fourth level, which is often combined with the third or excluded from the discussion, is that of commercial activities surrounding the retailing of energy (Crew & Kleindorfer, 1986; Wild, 2000). Though the traditional structure of the electric utility is that of a vertically integrated entity, competition could be introduced in most parts of the value chain, with a few exceptions. Technical constraints, efficiency considerations based on economies of scale, and the need for supply guarantees directly or indirectly require that the transmission and distribution functions remain as regulated activities occupied by (local) monopolies. Hence, during past years, governmental initiatives have been aimed at establishing competition at the generation and retail levels. The precondition for this is seen in the separation of the natural monopoly from the other activities (International Energy Agency, 2005): "For this reason, transmission and distribution networks must be operated independently of generation and retail" (International Energy Agency, 2005). Besides these new vertical organization options, utilities can choose along the horizontal dimension which additional services they want to provide to their customer base. The set of meaningful options is generally defined from the customer's perspective. Based on the assumption that customers like to satisfy a wide range of related demands via a single provider, other services that are required to maintain a household become the intuitive areas for diversification. Hence, gas, water and waste markets, which have also faced liberalization, are in the focus of electricity firms pursuing a multi-utility strategy (Schmidt, 2003). However, it is not the intuitive appeal of providing one-stop shopping for multiple services to the customers that drives such diversification, but the rigorous economic analysis of which service bundle a distinct utility company should optimally provide.

The diversification options offered by both dimensions build the frame for this question, which was already asked earlier in this chapter on a more general level. When adapted to the utility industry, the question of how companies can generate value by diversification translates into the question of how electricity-based utilities can generate value by vertical and horizontal diversification in response to the new market opportunities arising from the deregulation of the utility markets. The answer to the general question has been given above and also forms the basis for the answer to the industry-specific question: Economies of scope.

4.4.2   Sources of Economies of Scope within the Utility Industry

Economies of scope are induced by operations in different product markets and arise between or on the different vertical levels of the value chain that a company has internalized. Hence, both dimensions are of relevance. To structure the following analysis, the potential for the achievement of economies of scope will be explored in two steps. First, there will be a short discussion of the potentials relevant to the whole value chain. In the second, more comprehensive, step each stage of production will be individually analyzed to yield sources of economies existing specifically at each. For both steps, the following utility combinations are assumed to be relevant: energy and gas, energy and water, energy and waste disposal. Depending on the applicability for the respective production stage, the emphasis lies on one or more of these distinct combinations. The question of vertical diversification is disregarded, as a discussion focusing on economies of scope would be less constructive.

Sources of economies of scope, which are relevant for all stages of production, are more general than those that are relevant to the specific stages. They stem from market power and know-how. In an unbundled business model, each stage offers potentials arising from increased bargaining power if there are either common suppliers or common customers for the services provided. Shepard (1997) offers a detailed discussion on the specific means by which utilities can benefit from their market power. Similar benefits arise from know-how. Knowledge about suppliers, customers and technical knowledge may provide economies for multi-utilities if they can be shared between the different lines of business.

At production level, the utility combination of energy and gas in particular promises large economies of scope (Fraquelli et al., 2004). If the utility firm possesses a gas-fired power plant, the costs of the joint production of electricity and gas for the end-customer can be reduced by exploiting differences in the price fluctuations of gas and electricity. The operator of the gas-fired plant can benefit from rising gas prices by not using his stocked gas to produce electricity but selling it directly to his gas customers. To cover his customers' electricity demand he can then have recourse to the electricity market. Economically, such a plant provides the operator with a real option, allowing him to switch between different business models and take advantage of the so-called spark spread. Thus, this opportunity is named the spark spread option (Hsu & Quan, 1998). At the level of transmission and distribution, economies of scope arise from coordination of the infrastructural construction works that are necessary for the provision of the different services. Specifically pipeline-based services, such as gas and water, should be established in a joint effort in new areas. However, these economies of scope can be realized with no need for internalization of the services within one company. Market collaboration models between different providers are also able to realize such economies. Often, governmental institutions assist the coordination between the providers, as their interests are affected by the construction works (Thomas, 2006). At retail level a larger potential for economies of scope arises. Each contact with the costumer can be used to promote not only one service but several. Knowledge about the customer gained from one service business can be exploited in the others. Cross-selling initiatives, such as distinct pricing for service bundles, could increase overall sales and reduce the joint costs of production. In this sense, the customer bases of existing utility firms may prove to be a particularly valuable asset for other utility firms in their own growth strategies. This type of economy of scope, however, is reserved for diversification strategies that are implemented by means of acquisitions.

4.5   Conclusion

The objective of this book chapter is to explore the role of economies of scope within diversification strategies of firms on a general and on an industry-specific level. As such, it places the concept of diversification in the overall context of management and links it by production economics to the concept of economies of scope. As the concept of economies of scope stems from neoclassical economics, it is then complemented with some constraints that originate from management research. In this way, an understanding of all factors necessary for basing arguments on economies of scope is established. These factors include the different means by which the economies can be captured, the drivers of the costs that are associated with the different means, and the potential sources of economies of scope. Having established the relevant set of constructs and the relationships between them in a way that is of practical relevance, the chapter applies the ideas presented specifically to the utility industry.

The theoretical discussion in the chapter underlines the importance of economies of scope for diversification strategies. Yet it also suggests, particularly in the face of market imperfections, that there are alternatives to diversification. The potential sources of economies of scope are also crying out to be scrutinized. It has been shown that it is advisable to suspect public factors of actually being quasi-public factors. The application of these concepts to the utility industry provides further insights: First, the electricity industry's value chain generally offers a wide set of choices to define strategic positions. Furthermore, the relatedness to other utility services, such as gas, water, and waste disposal, means there are various sources of economies of scope that support the idea of the multi-utility business model. Overall, the chapter therewith underlines the relevance of economies of scope for diversification in general and for the utility industry in particular.

References

Andrews, K. R. 1971. The concept of corporate strategy. Homewood, Ill.: Dow Jones-Irwin.

Ansoff, I. 1957. Strategies for diversification. Harvard Business Review, 35: 113-124.

Bain, J. S. 1968. Industrial organization. New York: Wiley.

Bailey, E. E. & Friedlaender, A. F. 1982. Market structure and multiproduct industries. Journal of Economic Literature, 20: 1024-1048.

Barney, J. B. & Hesterly, W. S. 2006. Strategic management and competitive advantage: concepts and cases. Upper Saddle River, NJ: Pearson/Prentice Hall.

Baumol, W. J., Panzar, J. C., & Willig, R. D. 1982. Contestable markets and the theory of industry structure. New York: Harcourt Brace Jovanovich.

Bausch, A., Fritz, T., Werthschulte, S., Schumacher, T., Holst, A. & Schiegg, T. 2007. Wettbewerbsmarkt Energie – Managementkompetenzen werden Schlüsselfaktor für Erfolg. EW – Das Magazin für die Energiewirtschaft, 13-14: 34-39.

Bozem, K. 2004. Unbundling – Gesetzlicher Zwang oder Chance? In J. Grewe, D. Flandrich & N. Ellwanger (Eds.), Energiewirtschaft im Wandel: 101-110. Münster: Agenda Verlag.

Chatterjee, S. 1986. Types of synergy and economic value: the impact of acquisitions on merging and rival firms. Strategic Management Journal, 7: 119-139.

Chatterjee, S. 2007. Why is synergy so difficult in mergers of related businesses? Strategy and Leadership, 35: 46-52.

Collis, D., Young, D. & Goold, M. 2007. The size, structure, and performance of corporate headquarters. Strategic Management Journal, 28: 383-405.

Collis, D. J. & Montgomery, C. A. 1998. Creating corporate advantage: the key is learning how to differentiate truly great corporate strategies from those that are merely adequate. Harvard Business Review, 76: 70-83.

Crew, M. A. & Kleindorfer, P. R. 1986. The economics of public utility regulation. Cambridge, Mass.: MIT Press.

Datta, D. K., Rajagopalan, N. & Rasheed, A. M. A. 1991. Diversification and performance: critical review and future directions. Journal of Management Studies, 28: 529-558.

Faulhaber, G. R. 1975. Cross-subsidization: pricing in public enterprises. The American Economic Review, 65: 966-977.

Fraquelli, G., Piacenza, M. & Vannoni, D. 2004. Scope and scale economies in multi-utilities: evidence from gas, water and electricity combinations. Applied Economics, 36: 2045-2057.

Ghoshal, S. & Nohria, N. 1989. Internal differentiation within multinational corporations. Boston, Mass.: Division of Research, Harvard Business School.

Goold, M. G. & Luchs, K. 1993. Why diversify? Four decades of management thinking. Academy of Management Executive, 7: 7-25.

Goold, M. G., Campbell, A. & Alexander, M. 1994. How corporate parents add value to the stand-alone performance of their businesses. Business Strategy Review, 5: 33-55.

Hamermesh, R. G. & Roderick, E. W. 1984. Manage beyond portfolio analysis. Harvard Business Review, 62: 103-109.

Helfat, C. E. & Eisenhardt, K. M. 2004. Inter-temporal economies of scope, organizational modularity, and the dynamics of diversification. Strategic Management Journal, 25: 1217-1232.

Hitt, M. A., Ireland, R. D. & Hoskisson, R. E. 2003. Strategic management: competitiveness and globalization (5th ed.). Mason, Ohio: Thomson.

Hsu, M. C. & Quan, N. T. 1998. Spark spread options: linking spot and futures markets for gas and electricity. Public Utilities Fortnightly, 136: 26-30.

International Energy Agency (IEA). 2005. Lessons from liberalized electricity markets. Paris: OECD/IEA.

Jacquemin, A. P. & Berry, C. H. 1979. Entropy measure of diversification and corporate growth. The Journal of Industrial Economics, 27: 359-369.

Kanter, R. M. 1998. Seeking and achieving synergies. In A. Campbell & K. Luchs (Eds.), Strategic Synergy (2nd ed.): 146-170. London: International Thomson Business Press.

King, D. R., Dalton, D. R. & Daily, C. M. 2004. Meta-analysis of post-acquisition performance: indications of unidentified moderators. Strategic Management Journal, 25: 187-200.

Leland, H. E. 2007. Financial synergies and the optimal scope of the firm: implications for mergers, spinoffs, and structured finance. The Journal of Finance, 62: 765-807.

Lubatkin, M. & Chatterjee, S. 1994. Extending modern portfolio theory into the domain of corporate diversification: does it apply? Academy of Management Journal, 37: 109-136.

Markides, C. C. 1995. Diversification, restructuring and economic performance. Strategic Management Journal, 16: 101-118.

Markides, C. C. & Williamson, P. J. 1996. Corporate diversification and organizational structure: a resource-based view. The Academy of Management Journal, 39: 340-367.

Michel, A. & Shaked, I. 1984. Does business diversification affect performance? Financial Management, 13: 18-25.

Miller, D. J. 2006. Technological diversity, related diversification, and firm performance. Strategic Management Journal, 27: 601-619.

Montgomery, C. A. & Wernerfelt, B. 1988. Diversification, ricardian rents and Tobin's q. Rand Journal of Economics, 19: 623-632.

Müller-Stewens, G. & Lechner, C. 2005. Strategisches Management: Wie strategische Initiativen zum Wandel führen (3rd ed.). Stuttgart: Schäffer-Poeschel.

Müller-Stewens, G. & Brauer, M. 2009. Corporate Management im diversifizierten Unternehmen. In G. Müller-Stewens & M. Brauer (Eds.), Corporate Management (forthcoming).

Nelson, R. R. 1972. Issues and suggestions for the study of industrial organization in a regime of rapid technical change. In V. R. Fuchs (Ed.), Policy Issues and Research Opportunities in Industrial Organization: 34-58. New York: National Bureau of Economic Research.

Panzar, J. & Willig, R. 1975. Economies of scale and economies of scope in multi-output production. Unpublished Bell Laboratories Economic Discussion Paper (33).

Panzar, J. & Willig, R. 1981. Economies of scope. American Economic Review, 71: 268-272.

Peters, T. J. & Waterman, R. H. 1982. In search for excellence. New York: Free Press.

Porter, M. E. 1987. From competitive advantage to corporate strategy. Harvard Business Review, 65: 43-59.

Prahalad, C. K. & Bettis, R. A. 1986. The dominant logic: a new link-age between diversity and performance. Strategic Management Journal, 7: 485-501.

Prahalad, C. K. & Hamel, G. 1990. The core competence of the corporation. Harvard Business Review, 68: 79-91.

Prahalad, C. K. & Bettis, R. A. 1995. The dominant logic. A new linkage between diversity and performance. Strategic Management Journal, 7: 485-501.

PricewaterhouseCoopers (PWC). 2007. Power deals – 2007 annual review. PricewaterhouseCoopers.

Ramanujam, V. & Varadarajan, P. 1989. Research on corporate diversification: a synthesis. Strategic Management Journal, 10: 523-551.

Rumelt, R. P. 1974. Strategy, structure, and economic performance. Cambridge: Harvard University Press.

Schmidt, C. 2003. Multi-Utility – Erfolgsrezept für Energieversorger? EW – Das Magazin für die Energiewirtschaft, 102: 58-63.

Shepard, W. G. 1997. Market power in the electric utility industry: an overview. 12. National Council on Competition in the Electric Industry.

Sirower, M. L. 1997. The synergy trap: how companies lose the acquisition game. New York: Free Press.

St. John, C. H. & Harrison, J. S. 1999. Manufacturing-based relatedness, synergy, and coordination. Strategic Management Journal, 20: 129-145.

Teece, D. J. 1980. Economies of scope and the scope of the enterprise. Journal of Economic Behavior and Organization, 1: 223-247.

Thomas, T. W. 2006. Unternehmenszusammenschlüsse in der Energiewirtschaft: Empirische Analyse der Übernahmewelle der 1990er Jahre in Nordamerika und Europa. Wiesbaden: Deutscher Universitätsverlag.

Varaiya, N. & Ferris, K. 1987. Overpaying in corporate takeover: the winner's curse. Financial Analysts Journal, 43: 64-70.

Wild, J. 2000. Deregulierung und Regulierung der Elektrizitätsverteilung – Eine mikroökonomische Analyse mit empirischer Anwendung für die Schweiz. Zürich: Hochschulverlag an der ETH.

Williamson, O. E. 1975. Markets and hierarchies, analysis and antitrust implications: a study in the economics of internal organization. New York: Free Press.

Williamson, O. E. 1979a. Transactions-cost economics: the governance of contractual relations. Journal of Law and Economics, 22: 233-263.

Williamson, O. E. 1979b. Assessing vertical market restrictions: anti-trust ramifications of the transaction cost approach. University of Pennsylvania Law Review, 127: 953-993.

Willig, R. 1979. Multiproduct technology and market structure. The American Economic Review, 69: 346-351.

Wrigley, L. 1970. Divisional autonomy and diversification. Cambridge: Harvard University.

5 Innovation and Technology Management

Jürgen Hambrecht[1]

Abstract

Innovation is an essential driver for profitable growth and the key to our future. It enables us to meet future challenges and ensure sustainable development. In order to turn new ideas into market success, innovation management needs to balance two decisive factors: room for creativity on the one hand, and clearly structured processes on the other. Selecting the right key performance indicators is a crucial basis for evaluating performance achievement. As innovation issues become more complex, companies are becoming more receptive to open innovation processes and cooperating with academia as well as with customers. To enhance their innovative strength, companies need to establish a culture of innovation within their organizations. They also need to contribute to an innovation-friendly climate in society.

Keywords: innovation, market conditions, sustainability

---

[1] Dr. Jürgen Hambrecht is Chairman of the Board of Executive Directors of BASF SE, Germany.

A. Bausch and B. Schwenker (eds.), *Handbook Utility Management,*
DOI: 10.1007/978-3-540-79349-6_5, © Springer-Verlag Berlin Heidelberg 2009

5.1   Innovation – The Key to our Future

5.1.1   Pioneers of Modern Life

"Everything that can be invented has been invented", an official at the US Patent Office, Charles H. Duell, concluded in 1899. From today's perspective, this is a bizarre conclusion. How could people on the cusp of the twentieth century have been so blind to future innovation, with an era of unprecedented technological development just around the corner? And yet, the situation that obtained more than 100 years ago is not all that different from that we have today. Sustained decade-long industrialization had already revolutionized people's everyday lives. Processes foreshadowing major social and political changes had been set in motion. Times of change are times of great uncertainty. Some people have a tendency to cling fast to past achievements and close their eyes to future opportunity. Regrettably, this response pattern is as evident today as it was then.

Fortunately, now as then, we have enough pioneers in science and industry whose passion and will for research continues unabated. Pioneering thinking has brought us fertilizers and plastics, jet airplanes and satellites, television and computers, and countless other innovations, large and small. All these have made our modern lifestyle possible, and are an integral part of contemporary life.

In the same way, today's inventions and improvements will determine how future generations live. Our children's and their children's opportunity to live healthy and fulfilled lives depends on the innovations we initiate today.

5.1.2   Big Questions and Megatrends

Future trends looming ahead pose big questions and present difficult challenges. Innovation is the only answer.

What will the megatrends of the future be? The global population is set to rise to more than 9 billion (United Nations, 2007) by the middle of the century. Highly developed countries will see their populations aging. Urbanization is advancing rapidly, and a growing number of megacities have a total population in the range of tens of millions – larger than many of today's states. Rapid economic growth in newly industrializing countries is mirrored by soaring consumption of energy and resources. Advancing globalization and international division of labor largely determine the lifestyle of billions of people, with communications, mobility, consumer behavior, and work and leisure patterns undergoing massive change.

All these developments are associated with both opportunities and risks. We must succeed in putting science and technology to work in maximizing these opportunities and minimizing the risks.

One example is the issue of nutrition for a growing world population. The available arable farmland per capita was 4,300 m² in 1969. By the year 2030, less than half that amount of land will be available: 1,800 m² per person. The problem is compounded by the fact that an increasing global oil requirement is fueling demand for plant-based feedstocks. Substitution of just 10% of the oil requirement with renewable resources from plants required 320 million hectares of arable land in 2005. By 2030, that figure will have risen to 450 million hectares – 30% of what is available on this planet (OECD/FAO, 2007; BASF estimates). Given the increasing shortage of productive land, an innovation drive in agriculture is the only way forward. No other option will allow intensive farming while causing no harm to people or the environment.

Another example is the dramatic increase in energy consumption. Experts estimate that primary energy consumption will rise by more than 50% by 2030 if we continue on our current course. More efficient utilization of energy alone would limit the rise to 16% (IEA 2007; BASF calculations), with a related reduction in climate-damaging greenhouse gas emissions. Again, technological innovations will be crucial in balancing economic growth and rising quality of life with climate protection.

5.1.3   Innovations for a Future Worth Living In

The megatrends of the coming decades leave no doubt: We need innovations to produce a future worth living in for ourselves and coming generations. Growth and prosperity must not be at the expense of people and the environment. If they are, economic success will be undermined by ecological and social problems.

Our aim is to create a better quality of life for a growing population on a sustained basis. This aspiration applies especially when the challenges facing newly industrializing and developing countries are tackled, which will involve combating hunger and disease, creating humane living and working conditions, providing access to information and education, and boosting personal and social self-determination. To meet these aims, we need sustainable innovative solutions that foster the harmony of economic growth, intact environment, and a well-functioning society.

This is why it is so important to assess the sustainability value of a product, method or business model early in the development process. Businesses are well advised to factor sustainability into their innovation processes on a systematic basis. Dedicated tools (e.g., Eco-efficiency Analysis[2]) are available for early assessment of an innovation's likely economic benefit versus its potential ecological or social implications.

---

[2] For more about the BASF tools Eco-efficiency Analysis and SEEbalance®, see Section 5.3.10.

5.2   Innovation – an Essential Driver for Profitable Growth

5.2.1   The Changing Face of Industry

Every business enterprise aspires to long-term success in the form of sustained profitable growth and steady accumulation of economic value added. Globalization of markets and increasing international division of labor have revolutionized competition and growth scenarios in all industries. The chemical industry is a case in point, as a cross-sectional industry whose products and solutions are essential in just about every other branch of industry. Conversely, changes in other markets – automotive, textiles, IT – have an immediate impact on the chemical industry.

When client industries migrated to lower-cost production sites and new sales markets, the chemical industry followed in order to be able to serve its customers competitively in all major markets. Many chemical companies chose to specialize in narrowly defined areas, such as agrochemicals, pharmaceuticals, or paper and textile chemicals, in response to mounting pressure on margins and tougher competition. New competitors with access to low-cost resources and labor entered the arena. The advent of new technologies, such as biotechnology and nanotechnology, is revolutionizing the chemistry business.

Chemistry was and is the innovation driver par excellence in virtually all industries, a motor whose driving force must adapt continuously to keep pace with rapidly changing markets. Customers' increasing need for innovative solutions offers the chemical industry unique opportunities for profitable growth. The question is, how can a company make the most of these opportunities?

5.2.2   From Invention to Innovation

Every innovation begins in the mind. The passage from idea to innovation may be a long one. What makes an invention an innovation? It all depends on how the idea is put into practice and transformed into market success.

A famous example is the mp3 or digital decoding technology. Though invented in the 1980s by the Fraunhofer Institute in Germany, it took the computer company Apple to turn it into an innovation by combining digital decoding and streaming technologies with content licensing. The iPod's success was not due to technology alone, but also to usability and design – and, even more, to a clever marketing strategy.

Turning an invention into an innovation can be a tedious and costly process involving quite a number of failure risks. Technology push, or providing new technologies and creating a market demand, is no longer the only way to go. Market pull, that is, providing the technological answer to existing or, even better, future demands, has become an even more powerful innovation engine. The shift from technology push to market pull is due to a constantly changing and accelerating competitive environment.

Globalized, innovation-driven markets are highly dynamic. Speed and flexibility are essential if companies are to stay ahead. This means that companies must adapt or even reinvent their innovation processes in order to reduce time to market. They do this by building global research and development networks, partnerships between research institutes and industry, and/or close cooperation with customers during the development process, or by establishing open innovation processes.

In other words: Modern times call for modern innovation management. This is a complex topic, and every company has its own very specific requirements and approaches, which it would be impossible to address exhaustively in this paper. The selected real-life examples that follow show the innovation management concepts developed by BASF – The Chemical Company.

5.3   Elements of Innovation Management

5.3.1   Innovation as an Integral Part of a Company's Strategy

Innovation plays a crucial role for companies in an economic environment where competitive advantages cannot be gained by low cost alone, but rather by quality and superior technology. Thus, innovation is a vital element of the strategy in reaching the overall target of creating value and growing profitably. To ensure maximum return from innovation, a focused search for innovation opportunities is essential. Selecting the most promising market segments and dedicating resources to specific innovation projects are among the most important factors in innovation success.

The chemical industry contributes to almost everything that is part of contemporary daily living, but only 15% of its output is sold to end-consumers in products such as colorants or cosmetics. The bulk of chemical products are sold to and processed by downstream manufacturers in various industries to serve specific purposes. Typical examples are the construction business and the automobile industry. For chemical companies, the challenge lies in obtaining the relevant information on the end-user market. Meeting this challenge involves intensive contact with customers and customers' customers along the entire value chain.

To select the market segments with the highest innovation potential (i.e., focus areas), intensified evaluation of the inherent opportunities and risks is first necessary. Criteria for selecting market segments include:

- Innovation potential;
- Relevance of chemicals, especially regarding innovations;
- Market growth;
- Access to appropriate customers.

Portfolio management in the defined focus areas is an ongoing process. Promising new market segments may be added if they pass the screening process, while others are discarded if potentials do not materialize.

Partnerships are potential win-win situations. The customer benefits from an innovative partner, who provides a technical or commercial advantage by translating customer needs into chemistry. The product provider learns more about the focus market and profits from the customer's established market position.

5.3.2   Growth Clusters

BASF sees innovation as an essential driver of profitable growth. Accordingly, innovation driven by research and development (R&D) is an integral part of BASF's growth strategy. This approach is considerably strengthened by focusing on five growth clusters earmarked for special development and allocation of additional financial and human resources: energy management, nanotechnology, plant biotechnology, change of raw material(s), and white (industrial) biotechnology. These growth clusters were identified by strategic analysis of BASF's growth opportunities. BASF's existing R&D strength – which will be enhanced still further – makes the company ideally equipped for industrial development of the clusters into key drivers of organic corporate growth. The clusters will further reinforce BASF's future technological competence by identifying new scientific findings that are relevant to the company's business (see Figure 5.1).

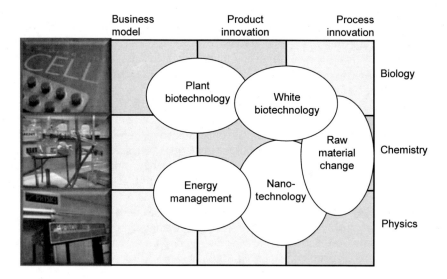

Figure 5.1: Technology trends that drive innovation

Growth cluster R&D will be conducted partly by BASF's technology platforms and operating divisions and partly in an open innovation environment with external partners.

5.3.3   Innovation Processes: PhaseGate™

The innovation pathway from an idea to a new product or solution is a process involving many selection stages. Typically, fewer than 1% of ideas result in a successful new product launch – a fact that makes R&D a high-risk investment.

To separate the wheat from the chaff, companies need a structured process based on defined stages and gates to manage their innovation projects. This principle, first introduced by Robert Cooper (Cooper et al., 2002), is established best practice in industry. BASF's PhaseGate™ process has five phases and six gates (see Figure 5.2).

The first phase, the generating and scanning of new ideas or opportunity fields, is an open and informal process. Its main focus is on obtaining a large number of top quality ideas. To be successful in this phase, companies need a well-established innovation culture with high awareness and commitment to innovation at all levels (marketing, sales, R&D, production, logistics, etc.). Important features of this early phase include the integration of external know-how (open innovation), tracking and evaluation of ideas with feedback to the idea generator, and the guidance provided by a well-communicated innovation strategy.

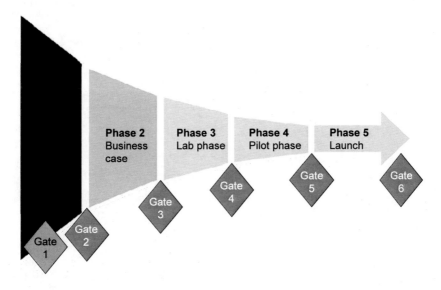

Figure 5.2: BASF's PhaseGate™ process

As soon as an idea has passed gate 2 – a decision to be taken by the gatekeeper responsible – a business case is set up, which will then result in an economic project evaluation.

Phases 3-5 (lab phase, pilot phase, launch) involve focused project work with clear stop/go criteria at the gates and transparent decision making.

One important criterion is that clear roles and responsibilities are assigned throughout the innovation process. The gatekeeper role is crucial. The gatekeeper is responsible for setting both clear targets and transparent and flexible decision criteria, and s/he acts as a coach or mentor for the project team. Interaction between the project manager and the gatekeeper is one of the key success factors for innovation projects.

5.3.4   Success Criteria: Key Performance Indicators

Measuring innovation means measuring success. However, there is little agreement on what the 'right' indicators for success are. Surveys indicate that quite a number of executives are not satisfied with measurement practice in their companies. The management literature offers a wide choice of metrics in the form of key performance indicators (KPIs). The two basic KPI categories are input and output measures, with further subdivision into different perspectives.

At this point we shall review a number of innovation-related KPIs (see Table 5.1), hoping the reader will find this useful as a basis for deciding which KPIs might best fit into their company's controlling (which is where they belong). It is important to remember that KPIs have two roles: to describe the current state of affairs and to exert an influence on the organization and its employees. In this respect, metrics are linked to value-based management.

Table 5.1: Innovation-related KPIs

	Finance	**Process**	**Employees**	**Market**
Input	• R&D expenditures and R&D intensity • Capital expenditures		• Employees in R&D • Number of ideas generated or realized	
Output	• NPV and ECV • Sales of new products, absolute and relative to R&D input • Return on investment • Cost savings	• Time to market (actual vs planned) • Number of successful projects • Number of projects stopped • Keeping milestones	• Idea transfer: from R&D; from customers to internal R&D • Employee satisfaction • Rewarding and tolerance of mistakes	• Growth of market share • Customer satisfaction • Sustainability (index) • Share of voice, brand image • Market penetration

There are a number of factors to be considered in selecting KPIs. First of all, the indicators should be relevant to the particular business unit or company. Accuracy, transparency, and care, should go into the generation of KPIs. To be successful, they need to be accepted and taken seriously by everyone involved in the process and should come with practical consequences. Obviously, to create value, the scorecard must be in line with the company's innovation strategy.

A typical evaluation tool used for existing businesses is the earning multiple. But how do you evaluate the future revenues and earnings of an innovation?

5.3.5   Project Evaluation

BASF's R&D evaluation procedure is aligned with the PhaseGate™ process described above. The decision tree analysis system used by BASF predicts the probability of an idea becoming a successful innovation. The probability and value of success are compared with the probability and value of failure.

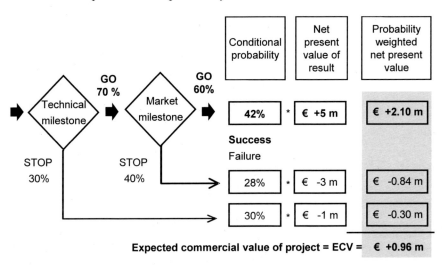

Figure 5.3: Decision tree analysis, potentially successful project

Figure 5.3 demonstrates the decision tree analysis for a R&D project. Here, the probability of solving all technical problems is put at 70% and the probability of a successful market launch is 60%. Success generates a net present value (NPV) of € 5 million; failure results in the spending of part or all of the R&D budget. The expected commercial value (ECV) is the total sum of the values weighted by their probability for all branches of the decision tree. A good project results in a positive ECV. The ECV of a R&D project rises if the project leader is able to address major risks at an earlier rather than a later stage. To get the best results from this evaluation approach, both the business plan and the probability of success need to undergo critical assessment by marketing and technology experts.

5.3.6   Open Innovation Processes

A common approach in R&D is to generate innovations with the input of internal departments and on the basis of a precise study of market requirements and customers' needs. In this 'closed model', a company's innovation success depends on the quality of market knowledge and on the ability to generate solutions that are appropriate to the problems identified.

Many companies use some elements of open innovation to increase the probability of success. Missing technologies and market intelligence can be sourced in. In the same manner, technologies that cannot be used internally can be licensed to competitors.

As companies increase their customer focus, they are tending to involve customers more actively in all phases of the innovation process, gathering and systematically exploiting their customers' knowledge along the way. Customers themselves are triggering innovation processes and contributing actively to the design of products and to the development of production processes. Examples are joint workshops, product/service business models, development alliances, and joint laboratories. The last is described in the next section, describing how scientists in the companies concerned are collaborating to generate new solutions and innovative products.

Open innovation processes need clearly defined agreements, especially with respect to intellectual property rights (IPR). Agreement from all the partners on sharing and utilizing IPRs is an absolute prerequisite for a collaboration that is open and trustful, and thus successful. Differences in the patent law between the US and most other states in the world are a major hurdle hampering open collaboration.

5.3.7   Managing Complex, Multi-level Innovation Processes

Chemical products may be only a small, though important, part of a complex, multistage innovation and value chain in the development of system solutions.

The 'organic photovoltaics' example illustrates a multistage innovation project. Projects of this kind present a particular challenge to the material developer at the start of the innovation chain. To be able to develop marketable products, the material developer must have a very precise knowledge of market requirements at a very early stage. This means either addressing the whole of the complex innovation and value chain single-handed, or finding a suitable technology partner early in the process. BASF chose the second option – a development alliance with such technology partners as Bosch, Heliatek, Philips, and Osram – for its activities in the fields of organic photovoltaics and organic light-emitting diodes (OLEDs).

The company can test the quality of its materials only on the basis of their device performance, i.e., in the photovoltaic cell or photovoltaic module. In many cases, material performance and device performance are inseparably linked. Component and module know-how is also essentially important to the technology partner. The obvious approach was to advance the development of materials and components in a joint lab in areas where interests overlapped.

This realization resulted in the setting up of the Joint Innovation Lab for Organic Electronics on the BASF complex in Ludwigshafen. Combining BASF material expertise with the partners' device and manufacturing expertise promises more effective and efficient development and also a shorter time to market. The expertise of partners in academia is recruited to ensure that the work done at the lab benefits from the latest academic findings.

Currently, twenty BASF employees are working in the lab, along with up to six alliance partners from industry and academia.

5.3.8   Venture Capital

Breakthrough innovations often come from young start-up companies. Typically, the entrepreneurial environment and specialized expertise of their founders enables start-ups to be very swift and productive in turning inventions into innovations. Successful young companies are particularly well represented in such areas as biotechnology and the software industry, which do not call for major asset investments up front.

Big business often participates in the innovation process of young start-ups by investing venture capital. 'Corporate venture capital' (CVC) means investments by a nonfinancial company with a strategic interest.

For CVC to succeed, it is important for a big corporation to weigh up the expectations of financial return against the strategic benefit to the company. Both aspects are essential to the corporate venture capital arm of a company.

To maintain the young start-up's independence and entrepreneurial spirit, the CVC investor's share should be no more than about 30%.

Big enterprises can support young start-ups in other ways than the strictly financial, such as by giving them access to a global network of market players and by sharing experience on similar projects. Other ways might be supplying urgently needed raw materials or providing legal or IP support.

The investor seeks a favorable, risk-adequate return on investment. Further benefits are:

- Knowledge of emerging markets and technologies;
- Benefits accruing from joint developments;
- Contacts with experts who can act as consultants;
- Options for further acquisition.

CVC is the ideal way to gather knowledge as a basis for future strategic decisions, especially if a big corporation wants to enter a unknown field. It is not uncommon for CVC investment to be the first step into a new market. If it succeeds, acquisition of the company may follow. If it does not, it is essential to have other options in place so that it is possible to exit the company with a risk-adequate return on investment.

Provided the do's and don'ts of CVC are addressed, this is a powerful tool for bringing innovation into a company. In a global economy with rapidly changing markets and emerging technologies, such as bio-, nano- and clean technology, a company simply has to include external entrepreneurs and young start-ups in its innovation strategy in addition to counting on the in-house R&D base.

5.3.9   Intellectual Property Rights

For their R&D to pay off, companies rely on protection of their IPRs. In the wake of globalization, industrial property rights (especially patents) are more important now than ever. Certain new players in global markets have been implicated time and again in massive IPR violations. The damage done to foreign investors has been particularly severe in some Asian countries.

Happily, major improvements are now in evidence. China, for instance, which joined the WTO in 2001, has created an extensive industrial property rights system in less than 25 years. This system provides for protection of registered rights, thus creating an attractive starting point for R&D. The Chinese patents office received more filings in 2005 than its European counterpart, with 50% of registrations coming from Chinese applicants.

This development shows that the creation of suitable legal systems helps to advance a country's research base. The growing research output in such countries gives them an ever larger self-interest in implementing applicable laws to protect IPRs. Overall, effective protection of IPRs creates significant incentives both nationally and internationally to invest in R&D in countries where such protection is in place (Zhang, 2005).

5.3.10   Ensuring Sustainability

Let us now come back once more to another very important issue: sustainable development. The demand for sustainable products and solutions is growing rapidly worldwide and has become a powerful driver for innovation and profitable growth.

Eco-efficiency analysis is a strategic tool developed by BASF for quantifying the sustainability of products and processes. It provides an assessment of the total costs and environmental impact that a product or process creates over its complete life cycle, starting with raw material extraction and continuing through to post-use disposal or recycling. Eco-efficiency analysis includes an in-depth comparison of the pros and cons of various alternative products, all of which meet the same need. It also includes an exploration of potential future scenarios to take account of potential future developments and assess imponderables. BASF experts have performed approximately 300 eco-efficiency analyses to date, both for BASF and for the company's customers. Their know-how has also been made available for studies outside BASF. The many examples include mineral water packaging, insulation materials, laminate flooring, and engineering plastics.

BASF added social factors to its eco-efficiency analysis (Schmidt et al., 2005) in a cooperation involving experts from Karlsruhe University, the Öko-Institut in Freiburg and Jena University. The intention was to enable the quantification of performance in all three aspects of sustainability – economic, ecological, and social – with a single tool. Called SEEBALANCE®, the new tool will be used at BASF to improve the company's product portfolio performance and manufacturing processes, and as an aid in marketing sustainable products. SEEBALANCE®

assesses the total cost, social impact, and environmental impact of a product or process throughout its life cycle.

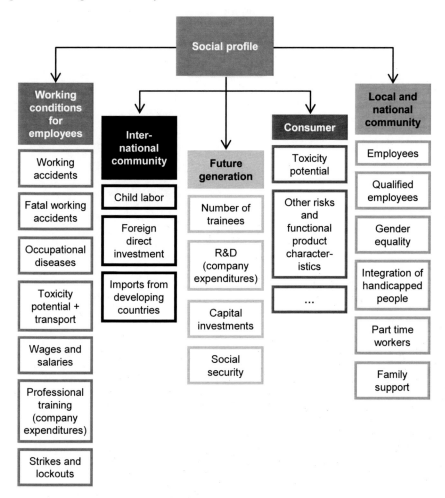

Figure 5.4: Categories of societal impacts (Kölsch et al., 2008)

The first step is to calculate the ecological data as set forth in the Life Cycle Assessment (LCA) regulations contained in ISO 14040 to 14043. The data are subsequently summarized into six main impact categories: consumption of raw materials, energy consumption, emissions to the air, water, and soil (wastes), toxicity potential of substances employed and produced, risk potential of misuse, and land use. These parameters are weighted and combined to give an overall impact score for the environmental performance of a product or process. The economic aspects of the alternative products or processes are represented in an overall cost calculation.

Social impacts are grouped into five stakeholder categories: employees, international community, future generations, consumers, and local and national community (see Figure 5.4). Measurable indicators are used for each of these stakeholder categories. Possible indicators for these categories are number of employees, occupational accidents occurring during production, and risks involved in the use of the product by the end-consumer. Social indicators are summarized in a social impact score in the same way as their environmental counterparts (Kölsch et al., 2008; BASF, 2008). The results are shown in a three-dimensional SEECube® (see Figure 5.5).

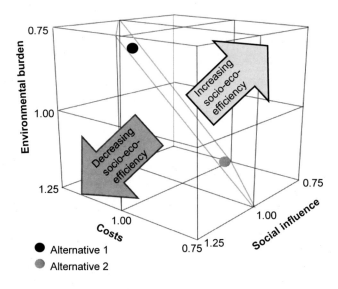

Figure 5.5: SEECube® (Schmidt, 2007)

5.3.11   Integrating Customers into the Innovation Process

Innovations are important in today's automotive industry, as a means of increasing market share, acquiring new customers, and justifying higher prices on the basis of unique value propositions. Marketing strategies build upon design, engine performance, environment and safety, and improved utility features.

Coatings, for example, have a very special role to play. A car's paint job contributes significantly both to preserving value (anticorrosion) and to product differentiation and emotional impact (color and effect). Premium car brands offer specially designed or customized paint jobs in addition to a range of standard presentations.

Car paint is supplied as a semi-finished product which achieves its final form and quality after processing in the coating plants of the automotive industry. The desired outcome is achieved only if the coating and the process are ideally matched. A new effect can be developed all the more successfully and speedily if there is close cooperation between the paint developer and the automotive customer's head of processing. The paint developer is the expert who knows most about the processing conditions for the new paint, and the head of the processing plant is the expert for the processing equipment's features and limitations. BASF has entered into strategic partnerships with automotive industry customers for optimum effect in terms of a rapid innovation process.

Partnerships of this kind allow critical issues (process modification, for example) to be addressed and resolved rapidly. Another advantage is that business-case issues can be answered in depth by the customer early on, culminating in a win-win situation at both ends of the strategic development partnership.

Close customer-supplier relationships have produced process innovations (in paint processing, for instance) as well as resulting in the development of new paints, effects, and performance profiles. New business models, such as payment per complete paint job rather than per kilogram of paint, result in cost and production benefits for both partners.

5.4   Innovation – a Cultural Issue

Preserving and strengthening a company's innovative power is one of the most important tasks of management. A company can survive and remain competitive in the long term only if it embraces change and does things differently on an ongoing basis, be that with respect to products, technologies, manufacturing processes, or business models.

Innovative strength stands and falls with the ability and motivation of the workforce to bring new ideas to the company and develop them successfully. This is why innovation management is very much more than the sum of the tools used to control individual processes. Whether a spirit of innovation is alive and well in a company depends on the leadership and corporate culture as a whole.

Innovativeness is also a matter of society's attitudes. Even the most innovative of companies can only be as innovative as the society in which it does business allows it to be. Public debate all too often tends to favor those who devote all their efforts to exposing the risks of innovative developments whilst blocking out their opportunities. Of course we have to identify and minimize potential risks in order to prevent damage to human health and the environment. This precautionary principle (EC, 2000) is a paramount concern of the chemical research community, and of industry in particular. Nevertheless, it would be nonsense to demand one hundred percent exclusion of even the remotest risk, for this is a basic scientific impossibility. Those who misuse the precautionary principle as a zero-risk principle not only risk paralysis and stagnation of today's societies but are also ruining the chances for future generations to achieve a better quality of life.

Innovations will blaze a trail more quickly and effectively in a society where curiosity and a passion for research are promoted from early childhood, where good educational and training opportunities are available to all and where people are receptive to science and technology. It is therefore in the interest of industry players to join in and influence the public debate and contribute toward a culture of innovation that embraces the whole of society. Both parties, industry and society, can only profit.

References

BASF. 2008. What is the SEEBALANCE®? http://corporate.basf.com/en/sustainability/oekoeffizienz/seebalance.htm, May 7.

Cooper, R. G., Edgett, S. J. & Kleinschmidt, E. J. 2002. Optimizing the stage-gate process: what best-practice companies do. Research Technology Management, 45: 21-27.

European Commission (EC). 2000. Communication from the Commission on the precautionary principle. Brussels: European Commission.

International Energy Agency (IEA). 2007. World energy outlook 2007. Paris: OECD/IEA.

Kölsch, D., Saling, P., Kicherer, A., Grosse-Sommer, A. & Schmidt, I. 2008. How to measure social impacts? What is the SEEbalance® about? – Socio-eco-efficiency analysis: the method. International Journal of Sustainable Development, 11: 1-23.

Organisation for Economic Cooperation and Development & Food and Agriculture Organization of the United Nations (OECD/FAO). 2007. OECD-FAO agricultural outlook 2007-2016. Paris/Rome: OECD/FAO.

Schmidt, I., Meurer, M., Saling, P., Reuter, W., Kicherer, A. & Gensch, C.-O. 2005. SEEbalance® managing sustainability of products and processes with the socio-eco-efficiency analysis by BASF. Greener Management International, 45: 79-94.

Schmidt, I. 2007. Nachhaltige Produktbewertung mit der Sozio-Ökoeffizienz-Analyse. Institut für Geographie und Geoökologie der Universität Karlsruhe, Karlsruhe.

United Nations. 2007. World population prospects: the 2006 revision.

Zhang, G. 2005. Promoting IPR policy and enforcement in China: summary of dialogues between OECD and China. Unpublished STI Working Paper 2005/1.

6 Entrepreneurial Orientation

Andreas Rauch[1]

Michael Frese[2]

Abstract

Entrepreneurial orientation (EO) describes firm-level strategic processes that firms use to obtain a competitive advantage. The dimensions of EO include innovativeness, risk taking, and proactiveness. The following chapter describes the conceptualization of EO and its underlying dimensions. Moreover, we summarize the empirical evidence relating to the relationship between EO and venture performance. We suggest a contingency approach and suggest moderator variables that affect the relationship between EO and venture performance.

Keywords: entrepreneurial orientation, business strategy, business performance

[1] Prof. Dr. Andreas Rauch is Professor of Entrepreneurship and New Business Venturing at Rotterdam School of Management, Erasmus University, The Netherlands.

[2] Prof. Dr. Michael Frese is Professor of Work and Organizational Psychology at University of Giessen, Germany, and the London Business School, United Kingdom.

A. Bausch and B. Schwenker (eds.), *Handbook Utility Management,*
DOI: 10.1007/978-3-540-79349-6_6, © Springer-Verlag Berlin Heidelberg 2009

6.1   Introduction

Both the scientific literature and the popular press have widely recognized that entrepreneurial activities make a positive contribution to countries' job creation, economic growth, and innovation (e.g., Birch, 1987; Minniti et al., 2006; OECD, 1996). While it is quite widely agreed that start-up dynamics produce positive economic effects, there is little agreement among scientists on any useful explanations of such effects. A wide range of theories, models, and typologies have been introduced, focusing on diverse scientific domains, such as theory of economic growth, ecological approaches, strategic management, and individual-level approaches. Moreover, different scientific domains frequently introduce new concepts to the domain of entrepreneurship without adequate examination of the evidence of previous ideas. As a result, there is little consensus about the status of concepts and evidence established in the field. However, without developing a consensus in the field it is difficult to suggest specific interventions and practice recommendations that are based on sound empirical evidence and to support entrepreneurship and wealth creation successfully.

One more promising set of concepts that has received consensus in the field of entrepreneurship focuses on firms' strategic posture: entrepreneurial orientation (EO). EO is concerned with the firm-level strategic processes that firms use to obtain a competitive advantage. This chapter focuses on the EO of business ventures and describes its conceptualization and its underlying dimensions. Moreover, we summarize the empirical evidence relating to the relationship between EO and venture performance, and also moderator variables affecting this relationship.

6.2   The Concept of Entrepreneurial Orientation

The concept of EO addresses strategic processes that help a firm to receive a competitive advantage. EO does not refer to individual-level variables that have been dominant in previous entrepreneurship theories, but addresses firm-level processes. Moreover, these processes are distinct from the strategic content/process distinction described by Chandler (1962) or Ansoff (1965), for example, which describe the type of strategy and its formulation and implementation. EO does not focus on distinct strategic decisions, but rather emphasizes the mindset of the whole firm, including processes such as a firm's decision-making styles and business practices, as well as many aspects of its culture, value system, and mission (Hart, 1992). Firms high in EO innovate frequently, make risky decisions, and act proactively on opportunities. Thus, EO focuses on obtaining a competitive advantage by seeking new opportunities, anticipating demands aggressively, taking risk, and positioning new products in markets (Lumpkin & Dess, 1996).

Accordingly, the salient dimensions of EO identified in the literature focus on innovation, proactivity, and risk taking (Covin & Slevin, 1986; Miller, 1983). Innovation involves a predisposition to engagement in creativity and experimentation through the introduction of new products/services and through technological leadership via research and development (R&D) in new processes. Risk taking involves taking bold actions by venturing into the unknown, borrowing heavily, and/or committing significant resources to ventures in uncertain environments. Proactiveness is an opportunity-seeking, forward-looking perspective characterized by the introduction of new products and services ahead of the competition and acting in anticipation of future demand. In addition to these original dimensions of EO, some authors have argued for two additional dimensions that are important in any discussion of the EO of business venture: autonomy and competitive aggressiveness (Lumpkin & Dess, 1996). Autonomy refers to independent action undertaken by entrepreneurial leaders or teams directed at bringing about a new venture and seeing it to fruition. Competitive aggressiveness involves attempts to outperform competitors and aggressive responses to competitive threats.

6.3   The Dimensionality of Entrepreneurial Orientation

There is intense discussion in the entrepreneurship literature about the dimensionality or the construct of EO and the interrelationships between the various dimensions of EO. EO was initially conceptualized as a unidimensional composite construct (e.g., Covin & Slevin, 1986) consisting of innovation, risk taking, and proactiveness (Miller, 1983). Consequently, the dimension of EO should covary. Others have argued that EO is a multidimensional construct and that the dimensions of EO can vary independently (Lumpkin & Dess, 1996). There is some agreement in recent theorizing that EO is a multidimensional construct (Lumpkin & Dess, 1996; Knight, 1997; Kreiser et al., 2002b). This being the case, a subsequent decision needs to specify whether EO represents a formative or a reflective construct (George, 2006). Some researchers have conceptualized EO as a reflective construct, implying that the dimensions of EO must covary and that a change in EO results in a change of innovativeness, risk taking, and proactiveness concurrently (Knight, 1997; Kreiser et al., 2002). In fact, most empirical studies have analyzed EO as a reflective construct (George, 2006). However, in his original work, Miller (1983) considered a firm as being entrepreneurial if it scored high on three dimensions of EO: risk taking, innovation, and proactiveness. It is important to note that Miller (1983) does not claim that the dimensions must covary, but rather proposes that EO is a formative construct. Two studies explicitly address this debate by analyzing the relationships between the dimension of EO; the authors conclude that it is more appropriate to conceptualize EO as a formative construct (George, 2006; Stetz et al., 2000). Thus, the dimensions of EO represent different aspects of the multidimensional concept of EO. This means, consequently, that correlations with antecedents or consequences of EO need to be studied at the level of the dimensions of EO. For example, the subdimensions of EO may have different relationships with certain strategic choices or venture performance.

6.4   Entrepreneurial Orientation and Firm Performance

Since Miller's (1983) and Covin and Slevin's (1986) initial work on EO, a considerable number of studies have addressed the EO–performance relationship. One study quantitatively compared 37 empirical studies and reported an overall effect size of r = .282 (Rauch et al., 2004). This is a moderate effect size according to statistical standards (Cohen, 1977), but comparatively high compared with effect sizes reported in the strategic process domain [r = .20 between planning and performance (Schwenk & Shrader, 1993)] or in the strategic content domain [r = .12 for the relationship between innovation and performance (Bausch & Rosenbusch, 2005); r = .13 for the relationship between internationalization and performance (Bausch & Krist, 2005)]. Thus, empirical results basically support the theoretical assumptions discussed above. Positive effects of EO on company performance have been found for various different performance criteria, such as accountant-based figures, growth, survival, and perceptual performance (Rauch et al., 2004). Thus, positive effects of EO are empirically well established. However, it is important to note that there is considerable variance in reported sizes of effects, ranging from nonsignificant results to relationships higher than r = .30. This heterogeneity of reported effect sizes and the theoretical arguments discussed above suggest that third variables moderate the relationship between EO and performance. Thus, we need to apply contingency theory to study EO of business ventures.

6.5   Contingency Theories

Accordingly, many authors decided to use a contingency framework to analyze the relationship between EO and performance. Unfortunately, no framework of moderator variables has been generally agreed upon for use in the field of entrepreneurship research. Lumpkin and Dess (1996) argued that environmental and organizational variables are key contingencies that affect the strength of the relationship between EO and performance. Recently, an increasing number of studies has addressed contingency variables. Most of these studies try to link specific contingency variables theoretically to the concept of EO.

6.6   Environmental Variables

Our literature search identified studies addressing different types of environmental variables, such as the task environment, the industry, and cross-cultural/cross-national differences.

The task environment refers to the way firms interact with customers, suppliers, and competitors. The task environment can be conceptualized along three dimensions: Complexity (heterogeneity, lack of information), dynamism (variability, predictability), and munificence (ease of getting finance and/or customers) (Dess

& Beard, 1984). Related to munificence, environmental hostility is another dimension of the task environment that describes unfavorable environments that are characterized by a high degree of competition in an environment. Some authors argue that the task environment is related directly to the EO of firms. For example, dynamic environments are characterized by constant changes arising from technological progress, competition, regulatory developments, and similar processes (Zahra, 1993). Therefore, dynamism should create new opportunities because it provides new niches and new markets. Moreover, dynamism requires ventures to innovate and renew themselves. EO should be positively associated with such an environment because EO focuses on proactively approaching new business opportunities. Indeed, a number of studies have revealed that there is a positive correlation between EO and environmental dynamism (e.g., Kreiser et al., 2002a). Similarly, it has been argued that munificence is positively related to EO, because munificent environments provide the resources to invest in process or product innovations. A positive relationship between EO and munificence was supported (Kreiser et al., 2002a). Finally, in hostile environments, businesses need to be innovative and invest in new markets in order to find new ways to compete and to receive competitive advantages (Miles et al., 1993). Thus, businesses make different strategic choices depending on their task environment.

However, the more interesting question is whether or not the task environment affects the relationship between EO and success. For example, successful businesses should have high EO in dynamic environments, because EO helps them to react quickly to new opportunities. Similarly, since hostile environments are highly competitive and provide fewer resources than nonhostile environments, successful firms will aggressively try to develop a competitive advantage, for instance by introducing innovations and being proactive. The empirical literature provides profound support for conceptualizing the task environment as a moderator in the EO–success relationship. We found several studies that empirically support the proposition that the EO–success correlations are higher in hostile environments (Covin & Covin, 1990; Covin & Slevin, 1989; Haiyang et al., 2000; Haiyang et al., 2005; Ibeh, 2003; Lumpkin & Dess, 2001; Zahra & Garvis, 2000) and also in uncertain environments (Weaver et al., 2002; Yusuf, 2002).

Type of industry is another moderator discussed in the literature, because different industries may require different strategic processes. For example, high-tech industries (e.g., computer software and hardware, biotechnology, electrical and electronic products, pharmaceuticals) involve the use of sophisticated and complex technologies and extensive research and development, and their business environment is typically dynamic and uncertain (Khandwalla, 1976; Utterback, 1996). In order to compete successfully in such an industry and to keep up with changes, firms need to have an entrepreneurial management style (Covin et al., 1994). Thus, high-tech environments are often quintessentially entrepreneurial. We identified a number of different studies addressing the effects of EO in a high-tech industry, and all of them reported positive relationships between EO and performance (Covin et al., 1990; Haiyang et al., 2005; Naman & Slevin, 1993; Tan & Litschert, 1994; Tan & Tan, 2005; Yoo, 2001). A meta-analysis shows that EO apparently relates positively to performance both in high tech and in non-high-tech industries; however, reported correlations are higher in high-tech industries (Rauch et al., 2004).

Although EO has been regarded as a vehicle for success and survival in an increasing competitive and global economy (Covin & Slevin, 1991), the concept of EO was originally developed in the US and may, therefore, be biased toward Western countries. Therefore, some studies have attempted to test the cross-cultural and/or the cross-national validity of EO. One set of papers reports tests of the validity of instruments across different countries. The eight-item measure by Covin and Slevin (1986) is the one that has been most frequently used in entrepreneurship research, because it has exhibited high reliabilities and validities in numerous studies. Confirmatory factor analyses support the cross-cultural validity of the Covin and Slevin scale across six countries (Kreiser et al., 2002b). Similarly, the nine-item scale by Khandwalla (1977) is reliable and valid in both English and French contexts (Knight, 1997). A second set of studies assumes that cultural values either converge or conflict with a society's ability to develop an EO (Lee & Peterson, 2000) and that, as a consequence, different cultures should have different levels of EO. Tan (2002), for example, found that the strategic orientation of mainland Chinese involves more risk taking and less future orientation than that of either Chinese Americans or Caucasian Americans. Moreover, Thai entrepreneurs are more innovative and proactive than Vietnamese entrepreneurs, while Vietnamese entrepreneurs score higher on risk taking than do Thai entrepreneurs (Swierczek & Ha, 2003). It is important to note that studies that address simple mean differences in EO are extremely vulnerable to biases, since many alternative explanations can affect mean differences in fixed group designs. Even though analysis of relationships may also suffer from biases, these are less problematic than mean differences. Accordingly, Mueller and Thomas (2000) compared individual-level EO across nine countries and concluded that there is a positive correlation between EO and individualism. The same study does not support the hypothesis that EO is negatively related to uncertainty avoidance. Finally, some studies have conceptualized cultural values as moderators affecting the relationship between EO and other outcome variables. For example, the relationship between EO and performance is higher in countries with high masculinity than in countries with low masculinity (Arbaugh et al., 2005). Another study compares German and Chinese entrepreneurs (Rauch et al., 2007). The authors argue for cultural universals and culture-specific effects and find that EO impacts positively on performance in both countries. However, since China is a collectivistic society that does not favor innovation, EO can be used as a tool to support innovation in Chinese businesses. In summary, we can conclude that researchers report the necessity of evaluating the cross-cultural validity of EO and that there are instruments available that can be used to study cross-cultural differences. However, empirical results on cross-cultural differences in EO and EO–success relationships are preliminary, and more studies are therefore required before more robust conclusions are possible. The moderating effects of task environment and of type of industry affecting EO–success relationships are well established and clearly support a contingency view that accounts for environmental variables.

6.7   Organizational Variables

Organizational variables that affect the relationship between EO and performance include organizational structure, age, size, strategy, and firm resources (network, competencies) (Lumpkin & Dess, 1996).

Covin and Slevin (1991) argue that the organizational structure, which consists of administrative relationships, formalization, and authority structures in an organization, can either support or inhibit entrepreneurial behavior and performance. Therefore, to affect business performance EO needs to be aligned with the organization structure. For example, an organic structure supports flexibility, informality, and expertise. A mechanistic structure, in contrast, is centralized, rigid, and has a formal bureaucratic structure. Since organic structures have a better information processing capacity and support innovation, they provide a better fit with an EO. Accordingly, several empirical studies have indicated that EO has positive effects on performance in firms with an organic structure, while there is a negative relationship between EO and performance in firms with a mechanistic structure (Caruana et al., 2002; Covin & Slevin, 1988; Covin & Slevin, 1989). One study analyzes the moderator effect of structure for the dimensions of EO separately (Wales et al., 2006). Results indicate that formalization negatively moderates that relationship between all dimensions of EO and performance. Centralization inhibits the relationship between innovativeness and competitive aggressiveness on the one hand and performance on the other. However, centralization has a positive effect on the relationship between competitive aggressiveness and success.

Age and size of business ventures are additional potential moderators that would be expected to affect the strength of the relationship between EO and performance. Age is important because the early years of new business ventures are the most critical for success and survival. An EO may help a firm to succeed in the early years and to gain a market share that makes it easier to maneuver the business. One study has found differential effects of age on the relationship between specific dimensions of EO and performance (Lumpkin et al., 2006). Since continuously high levels of risk taking are damaging to performance, risk taking is more beneficial for younger enterprises and, as a consequence, risk taking was more strongly related to the performance of young firms than of older firms. Similarly, young enterprises can reduce entry barriers in a market by introducing innovations and, therefore, innovation is positively related to performance in young firms. Nevertheless, both competitive aggressiveness and proactiveness are more effective in older ventures, probably because both require the availability of large resources. Other research indicates that EO is more effective in small companies than in larger enterprises, because smaller organizations are more flexible, allowing them to implement quick changes and to take advantage of new opportunities that may develop in the environment (Rauch et al., 2004).

Since EO is directly concerned with strategic processes in a firm, it is interesting to look at relationships between EO and other variables in the strategic process/content domain, such as planning, introduction of innovations, and differentiation strategies. It seems that EO is related to flexible planning that allows changing plans to adjust for environmental conditions (Barringer & Bluedorn, 1999). Moreover, EO is related to innovation in a firm (Atuahene-Gima & Ko, 2001; Hult et al., 2004). Most studies on the relationship between EO and strategy have focused on technological policy, which is related to innovative behavior. Accordingly, technological policy is related to EO (Salavou & Lioukas, 2003). One study indicates that the interaction between EO and innovation predicts performance in Chinese enterprises (Rauch et al., 2007). Although it seems obvious that EO is related to technological policy, because both concepts involve innovations, the two concepts are also conceptually distinct: EO accounts for a more general strategic orientation, while innovation is concerned with specific innovations and R&D investments. The interactions discussed above suggest that the introduction of innovations should be supported by the firm's EO. Moreover, since EO involves risk, it would be interesting to look how EO is related to radical innovations rather than incremental innovations: Radical innovations involve more risk because they require higher investments and may face more legitimacy constraints than incremental innovations.

Finally, some approaches have studied resources such as networks, knowledge, and capabilities, assuming that these resources are important if firms are to benefit from EO. Network approaches assume that venture success can be explained by the way ventures access resources in their environment through informal network ties (e.g., Aldrich & Zimmer, 1986). Two studies indicate that entrepreneurial orientation is closely correlated with success if firms can rely on networks that help to identify and exploit more opportunities (Lee et al., 2001; Walter et al., 2006). Regarding knowledge-based resources, different studies have modeled the indirect effect of EO differently. For instance, Wiklund and Shepherd's (2005) study indicates that EO is the moderator that helps to utilize knowledge-based resources and to pursue opportunities. Other studies indicate that competencies and capabilities moderate the EO–success relationship (Haiyang et al., 2005; Jantunen et al., 2005).

6.8   Combined Models of Venture Performance

Our review suggests support for a contingency approach and indicates that both environmental and organizational variables need to be considered for a complete exploration of the effects of EO. It is important to note that both early and recent studies have combined the effects of these two domains of moderator variables. For example, Miller and Toulouse (1986) have analyzed EO together with personality traits, organizational structure, and environment. Similarly, Naman and Selvin (1993) have shown that the fit between EO, environmental turbulence, organization structure, and mission strategy explain the performance of high-tech manufacturing firms better than the additive effect of the variables. Finally, an extensive study of Swedish small business owners supports a three-way interaction between EO, resources, and business environment (Wiklund & Shepherd, 2005): Performance was higher among firms with high EO, high financial resources, and dynamic environments than in firms with any other combination of the three variables. The implication of all these findings is that EO needs to be appropriately aligned with structure, resources, and environmental conditions.

6.9   Critique

There are a number of conceptual and empirical problems associated with EO that need to be discussed in more detail before we draw our specific conclusions. First, the concept of EO is relatively broad, as it refers to the decision-making styles, management behavior, and culture of the whole firm. It is important to specify how these broad orientations have translated into specific decisions and actions that, in turn, help in the successful running of a business. Although our review has identified a number of moderators, it would be interesting to specify mediating processes as well. For example, it may be that EO helps firms to apply flexible rather than rigid planning, which, in turn, helps them to exploit opportunities in the market more successfully. Thus, to develop a full theory of EO, we need to identify processes through which EO affects business outcomes.

Moreover, since we have concluded that it is necessary to analyze the dimensions of EO separately (see above), we need more studies analyzing the effects of individual dimensions of EO. The majority of studies have used a composite overall assessment of EO (Kreiser et al., 2002b), a fact that may be due to the extensive use of the Covin and Selvin (1986) scale, which regularly collapses into a single factor. Regarding EO measurement, this indicates the need to use more sophisticated instruments that provide reliable estimates of the subdimensions of EO. Future studies can use such instruments to test the differential relationships with the antecedents and consequences of EO.

A related issue is the number of dimensions that have been explored in the literature. The original conceptualization of EO assumed that EO consisted of three subdimensions (Covin & Slevin, 1986; Miller, 1983). Lumpkin and Dess (1996) recommended extending the number of dimensions to five. Another conceptualization uses six dimensions to describe EO: aggressiveness, analysis, defensiveness, futurity, proactiveness, and riskiness (Venkatraman, 1989). If EO is multidimensional and a formative construct, it is essential to identify the correct number of dimensions necessary to measure EO. Otherwise, we will repeatedly fail to specify the theoretical domain of EO correctly.

A number of authors have conceptualized EO as an individual-level rather than a firm-level construct (Krauss et al., 2005; Mueller & Thomas, 2000; Walter et al., 2006). In fact, most of the studies evaluating EO use individual-level data because they ask business owners or CEOs about their perceptions of their firms' management style. However, these perceptions may very well not reflect firm-level EO. More specifically, a firm-level construct requires the aggregation of data from multiple levels within the organization to the organization level (Klein & Kozlowski, 2000). Thus, in order to evaluate the strategic processes of a firm, studies need to be based on information provided by the employees, managers,

and CEOs of firms. To our knowledge, in only two studies have there been attempts to assess firms' EO by using multiple respondents from the firm (Lumpkin
& Dess, 2001; Rauch et al., 2007). Results indicate close correlations between
employees' and owners'/managers' perceptions of EO; however, these correlations are not high enough to justify the assumption that both assessments are
equally valid predictors of an EO in a firm.

It is also important to separate individual-level and firm-level entrepreneurship
because the two refer to distinct concepts. Personality traits, such as risk-taking
propensity, achievement motivation, and proactiveness are individual dispositions
that are caused by and may cause different processes than EO (Rauch & Frese,
2007). For example, individual-level entrepreneurship correlates with subjective
performance while EO correlates with financial performance in a meta-analysis
(Rauch et al., 2005). Moreover, individual-level entrepreneurship may help in
starting a venture that supports the EO of the firm. Therefore, EO may transmit the
effect of an individual's personality traits. Such a position is supported by Poon et
al. (2006), whose research shows that generalized self-efficacy influences performance through its effects on EO.

6.10   Conclusions

This review has identified some evidence that relates to the importance of the EOs
of business ventures and suggests both practical and theoretical consequences. We
have shown that EO focuses on strategic processes that are essentially important
predictors of business success. The effect sizes reported in the literature are moderately large. The overall correlation between EO and performance is $r = .242$
(Rauch et al., 2004), which is higher than effect sizes usually found in the innovation–success or the planning–success relationship, for instance (Bausch & Rosenbusch, 2005; Schwenk & Shrader, 1993). Importantly, these may be causal effects,
because two studies have indicated that EO affects performance over time
(Wiklund, 1998, Zahra & Covin, 1995). However, both the theoretical literature
and the heterogeneity of reported effect sizes indicate that this is not a direct relationship. EO is more efficient in some circumstances than in others, and a contingency approach is therefore the most appropriate for conceptualizing the effects of
EO. Moderating conditions identified in this review include both environmental
and organizational variables. Areas that still need to be addressed in future studies
include the number of different dimensions required to cover EO, the differential
impact of the subdimensions of EO on performance, and mediating processes.

In practical terms, business owners are well advised to fit their strategic orientation to their structure and their environment. More specifically, owners who rely
on high EO should run enterprises in high-tech industries and dynamic and unfavorable environments. Moreover, an organic structure also supports the effectiveness of EO.

References

Aldrich, H. E. & Zimmer, C. 1986. Entrepreneurship through social networks. In D. L. Sexton & W. Smilor (Eds.), The Art and Science of Entrepreneurship: 2-23. Cambridge: Ballinger.

Ansoff, H. I. 1965. Corporate strategy: an analytic approach to business policy for growth and expansion. New York: McGraw-Hill.

Arbaugh, J. B., Cox, L. W. & Camp, S. M. 2005. Nature or nurture? Testing the direct and interaction effects of entrepreneurial orientation, national culture, and growth strategy on value creation. In S. A. Zahra, C. G. Brush, R. T. Harrison, J. E. Sohl, P. Davidsson, M. Lerner, J. Wiklund, J. Fiet, C. M. Mason, M. Wright, P. C. Greene & D. Shepherd (Eds.), Frontiers of Entrepreneurship Research. Wellesley: Babson College Center.

Atuahene-Gima, K. & Ko, A. 2001. An empirical investigation of the effect of market orientation and entrepreneurship orientation alignment on product innovation. Organization Science, 12: 54-74.

Barringer, B. R. & Bluedorn, A. C. 1999. The relationship between corporate entrepreneurship and strategic management. Strategic Management Journal, 20: 421-444.

Bausch, A. & Rosenbusch, N. 2005. Does innovation really matter? A meta-analysis on the relationship between innovation and business performance. Paper presented at the Babson College Kaufman Foundation Entrepreneurship Research Conference, Babson, MA.

Bausch, A. & Krist, M. 2007. The effect of context-related moderators on the internationalization-performance relationship: evidence from meta-analysis. Management International Review, 47: 319-347.

Birch, D. L. 1987. Job creation in America: how our smallest companies put the most people to work. New York; London: Free Press; Collier Macmillan.

Caruana, A., Ewing, M. T. & Ramaseshan, B. 2002. Effects of some environmental challenges and centralization on the entrepreneurial orientation and performance of public sector entities. Service Industries Journal, 22: 43-58.

Chandler, A. D. 1962. Strategy and structure. Chapters in the history of the industrial enterprises. Cambridge, MA: MIT Press.

Cohen, J. 1977. Statistical power analysis for the behavioral science. New York: Academic Press.

Covin, J. G. & Slevin, D. P. 1986. The development and testing of an organizational-level entrepreneurship scale. In R. Ronstadt, J. A. Hornaday, R. Peterson & K. H. Vesper (Eds.), Frontiers of Entrepreneurship Research: 628-639. Wellesley, MA: Babson College.

Covin, J. G. & Slevin, D. P. 1988. The influence of organization structure on the utility of an entrepreneurial top management style. Journal of Management Studies, 25: 217-234.

Covin, J. G. & Slevin, D. P. 1989. Strategic management of small firms in hostile and benign environments. Strategic Management Journal, 10: 75-87.

Covin, J. G. & Covin, T. J. 1990. Competitive aggressiveness, environmental context, and small firm performance. Entrepreneurship Theory and Practice, 14: 35-50.

Covin, J. G., Prescott, J. E. & Slevin, D. P. 1990. The effects of technological sophistication on strategic profiles, structure and firm performance. Journal of Management Studies, 27: 485-507.

Covin, J. G. & Slevin, D. P. 1991. A conceptual model of entrepreneurship as firm behavior. Entrepreneurship Theory and Practice, 16: 7-25.

Covin, J. G., Slevin, D. P. & Schultz, R. L. 1994. Implementing strategic missions: effective strategic, structural, and tactical choices. Journal of Management Studies, 31: 481-503.

Dess, G. G. & Beard, D. W. 1984. Dimensions of organizational task environments. Administrative Science Quarterly, 29: 52-73.

George, B. A. 2006. Entrepreneurial orientation: a theoretical and empirical examination of the consequences of differing construct representations. Paper presented at the Babson College Kaufman Foundation Research Conference, Bloomington, Indiana.

Haiyang, L., Kwaku, A.-G. & Yan, Z. 2000. How does venture strategy matter in the environment - performance relationship. Academy of Management Conference Proceedings.

Haiyang, L., Zhang, Y. & Chan, T.-S. 2005. Entrepreneurial strategy making and performance in China's emerging economy - the contingency effects of environment and firm competencies. Journal of High Technology Management Research, 16: 37-57.

Hart, S. L. 1992. An integrative framework for strategy-making processes. Academy of Management Review, 17: 327-351.

Hult, G. T. M., Hurley, R. F. & Knight, G. A. 2004. Innovativeness: its antecedents and impact on business performance. Industrial Marketing and Management, 33: 429-438.

Ibeh, K. I. N. 2003. Towards a contingency framework of export entrepreneurship: conceptualization and empirical evidence. Small Business Economics, 20: 49-68.

Jantunen, A., Puumalainen, K., Saarenketo, S. & Kyläheiko, K. 2005. Entrepreneurial orientation, dynamic capabilities and international performance. Journal of International Entrepreneurship, 3: 223-243.

Khandwalla, P. N. 1976. Some top management styles, their context and performance. Organization and Administrative Sciences, 7: 21-51.

Khandwalla, P. N. 1977. Generators of pioneering innovative management: some Indian evidence. Organization Studies, 8: 39-59.

Klein, K. J. & Kozlowski, S. W. 2000. Multi-level theory, research, and methods on organizations. San Francisco: Jossey-Bass.

Knight, G. A. 1997. Cross-cultural reliability and validity of a scale to measure firm entrepreneurial orientation. Journal of Business Venturing, 12: 213-225.

Krauss, S. I., Frese, M. & Friedrich, C. 2005. Entrepreneurial orientation: a psychological model of success among Southern African small business owners. European Journal of Work and Organizational Psychology, 14: 315-344.

Kreiser, P. M., Marino, L. & Weaver, K. M. 2002a. Assessing the relationship between entrepreneurial orientation, the external environment, and firm performance. In W. D. Bygrave, C. G. Brush, P. Davidsson, J. Fiet, P. G. Greene, R. T. Harrison, M. Lerner, D. Meyer, J. Sohl & A. Zacharakis (Eds.), Frontiers of Entrepreneurship Research. Wellesley: Babson College.

Kreiser, P. M., Marino, L. D. & Weaver, K. M. 2002b. Assessing the psychometric properties of the entrepreneurial orientation scale: a multi-country analysis. Entrepreneurship Theory and Practice, 26: 71-94.

Lee, A., Lee, K. & Pennings, J. M. 2001. Internal capabilities, external networks, and performance: a study of technology-based ventures. Strategic Management Journal, 22: 615-640.

Lee, S. M. & Peterson, S. J. 2000. Culture, entrepreneurial orientation, and global competitiveness. Journal of World Business, 35: 401-416.

Lumpkin, G. T. & Dess, G. G. 1996. Clarifying the entrepreneurial orientation construct and linking it to performance. Academy of Management Review, 21: 135-172.

Lumpkin, G. T. & Dess, G. G. 2001. Linking two dimensions of entrepreneurial orientation to firm performance: the moderating role of environment and industry life cycle. Journal of Business Venturing, 16: 429-451.

Lumpkin, G. T., Wales, W. J. & Ensley, M. 2006. Entrepreneurial orientation effects on new venture performance: the moderating role of new venture age. Academy of management proceedings best conference papers.

Miles, M. P., Arnold, D. R. & Thompson, D. L. 1993. The interrelationship between environmental hostility and entrepreneurial orientation. Journal of Applied Business Research, 9: 12-23.

Miller, D. 1983. The correlates of entrepreneurship in three types of firms. Management Science, 29: 770-791.

Miller, D. & Toulouse, J.-M. 1986. Chief executive personality and corporate strategy and structure in small firms. Management Science, 32: 1389-1409.

Minniti, M., Bygrave, W. D. & Autio, E. 2006. Global entrepreneurship monitor 2005. Unpublished Report, Babson College and London Business School.

Mueller, S. L. & Thomas, A. S. 2000. Culture and entrepreneurial potential: a nine country study of locus of control and innovativeness. Journal of Business Venturing, 16: 51-75.

Naman, J. L. & Slevin, D. P. 1993. Entrepreneurship and the concept of fit: a model and empirical tests. Strategic Management Journal, 14: 137-153.

Organisation for Economic Co-operation and Development (OECD). 1996. SMEs and economic growth and change. In OECD (Ed.), Monitoring Job and Firm Dynamics from SMEs: Employment, Innovation, and Growth. The Washington Workshop: 10-17. Paris: OECD.

Poon, J. M. L., Ainuddin, R. A. & Junit, S. H. 2006. Effects of self-concept traits and entrepreneurial orientation of firm performance. International Small Business Journal, 24: 61-82.

Rauch, A., Lumpkin, G. T., Wiklund, J. & Frese, M. 2005. Who the entrepreneur is vs. what the entrepreneur does: comparing the empirical relevance of two dominant approaches. Paper presented at the 2005 Academy of Management Meeting, Honolulu, HI.

Rauch, A., Frese, M., Koenig, C. & Wang, Z. M. 2007. A universal contingency approach to entrepreneurship: exploring the relationship between innovation, entrepreneurial orientation and success in Chinese and German entrepreneurs. Unpublished Report, University of Giessen, Department of Work and Organizational Psychology, Giessen.

Rauch, A. & Frese, M. 2007. Let's put the person back into entrepreneurship research: a meta-analysis of the relationship between business owners' personality traits, business creation, and success. European Journal of Work and Organizational Psychology, 16: 353-385.

Rauch, A., Wiklund, J., Lumpkin, G. T. & Frese, M. 2004. Entrepreneurial orientation and business performance: cumulative empirical evidence. In W. D. Bygrave, C. G. Brush, M. Lerner, P. Davidsson, G. D. Meyer, J. Fiet, J. Sohl, P. G. Greene, A. Zacharakis & R. T. Harrison (Eds.), Frontiers of Entrepreneurship Research. Wellesley: Babson College.

Salavou, H. & Lioukas, S. 2003. Radical product innovations in SMEs: the dominance of entrepreneurial orientation. Creativity and Innovation Management, 12: 94-108.

Schwenk, C. R. & Shrader, C. B. 1993. Effects of formal planning on financial performance in small firms: a meta-analysis. Entrepreneurship Theory and Practice, 17: 53-64.

Stetz, P. E., Howell, R., Stewart, A., Blair, J. D. & Fottler, M. D. 2000. Multidimensionality of entrepreneurial firm-level processes: do the dimensions covary? In P. D. Reynolds, E. Autio, C. G. Brush, W. D. Bygrave, S. Manigart, H. J. Sapienza & K. G. Shaver (Eds.), Frontiers of Entrepreneurship Research. Wellesley: Babson College.

Swierczek, F. W. & Ha, T. T. 2003. Entrepreneurial orientation, uncertainty avoidance and firm performance: an analysis of Thai and Vietnamese SMEs. International Journal of Entrepreneurship and Innovation, 4: 46-58.

Tan, J. & Litschert, R. J. 1994. Environment strategy relationship and its implications: an empirical study of Chinese electronics industry. Strategic Management Journal, 15: 1-20.

Tan, J. 2002. Culture, nation, and entrepreneurial strategic orientations: implications for an emerging industry. Entrepreneurship Theory and Practice, 26: 95-111.

Tan, J. & Tan, D. 2005. Environment-strategy coevolution and coalignment: a staged-model of Chinese SOEs under transition. Strategic Management Journal, 26: 141-157.

Utterback, J. 1996. Mastering the dynamics of innovation: how companies can seize opportunities in the face of technological change. Boston: Harvard Business School Press.

Venkatraman, N. 1989. Strategic orientation of business enterprises: the construct, dimensionality, and measurement. Management Science, 35: 942-962.

Wales, W. J., Lumpkin, G. T. & Ensley, M. D. 2006. Linking new venture entrepreneurial orientation to firm performance: a multidimensional model of organizational structure moderation. In A. Zacherakis, S. Alvarez, C. Mason, P. Westhead & P. Davidsson (Eds.), Frontiers of Entrepreneurship Research. Wellesley: Babson College.

Walter, A., Auer, M. & Ritter, T. 2006. The impact of network capabilities and entrepreneurial orientation on university spin-off performance. Journal of Business Venturing, 21: 541-567.

Weaver, K. M., Dickson, P. H., Gibson, B. & Turner, A. 2002. Being uncertain: the relationship between entrepreneurial orientation and environmental uncertainty. Journal of Enterprising Culture, 10: 87-105.

Wiklund, J. 1998. Entrepreneurial orientation as predictor of performance and entrepreneurial behavior in small firms. In P. D. Reynolds, W. D. Bygrave, N. M. Carter, S. Manigart, C. M. Mason, G. D. Meyer & K. G. Shaver (Eds.), Frontiers of Entrepreneurship Research: 281-296. Babson Park: Babson College.

Wiklund, J. & Shepherd, D. 2005. Entrepreneurial orientation and small business performance: a configurational approach. Journal of Business Venturing, 20: 71-91.

Yoo, S.-J. 2001. Entrepreneurial orientation, environment scanning intensity, and firm performance in technology-based SMEs. Frontiers of Entrepreneurship Research.

Yusuf, A. 2002. Environmental uncertainty, the entrepreneurial orientation of business ventures, and performance. International Journal of Commerce & Management, 12: 83-94.

Zahra, S. A. 1993. Environment, corporate entrepreneurship, and financial performance: a taxonomic approach. Journal of Business Venturing, 8: 319-340.

Zahra, S. A. & Covin, J. G. 1995. Contextual influences on the corporate entrepreneurship performance relationship: a longitudinal analysis. Journal of Business Venturing, 10: 43-58.

Zahra, S. A. & Garvis, D. M. 2000. International corporate entrepreneurship and firm performance: the moderating effect of international environmental hostility. Journal of Business Venturing, 15: 469-492.

7 New Paradigms in Organizational Design

Denis Depoux[1]

Abstract

Since the early days of energy market liberalization in the late 1990s, almost all integrated utilities in Western Europe have undergone major organizational change. These changes have resulted from evolutions in the economic environment, regulations, or shareholder pressure, and they have impacted on all segments of the value chain. In this chapter, we discuss the various drivers of change over the past 10 years, from the liberalization of energy markets to the wholesale markets' regional consolidation. We also analyze the features of today's organizations to provide readers with keys to understanding the current organizational framework. We then examine the challenges and emerging paradigms in utilities' organizational design: leaner, simpler organizations, new, operational steering models, integration trends and synergies generation mechanisms, new centralized models, and the customized organizations designed to accommodate new activities, such as renewables or energy efficiency. Finally, we provide a brief outlook of trends in US utilities organization.

Keywords: utilities, organization, synergies

[1] Denis Depoux is Senior Partner and Head of Utilities Competence Center of Roland Berger Strategy Consultants, France.
This chapter benefited from contributions by Veit Schwinkendorf, Laurent Benarousse, Alexandre Bouchet, Marc Cibrario, Joao Saint Aubyn, Emmanuel Austruy and Jérôme Berthout, all members of Roland Berger's global Energy and Chemicals Competence Center. Jean-Louis Poirier, a Senior Advisor to Roland Berger in the US, provided his views on the US organization trends.

A. Bausch and B. Schwenker (eds.), *Handbook Utility Management,*
DOI: 10.1007/978-3-540-79349-6_7, © Springer-Verlag Berlin Heidelberg 2009

7.1   Introduction: Main Drivers Influencing the Organizational Framework of European Utilities

The organization of European electricity and natural gas utilities has been in a state of constant transformation over the past 10 years, creating huge challenges to change management, human resources, information technologies and managerial attitudes. This transformation has been fueled by a set of drivers pertaining to the transformation of the utilities industry itself:

- Regulation;
- Liberalization and the development of competition;
- Privatization and increased financial pressure;
- Organic development and consolidation.

7.1.1   Regulation as a Dominant Driver of Organizational Change in European Utilities in the Past 12 Years

The two European Union Directive packages (1996 and 2003) have mandated structural changes in the organization of electricity and natural gas utilities. The compulsory managerial and accounting changes, then structural unbundling of regulated activities (transmission and distribution networks) and competitive activities (generation, trading, supply) resulted in the creation of separate companies with distinct managerial responsibilities, the transfer of large amounts of staff from the predecessor company to the newly formed companies (transmission and distribution), and the definition of new organizations with their own support functions, in most cases resulting in additional, recurring cost on top of the cost of transformation. The magnitude of the transformation needed is such that most European utilities adopted a very slow pace of organizational change.[2] This pace may change over the next few years, even without a third EU Directive package.

Progressive unbundling of regulated and competitive activities, depending on the national implementation of EU Directives, now puts a lot of pressure on the resulting organizations:

- Regulated transmission and distribution companies or subsidiaries of large utilities have to face increased pressure from the national regulators to negotiate tariffs. The pressure by regulators on the cost to serve will increase, as a

---

[2] The starting position for most nation-wide or region-wide utilities is a grid of distribution centers combining technical distribution networks' operational activities with customer service activities. While it is reasonably easy to create a new, unified, marketing function at regional or national level, unbundling commercial retail activities from now regulated distribution network operations is a difficult endeavor: in France, the electricity and gas distribution organizations comprised more than 300 sites (agencies, technical centers) grouped in 100 management units that have to be unbundled; in Germany, unbundling of distribution system operators by RWE, E.ON or Vattenfall had to factor in local, regional, and cross-operators' shareholding interests.

result of their better understanding of the transmission and distribution net-works' cost structure and the progressive dilution of initial transformation costs. Most European regulators are also moving from single-year tariff ne-gotiation with transmission and distribution players towards multi-year con-tracts such as are already in place in the US, the UK, Austria, and Spain. These multiyear contracts will drive deeper organizational changes within regulated subsidiaries, to create performance improve waves at a pace that can beat that of RPI-x regulation, e.g., the creation of shared service centers across local or regional organizations, make-or-buy analyses resulting in in-creased contracting and outsourcing, etc.

- Stand-alone competitive supply businesses will no longer be able to benefit from the nice margin transfers from the regulated activities, thanks to in-creased regulatory pressure and more visible financial and human resources flows between parent companies and regulated and competitive subsidiaries. As a result, unbundling has also created a performance gap that has to be bridged, mainly in mass market retail activities. The organization of these ac-tivities had hence long been modeled on the distribution organization.

7.1.2   Liberalization of Electricity and Natural Gas Markets

The opening of wholesale and, later, retail electricity and natural gas markets is a key driver of organizational changes within European utilities. The development of wholesale gas and electricity markets and associated wholesale price transpar-ency in Western Europe drives the organization of generation asset portfolios along the lines of the market structure across the national and technical boundaries of electrical systems.

Business-to-business (B2B) retail market competition also drives the creation of marketing and sales organizations, progressively separating them from the gen-eration, transmission, and distribution organizations. In the late 1990s and early 2000s, sales organizations for very large electricity accounts[3] emerged, usually by transfer of the more technically oriented customer service teams that usually were part of the generation and transmission divisions of large utilities. A first wave of new appointments, usually from industrial B2B marketing departments, started to staff newly formed marketing and sales departments. These departments progres-sively shaped the new retail divisions of large utilities.

Business-to-consumer (B2C) retail market competition, as mandated from July 2007 by the 2003 EU Directive, led to the creation of national, bundled, electricity and natural gas retailing organizations within most European utilities. However, the pace of this evolution varied very widely, depending on national EU Directive implementation schemes (e.g., France did not open the residential market until 2007, while the German electricity and natural gas market had theoretically been

---

[3] Electricity end-users with an annual consumption over 100 GWh, which were open to competition by direct implementation of the 1996 EU Directive in 1999, as well as local distribution companies.

fully open to competition since 1998). Residential markets, in some countries, are still local or regional markets served by local or regional companies, even if these companies are part of a larger, European group. For example, until recently B2C retail organizations within RWE were managed at regional company level, with little if any marketing and sales coordination at national German level, while in France, EDF has had a national retail organization since 2003, with a progressive effort to minimize the number of regional B2C headquarters, which were once bundled with 100 distribution centers.

7.1.3   Privatization and Increased Financial Pressure

Financial markets played a significant role in shaping the organizational evolutions of European utilities, along several dimensions:

- First of all, energy markets are becoming increasingly financial, as a result of the development of wholesale markets' price references for several time scales beyond the spot markets, and the development of derivatives and structured products, either exchange or over-the-counter (OTC) traded. This increased the outside visibility of utilities' performance with respect to asset portfolio management, price spread management (wholesale–retail, oil/gas–electricity, etc.), and price position management for retail activities. The result of this has been the shaping of business units in such a way as to increase management accountability over the financial performance of each activity, so that it is now more easily comparable to that of other utilities.
- Privatization and subsequent initial public offerings (IPOs) of European utilities, starting in the UK in the 1990s and finishing with the privatization and IPOs of EDF and Gaz de France in 2005, combined with new IFRS reporting standards,[4] also led to increased financial pressure and demand from financial markets for visibility by way of portfolio exposure, business model, and margin creation mechanisms.

7.1.4   Organic and M&A Development and the Search for Growth Relays

After cash-affluent monopolies had diversified and invested heavily overseas in the early 1990s, European utilities focused on their new 'domestic' European territory in the early 2000s. The retreat of US players from Europe in the aftermath of Enron's bankruptcy, the emerging cross-national electricity and gas market structure in Western Europe, and increased competition and enhanced financial structures led to a new wave of consolidation in the sector (e.g., E.ON–Ruhrgas, failed E.ON–Endesa merger, subsequent acquisition of Endesa assets by Enel and E.ON, Gaz de France-Suez merger, British Energy acquisition by EDF, E.ON, RWE,

---

[4] Specifically market-to-market valuation and reporting alignment on organization and management structures.

EDF, ENEL and Gaz de France acquisitions in Eastern Europe). This wave of sizable mergers and acquisitions led to increasingly complex organizational structures combining historical organizations and new assets, with varying levels of integration.

Already dominant in their domestic markets, and in some cases in new markets (e.g., EDF in France and in the UK, E.ON–Ruhrgas in Germany and in Eastern Europe), European utilities have been searching for new growth paths beyond the traditional core business boundaries: renewables, energy services, energy efficiency services, natural gas or electricity for traditional utilities, upstream oil & gas, etc. These new developments have been pursued either through acquisitions or through organic development in existing territories, and have resulted in accrued organizational complexity, thus calling for change and optimization.

7.2   Keys to Reading the Current Organizational Framework of European Utilities

7.2.1   Significant Remnants of the Pre-liberalization Organization of European Gas and Electricity Utilities

Historically, the organizational framework of European utilities, pre-liberalization, had followed their technical development: there were local service territories within large utilities, or local utilities emerged around a distribution network center, serving local customers ranging from residential customers to local subsidiaries/plants of large corporations. Generation and transmission networks were often bundled in a single organization (e.g., within EDF in France, or CPTE, the predecessor company to Electrabel, in Belgium), again because technically it made sense to connect large generation units to a single grid and manage the supply–demand equilibrium accordingly.

Even though liberalization stormed these historical national or local organizations, the weight of several organizational features should not be underestimated in understanding today's organizations. As an example, political/administrative boundaries remain visible in today's organizational design of European utilities' distribution and retail activities; while the pressure on operational and financial performance has pushed for pooling resources at regional/national levels, local governments have been eager to maintain employment and public service presence across the territory, resulting in a relatively slow pace of transformation (e.g., France, Spain, Belgium and, to a certain extent, Germany).

The fast development of electricity and natural gas utilities in the 30 years after World War II also created very pyramidal and hierarchical organizations within both national and regional/local companies. Such organizations were badly needed to keep the fast pace of (re-)construction pace necessary to develop postwar transmission and distribution networks and hydro generation plants, then thermal and nuclear generation plants. After several waves of organizational changes, this pyramidal model, often coming with the standardization of local organizations and procedures across a large service territory, still prevails within most European utilities.

Other residual historical features include:

- The resilience of very local utilities (Germany, Austria, Switzerland) with dispersed shareholding and local interests, impeding integration and in some cases organizational change;
- The varying distribution networks technical standards across European countries, or in some cases within a single country, also hindering integration trends or performance improvement actions across geographies and electrical systems.

7.2.2   Current Organization of European Energy Utilities Can Be Read Along Three Dimensions

As a result of historical features, as well as the drivers presented earlier in the chapter, three dimensions usually characterize the organizational framework of European utilities today (see Figure 7.1). Understanding these dimensions is key to designing the next organizational paradigm, which may invert some of the dimensions.

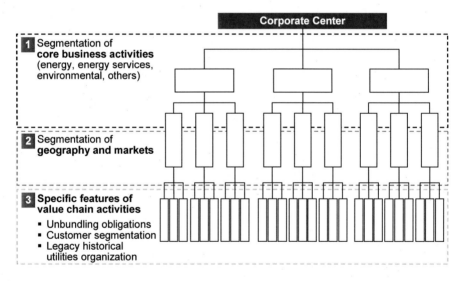

Figure 7.1: A schematic reading of the current organizational framework of European utilities

7.2.2.1   Dimension 1: Segmentation of Core Business Activities

All utilities clearly separate core business activities of different natures with specific characteristics:

- Energy activities are capital intensive and are characterized by a vertically integrated business model (or the willingness to vertically integrate), with long investment and return cycles and regulation being paramount in defining specific investment and return cycles for network activities (transmission and mostly distribution).

- Energy services and related services activities need little capital compared with energy activities, are often extremely segmented, owing to the variety of services required by industrial and commercial customers (combined heat and power, heating, ventilating, and air conditioning (HVAC), compressed air, facility management, internal network operations, energy efficiency, etc.). Synergies with electricity or natural gas supply are limited and are mostly concentrated on small and medium enterprises, where energy services are of limited profitability for major players. Business cycles can be short, depending on the overall economy, and costs should therefore be as variable as possible.

- Environment activities are capital intensive and create a lot of synergies with each other (water network operations, waste water treatment, etc.), while synergies with energy or energy services activities have so far been limited (local communities and industrials purchasing or outsourcing services considering energy and environment separately, from both commercial and technical standpoints).

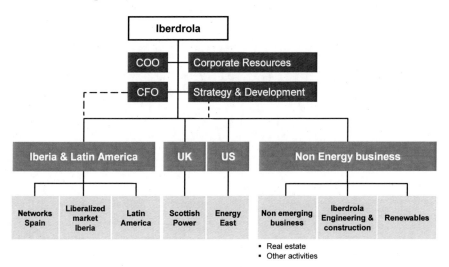

Figure 7.2: Iberdrola Group organization (2008)

Core business activities often define the boundaries of divisions at the first level of the organization, as can be observed in the organization of Suez (prior to the merger with Gaz de France in July 2008, but the separation at the first level, of energy services and environment activities remains in the GDF SUEZ organization) or the current organization of Spanish energy utility Iberdrola (see Figure 7.2).

7.2.2.2 Dimension 2: Geography and Markets

Both the organizational charts above also demonstrate that divisions focusing on core business activities, either national or global, have to co-exist, on the first level of the organization, with international divisions. These either regroup international activities across various regions, or are the result of a large acquisition, not integrated and directly reporting to the first level of the organization, for specific reasons such as:

▪   The size, and critical mass of the assets relative to the rest of the group, as is obvious in the case of EDF Energy, part of the first organizational level of the EDF Group. In the past, London Electricity, EDF's first acquisition in the UK, was a company belonging to the Western Europe, Mediterranean, and African Division of the International business line, together with other companies such as EnBW, then reporting to the Central Europe Division. The progressive build up of EDF's presence in the UK, with the integration of other distribution companies as well as generation assets led to EDF Energy being in the first rank division of the Group (see Figure 7.3), while other international activities and companies still report to a level 1 International Division.

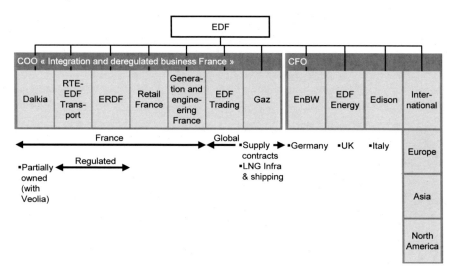

Figure 7.3: EDF Group organization (2008)

- Governance issues, mainly because of other shareholders. This is the case of EnBW, partly owned by EDF (45.01% alongside turbulent regional interests, sometimes impeding the enthusiasm of the French group in developing synergies and integration effects with its German 'subsidiary'). Then again, EnBW now is one of the level 1 division of the Group.
- The lack of obvious synergies with the rest of the Group, in the case of a distant overseas company or group of companies. This would best apply to E.ON UK, also one of the first level division of the E.ON Group, or the UK and US Divisions of Iberdrola group, which hold interests in Scottish Power and Energy East, respectively.

Spanish utility Endesa is the only one of the European utilities to develop a purely geographical organization at level 1, with three geographical Directorates General (Spain & Portugal, representing some 65% of Endesa's earnings before interest, taxes, depreciation and amortization (EBITDA) (Endesa, 2007), Europe, and Latin America). This organization is a result of very strong international growth, along with unbundling of distribution networks at home. The previous organization of Endesa, until 2004, was focused on the domestic market, with a typical generation-trading-retail and networks value chain-based lay-out, as represented in Figure 7.4.

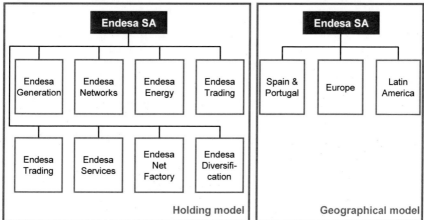

Figure 7.4: The transformation of Endesa's organization since 2001

Within the energy activities[5] of most European utilities, the size of the legacy domestic market often drives players to combine value chain structure with geography and shape domestic divisions along the value chain or regulated/competitive

---

[5] Energy activities designates the vertically integrated energy value chain segments: generation, wholesale trading and marketing, energy retailing.

activities at the first level of their organization, in order to maintain a strong coordination effect on the legacy markets.

Beyond large international assets, the domestic market can also be represented on the first level of the organization. EDF's organization, as shown in Figure 7.3, reflects an effort to recognize the share of the French market in the Group's revenues (54%) and EBITDA (65%) (EDF, 2007). Generation and Engineering, Optimization and Trading, and Commerce Directorates appear at level 1 of the organization and all report to a Chief Operating Officer (COO), clear number 2 of the Group, overseeing all unregulated activities, with a commitment to maintaining a high level of integration.

An increasingly significant variant of geography is the wholesale market structure, which drives organizational designs aimed at maximizing the value of a certain portfolio of physical and/or contractual assets within a relevant wholesale market. As a result, within an area that is relevant in terms of asset portfolio optimization, beyond the national boundaries, business units are aligned on value chain segments. As electricity wholesale markets are more fluid, transparent and structured than natural gas markets, they drive the layout of organizations aligned on markets for convergent utilities.

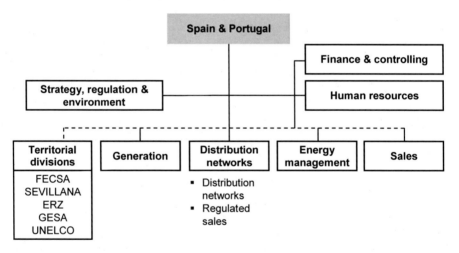

Figure 7.5: Current organization of Endesa for Spain and Portugal

Within the Spain & Portugal Directorate General (see Figure 7.5), Endesa has adopted a typical value chain-based organization for these countries, while maintaining a specific territorial representation,[6] a legacy of the pre-unbundling era and emblematic of the magnitude of the transformation that is at stake.

An organization of this kind can be adopted within a wider perimeter, such as Europe, with business units then covering a wide, integrated market, with a level of management centralization that is dependent on the specific features of the ac-

---

[6] No business management responsibility.

tivity (see below). RWE Group level organization, as represented in Figure 7.6, is emblematic of a very lean divisional organization aligned on the value chain segments (with the exception of RWE npower, the UK subsidiary).

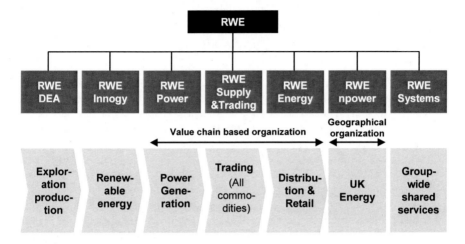

Figure 7.6: RWE Group level organization

Each of the divisions represented above oversees either centralized business units (e.g., in generation, trading and portfolio management in the case of RWE) or regional units for retail and distribution (German regional companies, to steer multiple shareholdings in distribution companies, organize retail at regional levels and create shared services, as shown in Figure 7.7).

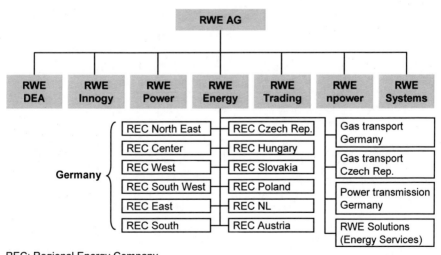

REC: Regional Energy Company

Figure 7.7: RWE energy organization

7.2.2.3 Dimension 3: Specific Features of the Activities

Specific features of value chain activities exert a heavy influence on the organizational design of utilities: customer segmentation-based organization of retail and various forms of distribution organization depend on unbundling schemes.

Customer segmentation is dependent on local energy markets. However, all European utilities' commercial organizations are converging toward a twofold structure:

- Mass market divisions, comprising residential customers, small enterprises, and small office, home office (SOHO) accounts. In all markets, the local or regional dimensions tend to give way to more standardized, centralized approaches (e.g., progressive reduction in the number of customer service centers, development of shared service centers, development of national or near-shore call centers, etc.).

- Business accounts divisions, often subsegmented into vertical industries segments (e.g., metal, pharmaceuticals, enabling the development of tailored offerings), massively multi-site accounts segments (often commercial/franchise accounts), which have highly specific and complex requirements for load aggregation, energy expenditure site-allocation, billing, etc., large accounts segments (industrial and commercial) and in some cases an additional key/giants accounts subsegment devoted to highly contributive electricity- or gas-intensive customers).

This more simple, more centralized, organization is a simplification coming from the legacy distribution-based structure. Attempts to pool marketing, if not the sales team, for the residential markets across countries, at least to a certain extent, have not yet succeeded. Language remain a key issue for customer service, but also for marketing purposes.

The effect of regulatory mandated unbundling on distribution networks depends on the level of pressure exercised by the regulator (if any: Germany, until recently, did not really have a regulator, resulting in very loose implementation of unbundling and continuing synergies between sales and network management organizations at local and regional levels).

Overall, we can summarize the evolution of distribution organization, under unbundling pressure, in three waves, the timing of which is dependent on the national regulatory schedule:

- *Wave 1:* Minimal organizational evolution at operational level, in order to safeguard, as much as possible, legacy synergies between distribution and sales on support functions.

- *Wave 2:* Strict separation, through the establishment of separate subsidiaries, at national and local levels, sometimes creating double organizations, in order to guarantee the absence of any financial flows related to shared services, service level agreements, or headquarters/overhead payment. As a result, the cost structure of the distribution companies may significantly increase, but regulators in several countries (e.g., France, Belgium) favor this clear-cut situation as new starting position.

- *Wave 3:* Once a reasonable level of transparency is established, tariffs/cost base more efficiently regulated, with multi-year regulation, synergies can again be considered, through transparent shared service structures.

EU's 2003/54/CE Directive defines regulated activities in distribution and stipulated how they must be unbundled:

- The Distribution System Operator (DSO) is responsible for operating, maintaining, and developing the system.
- The DSO must be legally independent of any other activities.

Only a limited number of activities had to be truly regulated as a result of these guidelines, at least in a strict sense: planning and budgeting of network operations/development, networks access pricing, supplier contract management, capacity/bottleneck management, management of security of supply. As a result, operations on networks or databases management are not regarded as regulated activities. Based on this directive, each country had defined its own detailed rules, which led to a variety of different regulation frameworks.

For instance, Germany had opted for a minimal application of the EU directive. This had led to cost-effective organizational structures that had enabled synergies between regulated and unregulated perimeters. In some German regions, RWE had bundled the minimal DSO functions detailed above within a dedicated subsidiary of the parent supply company. This had allowed synergies in client management (billing, collection, call centers, etc.), network O&M (maintenance, extensions, small works), and administrative functions (Human resources (HR), finances, IS, purchasing, etc.). In contrast, some countries had then chosen to apply strict separation of regulated and nonregulated activities in individual subsidiaries, with very few synergies or none at all allowed (e.g., the Netherlands or France). More recently, and under pressure to meet the next EU Directive 2007 deadline, RWE had set up, within the regional companies, two grid subsidiaries (networks O&M, regulated network operations functions), alongside an overhead organization (administrative functions, HR, finance) and a customer service subsidiary. To increase regulatory compliance, this latest structure evolved into regional companies functioning as the regulated grid companies, with sales subsidiaries.

7.3 Challenges and Emerging Paradigms in Utilities Organizational Design

European utilities have enjoyed a total shift in their environment and situation since 2005. Their financial leeway has greatly improved. As a result of divestments of non-core-business activities, their debt has been reduced and their cash situation has improved. European utilities are also more focused on energy and Europe, now that they have divested their overseas and diversification assets. As a result of the end of the power prices war in the early 2000s and the high fossil fuel prices, electricity and natural gas prices have also been constantly rising, restoring

European utilities' margins. Finally, European utilities now mostly enjoy stable and limited competition on their domestic historical markets.

Renewed financial leverage of European utilities pushed them back onto the merger and acquisition trail and into a scramble for size at both European and global levels, as is obvious in the recent wave of utilities mergers and acquisitions (M&A). This new era of European and overseas development should deliver:

- Operational excellence, as a result of scale effects where relevant (generation, trading, sales, G&A, etc.), wider pooling of resources, and increased opportunities for experience sharing.
- Performance jumps, related to the realization of operational synergies with newly acquired assets, after thorough optimization of existing assets.
- Enhanced financial performance management through the leverage of different regulation cycles/frameworks in different countries/regions for the transmission and distribution network activities.
- New activities intended to tackle new business areas (renewables, upstream oil and gas, electric vehicles, etc.) or to further integrate utilities business models (gas for electric utilities and conversely, upstream oil & gas, liquefied natural gas (LNG) infrastructure and shipping, nuclear, or renewable equipment manufacturing).

In contrast to the situation that prevailed in the pre-liberalization era, this new wave of development is under strong financial pressure and heavy shareholder scrutiny. The ongoing credit crunch and deteriorating economic conditions will only add to the pressure for acquisitions and new developments to be more accretive and generate more synergies.

7.3.1   Performance and Speed: Leaner and Simpler Organizations to Enable Profitable Growth

In this context, European utilities now have to face several complex organizational challenges:

- Their growth in size and geographical spread creates additional complexity and widens the span of control issues: how best to organize and manage activities diverse in size, financial and regulatory cycles, technology, and geographical distance from the headquarters? How to maintain operational excellence, often rooted in the technical background of utilities staff, while fostering economic performance?
- The emergence of structured regional wholesale markets[7] results in organizations aligned on the value chain segments in the relevant geography: upstream oil & gas, generation, trading and portfolio management, retail. Yet this organizational segmentation should not hinder the competitive advan-

---

[7] Such as France-Benelux with the coupling of Powernext, Belpex and APX, Iberia, the UK or North West Continental Europe as a whole, given the fluidity between France, Switzerland, Germany, Belgium, and the Netherlands.

tages related to vertical integration. Contractual frameworks have to be organized in between these entities to regulate volume and price transfer conditions, as well as risk limits, while empowering each entity to optimize its own stand-alone performance.

- The constant financial pressure on publicly traded companies, driving the need for more standardized organizations, enables a faster, more reliable and simpler reporting and consolidation.

While detailed responses vary among utilities, depending on their managerial maturity and the respective weight of the challenges above, a trend towards leaner and simpler organizations, with shorter management lines, can be observed.

Management structures and reporting lines tend to prevail over legal entities/theoretical shareholding structures. In fact, most European utilities have inherited complex, sometimes interlaced, shareholding structures as a result of series of regional, national, or international acquisitions. Diversification of activities, either organic or through acquisitions, also drove the creation of holding companies (E.ON, Suez, Iberdrola). While legal entities may remain, for tax optimization, regulatory or minority shareholding reasons, all players tend to promote managerial organizations structured across legal entities, and in some cases they are trying to align the legal structure on the managerial organization. As an example, in 2001, the territorial organizations of Endesa in Spain[8] have been dismantled and units spread across the management units of the group, with a value chain segment logic. The legal entities remain mainly for branding reasons. Likewise, Suez and newly formed GDF SUEZ maintain legal entities (Tractebel, Electrabel SA) that no longer appear on the group's organizational chart. RWE also systematically implemented a regional organization to encompass all sales and distribution activities (6 regions in Germany and 6 countries in North West and Central Europe).

These moves are intended to simplify reporting lines, enable faster decision-making processes, and ignore the complexity embedded with legal structures and associated representative bodies. In this context, employee representation, once multiplying, depending on the number of companies, are also pulled back to a minimum, encompassing a wider geographical or functional scope.

This also led to shorter management reporting lines, from the top of the group to the field operations. The number of management levels at EDF or Endesa, in their domestic service territories, could have been nine to twelve prior to the most recent organizational restructuring. It is now being reduced to seven (functional) to nine (operational) from field to Chief Executive Officer (CEO). Shorter reporting lines are often also getting leaner, with a return to more pyramidal models, empowering the management at each level. This is a reversal of attempts to implement semi-matrix organizations, for instance in the retail activities, to mix dimensions such as product, territory, and customer segment, and activity (customer relationship management (CRM), sales, marketing, etc.) in the organization, at national, regional and sometimes local levels. Such transversal dimensions, most useful during times of transformation, implementation of new organizations, in-

---

[8] Sevillana, ERZ, FECSA, GESA, Unelco.

dustrialization of practices, and less financially constrained organizations, are no longer needed with the same level of complexity and systematic duplication.

7.3.2 Control and Standardization: The New Operational Steering Model

Historically, utilities' organizational model was based on their generation and distribution backbones and was thus very pyramidal and hierarchical. The so-called historical operational model is characterized by:

- Heavy headquarters, historically the top level of the integrated generation-transmission-distribution monopoly, having evolved into a group headquarters while keeping a very operational steering role. This would include not only defining the overall strategy and the group financial targets, but also setting operational and economic performance objectives for all the group's businesses, playing a key role in the decision-making process, not limited to giving the final green light, but intervening several times at earlier stages.
- Business units responsible for economic performance within a constraining but negotiated budget framework, without significant strategic autonomy (e.g., new retail offerings, a new retail brand or a key generation maintenance framework contract would be reviewed at headquarters level).
- Systematic duplication of functions at all management levels of the organization, across the group, with little connection along the functional lines (HR, finance, IT, procurement, etc.).

The organization of Gaz de France, prior to privatization and the merger with Suez, was very emblematic of the pyramidal operational model. Electrabel, part of the Suez Group, prior to the unbundling of distribution system operations (direct or on behalf of Intercommunales, the local distribution companies) and the merger with Gaz de France also was steered in a very operational way. Both companies then had large headquarters with strong capabilities to intervene in operational, strategic, and financial decision-making at all levels and across all activities.

Such models then often evolved into so-called strategic management organizational models, characterized by:

- Reduced role of corporate level, positioned as strategic (as opposed to purely financial) holdings and focusing on setting up organization and management principles, group financial targets, strategic orientations. In this case, beyond setting objectives, headquarters also coordinates the group and fosters group synergies, despite not having much in the way of resources and capabilities to do this with.
- Business units enjoy wide operational autonomy, within the strategic boundaries set by the corporate level. Key projects, even though within a business unit, may be steered by or jointly with the corporate level (large transforming transactions, large investments, new activities/countries, etc.).

- Functional lines steered from the corporate level across all management levels of the group organization, with strong connection/coordination in between levels, ensuring reasonable visibility, by the corporate level, over the implementation of functional policies and projects within the group.
- Strong focus on shareholders' value at group level.

This evolution towards more financially oriented, more flexible strategic holding models served the growth of utilities well in the late 1990s and early 2000s. It also enabled them to keep most acquired units, as well as legacy domestic territory units, 'as is', with little, if any integration effect. This model is very emblematic of the Suez Group up to 2005, which also had to cope with control issues in some of its subsidiaries, such as Tractebel, which it did not own 100%. Financial markets pressure led to a first wave of rationalization within the strategic holding model, as demonstrated in the example of the Suez Group after 2005 (see Figure 7.8). The evolution of the Suez organization between 2002 and 2005 was aimed at the creation of homogeneous business lines, each focused on a single core business activity.

Strategic holding models, such as hybrid models between operation-driven & function-driven or purely function-driven models, have enabled a great deal of sophistication to recreate integration effects, in spite of the negative holding effects (high degree of autonomy, if not advocated freedom of subsidiaries/divisions, absence of group effects and corporate ownership behavior, etc.). As an example, the development of corporate controlled functional lines, with a high level of standardization across most of the Group's business lines and business units, has helped integrate the relatively unorthodoxly structured Suez Group after a continuous series of acquisitions.

Suez 2002   **Suez 2005**

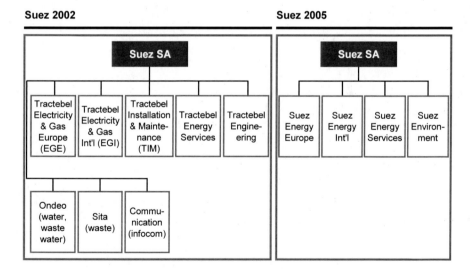

Figure 7.8: Group level organization of the Suez Group before/after 2005

Transversal performance improvement plans, such as the EDF Performance/Altitude Program (2003-2007) or Suez Optimax, were also putting homogeneous pressure on business lines/business units, which triggered some group effects. They also pushed the group divisions within their activity/territory to enhance performance through organization standardization, simplification, business and functional process reengineering, etc.

While these efforts have proved successful in fulfilling the expectations of shareholders in the past, financial markets now expect to see top- and bottom-line synergies as well as operational synergies from the recent race for size among European utilities. Analysts and shareholders want to understand the value of large transactions in adjacent or distant territories. Does size really matter? What organization can deliver transaction-related, then recurring, long-term operational improvements? While the performance gap between US and European distribution networks makes it obvious that proper management and consolidation by European players has the potential to improve the performance of US players, a recent Roland Berger survey of analysts' perceptions of synergies in European–European transactions demonstrates that European utilities have so far failed to provide convincing evidence that that they have put synergy-generating organizations and processes in place (Roland Berger Strategy Consultants, 2008).

As a result, we observe the development of a new operational steering model, coming back to the basics of a strong operational and financial grasp of utilities' activities by the top management. This new operational steering model is enabled by more focused, leaner, and simpler organizations, now that the transformation waves (unbundling, retail competition, wholesale market structuring, and development) are past. While keeping most of the features of the previous strategic management models, this new model is characterized by:

▪ The emergence, within the top management of European utilities, of COO, to whom the heads of value chain or geographical businesses report. Such positions appear at Iberdrola (COO also in charge of the Iberian Market Division), RWE, and E.ON. At EDF, the COO set-up was tried between 2002 and 2005 with limited actual control on the activities, owing to the strong 'baronies' in such business lines as Generation and Retail. While there is no actual Group level COO to-date, one of the two Deputy Group CEOs is in charge of all competitive French activities, thus steering four business lines.

▪ The development of group headquarters, in staff numbers and/or in capabilities, to actually oversee the operations of all business lines in all territories. This may not change the head count for heavy French or Spanish headquarters much, but definitely means a shift in competences. For leaner German headquarters at E.ON or RWE, competences and head count are at stake. Key areas concerned are controlling (with capabilities to better understand businesses and margin-generation mechanisms, and not limited exclusively to financial skills); strategy (with operational project management, business development oversight, wholesale market modeling capabilities).

▪ The development of very consistent functional lines steered by the group headquarters across the group's businesses and geographies. This enables group-wide policies in domains such as purchasing, IT, HR and group mobility, which can initiate synergies plans, while decision-making remains with the operational businesses.

- A strong focus on group synergies across regions in similar businesses, steered by both functional policies and a corporately sponsored synergies program and aggressive post-acquisition integration initiatives.

7.3.3   Integration: The Systematic Push Toward Realization of Group-wide Synergies

In leaner, more focused and more operationally controlled organizations, one of the promising performance improvement levers that is widely considered by European utilities executives is the realization of group-wide synergies. Most European utilities have articulated their quest for group synergies around:

- Aggressive post-acquisition approaches;
- Group-wide sharing of service centers;
- Group-wide functional policies;
- Transversal group programs, mainly focusing on performance improvement and continuous efficiency improvement;
- Transversal platforms for the generation of synergies, focusing on core business activities.

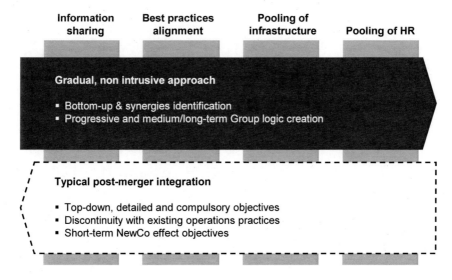

Figure 7.9: Different approaches to the realization of synergies

More aggressive post-acquisition approaches are one of the first levers to swiftly deliver synergies related to the reduction of redundancies, scale effects, and sharing of best practices. Approaches to the realization of synergies vary, as illustrated in Figure 7.9.

As an example, E.ON is very systematic and aggressive in its approaches to the identification and realization of synergies. The group organizational model is imposed on newly acquired objects, regardless of their size and culture. Such a straightforward approach makes it possible to focus on business issues and avoid relatively useless adaptation time. The analysis of the post-acquisition integration processes of Distrigaz Sud, acquired by Gaz de France, in Romania, and Distrigaz Nord, acquired by E.ON, two neighboring gas distribution utilities, is interesting, as the two approaches were totally symmetrical. Gaz de France initiated the post-acquisition effort with a slow, bottom-up, consensus-based process, to manage change with as much managerial and staff buy-in as possible. E.ON, in the same period of time, executed a 2-year, systematic, integration approach, with the help of both German experts and external consultants, to tackle the functional integration with the E.ON group and establish its standards at Distrigaz Nord, but also to profoundly restructure the distribution business, implement German best practices, etc. Both these European utilities have now reached quite a high level of restructuring and achieved significant performance improvement; the Gaz de France approach took longer to gain momentum.

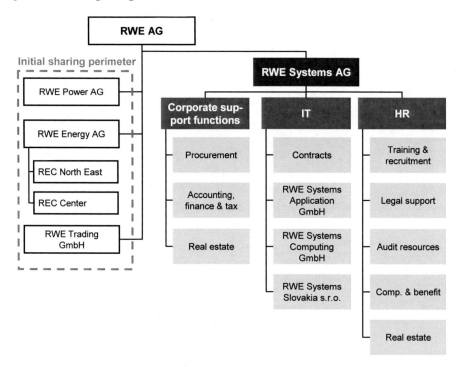

Figure 7.10: Bold approach to shared services: the case of RWE Systems

European utilities are also more systematically implementing shared service centers at all levels of the organization, across geographies, for support functions. Various set-ups co-exist and are highly dependent on the specific features of the companies involved. Some groups, such as RWE, have adopted very bold approaches towards pooling resources at national, or international levels. Figure 7.10 illustrates the scope and the organization of wholly owned subsidiary RWE Systems aimed at pooling resources mainly across German Regional Energy Companies, but also taking account of group-wide issues such as procurement or communication document production for Eastern European or UK activities.

The choice of a subsidiary with full-blown support functions enables strong empowerment of the management of the shared service company with detailed operational and financial objectives, to provide services at the lowest cost and optimize the shared services head count. Service level agreements enable transparency between RWE Systems and its clients, which is paramount when these are regulated network companies within the regional energy companies. GDF SUEZ subsidiary Electrabel has also developed shared services, at Belgian levels and across activities (generation, sales, and in some cases distribution network activities in the past), focusing on HR (payroll, recruitment, training) and accounting. Newly formed GDF SUEZ is now actively pursuing additional shared services opportunities, also bundling legacy Gaz de France and Suez shared service centers.

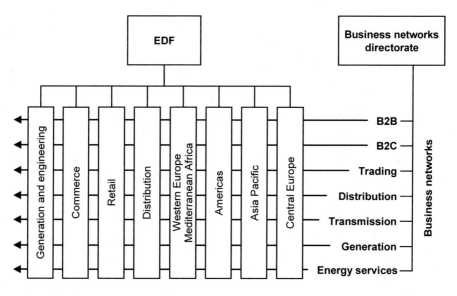

Figure 7.11: Business networks in the EDF Group[9]

---

[9] Figure 7.11 refers to a previous organization structure of EDF in 2004. However, these business networks are still structured and active in EDF's current organization under the international division.

Transversal operational coordination mechanisms are badly needed in refocused, more operationally controlled organizational structures. As an example, the newly formed GDF SUEZ has created a generation coordination group aimed at promoting best practices sharing, but also scale effects in initial design standardization, spare parts procurement, and maintenance contracting. EDF has long had a group synergies unit, with a small central support team and a matrix organization involving leaders in each of the business lines (nuclear generation, thermal generation, hydro generation, B2B and B2C retail, transmission, distribution). Typically, the development of these transversal platforms at EDF was incentivized through objectives set in the balanced score card of business lines (generation, trading, retail France, etc.) and divisions (nuclear, thermal, hydro, engineering, B2B, B2C, etc.). This approach, though relatively slow-paced and bottom up, achieved results such as a fleet framework agreement with a key CCGT spare parts contractor, performance benchmarking for eight thermal generation plants across Europe, multisites, cross-country sales to key accounts, which would not have been contracted otherwise (see Figure 7.11).

7.3.4   The Next Model: Value Chain-based Organization and Centralization

In the search for synergies in more focused, leaner organizational frameworks, some European utilities are moving toward systematic integration around value chain segments, across geographies. This eases the identification and steering of synergies in comparable activities, across regions, through a vertical management line, rather than more complex and longer transversal projects or coordination structures. Indeed, business line managers (generation, trading and wholesale marketing, sales) have oversight over all relevant assets and resources, across regions, that then structure the second level of the organization.

Such an organizational framework may also evolve into the centralization of some business activities, across regions, in order to maximize synergies. However, the ability to centralize depends not only on the organizational and managerial maturity, but also on the value chain segment itself.

Generation is mostly centralized, either at national or at European level, at least for asset management activities. Asset management activities include generation planning (technology, site and business planning), project management and engineering (engineering, procurement, construction, financing and management of EPC, etc.), operations and maintenance planning, and maintenance expertise/competence center. These functions are increasingly standardized and involve interaction with global EPC and O&M contractors. Critical size therefore makes a difference in terms of procurement, and also of exchange of best practices, technology watch, etc. As a result, these functions tend to be centralized at European, or sometimes global, level. Operations and maintenance activities are mostly organized in technology business lines, in which operational synergies can be maximized. While operations and maintenance activities are by nature local, both increasingly European or global contracting and the need for exchanging best practices and pooling scarce competences push either for centralization, or for the creation, on top of existing national organizations, of competence centers/ coordination groups, as described earlier. Electrabel created a maintenance competence center serving very operational field needs on the Belgian asset base, but also consolidating expertise and consulting with other Electrabel assets in the Netherlands, Germany, Spain and, in some cases, France (former Compagnie Nationale du Rhône hydro assets). E.ON and RWE, have also started to move toward centralization of certain generation activities, at least on a regional basis, through the creation of generation business units/divisions (or specifically in Market Unit Central Europe for E.ON, at group level, for RWE).

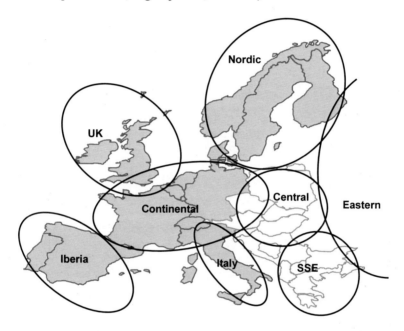

Figure 7.12: The emergence of regional electricity markets

Wholesale portfolio optimization, i.e., generation and gas supply contracts revenue management, trading, and sometimes retail portfolio optimization can be centralized. The key drivers for such centralization moves are:

- Market integration: at global level for oil, LNG, coal, and carbon emissions markets, at regional level, as illustrated in Figure 7.12, for power and gas markets in Europe.
- The identification and systematic harvesting of portfolio synergies across regions and commodities. The aim of creating the Global Gas and LNG business line of GDF SUEZ was to encompass all natural gas supply assets across all business units of the newly formed group, and it has a clear objective: to deliver synergies.

- Operational efficiency and excellence of the structure and the human resources carrying out these functions (IT, HR, quantitative skills, etc.). The
  short quote below is an extract from the 2007 RWE Group Annual report and
  illustrates these operational efficiency effects.

  "Another way we intend to enhance efficiency is through [...] the combination of RWE Gas Midstream and RWE Trading resulting in the new RWE
  Supply & Trading. Our goals are to avoid duplication of work, implement
  decisions more quickly, and pool market competencies. This division will
  thus be responsible for the commercial optimization of all our non-regulated
  midstream gas activities. These consist of the purchase, transmission and
  storage of gas as well as the LNG business. In addition, as Europe's largest
  energy trader, the company will be our hub for tradable commodities such as
  electricity, gas, coal, petroleum and CO_2 emissions allowances."

- Risk control and risk management.

As a result of these motivations, in recent years utility players have tended to:

- Centralize the management of the asset portfolio positions and associated
  commodity risks within a dedicated asset optimization unit allowed to make
  physical and financial buy-and-sell decisions.
- Set up internal transfer mechanisms to ensure that the production and commercial units sell or source energy to or from the performance objectives that
  reflect their responsibilities.
- Clarify the role of trading: Maintain a profit-driven trading group, either as a
  stand-alone business unit or as part of the asset optimization unit. Make sure
  the trading group supports the other company units as an internal market
  broker (market access, forward curves pricing support, etc.) and also as an
  adviser for portfolio management decisions.

Figure 7.13 illustrates some European utilities players' regional organization as
of 2008. E.ON is emblematic of this trend towards centralization of trading to
maximize value from cross-market and cross-commodity optimization. While
E.ON is still organized with geographical market units, it has systematically separated trading and portfolio optimization activities[10] from the regional companies,
to connect them with the central trading unit and in some cases purely to integrate
the activities. Hence trading and power portfolio optimization activities for the
Nordic, UK, Pan European Gas, and Central Europe Market Units of E.ON are run
through E.ON Energy Trading. Other European utilities, such as EDF, GDF
SUEZ, and Enel, already have trading business units whose reach extends well
beyond the legacy service territory of the utility. EDF Trading, as an example, is
active across European electricity and gas markets, and is also trading oil, natural

---

[10] This logic only applies to electricity portfolio optimization, while gas portfolio management is integrated on a European scale in market unit Pan European Gas, the core of which
is the former Ruhrgas. This is related both to the decision not to integrate Ruhrgas with
E.ON in Germany and Central Europe and the importance of gas supply contracts portfolio
management issues with Gazprom.

gas, LNG, and carbon globally, with local offices in Europe and overseas. It is optimizing the asset portfolio of EDF Energy in the UK, but has a limited grasp of EnBW trading and portfolio optimization activities, for which the German utility, being only partially controlled by EDF, runs its own trading unit. The recent merger between Gaz de France and Suez leaves GDF SUEZ with two main trading units, with Gaselys, a Gaz de France joint-venture with the French bank Société Générale, and Electrabel Trading, which was trading for Electrabel in France, Benelux, Spain, and Italy. There again, the centralization of trading activities across countries and business units might play a key role in reaching ambitious gas supply synergies (€ 180 million by 2013) and revenue synergies (€ 350 million by 2013) (GDF SUEZ, 2008). Portfolio management activities, as in other European utilities, may remain local, either to manage local generation assets more efficiently or to manage historical fuel supply contracts. A second level of optimization can, however, be organized at central level, within the trading business unit, as RWE Energy Trading has demonstrated in Central Europe.

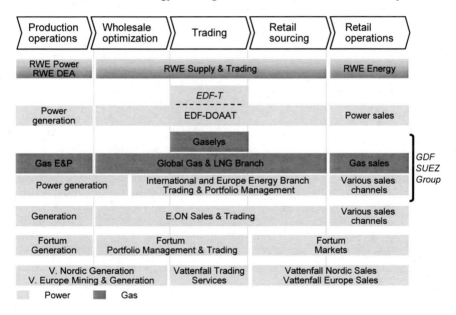

Figure 7.13: Trading and portfolio management organizations (Annual reports, Roland Berger analysis)

Retail activities have not been prone to centralization, given the differing retail market conditions on the one hand (retail pricing mechanisms and regulatory framework mainly, regardless of the market: B2B, B2C), and the demanded proximity to the clients on the other. Some European utilities (such as EDF and Electrabel) once thought of organizing international key account management units to serve very large, multi-site, multi-country industrial and services accounts. These customers, after widely benefiting from the Western European power and gas price war in the early days of market liberalization, started issuing European or multi-country RFP for energy in 2002-2003. This approach was unsuccessful, however, given the local nature of price-setting mechanisms and the complexity and differences between national sales contracts, including taxes. Last but not least, European utilities, though committed to trying to serve customers across regions to materialize commercial synergies between their various national subsidiaries, were not eager for their margins to deteriorate in a country where they were dominant, in order to gain market share in a country where the incumbent utility was better positioned to serve the sites of the customer. Thus, a central clearinghouse to accommodate such pan-European pricing mechanisms was rapidly deemed unnecessary. Most European utilities, after trying various cross-national organizations in order to position offerings with international accounts, tend to favor a well organized lead key account management process and associated organization.

Distribution networks are by essence local, even though, as discussed earlier in this chapter, some international synergies can be activated. The same applies to energy services, which require customer proximity. As an example, the Energy Services business line of GDF SUEZ then breaks down into country or regional business units, sometimes also taking into account activity segmentation (installation, facility management, asset outsourcing, etc.). Interestingly, the Tractebel Engineering business unit covers a cross-country/cross-activities scope, given the global nature of its underlying market for large infrastructure (networks, regasification, and generation). Likewise, French energy services group Dalkia, a subsidiary, is also organized through regional market units, combined with a set of specialized subsidiaries (public lighting, hospitals services, installation, etc.).

7.3.5 Empowerment: New, Customized Organizational Design for New Activities

Since 2005, European utilities, after refocusing on their new domestic European energy market, have regained sufficient financial leeway to go back on the development and acquisition trail, in order to tackle new business areas:

- To consolidate their European business model, with upstream oil and gas or nuclear assets, enabling strongly vertical integration;
- To diversify while remaining close to their core business and avoid shareholders' and financial markets' scrutiny, with renewables, energy-efficiency services, electric vehicle, etc.

Most European utilities adopt a relatively empowering, entrepreneurial stance, in order to organize these activities within their group structure. This posture is somewhat similar to the similar movement in the previous development wave, in the 1990s, with a more operationally and financially controlled model. Yet these developments benefit from a high degree of autonomy.

Renewable energies, as an example, have a very individual business model, which is quite distinct from core businesses:

- Specific technologies, with short evolution cycles, and very few common features compared with more traditional, centralized generation;
- Relatively small size of the unit investment, compared with centralized generation;
- Swiftness of the deal flow, also related to the ongoing boom, frequent technological breakthroughs and size of the deals;
- Specific nature of renewable development and entry strategies: pure greenfield, acquisition of technology, acquisition of predeveloped projects or project bundles, acquisition and integration of project and operations companies, upstream vertical integration in equipment manufacturing, technology, or manufacturing partnerships, etc.;
- Spectacular interest from financial markets and private investors, even in relatively troubled waters lately, in financing renewable activities and granting a strong stock premium, thus creating an incentive for market flotation of such activities. This strong, undeniable interest is also strongly related to the favorable regulatory and tariff regimen, guaranteeing long-term, steady revenues, which are quite appealing in times of credit crunch and difficult cash positions.

Several European utilities started 'incubating' renewable energy activities within either their corporate centers or their generation or regional business units. They soon realized that this was appropriate neither for business development at the right pace nor for the very compelling monetization of renewable units on financial markets. Thus, these players bundled all renewable activities in autonomous, in some cases public, business units overseen by the corporate center. This is the case for EDF with EDF Energies Nouvelles (which was earlier in the Development Branch of EDF in a previous organizational framework), with a very successful IPO in 2007. EDP with neo energia and Iberdrola with Iberdrola Renovables, and E.ON with Market Unit Climate & Renewables also adopted a centralized, autonomous approach to the development of renewable energy. Other utilities, such as Enel (with renewables developed within all business units nationally and internationally), or Endesa, with a specific business unit within the Iberia Division, put less emphasis on the development of renewables and also provide markets with less visibility.

Other relatively new activities, such as energy efficiency and electric vehicles services/solutions, may enjoy the same kind of autonomous approach, in order to foster innovation, financial/technical flexibility and entrepreneurial spirit. Interestingly, EDF, after trying out various set-ups to boost energy services for the residential and SME markets in France through units embedded in the retail divisions of the group, has recently structured two new business units: the 'Eco-Efficacité Energétique' unit is designing and marketing, directly and through the regular retail sales channels of EDF, bundled energy, energy services, efficiency services and renewable equipment offerings. Another business unit, called 'Downstream Industrial' aims to build the appropriate vertical integration in equipment manufacturing in order to enable EDF's strategy in that energy efficiency and customer-oriented renewable strategy. Both units are hosted by the Retail Division ('Commerce') a level 1 structure in EDF's organization.

The new wave of nuclear activities development will undoubtedly create additional organizational challenges for the European utilities involved:

- It is a large, capital-draining, core business activity, which will either contribute to reinforcement of the existing asset base in a regional market or help create a presence in that market, with an immediately significant generation presence.
- Nuclear project development is not project development with a nuclear touch. It is a very specific class of projects, with a long cycle and nuclear-specific features in all fields (financing, legal, regulatory, tax, insurance, risk management, grid connection, engineering, procurement, construction, etc.).

Most likely, European utilities that have few nuclear assets as yet (such as Enel and GDF SUEZ), and also nuclear utilities with large nuclear fleets, have to design specific units that are close enough to the existing assets, while combining the whole set of competences required to pursue new, international nuclear projects. As an example, GDF SUEZ (and its predecessor the Suez group) has a corporate level Nuclear Activities Department, reporting to a Deputy CEO and fully developed, with adequate technical, development, and support nuclear-specific resources.

7.4   An Overview of US Utilities Organizational Trends

In the US, similar organizational trends began to emerge in 1996-1997 and blossomed between 1998 and 2001. However, US energy utilities were hampered in their ability to develop or grow new business models, as deregulation in the US electric utility sector was incomplete and uneven. It was incomplete because the distribution and transmission sectors were essentially never open; and it was uneven because the opening of the supply sector remained state-specific, with only a fourth of all states having deregulated their retail customers and very few having opened the mass market (to date, under 2% of the residential sector can choose its electricity provider). Furthermore, retail deregulation was basically frozen when energy prices started to climb in 2004. As prices continued to climb in 2005, deregulation even regressed in some states. Regulators are also insisting on very strict codes of conduct for utilities that choose to have unregulated retail activities, particularly if they also serve customers in their own territory.

As a result, the only sector that is truly open is the wholesale power sector (generation and trading), and that only in regions where there is an organized marketplace (which covers about 70% of US demand, mostly in the northeast, mid-Atlantic, mid-West, Texas, and California). In the southeast, for instance, most deals continue to be bilateral.

In such a patchwork context, it is understandable that innovative business models are relatively scarce. For example, unregulated suppliers find it very difficult to source any substantial share of their open load from their own unregulated power generation assets (because many of these tend to be too far away). Even under some form of service contract, generators are generally forbidden to combine the dispatching and O&M operations of regulated and unregulated generation assets. Many state regulators also limit the ability to jointly manage regulated power and gas assets.

So far, the vast majority of utilities have stuck to an incumbent integrated model that focuses on their territory. This means that about 60 utilities represent about 60% of the total public investor-owned asset base, including mostly small and medium-sized utilities (with revenues in single-digit billions of US dollars). Only the larger utilities (about 15 in total) have a hybrid model that juxtaposes an integrated regulated model focused on their home base with an unregulated wholesale power activity that is regional or national. On average, the unregulated portion accounts for 25% of the second group's asset base. The more successful 'hybrid' companies, such as AEP, Constellation Energy, Dominion, Duke, Entergy, Exelon, FP&L, Progress Energy, PSE&G and Xcel Energy, can see up to 30-50% of their EBITDA stem from such unregulated activities. Hybrids have not developed their business models since the mid-2000s. Most of the changes have focused on sales and the purchase or trade of generation assets. Companies have generally refrained from substantially altering their organizational models. In fact, in 2005-2006, a 'back to basics' trend saw several medium-sized hybrids revert to being 'pure' integrated utilities. In the period between 2005 to 2007, all US utilities, regardless of whether or not they were hybrids, enjoyed strong stock performance (50% increase). Only a few hybrids have consistently done better through intelligent management of the balance between regulated and unregulated assets.

References

Roland Berger Strategy Consultants. 2008. Survey of European and US utilities sector transactions.

Endesa. 2007. Annual report. Madrid: Endesa.

EDF. 2007. Annual report. Paris: EDF.

GDF SUEZ. 2008. Prospectus prepared for the issue and admission for trading of GDF SUEZ shares resulting from the merger of SUEZ with and into Gaz de France. http://www.gdfsuez.com/fileadmin/user_upload/pdf/1_Prospectus_G DFSUEZ_en.pdf.

Part II:
Fundamentals in Utility Management

8 An Industry Overview – Strategic Groups and Critical Success Factors

Veit Schwinkendorf[1]

Abstract

This chapter provides an overview of current business models of European power utilities, which are classified into six major groups. Indications of future developments are also given for these strategic groups. Based on a recent global study conducted by Roland Berger Strategy Consultants, six major critical factors of success of power utilities are described.

Keywords: power utilities, business models, critical factors of success

---

[1] Veit Schwinkendorf is Partner and Head of the Energy & Chemicals Competence Center of Roland Berger Strategy Consultants, Germany.

A. Bausch and B. Schwenker (eds.), *Handbook Utility Management,*
DOI: 10.1007/978-3-540-79349-6_8, © Springer-Verlag Berlin Heidelberg 2009

8.1   Preface

Utility companies are typically defined as companies that produce, distribute and supply electricity, gas, heat and water – with a huge variety of business models around the globe working in very different environments ranging from national-ized (and still monopolistic) to privatized and fully liberalized.

As the European power sector is at the forefront of market liberalization within the utility sector, the following segmentation of business models is focused on European electricity or power utilities:

- On companies primarily active in the generation, transmission, distribution and supply of electricity. They may be engaged in all or only some parts of the value chain of this industry. They may also be active in the gas business or energy-related services.
- On companies that have their center of gravity in countries belonging to the European Union because of their common regulatory framework set by the relevant European legislation.

During the past 15-20 years the structure of the European power sector has changed significantly. Key drivers of this change process have been and still are:

- The EU efforts towards market liberalization and the creation of an internal market for electricity (notably EU Directives 96/92/EC and 2003/54/EC and also – for the future – the third package of legal measures currently under discussion).
- The privatization processes in almost all EU countries.
- The sector consolidation through countless mergers and acquisitions (M&As), at first more at national and currently more at European level.

In combination with an as yet increasing convergence of the European power and gas markets, this has resulted in the evolution of the existing integrated utility model and in the emergence of entirely new business models.

Against this background, this chapter aims at providing a segmentation (or ty-pologization) of current business models of European power companies and giv-ing some indications of future developments thereof, and in addition, at outlining critical factors of success for power utilities in general, based on a recent global study of Roland Berger Strategy Consultants.

8.2   An Industry Overview – Segmenting European Power Utilities

There are, of course, several ways to segment the European power utilities, e.g., by:

- Ownership structure (investor or publicly owned, cooperatives, nationalized entities);

- Presence along the value chain (fully or partially integrated, nonintegrated utilities);
- Lines of business (power, power and gas, etc.);
- Geographic presence (local, regional, national, multinational, or even global).

The following overview of the European power industry uses a segmentation approach that is based on the underlying strategic business model of the particular players (in other words on their strategic positioning along the value chain) according to Porter's concept of strategic groups.

In this chapter, European power utilities are seen and classified from a group perspective and not from the perspective of individual companies within a utility group. In reality, however, large groups in particular may adopt several business models simultaneously in different markets (e.g., being vertically integrated in core markets vs being a power generator only in others). For example, GDF SUEZ will be seen as a vertically integrated utility, although its division SUEZ Energy International acts as an independent power producer (IPP).

Overall, the following six major strategic groups or general business models can be differentiated.

8.2.1   Vertically Integrated Power Utilities

This strategic group of companies, present at all or most steps of the electricity value chain, is basically the business model inherited from the old monopolistic world. From today's perspective it still appears to be the most successful business model in the European power sector. The majority of the current top 10 European utilities by market size are vertically integrated utilities (EDF, GDF SUEZ, E.ON, RWE, Enel, Iberdrola, Endesa, CEZ).

Beyond the general logic of vertical integration, at least two different considerations are implicit in the power utility-specific idea of being vertically integrated:

(1) *From an energy industry perspective:* Because the electricity business – like all other energy businesses – is a cyclical one, having positions in generation and supply leads to more independence of wholesale market volatility. It is a common belief in the power sector that to benefit from this margin effect the retail position should be covered by at least 40-60% of own power production (or manageable power purchasing rights).

(2) *From an overall portfolio perspective:* Regulated businesses (transmission, distribution) will deliver a 'safe return' even in rough times and will therefore have a stabilizing effect on the financial situation of the vertically integrated company (generating value with a low risk, cash generation).

In addition to the vertical integration in the power business, some of the large players are already very far advanced in power and gas integration along the value chain.

The large vertically integrated players will still dominate the scene in the future; however, drastic change will continue to be high on the agenda:

- The current European consolidation process will continue, finally leading to three to four large vertically integrated power & gas utility groups dominating the business. In this process, all players will continue to round off their positions (along the value chain, in the gas business, and on a regional basis).
- The privatization process is also expected to continue, especially with regard to a (further) reduction of public shareholdings in large utilities (expected in 2009 for the Dutch players or Polish PGE, for example).
- Presence in the regulated businesses (transmission and distribution) will be (partly or wholly) sacrificed in favor of external growth opportunities in the unregulated business and/or for financial reasons (to fund growth investments or reduce debt). This can be illustrated with reference to a few examples: As long ago as in 1999-2001, National Power (now RWE npower) acquired the retail businesses of Midlands Electricity, Yorkshire Electricity, and Northern Electric in exchange for the respective distribution businesses to build up a leading retail position in the UK market from scratch. In 2008, E.ON agreed to sell off its German power transmission business within 2 years, and RWE did the same with its German gas transmission business. In addition, Enel is reportedly considering selling off its gas distribution networks to reduce debt in 2009.

8.2.2   Power Generators

Power generation is not only a capital-intensive business; it is also a very concentrated one. At national level, market shares of the top three generators usually range between 70% and 85%, with few exceptions (e.g., in the UK and in the Nordic market). In addition, European power generation is largely dominated by the above-mentioned integrated power utilities.

Nevertheless, there is a strategic group of companies whose business model is strongly focused on and structured around generation and asset-backed trading activities. These companies can be classed in the following groups:

- Some large IPPs such as UK's International Power (with about 21 GW of net installed capacity and power plants on five continents) or Evonik STEAG (9.5 GW, predominantly in Germany).
- Some large power generators such as British Energy (currently in the process of being acquired by vertically integrated EDF; with about 11 GW of mostly nuclear power generation), Austria's Verbund (8.5 GW, mainly hydro power), and Norway's Statkraft (12 GW, also primarily hydro), with some (but minor) activities or shareholdings in the supply business (Verbund is even the owner of the Austrian transmission system operator, APG).
- Many (usually) smaller power generators, often incorporated as joint ventures of regional or local utilities and heavily dependent on wholesale market developments.

- A still increasing number of nonutility generators, i.e., power plants owned and operated by industrial companies in sectors with high power and heat (or steam) consumption as well as financial investor-owned renewable energy generation assets.

These groups will persist in the medium-term perspective. Changes may include M&As (e.g., British Energy), stronger forward integration of the large power generators (e.g., Verbund), privatization of power plant operators that are still state owned (especially in Central and Eastern Europe) and/or a reduction of financial investor-owned renewable energy assets.

8.2.3 (Regional) Integrated Distribution & Supply Utilities

There are about 2,700 electricity distribution network operators (DNOs) in EU-27, many of which are very small with only a few thousand connections (as in Germany, for example). Almost all are integrated with a regional or local supply business. The larger distribution & supply businesses often belong to the above-mentioned vertically integrated groups, while smaller ones are often majority (or even fully) owned by public shareholders.

The integrated distribution & supply utilities have already gone through a long period of change, and this will continue, enforced and even accelerated by regulatory and competitive pressure. Major elements of this ongoing change process are:

- Privatizations and integration into vertically integrated groups;
- Mergers of regional utilities (in order to gain size);
- Backward-integration into power generation (on a stand-alone basis or in joint-ventures);
- Cooperation (joint ventures) with other regional and/or local utilities in all parts of the distribution & supply business (especially in energy procurement, grid operations, and customer operations).

8.2.4 (Independent) Grid Operators

This strategic group is a relatively young one, having basically been created in the EU energy market liberalization process (with the aforementioned EU Directives requiring the formation of transmission system operators (TSOs) by mid-2004 and DSOs by mid-2007). Today, there are still only a few independent grid operators. The following models can be differentiated:

- Of the more than 30 electricity TSOs in EU-27, only about 10 have actually implemented ownership unbundling, i.e., become independent TSOs. Most of the others are legal entities within larger integrated utility groups. The independent TSOs are publicly owned or investor owned, and some are even stock-listed; almost all are focused solely on power transmission in their home countries. A few of them do have shareholdings in transmission activities abroad, e.g., Italian Terna in Brazil or Spanish Red Electrica in Peru and Bolivia.

- 'Large' independent DNOs: These are companies that own and operate the electricity distribution network in a certain region and do not belong to a larger integrated group or have a supply business. The best-known examples are CE Electric UK (a company controlled through a subsidiary of Warren Buffet's Berkshire Hathaway) and Western Power Distribution, also in the UK (the only subsidiary of the vertically integrated US utility PPL Corp. in Europe).

- 'Small' independent DNOs: There is as yet only one significant example of a DNO in Europe: Electricity North West Limited (ENW). Created in December 2007, when United Utilities sold its electricity distribution network to North West Electricity Networks, a joint venture of Colonial First State (part of the Commonwealth Bank of Australia) and JP Morgan, ENW (with about 70 employees) became the licensed DNO for the North West of England, serving 2.3 million customers. United Utilities continues to operate, maintain, construct, and repair these assets on behalf of ENW.

- National Grid, the largest grid operator by market capitalization, with its activities in power and gas transmission and distribution in the UK and the US, and even some generation assets in the US, may be seen as an operator 'sui generis', being in a class of its own.

However, the picture may change soon: Ownership unbundling of TSOs is the preferred option of the EU commission (as against independent transmission operators or TSOs) within the third package of legal measures currently under discussion. Implementation would create more of the aforementioned independent TSOs. In addition, some of the European TSOs are rumored to be interested in taking over their German peers that are up for sale (TSOs of E.ON and Vattenfall). Such a move would signal the start of a European consolidation process in this strategic group, leading to the formation of large Pan-European TSOs. Also, more independent DNOs are about to emerge, for example in the Netherlands, through separation of distribution grids from generation and supply (prior to privatization of the large players) or through sales of distribution networks by large players. Last but not least, in 5 years from now, making ownership unbundling of distribution networks mandatory may even be considered.

8.2.5   Retailers

This strategic group is also a result of electricity market liberalization and – by definition – only comprises those companies that are independent of vertically integrated groups and of DNOs. The opening up of the market has attracted many new players trying to enter the market. At European level, more than 1,000 retailers have come on the scene, but not all of these are still active.

The challenges for these retailers are manifold: reluctant customers, still low churn rates (in most countries 3-8% p.a.), rather high cost-to-gain, rather difficult switching processes, rather thin margins, and increasingly volatile energy prices. Not surprisingly, some retailers have failed. The reasons for failure are diverse, however, as a few examples from one of the most highly developed retail markets, that in the UK, show: as long ago as in September 2000, Independent Energy, then the biggest of the new electricity and gas suppliers, with some 240,000 customers, collapsed after being overwhelmed by its mounting customer billing problems. And quite recently, in autumn 2008, two independent UK energy retailers (Bizz Energy and Electricity 4 Business, with roughly 40,000 customers each) reportedly ran into trouble after having problems with refinancing debt and struggling to cope with highly volatile energy prices, respectively.

To survive successfully in the long-run, retailers have to achieve their critical mass (industry estimate is about 1 m customers), to attain a high level of customer satisfaction, to be excellent in hedging, and to obtain a certain level of backward integration into power generation.

8.3   Critical Success Factors of Top-performing Utilities

In 2007 Roland Berger Strategy Consultants analyzed the financial and operational performance of 185 leading global power companies in 2002-2006. About 45% of these companies have their headquarters in North America (mainly US), about 30% are European, and the rest are based in Asia and Brazil.

A total of 55 top-performing companies were identified by application of the following criteria: above-median revenue growth (2002-2006) and above-median return on capital employed (2002-2006 and in 2006). In addition, 51 low performers were also identified. Among other things, the analysis revealed that:

- The average compound annual growth rate of all companies was 12% per annum in the period specified, whereas the return on capital employed (ROCE) average was slightly above 10%.
- The top performers' revenues were growing about 3.5 times as fast as the low performers' revenues.
- The profitability gap between low- and top-performing companies was huge: for example, in 2006 the (median) earnings before interest and taxes (EBIT) margin of the top performers was 1.4 times that of low performers.
- Furthermore, the gap is widening: for example, in 2006 the (median) ROCE of the top performers was 2.5 times the ROCE of low performers (as against 1.9 times in 2002).

In an attempt to gain an understanding of the drivers and patterns of sustained profitable growth, the top performers were studied in detail. Six critical factors of success were identified:

(1) *Size matters:* Size fosters economies of scale at all steps of the value chain as well as strong market positions in increasingly competitive markets. Size also leads to higher security and quality of supply (e.g., a larger plant portfolio is more robust against failure). Size also generates additional funds for

further growth, i.e., size drives growth to greater size. The study also found empirical evidence for the importance of size: the ROCE of the largest companies in the power sector was not only significantly higher (often by about 3-4 percentage points, and sometimes much more), but has also increased further over the last few years, whereas the ROCE levels of smaller companies (with revenues of less than $ 5 billion) have remained almost unchanged.

(2) *Balanced vertical integration is key:* It has already been mentioned that the business model of the vertically integrated utility is apparently the most successful. Balanced vertical integration has three different elements:

  (a) A competitive generation position, ideally characterized by a balanced and flexible mix of thermal energy (diversified fuel) and nuclear/hydro/wind power with an overall low carbon footprint (i.e., significantly below market average) and a balanced age structure.
  (b) Sufficient retail position coverage: Top performers are covering 100% (and more) of the position in the residential segment with their own electricity generation capacities (or manageable power purchase rights).
  (c) A sizable regulated business: To achieve lasting portfolio effects for the integrated group the regulated business should have a share of about 20-30% of the group's operating result.

(3) *Power & gas integration creates competitive advantages:* Having significant positions in both markets leads to economies of scope and scale. Synergies between electricity and gas can be utilized at practically each step of the value chain (gas-fired generation, multi-energy-trading, grid overlaps, customer base) and, in addition to the synergies, potential for differentiation can be realized in retail (dual fuel offerings) and trading (hedges). However, for full exploitation of the potential a large regional overlap is vital.

(4) *External growth is pivotal for achievement of above-average growth rates:* Of course, organic growth remains key for sustainable value creation. But as most European energy markets show only moderate growth rates, ranging between 2% and 5% per year, it proves difficult to achieve above-average growth (12% per annum and more). Only external growth (M&A) can close the gap. The potential for external growth (privatization, consolidation) in Europe is still huge, and even the question of what comes after European consolidation has already been answered by most of the top 10 utilities: they have been (and still are) expanding their activities outside Europe, primarily to North and South America and also to Asia.

(5) *Best practice transfer creates additional value (even in distant markets):* Managing assets in diverse markets offers opportunities for benchmarking as well as for sharing and spreading best practice within a larger group. Many of the large utility companies have introduced regular expert meetings or even established group-wide competence centers (e.g., for power generation or grid asset management) to share best practice. So far, however, only a few utilities have really implemented a uniform operating model on a group-wide basis (e.g., UK's National Grid, with its global operating model, or Austria's

EVN, implementing its operating model for distribution activities in its sub-sidiaries in Bulgaria and Macedonia). These are the only companies that are able to capture the value of uniform processes and supporting IT systems.

(6) *Performance improvement is a continuous effort:* The performance of the European power industry has increased over the past two decades (e.g., em-ployment in the power utility sector has halved in several countries). None-theless, competitors and regulators will continue to put pressure on the utility companies. Therefore, value-based management (margin before volume) and operational excellence programs remain high on the agenda of power utili-ties. Their challenge is constant improvement of operational performance (or outperformance of regulatory targets) while maintaining (improving) both availability and reliability of assets and quality of supply and services. The leading companies in the sector are conducting pretty large performance im-provement initiatives every 3-4 years. These programs have usually had cost reduction targets in the range of 1.7-3.5% (sometimes up to 4.5%) of the to-tal cost baseline (i.e., revenues minus earnings before interest, taxes, depre-ciation and amortization (EBITDA)). In addition to these larger programs, leading utilities have set up continuous improvement processes (CIP) with the emphasis on the permanent self-reflection of processes by employees, leading to the continuous identification and implementation of (incremental) efficiency improvements (using such methods as Six Sigma, Kaizen, and many others).

8.4   Conclusion

The structure of the European power industry has changed dramatically within the past 20 years and will continue to change. As a result of the formation of the Sin-gle European Energy Market new strategic groups (grid operators, retailers) have emerged and will develop further. However, the model of the vertically integrated power (and gas) utility is expected still to dominate the industry in the future, but even this strategic group will experience new challenges to its model, mainly driven by current and future (ownership) unbundling requirements and European consolidation. Overall, six major critical factors of success have driven the success of this model, and these are also expected to drive sustainable its success in the years to come.

References

ABS Energy Research. 2008. Electricity deregulation report global 2008.
Bundesnetzagentur. 2008. Monitoringbericht 2008. Entwicklung des Strom- und Gasmarkts.

Commission for Electricity and Gas Regulation (CREG). 2007. Annual report 2007.

Commission de régulation de l'énergie (CRE). 2007. Activity report 2007.

Energie-Control. 2008. Marktbericht 2008, Nationaler Bericht an die Europäische Kommission.

European Regulators Group for Electricity and Gas (EGREG). 2008. Obstacles to supplier switching in the electricity retail market, guidelines of good practice and status review.

Nederlandse Mededingingsautoriteit. 2007. NMa Annual Report 2007.

NordREG (Nordic Energy Regulators). 2008. Nordic market report 2008, development in the Nordic electricity market, Report 3/2008.

Office of Gas and Electricity Markets (OFGEM). 2008. Energy supply probe, initial findings report 2008.

9   The Utility Industry in 2020

Francesco Starace[1]

Abstract

"Energy is the very fuel of society and societies without access to competitive energy suffer." – Lee Raymond (past Chairman, Exxon Mobil)
The future major challenge to the European energy system is to ensure the security of supply of energy with a low environmental impact while maintaining a sustainable level of market competitiveness within the European economy.
The role of the utility industry is crucial to obtain the challenging but necessary balance between these three dimensions; the utility industry's task in the coming years will be to develop environmentally friendly technologies, to drive the energy interests, agreements and connections between different countries, and to find the way to let European customers be a responsible and committed part of this crucial change process.

Keywords: supply security, sustainability, energy policy

[1] Francesco Starace is Head and Managing Director of the Renewable Energies Division of Enel S.p.A, Italy.

A. Bausch and B. Schwenker (eds.), *Handbook Utility Management,*
DOI: 10.1007/978-3-540-79349-6_9, © Springer-Verlag Berlin Heidelberg 2009

9.1   Introduction

Energy policy is about industrial competitiveness, security of supply, environmental protection, and finally peace-keeping. Therefore energy management is the duty and responsibility of the industry, the energy-exploring, -transporting, -trading, -selling and -distributing industry, finding the most reliable, efficient and economic answers to the energy policy and the energy needs of their respective markets and clients. In today's debates about the future of energy the major issues, or better contradictions, and what we can do about the situation in the forthcoming decade are repeatedly tackled:

- Rising energy costs and prices against belief that energy costs too much (see Figure 9.1).
- Complete liberalization of demand against concentration on the offer side, and in particular, few primary energy suppliers (see Figure 9.2).
- Diversifying the current mix of energies and origins, against the hope that the solution of the near future will already be renewable (see Figure 9.3).
- Worldwide worrying about the future of the planet's climate against our everyday behavior in energy matters (see Figure 9.4).
- The evident need for long-term energy supply stability and related investment cycles against the increasing demand for short-term flexibility and pay-off (see Figure 9.5).
- Strong need for new production and transportation infrastructure both for power and gas against the poor performance in almost any country when it comes to defining and implementing procedures for construction permits.
- The increasing knowledge and decision power of individual clients against the widespread inability and the lack of automation in selling and delivering customized energy solutions of high quality.

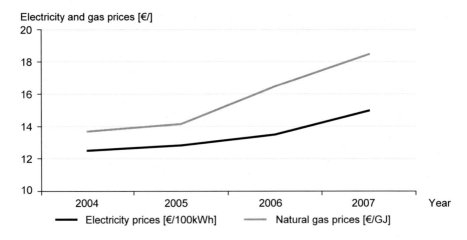

Figure 9.1: EU-25 electricity and gas prices to households 2004-2007 (Commission of the European Communities, 2007)

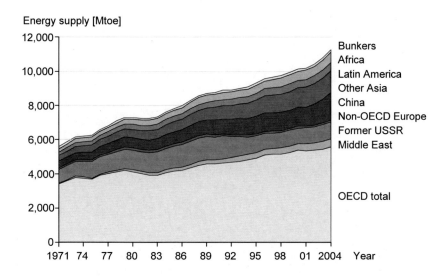

Figure 9.2: Evolution of world total primary energy supply from 1971 to 2004 by region [Mtoe] (OECD, 2007)

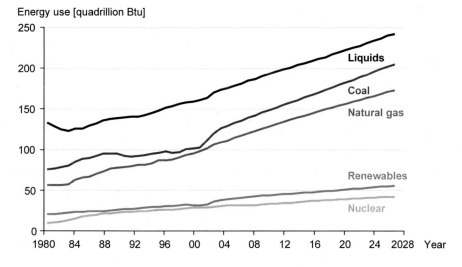

Figure 9.3: World marketed energy use by fuel type, 1980-2030 (IEA, 2007a)

There is no doubt, then, that in the coming decades the utility industry has to deal with big challenges that have to be managed using almost all the possible levers. Our goal is to use these pages to give a quick snapshot of the principal future topics and the industry's main answers.

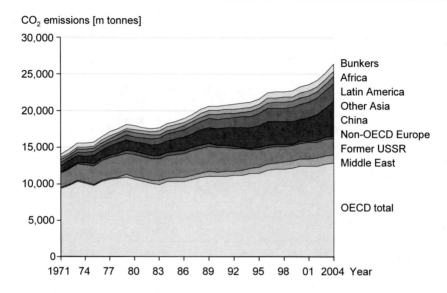

Figure 9.4: World CO_2 emissions from energy use, by region (OECD, 2007)

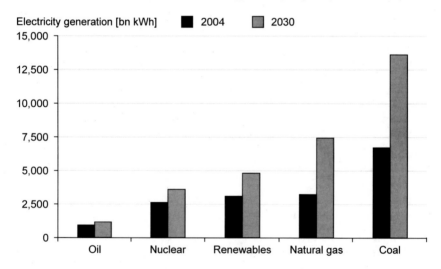

Figure 9.5: World electricity generation by fuel (IEA, 2007a)

The general framework is designed by the EU regulatory body with the EU Energy Package (10 January 2007). The EU aims for an integrated energy policy based on two major pillars. First the ambitious 20-20-20 reduction program: 20% reduction of the CO_2 emissions by 2020, 20% of renewables in EU generation in 2020, and 20% reduction of total primary consumption in 2020. Second a definitive legislative frame with growing competition in the European energy sector. The Commission focuses its attention on the needs of increasing fair access to transmission grids, finding the best and most effective solutions to be the full un-bundling (ITSO: independent transmission system operation) and the independent system operator (ISO) models. The regulator has corresponding wishes for the gas market, pushing for real third-party access to gas storage facilities and liquefied natural gas (LNG) terminals. They see increasing the transparency in the market as another important step on the way to strengthening the position of national regulators and creating an EU Agency with strong orientation and coordination tasks. Finally, the Commission understands the increasing importance and urgency of security of gas supply and aims to strongly stimulate solidarity between member states.

Otherwise, the industry is focusing its attention on mergers and acquisitions (M&A) strategies with a vertically integrated view, the objective of increasing the bargaining power in supply, and the ambitious aim of being at the same time international, national and local. While the industry is diversifying the primary energy needs to optimize the power mix by investing in new power generation capacity and in new interconnections, LNG and gas storage projects are considered priorities to balance profit maximization and supply risk minimization.

Again, investments and innovation are the principal answers to the problem of how to reduce the environmental impact. The first step must be investment in available 'carbon-free' or low-CO_2 emissions power production technologies such as renewables (wind, solar, hydro, etc.) and nuclear power; more or less in the same timeframe the second step to pursue is to prove and improve 'new frontier' technologies such as CO_2 capture and storage (CCS); (see Figure 9.6) nuclear fusion power plants, and hydrogen fuel.

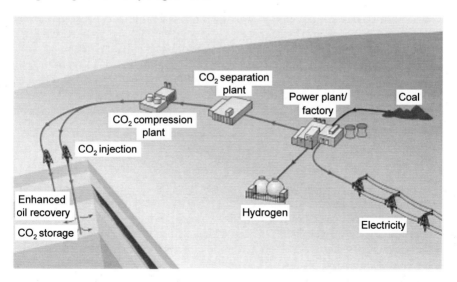

Figure 9.6: CO_2 capture, transport, and storage infrastructure (IEA, 2007a)

From a more operational point of view it is important to continue the cost reduction process. There is still room for further improvement in trading and risk management ability to develop a real, liquid, and unique European wholesale gas and electricity market and stimulate the power and gas exchanges' growth and the market coupling. At the same time, major utilities have a responsibility to drive the market liberalization by diffusing a culture of sustainable use of energy in terms of efficiency and stability with an appropriate product strategy (e.g., long-term, green, fixed-price- and daily/hourly price-driven products), by investing in the enabling technologies (e.g., smart metering, smart grids, and distributed generation), and by empowering clients and building up customer-centered organizations (industrialization of individualization) driven by strong use of new communication technologies.

To change the culture the companies have to put concerted efforts into implementing new management ways of thinking and models with the focus on innovation, internationalization, and efficiency. However, the common effort, and certainly the most ambitious goal, is to change the society mindset from 'NIMBY' (not in my backyard) to 'CERTOBY' (certainly somewhere in our common backyard), or, in order to permit and admit national and supranational decisions on our three principal dimensions. Let us look at all this in more detail, starting by analyzing the interests of the innumerable stakeholders.

9.2   Stakeholders in Utilities

The core business of utilities is supplying clients with primary or secondary energy and related services. The impact on planning stability and competitiveness of large parts of the entire industry and the responsibility for the environment and for security of supply for millions of homes makes the utility industry one of the most important stakeholder portfolios in terms of number and weight. The stakeholders in utilities are: clients, personnel, shareholders, the environment as well as society, the last represented by local, regional, national, and supranational authorities and also by governmental bodies.

Clients

For decades customers of the utility industry have taken the availability of secure and convenient energy for granted. They have associated these services with the very same basic concepts of freedom, technological advance, improvement in personal life style and well-being, to the extent that the very though of sudden or planned lack of energy for sustained periods of time is simply out of question. Over the same period of time, customers have been largely unaware of the costs and environmental implications associated with energy consumption and have been largely passive, captive recipients of a service passed on to them by the utility industry at a cost. Customers are now changing quickly from being unaware, irresponsible, and inactive, emerging as informed, conscious, responsible, and interactive clients who will be increasingly empowered and will exercise:

- Real freedom to choose supplier;
- Real freedom to choose primary energy or its mix;
- Active participation in demand-side management through digital metering and incentive pricing schemes;
- Participation in equity-like project schemes and in the long-term benefits accruing from renewable projects;
- Access to off-the-shelf home generation facilities (photovoltaic, fuel cells, mini-wind power, thermal solar power, efficiency kits, etc.);
- Participation in customized small- to-large scale on-site projects for combined heat and power (CHP), and, for industrial clients, direct equity-like participation in new technologies (nuclear, clean coal and CCS) and initiatives (renewable funds, international up-stream projects, new developments in rural and/or underdeveloped regions of the world).

In general it is safe to assume there will be a very strong increase in interest in the utility industry shown by this particular stakeholder, the customer.

Personnel

For utilities, the people working for them are the biggest lever and force in sustaining and accelerating the process of change in the industry; it is therefore vital for companies to revolutionize the mindset and culture of employees. Early talent scouting as the competition for very qualified resources becomes more intense and good career prospects have to be strongly connected with classic merit elements (line and staff experience, different business lines, different countries, and then: results, results, results), accompanied by intercultural and integration capabilities and life-long learning. Key business capabilities must be in-house; they should on no account be outsourced, and engagement in research and development (R&D) must be enforced.

Companies have to focus efforts on developing new competencies such as marketing, long-term supply, up-stream, IT, customer relationship management (CRM) research, multi-channel sales, efficiency and renewables consulting, internet sales and services, cross-market and cross-commodity trading, and related risk management.

In general, personnel in the utility industry will experience a massive change in composition, focus, training, career development, and remuneration, with reduction of job security in exchange for increased osmosis between utilities and other productive and service segments of the economy.

Shareholders

"A shareholder or stockholder is an individual or company (including a corporation) that legally owns one or more shares of stock in a joint stock company. A company's shareholders collectively own that company. Thus, such companies strive to enhance shareholder value" (N.N., 2007). Therefore, it is important to produce foreseeable results (deliver expectations), show credible (organic) growth paths, control volume and price risks, present sustainable solutions, be reliable, be a corporate citizen (CSR).

Another key point is to increase the capacity to manage communication and provide information steadily and transparently in both good and troubled times. Three major reasons for investors' interest are considered:

(1) Stable Regulatory Asset Base (RAB)-based remuneration of regulated grid activities (albeit with declining share owing to regulation and ownership unbundling).
(2) Predictable short- and medium-term remuneration from liberalized core business.
(3) Growth potential by total value chain management, through synergies, market integration, efficiency and organic growth, long-term vision about energy mix, security of supply, and M&A opportunities.

In general, investors will tend to have increasingly more understanding of and trust in the complexity of this capital-intensive industry, and to discriminate better between players that will lead the desired changes and those that will lag behind.

Environment and Society

Keywords are:

- *Sustainability:* "Future generations should be left no worse off than the current generation." (Tietenberg & Lewis, 2008)
- *Efficiency:* "The aim to use and manage depletable resources in an intertemporal and efficient way." (Tietenberg & Lewis, 2008)

The major issues in a world with increasing economic growth and energy demand, stimulated in particular from the 'two emerging giants', China and India are:

- CO_2 emissions and their consequences of climate changes and the consequent need to invest in low-emission and environmentally friendly technologies.
- Primary energy scarcity and the aim to manage it in an efficient way.

Utilities clearly have to be in the front line and to have the responsibility and the instruments to give a strong contribution to finding solutions for these major future issues. The major topics are to find the right trade-off between profit maximization and social welfare, and in general to educate the whole population, and in particular employees and customers, in the culture of respecting and living in harmony with the stakeholder and the environment.

To reach these ambitious goals, organizations have to be based on 'fair behavior' and a 'strong ethical approach', which means developing an ethical code with strong diffusion and rigorous control tools. Companies need to implement a corporate social responsibility model that takes account of the interests of society and of the companies' responsibility for the impact of all aspects of company activities not only on customers, employees, and shareholders, but also on communities and the environment. Ultimately, utilities should define and implement roles and incentive mechanisms for a more sustainable and efficient energy market by collaborating with the involved institutions and politicians (EU; national governments; parliaments, regulators) and providing substantial support to them in their work.

Our first consideration is that energy policy is one of the few areas left to single European countries' governments to steer the economy and general well-being of their countries. This will become increasingly difficult, as the EU will tighten its grip on this area too and will establish common rules with more detailed and more binding constraints. Local politics (at country, as well as regional and municipal levels) will face increasingly challenging times as it struggles to cope with EU's top-down detailed regulatory drive and with local constituencies' requirements. In general, politicians will have to dedicate more and more time to collaborating with the utility industry; failing to do so will result in a serious disconnect from the well-being of their home constituencies and in the collapse of their policies.

Second, utilities need to drive innovation into the entire system. In production, for example, we need to invest in power production technologies with low CO_2 emissions, such as nuclear, wind, solar, and hydro power, and develop such new frontier technologies as CCS, nuclear fusion power plants, and the use of hydrogen fuel. Other examples in transportation and distribution are lines with low visual and environmental impact and innovative networks, e.g., smart grids, to improve the capacity to drive and control the demand side.

When taking up investment opportunities in emerging countries it is vital to support their growth, both economic and social. Economic aid to local organizations and communities, or better still, stimulation of community-based development, investment in learning centers and education facilities to help educate the community's children, and also development of new skills for adults and a health education program are real initiatives that investing utilities can engage in and which will demonstrate their concern for sustainable growth.

Other perspectives are connected with the role of local utilities. In this case an important issue is to support citizens in managing the crucial resources and facilities of their city in a modern, efficient and sustainable way; another is to develop a sustainable relationship with the local communities living in the plant areas; the aim should be a 'best practice community' in terms of energy culture and economic growth, and the whole enterprise should provide a good example of national solidarity.

In general, stakeholders of utilities represent a large segment of society, and at the same time a large proportion of them also belong to other interest groups. In view of these aspects and the fact that our industry has a responsibility to manage primary resources with potentially high environmental impact, it is clear that the most important capacity that utilities have and should steadily develop is the ability to manage the multifaceted stakeholders and interests portfolio with a very good measure of common sense. The keywords here are equilibrium and stability.

9.3   Basic Drivers and Business Models

The basics of the utility industry in this period up to 2020 are being driven by the fundamental streams in world energy supply and demand accompanied by some of the major foreseeable socioeconomic developments.

We will define 'the utility industry' as all activity dedicated to exploring, producing, transporting, delivering, and serving energy with the ultimate goal of satisfying the energy needs of all segments of final consumers. The focus will, however, be on utilities that are active in Europe, as the degree of liberalization, the variety of national regulatory schemes, the dependence on energy imports, the efforts to save energy and fight climate change, and the importance of its final consumer market, some 450 million people, make it a reference case in several respects for many other regions in the world. At the same time, some elements providing answers to questions about the future of the utility industry are now already being provided by non-European regions and these too, of course, will be taken into account. While the elementary goals of the utility industry have in fact changed little over past decades, the respective weights of single goals have varied significantly. The elementary goals can be summarized as providing energy in a secure, affordable, efficient, socially acceptable, and environmentally sustainable way to all end-consumers. During the past two decades the weight of the goals at the end of the list has certainly increased against the weight of those at its beginning. The last 5 years, however, have given new weight in particular to the first two goals, security and affordability, and the strong interdependence between all of the goals mentioned has provoked new debates highlighting some of the major challenges of tomorrow's utility industry. These discussions are not only useful; they are definitely essential on the way to a holistic approach, a 'new common sense' overcoming simplistic and sometimes naive on-off solutions.

The Fundamental Drivers of the Energy Business

The growth of world population (see Tables 9.1, 9.2) and world GDP means there would be increased energy demand even if major efforts were undertaken to reduce waste of energy and increase efficiency.

Any reliable regional or supraregional supply strategy must be founded on a diversified mix of energy sources and origins (see Figure 9.7a, 9.7b). A leapfrog shift in technology or efficiency of energy conversion can hardly be planned and will therefore not be contemplated in this analysis. This does not in any way reduce the need for increased investment of effort in corresponding R&D activities.

The balance of power is between offer and demand, and this is also influenced by geopolitical considerations. The bargaining power of developed countries without adequate primary energy resources (in particular North America, Europe and Japan) will decrease over time, whereas the negotiation momentum of producers and their countries of origin will be gather force.

Table 9.1: World population growth in the reference scenario (average annual growth rates [%]) (IEA, 2007a)

	1980-1990	1990-2005	2005-2015	2015-2030	2005-2030
OECD	**0.8**	**0.8**	**0.5**	**0.3**	**0.4**
North America	1.2	1.3	1.0	0.7	0.8
United States	0.9	1.1	0.9	0.7	0.8
Europe	0.5	0.5	0.3	0.2	0.2
Pacific	0.8	0.5	0.1	-0.2	-0.1
Japan	0.6	0.2	-0.1	-0.5	-0.3
Transition economies	**0.8**	**-0.2**	**-0.2**	**-0.3**	**-0.2**
Russia	0.6	-0.2	-0.5	-0.6	-0.6
Developing countries	**2.1**	**1.6**	**1.4**	**1.1**	**1.2**
Developing Asia	1.8	1.4	1.1	0.8	0.9
China	1.5	0.9	0.6	0.3	0.4
India	2.1	1.7	1.4	1.0	1.1
Middle East	3.6	2.3	2.0	1.5	1.7
Africa	2.9	2.3	2.2	1.9	2.0
Latin America	2.0	1.6	1.2	0.9	1.0
Brazil	2.1	1.5	1.2	0.8	0.9
World	**1.7**	**1.4**	**1.1**	**0.9**	**1.0**
European Union	0.3	0.3	0.1	0.0	0.0

Note: These assumptions also apply to the alternative-policy and high-growth scenarios

Table 9.2: World GDP growth in the reference scenario (average annual growth rates [%]) (IEA, 2007a)

	1980-1990	1990-2005	2005-2015	2015-2030	2005-2030
OECD	**3.0**	**2.5**	**2.5**	**1.9**	**2.2**
North America	3.1	3.0	2.6	2.2	2.4
United States	3.2	3.0	2.6	2.2	2.3
Europe	2.4	2.1	2.4	1.8	2.0
Pacific	4.2	2.2	2.2	1.6	1.8
Japan	3.9	1.3	1.6	1.3	1.4
Transition economies	**-0.5**	**-0.4**	**4.7**	**2.9**	**3.6**
Russia	n.a.	-0.5	4.3	2.8	3.4
Developing countries	**3.9**	**5.8**	**6.1**	**4.4**	**5.1**
Developing Asia	6.6	7.3	6.9	4.8	5.6
China	9.1	9.9	7.7	4.9	6.0
India	5.8	6.0	7.2	5.8	6.3
Middle East	-0.4	4.2	4.9	3.4	4.0
Africa	2.2	3.0	4.5	3.6	3.9
Latin America	1.3	3.0	3.8	2.8	3.2
Brazil	1.5	2.6	3.5	2.8	3.1
World	**2.9**	**3.4**	**4.2**	**3.3**	**3.6**
European Union	n.a.	2.0	2.3	1.8	2.0

Note: These assumptions also apply to the alternative-policy scenario

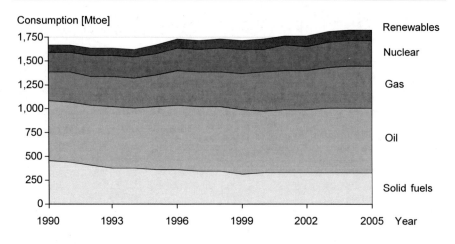

Figure 9.7a: Gross inland consumption – EU by fuel in [Mtoe] (Eurostat)

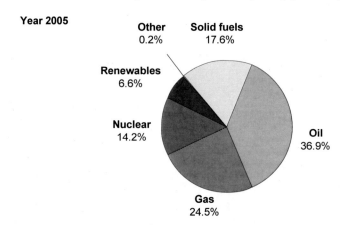

Figure 9.7b: Gross inland consumption – EU by fuel in [%] (Eurostat)

Climate change is as much of a threat as an opportunity to major developed economies. The danger, or threat, is that the efforts Europe is willing to undertake will not be shared by other major economies in North America and Asia, putting the overall emission reduction at risk and simultaneously hampering the competitiveness of Europe's economy. The opportunity for Europe lies in its ability to anticipate what is most likely to become an industry of world-wide impact: know-how and references in developing renewable energies, in efficiency excellence, CCS, fuel cell infrastructure, demand-side management, etc. In addition to the potential for economic and sustainable growth, these efforts will help Europe to reduce its energy dependence on fossil fuels and thus its vulnerability to producers' negotiating power.

In Europe, common energy policy and regulation will further streamline national market rules and regulations. Liberalization will remain in place, helped by truly independent transmission and distribution operators, standardized client switching procedures, increased room for cross-border trading supported by additional power interconnections, and new transcontinental gas transportation infrastructure.

Customers will become more powerful, for four reasons. Switching suppliers will become much easier over time, for both power and gas. Local generation facilities will become more and more popular, thanks to incentives and new technologies (see Figure 9.8).

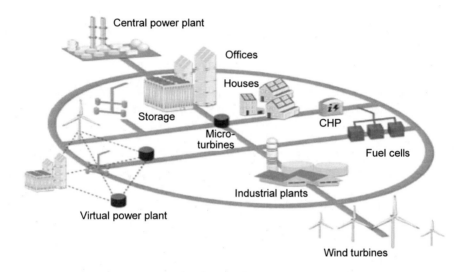

Figure 9.8: Functional scheme for distributed generation (Commission of the European Communities, 2006)

The installation of digital meters will become an industry standard in the next decade, driving operational efficiency (including demand-side management) and commercial options (prices and services) to new levels.

Internet will allow better use than any other means of communication of the three developments mentioned above.

The Business Models

The business models for utilities capable of shaping the industry in 2020 derive from the opportunities opened up by such major developments and can be summarized in the following three categories:

(1) Fully integrated utility (the super-utility) covering all major elements of the value chain, from investigations into transport, generation, trading, sales, and services down to distribution. The virtue of those utilities lies in the robust-

ness of their reach, profound business competence, and the diversification of risk. The importance of the transportation and distribution business will be shrinking, however, as the specific remuneration will at least be subject to long-term regulatory pressure, if not be separated out completely as a consequence of the unbundling efforts of the European Union.

(2) Specialized utilities with regional reach (the local utility), in particular municipalities and regional operators with strong local presences that are active in small-scale power production or tolling from multi-party generation facilities, with the main focus on sales and distribution of power, gas, heat, and in some cases water or waste management.

(3) Last, the more innovative model of specialized utilities concentrating on green energy and new services (the new green service utility); although true utilities of that kind do not yet exist, several of the new entrants can be observed to be putting their focus in that direction, and almost all super-utilities try hard to make contributions in both fields, i.e., service and green energy; true new green service utilities may see their time come when small-scale green energy production (from photovoltaic to small wind power and fuel cells), the trading of green energy, and the multitude of new green energy services (energy efficiency, small-scale integrated energy solutions for SME businesses and families) create open spaces that the existing utilities are not fast and/or credible enough to occupy.

Which combination of these models might be the one in the not-so-distant 2020 largely depends on the intensity with which some of the business drivers will prevail over others, and for that purpose we now examine two scenarios: first we present a more probable, evolutionary scenario based on an extrapolation of present trends, and then we take a quick look at a revolutionary one in which some disruptive technological innovations are introduced.

9.4   Evolutionary Scenario in the Utility Industry in 2020

Up-stream and Generation

The investment cycle of the world's current generation fleet is roughly between 20 and 40 years. This life-span can go on up to 60 years for nuclear power plants with appropriate maintenance and refurbishment if needed. Hydro power plants have an even longer life and can attain some 100 years.

The time-span of the investment cycle shows how much long-term planning is needed when scenarios for tomorrow's energy mix are designed. The investment in capacity new-build and refurbishment over the next decade is impressive in many countries or regions, and nevertheless will most probably not exceed some 10-20% of the fleets currently in use in developed countries.

The evolutionary scenario for power production up to the year 2020 therefore translates into a relatively smooth change of the three-dimensional generation mix made up of primary energies, origins, and plant technologies.

The first two dimensions impact on security of supply. Here, diversification is a must for all countries without direct access to large own resources. In 2020, super utilities will have gone further up-stream and successfully assured larger portions of long-term access to an equilibrated mix of primary energies and countries of origin. Those that have not will simply have stepped down from belonging to this exclusive and highly responsible category.

As regards technologies, important improvements have been made in terms of efficiency levels and unit cost for all conventional power plants over the past years. The overwhelming majority of plant new-builds in Europe over the past decade was still concentrated on gas-fired combined cycle turbines (CCGT) and on wind power. Coal-fired plants, which now attain over 45% of energy efficiency (as against some 36% in the current fleet) have suffered hefty permission setbacks and seen their competitiveness challenged by rising carbon emission cost. As coal is an essential baseload component of almost every country's energy mix, the only viable answer to this challenge is to continue investing in coal-fired generation accompanied by innovative emission-cleaning technologies as well as carbon sequestration and storage facilities.

Nuclear power will have been relaunched by 2020. The Evolutionary Power Reactor (EPR) technology will set a new standard for nuclear plant security and predictability of production cost and will make a significant contribution to the avoidance of additional carbon emissions. Yet the more important impact will stem from the life-time extension of the existing nuclear fleet. Many countries will have revised their exit strategies and allowed extension of the use of existing plants. The number of countries with new investment in nuclear power will constantly increase. Projects under way in Finland and France, Slovakia, Romania, Bulgaria, Russia, China, and the US, plus the recent political return to nuclear in the United Kingdom make this development already very tangible. Nevertheless, the share of nuclear power will presumably decline by the year 2020, as new production will not compensate for the closure of plants reaching the end of their technical and commercial life-time.

The share of small-scale generation will have grown steadily up to 2020, relying on wind power, in particular off-shore installations, small hydro facilities, photovoltaic and solar thermal plants, fuel cells, and small-scale CHP plants. As a large portion of this production and overall demand will increasingly depend on weather and climate conditions, the value of flexibility is set to rise. This will lead to additional investment in storage facilities for both power and gas. Although the impact of small-scale generation will be tangible, large-scale generation will continue to supply the predominant share of demand.

Transmission

The transportation of power and gas in Europe will have seen three major achievements by 2020:

(1) Higher cross-border transmission volumes generated by new power inter-connections and complementary transcontinental gas pipelines and a large number of new LNG terminals.
(2) Higher levels of internal supply security through elimination of regional bot-tlenecks and further improved coordination of short-term transmission man-agement (see Figure 9.9).
(3) Efficient and nondiscriminatory European-wide third-party access (TPA) to power and gas transportation networks accompanied by simple, standardized rules for capacity allocation and multinational cross-border transmission (market coupling).

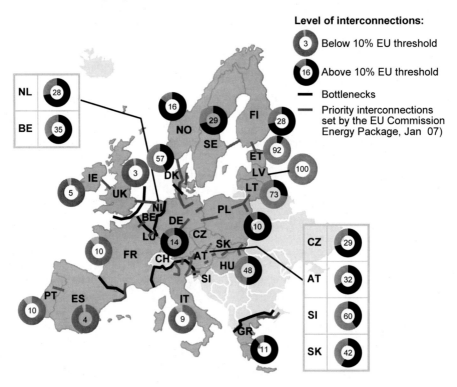

Figure 9.9: Level of interconnections, bottlenecks, and priority interconnections in 2006 (Capgemini, 2007)

Although these developments all appear feasible and their implementation only reasonable, it will certainly still be a challenge to achieve all of them. Integration of small-scale generation projects, for example, will require new planning of regional grid areas, and in the case of off-shore wind parks this will most probably lead to interconnected projects that are able to stabilize the power flows towards the main grid. The very important financial resources needed for additional power and gas transmission lines are evident. Private investment will ask for risk-adequate remuneration, and any TPA regulation will have to take this into account. Moreover, the primary energy owners' appetite for market share in the EU must be reconciled with the market owners' need for primary energy. Guarantees of reciprocal market access and comparable deregulation in the EU and non-EU countries concerned will be needed. This political dimension, and the rather poor track record of predictable authorization processes across the EU, may turn out to be the top challenge to intensified and better integrated transmission in Europe by 2020.

Trading

Trading of power and gas, as well as of the underlying commodities such as oil, coal, and emission rights, will expand further and will constitute a key competence of any significant player in the utility industry. With ongoing liberalization, a growing number of producers, increased numbers of interconnection and standard-ized access rules, and a general phase-out of state tariffs, market liquidity will be augmented and improved.

The development of financial services around the commodity markets will also contribute further to optimized resource allocation and risk management, again to the benefit of all client segments. Whilst wholesale prices are set to converge all over Europe, with gas as the marginal resource for peak and coal for off-peak pro-duction, the price solutions can be as various as the products: first and foremost they will depend on what exposure to risk and what duration of contract the client selects.

The physical day-ahead markets will have seen further integration across Europe by 2020, propelled by the grid operators' interest in maintaining high lev-els of short-term supply security and improving short-term cross-border optimiza-tion.

The forward markets will rely on consolidated power exchanges with strong fi-nancial services support and volume-driven complementary over-the-counter (OTC) markets.

The most prominent advantage of trading in the year 2020 will probably lie in the more efficient and wide-spread sharing of risk, with counterparties from all over the world, supported by financial services which guarantee competitively priced volumes, options, and contract durations.

Distribution

Successfully managing distribution networks both for power and gas will continue to involve two major components: cost efficiency and security of local supply. However, two additional tasks will join these at the top of the agenda: the ability to measure the power and gas consumption of every single client online and most precisely, and the flexibility necessary to absorb increasingly dynamic load-flows on the electrical network, which will result from a continuous rollout of small-scale generation. The development of smart grids with smart metering and the improved technologies to manage the growing distributed generation are the most important milestones on the way to achieving the necessary flexibility and to driving and controlling the demand side (DSM: demand side management).

From the regulatory point of view the industry needs to continue building up incentive mechanisms to stimulate virtuous system behaviors in terms of improved resource and allocative efficiency, reduced administrative and regulatory costs, investments, high-quality distribution, and introduction of new services. Examples might be the current performance-based regulations such as the now more classic revenue caps, price caps and sliding scales, and the newer menu of contracts (US) or the most innovative menu of sliding scales developed in the UK by OfGem.

Marketing and Sales

Competition will have strengthened in all client segments. The major advantages to all clients will be not only cost-efficient supply solutions, but the ability to consciously choose the most appropriate solution for every single dimension of supply, including service quality, security of supply, environmental impact, and duration.

The specific needs of large industrial clients will presumably concentrate on secure long-term supply of competitively priced power and gas reflecting the underlying cost of production, i.e., indexed to corresponding capacity, operation and maintenance (O&M) and fuel cost components, and tools for hedging forward contracts for different commodities and durations. The exposure to plant-related risk for permissions, construction, O&M, and fuel prices, but also taxation and environmental burden, will obviously define how close the supply cost comes to the investor's and operator's generating costs. With regard to the environmental cost element, super-utilities will take advantage of their international presence and offer long-term sourcing and/or hedging emission solutions to their most important industrial consumers. This activity will not only cover the supply of energy, but be extended to the emissions of the industrial complex itself.

The small and medium-sized clients will enjoy advantages arising from a variety of segment-specific price and profiling products, accompanied by the possibility of benefiting from local small-scale production of green energy. The same will apply to the most densely populated segments of small offices and residential clients, with more standardized offers which nonetheless provide every single consumer with the option of selecting from a variety of primary energies, price options, and service levels.

Branding for successful utilities will mean conveying the mission and convincing the stakeholders that they are competent and reliable suppliers of commodities, capable of providing services of high-quality and environmentally friendly energy solutions, and acting as a fair global and local citizen.

Marketing and sales techniques that are effective in extending market share or retaining portfolio clients will have reached the sophisticated levels familiar in other leading service industries. Co-marketing with complementary industries or service providers, segment-specific partnerships, and multi-channel sales forces will all be part of any strong commercial operator's toolkit.

The better product, the more effective sales technique, the quicker provision of advice and assistance, and the more accurate service and billing capabilities will make the difference not only between competing utilities but, in particular, between utilities and other service providers trying to enter the power and gas retail market.

9.5   Revolutionary Scenario in the Utility Industry in 2020

The revolutionary scenario can be built up in many different ways: we can assume unexpected limitations for primary energy supply, technical constraints on the offer side, technological breakthrough in generation, strong changes in demand, a U-turn on liberalization. Every single dimension has the power to drastically change the scenario, even when we consider that 2020 is rather close in terms of ordinary planning periods in the utility industry.

A U-turn on liberalization, or the return to state-controlled energy supply, is not a probable scenario, at least as long as primary energy supplies are not in danger. Nevertheless, the benefits of liberalization must be earned by the utility industry: they need to be worked out by competing utilities and continuously delivered to their final clients.

A more probable revolutionary scenario can be addressed in the following way: with environmental concern growing, lowered market entry barriers, new qualified service providers and perhaps top brands expanding to supplying power and gas, a massive roll-out of distributed generation, and intense use of innovative online services, there is suddenly ample space for different kinds of new utilities. One interesting symbiosis of some of the aforesaid developments is represented by the 'new green service utility'. This type may introduce itself to the market via the internet, for example, providing advice to people looking for credible and almost independent energy content, then start selling small-scale green energy generation and simultaneously launch the sale of green power and heat products, rolling out town after town, supported by suppliers of technology, top service providers and local businesses, delivering to the client the conviction that he is actively participating in the best choices for the future of his personal energy supply. The utility industry would start to be re-invented bottom-up. It might then come out that the top-down approach of super-utilities and local utilities are necessary to secure long-term supply to the country and competitiveness of its energy-intensive industry and the bottom-up-generated benefits of green power and service innovation simply provide a highly complementary picture of a more dynamic and competitive energy landscape.

9.6   Conclusion

To summarize, in this chapter we first go through the overall trends and principal aspects of energy supply and demand foreseen by the some of the main energy institutions for the next two or three decades and the differing and common interests of the stakeholders, after which we analyze the fundamental drivers of the industry and the possible upcoming business model, finishing with a quick overview of two possible scenarios for the immediate future, a more plausible evolutionary one and a more improbable revolutionary one.

We hope we have managed to stress the major challenges and the ambitious but necessary goal stated at the beginning of the chapter:

Secure, Sustainable and Competitive Energy for Everyone.

To sum up, the industry is changing in the following directions:

- A change from blissfully unaware consumers (power is always available and is what I get when I plug in) to aware and responsible citizens (power is a precious good, which I choose in full knowledge of its origin and price and which I consume but may also produce).
- A change from increasing consumption to 'less is more' (overall, and in any case).
- A shift from offline to online customers, empowering people, creating awareness, and providing clients with incentives to switch to sustainable energy consumption.
- A change from the top-down utility to a complementary mix of top-down and bottom-up strategies for the new utilities: security of supply, delivery of sustainable energy, energy efficiency in production and use, active participation of final clients in choosing energy mix and origin, long-term solutions and short-term flexibility in generation, trading, and sales, R&D, transparency in rollout, and delivery to all stakeholders.

Thus, utilities are forced to evolve, and we have identified as one of the principal forces, if not the most important one, the human lever: management and personnel. To finish we would like to give a snapshot of management guidelines for driving future development or hoped-for improvements. The management guidelines are the same regardless of whether the scenario is evolutionary or revolutionary.

First the industry needs to progress from a model focused on energy administration in monopoly times to an individualized one supplying and serving valuable energy to responsible clients.

Because of growing complexity and completely new scenarios, utilities have to increase their ability in business modeling, building cases around the different scenarios, and thorough management testing of them.

Another important need will be to improve power in providing reliability and stakeholder trust through applied professionalism and authentic management in times of increasing unpredictability and risk.

The capabilities to be further developed are therefore analytics, training in different cultures and communication skills, setting ambitious missions and objectives, with a consequent need for growing executive ability in different business cases and new environments, providing explicit room and process support to innovation and new investment or service ideas, stimulating team spirit and integration, and developing career paths for energy specialists and for holistic energy managers.

Hard times and big opportunities ahead for all of us!

References

Ambrosetti S.p.A. 2007. Energia elettrica domani. Milano: Ambrosetti.

Cambridge Energy Research Associates (CERA). 2006. OECD Europe electric power data 2006. Cambridge: CERA.

Capgemini. 2007. European energy markets observatory 2006 and winter 2006-2007, data set, 9th edition. Berlin: Capgemini.

Commission of the European Communities. 2005. Report on progress in creating the internal gas and electricity market 2005. Communication from the Commission to the Council and the European Parliament, COM (2005) 568 final.

Commission of the European Communities. 2006. Prospects for the internal gas and electricity market 2006. Communication from the Commission to the Council and the European Parliament, COM (2006) 841 final.

ENEA. 2007. Rapporto energia e ambiente 2006 – analisi e scenari. Roma: ENEA.

European Smartgrids Technology Platform. 2006a. Vision and strategy for Europe's electricity network of the future. Brussels: Commission of the European Communities.

Eurostat Database. Environment and energy, data 2005.

International Energy Agency (IEA). 2007a. World energy outlook 2007. Paris: IEA.

International Energy Agency (IEA). 2007b. Key world energetic statistics 2007. Paris: IEA.

Organisation for Economic Co-operation and Development (OECD). 2007. Factbook 2007: economic, environmental and social statistics. Paris: OECD.

N.N. 2007. http://www.bankruptcyworries.com/2007/11/22/shareholder-4/.

The Italian Regulatory Authority for Electricity and Gas. 2007. Annual report on the status of services and regulatory activities 2007. Milano: The Italian Regulatory Authority for Electricity and Gas.

Tietenberg, T. H. & Lewis, L. 2008. Environmental and natural resource economics. Boston: Addison-Wesley.

10 The Changing Structure of the Electric Utility Industry in Europe: Liberalisation, New Demands and Remaining Barriers

Reinhard Haas[1]

Christian Redl[2]

Hans Auer[3]

Abstract

Liberalisation of the electricity sector in various countries and regions worldwide as a precondition for the introduction of competition has faced electricity generators and suppliers, grid operators, governments, regulatory authorities and, finally, also consumers with new challenges. This chapter summarises this development with a regional focus on the European Union.

Keywords: liberalisation, electricity supply sector, European Union

[1] Prof. Dr. Reinhard Haas is an Associate Professor at the Energy Economics Group at Vienna University of Technology, Austria.

[2] Christian Redl is a Research Assistant at the Energy Economics Group at Vienna University of Technology, Austria.

[3] Dr. Hans Auer is Senior Research Assistant at Energy Economics Group at Vienna University of Technology, Austria.

A. Bausch and B. Schwenker (eds.), *Handbook Utility Management,*
DOI: 10.1007/978-3-540-79349-6_10, © Springer-Verlag Berlin Heidelberg 2009

10.1   Introduction

The restructuring of electricity markets in most European countries started in the late 1990s and is still going on. In the European Union (EU) this process was triggered by Directive 96/92/EC of the European Parliament and of the Council concerning common rules for the internal market in electricity. The major motivation for this directive was the conviction that liberalisation, price deregulation and privatisation would lead to competition in both generation and supply, resulting in lower prices for European consumers. As the main driving force, the European Commission's main expectation was that: "market forces produce a better allocation of resources and greater effectiveness in the supply of services" (European Commission, 1996).

However, these expectations were based on simplified assumptions about the behaviour of large incumbent players being reinforced by national politicians forcing national champions and European authorities allowing too much concentration within the electricity supply industry. In turn, the aforementioned directive was overruled in 2003 by Directive 2003/54/EC, which contains stricter provisions, especially with regard to unbundling. In 2007 the European Commission put forward the third legislative package, which includes a proposal for a new directive amending Directive 2003/54/EC – again containing stricter rules for the supply industry.

This chapter is organised as follows: The next section will summarise the organisation of the electricity supply industry (ESI) before liberalisation of the sector was implemented. Section 10.3 focuses on the implementation process and explains the main provisions of the first and second electricity directives. Price formation in liberalised markets is considered in Section 10.4. In Section 10.5 the performance of the markets will be analysed, while Section 10.6 discusses remaining barriers and problems associated with liberalisation of the ESI and the latest proposal of the European Commission. Finally, Section 10.7 gives the authors' conclusions.

10.2   The European Electricity Supply Industry
in Pre-liberalisation Days

In a perfect market, competitive prices ensure efficient resource allocation, which maximises social welfare. Yet, under certain constraints (e.g. monopolies, pollution) market forces alone cannot manage an optimal allocation, giving rise to state intervention by means of regulation.

The quick provision of an area-wide electricity supply was a socio-political high priority in the twentieth century. However, in the early twentieth century prices increased as result of the monopoly structure of the ESI. This monopoly structure arose from pronounced economies of scale in the generation sector, low investments in infrastructure and the network representing a natural monopoly. Hence, politics considered societally justifiable electricity prices ('fair' prices), security of supply and build-up of an infrastructure would best be reached via an ESI subject to tough regulation (price and/or ownership regulation).

Indeed, until the end of the 1990s, almost every electricity supply industry in Europe was largely vertically integrated with a captive franchise market, either state-owned (in the majority of cases) or under mixed private/public ownership (as in Belgium, Germany and Switzerland). Throughout Europe the ESI was price-regulated, the standard model being either average cost or cost plus regulation. Regulated area monopolies prevailed in all countries. Yet ownership structures and degree of vertical integration were different among the European countries.

Although electricity networks were typically synchronised over wide areas, interconnections of areas under different transmission system operators (TSOs) were frequently guided by security rather than by economic considerations. However, most trade in the past was due to economic benefits of arbitrage during off-peak and peak load hours.

To sum up, the standard model before liberalisation was "an effectively vertically integrated franchise monopoly under either public ownership or cost-of-service regulation" (Newbery, 2006).

10.3 Restructuring of the European Electricity Supply Industry

In the 1980s the role model of a vertically integrated regulated ESI was increasingly questioned by economists and politicians, among others. The key point of criticism concerned a supposedly inefficient electricity supply attributable to high prices resulting from high costs and a low service level. It is worth mentioning that this criticism was mainly aimed at the 'weak' regulatory authorities and their lacking capabilities to guarantee an efficient provision of electricity services.

To increase the economic efficiency of the utility industry three measures were proposed:

- Liberalisation;
- Introduction of competition and/or
- Privatisation.

The restructuring of EU Member States' electricity markets was finally triggered by a directive concerning common rules for the internal market in electricity, which came into force in February 1997. The main intention was to create a common competitive European electricity market. The major issues of this directive (Directive 96/92/EC, 1996) were:

- Minimal requirements for the unbundling of generation and transmission;
- Minimal market opening, expressed by the consumption size of 'eligible customers';
- Different approaches to access to the grid (negotiated or regulated, Third-party Access or Single Buyer).

Table 10.1: Milestones of reform of electricity markets in the EU

1996	EU-15	European Council of Energy Ministers and Parliament reach agreement on a market liberalisation directive
February 1997	EU-15	This Directive concerning common rules for the internal market in electricity (Directive 96/92/EC) becomes valid while waiting up to 2 more years for its implementation by countries
1998	Spain	Introduction of a Spanish centralised pool
1998	Poland	Introduction of TPA (market opening: 22%)
1998	Germany	100% market opening
February 1999	EU-15	Directive comes into force after a 2-year implementation delay: market opening attributable to the directive between 30% and 35% in Austria, Belgium, France, Italy, Spain, Portugal and the Netherlands
2001	Austria	100% market opening (in a second step)
2001	EU-15	Approval of the Directive of the European Parliament and the Council on the promotion of electricity from renewable energy sources in the internal electricity market (RES-E Directive) (European Parliament and Council, 2001 – Directive 2001/77/EC)
2003	EU-25	Approval of the Directive concerning common rules for the internal market in electricity (officially Directive 2003/54; usually named 'the Second Directive')
2003	Spain	100% market opening
2004	EU15+10	Expansion of the EU to 25 member countries, new CE member countries to open their market with 30% minimum
2004	EU 25	Electricity Directive 2003/54 due to be implemented by member states
		All nondomestic customers in the EU made eligible in July 2004
		An EU Regulation on cross-border electricity trade comes into effect (Regulation 1228/2003) in July 2004
2005	Portugal, The Netherlands	100% market opening
2007	EU 27	As result of Electricity Directive 2003/54, 100% market opening in all EU-27 countries in July 2007

However, each national government within the EU had to transpose the directive into national law, yielding rather different approaches. An overview of the major milestones is provided in Table 10.1. In practice, the major area of action within the European liberalisation project was 'Providing access to the market'. Aside from a minimal level of unbundling, the restructuring of utilities and the design of market places was not tackled comprehensively by governments in most countries (there were a few exceptions: Spain created a centralised pool, and Italy divested generation capacities). Also, provisions ensuring adequate generation and transmission capacity were given far less attention. Independent energy regulators were introduced in all countries except Germany (and Switzerland, but this country is not part of the EU). In addition, environmental issues were also treated very prominently.

The first important requirement for a competitive electricity market recognised in the electricity directive is nondiscriminatory access to the grid for new entrants. This means that access to transmission and distribution should be offered to all market participants at reasonable and nondiscriminatory prices. In turn, a precondition for competition is the unbundling of generation and supply from transmission. Unbundling is of crucial importance so as to avoid possible distortion, discrimination and cross-subsidies between different segments of the supply chain within the integrated incumbent. To achieve this, competitive segments of the supply chain (i.e. generation and supply) must be separated from noncompetitive segments (i.e. the grid). Figure 10.1 depicts this graphically.

According to the first directive, vertically integrated utilities had to keep separate accounts for generation, transmission and distribution activities (Directive 96/92/EC, 1996).

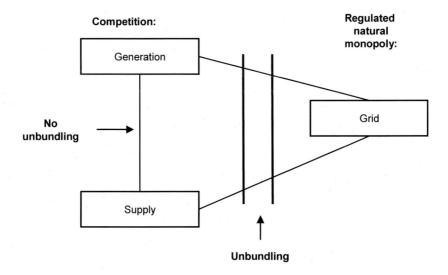

Figure 10.1: Separation of competitive from noncompetitive segments through unbundling

Member states could choose between negotiated or regulated third-party access or the single-buyer procedure when organising access to the transmission and the distribution network (Directive 96/92/EC, 1996). In all countries except Germany access to the grid was regulated by the directive. Finally, this was also introduced in Germany.

The third important issue in the directive concerns market opening: gradual opening in three steps (26.5% in February 1999, 28% in February 2000 and 33% in February 2003) was foreseen (Directive 96/92/EC, 1996). The geographically and temporally different opening of the markets led to at least some distortions regarding free choice of supplier. Some countries, such as Germany, the Netherlands, Spain, Portugal and Austria, opened their markets fully, while others, such as France, Luxemburg and the Czech Republic, opened theirs only partially.

As the directive only set minimal requirements, a rather diverse implementation in the EU's different member states was the consequence. Moreover, the economic and competitive performance of the national markets left much to be desired (see Section 10.5 for a detailed analysis). As a consequence, a second directive entered into force in 2003 and had to be implemented in national law by July 2004 (Directive 2003/54/EC, 2003).

This directive required legal and organisational unbundling of the transmission and distribution system (with exceptions for small distribution companies) from the vertically integrated company to ensure a proper separation of competitive segments from noncompetitive ones. Access to the network must be based on published, objective and nondiscriminatory tariffs, which must be approved by a regulatory authority. Since July 2004 all nonhousehold customers and since July 2007 all customers have had the option of choosing their electricity supplier (Directive 2003/54/EC, 2003).

10.4   Price Formation in a Liberalised Competitive Electricity Market

Before liberalisation, regulated electricity prices corresponded to average costs of power generation. In a liberalised competitive power market, prices are expected to equal short-run marginal costs. In the long run, the competitive price level should not exceed long-run marginal costs of new power plants. However, in a noncompetitive environment prices may exceed the former price level because of either mark-ups or strategic investment withholding. Figure 10.2 compares these different price development scenarios.

In competitive markets, marginal generation costs are relevant for price formation. In these markets, the wholesale price is determined by the generation costs of the marginal technology (i.e. the SRMC of the most expensive plant needed to meet demand – merit order principle): Generation costs of the various power plants are classified by rising generation costs resulting in a stepped supply curve with constant marginal costs up to the capacity limit of each plant. In addition, at least in the short term electricity demand can be modelled as price inelastic, resulting in an almost vertical demand curve. Figure 10.3 illustrates price formation in competitive power markets.

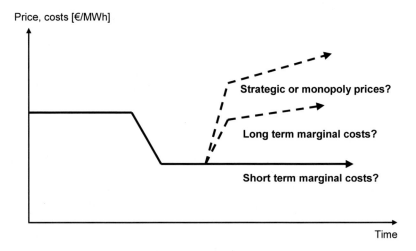

Figure 10.2: Price scenarios in liberalised markets

The intersection of supply and demand curves in Figure 10.3 implies that power plant types A, B, C and D are needed to satisfy electricity demand, where plant D is utilised only partly. Clearly, both supply and demand curves are subject to dynamic changes over time, resulting in varying system marginal costs and, hence, volatile patterns of wholesale prices. The concept of system marginal costs is reflected in uniform pricing auctions of wholesale markets. All inframarginal suppliers receive the system price as remuneration. Hence, the difference between total revenue and total generation costs – also called producer surplus – represents the contribution margin to cover fixed costs.

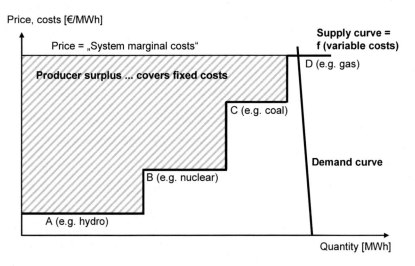

Figure 10.3: Price formation in electricity markets

The volatile pattern of prices shows various periodicities (from daily to yearly). Figure 10.4 shows an overview of electricity generation and consumption on a monthly basis in the core Continental European wholesale power market from January 1999 to December 2007.[4] Supply is clustered into nuclear power, conventional thermal power (lignite, hard coal, gas and oil), hydro power and 'new' renewables.

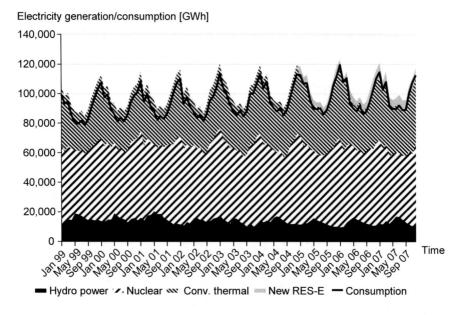

Figure 10.4: Development of electricity generation and consumption on a monthly basis in Western Europe (AT, CH, DE, FR) from January 1999 to 2007 (UCTE, 2008)

Figure 10.5 depicts a simplified supply and demand representation for the core Continental European wholesale power market. It is possible to identify a strong convexity of the merit order curve with a high slope of the supply curve approaching system capacity limit. Therefore, small fluctuations in demand or supply can yield significant price effects. More than 50% of total generation stems from power plants with low short-run marginal costs. These comprise run-of-river hydro power plants, new renewable plants that are subject to national support schemes and, finally, nuclear power plants. Generation costs of fossil-fuelled power plants are much higher, resulting in a huge jump in the merit order curve. The ranking of conventional thermal power plants changes depending on the prevailing fuel and CO_2 price level. Usually, new lignite-fired plants are the cheapest thermal generation source, followed by new hard coal- and natural gas-fired plants, with oil-fired plants being the most expensive generation technology. Nev-

---

[4] This market comprises Austria, France, Germany and Switzerland.

ertheless, distinctions between different technologies using different fuel types are not clear cut. Different ages and, hence, efficiencies of the plants and changing fuel and CO_2 prices result in a heterogeneous composition of the merit order curve.

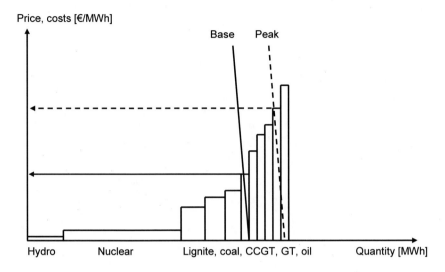

Figure 10.5: Stylised supply and demand curves for the Western European power market (AT, CH, DE and FR)

10.5   Performance of the Wholesale and Retail Markets

A major objective of liberalising the European electricity supply industry was and still is the creation of a single market. Nonetheless, this area currently consists of several submarkets separated by scarce transmission capacity and in access conditions to the grid. Another major obstacle for a joint competitive European market is a too-low number of competitors, resulting in a general lack of competition in virtually all local and national electricity markets both wholesale and retail, also because barriers to entry and incentives to collude remain too high. In addition, increasing horizontal integration with natural gas supply is observed. Hence, the paramount objective is still to construct competitive markets, while at the same time ensuring a reasonable level of grid reliability and supply adequacy (Haas et al., 2006).

Figure 10.6 depicts the average wholesale prices in these different submarkets in 2007, due to cross-border transmission bottlenecks or other exchange barriers (e.g. long-term contracts).

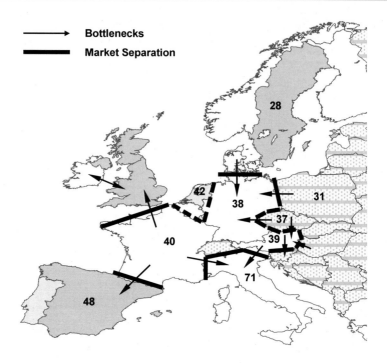

Figure 10.6: Average wholesale electricity prices in [€/MWh] and transmission grid bottlenecks in Europe in 2007 (APX, 2008; EEX, 2008; EXAA, 2008; IPEX, 2008; Nord Pool, 2008; OMEL, 2008; OTE, 2008; PolPX, 2008; Power-next, 2008)

Figure 10.7 shows the evolution of spot market prices in Europe from 1999 to 2007. With the exception of Italy a certain convergence of spot market prices is visible for 2004. Over the whole period virtually no price difference is observed between Germany, France, and Austria.

In 2007, again, increased convergence of Continental European spot prices was observed. First, implicit auctions between France, Belgium and the Netherlands were introduced, leading to coupling of these markets and thereby effectively removing the market separation in northwestern Europe. Moreover, Czech power prices almost reached Western European levels, for a number of reasons. CO_2 certificate prices fell dramatically during 2007, nuclear production decreased in the Czech Republic and more cross-border capacities became available owing to a reduction in the number of long-term contracts between Germany and the Czech Republic.

To assess the performance of a liberalised electricity market it is of prime importance to see how electricity prices have developed since restructuring. Therefore, a major question for further investigations is whether these prices are a competitive outcome; that is to say whether these prices really do reflect the marginal costs of generation or whether they are increased by some kind of market power.

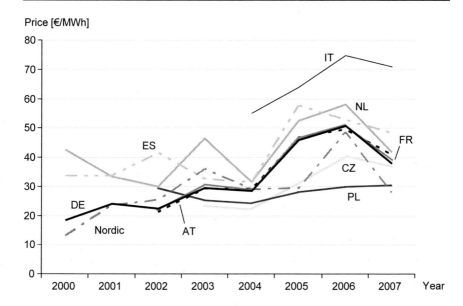

Figure 10.7: Wholesale electricity prices in selected European countries (APX, 2008; EEX, 2008; EXAA, 2008; IPEX, 2008; Nord Pool, 2008; OMEL, 2008; OTE, 2008; PolPX, 2008; Powernext, 2008)

Owing to the dominance of fossil-fuelled power plants in the EU power markets, primary energy prices and CO_2 emission allowance prices are crucial determinants of the development of power prices. Besides parameters directly affecting generation costs of thermal plants, production of inframarginal technologies (e.g. hydro run-of-river and nuclear power) also indirectly influences price formation.

Figure 10.8 shows the comparison of realised German EEX spot market prices and modelled system marginal costs. These prices are the relevant benchmark in the regional Western European power market, as depicted in Figure 10.6. The model shows a close correlation between prices and costs from 1999 to 2001, with a structural break in December 2001. Prices and costs diverge between 2002 and 2004. This mark-up led to the following interpretation. Müsgens (2004) argues in an analysis of the German wholesale market: "The difference between marginal costs and prices is attributed to market power. [...] there is strong evidence of market power in the second period from September 2001 to June 2003". In 2006 and 2007 prices again significantly diverge from the competitive benchmark model (London Economics, 2006; European Commission, 2007a; Hirschhausen et al., 2007).

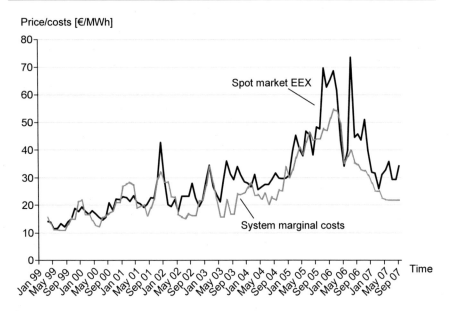

Figure 10.8: Evolution of electricity prices and system marginal costs in the regional Western European power market from 1999-2007 (BAFA, 2008; EEX, 2008; UCTE, 2008; authors' own calculations)

The industrial reference model for electricity changed completely between 1995 and 2001. It has shifted from a preference for vertical disintegration between generation, trading and sales to final consumers toward a preference for vertical reintegration of production, trading and final sales. However, for effective competition a large number of companies is required. This has been clearly demonstrated by the English and Welsh examples, where the number of generators has been increased several times by the regulatory authority. The 'merger-mania' within Continental Europe after the start of liberalisation indicates that the major strategy of the larger incumbent utilities is competing by merging so as to purchase market shares. These activities reached a numerical peak in 2003, 4 years after liberalisation started. As can be seen from Figure 10.9, of the 13 largest generators that existed in Continental Europe in 1999, only 9 remained 6 years later. Now in Continental Europe six large concerns dominate the market: EdF-EnBW, RWE, E.ON, Vattenfall, Enel-Endesa and Gaz de France-Suez-Electrabel.

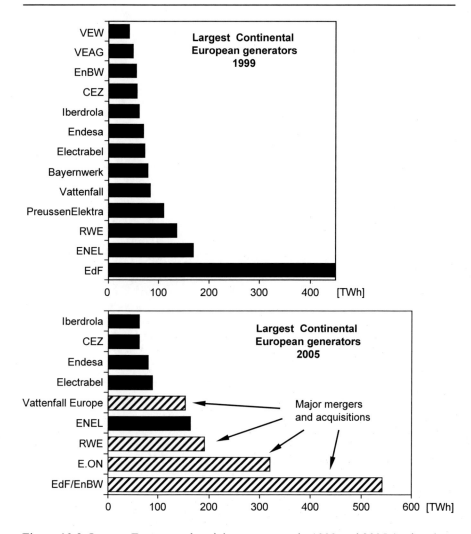

Figure 10.9: Largest European electricity generators in 1999 and 2005 (authors' own investigations)

The major expectation of final customers with respect to the liberalisation of electricity markets was that prices would drop substantially. Figures 10.10 and 10.11 depict the price evolution in some Continental European countries from 1999 to 2004 for industrial and household customers, respectively. As can be seen from Figure 10.10 large electricity users did indeed see lower prices, at least temporarily, but prices have been rising in most countries since 2002 or 2003. France is an exception, with a slightly decreasing price pattern ever since 1995. Eastern European countries show generally rising price patterns.

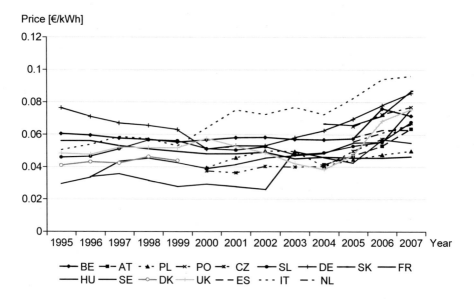

Figure 10.10: Evolution of large industrial customers' electricity prices in selected Continental European countries excluding taxes (EUROSTAT, 2008; average electricity consumption: 24 GWh)

Yet, as Figure 10.11 shows, households' electricity prices remained stable in the majority of the countries investigated after liberalisation was introduced and started rising in many cases from 2004 onward. Moreover, neither for households nor for industrial customers has there been any obvious price convergence. This was one of the expectations of the common European market. Household prices in Eastern European countries have been rising continuously.

Of course, there are many reasons for price increases, e.g. transaction cost of market creation (e.g. splitting of distributor into two legal companies: one for distribution and one for supply), new power plants that have to meet new ecological legislation (emission limits, minimum thermal efficiency etc.), which will mean utilisation of expensive technologies (especially in Eastern Europe), emission allowances for CO_2, consumer tax imposed on fossil fuels from 2007 (according to EU rules), fees for increasing share of renewables-based electricity (RES-E) production, and, finally, rising primary energy prices. Clearly, Figures 10.10 and 10.11 require more in-depth investigation.

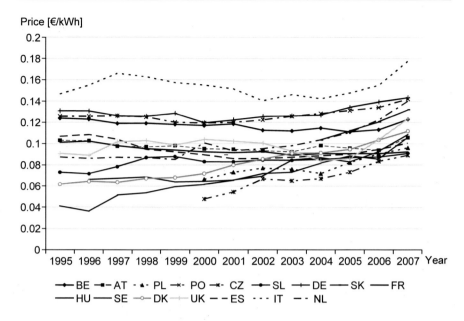

Figure 10.11: Evolution of households' electricity prices excluding taxes in selected Continental European countries (EUROSTAT, 2008; average electricity consumption: 3,500 kWh)

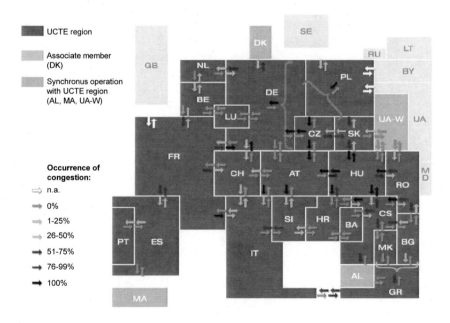

Figure 10.12: Cross-border congestion in Continental Europe for 2006 (UCTE, 2007)

Currently, transmission constraints have a substantial impact on the separation of submarkets in Continental Europe, which also limits competitive pressures from neighbouring markets. Hence, another important precondition for a sufficiently wide market would be that there is sufficient transmission capacity for supply to neighbour regions, increasing the number of potentially competing generators. Figure 10.12 depicts the situation at cross-border transmission lines for the year 2006.

The development of cross-border congestion (load flows divided by NTC) in winter and in summer over the period 1996-2005 is shown in Figure 10.13. Only borders with more than 85% congestion in at least one of the last 10 years are considered in Figure 10.13. In principle, it can be seen that there has been a continuous increase in aggregated congestion since the start of liberalisation.

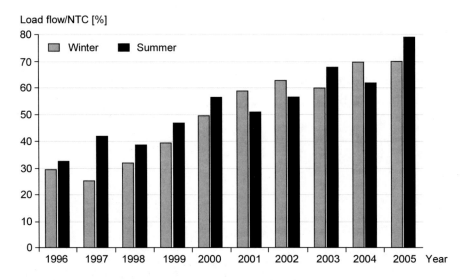

Figure 10.13: Development of aggregated cross-border congestion (load flows divided by Net Transfer Capacities) in winter and in summer over the period 1996-2005 (UCTE, 2008)

10.6   Remaining Barriers to Effective Competition

Meanwhile, the EU has successfully initiated the most extensive and ambitious project for building a new electricity market. However, there are no guarantees that the dynamics of this construction will not dissipate, as in the US, or that the internal market will not remain fractured in 'national or local blocks', which could persist for a long time (Glachant & Lévêque, 2005; Glachant & Finon, 2005). Moreover, as argued by Haas et al. (1997) and Haas and Auer (2001), the expectation of lasting competition in a 'free' market is based on highly simplified assumptions of the strategic behaviour of electricity generators and network operators. The caveats described by Banks (1996) are similar ("the market is a wonderful thing and it should be exploited as far as possible, but it also has its limits") to those of Newbery (2002), which are based on the experience in the UK and the Nordic market.

10.6.1 Decreasing Excess Capacities

As in many electricity markets that have been liberalised, most European countries started liberalisation with significant excess capacities in generation, which had built up in the time of regulated area monopolies. Indeed, it was a common motivation and driver for introducing competition. Nonetheless, excess capacity in generation plays a core role in the restructuring process of an electricity supply industry. If utilities compete with excess capacity in generation, which also depends on transmission capacity, the price they receive for electricity will be equal to their short-term marginal cost. In a situation of perfect competition without remarkable excess capacities the price will not rise above the long-run marginal costs of new technologies. However, if there is no competition or a too-tight capacity the price can be substantially higher than both marginal costs, especially when demand is inelastic relative to price. Figure 10.14 depicts this development graphically.

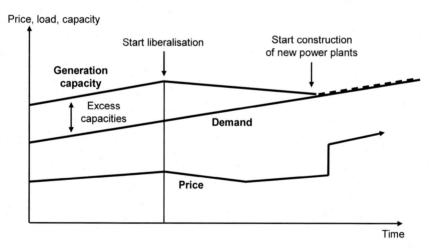

Figure 10.14: Decreasing excess capacities and corresponding wholesale prices

In fact, spare capacity has decreased continuously in recent years in the various submarkets (spare capacity = net capacity minus maximum load). In this context, variations and uncertainties in available capacities play a crucial role. Analysis of the effects of extending the core Western European regional market by the addition of Central and Eastern European EU member states indicates that no improvements can be expected in terms of security of supply. Adequate generation capacity is available for the foreseeable future; nevertheless, after 2012 when no new power plants have been or are being built and concentrated decommissioning of existing power plants (both nuclear and fossil-fuelled plants) is going on, this will have negative effects on security of supply. One remaining major uncertainty is the magnitude of demand growth (Haas et al., 2008).

Figure 10.15 depicts the developments currently looming in load and generation capacity. In recent years spare capacity decreased continuously in the core Continental European submarket consisting of Austria, France, Germany and Switzerland (spare capacity = net capacity minus maximum load). In Figure 10.16 the effects of extending the market by the Czech Republic and Poland are shown. Comparison with Figure 10.15 indicates that no improvements concerning security of supply can be expected from this market coupling.

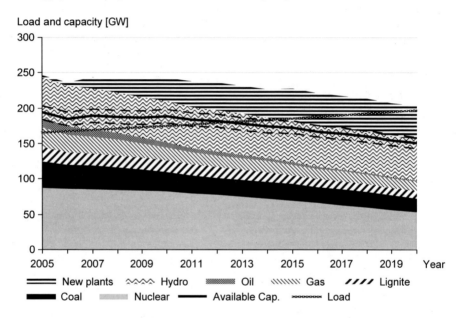

Figure 10.15: Trends in generation capacity and load in the Austrian, French, German and Swiss regional market (Platts, 2007; UCTE, 2007; UCTE, 2008; authors' own calculations)

Load and capacity [GW]

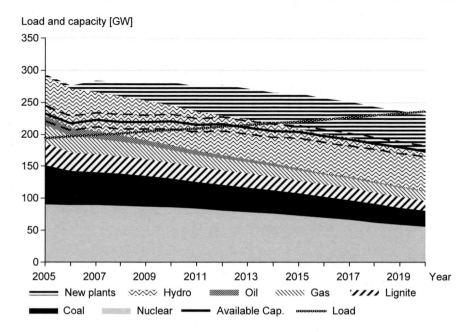

Figure 10.16: Trends in generation capacity and load in an integrated market consisting of AT, CH, DE, FR, CZ and PL (Platts, 2007; UCTE, 2007; UCTE, 2008; authors' own calculations)

10.6.2 Lack of Players

As mentioned earlier, the major obstacle to a common European market is the general lack of competition in national wholesale and retail electricity markets, reinforced by (at least) two other factors: (1) insufficient availability of transmission capacity between the submarkets and (2) increasing horizontal integration with natural gas supply.

This is recognised by the European Commission (2007b), which states: "far too many of the EU's citizens and businesses lack a real choice of supplier. Market fragmentation along national borders, a high degree of vertical integration and high market concentration are at the root of the lack of a truly internal market." Therefore, the third legislative package for the EU electricity and gas markets was presented in September 2007 (European Commission, 2007b).

As nondiscriminatory network access and sufficient incentives for investing in transmission grids cannot be guaranteed with the current unbundling rules, the Commission proposes ownership unbundling of the transmission system. As a second – though not preferred – option the Commission suggests an independent system operator (European Commission, 2007b).

10.6.3   Extending the Markets: a Solution?

In the light of market integration, removing cross-border transmission grid bottle-necks is not a straightforward issue. Besides lacking acceptance (which is also the case in the generation sector), the following questions arise: (1) Who will invest? (2) How can recovery of investments be ensured?

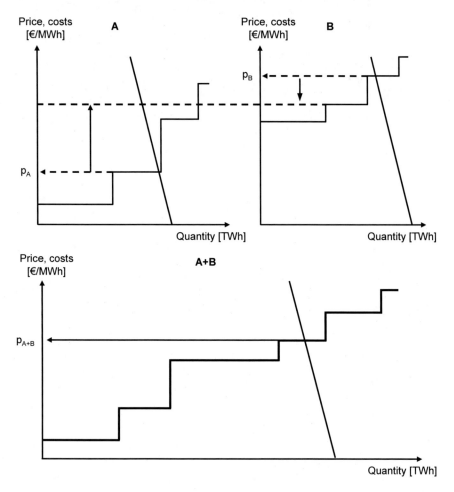

Figure 10.17: Effects of market extension in an electricity market

Currently, we do not see sufficient incentives for TSOs to invest in cross-border capacities within the present regulatory framework, especially with regard to legal unbundling. First, in the presence of a high wholesale price in the local market relative to the neighbouring markets the incumbent generator will be reluctant to increase interconnector capacity. Second, revenues from capacity auctions at congested cross-border lines have to be used for interconnector capacity investments or, in the absence of these investments, simply to reduce the cost base for deter-mining network tariffs, which constitutes a zero-sum game for the TSO.[5] In the light of unbundling provisions, the authors consider ownership unbundling as a means of resolving the aforementioned shortcomings.

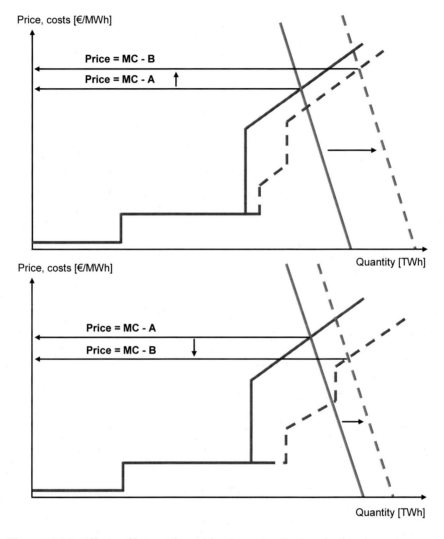

Figure 10.18: Effects of integrating a 'short' country (top) and a 'long' country (bottom) in an existing market

Figure 10.17 shows the theoretical result of market coupling of a low-price market A (with 'cheap' excess capacity, e.g. the Czech Republic) and a high-price

---

[5] See Regulation (EC) 1228/2003 for details (Regulation 1228/2003, 2003).

market B (with no cheap excess capacity, e.g. the Austrian, French, German and Swiss regional market). As a result, prices increase in market A and this goes along with an increase in producer surplus in market A, whereas prices decrease in market B, increasing consumer surplus in B. Of course, sufficient cross-border capacities must be made available at low costs.

Figure 10.18 depicts the effect of full market integration for two different cases. In the first case, adding a 'short' country B – a typical import country with demand exceeding capacities – results in price increases for the extended market relative to the former single market A. On the other hand, when a 'long' country B – where demand is less than installed capacities – is added prices decrease for the extended market relative to the single market A.

10.7   Conclusions

The European electricity markets are still under construction, but some conclusions are already possible on developments so far.

Liberalisation in Continental Europe started about a decade after the advances made in the UK and Norway. However, it seems that the Continental European countries had not learned much about conditions for competition from experience in the UK and Norway. Instead of divesting generation capacity and increasing the number of competitors (as recommended by Newbery & Pollitt, 1997), most countries pursued mergers (DE, NL), retained oligopolies (NL, ES, AT, CH) or a private monopoly (BE) or supported the concept of national champions (PO, FR).

Currently, the major obstacle to a common market that works reasonably well is a general lack of competition in virtually all local and national wholesale and retail electricity markets. Either the number of competitors is too low or barriers to entry or incentives to collude are too high. This situation is compounded by insufficient transmission capacity between the submarkets and increasing horizontal integration with natural gas supply.

Finally, it is stated that sufficient spare capacities in generation and transmission are currently still available in Europe. The definitive litmus test for liberalisation will come in every submarket in the EU at the point in time when the bulk of excess capacities have disappeared and demand has come close to available capacities. Current developments imply upcoming security of supply problems by 2012 in the Continental European markets investigated, even in the case of an extended multiregional market. The most important problem is how to provide long-term incentives for investment in upgrading and in new generation and transmission capacities, and also in demand-side efficiency and demand responsive measures. This issue is especially relevant in the context of decentralised vs further centralised development of the electricity supply system.

Moreover, to bring about the EU's goal of effective competition in a single integrated European electricity market and to avoid market power, the following structural conditions have to be fulfilled:

- Ownership unbundling of the transmission system from generation and supply as a means of both guaranteeing nondiscriminatory access to the grid and inciting and providing adequate transmission capacity to connect the single submarkets, thus creating a larger market with more potential competing players.
- With respect to the market structure, a rethink of structural remedies such as divestments or capacity payments.

References

APX. 2008. http://www.apxgroup.com/marketdata/powernl/public/monthly_avgpr ices_year/index.htm.

Banks, F. E. 2006. Economics of electricity deregulation and privatisation: an introductory survey. Energy, 21: 249-261.

Bundesamt für Wirtschaft und Ausfuhrkontrolle (BAFA). 2008. http://www.bafa. de/bafa/de/energie/index.html.

Directive 96/92/EC. 1997. Directive 96/92/EC of the European Parliament and of the Council of 19 December 1996 concerning common rules for the internal market in electricity. Official Journal – European Communities Legislation, 40: 20-29.

Directive 2003/54/EC. 2003. Directive 2003/54/EC of the European Parliament and of the Council concerning common rules for the internal market in electricity and repealing Directive 96/92/EC. Official Journal, L 176: 37-55.

EEX. 2008. http://www.eex.com/en/Market%20Information/Power/Hour%20Con tracts%20%7C%20Spot.

European Commission. 1996. Services of general interest in Europe. Official Journal, 96/C 281: 3.

European Commission. 2007a. DG competition report on energy sector inquiry SEC(2006)1724. Brussels: Commission of the European Communities.

European Commission. 2007b. Proposal for a Directive of the European Parliament and of the Council amending Directive 2003/54/EC concerning common rules for the internal market in electricity COM(2007) 528 final. Brussels: Commission of the European Communities.

EUROSTAT. 2008. http://epp.eurostat.ec.europa.eu/portal/page?_pageid=0,11362 39,0_45571447&_dad=portal&_schema=PORTAL.

Glachant, J. M. & Finon, D. 2005. A competitive fringe in the shadow of a state monopoly: the case of France. The Energy Journal, Special Issue on European Electricity Liberalisation: 181-204.

Glachant, J. M. & Lévêque, F. 2005. Electricity internal market in the European Union: What to do next? Contribution to the SESSA research project. www.sessa.eu.com, 19th May 2008.

Haas, R., Orasch, W., Huber, C. & Auer, H. 1997. Competition versus regulation in European electricity markets. Paper presented at the 2nd European IAEE conference, Vienna.

Haas, R. & Auer, H. 2001. How to ensure effective competition in Western European electricity markets. IAEE Newsletter, 3: 16-20.

Haas, R., Glachant, J. M., Keseric, N. & Perez, Y. 2006. Competition in the Continental European electricity market: despair or work in progress? In F. P. Sioshansi & W. Pfaffenberger (Eds.), Electricity Market Reform: An International Perspective: 265-316. Amsterdam: Elsevier.

Haas, R., Redl, C. & Auer, H. 2008. Mid-term perspectives for the Western/Central European electricity market. IAEE Newsletter, 1: 23-26.

Hirschhausen, C., Weigt, H. & Zachmann, G. 2007. Price formation and market power in Germany's wholesale electricity markets. Unpublished Electricity Markets Working Papers, WP EM 15b, Technische Universität Dresden, Dresden.

IPEX. 2008. http://www.mercatoelettrico.org/En/Statistiche/ME/DatiSintesi.aspx.

London Economics. 2006. Structure and performance of six European wholesale electricity markets in 2003, 2004 and 2005. Brussels: DG Comp.

Müsgens, F. 2004. Market power in the German wholesale electricity market. Unpublished EWI Working Paper, No. 04/03, Energiewirtschaftliches Institut an der Universität zu Köln, Cologne.

Newbery, D. & Pollitt, M. 1997. The restructuring and privatisation of Britain's CEGB: Was it worth it? Journal of Industrial Economics, 45: 269-304.

Newbery, D. 2002. European deregulation: problems of liberalising the electricity industry. European Economic Review, 46: 919-927.

Newbery, D. 2006. Electricity liberalization in Britain and the evolution of market design. In F. P. Sioshansi & W. Pfaffenberger (Eds.), Electricity Market Reform: An International Perspective: 109-144. Elsevier: Amsterdam.

Nord Pool. 2008. http://www.nordpool.com/system/flags/elspot/area/all/.

OMEL. 2008. http://www.omel.es/frames/en/resultados/resultados_index.htm.

OTE. 2008. http://www.ote-cr.cz/data-publication/statistic/month-report/daily-market-statistic.

Platts. 2007. Power in Europe. Issue 508 / September 10, 2007: 10-41.

PolPX. 2008. http://www.polpx.pl/main.php?index=223&show=38&lang=en&okres=dzien&s_data=30%2F07%2F2008.

Powernext. 2008. http://www.powernext.fr/index.php.

Regulation 1228/2003. 2003. Regulation 1228/2003 of the European Parliament and of the Council concerning on conditions for access to the network for cross-border exchanges in electricity. Official Journal of the European Union, L 176: 1-10.

Union for the Co-ordination of Transmission of Electricity (UCTE) (Ed.). 2007. System adequacy retrospect 2006. Brussels: UCTE.

Union for the Co-ordination of Transmission of Electricity (UCTE). 2008. Online Database. http://www.ucte.org/services/onlinedatabase/.

11 The Changing Structure of the Utility Industry from the Perspective of Regulation Authorities

Matthias Kurth[1]

Abstract

This chapter sets out the structural changes in the energy markets as seen by the Federal Network Agency for Electricity, Gas, Telecommunications, Post and Railway [Bundesnetzagentur]. It describes not only the changes identified in the period from the late 1990s to the end of 2007, but also the emerging trends for the coming years. Both national and European developments are included. The structural changes taking place in the European energy markets can be described in regulatory terms under the headings: redefinition of the markets, unbundling and technical integration of the networks.

Keywords: unbundling, regulation, liberalisation

[1] Matthias Kurth is President of the Federal Network Agency for Electricity, Gas, Telecommunications, Post and Railway, Germany.

A. Bausch and B. Schwenker (eds.), *Handbook Utility Management,*
DOI: 10.1007/978-3-540-79349-6_11, © Springer-Verlag Berlin Heidelberg 2009

11.1   Introduction

The greatest structural change in the utility industry began with liberalisation of
the energy markets in 1998. Liberalisation redefined the markets. Energy supply
was broken down into production/generation, wholesale trading, transport, distribution and energy supply (see Figure 11.1).

Market structure until 1998

- Regional monopolies of energy undertakings
- Vertically integrated market structures

Market structure 2007

- Regulation of natural monopolies on TSO & DSO level
- Wholesale market for energy as a new link in the energy value chain
- Upstream and downstream competitive activities

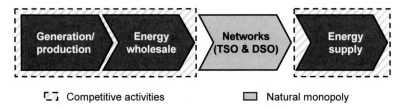

Figure 11.1: Market structures before and after liberalisation (Bundesnetzagentur,
2008)

The logical consequence of liberalisation was the regulation of the transport
and distribution networks as a natural monopoly. Regulation is a precondition for
competition in the upstream and downstream markets in the interests of consumers
in Europe. Also, regulation exposes this segment of the value chain to quasi-
competitive pressures that encourage the efficiency and innovation potential
needed by the network industry to manage supplies in the twentyfirst century and
to complete the European internal energy market. The main concepts here are: the
integration of new and more efficient, large-scale power plants, greater development of renewable energy sources, integration of wind energy potential with its
highly uneven regional distribution, enablement of congestion-free European trade

in energy and integration of European networks in which blackouts cannot be regionally contained.

When liberalisation began, the structure of the industry throughout Europe was predominantly vertically integrated. Ownership structure was – and still is – state controlled in many cases. This vertically integrated structure was fundamentally changed by the directives package in 1996/98 and in 2003.

The 1996 issue of a directive on the internal market in electricity (96/92/EC) and the 1998 directive on the internal market in natural gas (98/30/EC) were the first steps taken by the European Commission towards liberalising and restructuring the energy markets.

For the utilities, however, the requirements were more about behavioural obligations and less about structural issues. The aim of the first regulatory package was, first and foremost, to open the networks by making nondiscriminatory third-party access mandatory. Under the internal electricity market directive, there was the assumption of negotiated access. For the first time, member states were required to designate system operators (Articles 7.1 and 10.2) and to define their exact tasks (Articles 7, 8 and 11).

Accounting unbundling was the first form of unbundling introduced to secure commercially nondiscriminatory access (Article 14). Meanwhile, separate internal accounts for generation, transmission, distribution and other activities, the provision of notes to the annual accounts, a balance sheet and a profit-and-loss account for transmission and for distribution and information on the cost allocation of shared items are required.

Organisational unbundling, i.e. independent system operation, was envisaged for the transmission level only (Article 7.6). Also, the obligation to treat insider information, most notably on transport enquiries and contracts, confidentially was imposed on the staff of all vertically integrated undertakings concerned (Article 9).

The first directive on the internal market in natural gas, which basically reflected the requirements and obligations of the internal electricity market directive that preceded it, already contained special structural arrangements for the gas industry. Thus, it had no corresponding provisions on operational unbundling at transmission level.

The Commission's second energy package stemmed from the realisation that integrated undertakings had not developed competition at the pace required solely through behavioural rules. New wholesale and retail players that entered the market in 1998 had exited again by 2003. The second energy package thus contains a number of structural measures for unbundling different levels of the value chain. The directives address the legal separation of the transmission and distribution networks of the integrated gas and electricity undertakings. The network is to be managed separately in terms of legal form, organisation and decision-making powers from the integrated company's other areas of activity. In addition, the decision-making powers of the parent company are restricted by the transmission and distribution system operators having independent decision-making powers in respect of assets required for the maintenance, operation and rollout of networks. This is the purpose of the rules on management unbundling, on the introduction of compliance management – comparable only in essence with the compliance regime of financial service companies – and on dealing with operators' insider information.

Ownership remained untouched. This legislative reticence disappeared, however, with the proposals for a third energy package. In light of the beginning debate on the European Commission's unbundling proposals and their efficacy for low-priced energy supplies and greater investment in infrastructure, these proposals will not be considered here. Notwithstanding the outcome of the political debate, all the relevant structural changes in the utility industry for the regulatory authorities and for proper utility organisation are already on the regulatory agenda. Thus, the – politically inspired – idea of an independent network company based on the second package of directives differs but little in spirit from an independent system operator ('ISO') or full ownership unbundling model. For this very reason, it is right to ask whether ownership unbundling is an answer to all the problems of competition, as the debate at EU level would often have us believe. These models, too, need solutions to the problems laid out below, as seen by the German regulatory authority.

11.2   Structural Changes in the Utility Landscape in Germany

11.2.1   Radical Legal Changes

The Energy Industry Act 2005, which transposed the second regulatory package, brought a paradigm shift for the energy sector in Germany. For the first time, regulatory bodies were set up at both national and federal state level to oversee vertically integrated utilities.

Whereas transmission system operators had already begun putting the European requirements into practice before the Energy Industry Act took effect, most of the German supplies industry was dormant. Not until the regulatory authorities were created to execute the many new arrangements (see Table 11.1) were the desired effects achieved in every market segment.

One of the main consequences of the new provisions is the dissolution of the vertically integrated utility as a strategic unit to carry out the public service mandate. On the one hand, vertical integration delivers synergies that enable efficiency gains. On the other, it is susceptible to incentives for cross-subsidisation between the levels of value chain and for preferential treatment of the utility's own activities in matters of system connection and access. This potential for discrimination represents an economic disadvantage for the other market players, for consumers and for the national economy. The new legal framework is thus designed to make sure that the transmission and distribution network, as a natural monopoly, turns into a neutral unit within the vertically integrated utility.

Table 11.1: New binding rules for utilities since 2005 (Bundesnetzagentur, 2008)

Energy Industry Act *(EnWG)* – July 2005
- Legal, operational, information and accounting unbundling of the network from the competitive activities of the vertically integrated utility
- Specifying the tasks for the system operator, particularly in respect of expanding the network in line with demand
- General regulations on connection to the system
- Regulations on access to the system, particularly on approval by the regulatory authority of use of system charges
- Powers and possible sanctions the regulatory authority can impose, abuse cases, etc.
- Requirements on energy supply to final customers: basic (universal) supply, supply of last resort, content of contracts, etc.

Network Access Ordinance *(GasNZV & StromNZV)* – July 2005
- General requirements regarding the organisation of access
- Contractual forms of access
- Duty to publish information and to work with other system operators
- Balancing procedures
- Requirements for switching supplier, metering and congestion management
- Balancing services arrangements

Network Charges Ordinance *(GasNEV & StromNEV)* – July 2005
- Method for establishing use of system charges: types of cost, cost centres, cost unit accounting
- Benchmarking requirements
- Publication, documentation and notification duties for system operators

Low Voltage Ordinance *(NAV)* and Low Pressure Connection Ordinance *(NDAV)* – November 2006
- General requirements on system connection and use
- Rights of system operator in operating facilities

Electricity and Gas Basic Supply Ordinance *(StromGVV, GasGVV)* – November 2006
- General conditions for low voltage electricity and low pressure gas supply to domestic customers as part of basic supply at standard prices

Power Plant Connection Ordinance *(KraftNAV)* – June 2007
- General arrangements on connection of large-scale power plant
- Information duties and connection register

Incentive Regulation Ordinance *(AregV)* – November 2007
- Setting access charges by way of incentive regulation
- General provisions on incentive regulation: duration of regulatory periods
- Requirements for determining revenue caps
- Determining the revenue cap by benchmarking
- Quality of service regulation

Determination of the Regulatory Authority for supplier switching processes *(GPKE & GeliGas)*
- Defining uniform business processes (for contractual/legal supplier relationships)
- Determining the data format and information exchange

Metering Liberalisation Ordinance – expected in 2008

11.2.2   The Utility Landscape in Germany at a Glance

Liberalisation of the German gas and electricity market has brought about a fundamental change in the structure of the value chain. Whereas Figure 11.1 illustrated the changes observed in the utilities, Figure 11.2 shows the actual number of market players in each segment of the energy industry value chain today.

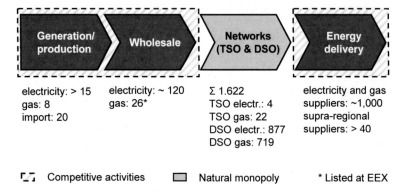

Figure 11.2: Market players along the energy value chain (Federal Network Agency, EEX, VDEW, Verivox, 2007)

Up to 1998, nine companies accounted for the entire value chain and some 900 were included at the levels of distribution and supply to final customers. Since 1998, however, the picture has changed greatly. On the one hand we find a concentration of the transmission system operators, so that today, four electricity companies provide the entire value chain. Yet new players are entering all the competitive markets. Large-scale power plant projects are being advanced by more than a dozen companies not previously seen in this segment. Currently, the four transmission system operators still generate around 90% of the produced electricity. On average, 120 companies take an active part in trading on the European Energy Exchange (EEX), and 26 are registered for gas trading on the EEX, which is just beginning. New gas and electricity suppliers are increasingly appearing to sell energy to industrial and domestic customers.

The results of this redefinition of the market have not yet filtered down satisfactorily to the consumers. Thus, the Monitoring Report 2007 of the Federal Network Agency for Electricity, Gas, Telecommunications, Post and Railway [Bundesnetzagentur] shows that consumer switching rates in 2006 tended to stagnate at persistently low levels, while wholesale electricity prices rose again. Despite these price signals from the wholesale market, announcements about the postponement of planned power plant projects are on the increase. However, this is also the result of factors outside the regulated area, deriving, for instance, from planning law or emissions trading. Yet trust in the neutrality and transparency of the infrastructure is essential if the good beginnings to more competition in the energy markets are to be built up on.

11.3   Unbundling Integrated Utilities

11.3.1   Model of an Independent Network Company

Effective unbundling creates clear conditions, allocates responsibilities and core competences to the network company, and gives it powers of disposal of the network and the necessary human resources.

11.3.2   Level of Implementation in Germany

For distribution system operators, legal unbundling was not made a requirement until June 2007. The transmission system owners began to separate their transmission systems before 2005, transferring them to legally independent network companies. This has revealed fundamentally different perceptions of the market in the gas and electricity industry. The electricity transmission system operators seem to have a greater recognition that the networks have a role of their own to play in the market, setting up companies that could perform system operator functions in their own capacity including the ownership of the network assets. For the gas industry, the networks were often a means to an end in competition for the sale of oil and gas, which is why strategic interests are associated more closely with the network here. This perhaps explains why even the vertically integrated gas undertakings in Germany are lagging with the transfer of the ownership of their transmission assets to their legally independent gas transmission system operators, but have chosen a lease solution instead. Interestingly enough, the Exxon/Shell and BEB group, the first gas transmission company to transfer network ownership into the transmission system operator, disposed of its network entirely in 2007.

11.3.3   Challenges Facing an Independent Network Company

11.3.3.1 Management Unbundling

Integrated utilities must free management of their network-related activities from all the conflicts of interest of a vertically integrated company (so-called management unbundling). Management unbundling concerns managers and the management board, authorised signatories and other senior executives in the network company. Depending on its exact form, however, persons below the first and second management levels might also be included. If the distribution of responsibilities within the system operator plans for further persons to have crucial influence on the planning and shaping of operations in an area of activity with potential for discrimination, these persons must also be assigned to the system operator and not exposed to any conflict of interest. This includes, for instance, network management, management of use and connection, strategic network planning and capacity allocation.

All those involved in management unbundling must be members of the network company and must not on any account be employed in companies of the vertically integrated utility with direct or indirect responsibility for production/generation or sales. This also applies to functions on management and supervisory boards.

A clear distribution of roles and allocation of management staff is vital here. Only in this way can the independence of the network operation management staff be secured and conflicts of interest avoided. Nearly every integrated utility has limited staffing resources for these qualified management and network activities, which is why management unbundling poses such great challenges. This is particularly the case when a utility is a combination utility with operations in water, heat and district heating as well as in gas and electricity. Here, tasks are sometimes performed in conjunction. Only utilities that actively shape the roles of asset owner and asset manager can meet the challenge of unbundling the regulated areas and operate the utility's infrastructure areas jointly from a joint infrastructure company.

11.3.3.2 Questions of Legal Form and Corporate Governance

In principle, a utility has free choice of the legal form for the network company. Yet some forms have restrictions that are incompatible with the operational independence required, resulting, for example, from the chief executive of a private limited company being bound by instructions and certain information rights of the shareholders. At any rate, such restrictions must be modified by contractual agreements in such a way that independence is given. It must be noted that the congruence of what is allowed by company law and what is allowed by energy law cannot be satisfactorily achieved except in the legal form of the joint stock company [Aktiengesellschaft]. Only in a joint stock company is the role of the shareholder adequately limited to operative activities and relations with the supervisory boards clearly defined. Yet this, too, must be qualified for listed companies. Thus the Transparency and Publicity Act 2002 required listed companies to specify cases of reservation of consent (cf. Section 111(4) second sentence of the Joint Stock Companies Act). The mixing of control and management tasks, explicitly advocated in the corporate governance debate, is not entirely applicable in the energy sector. As far as the corporate governance code can be applied to vertically integrated utilities at all, the legal unbundling requirements diametrically oppose the basic principles of the corporate governance code (greater meshing for 'better' management and 'preventative supervision'), and take precedence over these.

11.3.3.3 Efficiency Pressures and Fleshing out the Network Business

The pressure on companies to perform efficiently will increase with incentive regulation. Figure 11.3 aims to show that this pressure will also be felt strongly at the distribution level, which accounts for 90% of the electricity network costs.

Thus, it must be a particular concern for the many small and medium-sized distribution system operators to aim for efficient structures following the restructuring of the market. It is not only regulatory mistrust that leads to the lean lease network companies often found being seen as suboptimum solutions to the delivery of independent, efficient network operation.

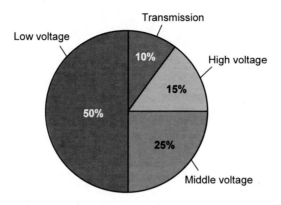

Figure 11.3: Repartition of the total network charges by the type of electricity grid voltage levels (example for a final customer with a yearly consumption of 4,000 kWh) (University of Aachen, 2005)

We are not likely to be overstating the case when we say that these companies will either fail in entrepreneurial terms, on account of their interface problems, or will put their faith, unlawfully, in the service providers within the integrated utility 'doing it themselves'. Incentive regulation will give every company the scope to decide on its structures for itself, within permitted limits. Yet the efficiency of the structures will be a factor in each regulatory period in determining the management possibilities of the network company and hence its overall efficiency. It is in line with what we have observed in Germany that it is not always the biggest units that are the most efficient. Thus, we find local utilities today that see their public service obligation in the provision of secure, cost-effective infrastructure that will also give them sustained returns if managed efficiently. Some of these utilities are also active players in the markets supplying final customers.

Of course, in network industries too we find critical mass and economies of scale. But in terms of regulation and competition it is not desirable, nor is it necessary, for unbundling and regulation to bring about yet greater market concentration. On the contrary, economies of scale can also be achieved by horizontal cooperation between small and medium-sized companies.

11.3.3.4 Compliance Management

The overarching aim of unbundling is to guarantee transparency and nondiscrimination in all aspects of network operation. Unbundling revolves around securing the nondiscriminatory treatment of information coming to the operator's notice in the course of business. Nondiscrimination must take the form of equal treatment. This requirement has considerable implications for future information management in vertically integrated companies. It is necessary to adapt all the internal structures and processes for both electronic data processing and staff management.

Irrespective of the size of the company, the management is responsible for effectively countering breaches of confidentiality of insider information on the network. It can only do so with the help of documentation and supervision of the network operation business processes. It is possible to integrate the requirements of information unbundling into an existing, externally certified quality management system. Management must be informed routinely and nonroutinely, by the internal audit unit or by the compliance officer or an external auditor, about compliance with unbundling regulations (compliance management). Suggestions for improvement must be assessed and management decisions documented.

11.4   Strategic Options for Utilities

As the last section made clear, utility unbundling is a building block for present and future structural change in the value chain in the energy sector. Full independence of the network business in an integrated utility will be achieved only as a result of actual – also emotional – emancipation of the network company from the parent company. Synergies will probably be reduced in the rest of the company as a result, and the strategic influence of the parent company will decrease. Utilities will have to develop new strategies against this background if they are to capitalise on the pressure for change in the industry. They have a number of options, such as:

- Going public;
- Opening up new fields of business at home and abroad;
- Cooperation projects within or across the industry;
- Mergers and acquisitions;
- Concentration on core businesses.

Adapting to the new framework will trigger a process of concentration in the regulated network business which, in the medium term, will lower the 1,100 or so network companies currently serving the public. A survey on cooperative network activities has shown that every third system operator, at least, in Germany is expected to disappear from the market in the long term (Werthschulte et al., 2007). Against this background the energy industry must use the regulatory pressure on the network industry as an opportunity for rethinking and for striking out on new paths, such as cooperative activities and mergers.

11.4.1   Cooperative Activities, Mergers and Network Sales

A future-proof option for network companies is merging with other network companies. Mergers can secure their economic efficiency and survival. Lower returns as a result of network regulation can be doubled or even trebled by the economies of scale cooperation brings (Werthschulte et al., 2007). Particularly against the background of the introduction of incentive regulation in 2009, through cooperative activities, network companies will be able to fully exploit the potential for synergies, which will contribute to the cost savings needed. The deeper the form of cooperation (acquisition, merger, joint venture) between companies, the greater the synergies potential.

Practical experiences have shown that the potential for synergies that derives from cooperative activity requires a certain minimum time before the gains kick in. The regulatory periods envisaged by incentive regulation thus take account of the timeframe for structural change. Particularly successful forms of cooperative activity appear to be those that consolidate locations and network areas and consistently harmonise processes and systems (Krötz, 2007).

It is probable that mergers are not, in themselves, a strategic option for every network company. In Germany there are very many, very small distribution networks which, despite cooperation projects in the network business, are not likely to reach the critical mass needed to create large synergies potential. Special arrangements for this group are already provided by the Incentive Regulation Ordinance. Small utilities must examine whether cross-industry activity could produce companies that are more future proof. Large network companies do not need mergers. We can expect the medium-sized network companies to benefit most from cooperative activity.

Another option is sale of the network. It may be an outcome of incentive regulation that owners of inefficient network companies will seek to sell their networks. This will attract not only financial investors, but also entrepreneurially-minded network companies. An efficiently structured and managed company will have further opportunity for growth through the acquisition of other networks.

11.4.2 Opening Up New Fields of Business or Concentration on Core Business

A further option for independent network companies could be to expand their service spectrum. There is no legal reason why they should have to restrict themselves to the legal minimum of a system operator. Provision of infrastructure services outside the regulated energy supply network has been mentioned several times. Besides traditional system operator activities, network companies could also offer specialised network services commercially. In light of their expertise, they could easily benefit from developments in new market segments (smart metering) if they position themselves as players early on.

Besides cooperative activities in the network business, utilities will also be able to concentrate on selected competitive fields of business. The major utilities will not necessarily regard the network business as their existential core business any more. Even for energy groups, the possibility that they will voluntarily sell their networks and invest the income in new fields of business at home and abroad cannot be ruled out. Often, psychological barriers prevent the creation of efficient structures. This can be observed with municipal utilities, in particular. From the point of view of the public shareholders, a multi-municipal utility without a distribution network is almost unthinkable. At the same time, the supply of energy to final customers is regarded as the purest of the public services of general economic interest, although in many cases there are no active supply strategies and marketing actions. Ultimately, only participation in production (power plant construction) can provide strategic scope as regards pricing and purchasing terms. Yet such large – and sometimes risky – investments presuppose a minimum company size and require cooperative activities. Municipal utilities that operate solely as resellers or distributors will perhaps succumb to pressures from third parties operating more efficiently in sales and accounting as a result of synergies and economies of scale. In the considerably fiercer competition for telecommunications services we clearly see that, as the telecommunications framework advances, food discount stores and the tabloid press have added the distribution of mobile services, for instance, to their operations.

11.4.3   Regulatory Perspective

Most important is the quest for sustainable, future-oriented restructuring solutions. One-off radical structural change followed by incremental adjustment will be more profitable for a utility than a number of minor short-term changes. Here, setting up full-service network operators, including the transfer of network ownership to the network operator, is one possible route to efficiency gains.

As long as the utilities industry is predominantly vertically integrated, effective separation of the network business from the competitive activities of the company as a whole is the quintessential structural change envisaged by regulation. The vertically integrated utility must develop new entrepreneurial strategies for all levels of the value chain if it is to benefit from the changed framework. Future-oriented planning also means not getting tied up in endless political and regulatory discussion about the most effective unbundling model. In regulatory terms, the adaptation strategies observed at system operator level must be assessed very differently. As set out in Section 11.3, the 'lean lease' model, the model most often chosen for the network area, gives rise to many problems and not acceptable in the medium term. By contrast, the route via cooperative activity is seen by the regulator as largely positive. In particular, independence of the network business can be achieved and maintained more rapidly internally and externally by, for example:

- Independent branding and communication of the network company engaging in cooperative activity through its own corporate identity (no immediate identification with the group it is part of);
- Credible independence in negotiations with the network owners and thus less potential influence on the network company's entrepreneurial scope;
- Cooperative activities beyond the regulated network business: network services as a new field of growth.

Cooperation projects are welcomed by the Bundesnetzagentur, as evidenced by, for instance, its tolerance of transitional solutions in network tariff approval procedures or in the implementation of operational and information unbundling.

11.5   Outlook

The structural changes in the energy industry are expected to alter the ownership structures of the utilities. Large network companies with ownership assets will increasingly use the capital market as a basis for refinancing. The excellent performance of listed transmission companies will reinforce this trend. Greater interlinkage between the listed European transmission system operators will follow the ever greater technical integration of the European transport networks. Energy policy will be confronted with massive challenges as a result of the manifold aims and projects of climate change (carbon dioxide emissions trading), development planning for renewables (25-30% of electricity generation is to come from renewables by 2020), and restructuring with respect to new power plants and decentralised elements of energy production, and greater trading activity. Use of network capacity will be more volatile; networks will need to be more flexible and to be expanded and upgraded as rapidly as possible in order to transport (for instance), electricity from offshore windparks to industrial centres of consumption. A clear regulatory framework is vital if the investment needed is to be made promptly. Network and incentive regulation will provide the right conditions for this to happen.

References

Anreizregulierungsverordnung (ARegV). 2007. Verordnung über die Anreizregulierung der Energieversorgungsnetze. Bundesgesetzblatt, 1, 62.

Directive 92/96/EC. 2003. Directive of the European Parliament and of the Council concerning common rules for internal market of electricity and repealing. Official Journal of the European Union, L 176/37.

Directive 92/96/EC. 2004. Directive of the European Parliament and of the Council concerning common rules for internal market of electricity and repealing. Official Journal of the European Union, L 236/10.

Directive 96/92/EC. 1997. Directive of the European Parliament and of the Council of 19 December 1996 concerning common rules for the internal market in electricity. Official Journal of the European Communities. Legislation L, 40: 20-29.

Directive 98/30/EC. 1998. Directive of the European Parliament and of the Council of 22 June 1998 concerning common rules for the internal market in natural gas. Official Journal of the European Communities. Legislation, 41: 1.

Directive 2003/55/EC. 2003:2004. Directive of the European Parliament and of the Council concerning common rules for the internal market in natural gas and repealing the Directive 98/30/EC. Official Journal of the European Union, L 176/56, L 2/ 55, L 16/74.

Elektrizitätszugangsverordnung (StromNZV). 2005. Verordnung über den Zugang zu Elektrizitätsversorgungsnetzen. Bundesgesetzblatt, 1, 46.

Energiewirtschaftsgesetz (EnWG). 2005. Zweites Gesetz zur Neuregelung des Energiewirtschaftsgesetz.

Gasgrundversorgungsverordnung (GasGVV). 2006. Verordnung über allgemeine Bedingungen für die Grundversorgung von Haushaltskunden und die Ersatzversorgung mit Gas aus dem Niederdrucknetz. Bundesgesetzblatt, 1, 50.

Gasnetzentgeltverordnung (GasNEV). 2005. Verordnung über die Entgelte für den Zugang zu Gasversorgungsnetzen. Bundesgesetzblatt, 1, 46.

Gasnetzzugangsverordnung (GasNZV). 2005. Verordnung über den Zugang zu Gasversorgungsnetzen. Bundesgesetzblatt, 1, 46.

goetzpartners. 2007. Wertanlage Stadtwerke II. München: goetzpartners.

Kraftwerks-Netzanschlussverordnung (KraftNAV). 2007. Verordnung zur Regelung des Netzanschlusses von Anlagen zur Erzeugung von elektrischer Energie. Bundesgesetzblatt, 1, 28.

Krötz, T. 2007. Horizontale Unternehmenskooperationen als Reaktion auf geänderte Rahmenbedingungen. Kronberg/ Köln: Accenture/ Energiewirtschaftliches Institut der Universität zu Köln.

Niederdruckanschlussverordnung (NDAV). 2006. Verordnung über Allgemeine Bedingungen für den Netzanschluss und dessen Nutzung für die Gasversorgung in Niederdruck. Bundesgesetzblatt 2006, 1, 50.

Niederspannungsanschlussverordnung (NAV). 2006. Strom Verordnung über Allgemeine Bedingungen für den Netzanschluss und dessen Nutzung für die Elektrizitätsversorgung in Niederspannung (BGBI. I S. 2477). Frankfurt am Main: VWEW-Energieverlag.

Stromentgeltverordnung (StromNEV). 2005. Verordnung über die Entgelte für den Zugang zu Elektrizitätsversorgungsnetzen. Bundesgesetzblatt, 1, 46.

Stromgrundversorgungsverordnung (StromGVV). 2006. Verordnung über allgemeine Bedingungen für die Grundversorgung von Haushaltskunden und die Ersatzversorgung mit Elektrizität aus dem Niederspannungsnetz. Bundesgesetzblatt, 1, 50.

Werthschulte, S., Kübel, M., Gold, H. & Getta, M. 2007. Neuordnung der Netzindustrie: Kooperationen und Zusammenschlüsse als Schlüsselkompetenzen. Energiewirtschaftliche Tagesfragen, 11: 64-67.

12 The Changing Structure of the Utility Industry from Its own Perspective

Werner Brinker[1]

Abstract

The framework within which the utility industry acts has changed enormously in recent years. Politics and increasing competition, growing demands for climate protection, and global competition for scarce energy resources necessitate new structures and strategies. Early on, EWE took the necessary steps to establish its strong competitive position in the energy and in the information and communications technology markets and, as a regional and international multiservice group, is actively helping to shape the transition to a sustainable energy supply for the future.

Keywords: EWE Group, regional supply, multiservice

---

[1] Dr. Werner Brinker is Chief Executive Officer and Chief Officer Sales and Marketing of EWE AG, Germany.

A. Bausch and B. Schwenker (eds.), *Handbook Utility Management,*
DOI: 10.1007/978-3-540-79349-6_12, © Springer-Verlag Berlin Heidelberg 2009

12.1   The Importance of Regional Utilities –
with EWE AG as an Example

12.1.1   EWE AG as Infrastructure and Energy Service Provider

Within the European distribution system, regional energy utilities are the link between long-distance and transport grid operators and local distributors. With the
operation of energy supply grids they help to fulfill important infrastructural preconditions in their supply regions. This chapter offers a brief look at the EWE
Group, its significance as a regional supplier, and its competitive position, and
also at its strategies for the future.

EWE AG supplies energy and telecommunications services in the northwestern
part of Lower Saxony, i.e. the region enclosed by the rivers Ems, Weser, and Elbe.
Beyond the Ems-Weser-Elbe region, the natural gas supply grid encompasses additional areas in the eastern part of Brandenburg, the northern part of Mecklen-
burg-West Pomerania, and parts of Poland. The electrical, natural gas, and telecommunication networks (see Figure 12.1) have a combined length of more than
165,000 km and are operated by EWE NETZ GmbH.

Almost 400 communities in the Ems-Weser-Elbe region receive their electricity
from EWE AG; in all, EWE serves roughly 1 million electric power customers,
including 22 municipal power companies. The EWE electric grid, with a downtime of less than 5 minutes per customer per year, is one of the most reliable in
Europe. To compare: in Germany, the power goes off for an average of
19 minutes; Italy lies in the middle with 76 minutes; the longest downtime, with
157 minutes per capita per year, is in Ireland. Ninety-eight percent of the EWE
power grid is underground and thus protected from the influence of weather.

EWE has constructed a comprehensive natural gas supply grid in the region;
more than 80% of all households are connected to the gas grid, which has meanwhile attained a length of approximately 54,000 km. EWE supplies a total of more
than 771,000 customers with natural gas and is one of the few providers in Germany that import their own natural gas and deliver it to private households without any further intermediaries. On a limited scale, EWE is also active in production. EWE is also one of the leading operators of natural gas storage facilities in
Germany. EWE AG operates cavern storage facilities in Nüttermoor and Huntorf
in Lower Saxony and in Rüdersdorf in the State of Brandenburg, with a combined
storage capacity of approximately 1.3 billion cubic meters. As a storage provider,
EWE rents out many of the caverns to other firms. The storage facilities contribute
substantially to the security of supply of natural gas; in addition, natural gas that
becomes available on the market and in favorably priced quantities can be stored
in reserve and called up as needed.

Building on its core strengths – the efficient management of complex electrical,
natural gas, and telecommunication networks – the EWE Group has developed a
broad multi-utility offering covering energy, water, environment, building management, and telecommunication and information technology.

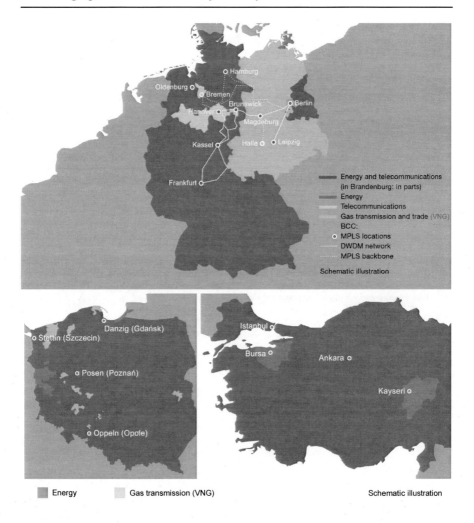

Figure 12.1: EWE grid area (EWE Group and major shareholdings)

12.1.2   Economic Significance of the EWE Group

With annual consolidated sales of € 4.7 billion and 4,700 employees, in 2007 EWE was one of the leading energy companies in Germany (see Figure 12.2). In Nord/LB's annual ranking of companies (e.g., Nord/LB, 2007), EWE ranks regularly among the strongest in terms of sales in Lower Saxony and, based on annual turnover, among the largest in the northwest region.

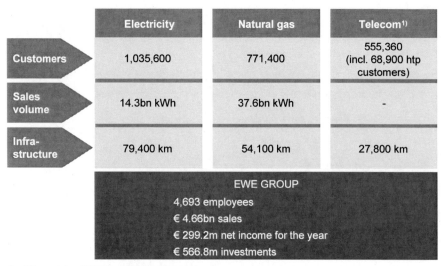

	Electricity	Natural gas	Telecom[1)
Customers	1,035,600	771,400	555,360 (incl. 68,900 htp customers)
Sales volume	14.3bn kWh	37.6bn kWh	-
Infra-structure	79,400 km	54,100 km	27,800 km

EWE GROUP
4,693 employees
€ 4.66bn sales
€ 299.2m net income for the year
€ 566.8m investments

1)   TC companies: EWE TEL, BREKOM, osnatel, Teleos
     The htp GmbH is an associated company (EWE`s share: 50 percent)

Figure 12.2: Key figures relating to the EWE Group in 2007

The EWE Group consists of the parent company EWE AG, based in Olden-burg, and numerous subsidiaries and majority and minority interests (see Fig-ure 12.3). They provide EWE services domestically and also in Poland and Tur-key. The largest EWE subsidiary is the network operator EWE NETZ GmbH, with approximately 1,400 employees. EWE NETZ GmbH is responsible for manage-ment and maintenance of and repairs and extensions to the grid infrastructure and operations. In addition, the subsidiary operates drinking water systems and a vast communications network for controlling and supervising the energy grid.

In 2007, EWE was among the largest municipal energy companies in Germany and the only regional energy company with exclusively domestic ownership. EWE AG is indirectly owned, through investment companies, by 21 cities and counties in the Ems-Weser-Elbe region. The shareholders count on annual returns in the millions from trade taxes, license fees, and dividend distributions for their gov-ernment budgets.

In July 2008, EWE AG's shareholders, Supervisory Board, and Board of Man-agement agreed to EnBW Energie Baden-Württemberg AG acquiring a 26% eq-uity share in EWE AG. Subject to approval by the German Federal Cartel Office in Bonn, this strategic partnership opens up opportunities for further sustainable development and growth.

EWE has strong commitments, both economic and social, to its grid areas; these include investment in an efficient infrastructure and involvement in the areas of research, development, and teaching; the creation and safeguarding of thou-sands of jobs; and, above and beyond its own requirements, job training for more than 270 young people. Socially, EWE is active above all in the areas of athletics and support of opportunities for youth. The EWE Foundation also supports regional projects and initiatives in the fields of art and culture, research and science, and teaching and education.

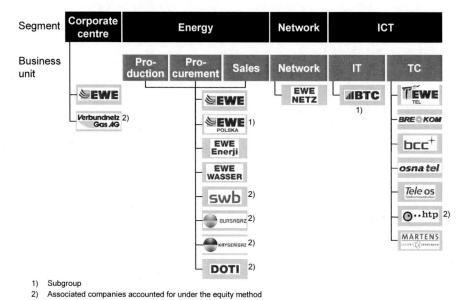

1) Subgroup
2) Associated companies accounted for under the equity method

Figure 12.3: EWE Group – including subsidiaries and major shareholdings

12.2   EWE's Strategies for Growth and Competition

12.2.1   Influence of Liberalization and Regulation on EWE's Development

The liberalization of the energy markets as the result of the EC internal market directives for electricity (1996) and gas (1998) and their incorporation into national law by amendment of the national energy law in April 1998 drastically changed the legal regulatory framework of the utility industry.

The internal market directives for electricity and gas were followed up by the so-called acceleration directives in 2003. In July 2005, the Energy Statutes Reorganization Act along with regulations governing grid access and fees came into effect; as a result, responsibility for regulation in the areas of electricity and gas supply was assigned to the Federal Network Agency. It is the Agency's task to guarantee open access to the grid and to supervise the grid fees charged by the operators.

Unbundling, the legal and functional separation of grid operations from the other functions of a utility company, is a fundamental ruling in this regard; to supply the communities and the region, EWE founded the network operator EWE NETZ GmbH, splitting off the division's employees into the subsidiary and transferring ownership of the grids to it. Unbundling involved considerable personnel and financial outlays. Also attributable to the introduction of the regulations are further burdens on the energy companies created by the establishment of regulatory management for the ongoing dialogue with the Federal Network Agency, new publication requirements for network operators, among others, and the general accounting and billing for electrical and gas transmission activities.

In 2006, for the first time, electric and gas network operators were required to seek approval of their grid fees. Grid costs, together with billing costs, make up about a third of EWE's total price for electricity and about 20% of the price of natural gas. In the first regulation period the Federal Network Agency reduced the fees EWE NETZ was charging for use of the electrical distribution grid in the 1-kV and 20-kV ranges by 9.9% and the natural gas grid fees by an average of 5.4%. Throughout Germany the Agency cut the charges applied for by an average of 12%, or a total of € 2.5 billion. In the second regulation round, in 2008, EWE NETZ's network access charges for electricity were reduced by an average of 4.7%. The gas charges for which EWE applied were not cut.

As of 1 January 2009, incentive regulation will replace the current rate regulation, which is based solely on cost considerations; it is intended to provide network operators with incentives by means of the attainable earnings within a regulatory period to improve the efficiency of their networks; however, they will not be compelled to take account of existing network quality until the second regulatory stage, starting in 2014. Operators of higher quality networks, such as EWE, will thus be at a disadvantage in a comparison of efficiency with other firms. These restrictions will make it difficult in the future for EWE to continue to invest to the same extent as hitherto in the high quality of its network.

In Germany liberalization has led to a series of business mergers at all levels of the utility industry; since 2006, consolidation at the European level has intensified. Shortly after the opening up of the energy markets, EWE AG merged with the neighboring Überlandwerk Nord-Hannover AG. With approximately 1 million electricity customers and almost a doubling of its grid area, the regional supplier thus reached a size in 1998 that made it a competitive concern and ensured its independence.

In recent years EWE has taken over or bought interests in several more municipal utilities. Of strategic importance was the 2004 acquisition of 49% of the voting rights for swb AG in Bremen and a 47.9% share of the Leipzig natural gas wholesaler VNG AG. EWE's participating interest in swb strengthened the regional market position of both groups, since the supply territory of the Bremen utility lies in the middle of the region that EWE supplies and the group operates its own power plants. Participation in the natural gas importer and internationally active wholesaler VNG contributes to preserving reliable procurement channels.

The ongoing liberalization of the European natural gas market also offers EWE new opportunities in the area of natural gas storage. With this in mind, EWE is expanding its existing capacity and setting up new storage facilities in strategically interesting locations. In cooperation with Wingas, EWE is building new storage caverns in Jemgum (county of Eastern Frisia), and in Moeckow (State of Meck-lenburg-West Pomerania) new storage facilities are planned near the site of the future receiving terminal for the projected Baltic pipeline.

Liberalization has also brought new business opportunities to the service sector. EWE has developed its own system for billing and customer care, which is being marketed to other utility companies and used to provide third-party billing services.

12.2.2   Positioning in the Competition for Electric and Natural Gas Customers

As a regional public utility, EWE stands out from other providers, which is attributable above all to its commanding presence in the region, its personal service, its wide range of products and services, and its active involvement in and commitment to the region.

Although at the start of liberalization only a small number of customers showed an interest in new electricity products or other providers, since the middle of 2007 more and more customers have begun switching suppliers, especially now that consumer organizations and politicians have started making effective use of the media to encourage this. The German Energy and Water Association (BDEW) has determined that, since the beginning of market liberalization, one out of every two private electricity consumers has changed suppliers or secured a new electricity supply contract with the old supplier; it is a similar picture for small and medium-sized firms. In the industry, all firms have meanwhile concluded new supply contracts. Since the start of the new grid access model, in October 2007, competition in the natural gas market has also increased markedly. According to the Federal Network Agency, some 50,000 customers switched natural gas suppliers in the first half of 2007.

EWE has also felt the effects of customers' increasing willingness to switch, but EWE's comparatively low prices and high customer loyalty have helped keep the changeover rate below the national average.

Increasing price sensitivity and a simultaneous rise in energy costs make it increasingly difficult to implement price adjustments that are really needed as a result of rising procurement costs and increasing government fees; the growing competitive pressure has also had an impact on EWE: up to the beginning of 2007 the net price of a kilowatt-hour of electricity from EWE for an average household never exceeded its 1996 level; from 2000 to 2004, it was even lower than in 1996. During this same period, purchase costs rose drastically, and the share of taxes and fees in the price of electricity doubled. Today about 37% of the amount paid for electricity by an average private household goes to the state in the form of EEG (Renewable Energy Sources Act) and KWKG (Cogeneration Act) fees, concession fees, electricity taxes, and value-added taxes.

EWE meets the demands of competition for market share in its home market by providing innovative, market-oriented products at competitive prices, maintaining an active presence throughout the region, and offering personal service and consulting. EWE's prices have traditionally been among the lowest in Germany and have served for years as a benchmark for the Federal Cartel Office in comparing providers. In comparisons of natural gas prices by the Association of Energy Consumers, EWE has also done well over the years as the most reasonably priced gas utility (VEA, 2007).

Since the beginning of 2008, in addition to its standard products EWE, as the first company in the German energy market, has offered electricity, natural gas, and telecommunications as a complete package. With this product offensive, EWE passes on its synergistic effects in the form of significant savings to its customers. The green power products of the EWE subsidiary EWE NaturWatt round out the electrical offerings of the regional supplier; since the end of 2007, the green power subsidiary has also marketed its products nationwide. With emission certificate trading and tranche-buying models, EWE also offers business customers such as municipal utilities and industrial groups the opportunity to optimize their electrical purchases in the energy market without having to function as traders themselves.

The 40 or so customer service locations in the region fulfill the conditions for a customer-oriented, multiservice offering. EWE advises both business and private customers personally on the more economical and efficient use of energy; to do this, EWE offers its customers suitable services: for natural gas heating, for example, EWE has developed a contracting product that includes an integrated service packet for the financing, planning, construction, and operation of a heating system.

An EWE poll of customers showed that despite increasing price sensitivity, a company's social commitment, especially to the creation and safeguarding of jobs and training in the region, remains a factor in the decision-making of many customers. This result is supported by an April 2007 survey by the VDEW (as of fall 2007: BDEW), in which almost every respondent viewed community involvement as one of the important tasks of the electricity companies (VDEW-Energie-monitor, 2007). From a customer standpoint, the regional factor comes into play most strongly for the green power subsidiary EWE NaturWatt.

12.2.3 Growth in the Information and Telecommunications Markets

The importance of the Group's information and telecommunications (ICT) business segment goes far beyond its – in comparison with the energy business – modest contribution to the Group's turnover. It contributes dynamically to growth and, furthermore, is a strategic core element of the EWE Group. The intelligent infrastructure provides a solid foundation for coping technically with the tremendous challenges of supplying energy in the future. In addition, the ICT subsidiaries, in their many decentralized locations, also offer interesting sales avenues for other products and services of the EWE Group.

The necessary conditions for successful development of this business segment were established early on: EWE was one of the first regional energy supply companies to implement its own remote technology for network control and to use its infrastructure for the development of new, market-ready telecommunication and

IT services. Since the 1980s, while expanding its natural gas grid, the company has also been laying empty pipe for the construction of an optical fiber network; the resulting line capacity far exceeds EWE's own needs. EWE AG's telecommunications network alone today encompasses 13,200 km of optical fiber and 14,600 km of copper cable, and is thus now one of the most capable and secure networks in Germany.

EWE's strong position in its domestic market also fostered the successful entry of EWE TEL into the telecom market. Trust in the EWE brand has served the subsidiary well: the 100% telecommunications subsidiary, founded in 1996, is now one of the largest regional telephone companies in Germany. After Deutsche Telekom, EWE TEL has the most direct access connections in the northwest. Utilizing EWE AG's telecommunications network, the subsidiary offers telephone, Internet, DSL, and mobile telephone services to more than 340,000 customers in northwestern Lower Saxony, the city of Bremen, and parts of Brandenburg.

In recent years, the TC business has also grown through EWE's participation in five other regional telecom firms that are active in other regions of Lower Saxony and have more than 210,000 direct subscribers. The strategic goal of the EWE Group is the construction of a high-quality telecommunications offering that fully covers all of Lower Saxony.

EWE's modern IT infrastructure also provides the foundation for a series of energy-related IT applications, which EWE has successfully marketed through its fully owned subsidiary BTC. Within just a few years, BTC AG has developed into the largest IT consulting firm in northern Germany. With 15 branch offices in Germany, Poland, Switzerland, Turkey, and Japan, the BTC Group provides IT and management consulting for companies in the energy supply, automotive, industrial, telecom, and public service sectors.

12.2.4   International Involvement

In order to continue to grow, EWE is relying increasingly on a strategy of internationalization. In the expansion of natural gas supplies in Poland and Turkey and the development of the respective regional markets, EWE is contributing its core expertise to the construction and operation of efficient networks.

The economic environment in Poland is developing dynamically; EWE has been active since 1999 in this market as the first foreign natural gas supplier through its EWE Polska subsidiary. In western Poland and in the region between Wrocław (Breslau) und Łódź, industry is prospering; many new firms are moving into the area. Business operations in this region and in regions lying further east in Poland are conducted by Media Odra Warta Sp. z o.o. (MOW), based in Międzyrzecz (Meseritz), in which EWE Polska has a 99.9% interest.

Since 2001, Turkey's economy has been undergoing a process of reform focused on liberalization. Along with the dynamic growth of its economy, prosperity is also increasing in Turkey; the demand for energy will increase greatly in the coming years. The Turkish natural gas market has not so far been divided up among the various large European energy groups, and thus also offers smaller foreign investors, such as EWE, opportunities for participation. With the purchase of 39.9% of the shares of Bursagaz A.Ş., in April 2007, EWE became the first German energy company to invest in a Turkish natural gas supplier. Bursagaz would like to establish natural gas as a source of energy in northwestern Turkey and in 2006 had sales of approximately 580 million cubic meters to natural gas customers in the Bursa region. In 2008, EWE enlarged its stake in the Turkish energy market by acquiring another 40.1% interest in Bursagaz and a 80% interest in the Turkish regional utility Kayserigaz A.Ş.

EWE also wants to expand its foreign involvement further in the future. In addition to natural gas, the ICT business offers new opportunities in this regard; BTC AG is already successfully doing business abroad, and EWE also wants to enter the Turkish DSL business. The goal is to transfer the experience EWE has gained over the past 10 years with the combination of energy, telecom, and IT services to Turkey's young, very dynamic market.

12.3   EWE Group's Strategy for Tomorrow's Energy Supply

12.3.1   Climate Protection – a Shared Responsibility

"The planet is becoming dangerously warm, the world's oil and natural gas reserves are running out, and the world's population will rise from 6.5 to 8.2 billion in 2030: electricity demand will double." This quote from the UN Climate Report 2007 underlines that demands for an energy supply for the future can only be met through international cooperation on the part of business, government, and science. The Intergovernmental Panel on Climate Change (IPCC), in its fourth climate report, came to the conclusion that it is already too late to halt global warming and that it can only be reduced (IPCC, 2007). At the same time, the International Energy Agency (IEA) predicts that the worldwide use of primary energy – and thus the emission of harmful greenhouse gases – from 2005 to 2030 will increase by an average of 1.8% per year; if governments around the world stick with current policies – the underlying premise of the IEA Reference Scenario – the world's energy needs would be well over 50% higher in 2030 than today (International Energy Agency, 2007).

In December 2007, almost 190 countries agreed on a road map for a new UN climate protection agreement, the so-called Bali Road Map. The Kyoto countries, among them Germany, want to reduce their emissions by 25-40% by 2020; some countries, however, among them the USA, the greatest emitter of greenhouse gases, in addition to such rapidly growing national economies as China and India, reject binding reduction goals; they have signed the climate framework convention that merely makes reference to the recommendations of the IPCC. A new climate protection agreement is intended to be negotiated by 2009 and will replace the Kyoto Protocol, which expires in 2012.

Every step toward any one of the three goals of climate protection, fair pricing, and security of supply has immediate consequences for the other two. Stricter regulatory and political measures have further intensified these correlations; one example is the trading of emission certificates as an additional cost element in energy production. The 100% accomplishment of all three goals simultaneously is thus not possible. Within this energy policy triangle, the goal of protecting the climate and the environment is not just one of three goals, but rather a critical bottleneck. It is CO_2 emissions, above all, that are held responsible for global warming. The weight of scientific opinion is that the increase in global mean surface temperature must be stabilized at no more than 2 °C above preindustrial levels if we are to prevent dangerous climate change. On this basis, the Advisory Council on Global Climate Change (WBGU) recommends that the concentration of CO_2 emissions in the Earth's atmosphere be stabilized at a maximum of 450 ppm (WGBU, 2003).

It is clear even now that Germany will exceed its 2010 goal of reducing CO_2 by 21%. Germany is playing a vanguard role in Europe in the area of climate protection and is a leader in many innovative technologies, including renewable energy. In an international ranking by the climate protection organizations Germanwatch and Climate Action Network, at the end of 2007 Germany was placed second, after Sweden, in a comparison of 56 industrial and emerging nations (Burck et al., 2007).

For years now, the utility industry has invested large sums in efficient, environmentally friendly technologies. In addition to these efforts, politicians have called on the industry not only to drastically reduce emissions during the production and provision of energy, but also to support energy consumers in their conservation efforts. Considerable potential for energy savings exist in the industry and building sectors; the local energy companies are helping to boost this potential by providing consultation and appropriate services and products. Additionally, in a pilot project conducted in cooperation with the county of Emsland, EWE is testing CO_2 certificates for private households. Up to 150 households will receive a one-time subsidy for energy consultation plus 20 €/ton of CO_2 saved annually. This project began in 2007 and will run for 3 years.

The climate protection and energy efficiency guidelines are ambitious; at the same time, pressure on the energy companies from increasing competition for worldwide resources is growing. The utilities are intended to provide secure and affordable energy; to do this, they need to secure access to existing resources for the long term, while developing new, preferably regenerative, energy sources. At the same time, the climate change necessitates innovative technologies that will make it possible to produce and transport energy in an environmentally friendly manner.

EWE is also meeting these challenges, and is investing in innovative technologies in addition to research and development. EWE is also taking an active role in the public debate; serving as the basis for this is a white paper that offers a vision for the energy supply in the year 2030, which EWE developed in collaboration with renowned scientists from the Fraunhofer Energy Alliance, the Technical University in Munich, and the Bremer Energie Institut. Its essential elements are ten assumptions from which recommendations for action can be drawn; the so-called Bullensee Assumptions (Luther et al., 1996) also serve as guidelines for

EWE's future strategic orientation. With a view to the future, it will be necessary to conserve even more energy, to increase energy efficiency significantly, and to expand renewable energy sources; these three points, abbreviated E³, form the heart of this strategy.

12.3.2   Renewable Energy and the Energy Mix of the Future

Worldwide, fossil fuels – oil, gas, and coal – make up more than 80% of our energy supply, and the demand continues to climb, above all in developing nations such as China and India. The competition for energy resources around the world is causing prices in the international supply markets to rise. Because technical advances now allow for the partial replacement of fossil fuel for producing electricity and heat, world energy demand no longer affects only the price of oil, natural gas, and coal, but also markets for renewable raw materials such as corn (maize), rapeseed, grain, sugar and other oilseeds, such as palm oil.

In Germany a good quarter of the electricity is generated from nuclear energy and about half from coal. Renewable energy, at 14%, already makes an important contribution to the domestic electricity supply and can replace an even greater share of the primary fossil fuels in the future; however, fossil fuel-fired electric power plants will still provide 70-80% of our electricity until 2020, according to the Federal Environment Ministry. The BDEW estimates that renewable energy will meet about half of our energy requirements in the year 2050.

Since Germany has very few energy resources available within its own boundaries, it needs to acquire more than 80% of the necessary primary energy through international energy markets. EWE ensures reliable long-term natural gas supplies by diversifying its procurement sources; in 2007, 46% of the natural gas came from domestic sources, 28% from the Netherlands, and 26% from Russia; to achieve this, the regional supplier concluded long-term contracts with both domestic and foreign suppliers and functions as a trader on the energy exchange in Leipzig. To a lesser extent, EWE also extracts natural gas from its own fields in the North Sea.

The future price of electricity in Germany is also a question of the nation's own production capacity. In Germany, adequate power plant capacity has so far been available to cover domestic demand for electricity; however, the BDEW estimates that, primarily because of the decision to stop using nuclear power, by the year 2020 about 40,000 MW of power-generating capacity in Germany will need to be replaced, which is more than a third of the currently installed capacity. According to a study by the HWWI Institute in Hamburg, even as soon as 2008 there could be a supply gap that cannot be filled by new power plants or power from renewable energy; by 2020, the gap could grow to 16% of the projected power demand (Bräuninger et al., 2007). The situation is made worse by drastically rising costs for raw materials and power plant construction; even EWE was forced, for economic reasons, to halt the planned construction of a coal-fired power plant, a joint project with swb and Essent; furthermore, in Germany at present there is increasing resistance, above all, to the construction of coal-fired power plants.

Since EWE's own production capacity remains very limited, the company secures its electricity purchases almost exclusively through long-term delivery contracts and, to some degree, on the spot market. Overall, EWE operates wind turbine, solar, and biomass/biogas installations with a total installed capacity of more than 100 MW.

In the coming years, EWE will expand its production capacity further, above all for the use of regenerative energy sources. In the field of biomass utilization, for example, the company has a 55% stake in the Emden biomass power station, operates a growing number of biogas plants, and provides vegetable oil cogeneration power stations under contract to customers. One of the largest projects is 'alpha ventus', the first offshore wind farm in the German Bight, which EWE is developing together with E.ON Energie and Vattenfall. Forty-five kilometers off the island of Borkum, the first of a total of twelve planned 5-MW wind turbines should be generating electricity by the beginning of 2009. The offshore farm, with a capacity of 60 MW, will be able to generate over 200 million kWh annually and supply about 50,000 households with electricity; at the same time, the wind farm should provide important knowledge for further development of offshore technology.

12.3.3   Investments in Innovative Technologies, Research, and Development

In the areas both of renewable energy and energy conservation and of increasing efficiency, there is still enormous potential for applied research and new technological developments; in coming years, therefore, EWE will intensify its investment in energy research. Presently the company is primarily engaged in the testing of fuel cells, the integration of wind turbines into the existing electrical grid, and the development of a decentralized energy management system (DEMS; see Figure 12.4). EWE is also working closely with the University of Oldenburg to build a research center that will open in 2008; in cooperation with EWE it will conduct fundamental practice-oriented research on the supply of energy.

In order to utilize the tremendous potential of renewable energy, it must be optimally integrated into system structures; this means that grid structure and load management must be adapted and storage systems for weather-dependent energy sources such as wind and solar light must be integrated in order to harmonize supply and demand. EWE is engaged on such research questions in several long-term research and development (R&D) projects.

With the frequent winds along its coastal areas, its wide range of renewable raw materials and biomass, and its abundant roof surfaces for solar applications, the northwestern area of Lower Saxony offers favorable conditions for the use of renewable energy. Thus, the current structure, with nearly 10,000 decentralized production facilities (mostly wind turbines), already quite closely resembles the structure of the future energy supply, and renewable energy infeeds are correspondingly high in the region: in 2006, about 4.7 billion kWh of electricity was fed into the EWE grid. This is already enough, theoretically, to satisfy one-third of the electricity demand of this region from renewable energy sources; accordingly, the percentage of electricity fed into the EWE grid from regenerative sources in 2006 (18.4%) was considerably above the national average of 12.0%.

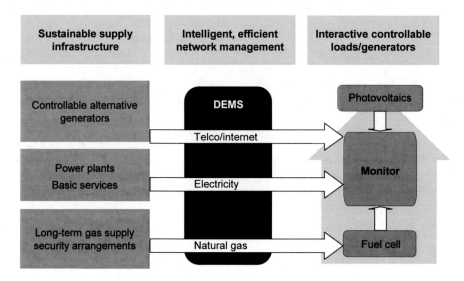

Figure 12.4: Decentralized energy management system (DEMS)

In practical terms for EWE, this means that for an increasing number of days each year the energy flow into the grid reverses, as the decentralized facilities feed in more electricity than is being used in the region at the time. Maintaining grid stability, a steady energy supply, and the most efficient distribution and use of the energy produced at decentralized locations is an enormous challenge for EWE NETZ; this is why one of EWE's key R&D projects is the development of a decentralized energy management system that will integrate these decentralized facilities for energy production and conversion into the existing supply structures and optimize and intelligently control the acquisition of electricity from various sources.

Storability also has a significant role in the integration of renewable energy into the energy supply. One possibility for storing electricity is the use of hydrogen; EWE supports the joint research project HyWindBalance, in which a number of companies and institutions are taking part. The project goal is to manufacture hydrogen from excess wind energy, then store it, and convert it back into electricity by means of fuel cells when needed. A further project in which EWE is taking part is concerned with the question of how the transport of liquid hydrogen and electricity can be combined.

Fuel cell technology is another key research emphasis of EWE; the company has been participating in field tests of fuel cells, which represent a possibility of efficient energy conversion, since 1998. In the course of the fuel cell program, 48 devices from various manufacturers have so far been installed. In addition, EWE has been involved with both national and international funding projects to encourage the introduction of fuel cell technology into the market.

Promoting regenerative energy also means making it marketable and competitive. The subsidiary EWE NaturWatt, one of the first German green power providers, sells wind, water and solar power throughout Germany. Since fall 2007, EWE has also directly marketed wind-generated power in cooperation with two regional firms on the energy exchange in Leipzig. In this way EWE wants to create an alternative in good time to power plants that, according to EEG rules, are no longer eligible for increased tariffs 20 years after commissioning. Every kilowatt-hour traded directly on the exchange is removed from the EEG feed-in tariffs and has the opportunity to earn a higher return on the exchange. With this in mind, electricity from wind farms with an initial installed capacity of approximately 2,000 MW is also bundled and offered on an hourly basis via EWE AG's trading floor on the exchange.

Biogas can also be marketed by feeding it into the natural gas grid. EWE has equipped a 2.5 MW biogas plant with a treatment and feed-in facility; since November 2007, it has been feeding up to 3 million cubic meters of biomethane annually into the local natural gas grid. Plant efficiency has thus significantly increased: the connected cogeneration station produces only the amount of electricity for which the resulting heat can be completely utilized. When this is not the case, the biogas is refined and flows via the distribution grid to other users. In the future, one option calls for the refined biogas to be blended in at more than 50 natural gas fuel stations operated by EWE throughout the Ems-Weser-Elbe region, thus further improving the CO_2 balance of the low-emission alternative fuel natural gas.

12.3.4   Outlook

In the future, the regulatory influences on the electricity and natural gas markets coming out of Brussels and Berlin will only increase, limiting the utility industry's room for maneuvering even more. EWE would also be impacted, for example, by the break-up of the energy supply companies that has been discussed, through the splitting off of the transport grids and the unbundling of natural gas storage. In addition, intense competition will make it increasingly difficult for municipal utilities and regional providers to succeed in the future.

With its entrance into new markets, EWE began opening up new growth sectors early on; the deployment of innovative technologies, and research and development efforts give the firm a technological advantage. Lean management, efficient networks, skilled employees, a pioneering spirit, and a long-term strategy for growth will all help to make it possible for EWE to continue its successful development. Furthermore, EWE will continue to take advantage of opportunities for domestic and international investment and use cooperation opportunities opened up by a strong strategic partner to gain an even better position for itself in the energy market for the long term.

References

Bräuninger, M., Kriedel, N., Schröer, S. & Hamburgisches WeltWirtschaftsInstitut (HWWI). 2007. Power für Deutschland – Energieversorgung im 21. Jahrhundert. Hamburg: HypoVereinsbank.

Bundesverband der Energie-Abnehmer (VEA). 2007. Erdgaspreisvergleich II/ 2007. Hannover: VEA.

Burck, J., Bals, C., Wittger, B. & Beck, M. 2007. The climate change performance index – a comparison of emission trends and climate protection policies of the top 56 CO_2 emitting nations. Berlin: Germanwatch.

Intergovernmental Panel on Climate Change (IPCC). 2007. Summary for policymakers. In S. Solomon, M. Manning, D. Qin, Z. Chen, M. Marquis, K. B. Averyt, M. Tignor & H. L. Miller (Eds.), Climate Change 2007: The Physical Science Basis. Contribution of Working Group I to the Fourth Assessment Report of the Intergovernmental Panel on Climate Change. Cambridge and New York: Cambridge University Press.

International Energy Agency (OECD/IEA). 2007. World energy outlook 2007. Paris: IEA.

Luther, J., Pfaffenberger, W., Wagner, U. & Brinker, W. 1996. 10 Bullensee assumptions and associated recommendations for tomorrow's energy supply. Oldenburg: EWE AG.

Nord/LB. 2007. Wirtschaft Niedersachsen – Die 100 größten Unternehmen in Niedersachsen – Analysen und Kommentare. Hannover: Nord/LB.

Verbandes der Elektrizitätswirtschaft (VDEW). 2007. VDEW-Energiemonitor. Mannheim, Berlin: VDEW.

Wissenschaftlicher Beirat der Bundesregierung Globale Umweltveränderungen (WGBU). 2003. Welt im Wandel: Energiewende zur Nachhaltigkeit. Berlin-Heidelberg: Springer-Verlag.

13 Mergers & Acquisitions from a Strategic Perspective

Wulf H. Bernotat[1]

Abstract

Intensive mergers & acquisitions (M&A) activity has been characteristic of the utilities industry for more than 20 years. This chapter outlines the rationale for these trends and discusses why mergers & acquisitions will continue to be of vital importance for the future strategic development of leading utility companies in Europe. Aside from providing a brief overview of the industry's M&A 'history', the chapter will touch specifically on how E.ON has developed by pursuing a strategy of acquisitive growth. Providing some of the key insights that E.ON has drawn from its own experience in this field, the chapter elaborates on success factors in M&A in the utilities industry. Furthermore, it describes how E.ON has positioned itself to be prepared for the challenges and opportunities ahead.

Keywords: mergers & acquisitions, strategic growth, utilities

[1] Dr. Wulf H. Bernotat is CEO and Chairman of the Board of Management of E.ON AG, Germany.

A. Bausch and B. Schwenker (eds.), *Handbook Utility Management,*
DOI: 10.1007/978-3-540-79349-6_13, © Springer-Verlag Berlin Heidelberg 2009

13.1   Introduction

Acquisitive growth is a well-known instrument in E.ON's strategic portfolio.
Mergers & acquisitions (M&A) activity has played a vital role in our company's
history. Ever since the merger of VEBA and VIAG in 2000, E.ON's development
has been crucially impacted by strategic considerations on acquisitive growth. For
E.ON, a sustainable and value-creating approach towards the market was always
closely linked to transforming the initial conglomerate structures of two traditional
German enterprises into a focused energy company. This has enabled us to pursue
the vision of becoming the world's leading power and gas company.

It took a lot of foresight and stamina to decide upon and implement these
changes once the key strategic decisions on our future market focus and business
model had been made. Between 2000 and 2007, we decided to carry out transactions of more than € 120 billion, which significantly changed our geographical
footprint and portfolio of activities. Our divestments and acquisitions were impacted by numerous internal and external factors – in most cases, several choices
were available and major decisions had to be made under time constraints. In addition, the prevailing political setting – from the regional to the European level –
had to be taken into consideration.

13.2   The Need for Acquisitive Growth
in the Utilities Industry

Basically, there are three factors that drive large utilities such as E.ON towards
inorganic growth: growth perspectives in European national markets are limited;
the goal of integration along the value chain can often be achieved best by acquisitions; and, finally, the ongoing conversion of the power and gas sectors also encourages M&A activity.

13.2.1   Limited Perspectives in European National Markets

Most major European markets have reached a level of maturity that will allow for
only rather moderate growth rates in the years to come. Since the beginning of this
decade, the electricity markets in Germany, France, Italy and Great Britain have
only grown at annual rates of between 0.5% and 2%. In Spain growth has been a
little faster, but still below 5%. We expect that this trend will continue until the
end of the decade and that some countries – such as Germany – may even experience negative growth rates. The situation is different in emerging markets, such as
Russia. Thus, these markets provide significantly better organic growth potential.

In addition, the margins of utilities have come under pressure owing to general
market liberalization in their home markets. Competition in many of the large
European markets has increased significantly since the mid-1990s. At the same
time, the increasing regulation of certain sectors in these liberalized markets has

aggravated the situation for utilities. Recently, there has been a political tendency to regulate particular market segments – grid access, price development, etc. – at European and national levels. This has corroborated the belief of many European utilities that international acquisitive growth is an important option in their corporate strategy.

Another aspect with respect to regulation is that the potential for national inorganic growth is limited. In many European countries, anti-trust laws have considerable influence on a utility's ability to grow. These regulations obviously reduce an enterprise's ability to purchase other players in the market. One key problem is that the European national markets are still regarded as separate spaces, with the consequence that a strong national presence quickly reaches a 'critical' level from an anti-trust perspective even though the utility's share on a European scale might still be relatively small. This aspect deserves to be discussed at national and European level – particularly when there are calls for more effective European market and cross-national competition.

13.2.2   The Requirement for Strong Positions along the Value Chain

In order to reach a decent level of self-sufficiency, balanced distribution of a company's assets along the value chain – in particular in the electricity generation, upstream gas, trading and retail segments – is of strategic importance. Since construction 'from scratch' and building up a significant customer base is a very costly and time-consuming exercise, acquisitions provide several advantages for utilities striving to achieve a balanced portfolio along the value chain.

This focus on increasing regional integration does not preclude functional units in the organizational set-up at the cross-national level. On the contrary: Such units can provide specialized services and concentrate the available expertise on topics that are similar in a number of countries. Recent examples at E.ON include the units Energy Trading, Climate & Renewables, our competence center for Generation Technology, and our freshly established New Build Unit, which bundles our planning and construction expertise.

13.2.3   Convergence of the Power and Gas Sectors

Past years have shown that providers of power and gas can achieve substantial synergies in certain segments of their businesses. In the retail segment, the ability to provide power and gas 'from a single source' has compelling advantages, because it helps to cut marketing and sales expenses, mainly in the business-to-consumer (B2C) sector. Moreover, substantial synergies can also be achieved in trading. A strong presence in both markets has proved to be a key competitive advantage and a driver of value creation. The convergence of the two sectors has created significant economies of scope, and M&A activities facilitate the ambition of utility companies to expand their assets and promote this convergence.

Based on this assessment of the outstanding role of acquisitive growth in the utilities industry, it is useful to take a brief look at the way utilities have performed mergers and acquisitions since this development gained momentum in the mid-1990s.

13.2.4   Integration of European Markets

The European Commission's political vision of a comprehensively integrated European market is of critical importance, since it affects the strategic set-up of utilities and the industry's overall consolidation process. Supported by the EU member states, the Commission has developed a convincing program to integrate national market segments and regional central markets into a single European market. E.ON proactively supports this integration process, which aims to establish a competition-based integrated market built on a regulatory platform. In our view, this is the most promising way to ensure a sustainable and secure future energy supply in Europe.

Some of the remaining obstacles hampering this process will soon decrease in importance as awareness of the need for sustainable, competitive and secure European energy supply increases. In any case, the development towards an integrated and fully liberalized energy market will intensify the need for utilities to have a certain critical corporate size in order to remain competitive in an international context.

13.3   M&A Patterns in the Utilities Industry

A key prerequisite for substantial acquisitive growth in our industry has been the opening of markets and the privatization of formerly state-owned companies. Many of the defining developments in our industry have been either directly triggered or critically influenced by the changes in the market setting and the ownership structure of European utilities.

13.3.1   Privatization and Liberalization

Starting from a mainly noncompetitive market situation, European utilities have been experiencing periods of privatization and market liberalization since the early 1980s. In Germany, this gained momentum when E.ON's predecessor companies were completely privatized in 1987 and 1988, respectively. Some European countries, such as the UK, started this process earlier; others, such as France and Sweden, are still lagging behind in this development. With Hungary at the forefront, Eastern European countries began privatizing their national utilities in 1992.

At the political level, major steps in EU member states included the European Union's Electricity Directive for a single European market in 1997. It liberalized the power sector, and its 1998 'sister directive' established the same objectives for the gas sector. However, the required liberalization also occurred at different speeds, as demonstrated by the very different developments in major economies such as Germany and France. Major consequences of this liberalization process for the business models of utilities can be seen in the fields of market access and pricing strategies. Providers of gas and electricity consolidated their positions by aligning fragmented markets and company structures in many EU countries.

13.3.2 National Consolidation and International Expansion

Another phenomenon that gained momentum in the late 1990s was the international expansion of utilities. Once national players had consolidated after the waves of privatization and liberalization, utilities began to look for opportunities outside their national borders. Most of today's major players in Europe have undertaken considerable M&A activities since the mid-1990s. Some of the most influential deals include the ongoing acquisition of Endesa by Enel and Acciona, EdF's takeover of Edison, and the purchase of Scottish Power by Iberdrola. Moreover, E.ON's acquisitions of Powergen, Ruhrgas, and OGK-4 are also significant examples of this process.

E.ON's home market of Germany has also been quite a popular place for foreign acquisitions. In 1997, Southern Energy landed one of the first deals by acquiring Berlin's remaining shares in the regional supplier Bewag, and in 1999 EdF bought a majority share in EnBW – thereby gaining a significant foothold in the German market. The same holds true for Vattenfall, which established its strong position in Germany with acquisitions between 1999 and 2002. On the other hand, German utilities have also secured major deals across Europe and beyond. Prominent examples are RWE's purchases and our own activities in the UK and in Eastern Europe.

13.3.3 Continuous European Consolidation

These phases of national consolidation and international expansion have blended into the ongoing period of European consolidation. A couple of large national energy players – often with significant assets across Europe – are striving to secure positions as European champions. Examples illustrating this tendency include our own company and most of our major competitors.

Occasional warnings that call into question the value of large champions at European level underestimate the advantages of these entities, particularly from a consumer's perspective. The largest providers of primary energy are state-owned companies concentrated in just a few countries. Large private counterparts ensure a certain balance in the European energy equilibrium, since they bring about a weight that is urgently needed in negotiations with state-owned players such as Gazprom or Statoil. Since some public companies have recently started establishing a foothold in the European power and gas sectors through integration along the value chain, large private entities are needed to balance their power.

As a very interesting side effect, this continuous period of European consolidation also demonstrates another conflict at the European level: The principles of the European market clash with national interests in major industry sectors such as the utilities industry. The European internal market remains a patchwork of different market structures and regulatory regimes. National borders are not yet sufficiently permeable, which is due both to inadequate transfer capacity and to government policies that distort energy prices and reestablish state control.

This most recent phase in the development of European utilities has been accompanied by the emergence of new business models. Driven by the compelling evidence of the threat posed by climate change, utilities are responding to this challenge by establishing units that promote the renewable energy business. Our own 'Climate & Renewables' unit is a prominent example of this trend. In addition, players from the utilities industry draw upon business opportunities provided by the Kyoto Protocol's flexible mechanisms, such as Joint Implementation (JI) or the Clean Development Mechanism (CDM). In any of these cases, inorganic growth can be a strategy to gain a foothold in the respective market segments, since building up the expertise and capacity for significant market activities is time-consuming and ties up human resources.

In many ways, E.ON's transformation from a highly diversified, mainly German, company to a focused international energy champion mirrors the general market development described above. On our way to attaining the vision of becoming the world's leading power and gas company, we have been through various phases in our corporate development.

13.4   E.ON's Development in the M&A Market

Our company's history has to be seen in the context of the development of our two German predecessor companies, VEBA and VIAG. Long before merging and becoming E.ON, both these companies were able to look back on a long tradition as utilities, but they also had significant positions in other industry sectors.

13.4.1   The Merger of VEBA and VIAG in Germany and the Transformation into a Focused Energy Company

E.ON was established in 2000, after the merger of VEBA AG – one of Germany's largest industrial groups at that time – with VIAG AG. Both our predecessor companies had a wealth of experience in the energy business. By establishing VEBA in 1929, the Prussian State consolidated its state-owned mining and energy interests. Following its transfer to the newly-founded Federal Republic of Germany after World War II, the company was successively privatized between 1965 and 1987. VIAG was also state owned for most of its history. Established in 1923, the company focused on electricity generation and the industrial use of energy. It was privatized in successive steps between 1986 and 1988.

After analyzing various cooperation plans with international utilities, VEBA and VIAG soon agreed that the best option in terms of synergies and their future business approach was provided in their common home market. They shared several similarities in terms of their structure and future core business. Both companies were conglomerates, had a solid capital base, and owned assets in the electricity, specialty chemicals and telecommunications sectors. VIAG first merged into VEBA, and the new entity was subsequently named E.ON to reflect the company's new approach after the merger. The boards of management of VEBA and VIAG had agreed to focus on energy and specialty chemicals as their core business. Other assets – held, for instance, in the fields of aluminum production, oil, real estate, logistics, electronics, or telecommunications – were to be divested after the merger. This divestment process can rightly be described as a success story, since the different assets were sold in deals that not only provided attractive returns for E.ON but also offered 'industrial logic' for the acquiring company.

In order to improve E.ON's capacity in the future core businesses, acquisitions played a major role in the process of transforming the newly merged conglomerate into a focused energy company. The 2002 acquisition of Powergen secured a foothold in the UK while making E.ON the largest investor-owned provider of power and gas worldwide. In addition, we strengthened our position in the Nordic countries and in Eastern Europe through further M&A activities. The next logical step was to optimize E.ON's position along the value chain of the gas business. We were convinced that an ideal target for acquisitive growth would be equipped with assets in the fields production, import, supply, trading, and sales. The German Ruhrgas AG fulfilled all of these requirements, and after a difficult negotiation process – mainly because of the complex shareholding structure of Ruhrgas AG – E.ON completed the acquisition of Ruhrgas in early 2003 and renamed the company to E.ON Ruhrgas in 2004. This enabled E.ON to achieve a more balanced portfolio comprising power and gas businesses.

These major acquisitions, which were designed to focus on energy as E.ON's core business, were followed by a period in our corporate development in which we concentrated on integrating the new assets and on consolidating our business.

13.4.2   Integration and Performance

In 2003, we reconfirmed that our growth would be focused on the integrated power and gas business. However, our previous acquisitive growth brought about challenges for the integration process and the future scope of our activities. Various interfaces between our market and business units had to be defined and differentiated from each other. Moreover, further inorganic growth had to be prioritized very clearly. To meet this challenge, we developed the on.top project in 2003, which placed strategic emphasis on our most powerful and promising market regions. Four integrated markets for the power and gas distribution and retail business were identified in Central Europe, the UK, the Nordic region, and the US-

Midwest. In addition, the supply, trading, and transportation of natural gas were combined in the pan-European gas market unit. In close cooperation with the corresponding market units, potential acquisitions were sorted according to strategic and financial categories. We decided to pursue inorganic growth projects only if they met strict strategic and economic criteria.

Further acquisitions that were in line with this prioritization included the UK power distribution company Midlands Electricity and assets of Sweden's fourth-largest utility, Graninge. Both of these acquisitions were motivated by synergies. The acquisition in the UK considerably improved E.ON's position along the value chain, making E.ON UK the second largest player in power production, distribution, and retail. In Sweden, E.ON Nordic had held a minority stake in Graninge, and significant synergies were achieved by acquiring the new assets which joined adjacent grid sectors. In addition, several regional utilities were acquired in Hungary, the Czech Republic, Romania, and Bulgaria so as to participate in the growth opportunities available in these new EU member states.

13.4.3 Growth in the Energy Business

Since 2005, we have enhanced our organic growth by investing mainly in new generation capacity. At the same time, we have continued to acquire small and medium-sized companies (including Caledonia Oil and Gas Ltd., licenses in the Skarv-Idun area, MOL Gas Trade and Storage). However, competition for such assets has increased because other large and medium-sized players are also focusing on M&A. Moreover, some markets have been practically closed or very expensive to enter owing to the limited number of potential targets. For this reason, we have also had to include larger options in Europe on our radar screen. All these activities have been implemented in accordance with our strict strategic investment criteria. In essence, this means that we only target acquisitions if both the target and the market are very attractive and if the material value creation potential is substantial.

Following our attempt to acquire Endesa in 2006 and 2007, we have secured an attractive asset package from Enel and Acciona, enabling us to enter, or to strengthen our position in, highly attractive markets such as Italy, Spain, and France. Once these transactions have been completed, no other energy company will match our broad European footprint. E.ON already has operations in nearly 30 countries, with leading positions in many key markets.

We successfully entered Russia's fast-growing electricity market by acquiring a majority stake in OGK-4, a major Russian power producer. OGK-4 operates four gas-fired power stations and one coal-fired station, with an aggregate capacity of about 8,600 MW. This is one of the most powerful and efficient asset portfolios in Russia. Over the next years, we intend to add 2,400 MW of technologically advanced generating capacity.

Another important aspect of our growth period is E.ON's increasing activity in the field of renewable energy sources. Expanding this business worldwide is one of our strategic priorities. At the beginning of 2008, our installed renewables capacity amounted to 1,400 MW worldwide, and we had about 3,000 MW of wind power under construction. We have achieved this position mainly through strategic acquisitions in Europe and the United States. By purchasing Energi E2 Renovables Ibéricas, our new Climate & Renewables Unit has added capacity in Spain and Portugal. The acquisition of Airtricity North America contributed to this development, and marks the first time that E.ON's renewables business has established a strong market position with substantial growth potential outside of Europe.

Based on our key beliefs in market success, we continue to pursue a clear strategic direction and business model, drawing on inorganic growth as an important instrument in our portfolio. E.ON focuses on leading market positions in the power and gas sectors with total value chain management and holds positions in infrastructure where they enhance market access and connectivity. Moreover, we have a clear geographic focus, have strengthened our leading positions in existing market units, and have entered new markets, particularly in Southeast Europe and Russia. Our investment rationale in new markets is defined by clear criteria: Emerging economies need to show strong economic growth, and the energy sector has to be a key industry. In addition, the energy industry needs to have substantial organic growth potential as a result of increasing demand. Finally, sharing experience and best practices with new markets and businesses is a key factor in value creation. E.ON has large store of experience in these processes, especially as a result of its acquisitions in Eastern Europe.

13.5   Success Factors and Organizational Line-up

13.5.1   Success Factors for Strategic Mergers

Even though it may sound trite, it is certainly worth mentioning that there are two key objectives for the successful integration of an acquired company: to minimize the disruption of your own daily business and to achieve synergies as soon as possible. For us, the most successful way was to comply with the success factors we have identified in our own M&A experience.

These success factors include strategic and financial investment criteria. While we have already elaborated on the strategic aspects, the financial criteria are equally important for a successful acquisition. The three most important financial criteria are: the target entity must enhance earnings within the first full year after the acquisition; returns must be in excess of the cost of capital within 3 years after the acquisition; and, finally, any acquisition must contribute to the overall Group's performance targets.

In addition, there are other factors that determine the successful outcome of an acquisition. Feeding back best practices and reverse synergies from an acquired company or asset is crucial to quick realization of the advantages of such an undertaking. Furthermore, speed makes all the difference. Quick and determined post-merger integration (PMI) is strategically and economically more successful than management of such a project in an average length of time. This also has a substantial impact on the work environment, particularly in the acquired company.

13.5.2 Conclusions for the Organizational Line-up

Establishing a unit within our company to focus specifically on the integration of acquired companies or assets has proved advantageous to our own activities. Similar in its set-up to other functional, cross-national units, the expertise condensed in this unit considerably facilitates the integration process. In addition to our M&A department, we have recently established an integration unit to plan and coordinate the main PMI activities across our Group. Its key responsibility is to coordinate and supervise integration projects Group-wide.

Our own experience has shown that it is crucial for the team that develops the concept for the integration process, decides on the staffing, and supervises the implementation to be made up of employees from all the company divisions concerned, to draw on external knowledge, and to include regional expertise. The acquired company has its own corporate culture, and the market one is entering as a foreign company also adheres to its own set of cultural rules. Taking all of these aspects into consideration is not just something that is 'nice to have' in an integration project; it is absolutely key to the successful incorporation of a new asset into a cross-national corporate culture.

13.6   Conclusion

The utilities industry has experienced major changes in the past decade. Our current market situation and current challenges were hard to anticipate in 1998 when the Kyoto Protocol had just been adopted and the EU Directive on a Single European Market for Gas had not yet been enacted. Like many of our competitors, E.ON has undergone radical changes. Two traditional industrial conglomerates were transformed into a focused international energy champion. Major entities have been integrated into our corporate culture while our strategy continues to develop and adapt to new challenges.

Many of our achievements have been largely determined by our M&A strategy. While most of our competitors have had to deal with acquisitive growth, E.ON has enjoyed an outstanding position owing to its own transformation, which required huge transactions across many geographic regions and industry sectors within the first few years after the merger of VEBA and VIAG in 2000. This gave us the tailwind to cope with future challenges in our industry. Our sound expertise has not only led to the most successful transactions, but also means that we are aware of the risks of bidding for companies in a difficult political environment. In this context, the experience we gained when bidding for Endesa has given us a critical insight into the political setting for cross-national M&A activities.

The future development of the utilities industry will not only be influenced by M&A activities; the success of its major players will largely depend on a sound portfolio development strategy. In a complex environment for worldwide investments, we believe that we are well prepared to achieve further progress on the way towards implementing our vision.

References

Bausch, A. & Fritz, T. 2005. Financial performance of mergers and acquisitions – a meta-analysis. Paper presented at the Academy of Management Annual Meeting, Honolulu.

E.ON. 2008. Strategy and key figures 2008. Düsseldorf: E.ON.

Gaul, H.-M. 2006. M&A-Aktivitäten zur Umsetzung der Unternehmensstrategie am Beispiel der E.ON AG. In B. W. Wirtz (Ed.), Handbuch Mergers & Acquisitions Management: 1303-1332. Wiesbaden: Gabler.

KPMG. 2003. M&A-Transaktionen steigern zunehmend den Shareholder Value. Hong Kong: KPMG.

KPMG. 2004. First hard evidence of recovery in global M&A: completed deal analysis shows growth worldwide. Hong Kong: KPMG.

KPMG. 2005. Erfolgreich größer werden, M&A im deutschen Mittelstand. KPMG EditValue, 1: 27-28.

Pautler, P. A. 2003. The effects of mergers and post-merger integration: a review of business consulting literature. Washington: Federal Trade Commission.

PricewaterhouseCoopers. 2006. Power Deals 2005: Fusionen und Akquisitionen im internationalen Strom- und Gasmarkt. Frankfurt am Main: PricewaterhouseCoopers.

PricewaterhouseCoopers. 2000. Speed makes the difference: a survey of mergers and acquisitions. Frankfurt am Main: PricewaterhouseCoopers.

Schenck, M., Finck, G. C. & Osterried, M. 2008. Übernahmen in Europa – Chancen und Hemmnisse dargestellt am Beispiel der Energiewirtschaft. In M. D. Kley, F.-J. Leven, B. Rudolph & U. H. Schneider (Eds.), Aktie und Kapitalmarkt: Anlegerschutz, Unternehmensfinanzierung und Finanzplatz; Festschrift für Professor Dr. Rüdiger von Rosen zum 65. Geburtstag: 327-342. Stuttgart: Schäffer-Poeschel.

Schiereck, D. & Thomas, T. W. 2006. Mergers & Acquisitions in der europäischen Energieversorgung: Eine empirische Analyse der Übernahmewelle der 1990er Jahre. In B. W. Wirtz (Ed.), Handbuch Mergers & Acquisitions Management: 1333-1355. Wiesbaden: Gabler.

Stahlke, N. A. 2006. Erfolg von Kooperationen und Fusionen in der deutschen Energiewirtschaft. Energiewirtschaftliche Tagesfragen, 56: 28-32.

14 What Next for European Power Utilities?

Gonzalo Garcia[1]

Wolfgang Fink[2]

Abstract

The European electricity sector has experienced significant consolidation over the last 10 years, but the era of mega-mergers is coming to an end. This chapter explores the main industry drivers behind the next wave of acquisitions, the implications for the super-utilities and the opportunities and challenges created. Unlike the consolidations of the past decade, the transactions over the next 10 years are likely to be shaped by rising oil prices, increasing environmental awareness, an increasing focus on unbundling of tariffs and ultimately assets, the emergence of financial asset owners and increasing nationalisation. The chapter explores how each of these factors poses challenges but also creates opportunities that will shape the strategies of all super-utilities in Europe.

Keywords: mergers & acquisitions, consolidation, European power market

---

[1] Gonzalo Garcia is Managing Director European Utilities and Infrastructure of Goldman Sachs, United Kingdom.

[2] Dr. Wolfgang Fink is Managing Director German Advisory of Goldman Sachs, Germany.

A. Bausch and B. Schwenker (eds.), *Handbook Utility Management,*
DOI: 10.1007/978-3-540-79349-6_14, © Springer-Verlag Berlin Heidelberg 2009

14.1   Introduction

Over the last 10 years, we have seen significant consolidation in the European power sector fuelled by the promise of a pan-European power market, borderless trading of energy and sector deregulation. Through a series of mergers and asset acquisitions, the top ten European power utilities ranked by market capitalisation now account for € 523 billion of the market capitalisation of the publicly traded universe of EU-27 utilities. Ten years ago, the combined market capitalisation of the top 10 European power utilities was a mere € 160 billion (see Figure 14.1). By comparison, the top ten US publicly traded companies (see Figure 14.2) only account for $ 271 billion (€ 201 billion) of the sector capitalisation for a market that is only marginally bigger (2006 US total power production was 3,900 TWh, as against EU-27 production of 3,710 TWh).

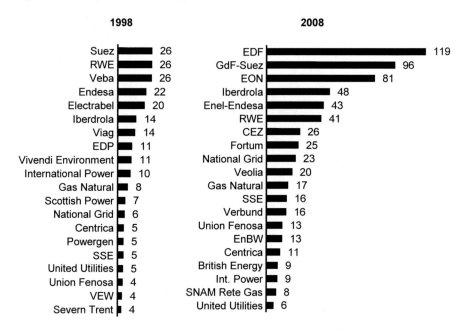

Figure 14.1: European utility landscape: 10 years ago and today (ranking by market capitalisation [€ bn]) (Bloomberg, Datastream, Factiva, copied at 31 May 2008)

Now roll the clock forward 10 years. While the same rationale as supported the rapid consolidation over the last decade is still there, it is difficult to foresee the same pace of privatisations, mergers and acquisitions and 'mega-mergers' among European utilities moving forward as we have seen over the last 10 years. A closer look at Figure 42.1 reveals a set of European super-utilities (roughly the top five or six by most metrics) that in our view is close to becoming a stable grouping; a shrinking group of mid-size utilities; and, off our chart, a very large group of small utilities (in Germany alone there are over 700 small municipal utilities). Furthermore, while most of the medium-size and smaller utilities remain strategically attractive acquisition candidates for the super-utilities, so far they have remained off-limits for reasons to do with regional politics and competition.

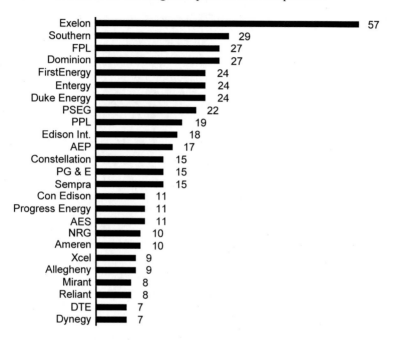

Figure 14.2: US utility landscape (2008 ranking by market capitalisation [\$ bn]) (Datastream, copied at 28 May 2008)

We believe that the era of the 'industry-shaping' mega-mergers in the European power utility industry is coming to an end; smaller 'bolt-on' acquisitions are becoming incrementally more difficult and expensive; and at the same time super-utilities are facing increasing investor scrutiny looking for sustainable growth and value creation. Against this background, the next 5 years pose an interesting strategic challenge for the sector, and in particular for the super-utilities of Europe. In this chapter, we explore what we see as the main industry drivers in the medium term, the implications for the super-utilities and the opportunities and challenges created. We believe that while mergers and acquisitions will continue to be an important component of the strategy of the super-utilities moving forward, the nature and size of value-creating transactions will be very different and the shape of the super-utilities 10 years hence may be very different as a result.

14.2   European Power Sector Key Drivers

In an attempt to frame our thinking, we have selected a limited number of drivers that we believe have a decisive influence on the way the sector evolves. The task is not made easy by the fact that each region of Europe is slightly different and there is no such thing as a 'standard' European power company. Even if we focus our attention on the super-utilities, the world looks very different for a brown coal generator in Central Europe than for a pan-European nuclear generator. It is also difficult to completely isolate each driver or distinguish cause and effect, and clearly most of the drivers we have picked out are interconnected. Nevertheless, we hope that to varying degrees most senior executives of the European super-utilities would agree in that in the medium term the sector will be shaped by an era of expensive oil, increasing environmental awareness, increasing focus on unbundling of tariffs and ultimately assets, the emergence of financial asset owners and increasing nationalisation. Let us look into each of these in more detail and consider the headline implications for super-utilities.

14.2.1   Expensive Oil

Let us leave the task of trying to predict the future to people more qualified than we are; the evolution of crude prices over the last 10 years is staggering: Brent has gone from under $ 20 to over $ 100 in less than a decade (see Figure 14.3)! Even in real terms, today's oil price levels are comparable in magnitude to those that provoked the Oil Shock of the 1970s. In a nutshell, we believe few people would disagree when we say we are in the middle of one of the biggest oil shocks in history.

Whilst oil and oil products are less relevant as a primary source of fuel for power generation in today's Europe, natural gas continues to be the price-setting fuel in almost every European market. With few exceptions, gas contracts in continental Europe, especially long-term ones, are directly or indirectly indexed to oil prices. Expensive oil therefore means expensive natural gas, and expensive natural gas means expensive power in Europe (see Figure 14.4).

In the short term, expensive power is good news for the majority of European super-utilities with large portfolios of coal, lignite and nuclear stations, especially as most of them have retained the ability to effectively pass on the cost of expensive power to their consumers. Expensive power also goes a long way towards explaining the surge in generation capital programmes across Europe aimed at renewing ageing plant that is bound to face environmental constraints in the near future.

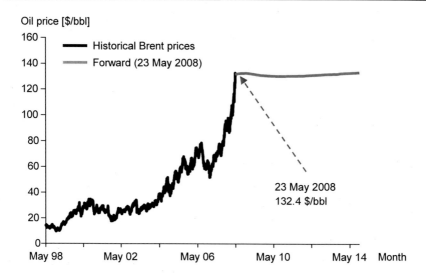

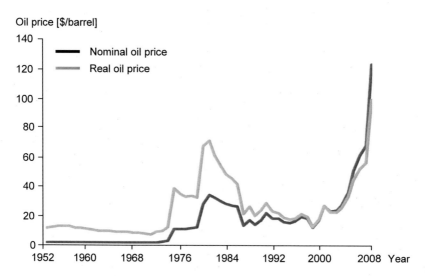

Figure 14.3: Oil prices (Datastream, copied at 28 May 2008)

In the long-run, however, it is not clear whether sustained high gas prices will be good news for all. A sustained high energy price environment will put pressure on margins, and the gradual move away from expensive oil may reshape the supply curve, especially as nuclear and wind power become more relevant in Europe. In our view, among other factors, long-term profitability for generators will be driven by the degree of upstream gas integration, embracing of nuclear power and embracing of trading expertise as an integral part of the generation and supply business.

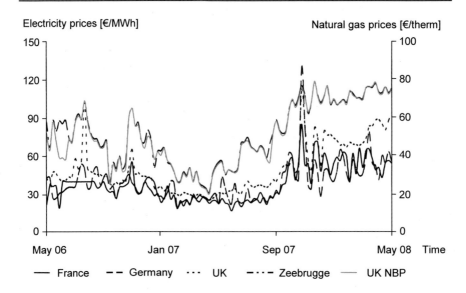

Figure 14.4: Gas and electricity prices (Bloomberg, copied at 30 May 2008)

14.2.2 Increasing Environmental Awareness

Europe is showing the world the way, and in our view will continue to do so, on increasing environmental awareness. Among other things we believe this translates into continuing strong commitment to the Kyoto Protocol, and as a result the power industry is bound to bear a high share of the cost of reducing CO_2 emissions. In the short term or until nuclear and/or other nonfossil fuel generation become a meaningful component of the overall generation mix, the cost of CO_2 has added and will continue to add to the cost of power (see Figure 14.5).

'CO_2 intensity' has become the buzz-word among industry analysts and executives. While it is difficult to see a clear direct correlation between CO_2 intensity and valuations so far, we believe that over time the CO_2 intensity or the 'greenest' of the generation portfolios of the super-utilities will become one of a handful of key value drivers. In the immediate future, we are beginning to see every single super-utility outlining its 'renewable strategy' and quickly catching-up with the industry leaders through major acquisitions in the space. CO_2 is in fact shaping the generation mix in Europe faster and more effectively than any other past policy.

As a side-effect, CO_2 is also accelerating the integration of so far relatively disconnected European power markets, as it is the only commodity that is genuinely traded and priced on a pan-European basis. We would argue that the more marked the impact of CO_2 on power prices, the faster European power markets will integrate through physical interconnections and/or pan-European trading platforms.

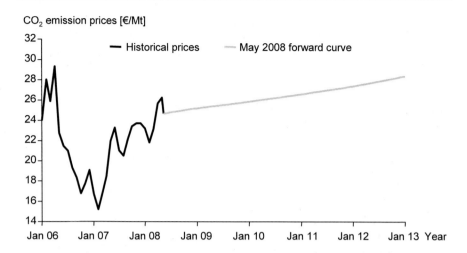

CO$_2$ emission prices [€/Mt]

— Historical prices — May 2008 forward curve

Jan 06   Jan 07   Jan 08   Jan 09   Jan 10   Jan 11   Jan 12   Jan 13 Year

Figure 14.5: CO$_2$ price development (Phase II) (JAron, copied at 28 May 2008)

14.2.3   Unbundling

A hugely controversial theme for many years, it seems that unbundling is finally leaving the list of nasty words for the industry as more and more companies seem to accept that generation and supply and networks are fundamentally different businesses that have been bundled together for convenience and historical reasons.

We believe there is a very strong rationale for keeping supply, generation, trading and possibly upstream as part of an integrated business. At its most basic, this business is about converting primary sources of energy (fossil fuel molecules, uranium, waterfalls, wind, solar light) into electric power conveniently delivered to people's homes at the lowest possible cost. It follows from this definition that there should be a strong rationale for upstream integration, portfolio diversification, trading and branding.

On the other hand, networks (pipes and/or wires) are a natural (and in most jurisdictions a legal) monopoly. As such, they need to be and are firmly regulated. In order to optimise the use of resources, there should be no discrimination among users of the networks, and by the same token ownership should not confer any strategic advantage vis-à-vis other users.

It follows from the above, at least in our view, that there are no obvious operational or commercial arguments for the users and the owners of networks to be one and the same and that there is indeed a strong logic to keeping them separate. This is particularly true in regulatory regimes, where tariffs and access to networks are strongly regulated. Although in theory ownership unbundling is not the only way to ensure optimal use of resources and separation in the way described above, it remains the easiest way of doing so.

Historically, there has been one very powerful argument for keeping bundled ownership, and that has to do with financial muscle and capacity to develop the networks, as huge sums of money and very long investment recovery periods are involved and traditionally only the utilities have been willing and able to make such commitments. The emergence of so-called infrastructure financial investors is changing all that.

14.2.4   Financial Players

With a few exceptions, traditional private equity houses have remained absent from the sector. While each situation is different and based on our individual experiences, we believe this to be driven by relatively low returns compared with stated return objectives of private equity funds, the limited (and relatively short) life of such funds and the need for an exit strategy and the long-term nature of significant capital commitments (e.g. 30 years plus for networks and 50 years plus for hydro plants). However, private equity houses are becoming increasingly comfortable with the commodity price risk.

Now, enter infrastructure financial players on the scene. By these we mean insurance companies, pension funds, sovereign wealth funds and aggregators/managers in the form of infrastructure funds. While it is difficult to generalise, they all have relatively long investment horizons (10 years plus), aim at relatively lower returns on equity (10-14% equity internal rate of returns), favour regulated and monopolist assets with stable returns and look favourably on large capital commitments once invested in a particular asset. In many ways they are the ideal owners of regulated networks.

From a structuring perspective, regulated networks are often suited to relatively high levels of debt/asset value ratios owing to the stable and regulated nature of income streams. More and more regulators across Europe are beginning to incorporate increasingly aggressive views on leverage in their tariff determinations so as to capture additional value, which in turns gets passed on to consumers through lower tariffs. Infrastructure financial players often structure their investments as stand-alone entities and look at leverage on the same basis. As a result, most assets owned by infrastructure financial investors tend to mirror or marginally exceed the leverage assumptions used by regulators. Utilities, on the other hand, are normally restricted in their ability to match the assumptions used by regulators, as they are constrained by corporate rating targets, structural subordination and overall more conservative capital structures, to allow them to cope with the higher risk profile of the supply-generation-trading part of their businesses. As a result, utilities normally struggle to get the full benefit of the tax and cost advantages of higher levels of debt for regulated assets, which makes it harder for them to match even 'allowed' returns. While to date most utilities have managed to compensate this impact through operational excellence and synergies as the networks become a more mature business and regulators, more aggressive, it is becoming increasingly challenging for them to compete on this basis.

Finally, there seem to be some interesting conclusions to be drawn from the analysis of the very few publicly listed network-focused utilities and their return on capital employed (ROCE) compared with that of the integrated utilities. The analysis seems to confirm the connection between risk and returns for the two groups. It also highlights the pressure to lower the cost of funding by optimising capital structure for the network-based utilities; thus, the heavy reliance on debt seems to be an inevitable consequence of this bifurcation of what we see as two distinct businesses.

Finally, it is interesting to note that the market seems to acknowledge the implicit lower risk of the regulated network companies compared with the broader universe. Figure 14.6 shows the ROCE of the very few publicly listed network-focused utilities compared with that of the integrated utilities. The ROCE for the former is clearly lower and within a tighter range than that for the latter, which also seems to confirm the connection between risk and returns for the two groups and highlights the pressure to lower the cost of funding by optimising capital structure for the network-based utilities, so that, again, the heavy reliance on debt seems to be an inevitable conclusion of this bifurcation of what we see as two distinct businesses.

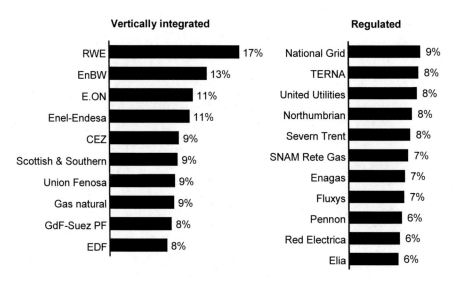

Figure 14.6: ROCE for vertically integrated and network utilities (Datastream, company financials)

14.2.5   Nationalism

Last but not least, for anyone following recent transactions in the sector or, perhaps more tellingly, attempted transactions in the sector, it is clear that politicians and governments (both local and national) are showing increasing willingness to openly flex their muscles and intervene to make their views known on what is acceptable and what is not around corporate transactions. This is particularly true in situations where governments retain ownership of utilities. In an increasingly polarised market with a handful of super-utilities with giant balance sheets and financial capacity and literally hundreds of small and medium-size utilities, transactions by the former for the latter are increasingly scarce and unwelcome.

14.3   Value Creation Transactions

To a greater or lesser degree, the above trends are shaping the strategies of all the super-utilities in Europe, and this is becoming increasingly transparent through their communication with the market on strategy, capital structure and announced transactions. Recent transactions also tend to support a common approach to these challenges. We have listed below the key components of what we see as an increasingly common approach among the super-utilities:

- Regional and ideally pan-European approach to generation, supply and trading with the aim of having a physical asset footprint, especially generation assets.
- Upstream integration through physical asset positions and/or long-term contracts.
- Decreasing CO_2 exposure through expansion of renewable portfolio and investment in new technologies. In the longer term we believe this will lead to the rapid expansion of Europe's nuclear generation asset base.
- Functional and legal separation of networks in accordance with EU directives. In the longer term we believe this will lead to the separation of the networks business from the upstream-generation-supply-trading business and a focus on the latter by the super-utilities, with networks slowly migrating towards private ownership by financial infrastructure investors.
- Move away over time from regional/geographical business units towards an organisational structure arranged along functions.
- Conservative capital structures with debt levels adequate to support strong ratings (A family).

One of the consequences of the increasingly common approach outlined above is that it is becoming progressively more difficult for super-utilities to engage in transactions with each other as their businesses develop into the same direction, to the point where the synergy benefits begin to be outweighed by the remedies to transactions imposed by competition authorities.

Against this background and as super-utilities adjust to the current challenges, we would expect to see more and more transactions in one or more of the following categories:

- Asset swaps;
- Sale of network assets to infrastructure financial players;
- Purchase and aggregation of renewable assets in hands of small developers and financial players;
- Investment in CO2-free technologies through investment in new start-ups or outright purchases;

- Strategic partnerships with smaller regional players;
- Selective expansion into new markets driven by growth prospects and potential gains from introducing operational improvements. Top of the list at the moment are Russia and Turkey.

We would also expect to see a period of high capital expenditure for the industry and heavy investment in the development of sophisticated trading and risk-management platforms and customer services systems.

Smaller utilities should be driven by the same considerations outlined above, and even though they may be constrained by size and the nationalistic sentiments of their owners, we believe they will seek to achieve similar aims through strategic partnerships and affiliations with the super-utilities that may stop short of full mergers.

Nonutility asset owners have quickly understood that the lack of growth opportunities in the utilities sector and similar strategies amongst super utilities together with growth ambitions of smaller utility players implies that intense competition for assets available for cash is almost guaranteed.

14.4   How the Sector Might Look in 10 Years' Time

Let us now turn the clock on 10 years; we believe the European power sector will be fully integrated by that time, with electricity and gas flowing freely across borders and price inefficiencies quickly eliminated through sophisticated pan-European trading systems. We believe Europe will maintain its commitment to CO_2 reduction and a bigger share of our electricity will come from renewable sources, but we also expect to see a bigger share of nuclear as base load and the emergence of clean coal technologies to replace existing coal and lignite fleets. Unless efficient electricity storage techniques can be developed, gas will continue to have an important role as back-up for interruptible sources and the marginal fuel in the system.

We would also expect to see an increasing role for financial infrastructure players and a growing proportion of network asset owned by them. This is likely to contribute to the expansion of cross-border capacity and facilitate the free flow of commodities across borders.

It is also likely, in our view, that the super-utilities group will not look so different but that all super-utilities will almost certainly be bigger as the result of a series of small/mid-size transactions and partnerships, and will have true pan-European footprints. While it is possible that smaller utilities will combine their businesses, we believe it is more likely that the sector will continue to have a large number of very small local players and a medium-size sector that will seek 'alignment' with the super-utilities or with each other through strategic partnerships.

15 Unbundling – Strategic and Organisational Challenges for Power and Supply Companies

Luis Atienza Serna[1]

Abstract

One of the most important consequences of liberalising the electricity sector has been the vertical unbundling of activities. The creation of companies specialising in transmission and system operation activities has become crucial in liberalised markets. The transmission system operation (TSO) model, in which the same company carries out both transmission and system operation activities, is the one more generally used in Europe. Compared with the independent system operation (ISO) model, where system operation and transmission are developed by different companies, this model presents many advantages in terms of efficiency and security of supply based on the synergies coming from the integration of functions within the same company. The independence of TSOs is essential to preserve efficient functioning of the electricity market. Ownership unbundling of TSOs is the most effective way to achieve such independence.

Keywords: unbundling, transmission, system operation

---

[1] Luis Atienza Serna is Executive President and Chief Executive Officer of Red Eléctrica de España, Spain.

A. Bausch and B. Schwenker (eds.), *Handbook Utility Management,*
DOI: 10.1007/978-3-540-79349-6_15, © Springer-Verlag Berlin Heidelberg 2009

15.1   Introduction

The supply of electrical energy exhibits a series of highly unique characteristics distinguishing it from other goods or services. Traditionally, these economic[2], social[3] and technical[4] characteristics favoured the perception that the economic synergies and the coordination advantages offered by the vertical and horizontal integration of the different activities surpassed any other organisational model, which led to the generalised adoption of a sectorial model of a public and monopolistic nature.

However, in the late 1980s and early 1990s, the earlier model was showing signs of obsolescence. Advanced techniques and experiences in other economic sectors precipitated liberalisation of the sector, which necessarily led to a rethink of the industrial organisational model, including:

- Vertical disintegration of the different activities involved in the supply chain;
- Horizontal disintegration, with the appearance of different companies (instead of just one company, as had been the case until then) in those activities where competition was possible, basically generation and end-user supply;
- Introduction of market mechanisms for the exchange of energy;
- Disinvestment and privatisation processes;
- With regard to the first of the points mentioned above, it is obvious that electricity supply, far from being a homogeneous activity, is the result of the coordinated integration of a group of activities, each with its own characteristics and peculiarities.

Hence, on the electricity supply chain there are various activities where competition is possible (generation and trading) and others which, owing to their naturally monopolistic characteristics, must be subject to nonmarket regulation. This includes operation of the system, and also transmission and distribution.

15.2   Transmission and Operation of the System in a Liberalised Environment

In a competitive environment, competitive activities (mainly electricity generation and wholesale trading) exist side by side with natural monopoly (mainly on transmission and distribution). It is extremely important to avoid any possible contami-

---

[2] Heavy investment, use of scarce resources, naturally monopolistic grid infrastructures, the importance of a safe and continuous electricity supply as input for other industrial processes.

[3] Essential service for quality of life and for the economic development of countries.

[4] Need to maintain an instantaneous and permanent balance between supply and demand; the impossibility of storing electricity; the need to control a series of technical parameters in real time and the fact that electricity is subject to the laws of physics and not of economics.

nation between the two (competitive activities and natural monopoly) in order to prevent the use of anti-competitive behaviours or strategies by competitors, which might exploit the natural monopoly (mainly grid access and grid availability) to their own benefit.

In the case of system operation, market power can be exercised in a number of ways given the central character of the activity and the information that is used in the course of business, while in the case of transmission, it could be manifested in the imposition of discriminatory conditions that restrict access to the grids by competitors, or in the form of cross-subsidies between activities, or in many other ways.

Consequently, if vertical integration is to be maintained in a liberalised environment, it will be necessary to establish complex regulatory measures that ensure the separation between businesses, forming veritable 'Chinese walls' between activities, and these measures must be easy for regulators to assess. This is something that is not easily achieved, partly because of the asymmetrical information between regulators and those being regulated.

One of the most important consequences of the process of liberalising the electricity sector, insofar as industrial organisation is concerned, has been the vertical disintegration of activities, and more specifically the creation of companies specialising in the different segments of the supply chain as an alternative to the development of complex regulations and surveillance.

The independence of transmission as against other activities is even more critical, to the extent that it has a central role and the agents who own the transmission system can therefore exercise market power or have a greater influence on its management or development.

It was precisely this need for greater independence of the transmission grids with respect to the competing businesses that gave rise to the appearance of companies specialising in electricity transmission, which started in the early 1990s; up to then this activity had lacked any clear industrial content since it was subordinate to other activities, such as generation or distribution.

This need for a company specialising in electricity transmission at the national level could be justified on the basis of the following points:

(a) *Uniqueness of the grid:* The transactions agreed between the market agents must ultimately be supported by the transmission grid, so that an inadequate, poorly developed, poorly maintained or poorly operated grid will result in excessive cost or limit the possible transactions, and may ultimately allow some agents to exercise control over the market.

(b) *Specialisation:* If the transmission activity is carried out in a vertically integrated company, it is highly likely that it will be marginal in nature from the point of view of the company's business and could be made subordinate to the rest of the company's activities or interests. In this case, we would be faced with the problem not only of cross-subsidies, but also of progressive degradation of the transmission grid.

(c) *Independence:* The possible use of the grid as a barrier to keep out new competitors or, in other words, the necessary nondiscriminatory treatment as far as access to the grid is concerned, and the need for the transmission not be treated as a marginal activity by the company responsible for it, but rather as an essential component of the electrical system overall, make it more than advisable for the transmission company to be independent of all the other agents operating in the sector, if not in terms of stock ownership, which would be ideal, then at least in terms of management.

(d) *Investment development:* The transmission business in a vertically integrated company can cause conflicts of interest with regard to investment in new transmission facilities. The interests of generation can run contrary to greater investments in transmission that could facilitate access by new generators competing with the integrated company.

In view of the above, the existence of a simple independent transmission company at national level that would be responsible for developing the grid on the basis of global criteria, while not guaranteeing the success of the liberalisation process, can contribute to it and can be an essential element in the achievement of efficient market functioning. It is a necessary, but not a sufficient condition.

There may be different opinions on the need to separate transmission completely from the rest of the vertically integrated company's business. However, in the case of system operations, owing to the importance of decisions for agents in the development of this activity, and particularly on generators, there should be no doubt whatsoever about the need for this activity to be completely independent of the liberalised activities, especially generation.

On the other hand, the fundamental functions of coordinating generation and transmission activities and maintaining an instantaneous balance between production and demand under safe conditions can only be effectively performed when to the extent that this function is performed in an exclusive and centralised manner in a particular geographical area, typically at country level.

Moreover, the necessary coordination between system operation and transmission, particularly in the case of highly meshed and extremely complex grids, means that there are significant advantages of performing the two functions jointly, as will be seen below.

15.3   Vertical Unbundling Alternatives – Independent System Operator and Transmission System Operator Models

As mentioned above, while efficient operation of an electricity system based on optimising costs certainly requires a properly sized, centrally operated transmission grid based on common criteria, operation of an electricity system under free market conditions requires, in addition, an organisation for these activities which guarantees:

- Free access to grids by all agents;
- Existence of regulated access tariffs to the transmission grid;

- Independence of the owner of the grids and the operator of the system with respect to the other competitive activities associated with electricity supply.

Hence, two different organisational models, both of which are recognised internationally, have been devised to make this possible.

15.3.1 Transmission System Operator

With the transmission system operator (TSO) model, there is a single publicly or privately owned company that handles both transmission and operation of the system.

In this case, the company responsible for both activities must be independent of the agents who perform other activities that are associated with electricity supply and which are incompatible with them. As far as ownership of the grid is concerned, while it would be most logical and desirable for the one company to own the entire transmission grid, there are cases where part of it may be in the hands of other companies, which normally also have interests in other activities.

This is the model generally used in liberalised systems that were formally national monopolies. It is also a system that is commonly used in highly meshed electrical systems such as the European systems.

15.3.2 Independent System Operator

With the independent system operator (ISO) model, system operation and transmission are two separate activities.

This model is organised so that there is one company responsible for operating the system and various transmission companies that own the assets.

The company responsible for operating the system is usually a public company or nonprofit agency, since this activity does not require large investments and is therefore unattractive from a business point of view, and very close to the regulator.

As far as the transmission facilities are concerned, they are normally split between several different owners who are usually specialised in transmission, thus enabling competition to exist in this area.

This model is common in countries with the following characteristics:

- Various independent transmission companies of a similar size or vertical companies that own transmission assets, with limited coordination between them;
- Immature and hence not highly meshed grids which are simple to operate;
- Need for foreign financing to develop the grids.

By way of summary, the principal functions of each activity and the party responsible for performing them are enumerated in Table 15.1.

Table 15.1: Principal functions of each activity and the party responsible for performing each (*x* primary role in performance of the function, *(x)* secondary role in performance of the function)

Function	Responsibility		
	TSO model	ISO model	
		Transmission Co.	ISO
Operates the electricity system in compliance with safety standards	x	(x)	x
Owns all of the transmission grid assets or a large part of them	x	x	
Plans and manages maintenance	x	x	(x)
Plans the transmission grid development	x	(x)	x
Develops the transmission grid	x	x	

15.3.3 Advantages of the Transmission System Operator Model

15.3.3.1 Economic Advantages

(a) *Economies of scale, scope, experience and other synergies:* Economies of scale and synergies are generated when transmission and operation are handled by the same organisation, primarily because of better management of the following aspects:

  - *Investment and expense:* There is a reduction in the number of control centres required and also in the amount of remote control communication, analytical software and other necessities.
  - *Financial management and cash requirements:* Both are optimised.
  - *Operation and maintenance of the transmission grid:* Some examples of optimisation in this area include the integration of processes, possible personnel synergies, reduction in the cost of information flows and faster maintenance processes.
  - *Coordination costs:* The extra-business costs (taxes, labour and finance), transaction costs (information, negotiation, guarantee), intra-business costs (management) and, generally speaking, all other items that can be influenced by centralised management are lower.

(b) *Optimization of the operating cost:* One of the immediate consequences of more efficient operation is lower electricity costs. The integration of functions makes it possible to optimise the investment and operating cost binomial, so that transmission activity is carried out in the most efficient way at all times. Optimising operating costs and investments leads to the development of new technologies and the most efficient expansion of the transmission system.

15.3.3.2 Advantages in Terms of System Security

One of the principal advantages of integrating transmission and operations into a single company is improved system security. This improvement is a consequence of:

(a) *Better knowledge of the transmission activity on the part of the system operator:* If the two activities are combined, the system operator has a thorough knowledge of the transmission system; if the two activities are separate, the system operator will have to hire personnel experienced in transmission, and even then there will always be an asymmetry of information in the transmission company's favour.

(b) *Better communications between the transmission company and the system operator:* Integrating the two activities means that more and better information is available and that the information can be accessed faster. This fast and reliable access to information is essential if system security is to be guaranteed during disturbances, when there is an immediate need for action by the system operator. Some of the advantages of this enhanced coordination include:

- Efficient management of discharges;
- Reduction of the propagation of disturbances and improved restoration processes;
- Greater management capacity in unexpected situations, in real time;
- Functional and business authority of the system operator over the transmission company (customer–supplier relationship).

(c) *Better long-term planning of transmission:* The transmission grid must be developed in such a way that it guarantees the adequacy and security of the overall system. Where there is no single company performing this function these aspects may be seriously jeopardised, since the investment in transmission facilities by other agents can respond more to the strategic needs of other business activities in which those companies are involved than to the goal of guaranteeing the suitability and security of the transmission system. For example, a less robust transmission grid might be developed with the aim of minimising the investment in distribution.

(d) *More efficient risk management:* The potential risks that can affect the system in the short, medium and long term and are inherent in such diverse factors as planning, maintenance, discharges and operations are more effectively and efficiently managed when the same company is responsible for transmission and operation. Risk management is improved because the efficiency of other processes, such as the exchange of information, coordination, operation and planning, is maximised.

15.3.3.3 Guaranteed Grid Development (Last-resort Transmission Company)

Only a company that is dedicated exclusively to transmission and also has the responsibility for operating the system assigned to it can make certain investments, which may be conflictive but are at once necessary to ensure safety or to provide access to the generators that compete with the disadvantages of the system; these are investments that no other company would be interested in making.

15.3.3.4 Transmission Independence of Agents

In a liberalised electricity system, it is essential to guarantee third-party access to transmission grids in order to ensure free competition and good market operations. Failure to combine the transmission and operation functions into a single company could mean the companies that own transmission assets in a vertically integrated structure could use this as a competitive advantage against those that do not own transmission assets or as a barrier to prevent other agents who wish to become active in the market (generation and commercialisation) from entering it. The regulation of access rights can very easily be dodged in a very passive environment that does not favour new transmission lines.

15.3.3.5 Avoidance of Conflicts Between Transmission Companies and System Operators

There are benefits to integrating the transmission and operation functions that disappear when the two functions are separated. On the one hand, there is a reduction of the potential claims and litigation that can arise between system operator and transmission companies as a result of operating decisions, and thus the economic costs that would be associated with these are also reduced. On the other hand, the TSO concept provides an appropriate forum allowing the resolution of regulatory disputes between the different agents involved in the market in an impartial and transparent manner.

15.3.4   Disadvantages of the Transmission System Operator Model

15.3.4.1 Discrimination When There Are Various Transmission Companies

There can be disadvantages to the involvement of various transmission companies, since there is a possibility of discrimination with regard to the transmission activities of other companies not associated with the operation of the system.

However, the economic effects of such potential discrimination are negligible, and a posteriori control by regulators is somewhat complex.

15.3.4.2 Risk of Overinvestment (Averch-Johnson effect)

The TSO, which is also responsible for planning the development of the grid, may tend to overinvest to maximise profits on the transmission business. This overinvestment in remunerative models based on return rates is also known as the Averch-Johnson effect. However, this risk can be mitigated as long as the regulator retains control over the last step in the planning process.[5]

15.3.5 Advantages of the Independent System Operator Model

While the TSO model has numerous advantages over the ISO model, in some cases regulators have no choice but to opt for the latter. These situations are described below.

15.3.5.1 Existence of Vertically Integrated Companies

When there are various vertically integrated companies in a country, normally private, and the country wishes to introduce competition, it can be difficult to oblige companies to sell their grids, as Spain did in 1985. In these cases, one solution is to allow the grids to remain in the hands of the vertically integrated companies and permit a certain amount of coordination of the overall electricity system through an ISO. The principal advantage of this is the fairness that the ISO concept may afford. However, in order for this to work it helps if the transmission companies are similar in size and independent of other phases in the value chain.

15.3.5.2 Privatisation Process and Grid Development

In some cases, the decision to maintain various transmission companies along with ISO, as in some liberalisation processes in South America, has been influenced by decisions of a strategic nature favoured by the limited development of the transmission grid (linear/radial), which is easier to operate than the meshed grids characteristic of mature sectors. This situation is analysed in more detail below.

15.3.6 Disadvantages of the Independent System Operator Model

The principal disadvantages of the ISO model encountered when various transmission companies are involved are as follows:

- *Higher system costs:* The separation of the two activities requires that a new company be created and therefore involves higher system costs. One of the consequences of this situation is also the duplication of facilities.

---

[5] Certain investments must be made in growing systems, which may at first seem unnecessary but are needed in the future to accommodate the growth of demand that occurs in these systems.

- *Operating criteria that focus exclusively on security:* A system operator that reports only to regulators may choose more stringent operating criteria that limit its own liability, to the exclusion of efficiency criteria that would result in lower overall system costs while guaranteeing the same level of security. Also, one possible result of ignorance of the grid associated with the nonownership of assets is that the system operator feels insecure about the decisions taken and those decisions therefore lead to the system's being less secure (i.e. the exact opposite of what bolstering the security requirements was intended to bring about).

- *Possibility of becoming an inefficient, bureaucratic body:* The fact that the system operator depends directly on the administration, which means that guaranteeing the safety of the system may become its sole objective, leads to a situation in which the drafting of procedures is an end in itself. This in turn reduces the operator's function to that of an inefficient, bureaucratic entity.

- *Inefficient information flows:* There is no doubt that the flow of information between two different organisations is less efficient than when the information resides in the same organisation. This is critical, particularly in emergency situations involving the system, when information must be obtained in real time.

- *Limited decision-making capabilities regarding third-party transmission assets:* Experience has shown that this occurs in cases where the system operator is not the owner of the transmission assets, as in the United States, where the ISOs do not have decision-making powers over certain key operating aspects.

- *Limited knowledge of the transmission grid:* The ownership, operation and maintenance of the transmission grid provide greater knowledge of the grid, which in turn facilitates system operations and contributes towards increasing the security of supply. This level of knowledge does not exist when these functions are not performed by the system operator.

- *Less coordination and asymmetrical information relating to the transmission companies:* The existence of various transmission companies and a different company to operate the system means that coordination between agents and between the agents and operators of the system is less efficient than when there is just one TSO. Similarly, the level of information coming from the different agents may not be the same (in quantity and/or quality) in all cases.

- *Insufficient entity and weight to avoid being 'captured' by the agents:* In order for the electricity system to operate correctly in a competitive environment there must be a neutral manager, who must, however, have enough negotiating power not to be 'captive' of the large agents.

- *Publicity given to conflicts with transmission companies:* Conflicts with transmission companies can multiply and take on greater significance than if they had been internal conflicts within a single organisation. The fact that these conflicts get more publicity has a negative effect on system operations.

To summarise the advantages and disadvantages of the two models, it can be said objectively that on balance and with due consideration for all the advantages and disadvantages, the characteristics of the TSO model are more beneficial in the electricity sector than is the ISO model or any possible combination of the two models.

15.4   International Experience

International experience has shown that the TSO model is the most commonly used in the European Union, while the ISO is more predominant in the United States, with some subtle differences (as will be seen below), and in South America, where the use of the ISO model is clearly justified.

15.4.1   The United States

The ISO model used in the US is not the same as that used in South America, i.e. one system operator co-existing with various independent transmission companies. In contrast, in most cases there are no transmission companies but rather vertically integrated companies.

Experience in the US shows that the principal problems with this model are related to the governance system, which is generally overseen by State authorities that are under political pressure and under which traditional electricity companies enforce their interests over those of new players, and to the fact that the system operator has limited decision-making capabilities over the transmission assets, which it neither owns or manages.

Another aspect that has fostered the existence of ISOs is the atomisation of the sector and its regulation, which has limited investment in interconnections, resulting in the existence of a multitude of loosely interconnected systems.

Notwithstanding other aspects, such as the regulatory complexities in this country, which are due primarily to the cross-competition between local, state and federal authorities, events such those that took place in California in 2000 and in the northern part of the country in August 2003 must be taken into account in any analysis of the implications of using this model in the US.

In the first case, the inability of the California ISO to make decisions on the transmission assets owned by other companies was one of the principal reasons why the planning and expansion of the grid were not done properly, causing restrictions that cost $ 141 million between May and August 2000 and adding to the already high price of energy during those months.

With regard to the blackout in the northern part of the country on 14 August 2003, the lack of coordination and control over the transmission grid by the ISO responsible for the area where the incident originated (Midwest ISO) was one of the principal reasons for the propagation of the incident through the system.

Following this important incident, and even before it happened, numerous opinions held by and recommendations made by the Federal Energy Regulatory Commission (FERC) had proposed the regional transmission organisation (RTO) model, in which the ISO concept would have absolute management capabilities over the transmission assets, which is not the case with the ISO model used there. The most salient features of the RTO model are as follows:

- The owners of the transmission assets are the members of the RTO.
- The RTO has greater management and decision-making capabilities over those assets.
- The geographical areas are larger than those controlled by ISOs, covering the markets in more than one state.

Implementation of the RTO model has been obstructed by the same problems as were previously faced by ISOs: regulatory diversity and companies' resistance to ceding control over their assets to third parties.

These problems led to a new regulatory amendment known as "Order 679 – Promoting transmission investment through pricing reform", which offers financial incentives for the creation of RTSs and electricity transmission companies (Transcos) and expands the control zones.

15.4.2   Latin America

In South America's case, the ISO model is a pure model, i.e., the system operator co-exists with various independent transmission companies. The use of this model is clearly justified by the conditions existing in these countries.

In effect, in some liberalisation processes in South America the option of maintaining various transmission companies along with an ISO has been favoured by decisions of a strategic nature influenced by the limited development of the transmission grid, which is composed primarily of radial-type, scarcely meshed lines. In this situation, system operation is simpler with this type of organisation.

The principal characteristics that have favoured the adoption of the ISO model in Latin America include:

- Systems composed of simple, scarcely meshed grids;
- Need for heavy investments in grid infrastructure;
- Inability of the State and/or nationalised companies to undertake these investments;
- Tendency to put the transmission lines out to international tender to attract foreign investment;
- Co-existence of various transmission companies.

As a result of these conditioning factors, the system operators in these countries have been given functions other than those inherent in operation of the generation/transmission system, converting this into an extension of the regulatory function. The main areas in which this symbiosis between ISO and regulator has occurred include, but are not limited to, grid planning, organisation and assignment of tenders and the establishment of penalties levied on transmission companies. This is what has happened in Bolivia and Peru, to name just two of the known cases. The principal functions assigned that were not directly related to the system operators' role as ISOs are as follows:

- The ISO also acts as the market operator.
- The ISO is responsible for planning the national grid.
- There is close collaboration between the ISO and the regulator.
- The ISO becomes the guarantor of national control over electricity transmission because of the fear of losing control over system operations.

However, despite the conditioning factors mentioned above, there are some countries in the region where the electricity sector has undergone a restructuring process and a TSO model has been chosen; these include Panama, Nicaragua and Colombia.

15.4.3   The European Union

The model that has generally been adopted by most countries in the European Union, and on which Europe's Internal Electricity Market is being constructed, is the TSO model, as can be seen from Figure 15.1.

While the concept of the TSO existed previously in some countries, including Spain, the first Directive on the Internal Electricity Market, Directive 96/92/CE, clearly established this concept in the European regulatory system. In this Directive the independence requirements for TSOs were limited to unbundling management from the rest of the activities of vertically integrated companies.

Seven years later, Directive 2003/54/CE, which amended and repealed the previous directive, established more stringent unbundling requirements, although these were still inadequate, as we shall see below. These requirements are currently in force and are limited to the legal, organisational and decision-making separation of the TSO activities from the rest of the activities performed by the same company. As discussed below, Directive 2003/54/CE is currently being revised.

Ever since this Directive came into force, not a single country has attempted to recast its TSO model as an ISO model. Rather, just the opposite has occurred. Conversely, all the countries that have adopted a TSO model are in compliance with the Directive.

Italy is one example of a country that has moved from an ISO to a TSO model. During restructuring of the electricity sector controlled by the public company ENEL, a transmission company called TERNA was created; this was owned by ENEL, as was a system operator that also performed the functions of a single buyer (GRTN). In 2005, the Italian government privatised TERNA, segregated the market operation functions from GRTN and merged the two companies, creating a TSO and so coming in line with the rest of the European countries.

It is also important to note that among the most highly developed electricity markets in Europe, the Nordic countries, which are pioneers in the liberalisation of electricity markets and the implementation of a multinational electricity market, have adopted the TSO model. In this case, there are four TSOs and a single electricity market, Nord Pool.

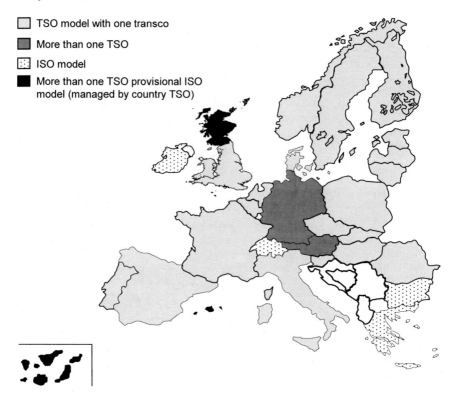

Figure 15.1: Situation in each of the 27 member countries of the European Union

There are several countries with TSO models in which various transmission companies co-exist. The most notable case is that of Great Britain, where the National Grid Transco (NGT), formerly the TSO for England and Wales, has also been appointed system operator for Scotland, thus establishing itself as a TSO that co-exists with two Scottish transcos.

NGT is an international reference for how electricity transmission and system operation can be carried out jointly by a completely private concern that is subject to strict oversight by regulators. Under the British model, the TSO is subject to oversight from both a quality point of view and a financial perspective (through what is known as ring-fencing).[6]

---

[6] Ring-fencing makes it possible for the regulator to be certain that the TSO has the financial capabilities it needs at all times to carry out the regulated activities it is licensed to perform in Great Britain. As long as the TSO remains within the established financial limits, it is allowed to carry out other activities outside the country, including transmission or distribution.

This regulatory scheme, which to date has worked well with very high-quality rates, has made it possible for NGT to develop new business elsewhere, primarily in the United States where it also acts as a distributor while performing its functions satisfactorily in Great Britain; these also include acting as the gas TSO following the merger with Transco, the former gas transmission system operator.

Germany and Austria are different from the rest of the countries in Europe since they each have various TSOs pertaining to vertically integrated companies, each of which is responsible for a different area of the country.

15.5   Upcoming Developments in the European Union – the Third Package

In part, the current situation of European energy markets is the result of how these markets have evolved in terms of the level of separation between TSOs and the rest of the activities inherent in the electricity sector. However, in some countries the independence of transmission and operation is still limited, since the TSOs are part of vertically integrated companies where the separation is merely legal (not separate ownership).

Aware of this situation, the European Commission, in its proposed amendment of Directive 2003/54/CE, has expressed its intention of separating transmission grids and system operations from all other electricity sector activities. This proposal was preceded by research carried out on the gas and electricity markets by the Competition Commission, which demonstrated the inability of third parties to have free access to grids and the limited investment (the lower the transmission capacity, the less competition there is) in those countries where transmission and system operation pertain to vertically integrated companies.

In this context the Spanish experience is noteworthy: complete independence of the TSO has made it possible to focus heavily on renewable energies in Spain, which is taking the form of large investments in transmission grids by the TSO and massive access to the system for generators of renewable energy. One example of this is seen in the fact that many projects whose characteristics indicate that they should be connected at distribution level nonetheless address access requests to the TSO asking for connection at transmission level because of the TSO's neutrality and independence.

To effectively ensure transmission independence, the Commission has explicitly established the TSO model with ownership unbundling as the best option. However, faced with the hesitance of some countries with large vertically integrated companies, the Commission has proposed the ISO model as the "second-best option" so that these companies do not have to relinquish their transmission assets. It must be emphasised that this second-best option is by no means the option of choice for European regulators, as they have been careful to say publicly on numerous occasions. All consider the TSO model to be the more effective for achieving the objectives being pursued, and the more efficient from a regulatory standpoint.

The Commission has upheld its preference for an independent TSO after analysing the results of experience with both models and in keeping with the advice of the ERGEG, the Commission's advisory body on regulatory matters related to the interior gas and electricity market.

In response to this, a group of countries, led by France and Germany, that oppose the European Commission's desire to guarantee complete unbundling of transmission and system operation from the rest of the activities has presented a third alternative in addition to the two proposed by the Commission. The "third way" proposed by these countries does not oblige vertically integrated companies to relinquish the ownership or management of their assets. The difference between this and the ISO model is that it proposes a series of more severe measures to guarantee the effective independence of the organisation and management of the TSO as a subsidiary company.

While experience has shown that liberalisation models are not directly exportable and that regulators cannot overlook the structure, history and particular circumstances of the sector when it comes to defining the liberalisation model, because of the indispensable independence, specialisation and uniqueness associated with the operation and development of the transmission grid so that the grid can accommodate the transactions agreed with agents and the market can function properly, the TSO model is considered the best option and is the predominant model in Europe.

References

De Quinto, J. 2001. Revisión del marco regulador de las actividades de Red Eléctrica en España: Comares – Fundación de Estudios de Regulación.

De Quinto, J. 2008. La posición de España (y de otros agentes del sector eléctrico) respecto a la independencia del transporte y la operación del sistema. Revista Electricidad n° 35 Julio – Agosto 2008.

European Union. Directive 96/92/EC of the European Parliament and of the Council of 19 December 1996 concerning common rules for the internal market in electricity, OJ L 27/20 of 30.1.1997.

European Union. Directive 2003/54/EC of the European Parliament and of the Council of 26 June 2003 concerning common rules for the internal market in electricity and repealing Directive 96/92/EC, OJ L 176/37.

European Union. Proposal for a Directive of the European Parliament and of the Council amending Directive 2003/54/EC concerning common rules for the internal market in electricity, 2007/0195 (COD), February 2008.

Red Eléctrica de España. 2005. El libro de los 20 años. Madrid.

U.S.-Canada power system outage task force. 2004. Final report on the August 14, 2003 blackout in the United States and Canada: causes and recommendations.

16 Convergence of Gas and Electricity Markets: Economic and Technological Drivers

Rolf W. Künneke[1]

Abstract

This chapter identifies different economic and technological drivers for the convergence of gas and electricity markets in the context of the ongoing market restructuring (i.e., liberalization). The analysis is based on a description of the economic and technological features peculiar to the gas and electricity value chains, and four different categories of market convergence. Market convergence can be related to products and services, regulation, business governance, and technology. Some implications of convergence for the market structure, industrial organization, and regulation are discussed.

Keywords: convergence, technology, regulation

[1] Prof. Dr. Rolf W. Künneke is Associate Professor at the Faculty of Technology, Policy, and Management, Section Economics of Infrastructures, Delft University of Technology, The Netherlands.

A. Bausch and B. Schwenker (eds.), *Handbook Utility Management,*
DOI: 10.1007/978-3-540-79349-6_16, © Springer-Verlag Berlin Heidelberg 2009

16.1   Introduction

In the past three decades the gas and electricity industries have been in a process of fundamental change. A process of market restructuring, often labeled liberalization, was initiated to allow for competition, introduce more private interest, and get policy at 'arm's length'. In addition, technology changed in this period. Gas turbine technology broke through in the electricity sector as an efficient means of generating power, not only in conventional large-scale units, but even as a distributed production technology (often combined heat and power (CHP)) within firms and commercial buildings or as district heating systems in residential neighborhoods. In addition, as compared with coal and oil, natural gas is quite an environmentally friendly fossil fuel to use for generation of electricity, as the CO_2 emissions are relatively low. This has added to the preference for gas as a primary energy source for electricity production, since there is growing public concern about environmental pollution, and hence more regulatory restrictions on 'dirty' generation technologies. Figure 16.1 illustrates the expected increasing use of gas between 2002 and 2030. After coal, gas is expected to become the second most important primary energy source for electricity generation by 2030.

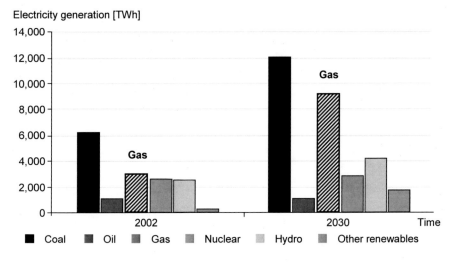

Figure 16.1: Primary energy sources for electricity generation in 2002 and 2030 (IEA, 2004)

These developments have changed the gas and electricity business quite significantly. Electricity producers have needed to become 'good in gas' for at least two reasons. First, purchasing gas at low costs was necessary to stay competitive in the new market regime. Second, trading gas on the wholesale market became an essential part of the electricity business, since long-term take-or-pay contracts did not always fit the actual needs. Besides that, it turned out that gas trading was also good for business. Sometimes selling gas on the spot market is more profitable than burning it and selling electricity (Baldwin, 2002). This was just the starting point towards convergence of the once separate markets for gas and electricity.

'Convergence' means a "tendency or movement toward union or uniformity" (Gove, 1986). This notion refers to a process of change that results in a situation in which there are fewer differences, or alternatively more similarities. With respect to gas and electricity, convergence is related to the "partial or full integration of the formerly separate infrastructure industries" (Toh, 2003). There are two different categories of 'convergence'. The 'joining together' of certain aspects of markets can occur either by substitutes or complements (Greenstein & Khanna, 1997). Convergence by substitutes means, for instance, that products and services become more similar and interchangeable. In the case of gas and electricity, both energy carriers might be used for space heating. Convergence by complements refers to a situation in which synergy occurs between parts of each industry. An example of convergence of complements is the increasing use of gas as a primary energy source for the production of electricity.

This chapter explores economic and technological drivers for converging gas and electricity markets in the context of the market restructuring and speculates on some implications for the market structure, industrial organization, and regulation. To start with, a brief characterization of the gas and electricity sectors provides some fundamental insights into the economics and technology of these infrastructures. Section 16.3 specifies four different categories of market convergence, i.e., products and services, regulation, business governance, and technology. Based on this classification, Section 16.4 identifies economic and technological drivers for convergence. Finally, Section 16.5 summarizes the main findings and speculates on the impact of convergence on the business organization and regulation of the gas and electricity markets.

16.2   Characterizing the Gas and Electricity Sectors

This section provides some economic and technological fundamentals of the gas and electricity sectors, based on a value chain approach. In addition to the present situation we also consider possible developments that might contribute to convergence in the future.

16.2.1   The Gas Sector

The value chain of the gas sector consists roughly of the seven elements depicted in Figure 16.2.

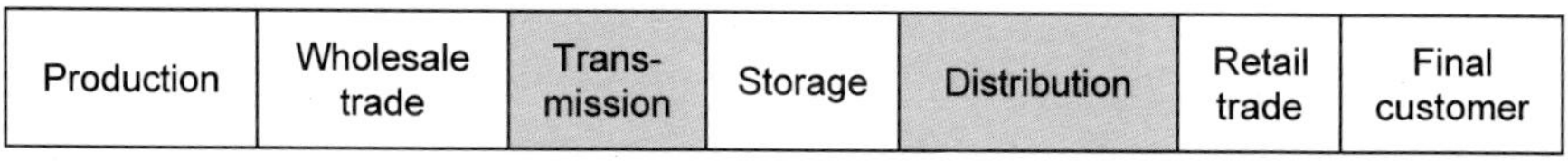

Production	Wholesale trade	Trans- mission	Storage	Distribution	Retail trade	Final customer

Figure 16.2: Value chain of the gas sector

The production phase entails the exploration and initial processing of gas to the required quality standards, for example with respect to the calorific value and possible contaminations.[2] Nowadays natural gas is the most common. This natural resource is only available at specific locations. The extraction is often on a very large scale and far distant from the consumers. Hence, long-distance transport is required to bridge this distance. In Europe about 85% of long-distance transport is accomplished through the high-pressure transmission system. The remaining 15% is transported by ship as liquefied natural gas (LNG). Other means of gas production include the gasification of coal, the fermentation of bio waste, and the electrolysis of water into hydrogen. Typically these 'new' gases can be produced in the customer's vicinity and on a comparably small scale. At present the market share of such new gases is marginal.

The pipeline system in the gas sector consists of the above-mentioned long-distance transmission and the local distribution networks. The distribution networks are operated at low pressure and serve most final customers.[3] It is important to note that transmission and distribution networks are only suitable for a certain quality of gas that meets the technical specifications of the customers' appliances. Hence, there are different gas networks for different gas qualities.

Storage is necessary to buffer production and consumption of gas. Typically gas is produced in quite a constant quantity that typically does not fit consumption patterns. Besides daily fluctuations in demand, there are also seasonal differences, or even unexpected events such as a sudden period of cold weather.

Wholesale, large-volume trade is located at the upstream part of the value chain, accommodated by either bilateral contracts or gas exchanges. Retail trade indicates the delivery of gas to final customers in conjunction with related services, the most important of which is storage.

An interesting future development is related to the possible use of the gas infrastructure for carbon capture and storage (CCS) to handle hazardous CO_2 emissions. According to the very ambitious goals for emission reductions, CCS seems set to become very important in the near future. A question currently under consideration is whether it is possible to use empty gas fields for the storage of CO_2 waste and to exploit a dedicated pipeline system for transporting this greenhouse gas. This would add an interesting new technical and economic aspect to the use of the gas infrastructure.

16.2.2   The Electricity Sector

The electricity value chain consists of six major elements (see Figure 16.3). Production is related to the conversion of primary energy sources into electric power. Natural gas is an important primary energy source, as are coal, oil, water, and uranium. In most cases electricity is produced in large-scale units, allowing for

---

[2] Different quality standards for natural gas include high- and low-calorific gas, and the Dutch Groningen standard.

[3] Some giant industrial users are directly connected to the transmission system.

economies of scale. However, there is now a trend towards small-scale decentralized production units, for many of which gas is an import fuel.[4]

Production	Wholesale trade	Transmission	Distribution	Retail trade	Final customer

Figure 16.3: The electricity value chain

Transmission refers to long-distance transport through high-voltage power lines. Distribution networks provide electric power at a low voltage level to final customers. As an important part of the transmission of electricity, various auxiliary services are needed. Since electricity cannot be stored efficiently on a significant scale, load balancing between production and consumption is essential to guarantee system reliability.[5]

The wholesale trading of electricity is conducted through bilateral contracts and power exchanges. Retail trade entails the delivery of power to the final customers. Other services, such as metering and billing, are related to this part of the value chain.

16.3   Categorizing Market Convergence

Markets can be characterized by at least four distinct features, i.e., the products and services traded, the regulatory regime, business governance, and technology. Accordingly, we distinguish four categories of market convergence:

(1) *Convergence of products and services:* Using this approach different markets for final and intermediate products are considered. The delivery of natural gas and electric power is an example of a final service. Intermediate services include the storage of natural gas or the exchange of electricity on wholesale markets. In the gas and electricity markets certain services might become more similar and hence converge; examples of these might be customer relations, billing, and metering.

(2) *Convergence of regulatory regimes:* Traditionally electricity and gas are perceived as basic infrastructure facilities that need to serve public interests. Accordingly, there is a long history of political involvement in these markets. Even under the conditions of liberalization, sector-specific regulation is perceived as necessary not only to create a level playing field for the competing

---

[4] Next to gas turbines, small-scale electricity production is often related to sustainable technologies, such as wind, tidal flows, or solar power.

[5] Other auxiliary services include disturbance response and voltage control. For a detailed overview see for instance Hirst (1997).

firms, but also to safeguard public values.[6] Regulation is also necessary to support technical control of the system so as to prevent malfunctioning or outages. This is especially the case for electricity and gas. These are very complex technical systems that need some centralized technical monitoring and control (Künneke & Finger, 2007). Both in gas and electricity, there is a need for a system operator that monitors certain critical technical functions. As a consequence, similar regulatory regimes have evolved, contributing to the convergence of the gas and electricity markets.

(3) *Convergence of business governance:* In attempting to gain competitive advantages, firms need constantly to redefine existing markets or create new markets, and hence to serve customers' needs even better. This can be done either by introducing new products (i.e., diversification) or by cost cutting and lower prices (i.e., cost leadership) (Porter, 1980). The internal and external governance of firms is an important instrument for readjusting strategic positions. What are the core competences, i.e., which products and services shape the firm? Which activities should be outsourced to enhance efficiency? Which contractual relations with suppliers contribute to innovativeness? These aspects of business governance determine the market position of firms and the kind of products and services they are offering. Gas and electricity have evolved into an energy business within which firms increasingly regard the supply of both energy carriers as their core business. Accordingly, firms redefine their business relations with suppliers, competitors and buyers, and hence redefine markets.

(4) *Convergence of technology:* The physical assets of firms determine the kind of products and services they are able to supply to customers. As mentioned in the Introduction, the increasing use of gas as a primary energy source for power generation has contributed significantly to the convergence of gas and electricity markets.

16.4   Drivers for Convergence of Gas and Electricity Markets

Based on the different categories of market convergence and the description of the value chains, it is now possible to specify the drivers for convergence of the gas and electricity markets in detail. Since convergence is a dynamic process, we not only refer to the present situation, but also reflect on possible future developments.

---

[6] These public values typically include accessibility to these services, affordability, sustainability, and reliability.

16.4.1 Convergence of Products and Services

For this case of convergence we need to consider whether different products and services throughout the gas and electricity value chains are 'joining together', i.e., becoming more similar (substitutes) or becoming increasingly intertwined (complementary). Traditionally, convergence occurs with respect to wholesale and retail trade. Wholesale trading of gas stimulates convergence with the electricity business in at least two respects. First, as mentioned in the Introduction, gas is an important primary energy source for the production of electricity. As a consequence, the wholesaling of gas is increasingly linked to the production of electricity. In order to guarantee the continuity of gas-fired electricity generation and keep costs down, long-term positions on the gas market have to be secured and short-term surpluses or shortages of gas need to be allocated on the spot market. Second, trading gas and electricity might even become substitutes on wholesale markets. There might be interesting trade-offs according to whether gas is to be used for electricity production or sold on a spot market. Energy firms can profit from short-term market fluctuations either in electricity or gas and can search for profit-maximizing opportunities.

On the side of retail trade, final customers perceive gas and electricity as comparable products that serve primary energy needs. In this case, convergence is related to such complementary services as metering, billing, energy saving, or customer care. If electricity is produced locally by decentralized production units, gas is often the primary energy source. In this case there is again a direct link between the use of gas and power production. There are expectations that increasingly even private households will be able to produce electricity using micro-CHP technology (Abu-Sharkh et al., 2006).[7] This could be an important future driver for convergence.

16.4.2 Regulatory Convergence

The gas and electricity markets were restructured in quite similar ways and in the same time period. Stimulation of competition and stronger involvement of private interests were important objectives. In addition, the European Union expected further integration of internal markets to follow when important infrastructures were liberalized. Before restructuring, gas and electricity firms were organized as regulated monopolies very closely related to political control and decision making. Liberalization appeared as a radical change of the regulatory environment in the 1980s and 1990s. The newly evolving regulatory regimes stimulated convergence between the gas and electricity markets. The changing 'rules of the game' forced market participants in both sectors to adjust their way of conducting business in a similar way. Gas and electricity firms needed to invest heavily in the development

---

[7] Micro-CHP's are very small combined heat and power production units that are operated on a household level. These units are heat driven and able to produce about one third to one half of the electricity needs of private households, as a joint product of space heating.

of new governance structures, arranging for a new 'play of the game' (North, 1990).[8] This includes establishing novel contractual relations, internal restructuring, and acquiring new activities such as gas and electricity trading on power and gas exchanges. These are large initial investments that exhibit characteristics of increasing returns. If these new governance structures can be applied to both the gas and electricity sectors, relative cost advantages can be obtained for the following reasons (North, 1990):

- *Economies of scale:* With a growing rate of application of similar institutional arrangements in the gas and electricity sectors the cost per unit declines.
- *Cumulative learning effects:* The more often certain modes of governance are applied in the gas and electricity market, the higher is the degree of cost efficiency through learning.
- *Coordination effects:* Cost advantages can be obtained if firms in gas and electricity markets apply similar institutional arrangements.

This process can be described as institutional convergence of gas and electricity markets. Through adaptive expectations this is a self-reinforcing process. The more popular certain modes of governance, the more they are expected to prevail in future. Hence, the similarity of institutional regimes in these markets is a stimulus for even stronger future convergence.

Genoud et al. (2004) describe the regulatory convergence of gas and electricity for the case of the European Union, not only between these sectors but also between countries. They argue that the various EU gas and electricity directives serve as catalysts to the convergence of market rules. Across the member states, very similar regulatory functions for gas and electricity have emerged. The functions and capacities of the national regulatory bodies for electricity and gas are increasingly harmonized. Often one single regulatory body is assigned to perform the sector-specific regulation, including the approval of ex ante access conditions and tariffs for the various networks. Very recently the EU proposed complete unbundling of transmission networks from commercial activities, both for gas and for electricity. There is also some convergence with respect to the public service obligations to be performed by the gas and electricity sectors. Among other aims, EU policy is oriented towards price transparency, development of trans-European networks, comparable tax policies, and investments according to the European Energy Charter. Accordingly, this regulatory convergence contributes to new business opportunities for energy firms and to the creation of opportunities for convergence (Section 16.4.3).

However, important differences between gas and electricity remain and should not be underestimated. Gas and electricity supplies serve as important national policy instruments. For instance, in gas-exporting countries there are such con-

---

[8] This argumentation is based on North (1990). 'Rules of the game' refers to changing formal legal arrangements and property rights. 'Play of the game' refers to the governance of firms and markets, such as contractual arrangements, internal and external organization, and the like.

cerns as maximizing state revenues, protecting national suppliers, enhancing political influence through the energy trade, and securing national energy autonomy.
This can result in different policy objectives for gas and electricity and hence different regulatory arrangements. Typically, sector re-regulation takes place at a
slower pace for gas than for electricity. This creates regulatory uncertainty and
might force energy firms to retreat from multisectoral activities (Toh, 2003).[9]
There might even be national policies strongly restricting convergence, as there
are in France, where the gas and electricity firms (GDF and EDF) are strictly separated. The French government has developed a national energy policy in which
energy security builds on a large share of nuclear power production in the electricity sector. Gas-fired electricity production would increase this country's dependence on gas imports.

16.4.3 Business Convergence

Business convergence is related to the strategic market positioning of electricity
and gas firms to secure long-term continuity and attain competitive advantages. In
general there are four ideal type configurations for gas and electricity firms, determined by the degree of vertical integration and sectoral configuration (see
Figure 16.4).

Vertical integration is determined by the degree to which the different activities
in the value chain are performed within the boundaries of a firm. A multisectoral
configuration depends on the degree to which the activities of different value
chains are unified within a firm. Obviously convergence only occurs in cases of
multisectoral configurations, culminating either as a multisectoral functional specialist or as a vertically integrated plurisectoral firm.[10]

In conditions of liberalized gas and electricity markets, there might be various
strategic considerations in favor of one or other of these configurations. Efficiency
gains are often expressed as an important driver for re-configuration of firms
(Jurewitz, 2001). From a transaction cost perspective the make-or-buy decision
depends on the degree of asset specificity of investments, the risk, and the frequency of transactions (Williamson, 1996). If gas becomes more important for the
generation of electricity it is reasonable to assume that more asset-specific investments are required and there are higher risks associated with the security of gas
supply. This is an important reason for convergence, since in these conditions a
multisectoral configuration contributes to a higher degree of cost efficiency. When
this cost efficiency objective is applied very strictly, the ultimate result of this
strategy is probably the multisectoral functional specialist. This specialization

---

[9] Toh (2003) refers to the case of Shell in the USA. This gas and oil company pulled out of
the retail of electricity in the USA because of the slow deregulation of gas markets in some
states.

[10] In this chapter we only focus on gas and electricity convergence. Hence, these cases refer
to vertically integrated multi-energy firms or sectoral functional specialists in gas and electricity.

would allow a cost leadership approach in which production and transaction costs can be minimized (Porter, 1980).

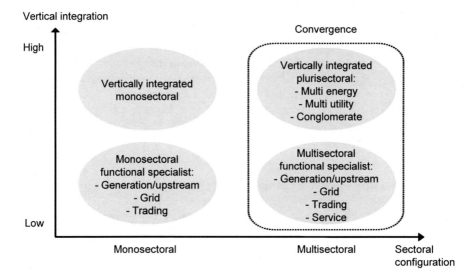

Figure 16.4: Four ideal type configurations (adapted from Finon & Midttun, 2004)

Market positioning is another reason for merging gas and electricity firms. Larger and more diverse firms are able to exaggerate market power and can thus fence themselves against competition. In the conditions of a tight oligopoly, market participants are able to control such important parameters as prices and service areas. In globalizing energy markets, a certain minimum scale might be necessary for it to be possible to stay independent. There are increasingly mergers and acquisitions, either friendly or hostile. Figure 16.5 illustrates this tendency. Under these premises, convergence most probably is manifested by vertically integrated plurisectoral firms. These firms are potentially larger than the functional specialists. Size is what matters, in this case.

From a public policy perspective the creation of national champions preserves existing market structures and safeguards political and economic power relations. Foreign takeovers can be perceived as threats to the national energy policy. In Europe, countries such as France, Germany, Belgium, Spain, and Portugal have a long tradition of national champions in the energy sector, fostered by tacit or explicit industrial policies (Finon et al., 2004). The recent controversial discussion in Europe on whether to allow Russian or Chinese state-dominated firms to take financial positions in the gas and electricity industry is an example of the strong political facets that are inherent to these essential infrastructures. Obviously there are limits to market forces and economic reasoning. Even in the conditions of liberalized markets, the national policy agenda is an important factor shaping the structure of the gas and electricity industry. With respect to the ideal type configurations the vertically integrated plurisectoral configuration serves these political objectives to a high degree.

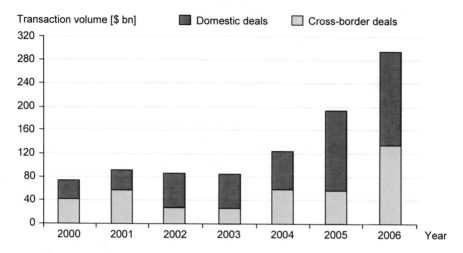

Figure 16.5: Electricity and gas deals by value (PricewaterhouseCoopers, 2006)

These are few examples of drivers of business convergence. Certainly other considerations are in play. In some cases this might even be "the simple satisfaction of management egos" (Jurewitz, 2001). This might end up in either of the ideal type configurations of the gas and electricity sector.

16.4.4 Technological Convergence

In the literature, technology is recognized as an important driver of convergence. Based on an historical analysis, Fai and Von Tunzelmann (2001) analyze technological spill-overs between different industries. Although many technologies are initially developed solely for one specific industry, there seems to be a tendency to absorb new modes of technological behavior into other industries. This pattern of convergence typically occurs in the second stage of the development of a technological trajectory, after it is settled and proven in an industry. Firms that are not able to perform this second move might degenerate into 'industrial dinosaurs' that have lost their initial competitive advantages (Fai & Von Tunzelmann, 2001).[11] According to Fai and Von Tunzelmann, convergence seems to be part of the evolution of technologies that broaden their scope of application through their lifetime.

In this chapter we interpret these technological spill-overs as responses to newly developing consumer needs or preferences in the energy sector. Illustra-

---

[11] Gambardella and Torrisi (1998) confirm this finding. They argue that better business performance is associated with technological diversification.

tively we identify three drivers of technological convergence between gas and electricity markets that now appear to be of some importance:

- Decentralization of energy production;
- Preference for clean and sustainable energy;
- Offering energy services to final customers.

16.4.4.1 Decentralization of Energy Production

The emergence of cost-efficient gas turbines contributed much to the resemblance of gas and electricity markets, as already mentioned in the Introduction. The gas turbine technology contributed significantly to the down-scaling of electricity generation, from traditionally a few hundred megawatts to a few megawatts or even kilowatts these days. Gas is the preferred fuel for these plants if the grid infrastructure is in place. Small-scale gas-fired plants are typically built in the final customer's vicinity, often as combined heat and power plants. This offers opportunities to provide new services to final customers based on the provision of gas and electricity (Section 16.4.1).

Another technical development of decentralization relates to the production and use of new gases. For instance, the bio-gasification technology is quite interesting for farmers seeking opportunities to use their waste products. Gases absorbed by landfills also fit into this category. Since these new gases have different technical characteristics than traditional natural gases, they cannot be fed directly into the gas pipeline system. Either they need to be refined to meet the existing gas standards (synthetic gas), or they could be utilized locally, for example for the decentralized production of electric power. These technical developments increasingly blur the distinction between the gas and electricity markets. Both energy sources are produced and utilized in close conjunction to each other.[12]

16.4.4.2 Preference for Clean and Sustainable Energy

Hydrogen is another new gas that seems very promising in our efforts to reduce CO_2 emissions. Since clean water is the only residual, this might be the ultimate energy source in a future sustainable energy system. Hydrogen can be used to produce electricity, preferably by using fuel cells.[13] Since hydrogen is not naturally available, it needs to be produced by electrolysis, i.e., separating water into hydrogen and oxygen. Hence, electric power is needed to produce hydrogen, preferably without CO_2 emissions. Options include nuclear power, clean coal power with CCS, and sustainable means like wind or solar power. The production of hydrogen offers novel opportunities for the storage of electricity. Electricity generators

---

[12] Biomass is not only used for small scale electricity production, but also in large centralized generation units operated by traditional electricity firms.

[13] Fuel cell technology converts energy sources (including hydrogen) into electric power by an electrochemical process. For more information refer for instance to en.wikipedia.org (2008).

could be operated at a constant base load level at which the production of hydrogen could serve as a buffer between peak and off-peak periods. If demand exceeds the base load, hydrogen-based fuel cells can be operated to fill the gap. This would be especially useful when the basic supply is produced from intermittent energy sources such as wind and solar light. These could always be operated at maximum level, with hydrogen as energy storage. This example illustrates how gas can be used to balance the electricity system. Gas can provide important auxiliary services, such as storage and load balancing, to the electricity system.

The ultimate hydrogen economy would ideally be based exclusively on clean and sustainable energy sources. However, fossil-fueled electricity generation is still expected to be needed for a significant period to supplement clean energy production, or to produce hydrogen (see above). However, coal belongs to the most environmentally unfriendly energy sources for the generation of electric power, since it causes significant CO_2 emissions. CCS is the envisaged technical solution to this problem. Obviously this requires fundamental technological innovations, since CO_2 has to be handled separately from other gases that are used as primary energy sources. In certain conditions, empty gas fields could be refilled with CO_2. Unused gas pipelines might serve new transport purposes, removing CO_2 from the polluting source and taking it to the final storage site. In this case gas flows would have to be handled in the opposite direction from today. If these technical developments materialize, there will be new cases of convergence not only with respect to power generation, but also for network and storage services.

16.4.4.3 Offering Energy Services to Final Customers

On the downstream parts of the value chains services, such as metering, customer care, and other dedicated energy services, are expected to converge even more than today. The cases of metering and customer care are straight forward, and now quite familiar. However, with the development of smart meters there are new opportunities. Although gas and electricity meters might be technically different, the information infrastructure required to retrieve and process the information they record is very similar. The same holds for customer care, billing, and the like.

New energy services might, for instance, be related to technical opportunities to produce electricity locally based on the micro-CHP technology. These micro-CHP installations could provide a significant part of the local electricity demand.[14] Using fuel cell technology, micro-CHP's could also be operated with hydrogen. There are even technical opportunities to produce and store hydrogen locally, offering possibilities for local load scheduling. If these developments materialize, auxiliary services that are currently closely related to the operation of gas and electricity networks could be provided locally. According to the preferences and needs of the customers, tailor-made energy services can be provided, for example with respect to reliability, costs, and environmental characteristics of power and gas.

---

[14] Based on the current technology about one third to half of residential customers' electricity need could be met in this way.

16.5   Conclusions

This chapter identifies different economic and technological drivers for the convergence of gas and electricity markets. The analysis is based on a description of the economic and technological features peculiar to the gas and electricity value chains, and four different categories of market convergence. Market convergence can be related to products and services, regulation, business governance, and technology. For each of these categories present and future drivers for convergence are identified.

The different drivers for convergence discussed in this chapter cannot be interpreted as isolated phenomena, being obviously more or less interrelated. It goes beyond the scope of this chapter to elaborate on this in detail. Take, for instance, the relation between technological and regulatory convergence. If it turns out in future that local electricity production suffices to meet the entire power demand, the universal service obligation for electricity needs to be reconsidered; the ability to consume electricity will no longer be strictly dependent on a direct connection to the public electricity network. In these circumstances a connection to the gas network serves the same needs. The regulatory framework needs to take these new technical opportunities into account, for instance by treating access to gas and access to electricity networks as alternative ways of meeting universal service obligations.[15]

The convergence of products and services has implications for the possible convergence of business strategies. As mentioned in the Introduction, the increasing use of gas as a primary energy source for power production has forced electricity firms to become 'good in gas'. A convergence of products and services is often fostered by technological advances, as in the case of micro-CHP technology.

These few examples raise the question of the implications of convergence for the market structure, industrial organization, and regulation. Some cases of convergence might have little impact, whereas others result in a fundamental restructuring of markets and industries. On a very general level it can be argued that convergence resulting from a change of the underlying technological or economic paradigm can be expected to have a deeper impact than changes of certain technological trajectories or business routines. The possible decentralization of the energy production can be considered as a paradigm shift away from the current model of centralized provision of gas and electricity. The associated convergence of gas and electricity markets will have major impacts on business strategies and governmental regulation. On the other hand, changing business routines, such as joint billing of gas and electricity supply, might have only slight repercussions.

Convergence of substitutes is expected to stimulate competition. This can be interpreted as an aspect of the Schumpeterian 'process of creative destruction' (Greenstein & Khanna, 1997), since there are new and possibly better ways of satisfying consumer needs. However, for gas and electricity markets, there are few examples of convergence of substitutes. The majority of cases presented in this

---

[15] This topic in technological and regulatory convergence is very current in the ICT sector. See for instance Zhang (2002) for the case of broadband industry regulation.

chapter fit the case of convergence of complements. This potentially stimulates cooperation between or even mergers of firms operating in different markets. Figure 16.5 illustrates this development by a growing number of mergers between gas and electricity firms. Firms acquire market power, resulting in barriers to market entry and strategic pricing. As a consequence, market structures become less competitive and there are fewer incentives for innovative approaches to convergence between gas and electricity markets. However, these potential economic barriers might be overcome by radical technical changes that undermine the market position of established firms. For instance, the upcoming micro-CHP technology is sometimes compared to the evolution of personal computers. At one time mainframe computers dominated the market, but ultimately the PC technology contributed to the radical restructuring of the ICT industry as we know it today (Greenstein & Khanna, 1997). If micro-CHP's can be installed in private dwellings as a 'plug and play' technology, this will potentially provide an opportunity for new and competitive converging market structures.

In these conditions regulation is a complex task. Convergence is the consequence of innovative activities and hence deserves support. On the other hand, the existing technical and economic structures of the gas and electricity infrastructures need careful maintenance in order to safeguard security of supply and the public service obligations of these fundamental services. There is little room for experimentation and 'creative destruction' of market players. Revealing some drivers for convergence, as was the aim in this chapter, is the first step in coping with these complex issues associated with the joining together of the gas and electricity markets. Convergence of the gas and electricity markets is just in its early stages and will reshape these industries in quite a fundamental manner in the years to come.

References

Abu-Sharkh, S., Arnold, R. J., Kohler, J., Li, R., Markvart, T., Ross, J. N., Steemers, K., Wilson, P. & Yao, R. 2006. Can microgrids make a major contribution to UK energy supply? Renewable and Sustainable Energy Reviews, 10: 78-127.

Baldwin, N. 2002. Competition, convergence, and consolidation: the new world. Power Engineering Journal, 16: 229-234.

en.wikipedia.org. 2008. Fuel cell – Wikipedia, the free encyclopedia. http://en.wikipedia.org/wiki/Fuel_cell. Date of access: April 28, 2008.

Fai, F. & Von Tunzelmann, N. 2001. Industry-specific competencies and converging technological systems: evidence from patents. Structural Change and Economic Dynamics, 12: 141-170.

Finon, D. & Midttun, A. 2004. Introduction. In D. Finon & A. Midttun (Eds.), Reshaping European Gas and Electricity Industries: 1-10. Oxford: Elsevier Science.

Finon, D., Midttun, A., Omland, T., Mez, L., Ruperez-Micola, A., Nucci, R. D., Soares, I. & Thomas, S. 2004. Strategic configuration: a casuistic approach. In D. Finon & A. Midttun (Eds.), Reshaping European Gas and Electricity Industries: 297-353. Oxford: Elsevier Science.

Gambardella, A. & Torrisi, S. 1998. Does technological convergence imply convergence in markets? Evidence from the electronics industry. Research Policy, 27: 445-463.

Genoud, C., Finger, M. & Arentsen, M. 2004. Energy regulation: convergence through multilevel technocracy. In D. Finon & A. Midttun (Eds.), Reshaping European Gas and Electricity Industries: 111-128. Oxford: Elsevier Science.

Gove, P. B. (Ed.) 1986. Webster's third new international dictionary of the English language unabridged. Springfield: Merriam-Webster.

Greenstein, S. & Khanna, T. 1997. What does industry convergence mean? In D. B. Yoffie (Ed.), Competition In The Age Of Digital Convergence: 201-226. Boston: Harvard Business School Press.

Hirst, E. 1997. Competition can enhance bulk-power reliability. Washington: Electricity Consumers Resource Council.

International Energy Agency (IEA). 2004. World energy outlook 2004. Paris: OECD/IEA.

Jurewitz, J. L. 2001. Business strategies evolving in response to regulatory changes in the US electric power industry. In A. Midttun & D. Finon (Eds.), European Energy Industry Business Strategies: 279-335. Oxford: Elsevier Science.

Künneke, R. W. & Finger, M. 2007. Technology matters: the cases of the liberalization of electricity and railways. Competition and Regulation in Network Industries, 8: 301-334.

North, D. C. 1990. Institutions, institutional change, and economic performance. Cambridge: Cambridge University Press.

Porter, M. 1980. Competitive strategy. New York: The Free Press.

PricewaterhouseCoopers. 2006. Power deals 2006 annual review: mergers and acquisitions activity within the global electricity and gas market. PricewaterhouseCoopers.

Toh, K.-H. 2003. The impact of convergence of the gas and electricity industries: trends and policy implications. http://www.iea.org/Textbase/publications/free_new_Desc.asp?PUBS_ID=918. Date of access: April 28, 2008.

Williamson, O. E. 1996. The mechanisms of governance. New York: Oxford University Press.

Zhang, B. 2002. Understanding impact of convergence on broadband industry regulation: a case study of the United States. Telematics and Informatics, 19: 37-59.

Part III:
Power Generation

17 Investing in Power Generation

Reinhard Madlener[1]

Rik W. De Doncker[2]

Abstract

In light of considerable political and market risk emanating from energy market liberalization, global warming, and rapid technological change, adequate investment in power generation capacity is of paramount importance for ensuring the security of electricity supply and a smooth transition to a more decentralized, energy-efficient and renewable energy system. Consequently, investors have to use more sophisticated approaches to determine optimal investment levels and technology choices than in regulated markets. In this chapter, we provide a discussion of relevant topics and issues in this context and some of the key literature. We also discuss the expected paradigm shift from centralized to more decentralized electricity generation, and the possible (re-)emergence of direct current grids, in light of the history of electrical engineering. Both phenomena, once manifested, would radically reshape the electricity system, with potentially severe economic consequences for existing real assets and new challenges for investment decision-makers, technical system operators, policy-makers, and regulatory bodies alike.

Keywords: risk management, paradigm shift, distributed generation

[1] Prof. Dr. Reinhard Madlener is Full Professor of Energy Economics and Management and Director of the Institute for Future Energy Consumer Needs and Behavior (FCN), Faculty of Business Administration and Economics / E.ON Energy Research Center at the RWTH Aachen University, Germany.

[2] Prof. Dr. Rik W. De Doncker is Full Professor and Director of the E.ON Energy Research Center at RWTH Aachen University. He leads the Institute for Power Generation and Storage (PGS) and the Institute for Power Electronics and Electrical Drives (ISEA), Faculty of Electrical Engineering and Information Technology at the RWTH Aachen University, Germany.

A. Bausch and B. Schwenker (eds.), *Handbook Utility Management,*
DOI: 10.1007/978-3-540-79349-6_17, © Springer-Verlag Berlin Heidelberg 2009

17.1   Introduction

As a consequence of the worldwide wave of deregulation of electricity markets, environmental problems caused by excessive use of both nonrenewable and renewable energy resources, and rapid technological innovation, policy-makers, utilities, and final consumers alike are concerned about the sustainability and security of future energy supply and the occurrence of substantial stranded investments in case of imprudent investment decisions. At the same time, owing to the often lacking incentives in liberalized markets to replace old and invest in new capacity in a timely manner and to the growing demand for electricity, reserve capacities have generally been dwindling rapidly. From a short-term production efficiency point of view this might be desirable, but given the long planning and construction lead times of many (especially large-scale) power plant projects, there is some danger of emergencies and involuntary rationing of electricity supply (brownouts, blackouts). In other words, power suppliers have to master the delicate task of balancing the short-term optimization of operation versus the economically optimal allocation of capital in the long run, both in the face of considerable risks and uncertainties.

In contrast to regulated monopolies, where utilities could pass on the costs and risks associated with investments in power generation to the final consumer, in a deregulated market environment utilities have to deal with uncertainty and tackle a number of risks that are often hard to quantify and transfer to other parties. One major uncertainty concerns electricity prices. The high volatility of electricity prices is attributable partly to low price elasticity of demand, accruing both from limited substitutability of electricity in many end-uses and the lack of information of many consumers (see Section 17.4.1 below on smart metering). Other market failures (e.g., abuse of market power, imperfect locational pricing) exacerbate the problem further.[3]

Uncertainty on the side of policy-makers leads to uncertainty about future policies and regulation, which can also discourage investment in new capacity. This is an issue particularly if poorly designed wholesale and retail markets, and constraints of electricity price volatility and upward price developments on the wholesale spot markets caused by government intervention, lead to situations where investors are either unlikely or unable to earn the capital investment and operating costs (Joskow, 2006).

---

[3] We do not deal with the issue of peaking plants, i.e., those plants that set the market price for peak power in the spot markets and are only run a few hours per year, since these only constitute a niche market in power generation (Frayer & Uludere, 2001). Another issue only briefly tackled in Section 17.2.3 is that of generation adequacy, i.e., whether power generation capacity is invested in a sufficient and timely manner in liberalized electricity markets, and the possible rise of power generation investment cycles (e.g., De Vries & Hakvoort, 2004; Joskow, 2006; De Vries, 2007; De Vries & Heijnen, 2008). For an analysis of policy strategies beyond the introduction of capacity payments, i.e., payments for providing peak power reserves at times of shortages in electricity supply, see Finon et al. (2004), among others.

Another issue that has received relatively little attention in the energy economics literature so far is that of financing considerations related to generation capacity. Harper et al. (2007) have studied the emerging financing structures in the wind power sector in the US, shedding some light on the challenges ahead in attracting sufficient capital and acceptable cost for rapidly rising power generation sectors (for a broader discussion of the huge global challenge of financing energy investments see IEA, 2003b, chapter 3). Older work, such as that of Jenkins (1985), has pointed out the inefficiencies of public-sector utilities resulting from their financing structure. The issue touches upon the more general one of the interrelatedness of financing of investments on the one hand and optimal provision of research and development (R&D), technological diffusion, and the impact of policy design on the other (Goodacre & Tonks, 1995; Stoneman, 2001).

Technological change in the electricity sector has many facets. One of them is the expected shift toward more decentralized production, which poses considerable risk to investors in long-lived large-scale power plants, since it is far from clear how the market shares, and thus also the economics of both small-scale and large-scale generation, transmission and distribution (T&D), and end-use technologies, will develop further. The International Energy Agency (IEA) has estimated the projected shares of capacity additions in OECD power generation capacity by energy source for the years between 1999 and 2030 (see Figure 17.1). As can be seen, it anticipated that natural gas-fired power generation will continue to be a preferred option, accounting for almost half of the capacity additions in the OECD countries and leading to a marked change both in the diversity of electricity supply and the primary energy mix. At that time, the IEA also raised the important question whether the 'short-termism' of investors could actually lead to economically inefficient solutions in the longer term, thus also touching upon the important issue of technological path-dependence (David, 1985; Arthur, 1989).

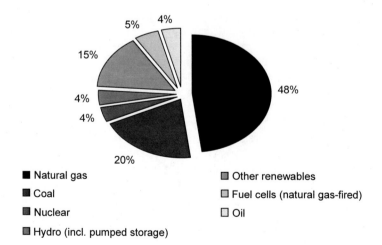

Figure 17.1: Projected capacity additions in OECD power generating capacity by fuel, 1999-2030 [%] (IEA, 2003a)

An issue related to the expected market shares of the different generation technologies and the capacity additions to power generation capacity is the enormous amount of capital needed for various infrastructure investments in the energy sector (IEA, 2003b). For example, it is estimated that in most developed nations (Europe and US) 80% of the electrical infrastructure needs to be replaced within the next 20 years. This represents major challenges, but also opens up a window of opportunity to explore new technologies that can more flexibly adapt the infrastructure to future needs (IEA 2003a).

The remainder of this chapter is organized as follows: Section 17.2 addresses the issue of investment in risky assets and methods that have been proposed in the literature to deal with risk. Section 17.3 first reflects on the historical development of the electricity sector and then tackles the changing paradigms expected by many experts as we pass from centralized to decentralized generation and related changes to the electric grid. Section 17.4 provides two illustrative examples of new technologies that may support the paradigm shift (smart metering and variable speed mini-turbines), and Section 17.5 gives our conclusions.

17.2   Investment in Risky Assets

17.2.1   Methods for Assessing Investment Projects Under Uncertainty

The simplest way to assess an investment is to calculate its expected net present value (NPV) in a deterministic setup. In regulated monopolistic markets, the costs of power supply were simply transferred to ratepayers, ensuring that costs could in principle be recovered whatever their level. In liberalized markets, in contrast, it is necessary to optimize returns (i.e., revenues minus cost) and risks, rather than only to minimize cost. In the presence of uncertainty, a risk premium may be imposed on the NPV calculation by employing some (typically arbitrarily chosen) risk-adjusted discount rate, and appropriate sensitivity and scenario analyses may be performed. In addition, the expected internal rate of return (IRR) is often also calculated, indicating the (implicit) discount rate that yields an NPV of zero. This is then often compared with some hurdle rate imposed by the investor for a particular type or class of project that makes sure that the risk taken does not lead to a reduction in the investor's credit rating, as this would raise the cost of debt financing (Gross et al., 2007).

In the presence of uncertainty and the often irreversible nature of power generation investment, standard NPV calculations are inadequate and therefore need to be complemented or replaced by improved methods. Two such complementary approaches, which are used more and more often in energy studies, involve the application of real options (RO) theory (Dixit & Pindyck, 1994; Trigeorgis, 1996) and mean-variance portfolio (MVP) theory (Markowitz, 1952). A useful survey on project valuation between traditional discounted cash flow (DCF) modeling and RO valuation has been provided by Mandron (2000), among others. For a useful review of the limits of traditional DCF approaches to deal with (multiple) uncertainties, (technological and/or managerial) flexibility and risk diversification, and the usefulness of probabilistic valuation models – such as Monte Carlo simulation – for assessing power generation technologies in liberalized markets, see for example Roques et al. (2006).

17.2.1.1 Real Options Theory

In principle, uncertainty may affect the optimal timing, the type, or the optimal size of an investment (van Mieghem, 2003). RO theory (sometimes also referred to as 'new investment theory') deals with situations of irreversible investments under uncertainty. In RO theory, the optimal timing of such an irreversible investment is influenced by the option value of waiting that arises from keeping the option to invest alive (i.e., from postponing the investment until better information is available that helps to reduce uncertainty). In this sense, project evaluations based on RO theory are more selective than standard DCF calculations, as the latter does not include the requirement that the expected return on an investment also has to compensate for the foregone value of waiting. Quantifying the value of the flexibility of investment alternatives proves useful in utility planning (Kaslow & Pindyck, 1994; Lu et al., 2006).

Depending on the circumstances and assumptions made, increased levels of uncertainty (measured by the volatility of influential variables, such as fuel input or electricity output prices) may actually accelerate investment, which at first sight seems paradoxical, especially if time to build is substantial or if there are important first-mover advantages (e.g., Driver et al., 2008).

The literature on power generation investment under uncertainty is growing rapidly. The idea here is not to provide an exhaustive survey, but rather to give a taste of the richness and diversity of studies that have been added to the literature in recent years. Botterud et al. (2005) and Botterud and Korpås (2007), for instance, introduce stochastic dynamic modeling, where the impact of uncertain load growth on electricity price is explicitly modeled and the impact of capacity payments is studied. Keppo and Lu (2003) study the case of a large producer that affects the electricity price in the framework of a RO model. They find that the price effect of dominant producers has to be accounted for if companies are unable to hedge this price effect in the financial markets and if there is a lack of competition on the investment opportunity. Murto et al. (2004) develop an investment timing model in an oligopolistic market for a homogeneous commodity and stochastic demand. In an asymmetry case, where one of the firms can only make lumpy investments, they illustrate the trade-off between the flexibility value and economies of scale. Other research has focused on the impact of operational characteristics (constraints) on the valuation of generation assets (e.g., Gardner & Zhuang, 2000; Deng & Oren, 2003). Specifically, Gardner and Zhuang (2000) focus on plant operation characteristics (e.g., minimum up and down times, minimum start-up time, minimum generation level, response time constraints, non-constant heat rate) as important influencing factors that make the plant valuation problem path-dependent and that determine the plant value and optimal operating policy. Pati et al. (2000) illustrate how RO valuation can be applied to distributed generation interconnection, while Siddiqui and Maribu (2008) study investment in power generation and heat exchanger equipment in a micro grid. In a decentralized power generation context involving renewables and uncertainty, Fleten et al. (2007) and Bøckman et al. (2008) show optimal investment strategies based on RO modeling. The latter investigates investments in small-scale hydro power plants when the electricity price is uncertain. The authors simulate the production size and investment costs, which are then used to find the value of the RO and the (unique) price limit where no investment would be made. Näsäkkälä and Fleten (2005) study the flexibility of an investor holding a license to build a gas-fired power plant with respect to the optimal investment timing and the choice of the production strategy (baseload or peakload). Chaton and Guillerminet (2007) model investment in power generation capacity under imperfect competition and compare EU emission trading versus feed-in tariffs (in the case of France). A particular feature of their analysis is that the investment options are sequential. Fuss et al. (2008) study the impact of market-driven price volatility combined with changing climate policy regimes and find that investors in carbon-saving technology might actually invest earlier than if the actual price path had been known beforehand, and later if policy uncertainty prevails. This is because if learning about policy commitment is more valuable than investing immediately in mitigation technology, then the option value exceeds the value of the technology, so that the investor prefers waiting for better information. Finally, Roques (2008) studies the optimal power generation technology choice for new entrants in liberalized markets, taking account of operational flexibility and contractual arrangements. In a comparative analysis of nuclear, coal, and gas technology, he finds that, in the absence of long-term fixed-price power purchase contracts, the combined-cycle gas turbine is the preferred option for new entrants, as with the close correlation between gas and electricity prices in many markets the cash flows are 'self-hedged'.

17.2.1.2 Risk-adequate Discount Rates – CAPM, Portfolio Analysis

Generally speaking, investment risks concerning the electricity supply system have to be considered from both an investor's (e.g., expected profitability) and a societal point of view (e.g., security of supply, environmental concerns). We look mainly at the investor's perspective here.

Investors increasingly take account of differences in risk levels when assessing the expected returns on different investments. Moreover, assets in the electricity supply industry are characterized by high asset specificity and long lead times for planning and construction, which increases the uncertainty about expected profits from such investments further. Hence, investors will ask for a risk premium, or risk-adjusted discount rate.

The capital asset pricing model (CAPM), introduced in the 1960s (Sharpe, 1964; Lintner, 1965), enables the use of such risk-adjusted, market-based discount rates in project valuation. Interestingly, the CAPM has long been used in financial markets, but its use is relatively new in the energy economics and energy finance literature (e.g., Awerbuch, 1993; Kahn & Stoft, 1993; Bolinger et al., 2002). In its simplest form, the CAPM states that the expected return on an individual asset above the risk-free rate is proportional to the systematic (or non-diversifiable) risk. The risk premium imposed on an asset is beta times the risk premium on the market portfolio, where beta measures the degree of co-movement between the asset's return and the market portfolio return. The simple model is at the same time compelling due to its simplicity and very restrictive, as it only applies if investors' access to capital (at a constant interest rate) is infinite, they hold perfectly diversified portfolios, and they do not face any transaction costs. The restrictiveness in the formulation, however, implies rather poor empirical estimates of the market risk premium, which has led to considerable criticism over the years (e.g., Fama & French, 1992; Kothari & Shanken, 1998). An important aspect for estimating the risk premium are expectations, which in rapidly evolving markets can be expected to change significantly. Advocates of the CAPM argue that it is better to estimate the risk premia and betas, despite measurement problems, rather than to assume some arbitrarily chosen values.

In addition to the CAPM, mean-variance portfolio (MVP) theory (Markowitz, 1952) may be used to find efficient portfolios and to explicitly account for the diversification effect arising from idiosyncratic risk mitigation by mixing assets with low or no correlation in their expected returns. For power generation analysis, an increasing number of studies has been added to the literature in recent years (e.g., Awerbuch & Berger, 2003; Awerbuch, 2006; Krey & Zweifel, 2006; Madlener & Wenk, 2008; Roques et al., 2008). Most of these studies demonstrate that new renewable energy technologies can be beneficial to generation asset portfolios even if they are more expensive than conventional ones or yield a negative expected return on investment if individually assessed.

17.2.2 Risk Management Strategies

Investors in power generation assets need to adapt to changing investment risks. While in the course of market liberalization it was expected that financial instruments would develop rapidly to provide investors with hedging opportunities against future electricity or fuel price developments, these markets have evolved rather slowly, forcing investors to seek for other means of hedging their risks. Apart from the portfolio approach described in the previous section, investors might also choose to hedge their risks by means of long-term contracts, by the integration of generation with retail business, by growing in size, and by mergers between electricity and gas companies (cf. IEA, 2003a, p.25). Note also that a firm's attitude to risk can have a decisive impact on the optimal investment strategy in the case of some irreversible investment under uncertainty (e.g., Bell & Campa, 1997). Other research, such as Deng et al. (2001), shows how so-called 'exotic' electricity options (e.g., spark and locational spread options) can be used to construct ROs valuation formulas for generation and transmission assets, thus providing an important new tool for risk management of power generation assets.

17.2.3   Investment Timing and Policy Impacts

As a final issue before moving on to the history of the electricity sector and the question of whether there is indeed a changing paradigm in sight, we briefly discuss the timing of investment and policy impact issues in a competitive market environment (Joskow, 2006; Finon et al., 2004; Gross et al., 2007). If flexibility exists to delay investments and if electricity prices are low, i.e., near the short-run marginal cost of power production, then there might be too little incentive to invest in generating capacity. Later, when capacity reserves diminish and the market becomes tighter and tighter, a boom phase may be triggered during which new capacity is brought on line in order to gain from the higher prices and to gain market shares. Overall, such boom–bust cycles can lead to cycles in both electricity prices and security of supply. Expected policy intervention may nurture these cycles (aggravated by the herding behavior of investors), and affect the planning and development of power generation projects especially if investors have to deal with power sales in multiple jurisdictions (Walls et al., 2007). Auctioning of reliability options has been suggested to mitigate the problem of such boom–bust cycles of capacity addition (Cramton & Stoft, 2008).

Ideally, policy-makers would take into account revenue and risk considerations of the investors (i.e., their optimal investment strategies under uncertainty, also with respect to action taken by competitors), rather than focusing solely on (levelized) cost minimization (cf. Thomas, 2007). Given that companies may follow different investment strategies even if they are exposed to the same market conditions (e.g., because of differences in risk attitude, capital endowment, or market strategy), however, it seems neither necessary nor practical for policy-makers to attempt precise anticipation of energy companies' investment plans. A further aspect is that policy instability, e.g., with respect to supportive public energy policies for particular investments, increases uncertainty and hence the risk premiums imposed by investors, thus causing additional barriers to investment and an incentive for 'gaming' (i.e., behavior aimed at strategically influencing the behavior of other players in the market). Finally, opportunistic behavior by regulators and regulated utilities in a regulated market setting where cost disallowances play an important role can also have a significant behavioral impact on investment in generation capacity (Lyon & Mayo, 2005).

17.3   Changing Paradigms?

Do we currently see signs of changing paradigms in the electricity supply and demand systems, or simply a return to the original electrical power generation and power distribution concepts? To answer this question, lessons learned from the more than 150-year history of electrical engineering must be revisited, as electrical power systems are not only large, but also very complex systems. Integrating new technologies into the existing infrastructure has, in many cases, been proven to be very difficult. Detailed analysis of its history shows that the current state of the largest and most expensive man-made network, i.e., the electrical alternating current (AC) power grid, depended first on technology breakthroughs, which enabled technically large-scale power transmission, distribution, and wholesale, but also on savvy investors who were willing and able to provide capital and take (a calculated) risk.

17.3.1 Historical Overview

Although electrical power generators were developed first for military and later for public (medium-voltage) arc-lighting applications in Europe, the commercialization of electrical power and implementation of its infrastructure was first realized in the US. These early units, first built by Edison, each comprised a direct current (DC) generator powered by a coal-fired steam engine (the latter had an efficiency of approximately 6%). The very first unit sold by Edison was taken into service in the home of J.P. Morgan on 8 June 1882. Today, such decentralized systems would be called micro-generators (power rating between 1 and 100 kW). To deliver electrical lighting to the masses and 'reach great fortunes' central stations had to be built soon after (Jonnes, 2004). Still, when Edison turned on the power switch of his first commercial central station, power was delivered to 300 of his newly developed (low-voltage incandescent) light bulbs from a central station where technicians ran steam engines driving 'dynamos', i.e., DC generators. This event also took place in the year 1882. J.P. Morgan was one of the investors in this costly grand project; apparently he had electrified his house as a test case, and he clearly understood that electric lighting could become a major disruptive technology competing against the widely used gas lighting systems. Clearly, as an investor, J.P. Morgan was trying to explore market opportunities for electrical technology in general (Jonnes, 2004). Today, these central stations would be considered (decentralized) mini-power stations (here defined by the authors as power generator units rated between 0.5 MW and 10 MW). However, the DC technology that was developed and implemented by Edison at that time had now reached its limits. Indeed, incandescent light bulbs represent low-voltage loads (115 V). Consequently, the DC generators had to produce low-voltage DC. To transport power, thick copper cables (Edison preferred cables for safety reasons, even when their installation came at a higher cost than overhead lines) were needed. Economically, this low-voltage concept only made sense for distances of up to half a mile. Hence, many 'central stations' were necessary to power a city or large city blocks. As soon as in 1883, newspapers were complaining about smoke and dust problems caused by these decentralized stations spread around cities. Note that the quest for lighting was so great that engineers did not consider using the waste heat from the steam engines, for instance for heating purposes, leaving a major economic advantage of decentralized power generation unexploited.

17.3.2 Paradigm Shift During Electrification of the US

A new technology, first demonstrated in Europe by Gaulard and Gibbs, but imported into the US and perfected by G. Westinghouse, would change the way electricity was produced and transported for ever. This technical innovation, which had nothing to do with power generation or consumer products, remained more or less invisible to the wider public and was initially called a 'secondary generator' or 'voltage converter'; today it is known as a 'transformer'. Using a Siemens AC generator, a step-up transformer and step-down 'converter stations', Westinghouse was able to demonstrate that distribution of electrical power through thin, low-cost copper (overhead) wires was economically viable. Based on this technology, Westinghouse would win the 1893 Chicago World Fair contract, under which the Westinghouse Electric Company installed 250,000 light bulbs. These light bulbs were lit from a distant machine hall. Based on this success, the company secured the contract for the Niagara Hydro-Power project, which was for many years the largest power generation station in the world. Hence, the transformer, a technical device capable of converting AC power from one voltage level to another, enabled the concept of centralized power production, transmission, and distribution. Interestingly, in the case of the Niagara Power Station, this first large power station used hydro-power, which was considered a 'clean' – i.e., low-pollutant and renewable – and low-cost power source. DC power stations were still built when electrical power needed to be converted into mechanical (motion) power using electromechanical power converters, i.e., electrical motors. The invention of the AC poly-phase machine, today called 'induction machine', by Tesla and the realization of the Ward-Leonhard AC-to-DC rotating converter would finally tip this balance in favor of AC centralized power stations and eliminate all decentralized mini-power systems. It was indeed more economical and efficient to produce AC power at the medium voltage (MV) level using large generators, e.g., driven by hydro power, convert this MV AC to high-voltage using transformers, transport this AC power over long distances, convert high-voltage AC back to the medium-voltage distribution level and, finally, step it down further to the low-voltage single-phase grid using transformers. Parallel to this development, metering and circuit breaker technology was developed to make AC power a reliable and safe energy carrier. As historian Jill Jonnes points out in her recent and very interesting book *"Empires of Light"*, this whole development came at a huge investment cost. Once electrical power technology was developed, it turned out to be so successful that a very large infrastructure and very large investments were needed to satisfy the growing markets. Interestingly, both key players, Edison and Westinghouse, would soon lose control over their electrical companies, partly because of rising material (copper) costs, an international economic downturn and – as a result of high investments made earlier – cash flow problems. Money was a medium that J.P. Morgan's firm had plenty of, and by 1900 J.P. Morgan ultimately held most of the stock (and thus control) in both companies, i.e., General Electric (Edison) and Westinghouse Electric.

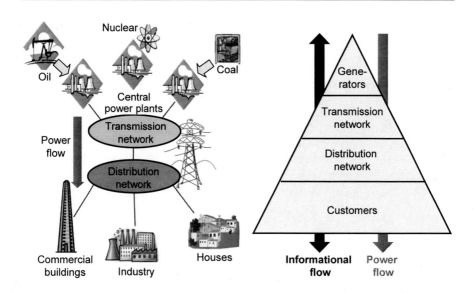

Figure 17.2: Classic electrical power grid

Today, the electrical power grid still follows the design originally laid out by Westinghouse and well-known electrical engineers of the 'first hour'. Classic electrical power grids are designed 'top down'. Large centralized power generation units generate electrical power, which is transported via a high-voltage transmission network and distributed locally using a medium-voltage distribution network to low-voltage loads at the consumer level (Iov & Blaabjerg, 2007). The current centralized, or top-down, system (see Figure 17.2) implements improvements such as GE's three-phase AC system, Brown's (co-founder of Brown, Boveri and Cie. or BBC, later ABB) high-voltage transmission system, Siemens AC generators, etc. The concept of centralized (top-down) power production was based on a key enabling technology, i.e., transformers, which are devices needed not only to convert power between voltage levels, but also to limit fault currents, enabling fault coordination. The fact that this is almost forgotten today, even by engineers, can be explained by the fact that transformers are electrical power converters. Consequently, they do not store or generate energy, which makes them very efficient, silent, and relatively small. In other words, the key enabling technology turned out not to be so spectacular. Today, transformers are a commodity product and are being produced in a very competitive market environment at near-marginal (i.e., mainly material) cost. Transformers require basically only three material types: silicon–steel alloys for the magnetic circuit, copper (or aluminum) for the windings, and insulation materials. In addition, to gain control over the market, only large investment firms could expect a major return on investment, because a large customer base had to be served (and metered). The initial investment in the centralized AC infrastructure and power stations was so high that even the largest companies at that time could not bear the cost alone. These large investments and the related economies of scale created monopolies, which soon after needed to be controlled by governments to guarantee fair prices and secure reliable power delivery. Consequently, the ambition of engineers to harness hydro-power in some (distant) locations as a cheap and 'eternal' source of primary energy came at much higher investment costs than anticipated at the outset. Until the development of nuclear power plants (in the 1950s), coal- and heavy fuel oil-burning plants became cheap alternatives (as they are still seen even today) for generating electricity, because their investment cost was much lower. Here too, as dust filter technology (electrostatic precipitators) would not be developed until the 1970s, to avoid adverse side-effects in densely populated cities caused by air pollution, distant, centralized power production seemed to be the only acceptable way. Even municipalities, which could use the waste heat from their power units, often had to follow this remote centralized power generation model.

17.3.3   Distributed Generation

Distributed generation (DG) refers to electricity production at or near the place of consumption (cf. e.g., Madlener & Wohlgemuth, 1999; Ackermann et al., 2001; CBO, 2003; Peperman et al., 2005). In contrast to centralized generation that usually feeds into the high or medium grid, DG is connected directly to the distribution network, either on the customer or the utility side of the meter. So far DG only accounts for a low share of the total electricity supply, although there is reason to believe that DG could meet a much larger share of future electricity demand (Pfeifenberger et al., 1998). Typically, DG means 'on-site' generation, owned and operated (not necessarily) by retail customers. Applications differ from the infrastructure for electricity supply used for decades (centralized system), and may range from a few kilowatts to several megawatts. A variety of technologies can be used, such as cogeneration, micro-turbines, steam turbines, Sterling engines, fuel cells, photovoltaics, or wind turbines (for useful reviews see, e.g., Madlener & Schmid, 2003; Onovwiona & Ugursal, 2006).

The economics of DG are somewhat hard to assess and generalize, owing to the many case-specific grid issues, but also to the performance characteristics of many new generation and grid components (for a simplified approach see Hoff et al., 1996). Also, it is quite impossible to assess the required DG investment costs and related system upgrade costs, and thus the potential net benefit of a transition toward DG. For instance, unitary capital costs are likely to be higher than for centralized technology, whereas transmission and distribution losses will be lower. Additional (potential) advantages to be mentioned are: modular design allowing sequential investment according to demand needs, peak-load shaving (reducing the variable cost of centralized generation), deferred investment in centralized generation capacity, and shorter planning and construction times. Recent work on modeling of the economics and market adoption of DG has been done by Maribu and associates (Maribu, 2006). The drivers of change toward DG are a mix of regulatory authorities on the one hand (transformation management) and market forces on the other (technological innovation, relative advantage of DG over centralized technology) (IEA, 2002).

Market liberalization, and in particular the fact that any power generation firm or municipality could now sell its electrical energy (expressed in kWh or MWh), and the fact that primary energy prices have soared have made alternative electrical power sources more attractive. Concerns about anthropogenic climate change, mainly attributable to massive burning of fossil fuels worldwide, have given additional impetus to the exploration of renewable power sources such as biogas, wind, and solar energy, including photovoltaic systems. Small-scale mini-power systems (ranging from 1 to 10 MW), for example in the form of combined heat-and-power generators, are being introduced again. These units take advantage of a feature that was lost early on when large, centralized power stations were built, namely that in addition to electrical energy consumption, the waste heat of the plant (based on a steam turbine, combustion engine, or gas turbine) can now be used for local heating or cooling (using heat pumps) of buildings, factories, or city quarters. Taking advantage of the fact that the large losses in long-distance transportation mean that heating and cooling always was and always will be a decentralized process, these mini-power units can achieve a higher exergy rating, i.e., a higher capability to extract useful energy from a given amount of primary energy. Renewable power sources, such as wind generators (approx. $0.5 \, \text{kW}_{\text{peak}}$ per m^2) and photovoltaic systems ($0.15 \, \text{kW}_{\text{peak}}$ per m^2) are characterized by their extremely low specific energy density. Hence, large areas (e.g., in terms of blades of wind turbines and PV module arrays) are required for these plants. Nevertheless, scaling laws and economic incentives (at about 50 €/MWh) have driven wind power generators up to the 5-MW class. Hence, they have become mini-power systems and are now connected to the MV distribution grid. Photovoltaic systems (economically viable today at about 450 €/MWh) are still more common in the micro-power range and are typically connected to the low-voltage grid. Most likely, this scenario will persist for a long time, even when subsidies diminish or disappear, simply because low-voltage (mostly residential) energy costs are evidently the highest (150-200 €/MWh) and can offset the higher PV cost more easily.

17.3.4 Economies of Scale and Technological Lock-in

Today, young engineers still learn about two major advantages of large centralized power plants and the top-down AC power grid. These can be summarized under the headings 'scaling laws' (in economics jargon 'economies of scale') and 'safety or coordination of protective gear'. The scaling law is based on the notion that larger machines (generators, transformers) and power plants can be built at higher efficiency and lower cost. This scaling law is based on the fact that, at full-rated power, the losses and the auxiliary power needed to operate (and cool) these units become relatively smaller compared with their net output power rating. Hence, higher efficiencies can be obtained by 'up-scaling'. This drove engineers to build generators rated from 350 MW (1950) up to their practical limits of 1.3 GW

(1980), while gaining just over 1% in (electrical) efficiency on generators and transformers. However, it is important to point out that these scaling laws are only valid as long as they are applied to the same type of machinery or power station concepts while operating at rated power. In a government-controlled or monopolistic electricity business that was growing this scaling model was taken for granted. However, nowadays, it is important for power engineers to look at the entire picture: most power stations are based on the so-called Carnot-type steam cycle, so that they have a (high-temperature) boiler and a (low-temperature) condenser, thereby creating a temperature difference that maintains a continuous flow of the medium (typically water and steam). Thermodynamics teaches us that the maximum efficiency of such a power plant (using a 100% efficient turbine) is equal to $\Delta T/T_{max}$. Today, single Carnot-cycle efficiencies of 'only' 45-47% can be economically achieved owing to material and construction limitations of furnaces and steam turbines. In contrast, electrical equipment today reaches efficiencies of up to 99%. Hence, improving the efficiency of transformers and generators by scaling for larger units can no longer be the key driver in future power plants, but rather cost reduction, in particular of the life-cycle cost, should become the main design goal. Actually, scaling electrical equipment to larger units becomes counterproductive, as they become impossible to transport and the investment risks and development and lead times are often too high and too long for today's business environment in a liberalized market. In addition, since fossil fuels as primary energy source became cheap after the oil crisis in the 1970s, over the past 25 years little has been spent on R&D directed at the potential use of higher temperature materials or alternative power station concepts that could realize higher efficiencies even at lower power ratings. Hence, it is clear now that the 'scaling law' became a self-fulfilling prophecy in the power engineering field. For example, combined gas and steam cycle power plants that reach efficiencies of up to 60% were not introduced into the market until the last 15 years, even though the concept was developed much earlier. It will be shown below that technological breakthroughs in the area of electrical energy conversion have now been overlooked for over 50 years, while these energy conversion techniques could have changed the way we produce and distribute electrical power to give more flexible and efficient systems. As new developments are in conflict with the omnipotent 'scaling law', and because primary energy was so cheap, it apparently made no sense to invest in these potentials or take the inherent investment risks, creating a situation of technological lock-in.

17.3.5 Safety Considerations

Maximum safety must be the goal of any engineering field. In AC systems, engineers take advantage of the alternating current zero crossing to extinguish the arc that occurs in circuit breakers or fuses when there is an attempt to interrupt the current. As a result, AC circuit breakers can be built smaller and at a lower cost than DC circuit breakers. Today, vacuum arc circuit breakers can interrupt a maximum short-circuit current of 60 kA (in practice, this current must be limited by the impedance of the transformer, another important feature of transformers). These safety functions are important to minimize the impact of a disturbance in the grid. Short circuits are one of the most frequent faults in power grids, and to guarantee safe operation of the grid with high power quality (few outages, no major voltage dips or frequency changes) circuit breakers or fuses play a key role. When a short circuit occurs on the low-voltage side (where it is most likely to happen), 'automatic' low-voltage circuit breakers or fuses installed close to the fault are supposed to clear this circuit from the supply (they can only do this at the zero crossing of the AC current, when the arc in the breaker is briefly extinguished). If they fail to extinguish the arc, the fault current keeps flowing. Hence, to prevent further hazards the main circuit breaker or the breaker that protects the feeder should now clear the fault (even though more consumers will lose power as a result). If the entire local low-voltage grid cannot protect itself, the MV circuit breaker of the transformer substation will respond (disconnecting even more consumers or loads). Clearly, coordinating transformer and line impedances with breaker ratings is a major engineering feat that was first solved economically in AC grids. Engineering experience has taught us that having redundancy at all levels (high-voltage, medium-voltage and low-voltage grids) in protection functions (also including ground fault interruptors) is key in making electrical power distribution one of the safest energy carriers today. No engineer will back off from these (international) standards, and any new technology should comply with them or offer even greater protection. Merging new technologies can become difficult when they cannot be coordinated with the existing infrastructure.

17.3.6   The Power Electronics Revolution

It should be pointed out that the use of renewable power sources has been made possible by a completely new energy conversion technology, mentioned above, that first saw the light of day in 1958, when the first power semiconductor devices were introduced into the market by the General Electric Company. Today, this engineering field is called power electronics. The Power Electronics Society of the Institute of Electrical and Electronic Engineers (IEEE) defines power electronics as an efficient electrical energy conversion means using power semiconductor devices. Whereas most people are well aware of the achievements made in microelectronics (e.g., Moore's law), few are aware of the fact that, since 1958, a similar revolution has taken place in the power electronics field. The power that can be converted and, most importantly, controlled dynamically by means of a single (silicon) power semiconductor device has steadily grown from 5 kVA to 60 MVA, and various approaches for improvements are likely to push this figure further upwards even based on conventional silicon technology (Köllensperger, 2006, 2007). Even in 1972, the first DC transmission systems were built using power semiconductors (silicon-controlled rectifiers or thyristors) with power ratings of 350 MW (IEEE Report, 1981). Today, power electronic converter stations are being built that transmit 6.4 GW of DC power at the 1.6-MV level (Astrom & Lescale, 2006). When gas is pumped from Norway to the Netherlands, for exam-

ple, this is done by compressors driven by 30-MW machines fed by power electronic converters, which in their turn control the speed of the compressor to control pressure at high efficiency. The variable frequency power of a wind turbine is
converted to fixed-frequency AC grid power using power electronic converters,
and the (low-voltage) DC power generated by PV cells is converted into AC using
DC-to-DC converters and DC-to-AC inverters. One can truly state that without
power electronics few renewable sources would function today. Furthermore, the
energy efficiency of many processes would decline dramatically without power
electronics. Once again, a technology that converts electrical power (voltage or
current and frequency) is delivering breakthrough concepts as the transformer (capable only of voltage or current conversion) did in the early history of electrical
power systems. Power electronics, as it matures and becomes more integrated and
standardized (commodity products), is now considered a key enabling technology
for future power generation, transportation, and distribution systems because it
enables us to convert AC to DC and vice versa. It is estimated by the Electrical
Power Research Institute (EPRI) that more than 50% of all electrical power flows
once through a power semiconductor, and not just copper (Hingorani, 1988)!
These power converters allow grid operators to eliminate several key problems
that arise in AC systems when more decentralized power generation is implemented (Meyer & De Doncker, 2004; De Doncker et al., 2007).

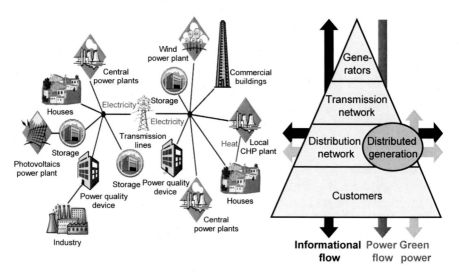

Figure 17.3: Decentralized power generation

In conclusion, the electrical grid will and can evolve into a system that from a
power flow perspective, is no longer top-down, but has more and more power
feeding in vertically, primarily at the (decentralized) medium-voltage level, as
Figure 17.3 illustrates. Decentralized power generators, currently mostly wind
energy and combined heat and power stations, can have profound effects on coor-

dination and stability of the medium-voltage distribution network (Iov & Blaabjerg, 2007). Today, this vertical feed-in of power is mostly from renewable power sources (as was the first large central power station at Niagara Falls). Appropriately, Frede Blaabjerg calls it the "green power flow" (Blaabjerg et al., 2004; Chen et al., 2006). Smart engineers and savvy business people have understood that scaling laws (of classic power plants) no longer offer the same economic benefits as they used to. In a competitive, liberalized market big is not always beautiful, and such goals as high exergy (attained by combining heat and power) or the utilization of renewable primary energies (avoidance of CO_2 certificate costs) are now pursued. We need to point out that this model holds as long as no other 'disruptive' technology comes along. One such disruptive technology, which is being researched intensively on a global scale again, could be nuclear fusion. As soon as fusion becomes economically viable (speculated to happen by 2050), large 2-GW power stations may become the norm again in densely populated, industrialized areas. However, decentralized vertical feed-in power will have been established by that time and will most likely remain, owing to its low investment costs and the fact that low-exergy power plants will probably remain the most economical option.

Owing to this vertical 'green power' influx, the classic AC grid is reaching stringent limits, and comparison with DC distribution grids is revealing some disadvantages of AC grids. At least six reasons can be identified:

(1) *Limits of protection:* The complexity of coordinating protective gear is reaching its limits owing to the many decentralized, dispersed power stations.

(2) *Excessive breaker currents:* Short-circuit currents in MV distribution systems now easily exceed the maximum rating of existing breaker technology when many generators are connected in parallel to a common point of coupling or feeder. The only way to deal with this problem is to install DC distribution systems or fast hybrid AC breakers. These breakers use fast power electronic devices to disconnect the fault before current can reach the short-circuit current. Studies have shown that this technology is cheaper in DC systems (having only two terminals) than in three-phase AC systems (e.g., Meyer et al., 2004).

(3) *Volatility of renewables:* Many renewable power sources cannot be controlled in the same way as classic power stations can (an exception is biomass). Their energy supply varies stochastically according to seasonal and meteorological circumstances and is difficult to forecast. Electrical storage systems (batteries, compressed gas, super-conductive energy storage systems, etc.) are very expensive devices and, except for pumped-storage hydro stations, are still under development. Hence, the AC grid, with little or no storage capacity of its own, as it was designed for a top-down controlled power flow, reaches limits in capacity and voltage stability especially at the distribution level. To maintain voltage control, reactive power (circulating power or reactive impedances, i.e., inductors and capacitors) need to be con-

trolled, and this so-called VAR compensation is relatively expensive. Power generation companies often like to ignore the cost of this infrastructure.

(4) *Grid capacity constraints:* Often renewable power, especially wind power, is generated at a considerable distance from the consumers. Hence, this power source appears not to be as highly decentralized as was initially planned. Offshore wind farms are actually large centralized power stations. The European AC high-voltage transportation grid was designed to keep the grid stable when a large unit (largest power units are about 1 GW) drops off line. As a consequence, HV AC transport lines can usually handle about 1-2 GW of power. One should understand that these are very narrow 'highways' for power transfer. For example, in Germany the total peak power of wind power now already reaches 24 GW (i.e., 30% of the total installed capacity of about 80 GW). Therefore, more transport capacity is needed to augment the wind power base, which can only be added to the existing power generation base (power is still needed even when no wind power is generated). Yet, few cities allow construction of HV overhead lines ('not in my backyard' (NIMBY) syndrome) and would prefer cable technology as it has a lower impact on the environment.

(5) *Lower losses in long-distance transport:* However, with cables, another disadvantage of AC versus DC becomes clear: AC power cannot be transported as efficiently with cables as DC power. Indeed, with power electronics, high-voltage DC (HVDC) transmission systems (DC current with thyristors or DC voltage with turn-off devices, e.g., transistors) not only can exceed the transmission power of AC systems, but have also turned out to be more efficient over long distances, since DC has no skin effect (i.e., electric current tends to flow more at and near the surface of an AC conductor) and eddy current losses (i.e., stray fields that induce circulating currents in the wires or in adjacent conductive materials). Most importantly, DC does not have to deal with the reactive voltage or current drop of AC lines and cables. Actually, the DC cable acts as a smoothing impedance, which helps voltage or current regulation.

(6) *Health impacts of electrosmog:* Aside from the visual impact on the landscape, the fact that the health impact of stray fields of AC transmission lines, in particular under unbalanced operation, remains a disputed topic has considerably limited acceptance of AC overhead lines in developed, densely populated areas. As humankind is constantly living in the earth's DC magnetic field, it is believed that DC stray fields (of lower magnitude) of DC cables are completely safe.

Taking these six arguments into account, it has become clear to the engineering community that future power grids should consider and evaluate more DC transmission and distribution systems using state-of-the-art power electronics and DC cable technology (von Bloh & De Doncker, 2000). Note that, with power electronics and improved cable technology, the electrical engineering field has come full circle on the way it can implement power generation and power transmission and distribution. Power electronics, which does not require AC for transformers to convert power, can integrate AC and DC power sources in a flexible manner and eliminates several shortcomings of AC grids (which were well understood by its developers, but no DC-based alternative pathway was possible at that time). Actually, the AC versus DC debate has quietened down with the advent of power electronics, as efficient conversion of one source into another is now possible. Figure 17.4 shows a possible concept for the future power supply of a city and how the DC distribution loops around cities, referred to as (medium-voltage) 'DC cells'. DC distribution cells are interconnected via efficient DC-to-DC converters to exchange energy and to tab energy from HVDC transmission systems, thus providing redundancy and secure power. Power electronic inverters convert DC to AC power at load points (substations). Battery energy storage systems (BESS) and pumped hydro storage systems (PHSS) provide storage capacity to support the grid at peak load.

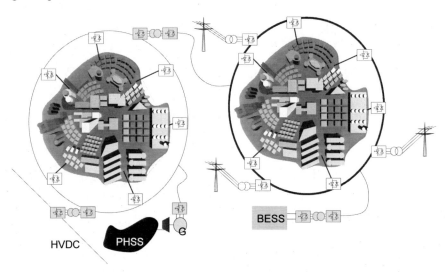

Figure 17.4: DC distribution as a part of the power grid of the future

DC-based systems are not only more energy efficient when more decentralized power generation is taking place, but are also easier to interface using power electronic converters to energy storage systems and renewable power generators (no need for ride-through functions or VAR compensation). As the grid infrastructure will need constant change (owing to aging and changing power requirements), power electronics technology will be able to merge steadily into the power grid. The choice of AC or DC will and can depend more and more on economic (investment costs and life-cycle costs) and ecological requirements. Of course, technical requirements such as safety, redundancy, efficiency, flexibility, and power quality will remain criteria that impact on the design of the infrastructure. As DC power distribution causes no eddy currents, future superconductive cables, which have zero losses only when they carry DC currents, may give the DC medium voltage cell-type distribution considerable cost- and energy-efficiency advantages, to the extent that high-voltage power transmission systems become obsolete.

Engineers are exploring the potential advantages that power electronic converters will bring and are not focusing their R&D on DC transmission alone, but exploring all facets that power electronics, communication, and information technology can bring. It is actually amazing that the pan-European AC power system, for example, runs synchronized at 50 Hz from Siberia all the way to southern Spain, and this with no communication at all! The information used by power stations to control active and reactive power is actually entailed in the AC waveform itself: namely, its frequency and voltage magnitude. Based on these signals, power stations can derive how much active and reactive power needs to be provided. Communication via telephone (dispatching) was only done to maximize efficiency. Nowadays, communication and measuring systems are being integrated on a large scale and at high cost. These systems are digital, much faster than telephone lines, but basically, in a liberalized market, they are used to help the operator to maximize profits by minimizing operating costs. One advantage of power electronic converters, which are needed for instance to stabilize the AC grid or to provide VAR compensation, is that they are equipped with an embedded digital control and communication unit to receive commands and to compute the complex control algorithms that need to be executed by the power converter. Usually, these units have plenty of processing power to diagnose assets in the grid. Linking these smart power converters (in the engineering community often referred to as 'power electronic building blocks' (PEBBs)) via communication systems provides new information on the state of the systems, enabling (for example) preventive maintenance and more efficient operation and control (Ericsen et al., 2006). It is believed that linking power electronics and communication in PEBBs will provide greater flexibility to the AC grid at lower cost (Schwartzenberg, 2003). In addition, on the consumer side, these PEBBs are implemented not only to convert energy but also to control processes, as has been done successfully over the past 25 years in factory automation. One of the main reasons for using power electronics was to gain flexibility (variable speed machine, robots, production of DC power, etc.) and thus to save energy. The first major application of power electronic converters was to vary the speed of the fixed-speed AC induction motor (invented by Tesla and touted by Westinghouse as the last missing stone in AC power systems) by varying its frequency. Many blowers, compressors, and pumps are driven by variable-speed induction motor drives to adjust electrical power to the flow of the medium, without wasting it in control valves, by-pass loops, or baffles. Modern heating, ventilation, and cooling systems are all equipped with AC inverters that control the speed of the compressor, enabling fast response and quiet whispering operation in steady state, a must in modern homes and hotels. In many applications, the pay-back period of the converters, compared with the fixed-speed solution, is less than 1 year (Steinke & Steimer, 2000).

17.4 Selected Examples

In the sections below, we briefly discuss two illustrative examples of technological change, based on communication and power electronics or PEBBs, that could have a profound impact on the future of the power sector: smart metering (Section 17.4.1) and micro-turbines with electronic gearboxes (Section 17.4.2).

17.4.1 Smart Metering

Traditionally, rising demand for electricity has by and large been met by expanding power supply capacity. The installation of so-called smart meters with displays where consumers can see their level of power consumption and its development over time, opens new opportunities for saving electricity and for providing incentives to change behavior.

Smart metering, combined with real-time pricing, can be expected not only to reduce overall electricity demand and to help shave demand peaks, but will also affect investment in power generation. If consumer behavior is affected by smart metering, demand can be expected to become more sensitive to price changes, and advanced electricity supply models should definitely endogenize load uncertainty. Bidirectional communication enables utilities to provide incentives for end-users to adjust consumption by shifting or reducing electricity demand, which can be used for active demand-side management (DSM), and it also allows improvements in the quality of demand forecasting. Taken together, it can lead to better capacity utilization of existing power plants, an improvement in the stability of the system (security of supply), and a better accommodation of fluctuating power supply from renewable energy sources (e.g., wind).

Unless regulators called for monthly billing, utilities or communal services have been reluctant to replace the classical Ferraris-wheel based energy meter with an electronic version. Indeed, apart from the considerably higher production cost of the electronic meter (about eight times more expensive), its installation cost and the cost of communication links (telephone modem, DSL or WLAN) have to be taken into account as well. In addition, communicating the data to a data center will cost as well and very few customers are willing to pay for this additional cost. Hence, to introduce electronic metering in developed countries (with classical metering systems in place) it is important that low-cost electronic metering and communication channels are developed. Of course, in large corporations, commercial buildings, business centers and office buildings electronic metering can be implemented more cost effectively, because the infrastructure to collect all data is already available. In this case, calibrated metering (0.1% accuracy) may not be needed when the metering is only used for internal billing and motivating specific user groups to save energy. Furthermore, it is technically possible to automatically switch on and off non-critical loads to avoid high peak power consumption ('peak-shaving'). Depending on contractual agreements, avoiding high peak power often leads to more attractive electricity prices, in particular for large energy consumers.

17.4.2   Variable Speed Mini-turbines with 'Electronic Gearbox'

Conventional gas turbines, owing to their operation at quasi-fixed speeds of rotation (as a result of their connection to the AC grid and its frequency), have low energy efficiencies at partial load operation, and their efficiency varies widely depending on the gas mix. Another disadvantage is the large volume and considerable weight of such systems. To maximize energy efficiency the speed has to be variably controlled (Kaikko et al., 2007). Power electronics not only facilitates safe and low-cost interconnection of DG technologies to the grid, it also provides an interesting opportunity to steer gas turbines via an 'electronic gearbox', and thus to uncouple the mechanical speed of the turbine completely from the frequency of the grid. Because the generator is directly connected to the turbine in this concept, there is no need for a mechanical gearbox and a transformer (Offringa & Duarte, 2000). This allows much higher speeds of operation and at the same time requires much lower volumes and lesser weight, which also potentially makes the technology economically more attractive (Davis, 2002).

During recent years, the increasing costs of fossil fuels and the impact of climate change have motivated more research on alternative supplies of electrical energy. As a result, the share of decentralized power systems in electric grids, the majority of which are based on volatile energy sources, such as wind power and photovoltaic, has increased significantly. A medium-size gas turbine system, being able to deliver power on demand, provides a means of compensating the fluctuating electricity production of renewable energy sources (Jardan et al., 2000; Jardan & Nagy, 2003).

Liberalization of the energy market has already augmented interest in the use of natural gas-, syngas-, and biogas-fired micro-turbines (up to 50 kW) to provide heat and electrical power locally (Pilavachi, 2002). Although these micro-turbines can deliver power on demand, they remain expensive and are too small to serve larger commercial facilities, industrial plants (1-5 MW), or communal energy sources economically. Furthermore, micro-turbines cannot easily stabilize the local distribution system of a medium-size city (~100 MW), because they represent too-low power and are connected typically to low-voltage networks. A fast-reacting, medium-size gas-fired power station is one solution to compensate fluctuating wind power in such a set-up. Basically, the concept of variable-speed micro-turbines, which consist of a low cost gas turbine that is speed controlled by an electronic gearbox (power electronic converter), are a potential solution for generating power 'on demand' when the concept is scaled up to the megawatt range. Besides the compensation of wind power, these systems could also be used for combined heat-and-power (CHP) production in industrial power grids.

In contrast to conventional turbine systems, these variable-speed turbine and generator (Vijlee et al., 2007) concepts have no mechanical gearbox. Furthermore, the medium-voltage transformer can be eliminated by using medium-voltage multi-level power converters. Hence, the entire system becomes lightweight and maintenance free (elimination of the bulky 50-Hz transformer and gearbox, the latter being prone to needing maintenance). The elimination of both gearbox and transformer also leads to a significant reduction in volume and weight, which simplifies transport and installation of the turbine system (plug-and-play). Moreover, the medium-voltage converter uncouples the generator speed from the grid frequency and therefore enables operation of the gas turbine at variable speed, leading to efficiency enhancements in part-load conditions. However, with regard to the envisaged output power range of several megawatts, the gearless topology leads to challenging specifications both for the generator (e.g., 15,000 rpm at 5 MW) and for the power electronic converter (Köllensperger, 2005).

17.5   Conclusions

In this chapter we have discussed aspects surrounding the topic of adequate investment in power generation in the light of risk arising from rapidly changing framework conditions and emerging new technologies that may lead to a paradigm shift in the power sector in the not-too-distant future. The major issues identified that are responsible for the changing boundary conditions are electricity market liberalization, problems affecting the environment and security of energy supply, which have arisen mainly from the excessive use of fossil fuels, technological change, capacity and other constraints, and policy and market risks emanating from these other developments.

Investors need to adapt and/or enrich their approaches to assess the adequacy of their investment projects and strategies. We have argued that new methods, such as the use of ROs theory and mean variance portfolio theory, are suited to complement traditional investment calculations based on simplistic NPV considerations. While RO theory helps to reveal the danger that high levels of uncertainty might be seen by investors as a reason to hang back for a very long time, thus fuelling supply security concerns owing to the resulting underinvestment in generation capacity and T&D infrastructure, portfolio analysis helps to identify the benefit of diversification, which is likely to foster renewables-based power generation units that typically feature much lower fuel price risk than, say, gas-fired power plants. Portfolio analysis also supports the idea of both adopting risk-adequate and technology-specific discount rates for investment calculations and searching for efficient portfolio choices (e.g., minimum risk for a given expected return level or, alternatively, maximum expected return for a given risk level).

Technically, DG poses new engineering challenges (e.g., voltage drops, line loadings, unbalanced networks). Substantial increases in DG also require changes to the electricity infrastructure if system reliability is to be maintained. Integration of increasing amounts of DG requires increased flexibility and operational management of the grid. Decentralized energy management systems will ease the balancing of distributed power sources against the load that has to be served. Regarding the expected paradigm shift, both towards a much higher share of DG and the establishing of 'smart grids' and 'smart metering', respectively, it remains to be seen how soon cost-effective new solutions can penetrate the market and what the eventual net benefits of these new technological solutions will be to the individual investors and to society as a whole. In line with the anticipated paradigm shift in the electricity system, there is no doubt that major investments will also be needed in innovation automation and distribution management systems.

Future investment in power generation will be burdened with high levels of risk and uncertainty, requiring increasingly sophisticated investment analysis, some of the forerunners of which (e.g., RO analysis, CAPM, portfolio analysis) and topics addressed so far in the energy literature have been discussed here. Finally, the tremendous investment requirements in the energy sector in decades to come, and in the electricity sector in particular, will also require enormous amounts of capital and tailored financing structures for the individual technologies concerned, and will thus likely attract much more attention to the so far largely neglected financing aspects.

References

Ackermann, T., Andersson, G. & Söder, L. 2001. Distributed generation: a definition. Electric Power Systems Research, 57: 195-204.

Arthur, W.B. 1989. Competing technologies, increasing returns and lock-in by historical events. The Economic Journal, 99: 116-131.

Astrom, U. & Lescale, V. 2006. Converter stations for 800 kV HVDC. Proceedings of the International Conference on Power System Technology 2006 (PowerCon 2006), Oct. 2006: 1-7.

Awerbuch, S. 1993. The surprising role of risk and discount rates in utility integrated-resource planning. The Electricity Journal, 6: 20-33.

Awerbuch, S. & Berger, M. 2003. Applying portfolio theory to EU electricity planning and policy-making. IEA/EET Working Paper No. EET/2003/03, IEA/OECD, Paris, February.

Awerbuch, S. 2006. Portfolio-based electricity generation planning: policy implications for renewables and energy security. Mitigation and Adaptation Strategies for Global Change, 11: 693-710.

Bell, G. K. & Campa, J. M. 1997. Irreversible investment and volatile markets: A study of the chemical processing industry. The Review of Economics and Statistics, 79: 79-87.

Blaabjerg, F., Chen, Z. & Kjaer, S. B. 2004. Power electronics as efficient interface of renewable energy sources. Proceedings of the 4th International Power Electronics and Motion Control Conference 2004 (IPEMC 2004), 14-16 Aug. 2004, Vol. 3: 1731-1739.

Bøckman, T., Fleten, S.-E., Juliussen, E., Langhammer, H. J. & Revdal, I. 2008. Investment timing and optimal capacity choice for small hydropower projects. European Journal of Operational Research, 190: 255-267.

Bolinger, M., Wiser, R. & Golove, W., 2002. Quantifying the value that wind power provides as a hedge against volatile natural gas prices. Environmental Energy Technologies Division, Report No. LBNL-50484, Ernest Orlando

Lawrence Berkeley National Laboratory, University of California, Berkeley, June.

Botterud, A., Ilic, M. D. & Wangensteen, I. 2005. Optimal investments in power generation under centralized and decentralized decision making. IEEE Transactions Power Systems, 20: 254-263.

Botterud, A. & Korpås, M. 2007. A stochastic dynamic model for optimal timing of investments in new generation capacity in restructured power systems. Electrical Power and Energy Systems, 29: 163-174.

Congressional Budget Office (CBO). 2003. Prospects for distributed electricity generation. Washington: The Congress of the United States, CBO.

Chaton, C. & Guillerminet, M.-L. 2007. Competition and environmental policies in an electricity sector. Paper presented at the AFSE Congress 2008. Paris.

Chen, Z., Hu, Y. & Blaabjerg, F. 2006. Control of distributed power systems. Proceedings of the CES/IEEE 5th International Power Electronics and Motion Control Conference 2006 (IPEMC '06), 14-16 Aug. 2006, Vol. 3: 1-6.

Cramton, P. & Stoft, S. 2006. The convergence of market designs for adequate generating capacity with special attention to the CAISO's resource adequacy problem. A White Paper for the Electricity Oversight Board, CEEPR Working Paper 06-007, Center for Energy and Environmental Policy Research, MIT, Cambridge, April.

David, P.A. 1985. Clio and the economics of QWERTY. American Economic Review, 75: 332-337.

Davis, M. 2002. Mini gas turbines and high speed generators: a preferred choice for serving large commercial customers and microgrids. I. Generating system. Proceedings of the IEEE Power Engineering Society Summer Meeting 2002, Vol. 2: 669-676.

De Doncker, R., Meyer, C., Lenke, R. U. & Mura F. 2007. Power electronics for future utility applications. Proceedings of the 7th International Conference on Power Electronics and Drive Systems (PEDS '07), 27-30 November 2007: K-1-K-8.

Deng, S.-J., Johnson, B. & Sogomonian, A. 2001. Exotic electricity options and the valuation of electricity generation and transmission assets. Decision Support Systems, 30: 383-392.

Deng, S.-J. & Oren, S. S. 2003. Incorporating operational characteristics and start-up costs in option-based valuation of power generation capacity. Probability in the Engineering and Informational Sciences, 17: 155-181.

De Vries, L. J. 2007. Generation adequacy: helping the market do its job. Utilities Policy, 15: 20-35.

De Vries, L. J. & Hakvoort, R. A. 2004. The question of generation adequacy in liberalised electricity markets. FEEM Working Paper 120.2004, Fondazione Eni Enrico Mattei, Milan, September.

De Vries, L. J. & Heijnen, P. 2008. The impact of electricity market design upon investment under uncertainty: The effectiveness of capacity mechanisms. Utilities Policy, 16: 215-227.

Dixit A. K. & Pindyck R. S. 1994. Investment under uncertainty. Princeton: Princeton University Press.

Driver, C., Temple, P. & Urga, G. 2008. Real options – delay vs. preemption: Do industrial characteristics matter? International Journal of Industrial Organization, 26: 532-545.

Ericsen, T., Hingorani, N. & Khersonsky, Y. 2006. PEBB – power electronics building blocks from concept to reality. Proceedings of the Industry Applications Society 53rd Annual Petroleum and Chemical Industry Conference 2006, Sept. 11 2006-Oct. 15 2006: 1-7.

Finon, D., Johnsen, T. A. & Midttun, A. 2004. Challenges when electricity markets face the investment phase. Energy Policy, 32: 1355-1362.

Fleten, S.-E., Maribu, K. M. & Wangensteen, I. 2007. Optimal investment strategies in decentralized renewable power generation under uncertainty. Energy 32: 803-815.

Frayer, J. & Uludere, N. Z. 2001. What is it worth? Application of real options theory to the valuation of generation assets. The Electricity Journal, 14: 40-51.

Fuss, S., Szolgayova, J., Obersteiner, M. & Gusti, M. 2008. Investment under market and climate policy uncertainty. Applied Energy, 85: 708-721.

Gardner, D. & Zhuang, Y. 2000. Valuation of power generation assets: a real options approach. Algo Research Quarterly, 3: 9-20.

Goodacre, A. & Tonks, I. 1995. Finance and technological change. In P. Stoneman (Ed.), Handbook of the Economics of Innovation and Technical Change: 298-341. Oxford: Blackwell Publishers.

Gross, R., Heptonstall, P. & Blyth, W. 2007. Investment in electricity generation – the role of costs, incentives and risks. UKERC, London, May.

Grund, C. E., Bahrman, M. P., Balu N., Bergstrom, L., Long, W. F., Newell, D. & Osborne, R. V. 1981. Dynamic performance characteristics of North American HVDC systems for transient and dynamic stability evaluations. Proceedings of the IEEE Transactions on Power Apparatus and Systems, 100: 3356-3364.

Harper, J. P., Karcher, M. D. & Bolinger, M. 2007. Wind project financing structures: a review and comparative analysis. Ernest Orlando Lawrence Berkeley Laboratories Report LBNL-63434, September.

Hingorani, N. G. 1988. Power electronics in electric utilities: role of power electronics in future power systems. Proceedings of the IEEE, 76: 481-482.

Hoff, T. E., Wenger, H. J. & Farmer, B. K. 1996. Distributed generation: an alternative to electric utility investments in system capacity. Energy Policy, 24: 137-147.

International Energy Agency (IEA). 2002. Distributed generation in liberalized electricity markets. Paris: OECD/IEA.

International Energy Agency (IEA). 2003a. Power generation investment in electricity markets. Paris: OECD/IEA.

International Energy Agency (IEA). 2003b. World energy investment outlook – 2003 insights. Paris: OECD/IEA.

Iov, F. & Blaabjerg, F. 2007. UNIFLEX-PM. Advanced power converters for universal and flexible power management in future electricity network – converter applications in future European electricity network. Deliverable D2.1

EC Contract no. 019794(SES6), February 2007, p. 171 (available online at www.eee.nott.ac.uk/uniflex/Deliverables.htm).

Jardan, R. & Nagy, I. 2003. Synchronous machine-turbine drive system with indirect speed control. Proceedings of the IEEE International Electric Machines and Drives Conference 2003 (IEMDC '03), Vol. 2: 1144-1150.

Jardan, R., Nagy, I., Nitta, T. & Ohsaki, H. 2000. Power factor correction in a turbine-generator-converter system. Proceedings of the IEEE Industry Applications Conference 2000, Vol. 2: 894-900.

Jenkins, G. 1985. Public utility finance and economic waste. The Canadian Journal of Economics, 18: 484-498.

Jonnes, J. 2004. Empires of light: Edison, Tesla, Westinghouse, and the race to electrify the world. New York: Random House.

Joskow, P. L. 2006. Competitive electricity markets and investment in new generating capacity. CEEPR Working Paper 06-009, Center for Energy and Environmental Policy Research, MIT, Cambridge, April .

Kahn, E. & Stoft, S. 1993. Analyzing fuel price risks under competitive bidding. Energy and Environment Division, Utility Planning and Policy Group, Ernest Orlando Lawrence Berkeley National Laboratory, University of California, Berkeley, February.

Kaikko, J., Backman, J., Koskelainen, L. & Larjoly, J. 2007. Technical and economic performance comparison between recuperated and non-recuperated variable-speed microturbines in combined heat and power generation. Applied Thermal Engineering, 27: 2173-2180.

Kaslow, T. & Pindyck, R. 1994. Valuing flexibility in utility planning. The Electricity Journal, 7: 60-65.

Keppo, J. & Lu, H. 2003. Real options and a large producer: the case of electricity markets. Energy Economics, 25: 459-472.

Köllensperger, P., Bragard, M., Plum, T. & De Doncker, R. W. 2007. The dual GCT – a new high-power device using optimized GCT technology. Proceedings of the 2007 IEEE Industry Applications Conference 2007, 42nd IAS Annual Meeting, 23-27 September 2007: 358-365.

Köllensperger, P. & De Doncker, R. W. 2006. Optimized gate drivers for internally commutated thyristors (ICTs). Proceedings of the 2006 IEEE Industry Applications Conference 2006, 41st IAS Annual Meeting, 8-12 October 2006, Vol. V: 2269-2275.

Krey, B. & Zweifel, P. 2006. Efficient electricity portfolios for Switzerland and the United States. SOI Working Paper No. 0602, University of Zurich, Switzerland.

Lintner, J. 1965. The valuation of risky assets and the selection of risky investments in stock portfolios and capital budgets. Review of Economics and Statistics, 47: 13-37.

Lu, Z., Liebman, A. & Dong, Z. Y. 2006. Power generation investment opportunities evaluation: a comparison between net present value and real options approach. Institute of Electrical and Electronics Engineers, 18-22, June 2006.

Lyon, T. P. & Mayo, J. W. 2005. Regulatory opportunism and investment behavior: evidence from the U.S. utility industry. RAND Journal of Economics, 36: 628-644.

Madlener, R. & Schmid, C. 2003. Combined heat and power generation in liberalised markets and a carbon-constrained world. GAIA – Ecological Perspectives in Science, Humanities, and Economics, 12: 114-120.

Madlener, R. & Wenk, C. 2008. Efficient investment portfolios for the Swiss electricity supply sector. FCN Working paper No. 2/2008, Institute for Future Energy Consumer Needs and Behavior (FCN), RWTH Aachen University, August.

Madlener, R. & Wohlgemuth, N. 1999. Small is sometimes beautiful: the case of distributed generation in competitive energy markets. Proceedings of the 1st Austrian-Czech-German IAEE Conference: Energy Market Liberalization in the Central and Eastern Europe, Prague, Czech Republic, 6-8 September 1999: 94-100.

Mandron, A. 2000. Project valuation: problem areas, theory and practice. The Current State of Business Disciplines, 3: 997-1017.

Maribu, K. M. 2006. Modeling the economics of market adoption of distributed power generation. PhD Thesis, Norwegian University of Science and Technology, Trondheim.

Markowitz, H. 1952. Portfolio selection. Journal of Finance, 7: 77-91.

Meyer, C. & De Doncker, R. W. 2004. Power electronics for modern medium-voltage distribution systems. Proceedings of the 4th International Power Electronics and Motion Control Conference 2004 (IPEMC 2004), 14-16 Aug. 2004, Vol. 1: 58-66.

Meyer, C., Schroeder, S. & De Doncker, R. W. 2004. Solid-state circuit breakers and current limiters for medium-voltage systems having distributed power systems. Proceedings of the IEEE Transactions on Power Electronics, Sept. 2004, Vol. 19: 1333-1340.

Murto, P., Näsäkkälä, E. & Keppo, J. 2004. Timing of investments in oligopoly under uncertainty: a framework for numerical analysis. European Journal of Operational Research, 157: 486-500.

Näsäkkälä, E. & Fleten, S.-E. 2005. Flexibility and technology choice in gas fired power plant investments. Review of Financial Economics, 14: 371-393.

Offringa, L. & Duarte, J. 2000. A 1600 kW IGBT converter with interphase transformer for high speed gas turbine power plants. Proceedings of the IEEE Industry Applications Conference 2000, Vol. 4: 2243-2248.

Onovwiona, H. I. & Ugursal, V. I. 2006. Residential cogeneration systems: review of the current technology. Renewable and Sustainable Energy Reviews, 10: 389-431.

Pati, M. E., Ristau, R., Sheblé, G. B. & Wilhelm, M. C. 2001. Real option valuation of distributed generation interconnection. prepared by M. C. Wilhelm Associates for the Edison Electric Institute (EEI), Washington, March.

Peperman, G. J., Driesen, D., Haeseldonckx, D., Belmans, R. & D'Haeseleer, W. 2005. Distributed generation: definition, benefits, and issues. Energy Policy, 33: 787-798.

Pfeifenberger, J. P., Hanser, P. Q. & Ammann, P. R. 1998. What's in the cards for distributed resources? The Energy Journal Special Issue. Distributed Resources: Toward a New Paradigm of the Electricity Business (Eds: Y. Smeers and A. Yatchew), 1-16.

Pilavachi, P.A. 2002. Mini- and micro-gas turbines for combined heat and power. Applied Thermal Engineering, 22: 2003-2014.

Roques, F. A. 2008. Market design for generation adequacy: healing causes rather than symptoms. Utilities Policy 16: 171-183.

Roques, F. A., Nuttall, W. J. & Newbery, D. M. 2006. Using probabilistic analysis to value power generation investments under uncertainty. Electricity Policy Research Group Working Papers, No. EPRG 06/19, University of Cambridge, Cambridge/UK.

Roques, F. A., Newbery, D. M. & Nuttall, W. J. 2008. Fuel mix diversification incentives in liberalized electricity markets: a mean-variance portfolio theory approach. Energy Economics, 30: 1831-1849.

Schwartzenberg, J. W. 2003. Application of AC switch power electronic building blocks in medium voltage static transfer switches. Proceedings of the IEEE Power Engineering Society General Meeting 2003, 13-17 July 2003, Vol. 3: 1372-1374.

Sharpe, W. F. 1964. Capital asset prices: a theory of market equilibrium under conditions of risk. Journal of Finance, 19: 425-442.

Siddiqui, A. S. & Maribu, K. Investment and upgrade in distributed generation under uncertainty. Energy Economics (forthcoming, available online 23 Aug 2008).

Steinke, J. K. & Steimer, P. K., 2000. Medium voltage drive converter for industrial applications in the power range from 0.5 MW to 5 MW based on a three-level converter equipped with IGCTs. Proceedings of the IEE Seminar on PWM Medium Voltage Drives 2000 (Ref. No. 2000/063), Vol. 6: 1-6.

Stoneman, P. 2001. Technological diffusion and the financial environment. EIFC Working paper No. 01-3, European Integration, Financial Systems and Economic Performance (EIFC), United Nations University, Institute for New Technology, Maastricht.

Thomas, S. 2007. Investment in new power generation in New South Wales. London: Public Services International Research Unit, June 2007.

Trigeorgis, L. 1996. Real options: managerial flexibility and strategy in resource allocation. Cambridge: MIT Press.

Turvey, R. 1968. Optimal pricing and investment in electricity supply: an essay in applied welfare economics. Cambridge: MIT Press.

Van Mieghem, J. A. 2003. Capacity management, investment, and hedging: review and recent developments. Manufacturing & Service Operations Management, 5: 269-302.

Vijlee, S., Ouroua, A., Domaschk, L. & Beno, J. 2007. Directly-coupled gas turbine permanent magnet generator sets for prime power generation on board electric ships. Proceedings of the IEEE Electric Ship Technologies Symposium 2007 (ESTS '07): 340-347.

Von Bloh, J. & De Doncker, R. W. 2000. Control strategies for multilevel voltage source converters for medium-voltage DC transmission systems. Proceedings of the 26th Annual Conference of the IEEE Industrial Electronics Society (IECON 2000), 22-28 Oct. 2000, Vol. 2: 1358-1364.

Walls, W. D., Rusco, F. W. & Ludwigson, J. 2007. Power plant investment in restructured markets. Energy, 32: 1403-1413.

18 Perspectives on Capacity Investment in Germany and Europe – The Future of Power-Mix Optimization

Ulrich Jobs[1]

Abstract

On liberalized markets, investment risks are now much greater than they were before liberalization. Prices and quantities are determined by international markets. In the energy supply area, too, we need sizable companies with the necessary risk-bearing capability. The efficient infrastructure in the electricity supply sector must be further developed in line with market conditions. In future as well, the power supply should be based on a broad energy mix consisting of coal, nuclear energy, natural gas, and renewable energies. With such a mix, technical and market-induced supply risks can be kept low. We need a political framework that is calculable in the long term and which takes account of the rules of the market and makes the necessary investment of billions in new environmentally compatible power plant technology defensible from a business angle.

Keywords: investment risks, market conditions, energy mix

---

[1] Dr. Ulrich Jobs is Chief Operating Officer of RWE AG, Germany.

A. Bausch and B. Schwenker (eds.), *Handbook Utility Management,*
DOI: 10.1007/978-3-540-79349-6_18, © Springer-Verlag Berlin Heidelberg 2009

18.1   The Underlying Conditions Have Changed Dramatically

In 2000 and 2001, there were temporary regional brown-outs on America's west coast, because power plants and grids were no longer able to meet demand. Given governments' current energy policy, do we in Germany and Europe have to fear similar developments? This chapter is designed to throw some light on a few aspects of the problem.

The underlying conditions for energy investment have changed radically in the past 10 years in Germany and Europe. With the amended energy-management act that came into effect in 1998, Germany now has a liberalized electricity market. Energy suppliers are in a state of free competition, power prices are formed at an exchange, and local supply regions have been lifted. The question now is: who, in these circumstances, is responsible for the security of supply? Is it the state, the power utilities or the market?

For a start, it must be noted that the efficient infrastructure that exists today in the electricity-supply field has been 'inherited'. It hails largely from the days of the supply monopolies. However, the capacity reserves available at that time have meanwhile been exhausted. After the so-called secondary market was formed in a first phase of liberalization, with the setting up of electricity exchanges and the emergence of significant trading in power, what matters now in the second phase is the further development of the actual primary market for the electricity supply, namely the generation and transportation of power.

18.2   The Power Plant Age Structure Needs Investment Running into Billions

This further development depends on a whole host of impacting parameters. These include market conditions, such as the price trends in fuels, CO_2 and electricity, but also company-specific factors, such as financial strength and know-how, and finally, the political framework.

Europe and Germany not only have a demographic problem: their power plants, too, have become elderly. There is a disproportionately high number of legacy power stations. Europe saw its most recent construction boom for coal-fired and nuclear power stations in the 1980s. Since then, the power plants built have been mostly gas-based plants (see Figure 18.1). One exception in the 1990s was the construction of new lignite-fired power stations in eastern Germany in the wake of reunification.

Some 40% of thermal and nuclear power plant capacity is more than 25 years old. This power plant capacity must be replaced by 2030. Add the fact that further rises in power demand must be reckoned with at European level, namely increases of about one third by 2030 – despite ambitious climate-protection targets. This is the conclusion reached in a study published by the EU Commission at the beginning of 2007 (European Commission, 2006).

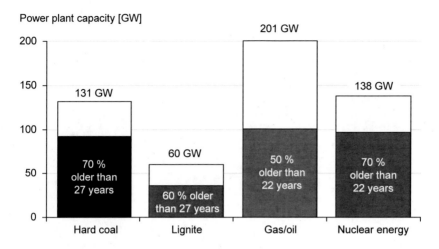

Figure 18.1: Outdated power plants all over Europe (RWE, 2007)

If we are to cover that higher demand, today's production capacity of some 800 GW needs to be increased to more than 1,000 GW by 2030. Both conventional and renewable energies must make greater contributions to power generation. Natural gas is witnessing the fastest growth of all. This is particularly true in view of more rigorous climate-protection measures.

Europe's dependence on energy imports will go on rising steadily. The share of imported gas, in particular, will grow, from a good 40% today to over 60% in the future. In Germany, the figure is already 83%.

By contrast, coal as an energy carrier is reliably available for long-term power generation. With its extensive lignite deposits, Germany has a low-cost potential for mitigating price and supply risks. Hard coal is abundantly available worldwide and is favorably spread geopolitically, so that it can in fact be provided at low cost and on a dependable basis in the long term. From the standpoint of mixed risks, therefore, further use of hard coal and lignite is called for. The best risk insurance against the growing dependence on gas and oil has so far been and still remains a balanced energy-source portfolio in Germany and Europe. We must retain and underpin this energy mix in upcoming investment projects.

The age-related shutdown of power plants and the rising electricity demand in Europe require a new-build of thermal power plant capacity on a scale of 400 GW by 2030. Germany, too, is facing huge challenges in underpinning its power supply. In the next two decades, numerous power stations will have to be replaced on age grounds. What is more, under the atomic energy act now in force, nuclear power stations are to be shut down, and this will leave an additional gap of 21 GW (see Figure 18.2).

Replacement capacities of some 45 GW – the power stations affected here are mainly plants operating in the base load – require investment of more than € 50 billion.

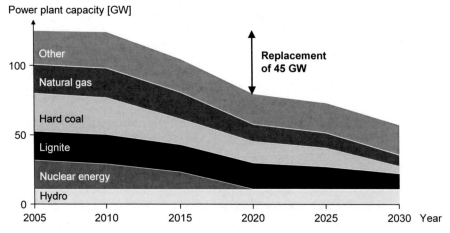

Power plant capacity [GW]

NB: incl plants under construction. Usual plant life span: 40 years. Shutdown of
nuclear-power stations in accordance with the nuclear-energy consensus Germany.

Figure 18.2: Age-related fall in existing power plant capacities, and nuclear phase-
out in [GW] (RWE, 2007)

Since worsening scarcity must also be reckoned with in neighboring countries,
an expansion of cross-border trade in electricity may alleviate the problem temporarily, but will not basically solve it.

Unlike the situation at European level, Germany can expect to see a trend toward stagnation in future electricity consumption. Although it is true that economic growth and the expansion of information and communication technology in
Germany, too, are driving up power consumption, successes in obtaining greater
efficiency have meant a far-reaching decoupling of growth in electricity consumption from general economic growth in recent decades. As shown in current studies,
this trend is set to continue in the next 20 years (Schlesinger et al., 2007; Prognos
AG, 2007; EWI/EEFA, 2007).

In view of the enormous replacement needs for power plants in Europe, it can
come as no surprise that a number of projects with different energy mixes have
been announced in every country. However, of the projects announced, involving
134 GW, a mere 60% are likely to be implemented by 2012. Is this a sign of market failure?

18.3   The Risks in Power Plant Investment Have
          Definitely Increased

For many years, the market lived off the excess capacities built up in the monopoly years. Electricity prices had fallen and for a long time moved at a level that –
at best – provided incentives for divestment, and not for new capital spending.

With liberalization, member states took the decision in principle to leave it to the market to handle investment in long-lived, capital-intensive supply facilities. Any investment is now subject to the usual market risk. The life span of conventional power stations is usually put at 40 years. The underlying conditions in the energy sector changed during this period and now harbor risks which before liberalization could be shifted onto consumers, in the same way as levies, as it were.

Until 2005, the imputed full costs were mainly construction and fuel costs. After that date, besides an increase in building and fuel costs, CO_2 outlays, too, had to be taken into account for the first time. These will be rising yet again, from 2007 on, owing to the expected lower allocation of emission certificates, so that the full costs of new coal-fired power plants have now reached a level of 80-90 €/MWh (see Figure 18.3). However, investors will only act if across the life span of the power plant concerned a sufficient return on investment can be expected on the basis of wholesale prices. This means that the electricity market must supply clear and unequivocal price signals if it is to trigger capital spending.

In the 1990s, few power plants were built in Europe. This development was further encouraged by liberalization. The capacities of Europe's plant builders shrank in this period. The plant-producer market has virtually dried up. With the rise in the electricity price in the last 4 years, the situation has undergone an abrupt change, and a number of power plant projects have been started or announced in Europe.

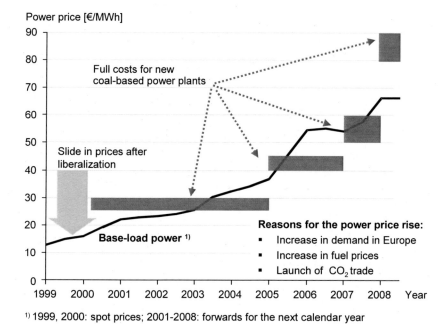

Figure 18.3: Developments in wholesale prices for power since liberalization (own calculations)

At the same time, the booming world economy – especially China's and India's – has triggered heavy demand among producers worldwide, and this has already led to supply bottlenecks and rising plant prices. In the wake of this development, the new-build costs of power stations have skyrocketed since 2005. The growth in demand for high-value plant parts has led to capacity log jams.

But it is not only rising prices in plant engineering that increase the risk; fuel-price risks, too, have grown significantly for investors. Smaller companies in particular are frequently overstretched here. Fuel markets are subject to high world-market price volatility (see Figure 18.4). Who can give a reliable forecast today of how the prices of natural gas and hard coal will evolve in the medium to long term? This, too, must be factored into investment planning, since fuel prices are a crucial parameter for the economic efficiency of future power plants. Owing to the long life spans of power stations, decisions have long-term consequences. A large company with a balanced power plant portfolio is in a position to deploy its coal- or gas-based power stations optimally depending on price developments in fuels.

The small enterprise often does not have this option. This being so, we need large companies in the energy sector that are able to shoulder market-price swings thanks to their broad-based energy mix. Only large companies have the financial clout to bear higher risks. Size is a necessary precondition if we are to keep up in the globalized energy market. Even the financing of new large-scale projects in the energy supply is a Herculean task that is simply beyond the means of smaller firms. This is also true of the research projects required.

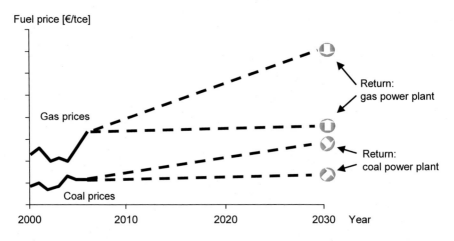

Figure 18.4: Future fuel prices are an investment risk and impact the economic efficiency of power plant projects (RWE, 2007)

Energy utilities not only compete on the European electricity market: they also compete for capital. We must convince our lenders of the economic efficiency of each investment. And we can only win them over for projects that promise a competitive return. So the investor restraint that can be noted is also due to a lack of size. Given this situation, any break-up or forced downsizing of German utilities – as repeatedly discussed at national and European level – must clearly be rejected.

18.4   Lack of Investment Means Higher Power Prices

It is a gross error of judgment when critics attribute rising electricity prices to the alleged market power of large energy utilities and to a supposed lack of competition. After 15 years of in-depth rationalization associated with painful job culls across all hierarchies, every employee in the energy sector by now knows what competition means. Germany's energy sector has done its homework in this respect.

Nonetheless, the EU Commission keeps on turning the spotlight on supposedly inadequate competition. In April 2007, for example, the Commission presented an analysis of the electricity markets in six European countries, including Germany. Responsibility for the analysis lay with the consultancy London Economics (London Economics, 2007). The study contains a criticism to the effect that prices on Europe's power market were excessive in the years 2003-2005. London Economics attributes this to a lack of competition and refers to what are said to be excessive prices in Germany and Spain. In actual fact, Germany's wholesale prices were among the lowest in Europe in the period under investigation.

In a detailed expert critique, Professor Ockenfels of the University of Cologne dealt scientifically with London Economics' study (Ockenfels, 2007). In doing so, he identified considerable errors as well as methodological weaknesses. Overall, he concludes that the central inferences drawn by London Economics are scientifically untenable. The allegations derived from this as regards competitive deficits on the German electricity market cannot be justified scientifically. According to Professor Ockenfels, the study cannot satisfy any claim to provide a sound basis for decisions on competition-policy or for regulatory measures. Hence, the rise in power prices has nothing to do with market clout. In fact, electricity prices will rise anyhow wherever capacities become scarce owing to a lack of investment.

18.5   Investment Program for Environmentally Sound Power Plant Capacities

To avoid this, RWE is investing substantially in new power plant capacities. The central, strategic element in this is the retention of a broad and balanced energy mix. One crucial component in RWE's power plant renewal program for lignite is the new lignite-fired unit with optimized plant engineering, BoA for short.

Once RWE had successfully commissioned the first 1,000-MW BoA unit at Niederaussem in 2003, we started building a twin BoA plant at Neurath in 2006. This also serves the needs of climate protection. For instance, construction of the twin lignite-based unit alone replaces existing legacy systems and yields a saving of some 6 million tons of CO_2 per year. What is more, with ultra-modern power plant engineering, we are setting a positive signal for Germany as a technology location. We will also be investing in hard coal-based power plants with a total capacity of over 1,600 MW in Germany. To this must be added the construction of a gas combined cycle gas turbine (CCGT) power station with a capacity of more than 800 MW at Lingen.

Also of importance to us are renewable energies. Throughout Europe, RWE has an installed capacity of some 2,200 MW today. We are planning to add capacity above all where the energy-sector and underlying geographic conditions are especially attractive. We will be making over € 1 billion available annually for this in the coming years.

In the medium and long term, we are pursuing the so-called clean-coal strategy, meaning the capture and storage of CO_2 in coal-based power generation. The beacon project in our climate-protection program is the world's first commercial-scale low-CO_2 coal-fired power station that we are planning with a capacity of 450 MW, which is due to go on stream in 2014. We have penciled in some € 1 billion for this.

In this way, by 2012 we will be spending more than € 5 billion on the construction of new power plants in Germany. We will invest a further € 5 billion or so in new production capacities, mainly in the UK and the Netherlands. These projects alone make RWE one of Europe's biggest investors.

18.6   Market Intervention by Energy Policy Slows Down Necessary Investment

However, such investment requires a dependable energy-policy framework that enables and helps justify the necessary high level of capital spending on the energy supply. In view of the higher risks, you might be forgiven for thinking that policy makers would offer the energy sector a robust planning basis by fielding a sound overall energy-policy concept. In spite of several energy summits mounted by the federal government in 2006 and 2007, though, this objective has been postponed yet again.

Despite liberalization, however, the electricity market is characterized more strongly than other markets by state intervention. Economic efficiency and a secure energy supply are being subordinated to regulation and a main focus on the concerns of climate protection. It is one of the federal government's declared aims, for example, to increase the share of renewables from today's 14% or so to 25-30% by the year 2020. The extra burden from Germany's Renewable Energy Sources Act (EEG) alone will amount to over € 4 billion in 2007. This does not take account of extra spending on grid extensions and on additional standard and reserve energy. Given the expansion targets, the extra strains will grow significantly in the years to come.

Thanks to the promotion of renewable energies and combined heat and power (CHP) plants, over 50% of the energy market will be regulated and subsidized in

2020. We will have two markets in Germany: one liberalized, the other regulated. Expansion of the regulated market segment heightens the risks for all other investment schemes, since the capacity utilization of fossil-fired generating plants is also indirectly co-determined by the utilization of renewable energy carriers. This can have an adverse impact on the profitability of conventional power plant investment. Or the prices per unit must increase to a point where the full costs, plus return on capital, are earned by the remaining operating hours.

Another risk is associated with a tightening of Germany's Law on Barriers to Competition (GWB). The supervisory authorities are being given an opportunity to interfere with the formation of market prices (see Figure 18.5). This is to prevent power producers from 'abusing' their market position. Irrespective of how the final shape of the new regulations will look in detail and how the envisaged set of instruments will be used in reality, the very mention of this measure has been generating a deterrent effect.

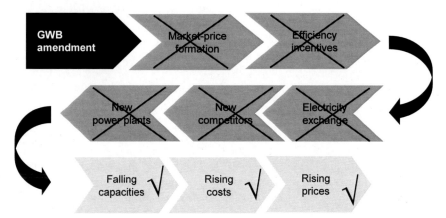

Figure 18.5: Amendment of cartel law (GWB) prevents competition and is unsuitable for lowering power prices (RWE, 2007)

The signal function of price formation and the incentive effect of the expected return on investment in power stations comes across only in a falsified form or, in the present case, in a much weaker form. Electricity prices capped by the state make investment less attractive, with the consequence that capital spending on power plants is deferred. Incidentally, this is not only a problem for established suppliers, but also and especially for new entrants. So, law makers must ask whether they can in fact achieve the objectives pursued with the amendment to cartel law, specifically more competition and falling prices.

Instead of improving the conditions for more competition, a relapse into the period before liberalization is foreseeable with state supervision of prices and investment. The search for cost-cutting potentials and increases in efficiency stimulated by liberalization would be vitiated. Indeed: efforts to tap rationalization potentials become pointless.

A current study by the Union for the Co-ordination of Transmission of Electricity (UCTE) makes it clear that the investor restraint in Germany and Europe will lead to the first bottlenecks in the energy field in 10 years' time (see Figure 18.6).

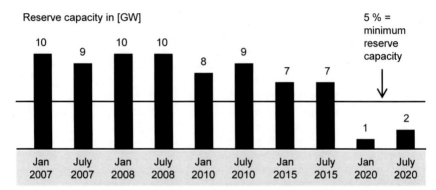

Basis: third Wednesday, 11:00 hrs
Power plant capacity in Germany: 122.3 GW (Jan 2007);
Estimated net power plant capacity for the period 2007-2020 (UCTE)

Figure 18.6: UCTE expects capacity bottleneck in Germany after 2015 (UCTE, 2007; RWE, 2007)

According to the study, the minimum reserve capacity regarded as necessary in Germany will fall below 5% of installed power-generation capacity after the year 2015, and it will be a mere 1-2% in 2020. The UCTE's assessment for developments in Europe is even more serious: here, no minimum reserve capacity is expected to be available after 2020. In fact, a shortfall of up to 10 GW is expected (UCTE, 2007).

18.7   Summary

We need investment in energy plants in larger dimension. Without this, we run the risk in 10 years' time of witnessing not only price problems, but also grave supply problems owing to capacity bottlenecks.

Especially in the energy supply area we also need large companies with sufficient risk-bearing capability. On the liberalized market, investment risks have become that much higher. Prices and quantities are determined by international markets. This being so, investment projects that run into billions, combined with the greater risks involved, require large, financially strong companies. Only they stand a chance of holding their own on the market thanks to the strategic risk management in their power plant portfolio.

Finally, we need a political framework that takes account of the three guiding principles in energy supply, which must be treated as equals wherever possible: security of supply, economic efficiency and ecological defensibility. Without the exclusion of specific energy sources on ideological grounds, we would then have a broad-based and balanced energy mix of coal, nuclear energy, gas and renewable energies.

The liberalization of the energy markets has yet to pass the acid test. Success will depend crucially on policy makers' refraining from interfering with markets. The political framework must not increase the risks. On the contrary: it must help ensure more calculability. Security of supply, competitiveness and environmental compatibility of power supply can only be achieved in the long haul if the underlying political conditions take account of the rules of the market.

References

European Commission. 2006. World energy technology outlook – 2050. Brussels: European Commission.

Energiewirtschaftliches Institut (EWI) & Energy Environment Forecast Analysis GmbH (EEFA). 2007. Studie: Energiewirtschaftliches Gesamtkonzept 2030, Erweiterte Szenariendokumentation. Cologne: EWI/EEFA.

London Economics. 2007. Study: structure and performance of six European wholesale electricity markets in 2003, 2004 and 2005. Paper presented to DG Comp, London.

Ockenfels, A. 2007. Measuring market power on the German electricity market in theory and practice – critical notes on the LE study. Energiewirtschaftliche Tagesfragen, 57: 12-29.

Prognos AG. 2007. Final report: the future role of coal in Europe. Berlin-Basel.

RWE AG. 2007. Fact book generation capacity in Europe. Essen: RWE.

Schlesinger, M., Hofer, P., Rits, V., Lindenberger, D., Wissen, R. & Bartels, M. 2007. Endbericht: Energieszenarien für den Energiegipfel 2007. Basel/Cologne: Prognos AG/ EWI.

Union for the Co-ordination of Transmission of Electricity (UCTE). 2007. UCTE system adequacy forecast 2007-2020. Brussels: UCTE.

19 Renewable Resources for Electric Power: Prospects and Challenges

Fritz Vahrenholt[1]

Abstract

Three factors are driving the expansion of renewables in the industrialised countries of the western world: the threat of climate change, dramatic shortages and price increases in conventional energy sources such as oil and gas, and the political situation in many of the remaining extracting nations, which puts ongoing security of supply for the importing nations in doubt. Energy providers, and increasingly politicians, in Germany are therefore looking to expand the use of renewables, and particularly the very promising area of offshore wind farms. Great advances in the performance, availability, and economic efficiency of these methods of power generation lead us to expect that in just a few years' time wind power will be profitable enough to justify the enormous investments it requires. These will, however, have to be supported by society as a whole, to trigger an injection of development funds into the required technologies.

Keywords: renewables, energy providers, offshore wind farm

[1] Prof. Dr. Fritz Vahrenholt is Chief Executive Officer of RWE Innogy GmbH, Germany.

A. Bausch and B. Schwenker (eds.), *Handbook Utility Management,*
DOI: 10.1007/978-3-540-79349-6_19, © Springer-Verlag Berlin Heidelberg 2009

19.1   Driving Forces Behind the Rethink in Energy Policy

Warning signs of climate change and the need to combat carbon dioxide emissions are key drivers of the trend towards sustainable energy supply solutions. The international scientific body, Intergovernmental Panel on Climate Change (IPCC), is predicting an average increase in global temperature of between 2 °C and 5.8 °C by the end of this century. This would have serious repercussions: displacement of animal and plant habitats, a rise in nonnative, invasive insect species, an increase in extreme events, such as flooding, heat waves, and drought periods – with major repercussions for the security of food supplies in many regions of Africa, Asia and Latin America. It should shake us out of our complacency to know that the Atlantic along the European coast has already heated up by 0.7 °C, that the winter season in Central Europe now begins 2-3 weeks later than before, that the glaciers have already receded by 10%, and that precipitation has increased by 10-40% in Northern Europe yet decreased in Southern Europe by 20%. We are on the brink of gigantic climate change, and our only option is to find ways to minimise the damage. This is why everything points to carbon-neutral energy sources in the long term.

Yet, increasingly, other compelling reasons for expanding the share of renewables are gaining prominence. For one thing, the scarcity factor. Our hugely energy-hungry world has led to erratic price rises in oil, gas and coal. In China alone, energy consumption is increasing every 3 years by about the same amount as is consumed by the entire Japanese nation. Then there is the fact that India and Brazil, and also other vast areas of the world, are developing industry, private consumption and mobility at a very rapid pace. Billions of people who have never had access to electricity now want to enjoy the same benefits of civilisation as we do. In addition, the world's population is expected to continue growing significantly through to the middle of this century, by an estimated 2.5 billion – which would be the equivalent of two more populations the size of China's. Furthermore, for many years now, we have been finding fewer new oil reserves worldwide, and this at a time when more and more oil is being consumed. For every three barrels of crude oil used today, only one is replaced by new oil finds. Four fifths of these currently tapped natural resources will have dried up by 2020. This means we would have to discover ten times the amount of oil currently available to us in the North Sea just to replace what we will lack a few years from now. Hardly any reserves that could be described as 'super-giants' are still being found. At best there are so-called 'mega-giants', such as the Doba Oil Field in Chad, where an investment of $ 3.7 billion promises reserves of some 900 million barrels. That will only cover global oil consumption for about 12 days. The constant rise in the price of oil and its increasing scarcity very closely mirror the trend in gas, which in many respects is also overstretched. It is supposed to heat our homes, cover part of our future mobility needs and supply a great deal of the impending power plant replacements in Europe. Yet North Sea gas, for instance, will run out in the second decade of this century.

A third driver of the high level of interest in renewable energy sources is political awareness. Governments are increasingly realising how vulnerable the geopolitical situation is and how quickly the dependence on oil- and gas-extracting nations can impact on the industrial societies of the OECD. The terrorist attacks of 9/11 and the continuing terrorist attacks on pipelines in Iraq and oil supplies in Saudi Arabia show how vulnerable the geopolitical situation is and how quickly the dependence on oil and gas-extracting nations can impact on the industrial societies of the OECD. After all, some 70% of all oil reserves lie in the strategic ellipse between Kazakhstan and the Persian Gulf. Saudi Arabia is another powder keg. The seeds of the Wahabbist dictatorship are bearing fruit. A fundamentalist youth with no prospects for the future may soon even turn against the royal house. Even worse are the increasing signs that the 260 billion barrels of oil reserves supposedly still available in the year 1990 are actually nonexistent. Ghawar (1948), Abuqaiq (1940) and Safaniyah (1951), the biggest oilfields in the world, now only produce oil with the aid of water injection, and increasingly produce water as well as oil. The situation with natural gas is not much better. After 2025, the Commonwealth of Independent States (CIS) and Iran will be the sole sources of reserves that can be supplied to Europe by pipeline. This means we are moving to a position of dramatic dependence on imports for our oil and gas. Without a doubt: security of supply, particularly from domestic energy sources, will become a higher priority.

19.2   Renewables in the National and International Settings

Germany's energy policy and research agenda should therefore include everything that produces less CO_2 and promises stable, sustainable pricing. Unfortunately, the fact that the German Federal Government halved energy research funding to a paltry € 400 million in the 1990s for the once influential energy research centres of Juelich and Karlsruhe is coming home to roost. Other nations, such as Japan, have doubled their efforts over the same period. Sweden intends to stop importing oil in 2020 and has decided to extend the operating time of its nuclear power plants to 60 years, while at the same time fostering a massive increase in the use of renewable, domestic energy resources. The UK has opted to expand renewables and also to revert to using nuclear energy. The US has devised an ambitious programme for clean coal usage, is planning to return to nuclear energy and is currently massively expanding bioenergy and wind power, which has led to a worldwide shortage of wind turbines. In Germany, by contrast, wind energy has long been scoffed at and even opposed as 'the windmill illusion'.

Yet, renewables are domestic energy sources and also carbon neutral. As a result, many energy providers have recognised the future potential of these forms of energy. To name but two such examples: the RWE Group is pooling all activities to do with renewables in a new company, RWE Innogy, and will be investing at least € 1 billion a year to put some life into the ambitious expansion goals of Germany and the EU. The company EDF has also set up its own subsidiary company and launched it on the stock market. It plans to invest in 1,000 MW of wind power a year.

19.3   Limited Potential of Geothermal Energy, Solar Power and Biomass

Some of the renewable energy sources here in Germany that have a comparatively small potential share of the energy mix are geothermal energy, solar power and biomass. Though the use of biomass will make up a large proportion of renewables worldwide, its potential in Germany is limited. Owing to the limited supply of timber, only 2-3% of our electricity consumption is achievable. Things look better on the fuel and heating side, as the Federal Government has set a target for biofuels of supplying 15% of our electricity needs by 2015. This includes synthetic fuels, bio-ethanol and rapeseed methyl ester. Here in Germany the potential of biogas has been underestimated. Even if only half of all animal excrement were converted to biogas in conjunction with fatty biomass, more than 5% of our electricity needs could be met.

Solar energy will pale into insignificance in Germany over the next two decades. Economic efficiency is still too far removed. Supporting the development of technology and mass production in Germany via a degressive funding formula was the right thing to do, for this technology is a decentralised form of generation in the rural areas of sunnier nations, where it is an elegant and more economical solution than it is in our climes, since it requires no grid connection costs. But it is doubtful whether even thin-film technology or cells with organic carrier materials could ever do more than halve costs in Northern and North-Eastern Europe, where there is a cable running through every street. After all, the conventional system costs make up 50% of the expense anyway. Even if the cell itself were free, the price of electricity would still be 25 euro cents. That is not sustainable, at least not here in Northern Europe. On the other hand, around 2 billion people in the world have no access to electric power or an electricity grid. Solar collectors may well be able to bring a little Western convenience to the rural regions of the southern hemisphere. That is where they belong – and not on the roof of detached family homes in Buxtehude or Unterhaching.

The particular strategic benefit of geothermal technology lies in the year-round availability of the resource. The technical feasibility of using it for heating and electricity generation is beyond question, but the economic viability of it here in Germany is still some distance away. Should increased productivity of geothermal power stations be made possible by innovative, reliable strike rates and stimulation methods, geothermal energy would certainly have a future in electricity generation. The first hot-dry rock power stations in Germany are expected to emerge within the next few years. However, the ratio of drilling investment (currently € 6-8 million) to output (1-2 MW) is still prohibitive at this stage.

19.4 Wind Power is the Most Promising Growth Segment

Consequently, if the goals of the EU and Germany (20% of all electricity from renewable energy sources by 2020) are to be achieved, the lion's share – apart from an increase in hydropower and a few additional percent contributed by biomass and biogas – will have to come from wind power. It has not escaped the notice of government and industry that wind power technology represents the most advanced form of electricity generation from renewable energy sources. In the past 15 years, engineers and technicians have succeeded in more than halving the cost of wind power. For some time now it has been decreasing by 2% every year. Now that government-backed wind power in the pioneering countries of Denmark and Germany has secured a significant share of the electricity supply market – in Germany currently almost 7% – it has blossomed from a once purely ecologically driven niche technology into a booming industry worldwide.

The gap between the oil or gas price and the hitherto higher cost of wind power is now closing. We anticipate today that some time between 2012 and 2014, wind power in suitable locations will generate cheaper electricity than the competing forms of power generation, for in the past few years a series of technological advances has led to a significant decrease of the cost of wind power in real terms. The mere fact that rotor blade diameters have doubled since the 1990s to between 80 and 100 metres has led to a fourfold increase in earnings from wind farms. In total their yields have risen 100-fold in just 20 years (see Figure 19.1).

The learning curve has also seen the average generator capacity per plant of 150 kW in the 1990s grow to 2 or 3 MW today. Engineering advances have meant that wind farms in high wind regions with more than 10 metres of average wind speed per second can be designed in such a robust way that they will last for more than 20 years. Wind turbines of the current generation are proving to be grid-friendly, and even have a stabilising effect in the event of temporary outages. And the first 5-MW turbines suitable for offshore use are now being added to the grid. The prospect of being able to generate electricity in high wind locations at 5 euro cents per kilowatt-hour in the future – making it more economical than coal or gas-fired electricity – has triggered a wind power boom in the US and China. After presenting its extraordinarily ambitious target of 20,000 MW of wind power by 2020 at the Bonn Environment Conference in 2004, China revised its targets upwards in the year 2005: 30,000 MW is the current plan. According to a reputable study by BTM Consult, the currently installed worldwide capacity of just 60,000 MW is expected to soar within 10 years to 230,000 MW. This represents an additional investment of € 150-200 billion.

Such perspectives are changing the producer market. While there were more than a dozen mainly small to medium-sized companies manufacturing turbines a few years ago, a series of takeovers and worldwide consolidation has reduced that number to some eight manufacturers of any note. Much more significant, however, has been the arrival on the market of multi-national power plant corporations, which only a few years ago viewed wind power as an ideological wallflower and in some cases opposed it accordingly. The emergence of GE, Siemens and

AREVA as wind power players shows that wind power is now an energy source to be taken seriously and one to be reckoned with in every sense of the word. These capital-rich companies are not only freeing up their own financial resources, but are also drawing the necessary financial muscle of banks and insurance companies into the sector. Local added value and job creation are a welcome side effect of this trend. About 50,000 people currently work in the wind power industry in Germany, with 60% of turnover coming from turbine construction and some upstream peripheral components even being exported. With sales totalling € 4.5 billion, the wind power industry is now one of the key sectors of the mechanical engineering industry.

Increase in capacity

In a mere 20 years, the yield of wind turbines has increased 100-fold. With the new 5 MW turbines, it will multiply another fivefold.

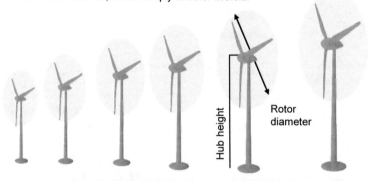

	1980	**1985**	**1990**	**1995**	**2000**	**2005**
Rated power	30 KW	80 KW	250 KW	600 KW	1.5 GW	5 GW
Rotor diameter	15 m	20 m	30 m	46 m	70 m	115 m
Hub height	30 m	40 m	50 m	78 m	100 m	120 m
Annual energy yield	35 MWh	95 MWh	400 MWh	1.25 GWh	3.5 GWh	17 GWh
Full load hours	1,170	1,190	1,600	2,000	2,300	3,400

Figure 19.1: Trend in wind power infrastructure from 1980 to 2005 (BWE, 2007)

There have also been developments on the investor side. While in the past it was primarily private investors or investment funds behind the development of wind power, it is increasingly energy providers themselves that are recognising the potential of wind power and investing in wind farms. The 7% of electricity in Germany currently generated by wind power is primarily in the hands of hundreds of thousands of private owners. Imagine if energy providers owned the wind farms as 'assets' and could operate them as virtual power plants. The potential for lever-aging further efficiencies would be immense.

19.5   The Offshore Mega-trend: Prospects and Challenges

Wind power has been getting a good following wind for some years now, and the mega-trend emerging from all this is offshore wind developments. All energy pro-viders are now involved in offshore projects: RWE, EDF, E.ON, Dong and Vat-tenfall. 'Sky 2000' was the name of the first offshore wind farm project of the 1990s. In Germany, however, wind power went the same way as many other ground-breaking projects involving energy technology, such as fusion power or the carbon-neutral coal power plant. Time and time again, the planned introduc-tion of new technology was postponed for yet another year. While some initial experience with offshore wind farms is being made in the UK and Denmark, the first German project is not expected to materialise before 2008. There are plans to construct the first German demonstration farm some 42 km north of the island of Borkum. The intention is to have twelve turbines of the 5-MW type constructed by Multibrid and REpower that will feed into the German grid.

There are a number of reasons why Germany is making heavy weather of adopting this future-proof option, which is now the preferred one for all key po-litical stakeholders. Consideration of flora and fauna protection concerns on the one hand and tourism interests on the other has led to projects only having a chance of approval if they are planned some 40-60 km off the coast in water 30-40 metres deep. This makes implementation much more complex, both techno-logically and economically. Cable costs, the increased expense of deep-sea foun-dations and also the higher service costs involved have tended to scare away in-vestors. It did not even help much that grid feed payments of 9.1 cents per kilo-watt hour would make earnings much higher than those of onshore alternatives.

Why go offshore in the first place? Well, the potential for onshore wind power has already been largely exploited, as the majority of areas with good wind condi-tions are now being utilised. Expansion in this field will focus primarily on replac-ing older, smaller equipment with modern large-scale turbines ('repowering'). There is, however, great potential in the long term for wind power generation of 70-100 TWh per year from off-shore farms. Further expansion of wind power will therefore centre on wind farms in the North Sea and the Baltic Sea. The additional costs of construction and connection to the grid are offset by much higher earn-ings. Moreover, owing to concerns about landscape protection and flight path se-curity, height restrictions placed on onshore wind farms means they rarely stand more than 100-120 metres high. Greater heights also promise better earnings and more consistent wind speeds – and a 5-MW 180-metre-high giant tends not to offend when stationed well out to sea.

These giants are also profitable. More than half the capital invested in offshore wind farms with conventional 2- to 3-MW turbines is accounted for by the cost of cables and foundations, making such investments uneconomical. This is one of the key reasons why REpower Systems AG opted in 2002 to develop a 5-MW facility, which more than halves these fixed costs. Cable costs and foundations – in 30-metre-deep water some 40 km off the coast – make up half the costs, which is why the highest possible volumes of electricity have to be generated per grid point. A 5-MW turbine works out to be about 1.5 euro cents per kilowatt-hour cheaper than the conventional 2-MW turbines we are used to seeing in the Baltic Sea. The amount of energy generated can be 40% higher than with the onshore alternatives, owing to the higher wind speeds and larger rotor blades involved, which also off-sets the higher capital cost. It is now a legal requirement in Germany that grid connection costs are carried by the transmission system operators, as is the case for other power plants. Moreover, grid feeder payments valid until 2014 have been raised again to 14 euro cents/KWh. Offshore wind power is about to take off here in Germany.

19.6   Integration into a National Energy Supply Concept

Further development of offshore wind power in Germany will depend on its integration into the existing electricity supply structure. The Germany Energy Agency (DENA), together with energy supply companies, representatives of renewable energy sources and the responsible federal ministries, commissioned a scoping survey (DENA-Netzstudie) on the subject (see Figure 19.2). The study shows that the expansion target of the German Federal Government of 10,000 MW of offshore usage (produced by 2000 turbines of the 5-MW type) is realistic.

Nonetheless, this will require enormous effort. In particular, owing to the geographical concentration on the North Sea and Baltic Sea, there will need to be an assurance that the electricity generated in the north can be transmitted to the consumption hubs in Central and Southern Germany. The transmission grid will also have to be adapted to this new requirement. Investment in the upgrade and expansion of the networks is required for other reasons as well, however: technical modernisation, appropriate strengthening of East–West connections and increasing electricity sales in the liberalised EU market. By the year 2020 at the latest, various sections of the grid totalling about 400 km will need to be upgraded. Some 850 km of new lines will also have to be built.

In addition, the grids will have to be upgraded, as the existing ultra-high-voltage grid needs extending by about 5%. The total investment required to complete this extension will run to € 1.1 billion. As part of this expansion of wind power, investment costs will be required to connect the offshore wind farm turbines to the grid via under-sea cables, which will be added as needed. According to the findings of the DENA study, the Federal Government is predicting investment costs of around € 5 billion by the year 2020. The export of offshore technology will become highly significant in the future. Numerous national regulations (in Germany, the Netherlands, the UK, Belgium, Ireland, Spain, France, Denmark, Greece and Sweden) point to substantial market growth occurring over the next few years. The 'Grand Coalition' in Germany even wrote the potential for offshore wind power into its coalition agreement:

> "An important element of our climate protection and energy policy will be the ecologically and economically sound expansion of renewable energy sources. [...] We will therefore be pursuing ambitious goals to expand them further in Germany, including raising the share of electricity generation from renewables by 2010 to at least 12.5 percent and by 2020 to at least 20 percent. [...] We will maintain the EEG [the renewables law] in its basic structure, while at the same time monitoring the economic efficiency of individual payment rates until 2007. [...] We will focus on upgrading old wind farms (repowering) as well as offshore wind power generation and improve the infrastructure for this development (by, for instance, expanding the electricity networks). [...]" (Coalition agreement CDU, CSU and SPD, 2005).

This is a clear description of a course by which the German Federal Government and also the energy industry will inevitably be measured.

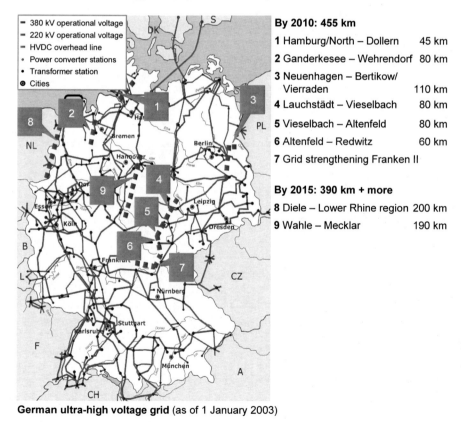

- 380 kV operational voltage
- 220 kV operational voltage
- HVDC overhead line
- Power converter stations
- Transformer station
- Cities

By 2010: 455 km

1 Hamburg/North – Dollern   45 km

2 Ganderkesee – Wehrendorf   80 km

3 Neuenhagen – Bertikow/
Vierraden   110 km

4 Lauchstädt – Vieselbach   80 km

5 Vieselbach – Altenfeld   80 km

6 Altenfeld – Redwitz   60 km

7 Grid strengthening Franken II

By 2015: 390 km + more

8 Diele – Lower Rhine region 200 km

9 Wahle – Mecklar   190 km

German ultra-high voltage grid (as of 1 January 2003)

Figure 19.2: Expansion of the German ultra-high voltage grid (DENA, 2005)

19.7   Outlook: The Right Social Framework Is Crucial

German energy providers have long since been at work on implementing offshore wind farms on a grand scale, as part of their overall renewables concept. Forward-looking companies have learnt that they will cease to operate as successful businesses if they do not meet the expectations that society as a whole has of them. But Germany also has to see this as a sociopolitical requirement for securing our future. The country has to reflect on its skill base and put engineering and the sciences back at the heart of educational policy. It needs to redouble the level of investment in energy research, which was halved in the 1990s. It has to return to making German energy research centres creative think-tanks, foster enthusiasm for technical solutions and guard against taboos such as those that have developed when it comes to putting thought and research into nuclear energy. Should fusion power – the true solar power – become available after 2030, major research policy efforts and political foresight will be required to hasten the viability of this form of energy generation. And why should we not be successful in doing this?

Of course, Germany needs to make a concerted effort to develop carbon-neutral coal power plants and to generate hydrogen from coal. The world is about to experience a coal renaissance anyway. And naturally, research into nuclear energy concepts with inherent safety mechanisms will have to be conducted. For even if renewables can meet 30% of our energy needs 20 years from now, we will still have to address the other 70% with equal vigour. Reducing the risks associated with coal power and nuclear energy is no less sustainable than developing renewables. At the same time, the structural disadvantage of renewables will have to be offset by:

- Developing storage technology for fluctuating renewable energy sources such as wind and sun;
- Constructing more transmission lines to improve the grid distribution of renewables, particularly connections to offshore wind farms;
- Making biofuels of the second generation ready to go to market;
- Researching new photovoltaic technologies to bring the cost down to 10% of what it is today.

We need a concerted campaign that will draw attention to the benefits of technology, a thirst for technical accomplishments and the motivation to excel at innovative engineering. In German schools the amount of science taught lags behind that of other countries. German mechanical engineering, with an export rate of 68% (worth € 87 billion) still leads the world in 19 out of 31 areas of mechanical engineering. At the same time, these small to medium-sized champions, with their high percentage of investment in research and development, are in danger of being bought up in the future by Russian oligarchies or Chinese, Indian or Arabic state funds in the wake of the private equity wave. Germany needs pro-active industrial policies that protect these capital-poor small and medium-sized enterprise (SME) champions. And it needs research policies that will substantially boost the engineering potential of this country as the basis for new top performances and the peak-performing products of CO_2-free technology.

References

Coalition agreement of CDU & CSU and SPD. 2005. Gemeinsam für Deutschland. Mit Mut und Menschlichkeit. 51.
Deutsche Energie-Agentur GmbH (DENA). 2005. Energiewirtschaftliche Planung für die Netzintegration von Windenergie in Deutschland an Land und Offshore bis zum Jahr 2020. Köln: DENA.
German Wind Energy Association (BWE). 2007. http://www.wind-energie.de/en/.

20 Emission Allowances – a New Production Factor in the Power Sector

Wolf Fichtner[1]

Abstract

The European CO_2 emission trading scheme results in a new input factor for CO_2 emission-intensive companies. Therefore, one of the objectives of this chapter is to characterise this new input factor. Emission trading and possible mechanisms of allocating allowances to existing and new installations are also discussed. Different effects of emission trading in general and of the European CO_2 emission trading scheme in particular are explained. Finally, the author shows how energy models can be used to develop consistent strategies for power companies within the framework of an emission trading scheme.

Keywords: emission trading, allocation of allowances, investment planning

---

[1] Prof. Dr. Wolf Fichtner is Professor of Energy Economics at Universität Karlsruhe (TH), Germany.

A. Bausch and B. Schwenker (eds.), *Handbook Utility Management,*
DOI: 10.1007/978-3-540-79349-6_20, © Springer-Verlag Berlin Heidelberg 2009

20.1   Introduction

Recent years in the European power market have been characterised by overca-pacities. Power prices at the energy exchanges have thus been based largely on the short-term marginal costs of existing power plants, and the construction of new capacities has not been realised owing to lacking profitability. However, with the electricity demand continuing to rise and the fact that significant amounts of ca-pacity will be reaching the end of their technical lifetime from 2010 onwards, power prices are starting to rise and planning activities with regard to new power plants are being intensified. The proper time to deal with these planning activities is now, as it takes years to build new power plants and many European power plants are rather old and will have to be replaced within the next 20 years (Pfaf-fenberger & Hille, 2004). In any analysis of the best technology to invest in, the new framework conditions of the power sector have to be considered. First and foremost this framework has changed because of the threat of global warming. Therefore, under the Kyoto Protocol of 1997, industrialised countries committed themselves to limiting their greenhouse gas emissions. The entire EU agreed to reduce its greenhouse gas emissions against 1990 emission levels by 8% in the period 2008-2012. This emission reduction objective was broken down into reduc-tion targets for each of the different countries in the EU in the so-called EU Bur-den Sharing Agreement. But as monitoring reports, e.g. those issued by the Euro-pean Environmental Agency, state, trends in greenhouse gas emissions indicate a significant compliance gap (Gugele et al., 2002). Therefore, the Commission de-cided to establish a European greenhouse gas emissions allowance trading scheme for CO_2-emitting installations. This emission trading scheme does not apply to all emissions produced in the EU; in sum the trading scheme considers less than half of the CO_2 emissions in the European Union. As energy activities are affected by the scheme and CO_2 is a joint product of fossil-fired energy production, the estab-lishment of such a greenhouse gas emissions allowance trading scheme will influ-ence the aforementioned investment strategies in this sector.

20.2   Characterisation of the New Input Factor Emission Allowances

Contrary to the emission trading approach mentioned in the Kyoto Protocol, which allows for a trade among nations, the European emission trading scheme is im-plemented with companies obliged to participate. Because companies affected by the European emission trading scheme have to hold sufficient emission allowances (EU Allowances (EUAs)), a new basic factor of production has in fact emerged, which will be characterised below by criteria typically used in business manage-ment (see Table 20.1; the sources mentioned refer to the criteria). In addition to this intangible and nonpersonnel input factor, the atmosphere – the place for the accumulation of trace gases – is, of course, still needed to run CO_2-emitting pro-duction processes.

Table 20.1: Characterisation of the new input factor CO_2 emission allowances

Criteria	Characteristics			Sources
Scheduling feasibility	Directing activity	Basic factor of production	Additional factor	Busse von Colbe & Lassmann, 1975, p. 68
Category	Personnel	Nonpersonnel		Gutenberg, 1966, p. 11ff.
Consumption	Potential factor of production	Consumable factor of production		Corsten, 1994, p. 9
Divisibility	Divisible	Indivisible		Kilger, 1975, p. 3098
Replaceability	Substitutional	Limitational		Heinen, 1970, p. 174f.
Variability	Long-term	Short-term		Beuermann, 1996, p. 1496
Marketability	Marketable	Nonmarketable		Haak, 1982, p. 139ff.
Repeatability	Possible	Impossible		Haak, 1982, p. 144
Integral part of the product	Direct factor	Indirect factor		Dinkelbach & Rosenberg, 2002, p. 11
Materiality	Substantial	Intangible		Kern & Fallaschinski., 1979, p. 17
Stage of production	Primary	Secondary		Bohr, 1979, p. 1483
Elasticity	Elastic	Inelastic		Haak, 1982, p. 139ff.

A CO_2 emission allowance is the right to emit the equivalent of 1 tonne of CO_2 – owing to the rather small quantity of 1 tonne this input factor can be characterised as divisible. Allowances lose their productive effect after the emission of the appropriate quantity of CO_2, and therefore allowances are consumable factors of production. By the end of April each year, the operator of each installation has to surrender the number of allowances corresponding to the total emissions from that installation during the preceding calendar year. Member states have to ensure that operators who do not hold sufficient allowances to cover their emissions are held liable and forced to pay excess emissions penalties. A way to substitute allowances would be a technology switch, for example to renewable energies to produce electricity. Owing to their homogeneity and their transferability, the purchase and sale of allowances can be varied at short notice; they are marketable, and a constant production quality can be guaranteed. Furthermore, CO_2 emission allowances are not an integral part of the product to be manufactured. Allowances are not intermediate products produced within the companies, but are received from outside the company and can therefore be characterised as primary input factors. Allowances can be used for completely different production processes: for electricity production in a bituminous coal power plant and for the production of cement clinker in rotary kilns, for example. Therefore, CO_2 emission allowances can be characterised as elastic. Another reason for this characterisation is the fact that there is a plan to enlarge the European CO_2 emission trading scheme into a European greenhouse gas emission allowance trading scheme by enabling conversion of greenhouse gases into CO_2 equivalents via calculation of their global warming potential.

20.3   Emission Trading

20.3.1   The Theory of Emission Trading

Under an emission trading scheme companies have the flexibility to meet emissions reduction targets according to their own optimal strategy, by reducing emissions or by buying emissions allowances on the market. On the assumption that emission reduction technologies are cheaper than emission allowances available on the allowance market, companies will invest in these technologies. To ensure this economic efficiency, all activities under the emission trading scheme need to receive a price signal depending on their emission intensity. In this way, nondistorted incentives for the economic appraisal are provided. At first glance the economic efficiency of an emission trading scheme does not depend on the allocation provisions chosen; the full cost of the emissions – including both the real costs for the purchase of emissions allowances and opportunity costs of the emissions allowances allocated free of charge – creates a nondistorted price signal (Matthes et al., 2005).

In addition to the economic efficiency, the desired environmental outcome will be achieved (environmental effectiveness) provided that reliable control mechanisms exist, since the remaining emissions are fixed by the overall cap, which sets the limit on the number of emission allowances to be allocated. Another advantage of an emission trading system is its innovation efficiency, as companies involved have an incentive to search constantly for new emission reduction technologies (Oberndorfer et al., 2006).

To realise such a promising scheme, oversupply of emission allowances has to be avoided, because without scarcity there is no trading and the entire system becomes obsolete.[2] Furthermore, as many emitters as possible should be covered by an emission trading scheme, in order to be able to benefit from differences in emission reduction costs. And, as long as there is no risk of so-called hot spots, such a system should have full temporal flexibility, implying that allowances can be borrowed as well as banked (Boemare & Quirion, 2002).

When such an emission trading scheme is developed, possible interdependencies with other environmental instruments have to be considered. For example, many countries have installed instruments to foster electricity production from renewable energy sources. Even if the installations to use renewable energies do not participate in emission trading, there might be strong interdependencies, because electricity from renewable energy sources reduces electricity production in power plants integrated into the emission trading scheme (Wissenschaftlicher Bei-

---

[2] The excess of allowances allocated in the period 2005-2007 led to the strong decline of allowance prices in the European emissions trading scheme.

rat, 2004). Therefore, at least the intended emission reduction by instruments fostering electricity production from renewable energy sources has to be considered in the calculation of how many emission allowances are to be issued.

20.3.2   The Theory of Allowance Allocation

In general the methods of allocating permits can be distinguished into auctioning, grandfathering and benchmarking. Auctioning of emission allowances may lead to a situation where the auction prices correspond from the very beginning with the marginal emission reduction costs. In contrast to this, approaches based on a free allocation of allowances can have problems in ensuring comprehensive and non-distorting incentive structures (Matthes et al., 2005). Other advantages of auctioning accrue from the simplicity of the system, since the cap is the only restriction to be determined. It is obvious that auctioning of emission rights is superior to any other allocation method (Cramton & Kerr, 2002). However, in order to promote the acceptance of an emission trading scheme an allowance allocation that is free of charge will often be chosen, because companies with existing installations are better off with such a scheme. Therefore, the choice of grandfathering sometimes seems to result from the political negotiation processes (Kehoane et al., 1998).

If grandfathering is used, emission allowances are allocated free of charge to existing plants based on their historical emissions. An extreme type of this allocation procedure requires that the allocation is strictly separated from plant operation and so leads to incentive structures equivalent to auctioning with respect to cost efficiency: Emission allowances are allocated to existing plants even if the plant has been shut down, whereas new plants do not get allowances free of charge. These rules ensure that the use of allowances produces opportunity costs, which are regarded as additional variable costs. Only if a second-best world with distorting taxes is assumed, the auctioning scheme can produce additional macroeconomic improvements if auction revenues are used to reduce taxes (Schwarz, 2006). Disadvantages of grandfathering are that there may be a bias against new companies entering the market, since existing installations get their permits free, and furthermore, that grandfathering can increase emissions if the companies are aware that larger current emissions will result in larger future allocations of emission allowances.

If benchmarks are used for allocation purposes, installations are given allowances free of charge according to a fixed emission-value per unit of output. Benchmarks in the energy sector can be differentiated into so-called fuel-specific benchmarks with different values for different fuels and in so-called product (or sector) benchmarks with only one benchmark for all fuels. If fuel-specific benchmarks are used for the allocation of emission allowances to existing and/or to new installations, power plants with higher specific CO_2 emissions receive more emission allowances than plants with lower specific CO_2 emissions. With product benchmarks the allocation is the same for all power plants; even installations with emissions lower than the benchmark receive the full benchmark allocation.

20.3.3 Allocation of Allowances According to the National Allocation Plans

Within the European CO_2 emission trading scheme member states have to develop so-called national allocation plans (NAP) for the different trading periods. These plans have to indicate how many emission allowances the state intends to issue during the corresponding trading period and how these allowances are to be distributed to the participating installations.

For the first and the second trading period most of the allocation plans developed by the member states grant allowances free of charge, although in the second period auctioning may also be found. Most countries allocate allowances free of charge according to the grandfathering rule on the basis of historical emissions or by using fuel-specific benchmarks. These fuel-specific benchmarks lead to the situation where power plants that use fuels leading to higher CO_2 emissions receive a more generous allocation than installations fired with fuels leading to lower CO_2 emissions. In addition, the allocation to a new installation might depend on whether it replaces an existing installation (so-called transfer rules). When emission allowances are allocated on the basis of historical emissions, updated reference periods are sometimes used.[3] Furthermore, most countries have introduced special provisions for combined heat and power (CHP) installations (e.g. double benchmarks: one for electricity production, the other for heat production) since this technology faces problems, because the trading scheme does not include all emission sources (e.g. heat boilers with a thermal capacity of less than 20 MW).

In Germany the method for allocating allowances to existing installations in the first trading period from 2005-2007 was grandfathering based on the average emissions in 2000-2002. New entrants received their allowances free of charge by an allocation with fuel-specific benchmarks. The quantity of the allowance allocated to new power plants was determined by the product of the installed capacity, the projected average utilisation and the fuel-specific benchmark (max.: 750 g CO_2 equivalent/kWh_e, min.: 365 g CO_2 equivalent/kWh_e[4]). If the utilisation during the operation of the installation was lower than the projected level, new entrants were subject to a so-called ex-post adjustment – they had to give back surplus allowances. This adjustment was realised to avoid selection by the operators of a too high projected average utilisation to ensure a generous allocation. In the second trading period from 2008 to 2012, allocating allowances to existing energy installations was switched to a benchmarking system (with the two benchmarks 750 and 365 g CO_2 equivalent/kWh_e), which rewards efficient installations. In contrast to the first allocation plan, installation-specific projections and the associated ex-post

---

[3] For example, the reference period for the second trading period in Germany is 2000-2005, which shows that the first year of the first trading period is part of the reference period of the second trading period.

[4] For power plants using fuels with a lower specific emission value than 750 g CO_2 equivalent/kWh_e the allocation should not exceed the requirements but was at least 365 g CO_2 equivalent/kWh_e.

adjustment have been avoided and general utilisation factors have been introduced. Furthermore, the transfer rule was deleted and around one-tenth of the total quantity of allowances is no longer allocated free of charge; instead these allowances are auctioned.[5]

20.4   Effects of Emission Trading

20.4.1   Theoretical Effects of Emission Trading

The shortage of a new production factor because of the cap of an emission trading scheme leads to additional marginal costs of production and in consequence inevitably to higher product prices. With pure grandfathering the corresponding rent is captured by the companies affected by the trading scheme, with auctioning the rent is socialised and can be used, for example, to cut existing taxes. According to the strong double-dividend hypothesis, auctioning could therefore even increase welfare (Boemare & Quirion, 2002). In competitive markets, companies are able to pass through the full costs of carbon to the wholesale prices, including the opportunity costs for allowances – even if these allowances have been allocated free of charge. Of course, the consequent windfall profits will be less significant if the allocation to installations is less generous (Matthes et al., 2005). The integration of opportunity costs of allowances into market prices of electricity is correct from an accounting point of view, since the allowances do have an economic value and could otherwise be sold. Moreover, emission trading cannot work without these price signals. The assumption that opportunity costs can only be passed on to customers in markets with little competition is not justified. Whereas the passing through of opportunity costs has been discussed intensively, it has gone almost unnoticed that in a fully competitive electricity market – in the long run – there might be times where electricity prices are lower in the case of an allowance allocation free of charge than in a situation with auctioning. This is because new power plants will only be built if there are some hours during the year where demand is higher than supply and the electricity prices are therefore above the short-term marginal costs. This is necessary for new power plants to be able to cover their fixed costs. During these hours the resulting electricity price is lower if the allowances have been allocated free of charge, because the benefits caused by this form of allocation will be handed on to the customers in a fully competitive market.

The incentives to reduce emissions from existing plants depend on the full costs of carbon, including the real costs for purchasing allowances as well as the opportunity costs of allowances allocated at no charge. Therefore, there seem to be no differences in the benefits from emissions reductions in existing installations, re-

---

[5] Because of the reduction factors due to auctioning and the efficiency standard and because there is no benchmark for lignite, the allocation to existing lignite power plants in Germany may lead to a considerable shortage of emission allowances in these installations.

gardless of whether auctioning, grandfathering or benchmarking has been used to allocate allowances.

In contrast to this, the economic incentives for investors to build new power plants with low emissions strongly depend on the allocation provisions. An operator analysing the replacement of an existing plant by a new installation will just compare the real costs of these alternatives. In this context it is essential to bear in mind that the real costs are reduced by a free allocation. Therefore, when allocating free of charge, the allocation provisions should be realised in such a way that the real costs reflect the carbon intensity; the real costs in installations with high emissions should be high, and in installations with low emissions they should be low. Fuel-specific allocation provisions can lead to erosion of the differences in real costs (Matthes et al., 2005). Fuel-specific benchmarks are sometimes supplemented by transfer provisions to establish an incentive to build low-carbon plants to replace existing installations, but these transfer provisions can result in fairness problems, because the amount of allocated allowances depends on whether the operator is an incumbent or a newcomer (Bode et al., 2005). The free allocation to new entrants based on product benchmarks can create carbon price signals equivalent to the case of auctioning.

Even if product benchmarks are used, however, there is still the question of the level of this benchmark to ensure incentives for the correct replacement decisions of power plants. The free allocation to existing and to new power plants has to be balanced to reflect their carbon intensity. If an existing power plant receives a rather generous allocation free of charge and a new installation does not, the operator may tend to extend the lifetime of the existing installations for as long as possible and to invest in lifetime expansion. On the other hand, a too-generous allocation to new power plants could lead to a too strong incentive for plant replacement or even to the establishment of overcapacities.

20.4.2   Effects of the European Emission Trading Scheme and the Corresponding National Allocation Plans

The current design of the European emission trading scheme has been criticised for various reasons. With respect to the ecological effectiveness it has often been quoted that the Kyoto targets are not considered sufficiently. Many countries seem to have shifted emission reduction obligations to sectors not participating in emission trading, further weakening the efficiency of the system by relaxing the reduction obligations without having well-defined strategies to ensure the reduction of emissions in the nontrading sectors (Oberndorfer et al., 2006). This could lead to high marginal abatement costs in sectors not participating in the European emission trading scheme (Böhringer et al., 2006). Furthermore, the insufficient harmonisation of allocation approaches and the very short time horizon of the emission trading scheme is criticised (Neuhoff et al., 2005). The rules of allowance allocation, and also the amount of granted allowances, are only known for the next 5 years, leading to extreme uncertainties for investment planning in the companies participating in emission trading, which seems to be critical, especially if the long lifetime of power plants is considered.

Whereas the allocation of allowances to installations was long seen as a pure distribution problem, the European scheme made it clear that some key provisions were implemented that could have negative impacts on the economic efficiency of the scheme (Matthes et al., 2005). Some NAPs managed to abrogate the rule that the allocation to existing plants normally does not change any incentives to de-crease emissions by introducing so-called ex-post adjustments, for example. As operators to whom these provisions apply have to give back surplus allowances, they will not consider possible opportunity costs, which eliminates carbon pricing. Furthermore, the economic incentives arising from the allocation to new installa-tions do not always reflect the different emission levels of new plants adequately. Many countries allocate emission allowances to new entrants with the help of fuel-specific benchmarks, reducing the intended incentive structures. If, for example, a bituminous coal power plant receives more emission allowances than a gas-fired power plant, the incentive to invest in bituminous coal plants increases.[6] Using one uniform product benchmark to allocate allowances to new installations leads to the situation that fossil-fired plants are now treated equally but the height of this benchmark can affect the intensity of plant replacement. Furthermore, updating the reference period has an essential drawback, as operators will become aware that today's generation influences the allocation of allowances in the next period. Hence, there is an incentive to alter one's own behaviour to increase one's future allocation of emissions allowances (Bartels & Müsgens, 2006). This can be seen as one reason why in the first trading period total costs of emission allowances have not been passed through totally to the electricity prices.

20.5   Consistent Strategies Under an Emission Trading Scheme

The introduction of an emission trading scheme and the corresponding shortage of a formerly free production factor results in additional requirements on power companies for extended analyses, not only of the power markets but also of the CO_2 emission allowance market. The identification of a reasonable investment strategy seems to be almost impossible, because slight modifications of the alloca-tion rules can lead to massive changes in the investment environment. Moreover, there are strong interdependencies between the power and the emissions allowance markets. For example, how advantageous one of the two totally different strategies for fulfilling emission reduction obligations is either by (1) reducing electricity production and selling corresponding surplus allowances or by (2) investing in new technologies and increasing electricity output, depends exclusively on a few

---

[6] There are certainly other reasons why there should be incentives to invest in coal-fired power plants in some countries, such as reducing dependence on foreign energy sources, but in this chapter only emission reduction is picked out as a the central theme.

assumptions concerning the energy-economic framework conditions. Therefore, energy system planning is often facilitated by the use of energy system models, which reproduce the existing supply system in a mathematical model. A common classification of models for electricity sector planning distinguishes between bottom-up models on the one hand and top-down models on the other. While top-down models are characterised by an integral approach considering the entire national economy at a high level of aggregation, bottom-up models employ a process-analytical approach, i.e. provide for a differentiated analysis of technological options at the microeconomic level.

Such models are usually used to analyse different scenarios (Bartels & Müsgens, 2006; Fichtner et al., 2007; Schwarz, 2006). To get an understanding of the impact of CO_2 emission trading on future power generation and capacity structures, it is necessary to study the expected development of this sector without CO_2 emission reduction obligations. Model results often indicate that without CO_2 restrictions electricity demand will largely be covered by fossil fuel-based electricity generation within Europe. The models indicate a rather diversified electricity mix; capacities fired by lignite, coal and natural gas would be built, as they provide the most attractive coverage of base, intermediate and peak load.

In a second scenario CO_2 emission trading with auctioning is normally set up, which serves as a reference for the comparison of different emission trading scenarios. If it is assumed that the Kyoto commitments have to be fulfilled, model results generally indicate a structural change to the less CO_2-intensive energy carrier gas all over Europe: at least until fossil-fired technologies resulting in hardly any CO_2 emissions, e.g. coal power plants with carbon capture and sequestration (CCS), are available and their investment costs decline drastically compared with the situation today, the construction of combined-cycle gas turbines is the dominating investment option. The electricity share of natural gas-fired power plants is growing even more strongly than their capacity share, showing that these units are operated at increased full-load hours. Furthermore, some model results have shown that in some countries, e.g. France, Great Britain and Finland, electricity production in existing nuclear plants is increasing and some new nuclear power plants are being commissioned (Fichtner et al., 2007).

Model results look different as soon as allocation with fuel-specific benchmarks is integrated: now the model results show that power companies would build more coal and lignite plants, while investments in gas are less attractive. If the same CO_2 emission cap is set, this leads inevitably to the operation of more technologies with hardly any CO_2 emissions, e.g. nuclear power plants or coal power plants with CCS. Finally, model results point out that emission reduction costs are higher if fuel-specific benchmarks are used to allocate emission allowances.

With regard to the different allocation procedures used in the different member states, the models also show that, for example, the different levels of benchmarks used to allocate allowances to new installations might create distortions between different states.

20.6   Summary

To reduce emissions of CO_2, the most important greenhouse gas, the EU decided to implement a community-wide emission trading scheme for power companies and energy-intensive production companies from 2005 onwards. Owing to this scheme, a new basic factor of production emerged for the affected companies. However, this trading scheme and the allocation rules implemented by the member states of the European Union do not fully fit into the framework of a perfect emission trading scheme. This chapter shows that the economic incentives to build and/or use installations with low emissions, which an emission trading scheme offers to investors, depend on the allocation provisions. Furthermore, the model analyses presented indicate that in a CO_2 emission trading scheme with perfect incentive structures attributable, for example, to the use of auctions to allocate emissions allowances, investments in combined cycle gas turbines are dominant, whereas under a trading scheme using fuel-specific benchmarks there will be much more investment in bituminous coal and lignite power plants.

References

Bartels, M. & Müsgens, F. 2006. Do technology specific CO_2-allocations distort investments? In International Association for Energy Economics (Ed.), Proceedings of the 29th IAEE International Conference. Potsdam.

Beuermann, G. 1996. Produktionsfaktoren. In W. Kern (Ed.), Handwörterbuch der Produktionswirtschaft (2nd ed.): 1494-1505. Stuttgart: Poeschel Verlag.

Bode, S., Hübl, L., Schaffner, J. & Twelemann, S. 2005. Ökologische und wettbewerbliche Wirkungen der Übertragungs- und der Kompensationsregel des Zuteilungsgesetzes 2007 auf die Stromerzeugung. Hamburg: HWWA-Report 252.

Boemare, C. & Quirion, P. 2002. Implementing greenhouse gas trading in Europe: Lessons from economic literature and international experiences. Ecological Economics, 43: 213-230.

Bohr, K. 1979. Produktionsfaktorsysteme. In W. Kern (Ed.), Handwörterbuch der Produktionswirtschaft: 1481-1493. Stuttgart: Poeschel Verlag.

Böhringer, C., Hoffmann, T. & de Lara Penate, C. 2006. The efficiency costs of separating carbon markets under the EU emissions trading scheme: a quantitative assessment for Germany. Unpublished Discussion Paper No. 05-06, ZEW, Mannheim.

Busse von Colbe, W. & Lassmann, G. 1975. Betriebswirtschaftstheorie Band 1: Grundlagen, Produktions- und Kostentheorie. Berlin: Springer-Verlag.

Corsten, H. 1994. Produktionswirtschaft (4th ed.). München: Oldenbourg Verlag.

Cramton, P. & Kerr, S. 2002. Tradable carbon permit auctions, how and why to auction not grandfather. Energy Policy, 30: 333-345.

Dinkelbach, W. & Rosenberg, O. 2002. Erfolgs- und umweltorientierte Produktionstheorie. Berlin: Springer.

Fichtner, W., Witt, M. & Baumert, S. G. 2007. Zur Analyse der Auswirkungen unterschiedlicher Zuteilungsverfahren von CO_2-Emissionsrechten. VDI-Berichte, 2018: 187-198.

Gugele, B., Ritter, M. & Mareckova, K. 2002. Greenhouse gas emission trends in Europe 1990-2000. Unpublished Report 7/2002, European Environment Agency, Kopenhagen.

Gutenberg, E. 1966. Grundlagen der Betriebswirtschaftslehre, Bd. I: Die Produktion (12th ed.). Berlin: Springer-Verlag.

Haak, W. 1982. Produktion in Banken: Möglichkeiten eines Transfers industriebetrieblich-produktionswirtschaftlicher Erkenntnisse auf den Produktionsbereich von Bankbetrieben. Frankfurt am Main: Peter Lang Verlag.

Heinen, E. 1970. Betriebswirtschaftliche Kostenlehre (3rd ed.). Wiesbaden: Gabler.

Kehoane, N., Revesz, R. & Stavins, R. 1998. The positive political economy of instrument choice in environmental policy. In P. Portney & R. Schwab (Eds.), Environmental Economics and Public Policy. London: Edward Elgar.

Kern, W. & Fallaschinski, K. 1979. Betriebswirtschaftliche Produktionsfaktoren (II). WISU (Das Wirtschaftstudium), 8: 15-18.

Kilger, W. 1975. Produktionsfaktor. In E. Grochla & W. Wittmann (Eds.), Handwörterbuch der Betriebswirtschaft (4th ed.): 3097-3101. Stuttgart: Poeschel Verlag.

Matthes, F., Graichen, V. & Repenning, J. 2005. The environmental effectiveness and economic efficiency of the European Union emissions trading scheme: structural aspects of allocation. A Report to WWF. Freiburg: Öko-Institut e.V.

Neuhoff, K., Grubb, M. & Keats, K. 2005. Impact of the allowance allocation on prices and efficiency. Unpublished Working Paper CWPE 0552, Cambridge.

Oberndorfer, U., Rennings, K. & Sahin, B. 2006. The impacts of the European emissions trading scheme on competitiveness and employment in Europe – a literature review. Mannheim: Centre for European Economic Research.

Pfaffenberger, W. & Hille, M. 2004. Investitionen im liberalisierten Energiemarkt: Optionen, Marktmechanismen, Rahmenbedingungen. Frankfurt: VWEW Energieverlag.

Schwarz, H. 2006. The European emission trading system and the present draft of the German national allocation law: A critical evaluation of the effects on electricity production and investment patterns. IWE Working Paper Nr. 05 2006.

Wissenschaftlicher Beirat beim Bundesministerium für Wirtschaft und Arbeit. 2004. Zur Förderung erneuerbarer Energien. Köln.

Part IV:
Energy Trading and Wholesale

21 Energy Trading, Emission Certificates and Risk Management

Ronald Huisman[1]

Abstract

One of the tasks of a utility company is to manage the risks that arise from the gaps between the obligation to make future deliveries of energy and the company's assets. The goal of this chapter is to provide insights into these gaps and to discuss some risk management concepts and instruments that can be used to actively manage these risks.

Keywords: risk management, energy derivative contracts, assets-liabilities management

[1] Dr. Ronald Huisman is Associate Professor at the Erasmus School of Economics, Applied Economics, Erasmus University Rotterdam, The Netherlands.

A. Bausch and B. Schwenker (eds.), *Handbook Utility Management,*
DOI: 10.1007/978-3-540-79349-6_21, © Springer-Verlag Berlin Heidelberg 2009

21.1 Different Roles of Energy Utility Companies in the Energy Markets

Before the process of energy liberalization started, utility companies were the crucial link in the chain between production and consumption of energy. Utility companies forecasted the future amount of energy consumption of their clients and managed a portfolio of delivery contracts in order to secure delivery. Examples of such contracts are own production facilities and long- and short-term contracts with power producers. Basically, a utility company used to manage a portfolio of delivery contracts to serve their regional clients, thereby managing the price and volumetric risks between producing and selling to customers. Examples of such risks are price fluctuations between purchasing and selling (in fact, variable fuel-related prices versus relatively fixed selling prices) and the differences between planned and actual consumption.

In the liberalized energy market, end-consumers are not obliged to purchase from their regional utility company, but may choose where to buy their energy from and do not need to limit themselves to only one energy company. For instance, they can purchase their energy needs directly in the market, from producers, from utility companies, or from some combination. These days, end-consumers manage their own portfolios of energy delivery contracts, and as a result, the focus of utility companies has changed towards helping their clients in optimally managing their own portfolio of delivery contracts by offering access to the marketplace and taking care of the actual physical delivery of the energy. As stock investors use banks and brokerage companies to purchase shares and other instruments in the equity markets, end-consumers use utility companies to buy energy delivery contracts that are traded on exchanges or some over-the-counter (OTC) contract structures. Examples of the latter are fixed-price contracts for one, two or three years, variable price contracts in which the price is linked to some market index (electricity price or oil prices or the price of some other commodity), and more advanced products such as one in which the price is variable but with a guarantee that it will not exceed a maximum or fall below a minimum. In the case of physical delivery, utility companies offer products to insure against risk in the imbalance market (the risk that occurs from differences between actual and planned consumption on the delivery day) or manage the clients' day-ahead positions.

In today's energy markets, utility companies offer products to service clients in optimally managing their own energy portfolio, recognizing that clients vary in terms of risk appetite and/or other characteristics. For instance, a risk-averse client is likely to buy a fixed-price contract, a risk-loving client has a preference for variable price contracts, and a chemical-producing company might have a preference for an energy price indexed to the price of some chemical commodity. Utility companies assist the end-consumers in optimally managing their portfolios by offering a variety of products. A thorough understanding of the markets is, therefore, crucial for a utility company to be competitive in the liberalized energy markets.

21.2 Overview of Energy Markets and the Contracts Being Traded

As a result of the liberalization process in the international energy markets, many energy markets have been established that facilitate trading all kinds of energy delivery contracts. Table 21.1 provides information on the volumes traded in power and emissions for the German European Energy Exchange (EEX) market, the Nordic Nord Pool market, and the European Climate Exchange (ECX) throughout 2007. The EEX market (formed from the merger of the Leipzig Power Exchange and the Frankfurt-based European Energy Exchange in 2002) is a major marketplace in the European Union where agents can trade spot and derivative contracts on power, gas, emission allowances and coal. During 2007, the EEX trade volume for power amounted to 1,374 TWh (spot and derivatives) and that for emissions to 23 million tonnes. The Nord Pool market, where trading in power and emissions contracts has been allowed since 1993 (following the Norwegian government's decision to liberalize energy markets in 1991), the corresponding volumes were about 1,351 TWh for power and 95 million tonnes for emissions (see Table 21.1). The ECX was launched in 2005. Here, emission futures and option contracts are being traded, and the 2007 volume was more than a billion tonnes. These are examples of the many different energy markets that have emerged since the start of liberalization. In addition to these market places there is an active OTC market, which represents all other transactions than those via the exchanges, between different agents. Energy trading has become a serious business and an international, multi-commodity affair.

Table 21.1: Traded volumes[a] in power and emissions over the whole year of 2007 (www.eex.de, www.nordpool.com, www.europeanclimateexchange.com)

Type of contract	EEX[b]	Nord Pool	ECX[c]
	Power [TWh]		
Spot	124	291	
Futures/options	1,150	1,060	
	Emissions [m tones]		
Futures/options	23	95	1,038

[a] Values represent traded (no clearing) volumes
[b] EEX – European Energy Exchange
[c] ECX – European Climate Exchange

In the markets presented above, we typically find spot, futures and option contracts. In the remainder of this section, the details of spot and forwards contracts are discussed, as these are the types most commonly being used by utility companies.[2] The focus will be on how the markets operate and on the price characteris-

---

[2] See Errera and Brown (1999) and Eydeland and Wolyniec (2002), among others, for a thorough overview of many other types of instruments.

tics. Section 21.3 will focus on how utility companies apply the contracts that are traded on the markets.

21.2.1   Day-ahead (Spot) Market

In financial markets, 'spot' refers to contracts that involve the soonest possible delivery moment. In energy markets, the term 'spot' is used for both the day-ahead markets and intra-day (imbalance) markets. The intra-day markets involve trading in contracts from which delivery takes places as soon as 15 minutes after the transaction (although the length of time differs for different exchanges). These markets are relatively thin and mainly used for balancing purposes to trade away the intra-day deviations between supply and demand. The day-ahead markets are more fluid, and day-ahead prices are used as reference prices in forward and futures contracts. For many traders, a day-ahead contract comes closest to spot delivery, and hence 'spot' is used to mean day-ahead in the rest of this chapter.

In day-ahead markets, one can trade power that will be delivered in the course of the next day. Traders can submit their bids and offers for each specific hour. For instance, one trader might submit that he is willing to deliver 3 MW of power tomorrow in hour 13. These markets function as an auction. The EEX day-ahead market closes at noon, and before this moment traders should have submitted their bids and offers for each hour separately.

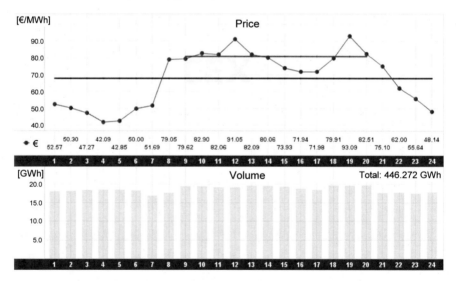

Figure 21.1: EEX day-ahead prices and volumes for delivery on 30 January 2008 (www.eex.de, 2008)

Figure 21.1 provides an example of the prices on the EEX for delivery on 30 January 2007. The market cleared at a price of € 52.57 for delivery of 1 MW in hour 1; the volume for that hour is about 18 GWh. The price for delivery at hour 12 is € 91.05. The figure shows clearly that prices are substantially higher during peak hours (between 08:00 and 20:00 for the EEX) than during the other (offpeak) hours. This reflects the higher demand for power during working hours, in which relatively expensive power plants are needed to supply the demand. The lower demand in the offpeak hours therefore results in lower prices. The two horizontal lines in the graph represent the base (the lower) and peak (the upper) prices for that day. The base price is the average price over the entire 24 hours; it is 67.83 €/WMh. The peak price is the average price over all peak hours; it is 80.93 €/WMh. The base and peak prices act as reference prices for future and forward, as will be discussed later.

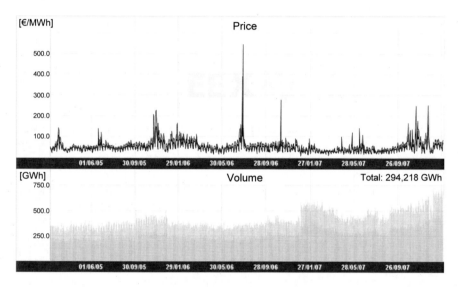

Figure 21.2: EEX base and peak day-ahead prices and volumes from January 2005 through January 2008 (www.eex.de, 2008)

Figure 21.2 shows the development of the daily base and peak prices over time for the EEX market. The characteristics that appear in the figure are typical for day-ahead prices in any market. The prices seem to revert around some long-term average price. This long-term average price relates to the marginal production costs of power. The prices are also very volatile. Volatility reflects price uncertainty; higher volatility implies more uncertainty about where prices will be tomorrow. Over time, the degree of volatility varies. Periods with relatively low volatility (spring 2005, autumn 2005 and spring 2007, for example) are followed by periods with high volatility, such as the winter of 2006 and 2007. In addition to the pattern of volatility varying with time, there are frequent spikes. Spikes are high prices that last for a relatively short time. Examples are easy to observe in Figure 21.2, with the spike in the summer of 2006 most noteworthy. Spikes are due to temporal imbalances in demand/supply conditions, for instance a breakdown of a power plant, a very hot summer with maximum use of air conditioning, or regulatory intervention.[3] An example of the last occurred in the Netherlands in the summer of 2003. The temperature of the water in rivers rose to such levels, due to the heat wave, that the Dutch government put a limit on the amount of cooling water that was allowed to flow into rivers. Indirectly, they restricted the maximum capacity at which power plants could run, and more expensive power plants had to come into operation. This event resulted in a spike. Power prices are also seasonal. In the winter months power prices are higher than average, and prices are more volatile in summer and winter months than in spring and autumn.

One of the implications of the above characteristics of power prices is that they are extremely uncertain. Energy purchasers might be willing to purchase a part of their energy needs on the day-ahead markets, but the volatile and spiky prices could become a serious risk. This explains the demand for different instruments that can be used to manage the price risk accruing from the day-ahead markets. Commonly used instruments are forward and futures contracts and options.

21.2.2 Forward and Futures Contracts

Forward and futures contracts are the same in essence. The single difference is that futures are traded on an exchange and forwards are not (they are so-called OTC traded). From here onward, the term 'forwards' is used to mean both forwards and futures, unless stated otherwise.

A forward contract is a contract in which the buyer agrees to purchase an amount of a commodity from the seller during a specified delivery period for a fixed price. The buyer and the seller agree on the price at the moment when they both enter into the contract. Consider Table 21.2, which contains the futures prices of 29 January 2008. When a trader buys one Feb 08 base contract, he commits himself to purchasing 1 MW of power in each hour of February 2008 against a fixed price of 61.65 €/WMh. If he were to sell one Feb 08 peak contract, he would be committing himself to delivering 1 MW in all peak hours on February 2008 and he would receive a price of 81.35 €/WMh. Thus, by trading a forward contract, a trader can fix prices.

As can be seen from Table 21.2, traders can buy and sell forwards and futures up to six years ahead. They can do so by trading monthly delivery contracts, quarterly delivery contracts (Q), and calendar year contracts (Cal). In the OTC markets, there are more forward contracts with all kinds of delivery periods, and delivery in peak, super peak, or single hours or some combination of hours. A purchaser of energy can therefore contract the delivery of energy up to six years ahead against prices that are fixed today. Entering into forward contracts helps these purchasers to manage the price risk they face from the day-ahead markets.

---

[3] See Huisman (2008), Mount et al. (2006), and Kosater (2006) for discussions of the origin and predictability of spikes in power prices.

Table 21.2: Prices [€/MWh] of EEX futures on 29 January 2007 (www.eex.de, 2008)

Delivery period	Base	Peak
Feb 08	61.65	81.35
Mar 08	57.00	75.50
Apr 08	56.00	73.00
May 08	52.00	68.00
Jun 08	56.49	79.97
Jul 08	60.50	87.50
Q2 08	54.80	73.56
Q3 08	58.83	84.54
Q4 08	64.75	91.50
Q1 09	68.34	93.45
Q2 09	54.25	73.45
Q3 09	57.75	82.52
Q4 09	63.94	90.04
Cal 09	61.05	85.50
Cal 10	60.20	85.70
Cal 11	60.80	85.96
Cal 12	60.85	86.25
Cal 13	63.50	88.00
Cal 14	63.25	88.25

As delivery takes place in a future time period, payment is also on delivery. This means that one can buy a Cal 14 forward contract (delivery in 2014) today and pay in 2014. However, this involves a credit risk for both the buyer and the seller of the contract. If the seller went bankrupt the contract would no longer be valid and the buyer would need to enter into a new forward contract at the moment of bankruptcy. At present the risk is that the market forward price might be higher than that specified in the previous contract. The opposite holds true for the seller. Therefore, companies demand collateral for taking on forward positions in order to protect themselves against credit risk. When trading a futures contract on an exchange, a trader is forced to enter into a so-called margining agreement (Errera & Brown, 1999). The essence of a margining scheme is that profits and losses on the contract are settled daily on a margin account. There are two types of margining: initial margin and variation margin. Directly after the transaction, a trader needs to transfer a fixed amount in euros to a margin account (typically this is about 5-10% of the underlying value). If the price of the future contract decreases during the next day, the loss is subtracted from the margin account and added to the margin account of the seller. If the contract price increases, the amount of price increase is taken from the margin account from the seller and transferred to the buyer. In addition to the initial margin, exchanges apply maintenance margins. When a contract suffers losses to the point that the amount of money on the margin account has decreased to a certain limit, the trader will receive a margin call and be required to deposit an amount to bring the margin account up to the initial margin level. The effect of a margin account in relation to credit risk is shown in the following example. Suppose a trader buys one Cal 09 base contract for the price of € 61.05 (see Table 21.2). The day after, the price of the contract increased to € 70.00. The trader then received an amount of € 70.00 (€ 61.05 = 8.95 times the number of hours in the delivery period on his margin account). If at that moment, the seller goes bankrupt, the buyer can buy a new futures contract in the market for € 70.00 and partly finance the deal with the settled profit of € 8.95 (times the number of hours in the delivery period), which is on his margin account. In effect, he still pays a net price of € 61.05 for delivery in 2009.

Futures contracts differ from forward contracts insofar as they are exchange traded and traders have to participate in a margining scheme. In forward markets, contract structures and collateral agreements are based on bilateral negotiations. Most emissions contracts are also futures and forwards. These contracts therefore involve a fixed price that a trader pays if he purchases the allowance to emit during a specific time period.

21.2.3   The Forward Price versus the Day-ahead Price

When energy purchasers think about how to purchase their energy needs, they can purchase on the day-ahead market or on the forward market or some combination. The optimal strategy for a purchaser depends on the price/risk tradeoff between the spot and forward markets. The day-ahead market brings uncertainty, but also a lower price, whereas a forward contract offers a fixed price against a premium. And, in making purchasing plans, is the current forward price for delivery in 2009 a good estimate for the expected future day-ahead price in 2009?

The relation between forward and spot prices in energy markets is not as straightforward as that in stock markets. This is due to the limited storability of energy. To show this, consider the following example. A stock is traded for € 100. Agents in the equity markets all expect that the stock will move to € 110 after one year, but the volatility of the stock return will be such that with 99% confidence the stock price will be in a range between € 70 and € 150 after one year. Furthermore, the market interest rate is 5%. What is the forward price for delivering one stock exactly one year from now? To answer this question, let us see what happens if the forward price were € 110 (the expected price after one year). As will be shown later, this price is too high. What happens is that if traders spot this too-high price, they will sell the forward. Assuming that they have no inventory of stocks or money in their pockets, they face the risk that the stock price will move beyond € 110 (remember that by selling the forward they commit to deliver against € 110). To protect themselves, they buy one stock against the price of € 100 and borrow the amount needed to finance the purchase. As a result, they are free of risk as they keep the stock in their portfolio and, after one year, deliver the stock to the buyer of the forward. The profit of this strategy is € 110 (forward price) – € 100 (initial stock price) – € 5 (borrowing costs) = € +5. Thus, whenever the price is above (and for similar reasons below) € 105, traders can make a risk-free profit, which they will exploit. Therefore, the forward price is € 105. For perfectly storable assets (such as stocks), the forward price is just equal to the current spot price plus interest. Surprisingly, neither the expected future value nor the volatility plays a role. This is an example of the theory of storage. Fama and French (1987) show that for storable commodities, the forward price equals the current spot price plus interest plus storage costs minus the convenience yield, where the latter is defined as all income one might derive from physically holding the commodity instead of having a forward contract. Following this theory, oil forward contracts do not reflect future price expectations. For electricity, this theory does not apply, because it is not directly storable. In this case, it is shown that the forward price is equal to the expected future spot price in the delivery period plus a risk premium. The risk premium can be seen as a markup for producers to commit themselves to fixed delivery prices. As a result, electricity forward prices reflect market expectations, whereas forward prices for storable energy do not.[4]

21.3   Trading From a Risk Management Perspective

The role of energy utility companies in the energy market has an impact on the risks these companies face. These companies face market risk from the fluctuations in prices of different commodities, credit risk from the counterparties and clients they deal with, and operational risks attributable to all kind of errors and changes in the environment. This section focuses on market risk and how it can be managed.

In order to put the risks of a utility company in perspective, it is helpful to think in terms of energy delivery assets and liabilities. The liabilities are the delivery and financial obligations of a utility company to its clients and other counterparties. The assets are the portfolio of contracts these companies have to supply clients, obtained from the markets of own production facilities. A gap between assets and liabilities occurs when utility companies have not (yet) bought sufficient assets to meet their liabilities. A gap causes risk. Table 21.3 is an example of how a report on gaps can be structured. It is a starting point for thinking, and not meant as the best report for all companies.

In Table 21.3, the report is structured around tradable forward contracts (see Table 21.2). For February 2008, the fixed-price delivery obligations of the utility company are expressed in terms of a Feb 2008 contract (in this table base and peak are taken together; reports for base or peak only can easily be prepared). The liabilities of February 2008 are equivalent to 150 MW Feb 08 forward contracts. On the assets side, it can be seen that the utility company has contracted only 90 MW (by own production or using forward contracts). This implies a gap of 60 MW over which the utility company faces market risk: when the price of energy (or fuels) increases, the profits of the Feb 08 period will decrease owing to the fixed price delivery obligations. Anyone wishing to reduce this risk should purchase 60 MW Feb 08 forward contracts. The gap report, then, provides insights

---

[4] See Eydeland and Wolyniec (2002) and Fama and French (1987), among others, for discussions on the predictability of forward prices for various commodities.

into gaps and, as it is structured around tradable forwards, also into the transactions that could be engaged in to reduce the degree of market risk faced. There can be various reasons for a gap. It may be speculative when people believe that prices in February 2008 will be low; it might be a deliberate strategy if it seems that clients might leave the company; or it might be due to some error. In any case, the gaps cause risk and it is up to the company to determine how much risk it is willing to take. This is where risk management comes in.

Table 21.3: A gap report example

	Gap report	
Assets	Delivery period	Liabilities
90	Day-ahead	100
90	Feb 08	150
130	Mar 08	130
125	Apr 08	125
125	May 08	125
115	Jun 08	115
100	Jul 08	110
121	Q2 08	121
100	Q3 08	110
100	Q4 08	140
85	Q1 09	140
85	Q2 09	121
85	Q3 09	110
85	Q4 09	140
85	Cal 09	120
80	Cal 10	150
80	Cal 11	130
0	Cal 12	80
0	Cal 13	75
0	Cal 14	60

The purpose of risk management is not to eliminate risk. The purpose of risk management is to identify the factors that cause risk for the company, to determine how much risk a company is willing to take (the risk appetite), to set limits for traders and gaps that are in line with the company's risk appetite, and to monitor and report the risks taken. A risk report may be structured in a similar way to a gap report, and a risk limit can be set as the maximum gap allowed in a certain time period. However, the most crucial element in risk management is that a company should know its risk appetite. Without this, a risk manager can set risk limits, but determination of the exact limits is meaningless without knowledge of what is and is not acceptable. As risk management is not an exact science, it is hard to tell what the best way is to express a risk appetite. However, Lam (2000) argues that a risk appetite should be expressed in terms of (1) loss tolerance, (2) risk-to-capital leverage, and (3) a target credit rating.

Loss tolerance specifies what the board regards as a 'normal' loss. The idea behind this is that companies make profits by taking risk and that a lower profit than expected or even a loss once in a while is part of doing business. However, the magnitude of the losses should not be too great and they should not occur too frequently. This is why loss tolerance is frequently expressed as a value at risk (VaR) number. A VaR number specifies the maximum allowed loss within a certain time with a specific amount of confidence. For a utility company, a one-year 95% VaR could be the maximum of allowed losses over one year at 95% confidence. For instance, if the board decides that the one-year 95% VaR should be € 10 million, the board announces that it will only allows a loss of more than € 10 million in 5 out of 100 years. Once such a number is set, a risk manager can calculate the actual VaR of the company daily and see whether it is in line with the VaR level set by the board. The exact VaR number depends on the amount of capital or equity available in the company and the expectations of shareholders.

Risk-to-capital leverage represents the link between capital and risk. If a company is willing to take a certain amount of risk (for instance a VaR of 10 million), it should have sufficient capital available to support this VaR, meaning that it should have a sufficiently substantial buffer of capital to survive even if the company suffers a loss greater than the agreed VaR. For financial institutions, the Basle II agreement states that banks should have a capital base available that is equivalent to at least three times the VaR number to support market risk accruing from open positions (gaps).[5] A number higher than 3 should be set in case the company does not have adequate risk management practices in place. The definition of a target credit rating is straightforward.

All risk reports should be structured so that they state the actual risk values and capital levels in relation to the risk appetite. If one of these numbers exceeds its limit, the company should hedge itself by closing gaps. This could be done by trading in the forward and futures, as described above, or by means of other instruments, such as options and swaps (see Eydeland and Wolyniec (2002) for a detailed presentation of such instruments).

21.4   Concluding Remarks

The emergence of international markets for energy and the new role for utility companies of assisting their clients in optimizing their energy portfolios make a thorough understanding of these markets of crucial importance. This chapter aims to provide some insight into the basic instruments for use in the field of electricity and emissions and discusses how companies could start thinking about structuring their risk management process.

---

[5] See the website http://www.riskglossary.com/link/basle_committee.htm and Jorion (2006) and Lam (2003) for references on Basle II and risk management.

References

Errera, S. & Brown, S. L. 1999. Fundamentals of trading energy futures & options. Tulsa: PennWell.

Eydeland, A. & Wolyniec, K. 2002. Energy and power risk management: new developments in modeling, pricing and hedging. New Jersey: Wiley Finance.

Fama, E. F. & French, K. F. 1987. Commodity futures prices: some evidence on forecast power, premiums, and the theory of storage. Journal of Business, 60: 55-73.

Huisman, R. 2008. The influence of temperature on spike probability in day-ahead power markets. Energy Economics, 30: 2697-2704.

Jorion, P. 2006. Value at risk (3rd ed.). New York: McGraw-Hill.

Kosater, P. 2006. On the impact of weather on German hourly power prices. Unpublished Working Paper, University of Cologne.

Lam, J. 2000. Enterprise-wide risk management and the role of the chief risk officer. ERisk.

Lam, J. 2003. Enterprise risk management. New Jersey: Wiley Finance.

Mount, T. D., Ning, Y. & Cai, X. 2006. Predicting price spikes in electricity markets using a regime-switching model with time-varying parameters. Energy Economics, 28: 62-80.

22   The Future of Liquefied Natural Gas Trade

Kenneth B. Medlock III[1]

Abstract

Previously disconnected regional natural gas markets are becoming increasingly integrated, largely due to liquefied natural gas (LNG) trade. Some factors are accelerating this trend, such as rapid demand growth, climate change policy, a desire to avoid transit country risks associated with pipelines, and seasonality in demand. However, other factors are acting to inhibit global market development, such as geopolitics, market structure, the emergence of unconventional sources of gas supply, and a move to alternative energy. The manner in which these forces act to offset or reinforce each other will be crucial to the nature of global LNG trade in years to come.

Keywords: liquefied natural gas, globalization, geopolitics

[1] Prof. Dr. Kenneth B. Medlock III is Fellow in Energy Studies, James A. Baker III Institute for Public Policy and Adjunct Professor, Department of Economics, Rice University, United States of America.

A. Bausch and B. Schwenker (eds.), *Handbook Utility Management,*
DOI: 10.1007/978-3-540-79349-6_22, © Springer-Verlag Berlin Heidelberg 2009

22.1   Introduction

In the past several years, developments in natural gas trade have been leading to growing interconnectedness among hitherto regional natural gas markets. Reports of deals being negotiated to transport natural gas supplies from places such as Russia, the Middle East, and Africa to consuming markets in North America, Europe, and Asia are now received with a high degree of regularity. Moreover, these deals are allowing for greater arbitrage opportunities, both directly and indirectly, between end-use markets in North America, Europe, and Asia. Pipelines, existing and potential, from Russia to both Europe and Asia can link prices back to the well-head in Russia, thereby establishing an equilibrium relationship based on transportation differentials between prices in Europe and Asia. Similarly, lique-fied natural gas (LNG) deliveries provide a linkage between prices in the Atlantic and Pacific basins by connecting those markets via exporting countries in the Middle East and the Pacific. In fact, since LNG cargoes can, in principle, be moved anywhere – as they are notional 'floating pipelines' – prices in every region of the globe have a strong potential to be linked.

The ability to divert LNG cargoes to the highest valued market has already begun to influence the manner in which natural gas is traded. As profitable arbitrage opportunities arise, LNG market participants seek to capture value, for example, through diversion of LNG cargoes from a low-priced region to a high-priced region. This effectively links prices globally by adjusting supplies and demands in various regions of the world until either no more gas can be traded or the value of the trade diminishes. The capability to divert cargoes to the highest bidder serves to mitigate future risks of investing in LNG infrastructures and, therefore, tends to accelerate growth of the industry. In all, there are significant forces pushing growth in global LNG trade. While the ability to capture value through diversion flexibility has captured the interest of players in the LNG business, it is, in fact, a derivative of fundamental forces such as the evolution of regional demand and supply balances.

Growing demand and reductions in the cost of transportation have created new opportunities for suppliers to monetize natural gas supplies. With each new infra-structure investment, the manner in which natural gas is traded is fundamentally changing, with natural gas becoming a more global commodity. The expansion of LNG trading, in particular, is perhaps the single most important driver of global-ization of natural gas markets. LNG allows trade between distant markets, thus allowing substantial distances – that often exist between regions with high demand and regions with substantial resources – to be bridged. Higher prices and reductions in LNG transportation costs have allowed owners of natural gas resources in all parts of the world to consider the possibility of monetization. This allows producers of oil, for example, to treat associated natural gas production as something of value that can improve the commercial evaluation of oil investments rather than as a nuisance by-product to be flared. It also allows resource owners to realize value from natural gas that has until now been 'stranded' as a result of prohibitive transportation costs.

Environmental pressures to move away from coal and petroleum products in power generation and economic growth are contributing to increases in demand. This is occurring despite production limitations in major consuming markets, which is forcing consumers to look to imports to meet their consumption needs. A vast majority of the world's natural gas resources are located far distant from regions with the greatest demands. For example, about 58% of the world's estimated natural gas reserves are in three countries: Russia, Iran, and Qatar. However, these same three countries account for only about 20% of global consumption, with a large majority of that demand in Russia. By contrast, the countries in North America, Asia, and Europe account for about 60% of global natural gas consumption, with the United States accounting for 20.7% and the countries of the European Union another 19.2%. Yet these regions collectively account for only about 14% of global natural gas reserves. The situation is compounded by the fact that although projections indicate that growth in North America and Europe will be strong, the countries in which most rapid growth is projected are China and India, which are also resource deficient. One potentially offsetting, yet relatively new factor, in the supply–demand balance equation is the emergence of shale gas production, especially in the United States. It is thought that shale, an unconventional source of natural gas, could ultimately provide up to 1,000 trillion cubic feet (tcf) of recoverable reserves, which could seriously diminish the need for LNG imports in North America and, in fact, potentially slow the pace of gas market globalization.

There is an obvious need for substantial infrastructure investment to facilitate the development and transport of natural gas from resource-rich areas to regions with high demand. The situation is complicated, however, when matters of energy security are considered. This is particularly true because the regions with the greatest concentration of supplies are regions that have historically been embroiled in conflict and political turmoil, or where resources are, at least to some extent, under the control of a state-owned firm. There are also other factors – such as deregulation of pipeline delivery networks in Europe, rate negotiations with transit countries, and strategic maneuvering to gain first-mover advantage in emerging and growing markets – that can also have an effect on global natural gas markets, and LNG in particular. In sum, there are many forces, both geopolitical and economic, that could act to hinder LNG market development. However, it is questionable whether these forces will be so significant as to offset the factors that are driving LNG market development.

This chapter is organized as follows. We begin with some brief background on LNG and follow with a discussion of the forces that are facilitating LNG market development. We follow this with a brief presentation of results from the reference case of the Rice World Gas Trade Model (RWGTM) in order to highlight the manner in which LNG market development may occur. Then we discuss the various risks that could alter the projected expansion of LNG trade and wrap up with some concluding remarks.

22.2   Liquefied Natural Gas

22.2.1   Some Background

LNG is natural gas that has been cooled to -260 °F at atmospheric pressure so that it is in a liquid state. Natural gas in its liquid state occupies about 1/600th of the volume of its gaseous state. Thus, LNG can be transported over great distances in large volumes in relatively small, albeit specialized, vessels. By liquefying natural gas, shipping it to an end-use market, and regasifying it so that it can be delivered to an end-user or injected into storage, value is captured that would otherwise be missed. The LNG 'value chain' is comprised of well-head production, a pipeline to a liquefaction facility, a liquefaction terminal, a specialized tanker for transportation of LNG, and a regasification terminal. The LNG value chain ultimately links remote, usually otherwise stranded, gas to consuming markets.

Developing an LNG delivery infrastructure is very capital intensive, typically more so than natural gas transport by pipeline. In the case of both LNG and pipeline delivery infrastructure, well-head development must first occur. Capital costs can vary at the well-head, depending on a number of factors, but they tend to differ substantially beyond the well-head. For LNG, after well-head production, the gas must be moved to a liquefaction plant, which can cost up to $ 3 billion to $ 5 billion per train. [2] Then, specialized LNG tankers, which can cost $ 150-250 million each, are needed for transport. Importantly, an LNG project requires multiple vessels to maintain a steady output flow, since voyage and delivery time must be considered. To deliver the LNG to a market, a regasification terminal, which can cost from $ 500 million to $ 1.5 billion, is required. Notably, the variability in cost is potentially very wide, and can be attributed to a number of factors, such as land costs, engineering and material costs, and costs related to port development. Other costs to complete the LNG delivery infrastructure might include pipeline infrastructure for delivery to the liquefaction terminal and/or from the regasification terminal.

The capital intensity of the LNG value chain typically requires that long-term contracts be in place to secure financing. Previously these contracts were usually take-or-pay and 20-25 years in duration, and they specified prices that were linked to crude oil or a basket of crude oil products. In addition, the terms of the earlier typical LNG contract did not provide for much flexibility in delivery. However, in the past few years some LNG project developers have withheld a portion of their supply from long-term contracts so that they can take advantage of short-term arbitrage opportunities. This behavior has led to the development, albeit small at this point, of LNG spot deliveries in both the Atlantic and Pacific basins.

A number of countries are already involved in LNG trade, with fairly rapid entry on both the liquefaction and the regasification sides of the value chain. In 2006, a total of 13 countries were LNG exporters – the United States, Trinidad and Tobago, Algeria, Egypt, Libya, Nigeria, Oman, Qatar, United Arab Emirates, Aus-

---

[2] The term 'train' is commonly used to describe the linear chain of equipment that lowers the temperature of the gas to the liquid point.

tralia, Brunei, Indonesia, and Malaysia – up from only 8 just 10 years earlier. Moreover, the list of LNG suppliers is likely to expand in the next few years, with Equatorial Guinea, Norway, and Russia all expected to begin exporting LNG by 2010 and several other countries that could also begin exporting LNG in the next few years, such as Angola, Iran, Peru, Venezuela, and Yemen. In addition, there are numerous plans for the development of additional export facilities in many of the countries already exporting LNG. Thus, the amount of LNG supplied to the global market will be significant, provided these projects move forward.

The number of countries importing LNG is seeing similar growth. In 2006, 17 countries were importing LNG: the United States, Mexico, Puerto Rico, the Dominican Republic, Belgium, France, Greece, Italy, Portugal, Spain, Turkey, the United Kingdom, China, India, Japan, South Korea, and Taiwan – up from only 9 countries in 1996. Several additional countries are expected to begin importing LNG in the next few years, and numerous greenfield and brownfield expansions are expected in countries already importing LNG over the next several years.[3]

22.2.2 Regional Developments

LNG trading has been going on in the Pacific for a few decades, driven primarily by demand growth for natural gas in Japan, which was born out of a desire to diversify sources of energy supply, and more recently also in South Korea. Since neither country has a sufficient indigenous resource endowment and there was no viable pipeline option for supply, both Japan and South Korea were forced to develop an LNG infrastructure.

In Europe and North America, however, LNG developments have moved much more slowly. In each of these two regions, adequate access to continental sources of supply and the development of extensive pipeline networks rendered LNG infrastructure largely unnecessary. As a result, North America, Europe, and Asia saw the development of regional markets that were more or less independent. A lack of LNG infrastructure to provide physical capacity linkages and contract rigidities that limited trading opportunities left little opportunity for arbitrage of price movements between these three regional natural gas markets.

Currently, Japan and South Korea are the largest LNG importers globally, consuming about 40% and 16%, respectively, of all LNG traded worldwide in 2006. However, rapid economic growth in China and India, along with rapid terminal expansion in Europe and North America, is expected to dramatically alter LNG flows in the next few years. Figure 22.1 depicts the LNG import terminal capacity, both existing and currently under construction, through 2010 in North America and Europe. North American import capacity is set to increase from less than 6 billion cubic feet per day (bcf/d) to almost 16 bcf/d by 2010, as terminals at Sabine Pass, Golden Pass, Cameron, and Freeport – all on the US Gulf Coast – begin operations. The trend in Europe is similar, with the UK, Spain, and Italy leading

---

[3] Note the term 'greenfield' refers to the construction of a new facility whereas 'brownfield' refers to expansion of an existing facility.

the way in new LNG regasification capacity investments. Import capacity in Europe is set to double by 2010. A large proportion of the new LNG supplies to both North America and Europe will be provided by liquefaction capacity expansions in Qatar, Nigeria, Algeria, and Egypt. In sum, these developments mark a significant increase in Atlantic Basin LNG trade.

In Asia, China and India are leading the way in LNG import capacity expansion, with total import capacity approaching 2 bcf/d by 2010 in both countries. In addition, there are proposals for additional capacity far in excess of this amount beyond 2010. While most of the growth is expected to come from these two countries, Japan's import capacity is by far the largest, and will remain so for the foreseeable future. In both Japan and South Korea, import terminals are built to handle peak demands, so that they are usually built much larger than baseload demands require.

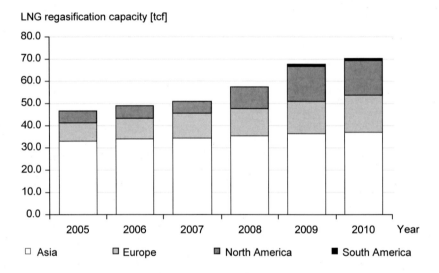

Figure 22.1: LNG regasification capacity to 2010 in North America, Europe, and Asia (Note: terminals indicated are either existing or under construction) (Data colleted from Platts LNG Daily's Terminal Tracker)

It should be noted that the import capacity expansions indicated in Figure 22.1 add up to a larger total than the liquefaction capacity being constructed globally. This is due in large part to the fact that some regions need to build import capacity to meet peak demands because there is very little storage capability and no alternative source of supply (from either pipeline or local production). These peak demands are not necessarily coincident across regions, so that liquefaction capacity need not match regasification capacity. LNG cargoes can be redirected to regions where demand is greatest.

22.3 Drivers of Current and Future Liquefied Natural Gas Market Development

22.3.1 Demand Growth

Demand growth in Europe, North America and Asia has been critical to encouraging both pipeline and LNG infrastructure development. Much of the recent growth in demand can be attributed to increases in natural gas-fired power generation capacity. These capacity expansions have, in turn, been driven by cost-reducing innovations in using natural gas to generate electricity (i.e., natural gas combined-cycle technology) and by environmental considerations, since natural gas combustion generally results in lower SO_x, NO_x, and particulate emissions than other fossil fuels. Natural gas is also less CO_2-intensive than other fossil fuels, so that future demand growth is to be exacerbated by policies that limit CO_2 emissions. However, a lack of indigenous supplies available at low cost in these regions has forced consumers, in the face of rising domestic prices, to increasingly look to imports to meet current and expected future demands.

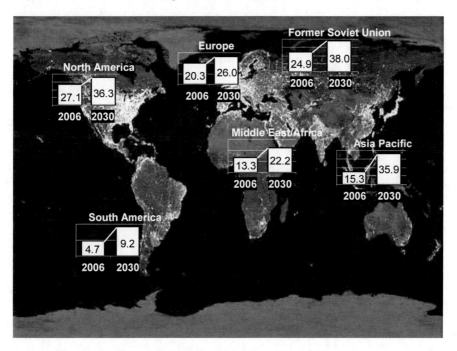

Figure 22.2: Global demand, 2006 and 2030 [tcf] (map available at http://www.cojoweb.com/earthlights.html, historical demand: US Energy Information Administration (www.eia.doe.gov), projected demand: the Rice World Gas Trade Model (available upon request from author))

Figure 22.2 is the famous 'earthlights' picture, which is a composite of satellite photographs on clear nights from around the world. Notably, Europe, Japan, South Korea, coastal China, the eastern half of the United States, and several other areas, are all relatively 'bright'. Layered over the picture are graphics of regional aggregates of data on recent and projected natural gas demand by region. The data provide, in particular, an indication of how demand in brighter regions in the figure might evolve through 2030. The regions of greatest demand, from highest to lowest, currently are North America, the countries of the Former Soviet Union (FSU), and Europe. However, economic development and an emphasis on cleaner-burning natural gas to generate electricity will cause the ordering to change. Demand in the United States, Western Europe, and Japan is among the highest in the world, but demand in China and India is growing fastest. To the extent that these regions' domestic natural gas resources are either lacking or in decline, each will look to imports, or adopt alternatives, to meet demand.

In the US, maturing production from conventional supplies and demand growth, especially for power generation, has catalyzed the search for new sources of gas supply. Nonconventional deposits are increasingly being exploited, such as coal-bed methane (CBM) and shale, but these supplies may only be enough to serve a portion of the incremental demand increases. This makes it very likely that the US will draw increasingly on supplies from abroad. LNG has been imported to the US gas market since the 1970s, albeit in small quantities. However, since 2000, LNG imports have increased substantially and import capacity has also begun to grow, first with the re-commissioning of terminals at Cove Point, MD, and Savannah, GA, then with expansions at existing facilities and on numerous greenfield sites. Thus, market participants are anticipating a dramatic increase in the importance of LNG as a source of supply.

Europe has a long history of reliance on Russia for natural gas supply by pipeline. Other pipeline supplies come from the North Sea (UK, Norway, and the Netherlands, primarily) and North Africa. However, the story in Europe is similar to that in the US. Major producing regions are experiencing declines and demand is growing, especially for power generation. This situation coupled with recent doubts about the reliability of Russian supplies – prompted by the recent Russia-Ukraine gas dispute as well as the declines experienced in major West Siberian fields – has led countries in Europe to look abroad for sources of supply. This has contributed with European interest in LNG development and pipeline development, the latter from North Africa and the Caspian regions.[4] Recent terminal developments in the UK, Spain, and Italy, in particular, are linked contractually to a diverse set of suppliers from West Africa, North Africa, the Middle East, and South America. These supplies allow growing demand to be met while providing some diversion flexibility that may be needed owing to seasonal demand swings, an especially important feature in a region where storage capacity is not very robust.

Economic development is the primary driver of demand growth in Asia and the Pacific region. In particular, China and India are the most rapidly developing

---

[4] The issue of diversification of supply away from Russia is one we return below.

countries in the region, and their energy demand growth does not belie that fact. Despite the heavy reliance on coal in both these countries, natural gas is viewed as an important part of the growing energy demand portfolio. In northeast Asia, China has an important role in determining investments in natural gas infrastructure. Specifically, if supply agreements can be reached with Russia, with China as an anchor consumer, then the development of a northeast Asian pipeline network to move gas from producing areas in East Siberia and the Sakhalin Islands to China, as well as to South Korea and Japan, is more feasible. However, to date such plans have seen no real progression. Hence, China, South Korea, and Japan have all been active in expanding LNG import capacity. As these regions bid for LNG supplies they will increasingly draw upon suppliers in countries in the Middle East, the South Pacific Rim, and Australia, as well as Sakhalin and Alaska.

Notably, demand growth is strong in regions where supply is relatively robust. For example, demand in the FSU and Middle East, regions which are home to over 70% of proven conventional gas reserves, is expected to increase by over 50% and 100%, respectively, by 2030. Contributing to this robust growth in demand is the fact that suppliers in both of these regions sell a substantial portion of their production to domestic consumers at subsidized prices. This, in general, promotes inefficient use of natural gas and encourages demand. In addition, since revenues from sales are lower than they would otherwise be, reinvestment in developing supply is made difficult. Eventually, it can become almost impossible to meet even domestic demand, despite a wealth of gas resource in place. The gas resource effectively becomes stranded because development becomes too difficult to finance. Ultimately, price controls must be lifted.[5] Such domestic pricing policies will have an impact on LNG trade. In fact, deals for LNG delivery from Qatar to both Kuwait and UAE are being discussed, even though the United States Geologic Survey (USGS) has assessed natural gas resources in both Kuwait and UAE that are high enough to avoid this outcome. This intraregional trade drives up competition for available supply, and can therefore have a profound impact on the availability and price of LNG to consumers in the Atlantic and Pacific basins.

22.3.2   Resource Rents, Transport Costs, Diversion Capability, and Seasonal Trends

The development of resources depends on the associated rents. These rents, in turn, are determined by the cost of field development, the transportation cost to market, and the market price. Project developers typically consider the 'netback' price when determining whether or not to proceed with project development. The netback price is determined as the price received from downstream sales minus the costs associated with moving gas to the market. Thus, the expected netback price

---

[5] In fact, the Russian government recently approved a phased increase of domestic gas tariffs, so that prices will eventually be at netback parity with those in Europe. This is deemed necessary by many, in order for Gazprom to increase its production and meet its current contractual obligations.

at the point of liquefaction must be high enough to justify project development, making transportation costs critical. For a given market price, even if the field development costs are very low, if the cost of transportation is sufficiently high the gas resource can remain undeveloped, or stranded. Netback prices can also influence short-term destinations. For example, if a cargo is not bound by contract to a specific port, it can 'chase' the highest netback. In other words, the cargo can be delivered in such a way that it fetches the highest value.

In general, LNG is a more attractive transportation option than a pipeline when the distance traveled is significant, the construction of a pipeline is not feasible, and/or there is significant transit-country risk. For example, a pipeline connecting resources in Algeria to North America is not likely, owing to both technical considerations and cost. However, LNG delivery infrastructure provides a technically feasible, economically competitive alternative, as long as market price in North America is high enough to yield a suitable netback price. Thus, both technical and economic considerations are crucial to determining the vehicle for gas monetization.

During the last several years, cost reductions in transporting LNG have provided an opportunity for natural gas producers to seek market outlets. For example, in places such as Nigeria natural gas has historically been treated as a nuisance by-product of oil production and flared at very high rates. The lack of a domestic market made substantial pipeline developments a subeconomic venture, and prohibitive costs made transport to major consuming markets via LNG unviable. However, rising global prices and declining costs of LNG transport have made accessing distant markets profitable. According to the International Energy Agency (IEA)'s World Energy Investment Outlook (WEIO), the pattern of LNG cost reductions from the early 1990s to the early 2000s saw liquefaction and transport capital costs decline by about 30% and regasification costs decline by about 20%. In all, this made the netback price necessary to support investment in the LNG value chain lower, effectively bringing suppliers and demanders closer together. Thus, cost reductions have greatly contributed to the ability of producers to monetize gas resources. Of course, any escalation in construction costs associated with rising material and labor costs can diminish resource rents and cause projects to be delayed or even cancelled.

The development of a global natural gas market depends crucially on a robust LNG trade. LNG trade allows price signals, and hence product volumes, to flow between markets that are not physically connected by pipelines. Importantly, this can only occur if LNG cargoes can be diverted at low cost from one destination to another. Although LNG project developments are usually anchored by long-term contracts, as the number of suppliers and demanders grows the average distance between market players is reduced and the likelihood of profitable swap arrangements increases. Developers of LNG projects recognize that this real option value of destination flexibility can improve profitability. However, this value can only be realized if a sufficient number of alternative supply sources and demand sinks emerge, thus diversifying market risk. Generally, by expanding the available market alternatives the risk of investing in infrastructure is reduced, which encourages further development. The resulting increase in liquidity could catalyze a rapid movement away from a world in which deliveries are dictated by long-term bilateral contracts to one of multilateral trading (Brito & Hartley, 2007). It is important to note that diversion capability does not render the LNG contract obsolete. In fact, the contract will likely remain a vital part of the LNG business as it provides the underpinning for financial support in a highly capital-intensive business. However, swap arrangements or destination flexibility clauses will enable market participants to fulfill their contractual obligations while minimizing transportation costs, thereby maximizing the rents associated with LNG.[6]

Diversion capability has already played a significant role in shaping LNG trade in the Atlantic basin. The National Balancing Point (NBP) price in the UK, the price at the Henry Hub in Louisiana in the US, and available storage capacity in both markets have played a role in trans-Atlantic arbitrage. During winter months, prices at NBP typically rise above those at the Henry Hub. This is coincident with the winter peak in demand in Europe. During this time, the price in Europe also usually rises because there is insufficient available storage capacity. In the US, however, storage capacity is very large (estimated at over 4 tcf). Thus, during the winter peak, LNG cargoes will flow to Europe and demand in the US will be met by withdrawal from storage. During periods of low demand in Europe, a lack of storage capacity means that any LNG cargo delivered to Europe will suppress prices. This should encourage diversion to a higher priced market, such as the US, where adequate storage capacity provides price support. Since LNG cargoes can be diverted, the US storage market (i) serves to balance supply and demand in the entire Atlantic basin, (ii) helps to smooth price (which is a normal function of market-based storage), and (iii) establishes a link between the prices in Europe and the US. In addition, by helping to keep price from experiencing extreme lows, especially in Europe, the US storage market helps to improve the netback value of natural gas sales, which in turn provides incentive for future supply development.

The pattern in Figure 22.3 is indicative of the seasonal arbitrage that is emerging in the Atlantic basin. LNG imports were higher in the US from March through August in 2007, when the Henry Hub price generally offered a better netback than prices in Europe. A similar pattern is evident in the figures for other years, although the exact timing of increased deliveries to the US varies slightly. In 2006, for example, the prices at Henry Hub offered better netbacks for a shorter period during the summer, and in 2005 there was even greater seasonal variation owing to price disruptions caused by hurricanes Rita and Katrina in the US. In 2008, strong natural gas demand in Asia associated with nuclear outages and strong growth in natural gas production in North America has resulted in many LNG cargoes being pulled out of the Atlantic basin, thus contributing to very low delivery to the US. In general, much of the variability in netback pricing is tied to weather-driven demands. Factors such as early or late winters, colder than normal

---

[6] This is the case in North American natural gas markets today, where the right to utilize pipeline capacity is bought and sold against firm contractual arrangements when it is profitable to do so. Without a significant number of market participants, the ability to trade capacity, and hence supply, would be severely limited.

winters and extremely hot summers can sometimes affect one side of the Atlantic but not the other and thus dramatically influence regional demand and price.

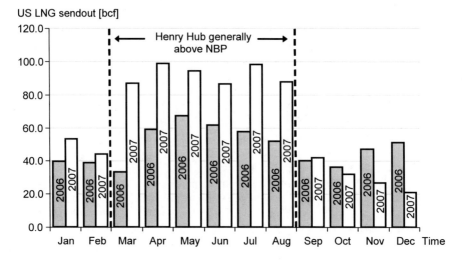

Figure 22.3: Monthly sendout from US LNG facilities (2006 and 2007) (LNG sendout data accessed May 15, 2008 from US Department of Energy Office of Fossil Energy (http://www.fossil.energy.gov/programs/gasregulation/publications/4th07ng.pdf); natural gas price data (not pictured) is available from NYMEX and ICE)

22.3.3   Transit-country Issues

Transit-country risks impose costs to both consumers and producers, and arise largely from the potential for supply disruptions. Rent-seeking behavior on the part of a transit country, via discounted pricing agreements or large tariffs, can reduce the profitability of exploration and production activities in the producing regions and hamper the competitiveness of natural gas as a primary source of energy in the consuming region. In addition, if any of the parties involved is dissatisfied with the status quo, drastic actions can sometimes be taken in an effort to improve the bargaining power of any one party. This can have dramatic, overarching effects. In particular, transit-country risks can encourage the development of LNG infrastructures, since waterborne supplies avoid third-party involvement.

Transit-country risk was recently highlighted in the gas pricing dispute between Russia and Ukraine. In an effort to force Ukraine to accept a different pricing arrangement that more accurately reflects the market value of natural gas in Europe, Russian gas monopoly Gazprom temporarily reduced its flow of natural gas to Ukraine in the winter of 2006. This greatly affected consumers in Ukraine and Western Europe, especially since the disruption occurred during a period when demand is generally very high, and it highlighted the vulnerability of European countries to the whims of a single large supplier. Moreover, the event sparked a wave of speculation that Russia could use energy as a tool for foreign policy in future dealings with Europe and has affected energy policy in the European Union, as some countries are actively seeking alternative sources of supply. Since the incident, several new LNG import terminal developments have accelerated, including terminals in the Netherlands and Germany. There has also been increased interest in securing pipeline supplies from countries other than Russia, such as those in North Africa and the Caspian region.

Another example of how the risks associated with a transit country can force alternative outcomes involves the proposed Iran-to-India pipeline. The proposed pipeline would traverse Pakistan, placing security of gas supply to India in the hands of a country with which there is a history of conflict. The potential costs involved with compromised energy security can, in turn, push the development of LNG import capacity, since this latter option avoids the transit-country risk associated with pipeline supply through Pakistan. Pakistan and Iran also bear costs from this. If the demand in India is not large enough, the economic feasibility of the pipeline is compromised. This would leave Pakistan having to develop LNG import capacity or paying higher tariffs to import gas via pipeline from Iran.[7] In addition, Iran would be forced to develop LNG export capacity to access the Indian market. Collectively, this would tend to be much more capital intensive than the pipeline option.[8]

In general, transit-country risk encourages consumers to seek alternative sources of supply. In the case of Europe, this ultimately works to the detriment of both Russia and Ukraine. Ironically, this should provide an economic argument for Russia and Ukraine to cooperate in order to avoid the costs associated with disruptions. Unfortunately, however, history indicates that disagreements over short-term rents can sometimes outweigh considerations of long-run profitability.

22.4 The Rice World Gas Trade Model Reference Case – One Possible Future

Having discussed some of the factors that will help to drive expansion of LNG trade and globalization of the natural gas market, we turn our attention to one particular modeling projection of the global natural gas market. Scholars at Rice University (Hartley & Medlock, 2004) have developed a dynamic spatial general equilibrium model of the world market for natural gas (hereinafter referred to as

---

[7] The argument that tariffs would be higher on a Pakistan-only pipeline from Iran is based on the fact that such a facility would likely have a much lower capacity than one that also delivered gas to India. Typically, as throughput capacity increases, the per-unit capital cost decreases, so that the tariff for capital recovery is lower.

[8] This of course does not even consider the fact that such a transport option for Iranian natural gas is strongly opposed by many western nations, so that there are other political costs to consider as well.

the RWGTM).[9] The RWGTM proves and develops reserves, constructs transportation routes and calculates prices to equate demands and supplies while maximizing the present value of producer rents within a competitive framework. By developing both pipeline transportation routes and LNG delivery infrastructure, the RWGTM provides a framework for examining the effects of critical economic and political influences on the global natural gas market within a framework grounded in geologic data and economic theory.

The resource data underlying the model is based on the World Resource Assessment of the United States Geological Survey (USGS) and on data for existing reserves from the Oil and Gas Journal Database. Long- and short-run capital and operating cost curves for resource development were derived using data from the National Petroleum Council (NPC). Demand for natural gas is determined endogenously as the equilibrium price of natural gas adjusts, although there are also exogenous influences such as economic development, the price of competing fuels, and population growth. The data used in estimating the demand relationship were obtained from the US Energy Information Administration (EIA), the IEA, the World Bank, and OECD. The costs of constructing new pipelines and LNG facilities were estimated using data on previous and potential projects available from the EIA and IEA and from various industry reports. The extent of regional detail in the model varies based primarily on data availability and the potential influence of particular countries on the global natural gas market. For example, large consuming and producing countries, such as China, the US, India, Russia, and Japan, to name but a few, have extensive subregional detail in order to understand the effect that existing or developing intracountry capacity constraints could have on current or likely future patterns of natural gas trade. In sum, there are over 280 demand regions and more than 180 supply regions. Output from the model includes regional natural gas prices, pipeline and LNG capacity additions and flows, growth in natural gas reserves from existing fields and undiscovered deposits, and regional production and demand.

The RWGTM generally indicates growing interconnectedness of the global market for natural gas. Natural gas suppliers in the Middle East and the Former Soviet Union, in particular, are poised to play a pivotal role in the growth of global natural gas trade. Geography places these regions as likely points of arbitrage between the major consuming markets in the Atlantic and Pacific, and geology has rendered these regions very well endowed with resources, making them likely points of origination for supplies to every region of the globe.

Table 22.1 illustrates the quantity of natural gas resources, both proved and potential, for major regions of the world. Apparent is the concentration of natural gas resource in the FSU and the Middle East, with more than 50% of the world's estimated natural gas resource in just four countries: Russia, Qatar, Iran, and Saudi

---

[9] The model is constructed using the MarketPoint software from Altos Management Partners. To be brief, a detailed description of the model is not included. For more detail on the RWGTM please see Hartley, P. and Medlock III, K. B., 2006a. (Note that 'Baker Institute' and 'Rice' are interchangeable.) Numerous working papers involving the RWGTM are also available online at www.rice.edu/energy.

Arabia. It is, therefore, reasonable to expect a concentration of global natural gas production in the future. Of course, factors such as geopolitics, domestic demand and pricing policies, and regional demand growth will shape whether and when such concentration might emerge. Another important factor could be the growth of unconventional supply sources. Since reserve data for shale, in particular, in the US is not currently known with high certainty there is much speculation as to the role production from this source will play.[10]

Table 22.1: Estimated natural gas resource by region [tcf]

Region	Proved reserves[a]	Undiscovered resource[b]	Share of total resource
Middle East	**2565.4**	**1294.7**	**34.4%**
Qatar	910.5	41.1	8.5%
Saudi Arabia	241.8	681.0	8.2%
Iran	971.2	314.6	11.5%
Former Soviet Union	**1952.6**	**1611.3**	**31.8%**
Russia	1680.0	1168.7	25.4%
Asia/Pacific	**391.6**	**688.9**	**9.6%**
Indonesia	97.8	107.7	1.8%
Australia[c]	27.6	338.4	3.3%
Africa	**485.8**	**330.1**	**7.3%**
Nigeria	184.7	123.2	2.7%
Algeria	160.5	49.0	1.9%
North America	**265.1**	**451.5**	**6.4%**
Central & South America	**250.8**	**421.0**	**6.0%**
Venezuela	151.4	101.2	2.3%
Europe	**200.7**	**312.4**	**4.6%**
Norway	84.3	183.0	2.4%
World Total[d]	**6112.1**	**5109.8**	

[a] Oil and Gas Journal as of 1 January 2006
[b] Compiled from USGS, ABARE and other national sources
[c] Includes assessed unconventional natural gas resources
[d] Does not include future growth in existing fields. USGS estimates the world total at 3305 tcf.

Figure 22.4 illustrates the RWGTM projection for exports of natural gas both by pipeline and as LNG. The figure indicates that LNG is projected to account for a growing proportion of global trade. This result is driven by the fact that increasingly remote locations become ever more crucial if the growing global demand is to be met, which favors LNG development. Also indicated in Figure 22.4 are projected global demand and the share of that demand that is met by internationally traded natural gas. For example, with global demand projected at 121.4 tcf in 2010, 27.3% of that demand will be satisfied via international trade. By 2040, the

---

[10] The reserve potential for shale gas in the US may be great enough to significantly alter projections for US LNG imports. We return to this point below.

internationally traded share of projected world demand (165.7 tcf) is expected to rise to 43.8%, with LNG trade responsible for the majority of this growth.

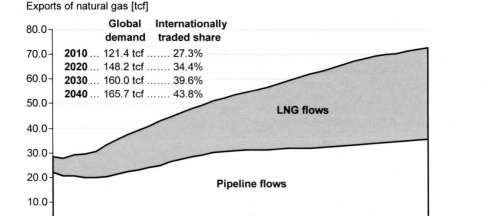

Figure 22.4: Global exports by pipeline and LNG (Data from the RWGTM run 14 February 2008 and is available upon request from author)

Figure 22.5 illustrates the breakdown of LNG imports and exports by major region, as predicted by the RWGTM. Among exporters, Australia emerges as the largest single LNG-exporting country in the long term, followed closely by Qatar. In fact, Australia does not take its position as the largest supplier until 2016. Until then, Qatar is the largest single supplier of LNG. Collectively, the countries of the Middle East ultimately account for the largest share of LNG supply. Much of the late growth in the Middle East is taking place as demand in North America grows beyond the capacity of indigenous supplies and the Atlantic basin LNG suppliers. Growth in North American imports also pushes expansion in Russia beyond the initial forays into LNG from Sakhalin and the Barents Sea. The latter location, in particular, begins to expand aggressively late in the model time horizon.

LNG demand is distributed across Asia, Europe and North America. In Northeast Asia, Japan and South Korea remain large importers, although some LNG is displaced in the reference case by the development of pipelines from Russia. The largest growth in LNG imports in the region is in China and India.

The decline in LNG net exports in Southeast Asia apparent in Figure 22.5 masks the developments in the region to some extent. LNG exports expand from Indonesia (from Bontang, Tangguh, and Donggi), Papua New Guinea, Malaysia and Brunei. However, imports grow in Singapore, Thailand, and Vietnam. The region remains a net exporter of LNG.

In Europe, Norway begins to export LNG, but does not expand beyond its initial development at Snohvit. Rather, the majority of future production is focused on exports by pipeline to Europe. Europe as a whole imports an increasing amount of LNG. Growth in LNG imports occurs in Spain, Italy, Germany, the Netherlands, France, and Greece. Diversity of supply to Europe as an economic phenomenon is apparent in the reference case, as pipeline expansions occur from Russia, North Africa, the Caspian region, and, later in the time horizon, the Middle East. In sum, Russia loses market share in Europe but remains a large and important supplier.

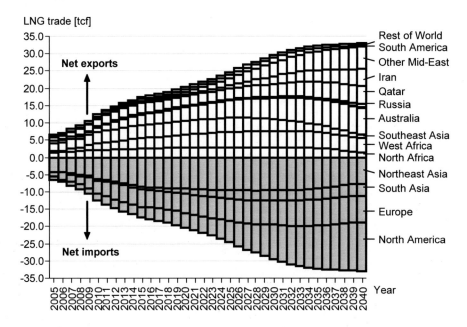

Figure 22.5: LNG trade (data is from the RWGTM run 14 February 2008 and is available upon request from author)

In North America, demand growth in Mexico is highest, and in fact, LNG imports to Mexico expand dramatically. While some of these LNG imports are directed at the US market, such as the facility in Baja to serve the US West Coast, expansions in other regions of Mexico are targeted to serve Mexican demand. In Canada, LNG imports to the Canaport facility in New Brunswick ultimately target the New England area. In the US, the facilities in the Gulf Coast expand most dramatically. This is a result of the fact that such expansions are generally lower cost, and there is ready access to already existing major pipelines that serve markets in the Middle Atlantic, Midwest, and New England.

As time progresses beyond 2010, North America, in particular the US, draws an increasing proportion of global LNG supply. Since the United States is separated by major oceans from the regions with the largest resource potential, it must rely increasingly on imported LNG. This is partly facilitated because the European market receives natural gas via pipeline from Russia, North Africa, and the Middle

East, and Asia receives natural gas via pipeline from Russia. Thus, those regions are able to receive a more diverse portfolio of supplies that includes both pipeline sources and LNG.

In Europe, although LNG imports grow substantially, the majority of imports to the region continue to be via pipeline. Existing and expanded pipeline infrastructure between Europe and Russia, Europe and North Africa, and eventually Europe and the Middle East offsets the need for even greater LNG imports. In Asia, LNG gains market share, but the development of pipelines from East Siberia to Northeast Asia mitigates the extent to which LNG imports increase.

Continued strong exports by pipeline along with entry to the LNG market in both the Atlantic and Pacific basins make Russia the largest single supplier of natural gas to global markets. Moreover, the ability to ship natural gas both east and west makes Russia a key arbitrage point between the Atlantic and Pacific basins. The Middle East as a region also increases its prominence in the global natural gas markets, primarily due to expansion of LNG exports. The result is that Russia and the Middle East play key roles in connecting markets in the Atlantic and Pacific. Again, geography and geology are critical determinants of this outcome.

Importantly, the results from the reference case of the RWGTM highlight various risks that can interfere with expanding LNG trade and, more generally, globalization of natural gas markets. Specifically, given the prominence of the US as a sink for LNG, anything that alters demand could have far-reaching impacts on LNG supply developments. Furthermore, any expansion of domestic production, perhaps from unconventional sources such as shale, could limit the need for LNG imports. These factors are important as lower global LNG demand would generally support fewer major LNG infrastructure projects.

Similar forces could also work in Europe and in Asia. Forces that inhibit pipeline developments to either region would favor LNG and likely strengthen the market position of existing suppliers. Thus, both international and domestic policies also have a role. Geopolitical conflicts such as the current standoff regarding Iran's nuclear ambitions and domestic policies toward fossil fuel use, in particular owing to CO_2 legislation, could also influence demand and available supply. Thus, although the RWGTM predicts a global gas future with fairly robust LNG trade, there are many factors that could delay, or even inhibit, such an outcome. These forces in general define the types of scenarios that can usefully be analyzed with the aid of such a modeling framework.

22.5 Various Risks to Liquefied Natural Gas Market Development

22.5.1 High Prices, Alternative Supplies and First-mover Advantage

The persistence of high prices in major end-use markets is at the center of most factors that could impede globalization. For example, high prices generally encourage exploration and development activities in areas that would not otherwise be considered attractive. In North America, high prices have encouraged rapid developments in unconventional natural gas supplies, such as shale gas.[11] There is also news of similar developments of unconventional supplies in Europe, China, and Australia.[12]

Development of these higher cost unconventional resources in certain regions is bolstered by other factors. These include delays in development of low-cost supplies in other regions, increasing costs for capital-intensive or technology-specific projects (such as LNG infrastructure), rent-seeking behavior by natural gas exporters (such as cartelization), and the development of alternative technologies. Thus, any of these factors can, each to varying degrees, affect the future of LNG.

Figure 22.6: Natural gas resource off limits to exploration and production (Hartley & Medlock, 2007)

Figures 22.6 and 22.7 indicate the extent of the resource that is either off limits owing to current policy or a frontier source of supply, such as shale gas. In a recent study, Hartley and Medlock (2007) showed that any relaxation of constraints to developing resources that are currently off limits in the US would greatly reduce LNG imports to the US. In fact, opening access to some 164 tcf of natural gas in regions in the Outer Continental Shelf and Federal lands in the Rocky Mountains would reduce US LNG import dependence by about a third in 2030. In

---

[11] Unconventional natural gas is typically defined as supplies that require alternative extraction methods, such as coal bed methane (CBM) and shale gas.

[12] The development of coal bed methane in Australia is actually targeting export markets, so it serves as a somewhat offsetting factor.

turn, this has ramifications for LNG developers, who would no longer be able to access the US market at favorable prices.

According to a recent study conducted by Navigant Consulting, Inc., shale gas potential (proved plus undiscovered technically recoverable) could amount to as much as 2,200 tcf. If that quantity proves to be commercially viable at reasonable production rates, the need for imported LNG will be greatly reduced, leaving LNG developers to sell their product in Europe and Asia. This, in turn, would significantly impact on the amount of LNG that is ultimately developed for export.

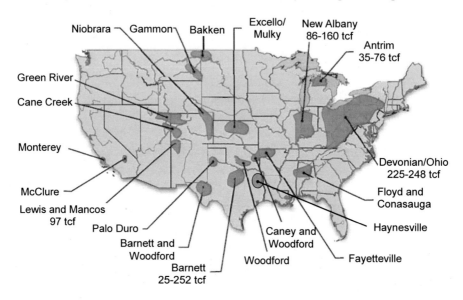

Figure 22.7: Major shale gas basins in the United States (Frantz & Valerie, 2005)

Other sources of supply include the development of methane hydrates and clean coal, and also nonfossil resources such as wind, solar, and nuclear power. With regard to methane hydrates, while the technology to develop hydrate deposits commercially is still in the testing phases, the resource potential dwarfs known conventional gas resources and, importantly, is located near major consuming markets. Thus, if methane hydrate development occurs at commercial rates, the need for LNG in countries such as the US and Japan could be dramatically lower. Clean coal also holds real potential, as the US is home to 27% of the world's coal reserves, with China holding another 12% and India about 10%. Given that the US is projected to be the largest LNG consumer, and China and India are among the fastest growing LNG consumers, any development that favors the expanded use of coal over cleaner burning natural gas could stifle LNG market development. Importantly, higher prices encourage the development of alternatives, which is why natural gas resource developers must be cautious about moving too slowly. If prices remain high for a long enough period of time, it is possible that an alternative source of supply will take the place of natural gas in the energy mix, highlighting the principle of first-mover advantage.

The principle of first-mover advantage is instrumental in the development of LNG markets, precisely because it plays on the backdrop of all the other risks mentioned above. Specifically, anything that tends to raise prices will ultimately beget two responses: development of new supply and/or reduction of demand. If developers are not able to move quickly enough to bring new LNG supplies to bear, then consumers will shift toward shale gas and/or alternative sources of energy supply. Once new capital is deployed and fixed costs are sunk, the ability of greenfield LNG projects to compete successfully becomes compromised, thus seriously delaying, or even prohibiting, projects at the margin.

22.5.2 Market Structure

Market structure can play a part in LNG developments, especially with regard to Europe. Anything that inhibits deregulation of the natural gas market could push large consumers toward LNG as a means of diversification. A pipeline network that is characterized by a secondary market in which capacity rights are openly traded could allow supply swaps and alleviate the need for some LNG infrastructure. The allocation of capacity based upon market considerations rather than take-or-pay arrangements reduces risk to consumers and encourages more efficient use of existing infrastructure. The lack of such an option on pipelines in Europe encourages the development of a high number of smaller scale LNG regasification terminals targeted to specific end-users, so that cargoes can be diverted to alternative destinations if they are not needed. In effect, the swaps that could occur on the pipeline grid must occur on the water. If there is no unified market it is likely that LNG regasification facilities will continue to be constructed to target specific customers and will be sized accordingly. Therefore, an open-access pipeline network will tend to favor fewer but larger LNG import facilities, where economies of scale can reduce average costs.

In the US, a secondary market for capacity rights has increased liquidity on the pipeline network. This has made it possible to construct larger scale LNG import facilities without a specific customer anchoring the construction. LNG can be delivered to a regasification facility even if there is no specific customer for the product. Pipeline shipments can then be modified through swaps and capacity release arrangements. This is possible due to the fungible nature of gas once it arrives to the pipeline network. While such a system may sound, in principle, as though it should be adopted in Europe, the task is burdened with other issues. Unlike in the US, where interstate transport is regulated by a federal body and there is no barrier to trade, countries in Europe must ultimately agree to a coordinated set of policies (even if a governing body exists in principle), because sovereign nations are involved. Nevertheless, if the European market evolves to something more similar in structure to that in North America, the nature of the LNG business in Europe will also change.

22.5.3   Geopolitical Forces

In general, international and domestic politics can significantly alter the outcomes such as those predicted in the RWGTM reference case. An example of domestic policy involves the United States NIMBY ('not in my backyard') issues spawned by environmental and/or terrorism concerns. In particular, prohibiting the development of import infrastructure could drive up prices and accelerate the adoption of alternatives to natural gas, such as expansion of shale gas production, the growth of coal gasification (as in integrated gasification combined cycle for power generation), and development of nuclear, wind and solar power. Furthermore, high prices for sustained periods could erode demand in certain sectors to a point that would discourage the development of import infrastructure.

As mentioned above, energy security concerns among countries in Europe regarding heavy reliance on Russian supplies that must transit multiple borders prior to reaching the end-user could push more rapid development of LNG and/or adoption of alternatives to gas. As consumers seek to diversify away from Russian supplies, their other pipeline options are North Africa and the Middle East and the Caspian Sea via Turkey, and these options also carry potential concerns of overreliance, particularly because pipelines are fixed point-to-point delivery infrastructures. LNG, however, provides a much more diverse set of potential suppliers, which tends to limit energy security risks.

Various political forces can also alter outcomes in Asian markets. For example, disagreements involving Russia and China can prevent the development of pipelines in Northeast Asia, which would increase the LNG import requirements in Asia above what it would otherwise be. This would certainly have effects around the globe as competition for waterborne supplies would generally be higher.[13]

Of course, the Middle East is a centerpiece of geopolitical risk. According to the USGS, Iran holds the second largest natural gas resource potential in the world, but political disagreements with the West may render much of that resource inaccessible. If nuclear proliferation conflicts escalate, then sanctions could effectively strand Iran's resources, which would have a significant influence on the long-run competitiveness of natural gas vs alternatives in all major markets. Furthermore, any conflict that compromises the ability of Qatar to maintain or even expand its LNG exports, perhaps a conflict involving the Strait of Hormuz, could do the same.

Environmental policies are also important, as regulation with respect to CO_2 and other pollutants could encourage gas consumption despite energy security concerns. This latter point applies to all regions, and is especially salient for Europe and North America, where legislation is both in place and progressing to impose restriction on CO_2 emissions. Environmental policies that penalize the use of carbon-intensive fuels will tend to favor the use of natural gas over coal. Thus,

---

[13] These types of scenarios have indeed been investigated. For one example please see Hartley and Medlock III, 2006b. The working paper, along with similar studies, is also available online at www.rice.edu/energy.

policy can drive an increase in demand and, therefore, affect the international gas trade.

The formation of a cartel in natural gas also looms as a possibility. The Gas Exporting Countries Forum (GECF) has already met numerous times, and while no concrete plans are in place for production agreements several member nations are seriously discussing coordination of production. Notably, representatives from Iran, Qatar and Russia recently met to discuss the possibility of coordinating their activities. Such a venture would likely have little success in the short to medium term, but as the concentration of supply increases, the ability of a cartel to success-fully manipulate price grows.[14] Moreover, if pending carbon legislation makes demand for natural gas greater and more inelastic then the ability of the cartel to operate successfully is enhanced. This comes about because there is no, or limited, substitution possibility in light of a lack of acceptable low-cost alternatives.

22.6   Concluding Remarks

The development of a global natural gas market is dependent on the expansion of LNG trade. Specifically, robust trade in LNG from many competing sources will increase market liquidity and accelerate a move to a more flexible market. Con-tracts will remain critical to project development, especially since the components of LNG value chain are very capital intensive. However, contracts will become less important in determining the direction of flow, as destination flexibility will provide value to producers seeking higher netbacks with the expansion of market alternatives.

The global gas market will be shaped especially by developments in Russia and the Middle East. This is a function of geology and geography. Geology is impor-tant because over 70% of the world's natural gas resource potential lies within these two regions. Geography favors these regions because each region can readily supply both the Atlantic and the Pacific basins. Russia currently accounts for al-most one quarter of world production of natural gas, and it has substantial re-sources that remain untapped. But Russia's position globally will ultimately de-pend on its ability to raise the capital it needs to develop resources in the Yamal peninsula, Kara Sea, and Shtokmanovskoye region, and to build new infrastruc-ture for delivery, either by pipeline or LNG.

Countries of the Middle East, especially Qatar and Iran, have substantial natural gas resources that position them to also become major players in shaping the global gas market. Middle East gas producers have a particular advantage in LNG developments, as they are well suited to serve growing markets in North America, Europe, and Asia.

Of course, various factors will influence Russia and/or the countries of the Middle East. Regional instability, impediments to investment, such as domestic price subsidies, cooperative rent-seeking by a select group of key suppliers, envi-

---

[14] More information is available from the author upon request.

ronmental concerns, and fears of terrorism can alter outcomes. At the very least, it is true that the resources are in place to shape a global gas market, and LNG trade will grow significantly, to the benefit of consumers and producers alike. Even if the various factors mentioned herein dominate, many of the futures that can be envisioned see LNG as a growing and important source of natural gas supply in the global energy future.

References

Brito, D. & Hartley, P. 2007. Expectations and the evolving world gas market. Energy Journal, 28: 1-24.

Frantz, J. H. & Valerie, J. 2005. Shale gas. Schlumberger White Paper, www.slb. com/media/services/solutions/reservoir/shale_gas.pdf.

Hartley, P. & Medlock III, K. B. 2006a. The Baker Institute world gas trade model. In A. Jaffe, D. Victor & M. Hayes (Eds.), Natural Gas and Geopolitics: From 1970 to 2040: 357-406. Cambridge: Cambridge University Press.

Hartley, P. & Medlock III, K. B. 2006b. Political and economic influences on the future world market for natural gas. In A. Jaffe, D. Victor & M. Hayes (Eds.), Natural Gas and Geopolitics: From 1970 to 2040: 407-438. Cambridge: Cambridge University Press.

Hartley, P. & Medlock III, K. B. 2007. North American security of natural gas supply in a global market. Rice University Energy Forum Working Paper, www.rice.edu/energy/publications/docs/natgas/ng_security-nov07.pdf.

International Energy Agency. 2003. World energy investment outlook.

Navigant Consulting Inc. 2008. North American Natural Gas Supply Assessment.

23 Cross-border Trading

Hilde A. K. Rosenblad[1]

Abstract

Within the integrated market of Norway, Sweden, Finland, and Denmark – the Nordic region – cross-border trading is handled implicitly in the day-ahead market clearing. The capacity on all connections between the four countries, and partly also the capacity on the connections between Denmark and Germany, is included in the Nordic price calculation. This chapter aims to describe how the exchange of power across the borders between the Nordic countries comes about and how the Nordic model ensures socioeconomic utilization of generation and transmission resources within the Nordic region, allocating the power flow from the surplus areas to the deficit areas.

Keywords: electricity trading, cross border, Nordic power exchange

---
[1] Hilde A. K. Rosenblad is Senior Adviser at Nord Pool Spot AS, Norway.

A. Bausch and B. Schwenker (eds.), *Handbook Utility Management,*
DOI: 10.1007/978-3-540-79349-6_23, © Springer-Verlag Berlin Heidelberg 2009

23.1   Introduction

Within the integrated market of Norway, Sweden, Finland and Denmark – the Nordic region – cross-border trading is handled implicitly in the day-ahead market clearing. The capacity on all connections between the four countries, and partly also the capacity on the connections between Denmark and Germany, is included in the Nordic price calculation. This chapter aims to describe how the exchange of power across the borders between the Nordic countries comes about and how the Nordic model ensures a socioeconomic utilization of generation and transmission resources within the Nordic region, allocating the power flow from the surplus areas to the deficit areas.

Transmission capacity that is not utilized in the day-ahead market is made available for the intraday market. Throughout Finland, Sweden, Denmark, Germany, and soon also Norway, participants can buy or sell power across the borders until 1 hour before delivery.

Capacity limitations on transmission lines may cause price differences between the countries. In the financial market there are instruments that give the participants the opportunity to hedge their risk against a Nordic Elspot reference price, called the system price, and in addition the area price differences that may occur via so-called contracts for difference (CfD). The financial contracts linked to the system price and the complementary CfD are described in this chapter.

23.2   The Nordic Power Exchange – The Nord Pool Group

The Nord Pool Group operates marketplaces for trading and clearing physical-delivery and financially settled power contracts in the Nordic region. Together the Nord Pool Group provides Europe's most liquid wholesale marketplace for power. Its main physical market, the day-ahead Elspot Market, accounts for about 70% of the Nordic region's power consumption (and production).

The Nord Pool Group comprises the parent company Nord Pool ASA with its wholly owned subsidiaries Nord Pool Clearing ASA and Nord Pool Consulting AS.[2] Nord Pool Spot AS and its wholly owned Nord Pool Finland Oy are also part of the Nord Pool Group. Nord Pool ASA is owned 50-50 by Statnett SF and Svenska Kraftnät, the Norwegian and Swedish transmission system operators (TSO). Nord Pool Spot AS is owned by the four Nordic TSOs and Nord Pool ASA, with equal shares of 20% each.

Nord Pool ASA provides a marketplace where exchange members can trade financially settled electricity contracts, futures, forwards, and options up to 6 years ahead. Nord Pool ASA also offers trading with European Union Allowances, Certified Emissions Reductions, and Swedish green electricity certificates. All con-

---

[2] As of December 21, 2007 press release: OMX is acquiring Nord Pool ASA's clearing and consulting operations and international derivatives products and establishing a business unit for international energy derivatives headquartered in Oslo.

tracts traded on Nord Pool ASA's marketplace are cleared through its daughter company Nord Pool Clearing ASA.

Nord Pool Spot organizes and offers trading platforms for both day-ahead and intraday trading of electricity for physical delivery. The day-ahead market Elspot covers the Nordic region and the TSO area of Vattenfall Europe Transmission GmbH in Germany. In addition, Nord Pool Spot operates the intraday market Elbas in Finland, Sweden, Denmark, and Germany. During 2008 Elbas will also be extended to cover Norway. Nord Pool Spot provides a market place to producers, distributors, industrial companies, energy companies, trading representatives, large consumers, and TSOs on which they can buy or sell physical power. Nord Pool Spot is the central counter party in all trades guaranteeing settlement for trade and anonymity for participants.

The Nord Pool Group has operations in Oslo, Stockholm, Helsinki, Fredericia, Berlin, and Amsterdam.

23.3 The Common Nordic Power Market

A well-functioning power market ensures that electricity is generated wherever the cost of generation is lowest at any time of the day. Increases in demand will be balanced against more expensive modes of generation.

The benefits of the Nordic power market derive from the opportunity it provides for Finland, Sweden, Denmark, and Norway to assist each other when additional electricity supplies are required. If one country is unable to satisfy demand from its own output it can import the necessary power from a neighbor. The common Nordic market primarily involves electricity generation from such resources as hydro, nuclear, coal, natural gas, biofuel, and wind power. Since the generating modes differ and are distributed differently in the various countries, the need for additional power will vary from country to country and at different times. This makes it possible to share Nordic power resources. A common Nordic resource pool for electricity helps to optimize the use of available power and reduce local deficits. This allows the various countries to make socioeconomic gains. For the longer perspective it also gives the market an indication of what it would take to establish new generating capacity.

Participants from outside the Nordic countries who want to import from or export to the Nordic market trade on the same terms within the exchange area and through individual 'capacity windows' procured either through a capacity auction or through long-term rights to usage of interconnections.

The presence of a power exchange has contributed to the high level of trade activity in the Nordic power market and is also beginning to prove to be an important element in the design and trading activity emerging in a competitive European market.

The key features of the Nordic Elspot day-ahead market concept are: auction trading; bidding areas; implicit auctioning of the grid capacity; the area prices; and the system price.

23.3.1 Auction Trading

On Nord Pool Spot's day-ahead market, hourly power contracts are traded daily for physical delivery in the next day's 24-hour period. The price calculation is based on the balance between bids and offers from all market participants, finding the intersection point between the market's supply curve and demand curve. This trading method is referred to as equilibrium point trading, auction trading, or simultaneous price setting.

23.3.2 Bidding Areas

In order to handle grid congestions, the Nordic exchange area is geographically divided into bidding areas or trade zones. Participants must make bids according to where their production or consumption is physically connected in the Nordic grid. Thus, the transmission capacity between each possible pair of bidding areas is auctioned implicitly in the Elspot price calculation. Internal grid congestions within a bidding area are handled by the TSOs using other methods such as countertrading.

In general, the bidding areas are consistent with the national borders in the Nordic region. In addition, the grids in Jutland and Zealand are not physically connected, giving two bidding areas in Denmark. In the Norwegian grid there can be several bidding areas. It is the Norwegian TSO who determines how to split the Norwegian grid into bidding areas on the basis of physical conditions.

23.3.3 Implicit Auctioning of Trading Capacity

All trading capacity between the bidding areas is dedicated to the Nord Pool Spot day-ahead market. This gives the market an advantage, since the capacity may be utilized based on the actual situation in the market, which can be read from the aggregated bid curves submitted by the participants. There are no explicit capacity auctions on these connections, and no single party has sole access to any of the trading capacity.

The price mechanism in Elspot adjusts the flow of power across the interconnections – and also on certain connections within the Norwegian grid – to the available trading capacity given by the Nordic transmission system operators. Thus, Elspot is a common power market for the Nordic countries, with an implicit capacity auction on the interconnections between the bidding areas.

23.3.4 Area Prices

If the contractual flow of power between bid areas exceeds the capacity allocated for Elspot contracts by the TSOs, area prices will be calculated. At the interconnections between the Nordic countries and within Norway, price mechanisms are used to relieve grid congestion (bottlenecks) by introducing different Elspot area prices. A price area may consist of one, two, or several bidding areas, depending on where the congestions occur.

The solution for the area price calculation is sought to optimize the social surplus in the market. The transmission capacity between the high-price (deficit) area and the low-price (surplus) area is utilized to the maximum. In this situation the flow of power will always go from the lower price areas towards the higher price areas.

23.3.5 System Price

The Elspot market's system price is also referred to as the 'unconstrained market clearing price'. This is because the system price is the price that balances sale and purchase in the exchange area while no transmission constraints within the Nordic Area are factored in.[3] When there are no constraints between the bidding areas, the area prices are all equal to the system price.[4]

Nord Pool Spot's system price is the reference price for futures, forwards, and options contracts traded on the exchange with Nord Pool ASA. The system price is also the reference price for the Nordic over-the-counter (OTC)/bilateral wholesale market.

23.4   Price Formation at Nord Pool Spot

The primary role of a market price is to establish equilibrium between supply and demand. This task is especially important in the power markets, because of the impracticability of storing electricity and the high costs associated with any supply failure. The spot market at Nord Pool Spot is an auction-based exchange for the trading of promptly physically delivered electricity. It is the central marketplace for Nordic Electricity. The spot market carries out the key task of balancing supply and demand in the power market, with a certain scope for forward planning.

The 'invisible hand' that creates equilibrium in most other markets is replaced in the power markets by a concrete visible hand. This is the Elspot market, which receives bids and offers from producers and consumers alike and calculates an hourly price that balances these opposing sides. Nord Pool Spot publishes a spot price for each hour of the coming day in order to artificially balance supply and demand.

---

[3] Note that the system price is the unconstrained price within the Nordic region, the influence of the German bidding area to the system price is limited to the effect of the exchange of power between Denmark and Germany.

[4] Exceptions occur due to different selection of bids that influence the price in several hours in the system price calculation and the area price calculation.

The primary function of an organized spot market for electricity is to maximize cost efficiency by supplying the demand for power from the most economic source available. It is difficult to achieve such optimization without a continuous price-setting mechanism producing a transparent equilibrium price. The large differences in production costs for the different generating units entail a high risk for losses of efficiency stemming from a poorly functioning pricing system. In addition, a much greater reserve capacity would be necessary to guarantee supply in a system without a successful spot market.

Every morning Nord Pool participants post their orders to the auction for the coming day. Each order specifies the volume in megawatt-hours per hour (see Figure 23.1) that a participant is willing to buy or sell at specific price levels (€/MWh) for each individual hour in the following day.

A well-functioning and competitive power market produces electricity at the lowest possible price for every hour of the day. The balance price represents both:

- The cost of producing one kilowatt-hour of power from the most expensive source that needs to be used in order to balance the system – either from a domestic installation or from external imports; or
- The price that the consumer group is willing to pay for the final kilowatt-hour required to satisfy demand.

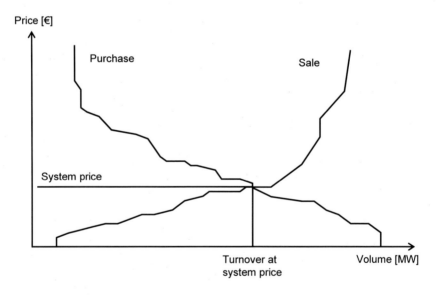

Figure 23.1: Price calculation one area – system price calculation

As soon as the noon deadline for participants to submit bids has passed, all purchase and sale orders are aggregated into two curves for each delivery hour; an aggregate demand curve and an aggregate supply curve. The system price for each hour is determined by the intersection of the aggregate supply-and-demand curves, which represent all bids and offers for the entire Nordic region.

Calculation of Area Prices – and the Cross-border Flows

Whenever there are grid congestions, the Nordic Exchange area is divided into two or more price areas (see Figure 23.2). Assume the calculation of price for two areas with limited capacity to transport power from the surplus area to the deficit area. The participants' bids in the bidding areas on each side of the congestion are aggregated into supply-and-demand curves in the same fashion as in the system price calculation. A volume corresponding to the trading capacity on the constrained connection is added as a non-price-dependent purchase in the surplus area and a non-price-dependent sale in the deficit area. In the deficit area the sale will give a parallel shift of the supply curve, while in the surplus area the additional purchase will give a parallel shift of the demand curve.

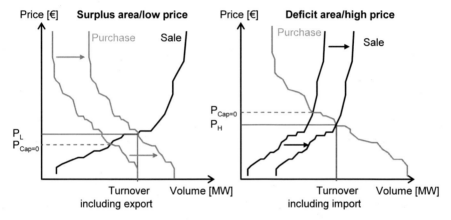

P$_L$ and P$_H$ → Prices for each area when full utilization of trading capacity
P$_{Cap=0}$ → Price in area with isolated price calculation.

Figure 23.2: Price and flow calculation – two areas

The area price in the surplus area and the deficit area is found in the new equilibrium points given after addition of the flow between the areas as purchase and sale, respectively. The price is relatively lower in the surplus area and relatively higher in the deficit area.

The logic can be summarized as follows: when the price is increased in the deficit area, the participants in this area will sell more and purchase less, while in the surplus area a lower price will lead to more purchase and less sale.

In a two-area model there are two possible solutions: either there is one common price and no constraints in the transmission or there are different prices in the two areas and full utilization of the capacity, with power flowing from the lower priced area towards the higher priced area.

In the Nordic Exchange area there are several bidding areas, and several solutions giving balance between supply and demand in the market may be found. The sustainable energy systems analysis model (SESAM) algorithm, doing the price calculation at Nord Pool Spot, is based on application of the social welfare criteria in combination with market rules.

For every bidding area the participants' bids are aggregated into a purchase-and-sales curve (see Figure 23.3). The demand curve indicates the value of each megawatt bought by the buyers in the market. Thus, the area below the demand curve to the left of the intersection point represents the total utility for the buyers in the market. Correspondingly, the supply curve indicates the sellers' estimated value of each megawatt that will be delivered and consumed in the market. Thus, the area below the supply curve on the left side of the intersection point represents the 'cost'[5] of each megawatt consumed.

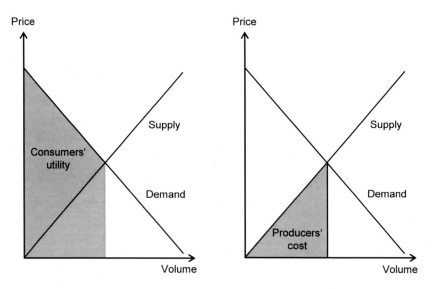

Figure 23.3: Consumers' utility and producers' cost at balancing price

Optimizing the economic welfare means finding the solution that maximizes the area between the supply curve and the demand curve. The solution of prices and flows is found where the total social surplus taking account of all the bidding areas and all the 24 hours together is at its maximum (see Figure 23.4).

There are several market rules that set additional requirements to the solution found in the price-and-flow calculation. These requirements are related to capacity limitations set by the TSOs, balance of supply and demand, the Elspot products offered at Nord Pool Spot, etc. Simplified, they may be described as follows:

- There is a balance between demand and supply within each bidding area.
- For each bidding area the demand price is equal to the supply price.

---

[5] The cost is the value that the sellers ascribe to each unit considering also the alternative cost in the market.

- Transmission capacities set by the TSOs are not exceeded. This includes limitations on ramping (max. change of power flow from one hour to the next) on certain high-voltage direct current (HVDC) connections.
- Price and volume conditions set by the participants in the individual bids – within the standard product range in Elspot – must be satisfied.
- If the Elspot prices differ between two areas, then the transmission capacity between these areas is fully utilized towards the area with the higher price.

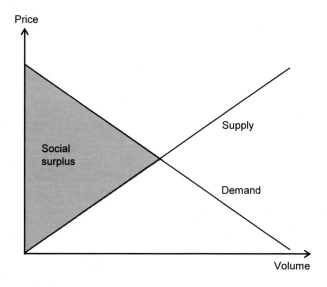

Figure 23.4: Social surplus (consumers' utility – producers' cost)

23.5   Handling of Internal Grid Limitations

Congestion in transmission of power is possible, naturally, on any line in the grid, and also within the bidding areas. Cases of internal congestion within bidding areas are normally handled by the TSO responsible countertrading on each side of the congestion. Countertrades are done outside of NPS and independently of the Elspot price-and-flow calculation and are thus not shown in the Elspot calculation and results.

There are, however, two internal cuts in the Nordic region that are handled differently; the trading capacity across cut 2 in Sweden and cut B in Jutland. Cut 2 in the Swedish grid limits the amount of power that can be transported from the north to the south of Sweden, and cut B in Jutland limits the amount of power it is possible to transport between the southern and northern parts of Jutland.

Instead of dividing Sweden and Jutland into two separate bidding areas on each side of these cuts – as, for instance, in the Norwegian grid – the capacity limits in these internal cuts are handled as additional constraints in the SESAM model. The sum of flow on the connections from/to one part of the bidding area on one side of the limiting cut must not exceed the capacity given on the internal cut. For instance, the sum of flow on the Skagerrak cables and the Kontiskan cables must not exceed the capacity limit given on cut B in Jutland. Thus, the internal capacity limit in cut B may actually reduce the power flow between Jutland and Norway/Sweden.

The alternative to using an extra internal capacity limit in the Elspot price[6]-and-flow calculation would have been for the TSOs to limit the exchange capacity on the connections from/to these areas i.e., the connections from Sweden to Norway and Denmark, directly. This would naturally have given a less than optimal solution for the market. Taking the internal capacity limitation into account in the Elspot calculations gives the SESAM model the opportunity to optimize the use of the connections from/to the area in situations where there is import on one connection and export on another.

Owing to this method of handling internal capacity limitations, certain situations may be observed from time to time during some hours in the Nordic market. Two examples are given to illustrate these:

Example 1: There is a price difference between Sweden and Denmark East, but the trading capacity between the two areas is not fully utilized.

If the internal capacity limit is congested – or fully utilized – there may still be available capacity on the export/import connections, but the flow is limited by the internal capacity limit. The internal capacity limit prevents an adequate power flow between the areas to achieve total convergence of the area prices. A look at the price difference and the flow between the two areas isolated suggests that the market rules are not followed. However, the inclusion of the internal capacity limit in the calculation model leads to better utilization of the overall grid and production/consumption resources than if the limitations on the internal cut had to be reflected on the capacity given for the connections between the areas instead.

Example 2: The direction of power flow is from southern Norway to Sweden, but the price in Norway South is higher than the Swedish area price.

Again, a look at the price difference and the flow between these two areas in isolation does not give the full picture. In this situation, without exception, the power imported from Norway South to Sweden is always transported further on to a third area (Denmark East or Denmark West), which has an even higher area price than Norway South. Power is moved from a lower priced area (Norway South) to the higher priced area, but the power flows through the area with the lowest price. Optimizing the utilization of capacity subject to the internal capacity limits allows for more power to be exchanged between Norway and Denmark than would have been possible if the limitations on the internal cut had to be reflected in the capacity given for export from Sweden to Denmark instead.

---

[6] Technically the division of Sweden and Jutland into two (or several) bidding areas (as in Norway) is possible but there are political arguments for keeping a common price within these areas.

23.6   Cross-border Optimization Between Denmark West and Germany

Cross-border optimization (CBO) is a service offered by Nord Pool Spot to improve the efficiency of the cross-border trade between Jutland and Germany. The main purpose of the service is to ensure that the power flow across the border is responding to price signals from the two markets. Traders have the option of handing over administration of the capacities bought at the daily auctions at the border between Germany and Jutland to Nord Pool Spot. Nord Pool Spot will ensure that the power flows from the low-price area to the high-price area.

Working Principles of the CBO Service

At the daily auction, a participant buys capacity at the Jutland–Germany border for one or more hours of the next day. Then he transfers administration of the capacity to Nord Pool Spot. Nord Pool Spot includes transferred capacity from all participants in the price calculation in Elspot, as it does the capacity on all other connections, and calculates the power prices and the flow between each bidding area for the next day.

The calculated power flow between Nord Pool Spot's bidding area DK1 (Western Denmark) and Nord Pool Spot's German bidding area KONTEK is decided according to the market rules and will thus always go from the lower priced area towards the higher priced area, or lead to price convergence between the two areas. The capacity will not be utilized in the opposite direction.

When there is a price difference between the two areas the participant who has handed over capacity from the explicit capacity auction will receive the congestion rent.[7]

23.7   Financial Products Related to Cross-border Trading

The products traded on Nord Pool's financial market are power derivatives. They are categorized as base and peak load futures, forwards, options, and CfDs. These contracts are used for trading and risk management purposes, and have a current trading time horizon of up to 6 years. The contracts listed are for days, weeks, months, quarters, and years. There is no physical delivery of financial market power contracts. Cash settlement is made throughout the trading and/or the delivery period, starting at the due date of each contract, which depends on whether the product is a futures or forward.

The reference price for forward and futures contracts and options in the financial market is the Elspot system price. Actual physical-delivery purchase costs are determined by actual area prices. When there are constraints in the transmission

---

[7] Congestion rent is the price difference between the two areas multiplied with the utilized capacity.

grid, the area price differs from the system price; CfDs that are offered for trading in the financial market organized by Nord Pool ASA allow participants to hedge against this area price risk.

A perfect hedge using forward or futures instruments is possible only in situations when there is no transmission grid congestion in the market area, that is to say when area prices are equal to the system price. Hedging in forwards or futures therefore implies a basis risk equal to the difference between the area price at the member's physical location and the system price.

CfDs were introduced to provide the possibility of a perfect hedge even when the markets are split into two or more price areas. New forward contract types based on the area prices would have been another way to accomplish this goal. However, this method would have split the total liquidity among several products, and it was therefore rejected. This separate product, the CfD, was therefore introduced.

To create a perfect hedge that includes the basis risk when area prices are not equal to the system price, a three-step process using CfDs must be followed:

(1) Hedge the required volume using forward contracts.
(2) Hedge any price difference – for the same period and volume – through CfDs.
(3) Accomplish physical procurement by trade in the spot market area of the member's location.

Nord Pool ASA provides trading in CfDs for the following area price differentials:

CfD name and reference area	CfD definition
Norway	ΔP = Oslo area price minus system price
Sweden	ΔP = Stockholm area price minus system price
Finland	ΔP = Helsinki area price minus system price
Denmark West	ΔP = Aarhus area price minus system price
Denmark East	ΔP = Copenhagen area price minus system price
SYGER	ΔP = Phelix price Germany minus system price (NP)

A CfD (see Figure 23.5) is a forward contract with reference to the difference between the area price and the Nord Pool Spot system price. The market price of a CfD during the trading period reflects the market's prediction of the price difference during the delivery period.

The market price of a CfD can be positive, negative or zero. CfDs trade at positive prices when the market expects a specific area price to be higher than the system price (i.e., the selected market area is in a net import situation). CfDs will trade at negative prices if the market anticipates an area price below the system price (the market area is in a net export situation).

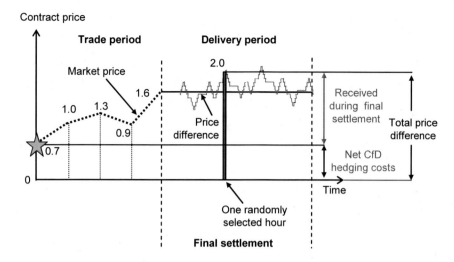

Figure 23.5: Contracts for difference (CfD)

In this example, an exchange member/clearing member purchased a CfD at a price of 0.7 €/MWh and no forward market hedge of the power volume was made. During the trading period, the market price of the CfD increased to 1.6 €/MWh. For the randomly selected hour during the delivery period shown in the illustration, the member receives (2.0-0.7) €/MWh = 1.3 €/MWh. Spot market purchase cost over the system price for the specified hour is 2.0 €/MWh. However, the member's net cost is equal to the hedging cost of 0.7 €/MWh.

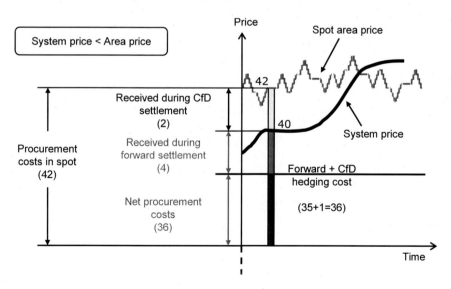

Figure 23.6: CfD together with forward contract – system price < area price

The next example illustrates a perfect hedge using CfDs and forward contracts. Here, the Exchange member has carried out the two steps required to make a perfect hedge of area prices. He has purchased a forward contract (at a cost of 35 €/MWh) to hedge the Nordic Power Exchange spot market price, and a CfD (at a cost of 1.0 €/MWh) to hedge any area price differential. Total hedging costs are 36 €/MWh.

The financial results of using CfD hedging can be illustrated in a comparison of two delivery hours. In one case, the system price is less than the area price, while in the second example the system price is higher than the area price.

In Figure 23.6, the area price for the selected hour is 42 €/MWh. The system price is 40 €/MWh.

In the forward settlement during the delivery period, the member receives 4 €/MWh, and in the CfD settlement, 2 €/MWh.

Net procurement cost is 36 €/MWh, which equals the initial hedging costs of the forward, plus the CfD.

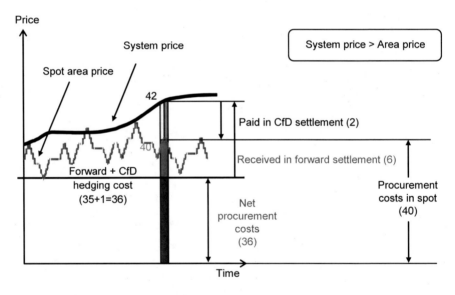

Figure 23.7: CfD together with forward contract – system price > area price

In Figure 23.7, the area price for the selected hour is 40 €/MWh. The system price is 42 €/MWh. In the forward settlement, during the delivery period, the member receives 6 €/MWh, and in the CfD settlement he is charged 2 €/MWh. Again, the net procurement cost is 36 €/MWh, which equals the initial hedging costs of the forward and the CfD.

23.8   The Intraday Market – Elbas

The Elbas market provides continuous power trading with contracts that lead to physical delivery for the hours that have been traded on the Elspot market and are more than 1 hour from delivery. The trading platform is available for trading 24 hours a day, 7 days a week. The traded products are 1-hour-long power contracts or block contracts of several consecutive hours.

The time span between the day's Elspot price fixing and the actual delivery hour of the concluded contracts is quite long (36 hours at the most). As consumption and production situations change, a market player may have a need for trading during these 36 hours.

The Elbas Market enables continuous trading

The participants are power producers, distributors, industries, and brokers. The Elbas market is currently open in Finland, Sweden, Denmark, and Germany, and it will also be opened in Norway during 2008.

Nord Pool Spot AS acts as counterparty in all contracts traded on the Elbas market, and all trades are physically settled with the respective TSOs.

Elbas Cross-border

As long as there is available capacity between the bidding areas that are covered by Elbas, the participants may trade freely on the available bids and offers in the system – including those across the borders between the areas/countries. An essential point in the Elbas market is managing the trading capacity between the bidding areas. After a cross-border trade has been concluded, the capacity between the bidding areas is automatically updated. If the connections are congested, the market area is automatically divided so that contracts that would have to be delivered across the congested connection are not visible in the Elbas trading system to the participants trading in the area on the other side of the congested connection.

References

Hjalmarson, L. 2007. Price formation at Nord Pool Spot. Oslo: Nord Pool Spot AS.

Houmøller, A. P. 2006. The Nordic power exchange and the Nordic model for a liberalised power market. Oslo: Nord Pool Spot AS.

Nord Pool ASA. 2006. Annual review 2006. Oslo: Nord Pool ASA.

Nord Pool ASA. 2007a. Nord Pool power markets – basic information. Oslo: Nord Pool ASA.

Nord Pool ASA. 2007b. The Nordic power market. Oslo: Nord Pool ASA.

Nord Pool ASA. 2007c. Product report: Derivatives trade at Nord Pool's financial
    markets. Oslo: Nord Pool ASA.
Nord Pool Spot AS. 2006. Annual review 2006. Oslo: Nord Pool Spot AS.
Nord Pool Spot AS. 2007. Product report: The spot market. Oslo: Nord Pool Spot
    AS.

24 The Future of Gas Supply in Europe

Jonathan Stern[1]

Anouk Honoré[2]

Abstract

In 2006, Europe imported 43.5% of its gas consumption. This share is expected to rise sharply, creating new challenges and raising serious political concerns about security of supply. The short to medium term is more likely to see a period of easy supply rather than shortage, but problems may appear post-2015/2020. The source of the next 50-100 bcm/year of supply is not obvious, because of geopolitical problems between Europe and its principal suppliers, and if the situation does not improve in the coming years, there are significant uncertainties from where Europe will receive substantial additional gas supplies.

Keywords: natural gas, import dependence, geopolitical environment

---

[1] Prof. Dr. Jonathan Stern is Director of Natural Gas Research at the Oxford Institute for Energy Studies, United Kingdom.

[2] Anouk Honoré is Research Fellow at the Oxford Institute for Energy Studies, United Kingdom.

A. Bausch and B. Schwenker (eds.), *Handbook Utility Management,*   401
DOI: 10.1007/978-3-540-79349-6_24, © Springer-Verlag Berlin Heidelberg 2009

24.1   Introduction

Europe[3] imported about 43.5% of its gas consumption in 2006 (IEA, 2007a). The maturity of the resource base in most European countries means that indigenous gas production will level off and then decline over the next decade and beyond. An increase in gas imports will be needed to cope with increased demand. The reliance on external supply is expected to rise sharply, creating a new situation and challenges for many gas-consuming countries in Europe. Growing fears about rising import dependence and market power of exporters in general, and Russia in particular, is even leading governments to question whether gas is a desirable fuel whose growth should be encouraged.

This chapter is structured as follows: Section 24.2 provides an outlook for supply to 2015, with particular emphasis on the likely development of pipeline and liquefied natural gas (LNG) supplies and import dependence. Section 24.3 deals with security of supply and the worsening geopolitical environment for natural gas trade around Europe, with a particular focus on Russia and the Middle East. The final section draws together these different factors into a conclusion.

24.2   Supply Outlook to 2015

24.2.1   Indigenous Production

European gas resources and production are declining. UK production, which has been the largest in Europe, is already in a decline. It is projected to deepen with the country, becoming up to 50% dependent on imports in the early 2010s, rising to as much as 80% by 2020 (Parliament of Science and Technology, 2004). Dutch production can hold level until 2010-15, with output from the Groningen field compensating for declines in the smaller fields. However, after 2015, all fields will experience accelerating decline. Elsewhere in Continental Europe, most countries will experience a gradual decline in production. The only exception to the trend of declining gas production in Europe is Norway, which exported 85 billion cubic metres (bcm) of gas to the Continent and the United Kingdom in

---

[3] In any discussion about 'European' gas markets, it is important to be precise about the geographical region under consideration. The most common definitions of Europe are the 27 countries included in the European Union or the 23 countries of OECD Europe. However, in gas terms it is important to look at 'Europe' as a group of countries interlinked by pipelines through which gas is exchanged. In this chapter 'European gas markets' include 35 countries, stretching from the Atlantic Ocean in the west almost to the CIS countries in the east: Albania, *Austria, Belgium,* Bosnia and Herzegovina, *Bulgaria,* Croatia, *Czech Republic, Cyprus, Denmark, Estonia, Finland, France, Germany, Greece, Hungary, Ireland, Italy, Latvia, Lithuania, Luxembourg, Malta, the Netherlands,* Norway, *Poland, Portugal,* Republic of Macedonia, *Romania,* Serbia and Montenegro, *Slovakia, Slovenia, Spain, Sweden,* Switzerland, Turkey *and the United Kingdom* (the countries in italic are members of the European Union).

2006 (Ministry of Petroleum and Energy, 2007). The Langeled and Tampen (via Far North Liquids and Associated Gas System) pipelines will increase export capacity to 130 bcm/year in 2010, where it will level off and, without additional resource discoveries, decline.

24.2.2 Supplies in 2006

Traditionally, Europe has relied on four main sources of gas, two European – the Netherlands and Norway – and two non-European – Russia and Algeria. In 2006, Europe 35 imported about 37% of its gas demand from Russia and Algeria (see Figure 24.1).

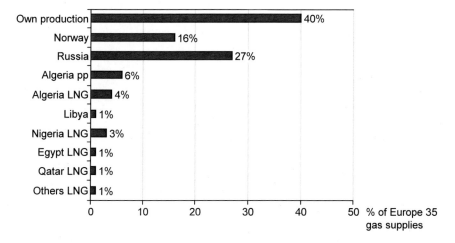

Figure 24.1: Europe 35 gas supplies in 2006 (total: 571 bcm) (IEA, 2007a)

In 2006, Russia was the largest single supplier to Europe, with more than 151 bcm gas to 21 countries – around 25% of European gas demand. All this gas was exported by the dominant Russian gas company Gazprom via its export subsidiaries, principally Gazprom Export.[4] Dependence on Russian gas is not uniform throughout Europe: some Central and East European countries are totally dependent on Russian gas, and there is significant dependence in North-West Europe. But the Iberian Peninsula imports no Russian gas, and the UK (Europe's largest gas market) has so far imported only relatively small quantities on a short-term basis.[5] The Nord Stream Gas Pipelines will create an additional 55 bcm/year of Russian export capacity to North-West Europe by the mid-2010s.

---

[4] Before November 2006, this subsidiary company was named Gazexport.

[5] Gazprom exports to the UK in 2005 were 3.8 bcm or around 4% of total demand (Gazprom, 2005).

Algeria exported 59 bcm of gas to Europe in 2006 (pipeline and LNG). Its two export pipelines to Europe have a combined capacity of 34 bcm. There are two new pipeline projects: the Medgaz line to Spain, 8 bcm/year with a projected start date of 2008, and the Galsi line to Italy via Sardinia, 8 bcm/year with a projected start date of 2009.

In the 2000s, Europe developed a huge enthusiasm for LNG, with numerous proposed projects. For many companies and governments, LNG has advantages over pipeline gas. First, the more border crossings that a pipeline needs to make, the greater the commercial and political risks. Therefore, the likelihood that new gas pipelines to Europe, such as Nabucco, will have to cross numerous borders favours LNG. Second, LNG can also provide supply diversification and potential competition. This is a huge change compared with prospects for LNG a decade ago: both long-term and traded LNG volumes are increasing, and will become a more and more important source of Atlantic Basin gas supply. In addition, LNG helps companies overcome problems of obtaining access to networks in Continental Europe.

Table 24.1: LNG supplies in Europe in 2006 (Cedigaz, 2007)

From To	Oman	Qatar	Trinidad	Algeria	Libya	Nigeria	Egypt	Total
Belgium		0.36	0.16	3.35		0.16	0.25	4.28
France				7.35		4.23	2.30	13.88
Greece				0.45			0.04	0.49
Italy				3.00			0.10	3.10
Portugal						1.97		1.97
Spain	1.00	5.00	3.00	2.80	0.72	7.10	4.80	24.42
Turkey				4.60		1.12		5.72
UK			0.60	2.00			0.96	3.56
Total	1.00	5.36	3.76	23.55	0.72	14.58	8.45	57.42

European LNG imports jumped by 21% in 2006, to 57 bcm (see Table 24.1). There was double-digit growth across Europe except in Greece and (curiously) France, where imports almost stagnated. The UK showed the biggest increase with 3.5 bcm received in 2006 as against 0.4 bcm in 2005.

LNG will become a major contributor of incremental gas supply in Europe over the next two decades. This will particularly be the case in Spain, Italy and the UK.[6] LNG will also expand in France and Belgium. Within a decade LNG terminals are likely to be built in Germany, the Netherlands and some central and East European countries.

In 2006, seven countries delivered LNG to Europe. In 2006, Europe received 27% of world LNG deliveries, the US and Caribbean 9%, and East Asia plus India

---

[6] The UK alone has seven new LNG terminals in various stages of development: Grain, Dragon, South Hook, Teeside (Excelerate), Teeside (ConocoPhilips), Canvey Island, Milford Haven (Amlwch Anglesey) and Port Talbot.

64% (Cedigaz, 2007). The rate of growth in the Atlantic Basin is even outpacing Asia Pacific, the historical focus of LNG marketing.

The numerous regasification facilities announced in the Atlantic Basin emphasize the rapid growth and changing market conditions. This geographic region includes seven exporting countries (Algeria, Libya, Egypt, Nigeria, Oman, Qatar and Trinidad) and 10 importing countries (USA, Mexico, Spain, France, Italy, Turkey, Greece, Portugal, UK and Belgium). Norway, Equatorial Guinea and Angola will join the list of exporting LNG countries, while Russia is expected to eventually be a major LNG exporting country. Brazil, Germany, the Netherlands and Poland may join the list of importing LNG countries in the next 5-10 years.

24.2.3 Future Supplies

Because of political concern about security of Russian gas supplies (see below), diversification of supply has become an important priority.[7] The obvious regions from which substantial supplies could be made available are North Africa, the Middle East and the Caspian Region. As far as the Middle East and North Africa (MENA) is concerned, the potential exists to increase exports four-fold by 2030. In absolute terms, this would require an increase in total exports of nearly 350 bcm/year, of which the majority (over 200 bcm) would need to come from the Middle East. In 2006, Middle East gas exports had reached only 57 bcm which had been achieved 25 years after the start of exports (IEA, 2005). This is not because of any lack of resources, project proposals or interest in developing gas exports. North African projections foresee exports from that region increasing more than 3-fold to 200 bcm/year over the next 25 years, when around 40 years were required for exports to reach the 2006 level of 87 bcm (Cedigaz, 2007).[8]

These levels of gas exports could certainly be sustained by known proven reserves (let alone what may be discovered in these countries over the next three decades), although a significant number of new fields will need to be developed.[9] New LNG and pipeline projects, both under construction and in advanced stages of planning, would support the projections to 2010. Cost increases in LNG (and to a lesser extent pipeline) projects over the last 2-3 years mean that the economics of any project under discussion have changed, and projects are being delayed.[10]

There are other serious doubts about whether such a huge rate of increase in exports, sustained over a 25 year period, is realistic: economically, institutionally, politically and geopolitically. Virtually all countries which currently export gas, or are projected to do so in the future, are experiencing significant increases in do-

---

[7] The next two sections are drawn from Stern 2006c.

[8] Algerian LNG exports commenced in 1964, and pipeline exports in 1987; Libyan exports only became significant with the start of pipeline trade in 2004.

[9] For example, by 2030, less than 40 bcm out of an anticipated total of 200 bcm of Algerian gas production will come from fields currently in production (IEA, 2005).

[10] New LNG projects under construction are being delayed by 1 year on average (IEA, 2007b).

mestic consumption of gas, either for their domestic industry and power sectors or for reinjection in oil fields, which seems set to curtail incremental availability of gas for export. This already applies to Russia, Algeria, Nigeria, Egypt, Iran and other countries in the Middle East (Hallouche, 2007). Furthermore, very substantial increases in export prices since 2003 have significantly reduced the financial pressures on these countries to expand gas exports significantly.

In Russia, gas demand increased at 3-4% per annum in the mid 2000s due to very strong economic growth. This will probably fall as major efficiency improvements are introduced as a consequence of increases in domestic prices, which are intended to rise to parity with export prices to Europe by 2011. However, once those levels of domestic prices are achieved, it will be as profitable for Gazprom to deliver gas to the domestic market as to export it to Europe. Hence incentives to increase exports to Europe, beyond current contractual commitments, will be significantly reduced.

In Algeria, a combination of rapid increases in domestic demand and reduced supply availability due to maturing of existing fields, together with the relatively slow pace of bringing new discoveries into production, threatens further expansion possibilities. The new Algerian Hydrocarbon Law passed in 2006, which restricts foreign participation in upstream development, may present a further obstacle to resolving this situation.

In the 2000s, West Africa emerged as an important LNG-exporting region, with Nigeria as the major supplier and Equatorial Guinea and Angola likely to start deliveries over the next few years. After more than 30 years of discussion and disappointment, the Nigeria LNG (NLNG) project began exports in 1999. But within a decade of starting these exports NLNG will have six trains in operation delivering more than 30 bcm/year of supplies to the Atlantic Basin. Two more Nigeria LNG trains are planned, which would add a further 22 bcm of export capacity. In addition, three more projects are in various stages of planning and, if realised, would provide up to another 47 bcm of LNG export capacity, bringing total export capacity to nearly 100 bcm/year – in the same range as Qatar and Algeria – to make the country one of the world's leading gas and LNG exporters. In addition, Equatorial Guinea and Angola may add up to another 12 bcm of exports per year. West African gas export potential currently appears somewhat less than either North Africa or the Middle East, but additional discoveries could significantly expand current expectations.

In the early 2000s, significant emphasis has been placed on creating a new pipeline route to Europe via Turkey, carrying supplies from a number of Middle East and Caspian countries: Azerbaijan, Turkmenistan, Kazakhstan, Iran, Iraq and Egypt. None of these countries currently has thus far shown inclination to commit substantial piped volumes to the European market, and it is uncertain whether some could be considered secure suppliers, but diverse sources of supply flowing through a single pipeline would decrease the importance of any individual source. This appears to be the concept underpinning the Nabucco pipeline currently being promoted by a number of Central and South-East European utilities and the European Commission.[11] Such pipelines from the Middle East/Caspian region are strongly endorsed by governments in the US, European Union, and South-Eastern Europe to promote diversification away from Russian gas supplies and transport routes. However, two points should be recalled in relation to pipeline gas from the Middle East and Caspian region:

- In no way can such pipelines be considered a new idea. There have been regular initiatives to create such projects for at least the past 30 years without success.
- It is not clear – given the number of borders they will need to cross and the potential for problems within and between countries along the route – whether such pipeline routes can be considered more reliable than existing and new supplies from and through Russia, which they are intended to displace.

The IEA has projected that the share of total MENA gas exports delivered to European markets will increase to more than one third by 2010, and to nearly one half by 2030. Out of a total of 270 bcm of MENA LNG exports in 2030, the IEA believes that Europe will capture a minimum of 113 bcm or 42%, and perhaps up to 50%.[12] This suggests that Europe largely 'wins the battle' for global LNG supplies with the US and the Pacific Basin for both Middle East and North African LNG. This is a very optimistic projection for Europe and, given recent developments in the North American, and particularly Pacific, gas markets and prices it is impossible to be certain whether it is realistic.

24.3   Security of Supply

Security of gas supply, expressed as current and projected national or collective dependence of European countries on supplies from individual suppliers (or groups of suppliers) over the next 15-25 years, has become an increasingly important subject in the twenty-first century. Even before the cuts in Russian supplies to Ukraine in the first days of 2006, restricting the availability of supplies to some European countries and bringing the subject of gas security to the attention of politicians and public, the European Commission had already published a Green Paper on the subject and passed a Directive on gas security (EC, 2004). In March 2006, the Commission published another Green Paper on security (as well as sustainability and competitiveness), in which it projected that the share of imports in EU gas demand would increase to 80% by 2030 (EC, 2006).

---

[11] Commissioner Piebalgs welcomes agreement to accelerate Nabucco gas pipeline project. Press Release IP/06/842, Brussels, 26 June 2006. This mentions a scenario in which 10-15% of EU gas supplies would come from the Caspian region by 2025, suggesting two or three Nabucco-sized pipelines by that date.

[12] Calculated from the statements in IEA 2005 that the share of LNG in total MENA exports will not exceed 60% (IEA, 2005).

Even if these projections of future dependence are believed to be correct, they form only a small part of a security environment that includes a cluster of short-term and long-term issues, including: resource availability, technical breakdown and accident, terrorist attack, political instability, lack of investment and disagreements in relation to existing and future supplies, transit and facilities.

The trend towards declining European gas production and resource discovery has been discussed above. A major question is whether, as most commentary assumes, rising import dependence should be automatically regarded as equivalent to decreasing supply security.

24.3.1   Russia

European gas security concerns have focused on the role of Russia (and prior to 1992, the Soviet Union). This is not a new subject, but what has changed in the present century is the pan-European scope and the much larger volumes of Russian gas supplies.[13]

Irrespective of national positions, the crisis on 1-4 January 2006, which saw Russia cut gas supplies to Ukraine, with the consequence that Ukrainian consumers diverted substantial quantities of gas in transit through their country to Europe, produced a huge negative reaction from governments and commentators on both sides of the Atlantic.[14] Gazprom's imposition of steep increases in gas prices on CIS importing countries since 2005 has been interpreted both within and outside those countries as politically motivated, despite the continuing gap between those prices and the corresponding EU import price. CIS governments (as well as some in Central and Eastern Europe) appear to believe that, if they could only obtain access to non-Russian supplies of pipeline gas and LNG, they would be able to import such supplies on more favourable terms and improve their security of supply.

The 2 months immediately after these events saw a period of exceptionally cold weather in both Russia and many parts of Europe, Moscow experienced temperatures well below minus 30°C for an entire week. This raised gas demand in Russia and much of Central/Eastern Europe to extremely high levels, placing a huge strain on Russian gas and power networks. During this period, there were again diversions of Russian gas in transit to European countries through Ukraine. These diversions, which were mostly not disputed by the Ukrainian government, prevented Gazprom from being able to meet the very high demand requirements of some European customers. Buyers in Poland, Hungary, Italy and Austria reported that deliveries were 10-35% below requested volumes on a substantial number of days in January and February.[15]

---

[13] A very brief overview of the past 25 years of this debate can be found in Stern 2005, pp. 140-144.

[14] For details of this crisis and the subsequent reaction see Stern 2006a and b.

[15] In the Italian case, deliveries were still up to 15% below nominations at the beginning of March 2006.

The overwhelming conclusion of the political and public commentary throughout Europe on these episodes was that, by this action, Russia was exerting political pressure on the Ukrainian government and president in order to reassert its influence on a country attempting to make a decisive move towards the European Union and NATO and away from Russian political influence. The lack of any public official European censure of Ukraine for taking gas supplies to which it was not entitled clearly demonstrated where European politicians believed the blame lay for this episode.[16]

Irrespective of the contractual situation (i.e. legal obligations in respect of entitlements, prices and payments), the January/February 2006 episodes, and ongoing problems and uncertainties in the Russian-Ukrainian relationship, raised serious doubts in the minds of European politicians as to whether Russian gas can be considered reliable. There have been suggestions that the Russian government was – by this action – 'sending a signal' to Europe that it had the power to cut off gas supplies should it choose to do so and that, should European countries act in ways which it did not like, it might well choose to do so. This is based on an increasingly popular view of Russian foreign policy, which holds that the Putin Administration sees energy trade as an important means – and perhaps the principal means at Russia's disposal – of projecting its political power and influence internationally.[17] In this view, the Ukrainian crisis is seen as a 'trial run' for what Europe might suffer in the future, particularly if there should be a significant deterioration of its political relationship with Russia.

The March 2006 EU Green Paper on energy security envisaged a deepening of the existing energy partnership with Russia and argued that the G8 should intensify efforts to secure Russian ratification of the Energy Charter Treaty and its Transit Protocol (EC, 2006). But these suggestions were not new, and the failure of European Commission to play any significant role during or after the events of 1-4 January 2006, using the institutions of the EU-Russia Energy Dialogue and the EU-Ukraine Summits, did not inspire confidence in its role in any future crisis management.[18]

European concern about Russian gas security was echoed by the US Administration both in January 2006 and later in the year; Vice President Cheney, in a speech to a conference of European leaders in Lithuania, noted:

---

[16] There are indications that confidential letters were sent from both the EU and the Energy Charter Secretariat to the Ukrainian government pointing out shortcomings in the latter's behaviour, but even if these existed they stood in sharp contrast to the harsh and very public condemnation of Russia.

[17] Section IV.3 of the 2003 Russian Energy Strategy (Energeticheskaya Strategiya Rossiya na period do 2020 goda; confirmed by the Russian Government on August 28, 2003) states that one of the strategic aims of gas industry development is to "secure the political interests of Russia in Europe and surrounding states, and also in the Asia-Pacific region". Many believe that President Putin's PhD Dissertation also supports such a policy (Balzer, 2006).

[18] For the history of the EU-Russia Dialogue and the Energy Charter Treaty in relation to Russian gas trade with the EU see: Stern 2005, pp. 134-139.

"No legitimate interest is served when oil and gas become tools of in-
timidation or blackmail, either by supply manipulation or attempts to
monopolize transportation." (The White House, 2006)

The International Energy Agency subsequently made a direct connection between Gazprom's export monopoly and security, and cast doubt on Gazprom's
ability to honour its long-term contracts with European customers:

"[…] the IEA is worried about the increasingly monopolistic status of
state-controlled Gazprom. Europeans cannot import gas from Russia
unless Gazprom agrees. This restriction undermines European energy
security." (IEA, 2006c)

"Current IEA projections suggest that Gazprom could face a gradually increasing supply shortfall against its existing [European] contracts beginning in the next few years if timely investment in new fields is not made."
(IEA, 2006b)

24.3.2 A Worsening Geopolitical Environment

Just as there is a common assumption that the principal threats to European gas
security are externally focused, so there is a common assumption that within that
external focus, the policies of exporting countries and/or political events which are
likely to happen within exporting countries will be the principal threats to European gas security. Thus, in respect of both Russia and the Middle East, much
European commentary is focused on the general political and economic policies of
governments, as well as narrower (oil and) gas policy frameworks, which are believed to 'threaten' European (and possibly OECD) gas security. Some part of this
stronger recent sensitivity towards exporting countries is the product of a new assertiveness of (oil- and) gas-producing and -exporting countries in the wake of the
post-2003 increase in prices and a widespread perception (whether or not correct)
that such price levels will be at least a medium-term phenomenon. This new assertiveness – often termed 'resource nationalism' – has produced significant commercial challenges to both international oil and gas companies and OECD government
policies in countries as geographically diverse as Venezuela, Bolivia, Russia and
Iran, combined with a desire and an ability to challenge the political and geopolitical status quo, which they see as imposed by the US and EU governments.

Geopolitical scenarios, such as the Clingendael Institute's 'Regions and Empires' and Shell International's 'Low Trust Globalisation', have produced comprehensive storylines which are strongly negative for geopolitical energy trends
(Clingendael, 2004; Shell, 2005). Correlje and Van der Linde have observed that
under 'Regions and Empires' there is likely to be, "[…] a slowly emerging [gas]
supply gap, as a result of lagging investments as a consequence of ideological and
religious contrasts, particularly with regard to the North African suppliers, the
potential supplies in the Persian gulf and the Caspian Sea region" (Correlje & van
der Linde, 2006). The mid-2000s is witnessing a worsening of international energy

relations owing to worsening of international relations attributable to increasing producer/exporter assertiveness and increasing concern of OECD countries, which believe they are faced by a range of commercial threats, including deprivation of access to resources for international oil and gas companies (IOGCs), demands by host governments and national energy companies for increasing shares of the rent from any joint activities with IOGCs, and competition for energy exploration opportunities and resources with (particularly) Chinese and Indian companies. Overlaying all of these commercial developments are trends that have potentially serious consequences for European gas supplies:

- Increasing bilateral and geopolitical tensions between Russia and both the US and European governments, because of what the latter perceive to be weakening commitments to democracy and economic reform in Russia.
- Continued deterioration of political stability in the Middle East region as well as increasing tensions between potential gas exporting countries, such as Iran, and US and European governments. Six countries account for more than 90% of MENA gas exports in the period 2010-2030; two countries – Algeria and Qatar – account for 70-90% of total exports.[19] Should any political or geopolitical problems prevent these two countries from developing exports as anticipated, the consequences for European gas supplies and the Atlantic Basin (and global) LNG market will be significant.
- Uncertainty about political stability in West African LNG-exporting countries, especially Nigeria.

24.3.3 Security and Import Dependence – Empirical Evidence and Legislation

The traditional inclination among politicians and the media in OECD countries is to regard energy supplies which are produced domestically as 'secure', and supplies which are imported as 'insecure'. Most security planning is predicated on disruptions of imported supplies.[20] Summarising the security incidents which have occurred over the past 25 years in Europe: there have not been very many; those that have occurred have been divided between the three main causes (source, transit and facility), but facility incidents appear to have increased over recent years. In particular as far as the UK is concerned, the risk of facility incidents became increasingly problematic in the mid-2000s owing to the tightness of the supply/demand balance and the lack of storage capacity (Stern, 2004). Despite the constant references to the EU of the problems of importing gas by 'regions threat-

---

[19] The other four countries are Iran, Iraq, Libya and Egypt.

[20] For example, the EU Gas Security Directive (Article 2), which defines a major supply disruption as "a situation where the Community would risk to lose more than 20% of its supply from third countries".

ened by insecurity', it is difficult to think of any historical incident involving political instability which has prevented gas from being delivered to Europe.[21]

There is no evidence from Europe or anywhere else in the world that imported gas supplies have been – or are necessarily likely to be – less secure than supplies of domestically produced gas. Indeed, history suggests that all serious security incidents, i.e. where customers have lost gas supplies for a considerable period of time, have stemmed from failure of indigenous supplies or facilities. No empirical experience would lead to the conclusion that a country with substantial dependence on imported gas supplies would be necessarily less secure, i.e. more prone to disruption, than one which was self-sufficient. Increased security, whether for domestically produced gas or imports, requires increased diversity of: sources, transportation and transit routes, and facilities. These facilities include: pipelines, LNG terminals, processing plants and storages. Clearly the higher the percentage of gas in a country's energy demand, the greater is the importance of diversity as protection against security incidents.

Exporting countries have a very strong incentive to maintain continuous and secure deliveries due to the revenues which they earn and the importance of those revenues to corporate and national budgets. For most non-OECD gas exporting companies and countries, earnings from gas export revenues are not only very significant in absolute terms, but also as a proportion of their total revenues. Even for a company as large as Gazprom, gas export revenues in 2005 were around 55% of the company's total receivables and around 17% of total Russian foreign trade earnings outside CIS countries.[22] This is a long-term stream of earnings that would not be lightly jeopardised by an exporting company or government and which could not easily or quickly be replaced by any other commodity.

Two dimensions of European gas security that are only just beginning to receive the attention they deserve are the potential problems which can be caused by infrastructure breakdown, and how to ensure adequate gas storage in liberalised markets. The fire at the Rough storage site in February 2006 deprived the UK of access to around 80% of its stored gas for more than 3 months. Had the incident happened any earlier (or later) in the winter, the consequences might have been substantially more serious than the price spikes the market experienced in the few weeks before temperatures rose and demand declined.

While significant investments in both new supplies and new storage are under way, these will arrive several years later than the market needed them. Even when all of the storage capacity which UK investors are currently seeking to build is

---

[21] This may of course depend on the exact definition of 'political instability'. Political instability has delayed or prevented a number of contracts from being concluded, but the only example of political instability – meaning inability of central government to maintain political control over a region – which this author can recall that caused any protracted disruption of supplies in an ongoing contract was Indonesian LNG deliveries from Aceh (Sumatra) to Japan and Korea in 2001.

[22] Although for Gazprom, European earnings fell from around 63% of total receivables in the early 2000s, which, given the huge increase in European gas prices and volumes post-2004 is significant and shows the importance of increased domestic and CIS gas prices over the same period.

complete, this will only equate to around 10% of annual demand, substantially less than is available to other major markets in Europe. The Italian case provides a useful comparison where a combination of problems with Russian gas and very cold weather in the winter of 2005-06 forced the use of strategic storage. The Italian government considered that they had a narrow escape with 3.9 bcm of strategic storage remaining on 22 March 2006 (Garriba, 2006). But this volume is roughly equal to the total available storage in the UK – a much larger gas market than Italy. Both these cases, but especially that of the UK, raise important issues about the ability of liberalised gas markets to provide market-based security investments when these are needed (Van der Linde et al., 2006).

They also raise the issue of whether EU security standards, particularly in relation to gas storage, require more centralised coordination from Brussels. Stringent standards were proposed by the original draft of the Gas Security Directive, but not accepted by either gas utilities or their governments.[23] The eventual Directive (Article 3.1) required the establishment of policies and definition of roles and responsibilities to ensure adequate minimum levels of gas security, but nothing more specific. In relation to protection of customers, the Directive went no further than to set security of supply standards (Article 4), which conformed to those which already existed in most countries. It encouraged (rather than required) member states to: develop national storage, enter into bilateral storage agreements with other countries, and publish targets for the future contribution of storage to security. This was as far as member states were prepared to go in relation to cooperation in gas storage. The only new institution created by the Directive (Article 7) was the Gas Coordination Group – which met in January 2006 following the Russia-Ukraine crisis – but this fell somewhat short of the European Observation System with wide-ranging duties and powers in the event of a crisis, which was proposed in the Draft Directive.

24.4   Conclusions: a Constrained Future for Gas in Europe?

By mid-2007, the future prospects for gas were much less bright than they had seemed a few years previously, for two main reasons:

- Demand is likely to increase more slowly because of the reduced attractiveness of gas-fired power generation caused by high prices.
- Ongoing depletion of indigenous resources and increasing import dependence has raised serious political concerns about security of supply.

While ample reserves of gas could potentially be available by pipeline to Europe from CIS, Caspian and Middle East countries, serious uncertainties have

---

[23] Proposal for a Directive of the European Parliament and the Council concerning measures to safeguard security of natural gas supply, August 2002. For a sample of the opposition from industry to the original proposals see: Eurogas Response to the Proposed Security of Natural Gas Supply Directive, February 2003.

developed around the economic politics of their development and transportation. In addition, although LNG will become a more important source of imports for many European countries, the latter will face competition from both North America and the Pacific Basin, especially for Middle East LNG.

These problems will not create a shortage of gas in Europe over the next 5 years; indeed the short to medium term is more likely to see a period of surplus than of shortage. In this time frame, at least as much, and probably more, attention should be devoted to dealing with the risk that end-users could be deprived of supply due to a combination of domestic infrastructure failure and insufficient storage to meet extreme weather conditions. Security of domestic supplies and infrastructure, particularly for countries such as the UK, which have limited storage capacity relative to the size of their markets, will be of paramount importance.

However, if Europe requires a significant increase in gas-fired power generation supply, problems may arise after 2015, and particularly after 2020. The source of the next 50-100 bcm/year of supply for European markets is not clear because of:

- Economic and energy, specifically gas, developments within the major current and potential gas exporting countries;
- Political and geopolitical problems between Europe and its principal gas suppliers.

These observations apply particularly to Russia and Algeria, but also to Nigeria, Egypt and Iran. At present, there is no sign that these problems will be resolved quickly. In the mid 2000s, European international gas security discourse was dominated by commercial and political difficulties between Russia and the CIS countries which transit its gas to Europe. It would be comforting to think that established EU institutions – such as the EU-Russia Energy Dialogue – could take some role in helping to resolve them. Whether justified or not, there is likely to be considerable nervousness in Europe about Russian supplies for the foreseeable future. A combination of heightened European security concerns and a worsening geopolitical environment may mean that a political limit on Russian gas supplies is likely to be reached following the completion of the two Nord Stream pipelines in the early 2010s.

Political developments within the main alternative gas suppliers to Russia, and relations between those countries and Europe, are similarly discouraging. Producers and exporters in the Middle East, North and West Africa, Central Asia and the Caspian have alternatives to dedicated pipeline gas supplies to Europe; and the routes that such pipelines could take are either dominated by Russia, fraught with political complications, or commercially unattractive compared with pipeline or LNG alternatives.

The future of the European gas supply depends largely on whether the geopolitical environments between Russia and Europe and between the Middle East and Europe will improve, thereby encouraging additional pipeline connections.

If the situation does not improve in the coming years there are significant uncertainties about where Europe will be able to source substantial additional gas supplies post-2015/2020.

References

Balzer, H. 2006. Vladimir Putin on Russian energy policy. Energy Politics, 9: 31-39.

Cedigaz. 2007 Cedigaz, Natural gas in the world: trends and figures in 2005. www.cedigaz.org.

Clingendael International Energy Programme. 2004. Study of energy supply security and geopolitics. http://www.clingendael.nl/publica-tions/2004/20040 1000_ciep_study.pdf, 5th May 2008.

Correlje, A. & Van der Linde, C. 2006. Energy supply security and geopolitics: A European perspective, Energy Policy, 34: 532-543.

European Commission (EC). 2004. Council Directive 2004/67/EC of 26 April 2004 concerning measures to safeguard security of natural gas supply, Official Journal of the European Union, 29.4.2004, L127/92.

European Commission (EC). 2006. Green paper: a European strategy for sustainable, competitive and secure energy, COM(2006)105 final, Brussels: EC.

Garriba, S. 2006. Dealing with gas supply disruption in Italy during winter 2005-06 and its aftermaths. Paper presented at the IEA Gas Security Workshop, Paris.

Gazprom. 2005. Annual report 2005. http://www.gazprom.com/documents/Annual _Report_Eng_2005.pdf, 5th May 2008.

Hallouche, H. 2007. Algeria's gas future: between a growing economy and a growing export market. Unpublished Research Project, Oxford Institute for Energy Studies (OIES), New York.

Honoré, A. Forthcoming 2009. European gas demand, supply and pricing: cycles, seasons and the impact of prices arbitrage. Unpublished Research Project, Oxford Institute for Energy Studies (OIES), New York.

International Energy Agency (IEA). 2000. World energy outlook 2000. Paris: OECD/IEA.

International Energy Agency (IEA). 2003. World energy outlook 2003. Paris: OECD/IEA.

International Energy Agency (IEA). 2004. World energy outlook 2004. Paris: OECD/IEA.

International Energy Agency (IEA). 2005. World energy outlook 2005. Paris: OECD/IEA.

International Energy Agency (IEA). 2006a. World energy outlook 2006. Paris: OECD/IEA.

International Energy Agency (IEA). 2006b. Optimizing Russian natural gas: reform and climate policy. Paris: IEA.

International Energy Agency (IEA). 2006c. IEA top stories and comments. http://www. iea.org/journalists/topstories.asp, 23rd May 2006.

International Energy Agency (IEA). 2007a. Natural gas information 2007. Paris: IEA.

International Energy Agency (IEA). 2007b. Natural gas market review 2007. Paris: IEA.

Ministry of Petroleum and Energy. 2007. Facts 2007 – the Norwegian petroleum sector. http://www.npd.no/NR/rdonlyres/4E929265-F111-4578-ADF320480C A09E0A/0/Facts_2007_engelsk.pdf.

Parliament of Science and Technology. 2004. The future of UK gas supply. Post-note, 230.

Shell International Limited. 2005. The Shell global scenarios to 2025. http://www.shell.com/static/aboutshellen/downloads/our_strategy/shell_global _scenarios/exsum_23052005.pdf, 5th May 2008.

Stern, J. P. 2004. UK gas security: time to get serious. Energy Policy, 32: 1967-1979.

Stern, J. P. 2005. The future of Russian gas and Gazprom. New York: Oxford University Press.

Stern, J. P. 2006a. The Russian-Ukrainian gas crisis of January 2006. http://www.oxfordenergy.org/pdfs/comment_0106.pdf, 5th May 2008.

Stern, J. P. 2006b. Natural gas security problems in Europe: the Russian-Ukrainian gas crisis of 2006. Asia-Pacific Review, 13: 32-59.

Stern, J. P. 2006c. The new security environment for European gas: worsening geopolitics and increasing global competition for LNG. http://www. oxfordenergy.org/pdfs/NG15.pdf, 5th May 2008.

The White House 2006. Vice President's Remarks at the 2006 Vilnius Conference, http://www.whitehouse.gov/news/releases/2006/05/20060504-1.html.

Van der Linde, C., Correljé, A., de Jong, J. & Tönjes, C. 2006. The paradigm change in international natural gas markets and the impact on regulation. http://www.clingendael.nl/publications/2006/20060600_ciep_misc_wgc-regulation-report.pdf, 5th May 2008.

Wright, P. & Oxford Institute for Energy Studies. 2006. Gas prices in the UK: markets and insecurity of supply. Oxford; New York: Oxford University Press for the Oxford Institute for Energy Studies.

25 Strategic Use of Gas Storage Facilities

Reinier Zwitserloot[1]

Anke Radloff[2]

Abstract

This chapter gives an overview of the fundamentals of gas storage and explains the importance of gas storage facilities for the European market. Taking into account the current gas market development, the strategic relevance of using storage becomes an increasingly significant issue for gas market players. Storage provides security of supply and flexibility. Both are essential to reliable and sustainable success in the European gas market. Access to storage facilities generates competitive advantage through physical and commercial portfolio optimisation, which in turn has a positive effect on the efficiency of the gas market as a whole. To provide sufficient storage capacity for the European gas market, a stable political and regulatory framework is required to encourage the investments needed.

Keywords: gas, storage, flexibility

---

[1] Reinier Zwitserloot is Chairman of the Board of Executive Directors of the Wintershall Holding AG, Germany.

[2] Anke Radloff is responsible for gas market analysis within Strategic Planning at the Wintershall Holding AG, Germany.

A. Bausch and B. Schwenker (eds.), *Handbook Utility Management,*
DOI: 10.1007/978-3-540-79349-6_25, © Springer-Verlag Berlin Heidelberg 2009

25.1   Introduction and Fundamentals of Storage

25.1.1   The European Gas Market and the Role of Flexibility

Natural gas is, after oil, the second largest primary energy source in Europe (BP, 2008), with a 25% share of prime energy consumption. With approximately 1.4% p.a. (2004-2030) it has the highest consumption growth rate in the European Union of any conventional energy source (IEA, 2007).

In 2006 about 550 bcm of natural gas were consumed in the EU 27. Natural gas is widely used in the residential sector (~40%), for power generation (~31%) and in the industrial sector (~22%) (Eurostat, 2008).

Today about 55% of the annual European[3] natural gas demand is covered through indigenous production. The remainder has to be imported from outside Europe via pipeline or by ship as liquefied natural gas (LNG; in 2007 approx. 21% of all imports). The Russian Federation (~60%) and Africa (~35%) hold the largest share of imports (BP, 2008). It is expected that short- and medium-term demand for natural gas, the most environmentally friendly hydrocarbon, will continue to grow, particularly in the power sector, while at the same time indigenous production is set to decrease substantially. The resulting gap will be filled by increased imports, especially from the Russian Federation and the Caspian region, and by LNG from Africa or the Middle East.

The supply of natural gas from the well-head to the final consumer requires production, import, transport and distribution to the end-customer. Some companies now focus on operating just one level of the supply chain, while others follow a more integrated approach and are active on many or all levels of the supply chain. In the not-too-distant past, the European gas market had a monopolistic structure, with one company often being the sole gas supplier for a country and controlling several parts of the supply chain. Liberalisation of the UK gas market was followed by the first Gas Directive of 1998 and the second Gas Directive of 2003, which set the course for market liberalisation in the continental EU also. The goal of the EU Commission was to open the market to competition by providing nondiscriminatory third-party access (TPA) to the pipeline grid and to storage facilities. To implement the Directive, the EU member states have the option of choosing between regulated and negotiated TPA, so that the access regimes vary across the EU. Overall, liberalisation has started to make progress and begun to change the European gas market.

One specific characteristic of the gas market is that supply of and demand for natural gas often diverge significantly (see Figure 25.1). Whereas electricity can be produced in close vicinity to its consumption, the sources of Europe's imported natural gas are located hundreds or thousands of kilometres outside the EU (Russian pipeline gas about 4,000 km, some LNG sources up to 10,000 km) and once over here the gas has to be further distributed within the EU. Naturally, long-distance gas transport is most cost efficient when gas flows are constantly at high

---

[3] EU 27 and Albania, Bosnia Herzegovina, Croatia, Former Yugoslav Republic of Macedonia, Iceland, Montenegro, Norway, Serbia, Switzerland, Turkey.

utilisation rates. On the other hand, demand varies considerably, some variations being predictable and others occurring unexpectedly. Particularly in the residential sector, demand follows strong seasonal and daily volatility. Since natural gas is largely used for heating, the gas consumption is highly dependent on temperature; e.g. households in Germany consume about 90% of their overall gas demand in the winter. In North Western Europe[4] approximately two thirds of the total gas volume is consumed from October to March (Höffler & Kübler, 2007). Hence a wide 'swing' between low summer demand and high winter peaks has to be taken into account when delivering gas to final consumers. To balance these variations between supply and demand, the supplier has to be able to react flexibly.

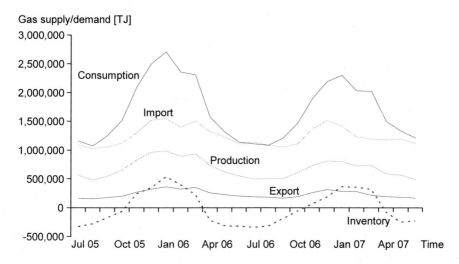

Figure 25.1: Monthly gas supply and consumption in the EU (Eurostat, 2008)

Traditionally, there are several sources of physical flexibility to balance the gas deliveries as required by the market (IEA, 2002).

The gas production might provide some flexibility, depending on the fields' nature; the Groningen field in the Netherlands is a well known example of a 'swing producer'. But since the infrastructure has to be sized to peak rather than average production, flexibility is costly. Moreover, this swing production can only provide flexibility for a local market around such production areas, since long-distance transport infrastructure needs to be operated with a rather high utilisation to provide the returns needed for the high pipeline investments.

A further source of flexibility is the conclusion of traditional supply contracts. Natural gas is often sold under long-term contracts, especially if the deliveries are related to new, specific investments in field development and infrastructure. These supply contracts often include 'Take-or-Pay' (ToP) clauses to guarantee the sup-

---

[4] North West Europe here comprises Belgium, Denmark, France, Germany, the Netherlands, Switzerland and the United Kingdom.

plier a certain minimum annual revenue flow. Hence the risk of high-capital projects is shared between producer and importer; the price risk is typically taken by the seller and the volume risk, by the buyer. In Europe a yearly minimum take of 80-90% in combination with defined daily minimum and maximum volumes between which the buyer can choose is common practice at the import level, which means that some flexibility can be used for balancing supply and demand.

Flexibility instruments have also been developed on the demand side to avoid peaks and increase efficiency. Such instruments are, for example, interruptible contracts, which can be concluded with industrial customers who have the ability to switch to alternative fuels for their production processes. The supplier is entitled to interrupt the deliveries; in return the customer receives a discount on the price.

Another important flexibility tool for aligning gas supply and demand is the use of gas storage. Depending on their physical and economic characteristics, various types of gas storage exist, providing for both seasonal and short-term swing.

Since the mid-1990s, another flexibility provider has been emerging, first in the UK and later also on the mainland of Europe: the spot market. With the progress in market liberalisation in the gas sector, gas hubs have developed where gas is now traded like any other commodity. Well-known examples are the NBP in the UK and the Zeebrugge Hub in Belgium; here a surplus can be sold and shortfalls can be covered. At the hubs, gas supply and demand are balanced by price. Spot markets differ from the above-mentioned flexibility instruments in that they are a source of flexibility despite not providing additional liquidity to the overall pipeline grid. With the emergence of trading hubs, the role of flexibility has started to evolve, since forward spot prices indicate a value for flexibility. This allows flexibility to be 'traded'. As a result flexibility is no longer based on physical needs alone, but rather has a high commercial aspect.

25.1.2   Use of Storage

25.1.2.1 Flexibility

Physical Portfolio Optimisation

The traditional, and still most important, role of gas storage is to match supply and demand. As already mentioned, natural gas is a fuel with a highly volatile demand, while production and supply over long distances are relatively inflexible. Storage facilities therefore provide an opportunity to balance the transportation system. Excess supply produced or imported during the summer months is injected into storage and during winter it is made available to meet increased demand. Therefore, being relatively close to the market is particularly important for a storage facility, as the transportation system to the storage facility can be utilised with an optimally high load factor. Hence storage helps to optimise the physical transportation system, allowing for a suitable grid design and enhancing the cost effectiveness of the whole gas supply chain.

On the purchase side, an importing company can reduce the cost of supply by accepting a high take-or-pay obligation in return for a lower purchase price under an import contract by generating flexibility through access to storage capacity. Gas prices at distribution level in continental Western Europe are traditionally made up of a price for the gas itself (commodity price) and a price for the yearly maximum usage of the infrastructure (e.g. storage, pipelines) needed for deliveries to the customer (capacity charge). Hence a distribution company has an efficient way of reducing its costs by cutting its demand peaks through its own access to storage capacities.

On the sales side, using storage allows adjustment to seasonal swing, but also enables the storage user to react to short-term demand fluctuations. Short-term volatility means e.g. differences between night and day and between working days and weekends, and demand fluctuation resulting from sudden weather changes.

Commercial Portfolio Optimisation (Arbitrage)

Since the development of gas-to-gas competition and the emergence of spot markets, gas storage both for commercial optimisation and for speculation is becoming more important. As the spot market is a price marker for the scarcity of gas, the spot prices follow quite a predictable seasonal cycle, with generally high prices in winter and low prices in summer. Thus, a storage user can benefit from the opportunity to buy cheap gas in summer, store it and sell the gas at high prices in winter. If the difference between buying and selling is higher than the costs of physically storing including transportation or entry/exit expenses, seasonal arbitrage is possible. For short-term price fluctuations an analogous transaction is possible, allowing the storage user to benefit from short-term arbitrage.

In general, arbitrage means taking advantage of price discrepancies of identical or similar alternatives with little risk or even none at all. In fully functioning, efficient markets, though, arbitrage should not be possible, since the risk-free profit would immediately be realised and the price be adjusted to the same level for both alternatives (Clewlow & Strickland, 2000).

In reality, markets are rarely perfect, but utilising arbitrage opportunities is the first step towards minimising inefficiencies. Consequently, the availability of sufficient storage should have a damping effect on price volatility.

25.1.2.2 Security of Supply

Another essential task of storage is providing security of supply. Owing to the growing dependence on imports from distant fields, this issue has become increasingly important for Europe. Although delivery interruptions are rare, the possibility of difficulties in the pipeline network or on the production side may be remote, it can never be completely excluded. Therefore, a prudent supplier needs to take the necessary precautions. Here again it is efficient to use storage facilities close to the market to make a quick reaction to unforeseen shortfalls possible. From a gas supplier's perspective, it is very much a market- and customer-driven reason to take care of security of supply. The supplier has a vital commercial interest in being viewed as reliable, as otherwise he will not be able to compete in the market. Hence most companies hold a sufficient amount of working gas volume to cover an extremely cold winter in storage. In addition, gas suppliers normally secure deliveries by diversifying their supply portfolio and through long-term partnerships based on a balance of interests.

Since natural gas is in competition with other energy sources and gas-to-gas competition has arrived, a competitive structure for the storage market supersedes the need for legislation or regulation that enforces the maintenance of storage volumes for national or European energy security. Nevertheless, in the European Union ideas are being floated about forcing member states to hold some amount of natural gas in storage, so-called strategic gas stocks. So far, no such obligations exist at the European level. However, at the national level some EU member countries have already enacted legislation with regard to strategic storage. In Italy, for example, gas suppliers have to store 10% of their annual imports from non-EU countries as strategic reserves. In other North West European countries, such as Belgium, Denmark, France, the Netherlands and the UK, there are also storage obligations, but they are meant as a compulsory buffer against extreme weather conditions. The disadvantage of such obligations is that they block storage facilities, which therefore cannot be used to balance swing demand. In addition, it is questionable whether such an intervention from a government is more efficient than leaving the issue to the market. As explained above, in a competitive market there is enough incentive for the market participants to provide security of supply. That the market is competitive is shown by the high number of storage operators; in Germany, for example, 25 different storage operators are active. Furthermore, the fact that no shortages for West European customers have occurred in the past can be seen as a signal for a well-functioning market (Höffler & Kübler, 2007; IEA, 2004).

25.1.3   Storage Facilities in Europe

25.1.3.1 Types of Storage

In principle there are two types of facilities: below and above ground. Gas can be stored underground in porous rock formations that have previously held oil, gas or water and in artificially created caverns such as hollowed out salt layers or residues from former mineral mining. Above ground it can either be liquefied and stored in insulated tanks as LNG or in its gaseous form in tanks (gasometers), and also in the pipeline grids themselves as so-called line pack. This chapter provides an overview of possible storage facilities, although underground storages play by far the most important role and our focus will therefore be on these in the rest of this section.

Porous Rock Storage

Porous rock storage uses existing geological underground formations that are able to retain gas. Storing gas in depleted fields is the most widespread method. It is comparatively simple, because a reservoir which formerly contained gas or oil is likely to satisfy the permeability and porosity conditions required for holding natural gas. Using depleted former production fields is relatively inexpensive, since an existing infrastructure, such as wells, gathering systems and pipeline connections, can often be reused. Aquifers are rock formations that also meet the requirements with regard to permeability and porosity, but these were originally filled with water. An aquifer needs a greater investment of effort for exploration and development, which leads to higher investment costs than when depleted fields are used (Rojey & Jaffret, 1997; Cerbe et al., 1999). Porous rock storage provides large storage volumes. This applies to the so-called cushion gas, which always remains in storage to ensure minimum reservoir pressure and to the 'working gas', which is the volume available for repeated injection and withdrawal. A disadvantage of most porous rock storage is its limited injection and withdrawal rate. Owing to their relatively low withdrawal rate, porous rock storages are basically used for seasonal storage with only one storage cycle per year (Cerbe et al., 1999; Rojey & Jaffret, 1997; Sedlacek, 2007).

Cavern Storage

Caverns are geological rock or salt formations suitable for building gas-holding hollows. Most caverns are carved out of large underground salt formations by injecting water and dissolving the salt. The resulting salt caverns are filled with gas. Relative to porous rock storages the development cost of salt caverns is higher, but on the other hand considerably less cushion gas is required. Salt caverns have a relatively high withdrawal rate compared with total inventory volume. In addition, the flow mode can be switched rapidly from injection to withdrawal and vice versa. Hence salt caverns provide short-term flexibility for peak shaving and are often cycled several times a year (Cerbe et al., 1999).

LNG Storage

When gas is chilled to minus 160 °C it becomes a liquid and in this state can be stored in tanks or transported as liquefied natural gas (LNG). LNG is usually stored at LNG import terminals prior to being regasified and fed into the pipeline grid. Some importing countries hold LNG storages, especially where geological options for development of underground storages are rather limited (IEA, 2002). LNG has the advantages of requiring significantly less space than gas stored underground, needing no cushion gas and providing a high withdrawal/injection rate at very short notice. Hence LNG storage is appropriate to cover peak demand. However, LNG facilities are more expensive to build and operate than underground storage facilities, since the processes of liquefying gas and its subsequent regasification are very energy-intensive and thus expensive processes.

Gas Tanks

Gas can also be stored in tanks under low or high pressure (Cerbe et al., 1999). This is not economical for high volumes and only has a role for local cover of peak demand for municipalities.

Line Pack

Line packing refers to the storage of gas inside gas transportation pipeline networks by significantly increasing the line pressure above the minimum delivery pressure. It can be used to balance supply and demand fluctuations during the day. Hence the transportation grid itself contains a certain degree of diurnal storage as line pack (IEA, 2002).

25.1.3.2 Allocation of Storage

In 2006 70 bcm of working gas volume was available in storage facilities in the EU (ERGEG, 2006). The mix of storage types differs widely from region to region: worldwide 82% are depleted oil/gas fields, 14% are aquifers and 4% are salt caverns. In Western Europe[5] the share of storage capacity in depleted oil/gas fields is relatively lower, at 66%, while aquifers (22%) and caverns (13%) have a more important role. The storage size also differs considerably: 72% of all gas storages worldwide are located in the USA and only about 14% in Western Europe, although in terms of volume only 35% of working gas capacity is located in the USA and almost 20% in West Europe (IGU, 2006). In the EU the country with the largest working gas volume of almost 20 bcm is Germany, followed by Italy (~13 bcm) and France (~12 bcm) (ERGEG, 2006). Taking into account the individual market size (see Figure 25.2), Austria has the highest working gas-to-gas demand ratio in West Europe, with ~29%, while the UK has the lowest ratio with ~4% (ERGEG, 2006; BP, 2007).

It is obvious that countries with a larger share of indigenous production, such as the UK and the Netherlands, tend to have less storage capacity than heavily import-dependent countries. Certainly the local climate and alternative sources of flexibility also have an influence. Hence Spain has a relatively low working gas-to-demand ratio (~7%) although it is highly import dependent. But since seasonality is relatively low in Spain it can satisfy swing demand through flexibility from its relatively high share of LNG imports.

---

[5] West Europe is defined as Austria, Belgium, Denmark, France, Germany, Ireland, Italy, the Netherlands, Portugal, Spain, Sweden and the United Kingdom.

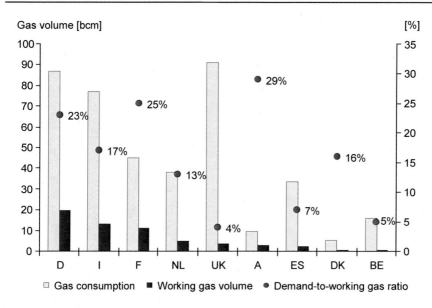

Figure 25.2: Demand-to-working gas ratio in West Europe 2006 (ERGEG, 2006; BP, 2007)

25.1.4 Value of Storage

As explained above, the main value of access to storage is flexibility. The value of storage facilities can therefore be derived by looking at alternative ways of generating the same flexibility.

On the European continent, a market player planning to use storage instead of a supply fully adjusted to demand has to take into account its alternative costs of flexibility, such as the transportation and capacity charge under its supply contracts. As explained in Section 25.1.2.1, this charge is determined by the maximum peak load a buyer needs. Since it is normally fixed on an annual basis, the charge is constant over the whole delivery year. The same applies to a continental gas market player at the import level. The supplier compares the cost of usage of gas storage with the embedded price for flexibility achievable through a take-or-pay supply contract with defined minimum and maximum take.

In the UK a storage user who has the opportunity to trade on a liquid spot market will take another approach. In this market storage capacity can be seen as an option for realising arbitrage potential between gas price spreads. For this purpose there are two components that need to be examined: the intrinsic value and the extrinsic value of storage. The intrinsic value is related to the volume of gas that can be injected into the facility in summer and later withdrawn in winter. It is effectively the maximum market value of a single cycle of storage and is derived from the price during the injection period versus that during the withdrawal period. Thus the seasonal spread in the forward price curve at the time of storage capacity booking determines the intrinsic value. The intrinsic value can be unlocked at relatively low risk, since the value can be immediately realised by price hedging. The extrinsic value is the ability of the storage user to utilize the storage volume or parts of it more than once during the contract period in response to short-term price volatility. It is an optimisation of the volumes injected and withdrawn, on the basis of the available gas in storage and the changing spot prices (Ronn, 2002).

In addition, the value of storage also depends on technical constraints. Porous rock storage basically has an intrinsic value, since it has low injection/withdrawal rates and cannot be cycled several times a year. Caverns provide more operational flexibility as the flow direction can be more easily changed, which generates an additional extrinsic value. Factors such as reliability or flexible nomination rights may also influence how much of the intrinsic value users are likely to pay. When demand for capacity is very high the storage may cost more than the basic intrinsic value, but it is rare for users to pay the extrinsic value unless a site can be cycled a significant number of times during the contract period.

The spot market base and the traditional continental pricing systems for flexibility have started to converge as a result of increasing transit pipeline capacities between the UK and the mainland of Europe, such as the Interconnector or the BBL. Currently, the market is in a transition phase where both systems coexist in parallel. Because the prevailing pricing systems differ significantly the possible alternatives depend on where in the supply chain a company is active and where its market is located.

25.2 Current Gas Market Development and Implications for Gas Storage

Although the expectations for gas demand growth are currently adjusted downwards, the demand in the EU is still predicted to increase by approximately 40% by 2030 (IEA, 2007). Most of this growth is expected to come from the power generation sector. To reduce CO_2 emissions there is a trend in power generation to low carbon content fuels, such as natural gas. The development of oil and gas prices and the outcome of the discussion on the phase-out of nuclear power will determine whether this trend is more or less pronounced (European Commission, 2006). As long as nuclear power generation or coal-fired power plants cover the base load power demand in many European countries, gas will mostly be used to produce the medium and peak load demand. Consequently, the incremental gas demand will be volatile. Since at the same time indigenous production will be decreasing, the European import dependence will increase to about 70% in 2030 (IEA, 2007). This will have a negative effect on the availability of supply and transport flexibility, as imports from distant fields are less flexible than indigenous production close to the consuming markets. Most existing import pipeline corridors already have very high capacity utilisation, and new projects tying in remote production areas are very capital intensive, thus requiring very high pipeline utilisation immediately after the project completion date. Based on the increasing import dependence the demand for flexibility measures within Europe itself will grow substantially, along with increasing import volumes. The storage gap is expected to amount to more than 20 bcm in North West Europe in 2030, assuming existing capacities can meet current demand (Höffler & Kübler, 2007).

The decreased indigenous production will partly be compensated for by an increase in LNG imports, which can offer additional short-term supplies if the price in Europe is comparable with prices in other LNG-importing regions, in particular the USA (IEA, 2002 & 2004 & 2006). Initially, short-term LNG deliveries can be a valuable source of physical flexibility, because the growth in the market for spot cargoes provides LNG buyers with the means to diversify imports and eventually to balance supply and demand by using the LNG spot market. However, it should be kept in mind that LNG is following global economic drivers and that it might therefore be difficult to lay hand on, or expensive, or both. Thus, LNG may also be a reason to increase storage capacity to account for periods of highly divergent global gas prices, e.g. between the USA and Europe.

Market liberalisation may also offer new opportunities for dealing with flexibility requirements. TPA allows new market players to enter the market, and hence gas-to-gas competition emerges and trading hubs develop. In addition, regional markets begin to converge, since companies start to operate across borders. This triggers several new developments, such as the trend for new pricing mechanisms, shorter contract durations and smaller contract volumes. In addition, new products begin to evolve, e.g. separate services such as additional annual, daily or hourly flexibility or a complete balancing service. While these new tendencies make the gas market more flexible by providing more alternatives, they do not reduce the underlying physical need for flexibility. However, a mix of different pricing systems for flexibility is emerging, which provides the storage user with more alternatives for generating value (IEA, 2002).

The development of the current spot price forward curve as price marker shows an increasing summer–winter spread. This means, on the one hand, flexibility bought at the spot market becomes increasingly expensive, but, on the other, one can also conclude that even today Europe is short of storage capacity. The very fact that there is a market for flexibility will not reduce the need for physical storage capacity, but will rather create a more competitive environment for the usage of these capacities. This is essential for an effective and integrated gas market, since storage is an important tool in providing flexibility and physical security of supply. Thus, storage capacity plays a key role in the sustainable development of gas competition across Europe.

Therefore, it is important to create a framework that encourages new investment. Considering that the development of storage capacity requires significant capital investment, a reliable, appropriate and stable investment framework needs to be provided. Everything else the market will take care of, since in a competitive market investments are directed where they are most efficient. In the case of storage, competition already exists today: gas storage is in competition with other sources of flexibility, such as supply swing, demand-side management and spot market products, and in addition there is competition between storage providers.

The storage market is not a natural monopoly, since storage can and will be built by anybody deeming it economic. Several new European storage projects that are currently in the planning or construction phase show the functioning of the gas storage market, e.g. the extension of Epe or planning of Jemgum in Germany, the development of a facility in Haidach (Austria) or the construction of a storage facility in Saltfleetby (UK) (GSE, 2007; Sedlacek, 2007). This trend should not be undermined by overregulation but supported by a regulatory and political framework that encourages investment to meet the growing demand for storage (IEA, 2002 & 2004; Höffler & Kübler, 2007; Monopolkommission, 2007). The regulation of the storage market proposed by the European Commission in their third legislative package of September 2007 is a step in the wrong direction. Based on the competitive market structure for flexibility a regulatory intervention such as legal unbundling of storage business is unjustified.

25.3   Strategic Use of Storage for a Gas Market Player

25.3.1   Access to Storage Facilities

From the perspective of a gas supplier or customer in a liberalised market gas storage can play various parts in a company's strategy. For instance, the use of storage can be part of an integrated sales strategy or have a key role in a purchase strategy. In any case, having access to storage facilities is the basis for generating added value.

The availability of storage capacities supports a company's strategy fourfold: it provides security of supply, it increases the efficiency of the supply chain, it offers flexibility at predictable costs and it enables commercial portfolio optimisation. These advantages distinguish a company with access to storage from a pure gas trader without access to storage. The first three items listed above create competitive advantage by securing reliable and cost efficient physical supply.

First, a gas market player who has access to storage capacity close to the market receives or can provide secure physical deliveries independently of the liquidity situation of the spot market. This is the key point in security of supply and an essential element in any successful gas supply strategy.

Second, as explained in Section 25.1.2.1, use of storage facilities close to the customer can significantly reduce the cost of supply by optimising the efficiency of the entire supply chain. Hence storage is a means of creating significant value for the gas supplier and also for the customer.

Third, it is a source of flexibility at predictable costs, avoiding unexpected price peaks. Whether the prevailing price system for flexibility is the traditional one based on load factors, or one based on the spot price, the costs of storage usage can be foreseen. They are based on a set storage tariff. Hence the flexibility price risk is limited.

The fourth point provides value added through using of price spreads for purposes of commercial optimisation of a supply and sales contract portfolio. Access to storage facilities allows the opportunity to benefit from gas price or flexibility price arbitrage.

As already mentioned, with the development of liquid spot markets a new gas pricing system emerged on the European continent. Since the price develops based on supply and demand, this can lead to very volatile prices, which provides the opportunity for gas price arbitrage. Most evident is arbitrage between different time points at which different gas prices prevail. This creates intrinsic and extrinsic value of storage, as described in Section 25.1.4. A trading company without access to storage cannot realise this arbitrage potential without taking substantial risks, since it lacks the physical availability of gas to sell and the capacity to store gas.

In addition, different instruments exist to generate flexibility, but the pricing mechanisms differ. This allows for additional arbitrage opportunities: if an alternative source of flexibility is more attractive than using the storage facility, the storage capacities can be sold and vice versa. Hence a company that can choose between those different flexibility pricing systems can generate advantage through flexibility price arbitrage. This of course works only as long as there is no prevailing price system for flexibility. If the price for storage is exactly determined by the spot price differential, for example, no arbitrage will be possible between using storage and generating flexibility at the spot market. For a company that can base its business on different pricing mechanisms, access to storage facilities provides new business opportunities, since flexibility services can be separately promoted.

Companies nowadays are often active in a rather wide geographical area. They act across European borders and are no longer focused on covering the demand of only one region. With the supply of gas to or from different countries, the use of storage can no longer be viewed just from a national perspective, but takes on a multinational dimension. Storage is most efficient when located near the customer; hence a multinational sales strategy needs a multinational storage concept. Such a storage portfolio provides even more opportunities for physical or commercial optimisation.

25.3.2   Investment in Storage Facilities

Since storage capacities are in short supply, access to existing facilities is not always available. Hence investment in new capacities is an alternative way of realising a competitive advantage provided by access to storage. Theoretically, this could be done by every company, although it should be kept in mind that special know-how and a strong financial background are necessary, since the development of new storage facilities is technically sophisticated and requires significant capital investment. Besides this, the planning phase of a new facility takes several years and is subject to a number of geological and technical risks and approvals by local and national authorities. Therefore it is essential to provide a stable investment framework, rather than creating further uncertainty through the threat of ever increasing legislation and regulation.

Another precondition is the existence of appropriate geological and geographical conditions and a match between the two. In some parts of Europe, e.g. in Germany, the geology meets many of the requirements for developing underground storage, whereas in other regions it does not. In addition, the geographical location plays an important role, since storage should be located close to the demand centres. Again, Germany is a good example, owing to its location in the middle of Europe. Hence, given sufficient storage beyond local and national demand, it could be a storage provider for neighbouring countries.

If all preconditions are fulfilled and the economic incentive to invest in new facilities is sustainable, investments will be made. Currently, storage capacity is scarce and the demand for flexibility is expected to grow further. Thus, assuming a stable political and regulatory framework, storage can deliver sustainable value to the investor.

Since liberalisation may enable companies to embark on an expansion strategy, the availability of storage capacities will become even more important. Because reliable, cost-efficient supplies are a basic requirement of any market entry strategy, investment in storage is a suitable way of generating access to capacities and thus permits the owner to unlock the above-mentioned strategic values (Höffler & Kübler, 2006; Monopolkommission, 2007).

25.4   Conclusion

Wide demand fluctuations require flexibility in the supply of gas. This need is expected to grow in Europe, since against the background of growing total demand indigenous swing production will be replaced by less flexible imports from faraway sources. For the year 2030 an additional demand for storage of 20 bcm is expected in North West Europe.

Even though storage is an essential means of achieving flexibility, it competes with other instruments such as production swing, ToP or interruptible contracts, and spot market flexibility. However, the other sources have limited potential, are inefficient or leave the supplier extremely exposed to price volatility. Using flexibility offered by storage enables cost-optimised supply by providing physical volume balancing close to the market. Hence storage is an adequate tool for efficient management of the entire supply chain and has a sustainable role in providing European customers with secure, reliable and suitable natural gas at predictable costs. Emerging spot markets in Europe offer a second price marker for the value of storage besides the traditional capacity charge-based storage price concept in mainland Europe. In combination with spot markets, storage capacity enables commercial optimisation opportunities. Access to storage allows the using of spreads between seasonal gas prices, as well as spreads between prices for different sources of flexibility. This arbitrage potential together with the efficient and reliable physical flow optimisation significantly enhances the competitive position of a gas marketer having access to gas storage facilities, in particular compared with an 'asset-free' trading company.

Since storage capacity is tight, it is important to encourage investment in new storage facilities. This is most efficiently achieved by allowing the market to optimise the allocation of investments in flexibility. Competition of gas with other sources of energy, gas-to-gas competition and operation of storage facilities subject to market mechanisms are what is needed for the storage demand to be met. The pure interest of the gas marketer in being able to deliver to its customers in any circumstances will trigger investment into flexibility. The storage market in Germany is a good example of how a competitive market structure stimulates investment in additional storage even though the ratio of total demand to working gas capacity is already one of the highest in West Europe. For this mechanism to function, liberalisation is essential, but any regulatory intervention, e.g. legal unbundling, has the potential to lower investment and to harm the existing competitive structures of the markets for storage and for flexibility in Europe. Mandatory strategic gas stocks for each single member state of the European Union, as discussed in Section 25.1.2.2, would lead to inefficient results and would not enhance security of supply. Other flexibility sources, e.g. the summer–winter spread in the spot price curve, indicate that storage has a high value for all participants in the gas market, which automatically leads to investment since companies will seek to obtain a competitive advantage by securing their access to storage facilities.

References

BP. 2007. BP statistical review of world energy June 2007. London: BP.

BP. 2008. BP statistical review of world energy June 2008. London: BP.

Cerbe, G., Carlowitz, O., Kätelhön, J. E. & Köhler, H. 1999. Grundlagen der Gastechnik: Gasbeschaffung, Gasverteilung, Gasverwendung. München: Carl Hanser Verlag.

Clewlow, L. & Strickland, C. 2000. Energy derivatives: pricing and risk management. London: Lacima Group.

European Commission. 2006. European energy and transport: trends to 2030 – update 2005. Brussels: European Communities.

European Regulators' Group for Electricity and Gas (ERGEG). 2006. ERGEG final 2006 report on monitoring the implementation of the guidelines for good practice for storage system operators (GGPSSO). Brussels: ERGEG.

Eurostat. 2008. http://epp.eurostat.ec.europa.eu/portal/page?_pageid=0,1136239,0_45571447&_dad=portal&_schema=PORTAL, 1st August 2008.

Gas Infrastructure Europe (GSE). 2007. http://www.gie.eu.com/maps_data/downloads/GSE_STORAGE.pdf, 1st August 2008.

Höffler, F. & Kübler, M. 2007. Demand for storage of natural gas in Northwestern Europe: trends 2005-2030. Unpublished MPI Collective Goods Preprint, Max Planck Institute for Research on Collective Goods, Bonn.

International Energy Agency (IEA). 2002. Flexibility in natural gas supply and demand. Paris: OECD/IEA.

International Energy Agency (IEA). 2004. Security of gas supply in open markets: LNG and power at a turning point. Paris: OECD/IEA.

International Energy Agency (IEA). 2006. World energy outlook 2006. Paris: OECD/IEA.

International Energy Agency (IEA). 2007. World energy outlook 2007: China and India insights. Paris: OECD/IEA.

International Gas Union (IGU). 2006. Basic UGS activities. Paper presented at the 23rd World Gas Conference, Amsterdam.

Monopolkommission. 2007. Strom und Gas 2007: Wettbewerbsdefizite und zögerliche Regulierung. Sondergutachten gemäß § 62 Abs. 1 EnWG. Bonn: Monopolkommission.

Rojey, A. & Jaffret, C. 1997. Natural gas: production, processing, transport. Paris: Edition Technip.

Ronn, E. I. 2002. Real options and energy management: using options methodology to enhance capital budgeting decisions. London: Risk Books.

Sedlacek, R. 2007. Untertage-Gasspeicherung in Deutschland. Erdöl Erdgas Kohle, 123: 422-432.

Part V:
Transmission and Distribution

26 Regulation of Network Charges

Gert Brunekreeft[1]

Abstract

This chapter indicates that we seem at present to be facing a paradigm shift in network regulation, from pure price-based approaches to hybrid models with cost-based elements. The driver behind this move is the need for adequate network investment. Price-based approaches, such as price or revenue caps, designed to increase incentives for short-run efficiency improvements, are successful. However, it appears that when timely and adequate long-run investment is the policy aim (which is not the same as efficient investment), cost-based approaches are more effective than price-based regulation. One of the more prominent examples of a sophisticated hybrid form is the introduction of an 'incentive mechanism' with a menu of sliding scales for the promotion of investment in the electricity distribution networks in the UK in 2005. This appears to be a promising way forward.

Keywords: monopoly, network, regulation

[1] Prof. Dr. Gert Brunekreeft is Professor of Energy Economics at Jacobs University Bremen and Director of the Bremer Energie Institut, Germany.

A. Bausch and B. Schwenker (eds.), *Handbook Utility Management,*
DOI: 10.1007/978-3-540-79349-6_26, © Springer-Verlag Berlin Heidelberg 2009

26.1   Introduction

Liberalisation of electricity markets can meanwhile look back on two decades of experience in (for example) the UK, Norway and parts of the USA, and something over 10 years in many other parts of Europe. It is by now also well established that competition can be effectively introduced in some parts of an electricity sector: generation, trade and retail. In these parts, with appropriate market design and due control by competition agencies, competition can develop with varying degrees of success. It is also well established that competition cannot effectively develop in the monopolistic parts of the sector: at least for the foreseeable future, both the high-voltage transmission network and the low- and medium-voltage distribution networks will remain as (regional) natural monopolies. Therefore, in order to compete, potentially competitive commercial businesses need access to the same monopolistic network. The regulatory framework guiding and promoting competition on the networks relies on two main factors:

- Nondiscriminatory access for third parties;
- Regulation of network access and network charges.

Nondiscrimination includes a wide field. First, third-party access to the network should be warranted. This can be enforced by competition law under the essential facilities doctrine, but it is normal to have an ex ante third-party-access provision in sector-specific law. Secondly, access should be nondiscriminatory. Many rules and provisions seek to guarantee that the network operator cannot effectively discriminate against third parties. Part of this is what is called legal or functional unbundling of network and commercial activities. Thirdly, the underlying assumption is that the network operator is or can be vertically integrated in the commercial businesses. The current debate at European level is concerned with the idea of unbundling the network from the commercial businesses in ownership. The underlying reasoning of the European Commission is that current arrangements of legal unbundling are not adequate to address the problem of discrimination fully.[2]

The second main factor mentioned above is the focus of this chapter: the (economic) regulation of network access charges. Regulation of charges, revenues or profits aims to achieve two goals:

- Promotion of competition on the network (generation and retail);
- Protection of the consumer and economic welfare.[3]

---

[2] The interested reader is referred to the research project Unbundling of Energy Companies (UNECOM) www.unecom.de. Brunekreeft (2008) provides a social cost–benefit analysis of unbundling of the TSOs in Germany.

[3] It is important to realise, but beyond the scope of this paper to go into detail on this matter, that these two factors are mutually dependent. Regulation of the network charges strengthens the incentives for leverage of market power, implying that the necessity for vertical unbundling gets stronger with regulation of the network charges. For a more detailed analysis see Brunekreeft (2003).

At the same time, the regulatory framework must consider two constraints:

- Regulated charges should be sufficient to allow full cost recovery and thereby allow adequate new investment.
- The framework should set incentives for the network operators to maintain and improve efficiency of production. Or in other words, the regulation should not create incentives for low efficiency.

The latter constraint has been the driver behind a paradigm shift in regulation theory and practice. It is the paradigm shift from cost-based to price-based regulation that started during the mid 1980s and has continued up to now. Meanwhile, many electricity networks worldwide are regulated with a price-based scheme with names such as price caps, revenue caps, RPI-X and even yardstick regulation.

This chapter will give a concise, largely theoretical, overview of the main types of regulation and thereby contrast cost-based and price-based regulation on their short-run versus long-run effects. Price-based regulation sets strong incentives for short-run efficiency (i.e. cost cutting), but may be less effective for long-run investment. It seems that as new investment is gaining relevance and short-run post-liberalisation efficiency gains are becoming exhausted, cost-based regulation is regaining ground relative to price-based regulation. One of the more inspiring adjustments to the investment problem is the introduction of a menu of sliding scales for the electricity distribution network in the UK in 2005. This new development will be discussed in Section 26.4. Section 26.5 concludes the chapter.

26.2   Cost-based Regulation

Cost-based regulation has a long tradition in monopoly regulation, especially in the USA. The European answer to the monopoly problem has long been to nationalise the industries and have them managed by the ministries. Because a ministry's raison d'être is to serve the public interest, regulation of any such monopoly was largely assumed to be unnecessary. The utilities in the USA were predominantly privately owned, and hence monopoly regulation was required.

Cost-based regulation can have different variations, two of which stand out:

- Rate-of-return regulation, where the regulatory cost base is capital expenditure (CAPEX);
- Mark-up regulation, where the regulatory cost base is total costs (total expenditure (TOTEX)).

In the rest of the chapter we concentrate on the rate-of-return regulation.[4]

---

[4] For mark-up regulation, the reader is referred to Finsinger and Kraft (1984) and Borrmann and Finsinger (1999).

In essence, rate-of-return regulation allows a 'fair' rate of return on capital employed (Joskow, 1974 & 1989). The basic formula is:

$$REV = OC + d \cdot (KT - CD) + s \cdot (KT - CD) + T \quad \text{(eq. 1)}$$

where

- REV   is revenue;
- OC   is operating costs;
- KT   is historic capital value;
- CD   is cumulative depreciation;
- T   is taxes;
- d   is depreciation rate;
- s   is allowed rate of return on capital;
- r   is cost of capital.

The allowed rate of return s is to be determined by the regulator. If $s = r$, then the allowed rate of return would exactly match investors' idea of the cost of capital. Usually, we would expect s to be somewhat larger than r as the bargaining outcome between regulator and regulated firm. The allowed revenues are calculated from the regulatory cost base: the asset base, operating cost and taxes. Note that the regulatory asset base is ambiguous (or even arbitrary), as it depends on depreciation rules, which in turn are set by the regulator.

In theory, the regulator sets s and all else follows from this. In particular, the firm would have to calculate its own prices and revenues following the costs in such a way that the rate of return does not exceed s. Therefore, if the costs change, the revenues have to be adjusted to fulfil the regulatory constraint. As has been well explained by Joskow (1974 & 1989), in practice the regulation is subject to a regulatory lag. The regulator deduces the allowed revenues from the allowed rate of return s, and quite often also determines individual prices. These allowed revenues and prices then remain valid until either party (regulator or firm) requests a rate review to change the regulation or, if this does not happen, rate reviews take place after a predetermined period. As long as a review does not take place, there is no guarantee that the actual rate of return does not exceed s. This period between two reviews is called the regulatory lag. The regulatory lag may thus be defined as a period in which allowed revenues are de-linked from underlying (own) costs. For cost-based regulation it follows that the regulatory lag is endogenous, and as a rule relatively short. Rate-of-return regulation is simple and straightforward, but suffers from the following four drawbacks.

In practice we find that regulators are not restricted to controlling fulfilment of the rate-of-return constraint. The allowed rate of return might be more appropriately seen as the starting point after which the allowed future revenues and prices are deduced. Although there is no need to do this, in practice we find that regulators often set individual prices and thereby determine the price structure. In the past, this has been inspired by socio-political goals (e.g. low electricity prices for the socially vulnerable, or development of rural areas) at the expense of efficiency. During the 1980s, this policy went out of fashion, which triggered awareness that the price structure could be left to the firm, while the regulator could then concentrate on the price or revenue level. The theoretical argument behind this reasoning is that whereas a monopoly may set a too-high price level, simultaneously it will seek an optimal price structure. If the firm and the regulator were seeking the same price structure, it might as well be left to the firm and the regulator could then concentrate on the price level.

The information requirement under rate-of-return regulation is high for two reasons. First, as noted above, if regulators set individual prices they will need information about demand. To the extent that such information is available at all, we would expect the firm to have better information. Secondly, the rate-of-return regulation relies on underlying costs, because the regulatory costs and allowed rate of return determine allowed revenues. To set prices, the regulator will have to know the cost. Clearly, the regulator is at a strong informational disadvantage compared with the firm. The informational asymmetry has been the strongest driver of the paradigm shift towards more refined incentive mechanisms, which try to repair the informational imbalance.

A third problem has come to be known as the Averch-Johnson (AJ) effect (Averch & Johnson, 1962), also known as gold-plating or overcapitalisation. The AJ effect is typical for rate-of-return regulation and does not apply to cost-based regulation in general. The rate-of-return regulation restricts the rate of return on capital employed while operating expenditure is subject to a straightforward 'cost pass-through'. If $s > r$, it pays to inflate the capital base at the expense of operating costs, because the capital base determines allowed profits under rate-of-return regulation. In other words, for a given level of output, production will be inefficiently capital intensive relative to noncapital inputs. In still other words, under rate-of-return regulation it would be attractive to invest in new lines instead of maintaining the lines if the latter qualifies as an operating cost. Note, however, that the capital is not 'wasted' and is actually used; the inefficiency lies in the distorted ratio of CAPEX versus operating expenditure (OPEX).[5] To avoid automatic pass-through of unnecessary new capital-intensive investment, regulators in the USA apply a so-called use-and-useful rule. Capital expenditure can be excluded from the capital base if the use-and-useful criterion is not fulfilled, in which case the capital expenditure must be borne by the shareholder instead of by the consumer. In the 1980s, substantial nuclear assets were subject to the use-and-useful rule (Lyon & Mayo, 2000). Whereas this rule manages to discipline firms and prevent them from making capital expenditure too easily, it also increases regulatory uncertainty if the rule is applied too easily by the regulator.

A fourth problem is the low-powered incentives of rate-of-return regulation, which holds for cost-based regulation in general. Assume that the cost-based regulation is strict and thus the regulatory lag is zero; in other words, assume that the rate-of-return requirement must be fulfilled at each moment. If the management of the firm now puts effort into cost reduction, it will have to reduce prices immedi-

---

[5] It should be remarked that although the AJ effect is widely accepted in the theoretical literature, empirically it is controversial and it has not been convincingly shown to exist (Borrmann & Finsinger, 1999).

ately to fulfil the regulatory constraint. The reverse argument also holds; additional costs (slackness) can be passed on to consumers immediately. In both cases we should expect that the incentives to control costs are low. This problem can be embedded in the literature on asymmetrical information and would relate to the phenomenon of moral hazard (also known as 'hidden action'); the regulator cannot effectively observe the firm's effort, and in response, following the incentives set by the regulatory framework, the firm reduces effort. This problem of low-powered incentives to reduce costs was considered a particularly strong problem for the phase of liberalisation of the European utilities, which were considered to be inefficient. Therefore, a low-powered regulatory framework was seen as a hurdle to be overcome prior to the achievement of productivity gains.

An extension to the AJ effect, combining the third and fourth points above, comes from Bawa and Sibley (1980). The outcome of the AJ model as described above is ambiguous if the allowed rate of return s is equal to the cost of capital r. Bawa and Sibley (1980) apply regulatory threat as a way out of the ambiguity. Assume, as described above, that allowed revenues (irrespective of underlying costs) remain unchanged as long as no regulatory review is requested. Assume further that a regulatory review is triggered if profits in excess of allowed rate of return s are too high. Assume lastly that if a review takes place, then the allowed revenues will have to be brought back to a level that corresponds to an allowed rate-of-return level s. The result now is that if s is close to r, the AJ effect unambiguously ceases to exist. The argument is as follows. If s is much larger than r, then there is a lot to be gained with gold-plating and the firm will not want to trigger a review by having a higher rate of return than s. However, if s is close to r, the gains from gold-plating are small and hence it is more appealing to ignore the constraint (make profits by reducing costs) and risk a review. If the constraint is 'ignored', gold-plating would decrease profits (as if there were no regulation) and hence we conclude that gold-plating does not take place. At the same time, however, if the probability of triggering a review is very high, the incentive to reduce cost will be low as the reward is small, and thus we expect low-powered incentives if s is close to r.

26.3   Price-based Regulation

In 1983, Professor Stephan Littlechild was asked by the British government to assess different regulatory regimes for the regulation of British Telecom, which was then to be liberalised and privatised. This resulted in what is now seen as a paradigm shift. Littlechild was quite critical of cost-based approaches and suggested to follow price-based models instead (Littlechild, 1983). The British government followed this advice and implemented what came to be known as RPI-X regulation (or, price cap regulation). Soon afterwards, price-based models gained popularity in both practice and theory. The literature on price-cap regulation is vast. Even in the USA, in many sectors, price-based models have replaced cost-based models.

Beesley and Littlechild (1989) set out the main reasoning very clearly. As outlined above, cost-based approaches suffer from the following main flaws:

- Setting of individual prices and thereby the price structure;
- The high informational requirement;
- Low-powered incentives for cost reduction.

Obviously, price-based models should have the reverse points as relative merits. The pros and cons of the approaches have been extensively studied, and presumably the most important insight to emerge from the debate is that cost-based and price-based models are the extremes on a scale, while in practice neither extreme exists. In fact, as especially Joskow (1989 & 2006) argues, in practice the difference between the two may be quite small. Cost-based regulation has a price-based component through the regulatory lag, while price-based regulation has a cost-based component through the reviews, at which a reasonable relation to underlying costs is restored.

26.3.1 Price and Revenue Caps

The key point of price-based models is to de-link allowed revenues from underlying costs. This mimics a competitive outcome as prices in a competitive setting are determined by the market (i.e. demand and supply of all firms) and not by the individual firm. The theoretically purest form of price-based regulation is price capping or the 'tariff-basket', which is formally described as follows (Cowan, 1997):

$$\sum_{i=1}^{n} p_{i,t} \cdot Q_{i,t-1} \le \sum_{i=1}^{n} p_{i,t-1} \cdot Q_{i,t-1} \cdot (1 + RPI - X) \qquad \text{(eq. 2)}$$

where $p_{i,t}$ is the price and $Q_{i,t}$ is the quantity of good i ($i = 1,..,n$) in period t, RPI is retail price index (say, general inflation) and X is (estimated ex ante) productivity increase. In words, the average price level is calculated by weighing the prices with the quantities of the previous period.[6] The periods t are normally years within a regulatory control period of 3-5 years. This rule is applied within the control period and all variables change accordingly, but the rule itself is not changed. Prices should follow this rule. Only at a regulatory review, which takes place at a predetermined moment, can the rule itself be changed. It will be clear that the regulatory control period is the same as the regulatory lag, as described in Section 26.2. The difference in the regulatory lag between the cost-based and the price-based regime is gradual; in a price-based regime the regulatory lag is exogenous, predetermined, predictable and reasonably long.

In the equation for the tariff basket the following points should be noted. In the equation, the 'revenues' (or, more precisely, quantity-weighted average prices)

---

[6] The equation relies on the Laspeyres price index. If for convenience (RPI-X) is assumed to be zero, the constraint says the consumer should be able to purchase the previous period's bundle of goods in the current period with at most the same amount of money as in the previous period.

bear no relation to underlying costs. The path of the prices is determined in particular by the X-factor. The X-factor, which represents expected productivity increases, is subject to strong debate, which centres around the question of how to de-link X from own underlying costs. Basically, the main alternatives are to use long-term industry trends in productivity growth and to use efficiency data of the other firms (i.e. benchmarking).[7] De-linking allowed revenues from underlying own costs implies high-powered incentives to reduce costs. If the regulated firm manages to reduce its cost during the control period by more than what is expressed in X, it does not have to reduce prices for the additional cost reduction, but can instead keep these profits. This is precisely what sets the incentives to reduce costs in the first place. There is by now ample evidence that this effect is strong.

Secondly, note that price cap or tariff basket regulation as in eq. 2 does not regulate individual prices. It sets a constraint on the overall (price) level of a basket of different goods (or consumers): The left-hand side is a construction of prices weighted by the goods, and only the overall level is constrained. What happens within the basket is left for the firm to decide. Hence, it is left to the firm to decide whether to have a high price for one good and a low price for another good or the other way around, as long as the weighted average is not violated. This follows the logic set out above: the profit-maximising firm seeks the same price structure as the regulator, and it is therefore enough for the regulator to constrain the overall level and leave the structure to the firm. Note in this respect the lagged structure in eq. 2. This period's average prices (t) on the left-hand side are weighted against quantities from the previous period (t-1), whereas the constraint consists of revenue in the previous period (t-1). Hence, in this period the quantities (t) are free (although constrained by the prices). However, this period's quantities flow into the constraint for the next period and so on. This triggers a chain of adjustment that can be controlled by the firm. The result of the adjustments is a rebalancing of tariffs, which closely resembles what the regulator would do with the tariff structure (cf. in particular Bradley & Price, 1988 and, more generally, Vogelsang & Finsinger, 1979). Thus, the flexibility of the tariff basket can be explicitly used to avoid the necessity for the regulator to interfere in the price structure, leaving him free to concentrate instead on the price level.

Thirdly, and putting the first two points together, we find that strictly speaking the informational requirement of price capping is low. If allowed prices or revenues are not linked to underlying own costs, then firms will have an incentive neither to manipulate information nor to withhold information. If de-linking the allowed prices from the underlying costs also sets high-powered incentives to reduce costs, then the informational asymmetry caused by the fact that the regulator cannot observe the firm's effort to reduce costs (moral hazard) would be addressed effectively. Lastly, if the regulator can refrain from setting individual prices, the informational burden will be shifted to the firm, which can be expected to have superior information.

---

[7] This issue will be left here and the reader is referred to e.g. Makholm and Quinn (1997) and Jamasb and Pollitt (2000) for more detail.

In practice, we find two main deviations from the theoretical world outlined above. First, there are many variations of the tariff basket described above. A prominent variation is the revenue cap, which looks like this:

$$\sum_{i=1}^{n} p_{i,t} \cdot Q_{i,t} \le R_0 \cdot (1 + RPI - X) \quad \text{(eq. 3)}$$

The notation is as in eq. 2, while R_0 is some initial level of revenues. Although the revenue cap has theoretical drawbacks, it does have two powerful practical strengths compared with the tariff basket. First, it stabilises the stream of revenues, which reduces the risk to the firm (as long as costs are stable). Second, it is easy to implement. To implement the revenue cap, only aggregate values (total revenue) are required and there is no need to go into individual goods. In other words, the regulator does not even need to know the contents of the basket. The second main deviation is linking revenues and costs. At the latest at the review moment, allowed revenues are brought back to underlying own costs. In other words, allowed revenues are hardly ever completely de-linked from own costs. In the next section we will present yardstick regulation as a form of price-based regulation which can potentially completely de-link revenues from own costs. The reason for having review periods and trying to relate revenues to underlying costs is straightforward. The result of complete de-linking may be unreasonable. Either it may turn out that the allowed prices are actually far too high, which questions the effectiveness of the regulation, or, what is worse, the allowed prices may be too low to recover full costs or warrant new investment. The review period gives the regulator the possibility of controlling the degree of reasonableness. This particular problem of the reasonable level implies a second problem of asymmetrical information: the regulator will not know whether a firm has high or low costs. If, however, the price level should be such that firms are allowed full cost recovery, then the regulator must set a relatively high price cap to take account of the possibility of dealing with a high-cost firm. In information theory this is called the problem of adverse selection (also known as 'hidden information').

26.3.2   Yardstick Regulation

As discussed above, the key to the efficiency incentives is the link between price and/or revenues and own costs. The extreme form of yardstick regulation, which was developed by Shleifer (1985), completely de-links the allowed prices from own costs. Unfortunately, there is no consensus on the name: the terms yardstick regulation and yardstick competition are both widely used to describe the same phenomenon. We use yardstick regulation. Following the notation in Jamasb and Pollitt (2000, p. 6), yardstick regulation can be defined as follows:

$$P_i = \alpha_i C_i + (1 - \alpha_i) \sum_{j=1}^{n} (f_j C_j) \quad \text{(eq. 4)}$$

where

- P_i is the price cap for firm i;
- α_i is the share of the firm's own cost information ($\alpha = 0$ represents pure yardstick);
- C_i is the unit cost of firm i;
- f_j is the revenue or quantity weighting for peer group firms j;
- C_j is the unit cost (or prices) for peer group firms j;
- n is the number of firms in the peer group.

The price cap under the yardstick as generally defined in eq. 4 is a function of own costs and costs of other firms. In the most extreme case, α would be zero, meaning that the allowed price bears no relation to own costs at all. The allowed price would only be determined by external factors. For a high value of n, the next-to-extreme case is that firm i's own costs are simply a (small) part of the average unit costs of all firms. If only the costs of others determine the level of the cap of firm i, then it will have a strong incentive to improve its efficiency and thereby lower its costs. As this is true for all, the result is that the industry unit cost and thereby the yardstick are lowered. Therefore, the mechanism dynamically converges on lowest costs equilibrium. This mimics the outcome under perfect competition. Indeed, in perfect competition the price in the market is determined by the collection of the suppliers and is independent of individual behaviour.

Note the technical relation to more general price-based regulation. Within the regulatory control period, price-based regulation is the same as yardstick regulation. Critical is what happens at the regulatory review. If the regulatory rule is then adjusted to own underlying costs, yardstick regulation and the more general price-based regulation start to diverge. If, however, the regulatory rule is adjusted only to benchmarking of the costs of others and not to underlying own costs, then price-based regulation and yardstick regulation are actually the same.

The strength of the yardstick regulation is the high-powered incentives for efficiency. The yardstick and thereby the allowed revenues can be completely de-linked from own costs, and therefore, any efficiency gain can be fully retained by the firm. The system also has downsides. We mention three. First, since there will be no adjustment to underlying own costs, the results may become unreasonable. Firms may end up with high profits or with large losses. Of course, this is normal in the competitive environment, but we are dealing here with an artificial world with a regulatory framework designed by men. Second, and this strengthens the first point, the outcome depends strongly on the benchmark. To push the analogy with competition a little further, we would typically look for a weighted average of the x most efficient firms. This, however, assumes that the firms (comparators) can actually be compared, which is not always the case. Third, there is a danger of collusion. If a few firms can tacitly agree not to reduce costs and so keep the yardstick at a high level, they can by-pass the system and keep the pressure off. However, as in the case of normal collusion, such an agreement is unstable as each party has an incentive to cheat.

26.3.3 The Investment Incentives

Experience strongly suggests that price-based regulation is unambiguously good for short-term cost reductions and efficiency improvements. However, theoretical reflections suggest that price-based regulation may be less effective for long-term investment incentives. As the experience with price-based models and the duration of repeated cost reductions continue, we expect that the strong emphasis on price-based models will decrease and that cost-based components are included in the price-based models. Below we discuss four reasons why price-based models may have limited effectiveness on investment incentives.

Cost of Capital: Risk-adjusted Rate of Return

The 'buffering hypothesis' put forth by Peltzman (1976) explains the effect of market risk on the regulated firm: "Regulation should reduce conventional measures of owner risk. By buffering the firm against demand and cost changes, the variability of profits and stock prices should be lower than otherwise. To the extent that the cost and demand changes are economy-wide, regulation should reduce systematic as well as diversifiable risk". The crucial factor is how much of the shocks can be passed through to customers. Profit-maximising prices of a firm with market power pass through only some of the demand and cost shocks, absorbing the remainder; consequently, profits vary with demand and cost shocks. Under an extreme notion of rate-of-return regulation (i.e. with a zero regulatory gap), the firm passes through all of the shocks in order to stick to the allowed rate of return. The investment in the rate-of-return-regulated firm gives moderate, but safe returns.

It is a different story for firms regulated with a price cap. Restricting attention to systematic, nondiversifiable risks, Wright et al. (2003) examine the case of price caps in detail. They conclude that the cost of capital is higher under price-cap regulation than for an unregulated firm if there is cost uncertainty. This is intuitive because if costs change while prices stay the same, the variability in profits will be strong. With demand uncertainty, the cost of capital is lower under price-cap regulation than without regulation. In this case, the price cap works as the buffer under rate-of-return regulation. The fact that the firm is not allowed to increase the price (to adjust to a demand increase) and, with a binding cap, does not wish to decrease the price (to adjust to a demand decrease) means that the volatility of profits is less under the price cap than it would be if the firm freely adjusted to demand changes.

To conclude, price-based regulation increases risk of cost or demand uncertainty more for the regulated firm than for firms subject to cost-based regulation. The consequence of this is that different types of regulation should apply a different risk-adjusted rate of return on capital to reflect the appropriate cost of capital of the investment (Grout & Zalewska, 2003).

Time Inconsistency

Time inconsistency means that an agent has conflicting short-run and long-run goals. The best economic example is monetary policy. In the short run, politicians will be tempted to reduce unemployment at the expense of (short-run) higher inflation. In the long run, this achieves nothing but higher inflation. In the long run, a low inflation target basically ignoring effects on national output and employment is best. Hence, the time inconsistency is that the long-run policy of a low inflation target is overrun by the short-run, low-unemployment, high-inflation trade-off.

For the context of regulation, it is claimed that time-inconsistency is higher under price-based regulation than under cost-based regulation. Basically, the argument is that cost-based regulation follows a reasonable rate of return, whereas price-based regulation has no such reference. Therefore, the regulatory commitment to long-run, sunk investments is lower and regulatory risk is higher, and thus we would expect a detrimental effect on investment activity.

The precise line of argument relies on one-sided upward capping and is best illustrated by Gans and King (2003). We illustrate with an example. Assume an investment project with sunk costs and high demand uncertainty; the project can be a success or a failure. Assume that these events have the same probability (0.5). Assume further that unregulated rate of return in case of success would be 12% and in case of failure, 8%. The expected rate of return will thus be 10%. Now assume that the project will be price cap regulated, aiming at 10%; in the case of good demand, the cap binds and the rate of return will be 10%, while in the case of poor demand the cap does not bind and rate of return will be 8%. The expected rate of return under the price cap regulation is thus 9%. If investors require 10%, then the investment will not take place. The problem is one-sided upward capping and downward market risk. Principally, the problem could be solved by allowing a 12% rate of return in good times. But here is the regulatory commitment problem. The 12% rate of return only bears any relation to ex ante risk expectations (which may be quite far in the past); it does not relate to actual underlying costs and as a 'real' cost benchmark is lacking, the regulator will have difficulty justifying this. Alternatively, if the sunk investment has been made irreversibly, an opportunistic regulator may be tempted to simply ignore the past expected value and decrease regulated rates to real costs in times of good demand. Even if the regulator does not actually do this, the investors may not believe it before the investment is made; in other words, it is difficult to achieve a credible regulatory commitment. To sum up the problem of time inconsistency, the (pre-investment) long-run policy should be to regulate at a level which allows new investments (thus taking proper account of risks), whereas in the short run (post-investment), regulators may be tempted to lower charges, ignoring ex ante risk and exploiting sunk costs.

Quality of Service and the Reduction of Gold-plating

There is justified concern that price-cap regulation impedes investment in quality of supply (QoS), which is an important indicator of network adequacy (and reliability). The incentives for a monopoly to invest in quality under different regulatory regimes have been studied extensively by Spence (1975). First, it should be noted that an unregulated monopolist need not but can have incentives to set optimal quality; the details depend on the effect of quality changes on the demand function. To be precise, the change in quality should not alter the slope of the demand function. Secondly, note that quality can be too high. As the classic form of rate of return regulation is said to induce excessive quality, one might expect quality to go down in many cases as a result of implementing price cap regulation, but this would not mean that quality would be too low. Thirdly, note that quality changes can be triggered by investment, which is CAPEX, or alternatively by improving and maintaining existing assets, which would be OPEX. In regulatory practice, capital and operating expenditure can be treated entirely differently, and hence the incentive on quality may differ. Fourthly, quality changes may require research and development, leading to literature on the relation between regulation and innovation. Insofar as innovation is involved, the usual free-rider problem may occur: firms may want to downsize on research and development when faced with pressure to cut costs and leave innovative research to others; obviously, if all do this, then the overall level of innovation will be too low.

What does the literature suggest? With fixed prices, quality will be lower than optimal (Spence, 1975). In economic terms, a quality improvement shifts the demand function outward; with a price increase, part of this additional demand (willingness to pay) can be captured in additional profits. A price cap does not allow this price increase, and as a result the quality improvement does not take place to its full extent. In the short run, price caps set a rather straightforward incentive to cut costs at the expense of quality. In the long run, as prices and demand adjust (i.e. as price-based regulation starts to be cost-based regulation) these effects are mitigated.

Timing of Investment

Much of the analysis on investment covers the capacity, quality and whether-at-all questions, whereas the issue on the timing of investment is short of attention. Relying on formal set-ups in Gans and King (2004), Brunekreeft and Newbery (2006), and Katz and Shapiro (1987), Borrmann and Brunekreeft (2007)[8] develop a formal approach to study the effects of different types of regulation on the timing of monopoly investment. The main comparison in the analysis is price-based versus cost-based regulation, with a focus on yardstick regulation as an extreme form of price-based regulation.

Timing of investment, and in fact investment at all, only makes sense if something changes. Borrmann and Brunekreeft (2007) work with two types of dynamics. First, wear and tear causes variable production costs to increase over time. An investment lowers the variable production costs at the expense of higher cost of capital. Second, demand growth implies that at some point in time it may be profitable to expand capacity. Note that without such or similarly dynamic assump-

---

[8] This paper is available as a mimeo from the authors upon request.

tions, there will be no reason to invest in the first place. Using these two types of dynamics, two types of investment can be examined. First, 'replacement investment', which follows from wear and tear, and second, 'expansion investment', which follows from demand growth. The effects of regulation on the timing of investment are different for replacement and expansion investment. In the next section we define yardstick regulation in such a way that the price cap does not change as a result of investment; hence, despite cost changes, the allowed price (i.e. the price cap) is fixed. Below we summarise the main insights.

- *The benchmark case:* The timing of investment for the unregulated monopolist is always later than with social-welfare maximization. This is a well-established result, and serves as our benchmark case.

- *Replacement investment:* For replacement investment (the case of wear and tear), the timing of investment under yardstick regulation moves, roughly speaking, between a relatively early investment date (possibly earlier than under welfare maximisation) on the one hand and the investment date of the unregulated monopoly on the other hand. More precisely, the investment date is accelerated with a lower yardstick price. However, this only holds as long as the yardstick price recovers full costs; otherwise the investment will not be done at all.[9]

  Things change if the yardstick price is broken up in a price cap before the investment and a price cap after the investment. Assuming that the post-investment price cap is higher than the pre-investment price cap and assuming, for reasons of comparison, that the average of these two is equal to the hypothetical yardstick, we find that the investment timing is accelerated relative to a strict yardstick. Note, however, that the investment moment might be inefficiently early. This case of the broken-up yardstick is equivalent to cost-based regulation, as the underlying principle is that the price cap increases with higher post-investment costs reflecting higher CAPEX. Hence, if the policy aim is to promote early investment, then a cost-based approach helps.

- *Expansion investment:* For expansion investment we assume the following regulatory procedure. For reasons of comparison, we assume that capacity is constrained before the investment. With investment (adding new capacity, thereby relieving the capacity constraint), the regulatory constraint affects the entire capacity equally and not separately for the existing and the additional capacity.

  For expansion investment and under yardstick regulation, the investment moment is accelerated with a higher price cap level. Reversing the same claim, a lower yardstick delays the investment inefficiently and even more than the unregulated monopolist. This is immediately clear if we consider a very small initial capacity, say zero, which is the same as saying that there

---

[9] To be precise, for inelastic demand, the level of the yardstick price does not have an effect on the timing of the investment (as long as the level is high enough to support full cost recovery). It is precisely the fact that under elastic demand, output increases with lower prices which drives the claim above.

was no output (and hence nothing to lose) before the investment and the only thing that matters is the potential profit after the investment; obviously, a higher allowed price increases the post-investment profits and thereby accelerates the investment moment. The same principle holds for positive, but constrained pre-investment capacity. This in turn implies in a straightforward way that if the pre-investment price cap is low and the post-investment price cap is high, the investment moment is accelerated. Again this implies that if timely investment is the policy aim, then a cost-based approach helps.

To back up these claims, we note that in practice we do find numerous examples of so-called cost-based adders in addition to price-based regulation. These cost-based adders serve one purpose only: promotion of investment.

26.4   Further Developments in Network Pricing – a Menu of Sliding Scales

In the UK, price-cap regulation for the distribution networks (DNOs) started in 1990, and thus has now been in force for about 18 years. With the fourth regulatory control period, which started in 2005, the regulatory regime changed quite dramatically. It was felt that investment in the distribution networks had been worryingly low, and the DNOs claimed it was necessary to improve investment incentives. The UK regulator, Ofgem, faced the problem that different DNOs had widely different views on how much new investment they needed. Ofgem (June 2004, p. 88) notes: "[…] significant differences from the CAPEX for […] DNOs", and a severe lack of information about them. The dilemma faced by Ofgem was how to allow sufficiently high revenues to avoid frustrating new investment, while at the same time not letting them be so high that regulation would become ineffective and inefficient. Hence, Ofgem wanted to allow CAPEX pass-through in case CAPEX overspend should be necessary and thus hesitated to use a strict price cap. On the other hand, Ofgem wanted to avoid automatic cost-pass-through and thus hesitated to use strict rate-of-return regulation. The obvious solution, then, is to find the middle way, which is a sliding scale: a sliding scale is a mixture of price-based and cost-based regulation. The novelty introduced by Ofgem was not the sliding scale itself, but the menu of sliding scales, which is an 'incentive mechanism' in a pure sense. As an aside, the real novelty is the implementation of such a scheme for the regulation of an electricity network; the principles of incentive mechanisms have long been known in theory and in fact are quite normal in the insurance industry and more generally in pricing strategies involving multi-part pricing.

As pointed out above, Ofgem rightly noted its informational disadvantage. It did not know which DNO had a high investment requirement and which a low one. This leads to the theory of asymmetrical information and, at a more advanced level, incentive mechanism design. The menu addresses the informational problem by introducing a self-selection component. The idea of a correct scheme is that a firm with a high probability that allowed CAPEX suffices for actual CAPEX chooses price cap, and a firm with a high probability that allowed CAPEX does not recover actual investment requirements (and thus capital overspend would be likely) chooses cost pass-through. In this way, the price cap can be reasonably low while still setting incentives to be efficient, and at the same time capital overspend (if necessary) is not frustrated.

We can embed this more formally in the theory of informational economics, which relies on Laffont and Tirole (1994) and has been well applied to the regulation of electricity networks by Joskow (2006). The regulator's constraint is to avoid bankruptcy of a firm. Regulated prices should take account of the possibility of high costs. Two polarised cases follow. First, pure price-based regulation addresses the moral-hazard problem, but not that of adverse selection (allocative inefficiency); in other words, price-based regulation sets high-powered incentives for being efficient. Second, pure cost-based regulation addresses adverse selection, but not moral hazard (X-inefficiency); this means that under cost-based regulation the incentives to be efficient are low, but the risk of setting too-low charges for a high-cost firm is low. The compromise is an incentive mechanism that tries to strike a balance between the two polarised cases: a self-selecting mix of cost-based and price-based regulation.

Consider the following small model, which also underlies the case of the menu of sliding scales in the UK. Assume:

- β is the inherent cost, which can be low or high and which is known to the firm but not to the regulator.
- c is the realized or actual cost.

Assume that the firm receives a transfer payment, t, in excess of realized costs, c (which, of course are also reimbursed):

$$t(\beta, c) = A(b(\beta)) - b(\beta) \cdot c \quad \text{(eq. 5)}$$

Total allowed revenue $R = t + c$, which can be rewritten as:

$$R = A(b(\beta)) + (1 - b(\beta)) \cdot c \quad \text{(eq. 6)}$$

In words, allowed revenue is a function of some fixed component (independent of actual costs) and actual costs. Therefore, allowed revenue is a sliding scale between a price cap and cost pass-through. The balance between these two components is determined by the factor b, which is the sliding scale factor. In a normal sliding scale b is unique, fixed and determined by the regulator. For a menu of sliding scales there are multiple b's, and the firm chooses its preferred b. The fixed component (the price cap), A, can be defined as:

$$A = a(b) \cdot b(\beta) + \gamma(b) \quad \text{(eq. 7)}$$

In eq. 7, both a and γ are factors set by the regulator, who calculates the allowed revenue. The key important point is that these two factors should be such that the overall scheme is 'incentive compatible'. Note that A is independent of observed c. Importantly, assume that the level of the price cap, A, is an increasing function of b: $\frac{\partial A}{\partial b} > 0$. In words, opting for a stronger reliance on the price cap implies that the fixed component is higher. Note that:

- $b = 0$: this is the case of full cost pass-through, and A will be low (or even zero).
- $b = 1$: this is the case of a strict price cap, and A will be high.
- $0 < b < 1$: this is the case of the sliding scale: additional costs/profits are partially borne/kept by the firm and partially passed through to the end user.

The menu is $A(b)$, which is designed and set by the regulator. The firm then chooses b and thereby, implicitly, A. The firm's choice of b depends heavily on β, the inherent costs, which are not known to the regulator. This expresses the informational asymmetry. The regulator would like to set a reasonable price cap but does not know whether the firm is a high-cost or low-cost firm (i.e., whether β is high or low). The regulator can, however, design an incentive scheme of A, relying on b, so that the firm will always want to report the true value for β. An optimal incentive mechanism will secure truth-telling self-selection, such that the:

- High-cost firm (β high) selects low b (cost pass-through).
- Low-cost firm (β low) chooses high b (price cap).

Hence, by clever design of the sliding scale, the regulator avoids setting a too-low price cap for high-cost firms (as these will choose a cost-pass-through element) and also avoids setting a too-high price cap for low-cost firms (as these will opt for a price-cap element).[10]

The regulator scheme for the electricity distribution networks in the UK that started in 2005 is an excellent example. The scheme is depicted in Table 26.1. We can interpret Table 26.1 in terms of the small model above:

- Marginal incentive = b;
- Allowed CAPEX = a;
- Additional revenue = γ;
- Marginal incentive * allowed CAPEX + additional revenue = (b*a) + γ = A.

A marginal incentive of 40% says that 40% of capital overspend (in excess of allowed CAPEX) is borne by the firm (and thus 60% can be passed through) and 40% of capital underspend can be kept by the firm (and thus again 60% of the avoided expenses should be passed through). The procedure is as follows. The firms are asked about their investment requirement; these numbers are checked by Ofgem's consultants, who then also make a shadow calculation for each firm, after which the firm has opportunity to revise their numbers if they wish so. The ratio of the firm's estimate over the Ofgem's estimate is the top line (DNO/PB Power ra-

---

[10] The terms 'high-cost' and 'low-cost' are actually not accurate. From the perspective of the regulator (and in line with informational economics) the terms 'high-risk' and 'low-risk' are more to the point.

tio). If the ratio is 100, this implicitly says that the firm and Ofgem agree on the required expenditure. If the ratio is high, then Ofgem thinks that the firm does not need so much as it claims, thereby running the risk of frustrating necessary investment if Ofgem turns out to be wrong. In these cases, a regulator will want to allow capital overspend if necessary, while at the same time ensuring that this is only done if true.

Table 26.1: Regulator scheme for the electricity distribution networks in the UK (Ofgem, 2004; Distribution Price Control 2005-2010; June 2004, table 6.9)

DNO/PB Power ratio [%]	100	110	120	130	140
Marginal incentive	40%	35%	30%	25%	20%
Additional revenue	5	4	2.8	1.5	0
Rewards and penalties:					
Allowed CAPEX [%]	105	107.5	110	112.5	115
Actual CAPEX					
70	19	17.1	14.8	12.1	9
80	15	13.6	11.8	9.6	7
90	11	10.1	8.8	7.1	5
100	7	6.6	5.8	4.6	3
105	5	4.9	4.3	3.4	2
110	3	3.1	2.8	2.1	1
115	1	1.4	1.3	0.9	0
120	-1	-0.4	-0.3	-0.4	-1
130	-5	-3.9	-3.3	-2.9	-3
140	-9	-7.4	-6.3	-5.4	-5

Denote actual CAPEX as ACC and allowed CAPEX as ALC. The numbers in the cells denote the additional revenue in the case of spending less than allowed CAPEX corrected for the sliding scale (marginal incentive). Total revenue is then calculated as:

$$R = ACC + \gamma + [(ALC - ACC) \cdot b] \text{ (eq. 8)}$$

which can be rewritten as:

$$R = b \cdot ALC + \gamma + (1 - b) \cdot ACC \quad \text{(eq. 9)}$$

which is equal to eq. 6 above and exactly illustrates the sliding scale.

The precise level of the numbers is important, as this determines incentive compatibility: Low-cost firms should opt for high b and vice versa. Whether they actually do depends on ALC and γ. A look at Table 26.1 reveals that the highest additional pay-off is always at the point where actual CAPEX is equal to the ratio (these are grey in Table 1). Suppose a DNO knows it will have actual CAPEX of 100 and suppose it chooses a ratio of 120 (or equivalently, it chooses a marginal incentive of 30%) and will thus be allowed CAPEX of 110. As can be seen from Table 1, it is best not to spend the 120, but indeed go down to 100, in which case the additional pay would be 5.8. It seems that the firm has gained by overstating its investment requirement. However, this strategy is less than optimal. The firm should have stated 100 in the first place, resulting in a ratio of 100, a marginal incentive of 40. With an actual CAPEX of 100, the additional payment would have been 7, which is more than 5.8. Now suppose, as an alternative, for the same firm that actual CAPEX is indeed 120 (which means that Ofgem has underestimated the investment requirement). In this case, a statement different from 120 would have resulted in an additional loss greater than 0.3. If the firm is serious it should stick to a high ratio. Given the expectations of Ofgem (the other side of setting the ratio) it is optimal to stick to the truth. The result is that firms for which capital overspend is likely opt for a high b (cost-pass through) and reverse.

As may be clear by now, a system like this has the enormous advantage of bypassing the informational disadvantage to the regulator. Yet, despite all its elegance, there is one unresolved issue. The outcome depends on the DNO/PB power ratio, which depends in turn on Ofgem's estimate of the investment requirement, which is of course the original problem. The firm can set a high estimate and try to make Ofgem believe this to be true. If it succeeds, the ratio will in fact be low, and the firm would end up in the left column with low actual CAPEX (and thus high rewards). It follows that we should expect the following. If, in the real case, Ofgem's estimates are conservative (i.e. cautious), then we will find that the estimates of CAPEX are inflated and many firms opt for price caps (high marginal incentives), whereas in many cases it will turn out that there is quite significant CAPEX underspend. The key is that no firm will want to be below Ofgem's estimate. The counterstrategy would be to be tough and enforce a high ratio. Two things can happen. Either the firm was right and will thus stick to a low marginal incentive, but at least then it will have a high cost-pass-through factor (hence, Ofgem's wrong estimate would not have any serious consequences), or the firm was gaming and will revise its own estimate.

Overall, the menu of sliding scales is a promising way forward. Also, it illustrates very strongly the point made in this chapter. Strict price-based regulation may have drawbacks for the investment incentives. Introducing cost-based elements mitigates this problem. A menu of sliding scales strikes a balance.

26.5   Concluding Remarks

In this chapter the author argues that we currently seem to be facing a paradigm shift in network regulation. Up to the mid-1980s cost-based models were at the regulatory front. From the mid-1980s onward, price-based models, most prominently price-cap regulation as developed in the UK, took over the leading role. In strictly cost-based models, prices and revenues should follow underlying cost developments. As a result, cost reductions do not lead to additional profits, so that the incentives to put effort into cost reduction are low. With the liberalisation of network industries that started on a large scale in the UK of Margaret Thatcher in the 1980s, the efficiency of firms in these sectors was considered to be low and substantial efficiency gains were expected. Therefore, the search was for a regulatory scheme that would stimulate efficiency improvements and cost reductions. This search led to the price-based approaches, the idea being to make revenue or price constraints independent of firms' own underlying costs as far as reasonably possible. There are several ways to achieve this. One way is to make an allowed price path exogenous and ex ante for a long time, i.e. to incorporate an exogenous, predetermined and long 'regulatory lag'. Another way would be to rely completely on external factors (such as comparable firms) for price constraint, which leads to benchmarking and yardstick regulation. In either case, efforts to reduce cost lead to increased profits, resulting in strong incentives. Importantly, the strict forms as outlined above only exist on paper; in practice we find only less extreme forms and hybrids, including cost-based approaches with price-based elements and vice versa.

The price-based approach to increasing incentives for efficiency improvements is successful. However, it only works as long as efficiency improvements can reasonably be made. As firms are subject to price-based regulation for a longer time in succession, the potential for improvements decreases. Consequently, the need for a regulatory scheme that relies on setting strong incentives for cost-reductions decreases. More importantly, for a variety of reasons, the incentives for adequate investment may not be strong under price-based approaches. Indeed, it appears that as far as timely and adequate investment is the policy aim (which is not the same as efficient investment), cost-based approaches seem to be more effective than price-based regulation. As a result, the current shift in regulation theory and practice appears to be a shift from pure price-based approaches aiming predominantly at short-run efficiency improvements to inclusion of cost-based elements into price-based regulation to promote investment.

One of the more prominent examples is the introduction of an incentive mechanism with a menu of sliding scales for the promotion of investment in the electricity distribution networks in the UK in 2005. A sliding scale is a mixture of cost-based and price-based regulation. The novelty is the menu; the firms themselves choose the mixture from a set of options designed by the regulator, so that with this, they are themselves choosing the extent to which the regulation they are subject to is cost-based or price-based. The menu is novel in regulation practice, but it is well established in the theoretical literature and can be found in other parts of the economy. In essence, the idea is that if a firm expects that it needs more investment than the regulator expects it will choose a cost-based approach and if the firm's expectations are in line with the regulator's expectations it will tend to opt for a price-based approach. In this way, the regulator avoids frustrating necessary investment, while at the same time keeping regulation effective. This type of incentive mechanism is a promising way forward.

References

Averch, H. & Johnson, L.L. 1962. Behavior of the firm under regulatory constraint. American Economic Review, 52: 1053-1069.

Bawa, V. S. & Sibley, D. S. 1980. Dynamic behaviour of a firm subject to stochastic regulatory review. International Economic Review, 21: 627-642.

Beesley, M. E. & Littlechild, S. C. 1989. The regulation of privatized monopolies in the United Kingdom. Rand Journal of Economics, 20: 454-472.

Borrmann, J. & Finsinger, J. 1999. Markt und Regulierung. München: Vahlen Verlag.

Borrmann, J. & Brunekreeft, G. 2007. Regulation and the timing of monopoly investment. Paper presented at the Infraday, Technical University Berlin.

Bradley, I. & Price, C. 1988. The economic regulation of private industries by price constraints. Journal of Industrial Economics, 37: 99-106.

Brunekreeft, G. 2003. Regulation and competition policy in the electricity market; economic analysis and German experience. Baden-Baden: Nomos.

Brunekreeft, G. & Newbery, D. 2006. Should merchant transmission be subject to a must-offer provision? Journal of Regulatory Economics, 30: 233-260.

Brunekreeft, G. 2008. Ownership unbundling in electricity markets – a social cost benefit analysis of the German TSO's. EPRG Discussion Paper 08-16, University of Cambridge and UNECOM Discussion paper 2008-05.

Cowan, S. 1997. Price-cap regulation and inefficiency in relative pricing. Journal of Regulatory Economics, 12: 53-70.

Finsinger, J. & Kraft, K. 1984. Pricing and firm decisions. Journal of Institutional and Theoretical Economics, 140: 500-509.

Gans, J. S. & King, S. P. 2003. Access holidays for network infrastructure investment. Agenda, 10: 163-178.

Gans, J. S. & King, S. P. 2004. Access holidays and the timing of infrastructure investment. Economic Record, 80: 89-100.

Grout, P. A. & Zalewska, A. 2003. Do regulatory changes affect market risk? Unpublished LIFE Working Paper 03-022, Maastricht University, Maastricht.

Makholm, J. & Quinn, M. 1997. Price cap plans for electricity distribution companies using TFP analysis. Unpublished NERA Working Paper.

Jamasb, T. & Pollitt, M. 2000. Benchmarking and regulation of electricity transmission and distribution utilities: lessons from international experience. Cambridge: Dept. of Applied Economics, University of Cambridge.

Joskow, P. L. 1974. Inflation and environmental concern: structural change in the process of public utility price regulation. Journal of Law and Economics, 17: 291-327.

Joskow, P. L. 1989. Regulatory failure, regulatory reform, and structural change in the electric power industry. Cambridge: Massachusetts Institute of Technology (MIT), Department of Economics.

Joskow, P. L. 2006. Incentive regulation in theory and practice: electricity distribution and transmission networks. Cambridge: MIT Center for Energy and Environmental Policy Research.

Katz, M. L. & Shapiro, C. 1987. R&D rivalry with licensing or imitation. American Economic Review, 77: 402-420.

Laffont, J.-J. & Tirole, J. 1994. A theory of incentives in procurement and regulation. Cambridge: MIT Press.

Littlechild, S. C. 1983. Regulation of British telecommunications' profitability. London: Department of industry.

Lyon, T. P. & Mayo, J. W. 2000. Regulatory opportunism and investment behavior: evidence from the US electric utility industry.

Office of Gas and Electricity Markets (Ofgem). 2004. Electricity distribution price control review; Initial proposals. pp. 90/91. London: Ofgem.

Peltzman, S. 1976. Toward a more general theory of regulation. Journal of Law and Economics, 19: 211-240.

Shleifer, A. 1985. A theory of yardstick competition. Rand Journal of Economics, 16: 319-327.

Spence, A. M. 1975. Monopoly, quality and regulation. Bell Journal of Economics, 6: 417-429.

Vogelsang, I. & Finsinger, J. 1979. A regulatory adjustment process for optimal pricing by multiproduct monopoly firms. Bell Journal of Economics, 10: 157-170.

Wright, S., Mason, R. & Miles, D. 2003. A study into certain aspects of the cost of capital for regulated utilities in the U.K. London: Smithers & Co.

27 Transmission Management and Pricing

Christoph Riechmann[1]

Dan Roberts[2]

Abstract

Transmission system operators (TSOs) face new operational challenges: they need to integrate new generation, such as intermittent wind and embedded generation. They are also expected to enhance interconnectivity with neighbouring operators and countries. TSOs need to optimise their strategies subject to regulatory and market constraints and ensure system reliability while also improving operating and investment efficiency. TSOs which are vertically bundled with generation face a further challenge of vertical separation (unbundling). Their interaction with stakeholders, such as generators, traders and retail suppliers, has to evolve into a market-based or regulated coordination.

In this chapter we outline the tasks of TSOs; the operating environment and key value drivers of transmission operation; possible management actions and tools to inform management decisions; possible organisational responses; and implications for the pricing of transmission services.

Keywords: transmission, unbundling, regulation

---

[1] Dr. Christoph Riechmann is Director at Frontier Economics Ltd., Germany.

[2] Dan Roberts is Associate Director at Frontier Economics Ltd., United Kingdom.

A. Bausch and B. Schwenker (eds.), *Handbook Utility Management,*
DOI: 10.1007/978-3-540-79349-6_27, © Springer-Verlag Berlin Heidelberg 2009

27.1   Introduction – the Tasks of Transmission System Operators

Transmission system operators (TSOs) are responsible for connecting energy production and demand centres and transporting the energy from source to sink in extra-high-voltage or high-pressure systems. Electricity TSOs operate, maintain and expand the extra-high-voltage power systems (typically at voltage levels of 220 kV and above), which are composed of lines and transformer stations. The precise tasks allocated to TSOs vary by jurisdiction. However, across most jurisdictions there are a number of core tasks that a TSO must undertake. One way of categorising these core tasks is shown in Figure 27.1.

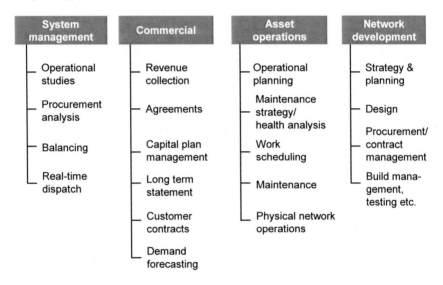

Figure 27.1: TSO tasks (Frontier Economics, 2007)

The tasks vary from those relevant to the short term to those which are more forward looking:

- System management involves activities based on the existing grid leading up to the physical real-time dispatch of the system – directing generation production and network switching. These tasks involve receiving nominations from production and demand connected to the network, undertaking an analysis of the balancing and other ancillary services required and then procuring ancillary and balancing services (including management of congestion through redispatch).
- Commercial tasks involve what could loosely be described as 'market'- or 'customer'-facing activities – including collecting tariffs from system users for their use of the network, managing customer contracts (e.g. for connec-

tions), projecting demand and considering different generation scenarios for the future.

▪ Asset operations involve activities related to maintaining the existing network – gathering the information required to manage the assets effectively and managing the work of the field force undertaking physical network maintenance. There is clearly a strong linkage between asset operations and system management, as when lines or substation assets are out for maintenance it can have a significant effect on the way the system needs to be operated.

▪ Network development involves the extension and reinforcement of the network – undertaking an assessment of need, considering different design options, procuring the work and then project-managing the construction on the ground.

Depending on the jurisdiction in question, there are a number of additional tasks that may be taken on by the TSO:

▪ *Procurement of losses:* Purchasing electricity to replace the cost of electricity lost in the transport system.

▪ *Market operation:* In some countries the transmission operator may also be responsible for organising the electricity wholesale market or it may at least be the major shareholder of a power exchange. This may involve operating the IT systems and processes which support the electricity wholesale market (e.g. nomination of intended generation schedules, calculation of metered output, levying imbalance charges, etc.).

▪ *Data service provision:* Transmission operators may have certain roles in data provision, for example for settlement purposes in the energy wholesale market.

▪ *Wind offtake:* In Germany, for example, transmission operators are obliged to take up and remunerate generation from wind plants. They are further required to resell this power by complementing it with power purchases that smoothen the intermittent production profile of wind generators and sell these bands of power in the wholesale market.

27.2 Value Drivers and External Influences

We first describe the external operating environment of TSOs before highlighting key value drivers within this environment.

27.2.1 External Environment

TSOs must fulfil their remit against the background of a relatively complex external environment. While transmission operation has always been an integral part of energy supply, transmission operators today are facing new and sometimes previously unknown challenges:

- *Globalisation:* In the developed world energy production and demand are increasingly dislocated as indigenous supplies run out and new sources need to be connected. For example, new power stations are often built near sea ports, where it is easier to land imported fuels, while demand centres do not move; historically, demand had moved to the sources of indigenous production, e.g. of coal or gas. Such restructuring of supply relative to demand can increase transportation requirements and creates uncertainty about future transportation patterns.

- *Competition and market integration:* Legal changes at the EU level, for example through the Electricity Directive 2003/54/EC and the Cross-Border Regulation EC 1228/2003, bring about strategic and operational changes:

  - *Investment expectations:* Policy makers expect TSOs to further invest in the network infrastructure in order to reinforce physical and commercial transmission connections between countries, thereby creating wider cross-national markets for energy supply.

  - *Changes in flows and transits:* Wholesale markets are developing across Europe, leading to a requirement for TSOs to participate in activities that could carry a greater level of risk than was previously the case. For example, the closer coupling of markets between European countries is likely to result in greater cross-border flows and the need for greater co-operation between TSOs than previously, in order to ensure that events in one system do not 'cascade' and cause problems across a wide geographic area. In Europe the so-called third EU energy package is aimed at further enhancing cross-border competition and flows, and transits can be expected to change further.

- *Unbundling:* Further market reform is envisaged: the third energy package is clearly a major potential driver of change for all TSOs. At the centrepiece of the new legislation is ownership unbundling. For those TSOs which are currently vertically integrated, this could mean a major transformation from a division within a corporate group to a stand-alone entity, with its own management and shareholders. However, the changes may not stop there: as for TSOs which are already unbundled, ownership unbundling would potentially bring with it new opportunities for consolidation and the development of a supra-national geographic footprint.

- *Environmental pressures:* Policies to address problems of climate change are also a major driver of new activity (and new risks) for TSOs. On one hand, the policy responses relating to climate change (e.g. financial support for renewables and distributed generation) often mean:

  - *Grid extension:* The grid has to be extended to new areas (including offshore) and many new connections managed.

  - *Change in grid utilisation:* The EU uses a 'cap and trade regime' to limit overall emissions. Rights to emit carbon gain a commercial value, and power generators factor in the direct or opportunity cost of carbon when making their plant dispatch decisions. In the short run this leads to structural changes in plant dispatch profiles and flow patterns on the system, which the TSO must manage. In the medium to long run it can lead to early closures of less efficient plants and the construction of new plants, possibly in new locations.

- *Change in grid utilisation:* The EU uses a 'cap and trade regime' to limit overall emissions. Rights to emit carbon gain a commercial value, and power generators factor in the direct or opportunity cost of carbon when making their plant dispatch decisions. In the short run this leads to structural changes in plant dispatch profiles and flow patterns on the system, which the TSO must manage. In the medium to long run it can lead to early closures of less efficient plants and the construction of new plants, possibly in new locations.

- *Underutilisation:* Equally, the reduction in significance of conventional, large-scale thermal generation may mean some transmission assets are used significantly less than previously, with the potential risk of regulatory stranding.

- *Intermittent generation:* Wind energy is seen as a key source of cleaner energy production. Wind generation, however, is strongly contingent on wind availability, and supplies can be highly intermittent. TSOs need to ensure that the system still works even if wind generation is momentarily not available.

- *Generation connections outside TSO control/embedded generation:* Other sources of environmentally friendly supply operate on a small scale and are often connected to local distribution networks. Such production offsets demand from the central transmission grid while being outside the direct control of the transmission operator.

- *Revenue regulation:* Legal changes also imply new approaches to regulation of the operation of transmission operators, which often constitute natural monopolies. Relevant developments relate to:

  - *How revenues are capped and prices are set for the regulated services:* Regulators are typically moving away from 'cost plus' regulation to forms of regulation which provide more of a financial incentive for operational efficiency. These may include the RPI-X style incentives (as used in the UK market since the early 1990s) and also the establishment of 'efficient' levels of cost through benchmarking (see e.g. the ARegV Decree [Anreizregulierungsverordnung] in Germany).

  - *Which services are provided under a regulatory and which under a competition regime:* These regulatory changes can also affect how the capital markets judge investments and whole corporate entities.

  - *What incentive gearing is applied to regulated activities:* Regulators may increasingly be looking to expand the scope of activities for which TSOs take financial responsibility. For example, in the UK market the TSO has been incentivised to manage the cost of congestion for many

years. Similar arrangements are under discussion now in the German
market, in order to incentivise network investment and operational efficiency.

- *Technological developments:* These are driving new opportunities for efficiency; it is now economically more feasible (particularly for new assets) to
  deploy many more asset-monitoring devices from which information on the
  status of critical components can be collected remotely (e.g. using GPRS or
  power line carrier technology). This can remove the need for intrusive inspection of assets, which in turn increases their availability and reduces the
  risk of the inspection process resulting in component failures. The mass rollout of such assets has yet to occur. However, their deployment for new assets
  is more common, and by making more data available, makes the asset operation tasks of the TSO more complex.
- *Pressures from capital markets:* These are also driving the pace of change,
  with increasing levels of interest being shown for infrastructure asset classes.
  In particular, the growth in significance of financial investors (private equity
  operations or infrastructure funds) has increased the pressure on TSOs to ensure that attention is paid both to operational efficiency and to efficiency of
  financing.

TSOs need to respond with new business models and business tools to these
new challenges. This chapter gives an overview of possible approaches.

27.2.2   Value Drivers

Within this environment of external change, the value drivers for TSOs are relatively clear. Within a mature regulatory framework, TSOs typically drive value for
their shareholders through a relatively small number of routes:

- Financing activities efficiently, and in particular ensuring that their actual
  weighted average cost of capital is below that allowed by the regulator.
- Managing operations efficiently, in order to equal or beat peer performance –
  this should help to ensure that outturn operating costs are below those foreseen by the regulator, and that in future price controls, regulators set achievable operational targets.
- Managing market risks, where they exist as a result of the regulatory regime,
  in order to ensure that market exposures add to shareholder value without
  creating unacceptable risks for a company whose return will continue to be
  dominated by low-risk network activities.
- Securing quality of supply, in order to ensure that customers, regulators and
  governments (within the jurisdiction and, if growth strategies are being considered, in other jurisdictions) continue to trust the TSO to operate critical
  national infrastructure.
- Leveraging management capability and economies of scale, in order to secure value-enhancing growth. This may come through growing the network

asset base organically (i.e. managing a bigger national network), diversifying into other related activities (e.g. merchant interconnector development) or acquiring other network businesses (e.g. other TSOs, distribution operators, gas networks, etc.).

It is perhaps not surprising for a natural monopoly activity that the majority of these value drivers relate, in one way or another, to the ability to shape the regulatory agenda and secure the right regulatory deals. Effective regulatory management is clearly at the core of value creation for a regulated utility.

27.3   Management

For TSO management, therefore, the key challenges to ensure that all activity is effectively targeted towards value creation are understanding:

- How individual activities and capabilities map to these value drivers.
- The relative strength of each of the value drivers, and hence the prioritisation of effort and management focus among them.
- The tensions between the value drivers, and hence the relevant considerations when particular decisions are being considered.

Some examples of the possible questions facing management structures may make this more concrete.

27.3.1   Mapping of Activities and Capabilities to Value Drivers

We have described above the tasks which typically fall within the remit of a TSO. However, TSO management teams need to understand the linkage between the way in which these activities are undertaken, the capabilities built within the organisation, and these value drivers.

For example, as we have already indicated, the way in which network planning and maintenance are undertaken can have a major impact on congestion management and balancing costs, and hence on the performance of the TSO in relation to areas of market risk exposure. Understanding this interaction and the ways in which the two activities can more effectively be undertaken is important.

Similarly, many TSOs undertake significant work in relation to understanding new technologies – remote asset monitoring devices may be one such example, but there are many others. Understanding how the further development and eventual rollout of these technologies will impact on value drivers is clearly important.

27.3.2   Prioritisation Among Value Levers

Traditional TSO management structures come from a utility background – and management may therefore tend to focus on operational factors and on ensuring efficient and effective operation. Few would dispute the importance of this. However, any management team has limited resources, and a focus on operational effectiveness must come at the expense of less focus on other aspects of the business. An analysis of the source of earnings of network businesses in mature markets reveals that, in addition to having a bearing on operating costs, efficient financing can be as important a contributor to total earnings: Table 27.1 shows the extent to which recent utility transactions have been geared up, in particular by purchasers with a financial background. These gearing rates are significantly above those maintained by TSOs, which have until recently been subjected to relatively loose competitive and regulatory pressures.

Therefore, if focus on operating costs 'crowds out' consideration of an effective financial structure, value will be sacrificed.

Table 27.1: Levels of gearing seen in recent utility transactions (analyst, bank and frontier estimates)

Target	Acquirer(s)	Gearing (debt/ enterprise value)	Gearing (debt/RAV*)
Thames Water	Macquarie consortium	Approx. 75%	Approx. 90%
Wales & West Gas Network	Macquarie consortium	Approx. 75%	Approx. 85%
Anglian Water	3i consortium	Approx. 70%	Approx. 85%
Scottish & Southern Gas Networks	SSE consortium	Approx. 65%	Approx. 75%
BAA	Ferrovial consortium	Approx. 65%	Not available
Northern Gas Networks	United Utilities consortium	Approx. 60%	Approx. 70%

* Note: RAV – regulated asset value

27.3.3   Tensions Between Value Levers

As well as ensuring an appropriate prioritisation and focus across different value levers, it is also important to understand and manage the tensions between them. For example, there are likely to be tensions between:

- Managing operations efficiently;
- Securing quality of supply; and
- Leveraging management capability and economies of scale.

While a very-low-cost operation may not jeopardise security of supply, it is likely that it will deliver less in relation to some of the 'softer' measures of customer service than other utilities. This may have the result that regulators and governments perceive the utility as a low-quality operation. This may impact on the utility both within national boundaries (e.g. it may do less well in relation to customer service incentive schemes) and in other jurisdictions (where regulators may not see the management team as natural partners in ensuring high-quality customer service).

Such tensions will always exist between value drivers – the important thing is that they are considered by the TSO management and that decisions are taken with a full understanding of the different impacts they can have throughout current and potential business activities. Otherwise, a drive towards 'best in class' operating cost levels could have a short-term payoff, but could result in a long-term downturn in the growth opportunities faced by the utility.

TSO management teams also face challenges in relation to potential changes to organisational structures, which we address next.

27.4   Organisation of Transmission Operations

The organisation of TSOs, together with the third energy package, is very much a hot topic of debate in Europe. The immediate debate triggered by the legislative proposal relates to the ownership separation of national transmission networks from vertically integrated businesses. However, in many ways, this begs further questions in relation to TSO structure (Frontier Economics, 2007):

- Whether the alternative structural models – e.g. the so-called independent system operator (ISO) – proposed by the EC make sense;
- Whether the focus on national unbundling is appropriate.

27.4.1   What is in an Independent System Operator?

The ownership unbundling solution has been proposed as one possible model to be adopted in Europe, the alternative being an ISO. In an ISO model a vertically integrated company may retain ownership of the grid, although different activities may be subjected to an independent system management to avoid the potential risk of the system operator not treating his related generation branch and third-party generators in a nondiscriminatory manner.

The EC in their recent proposal have defined a relatively 'thick' ISO taking on, practically speaking, all activities save asset ownership. This is a model with no significant precedent internationally – where ISOs have been implemented, they have typically been thinner (see Figures 27.2-27.4).

ISOs in other jurisdictions tend not to take on tasks involving major elements of controllable operating costs, as their usual not-for-profit status makes it relatively difficult to hold them financially responsible for their actions. If the entity responsible for all network maintenance cannot be held financially responsible for the costs involved, this may result in a significant additional cost to the consumer; the management team will not have strong incentives for operational efficiency and, in addition, may perceive significant personal cost associated with reputational damage resulting from power interruptions. This may drive up the operating costs of European grids substantially.

Such concerns typically drive policy makers to minimise the scope of the ISO, subject to meeting concerns regarding ensuring nondiscriminatory access to the network. At least from this perspective, the choice of a very thick ISO model – and the failure to consider alternative models in the impact assessment accompanying the legislation – may be unwise if we assume the intention was not to make it deliberately unattractive to national policy makers.

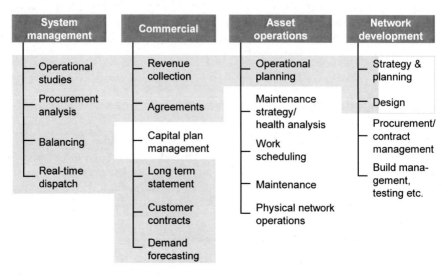

Figure 27.2: Scope of GB system operator (Frontier Economics, 2007)

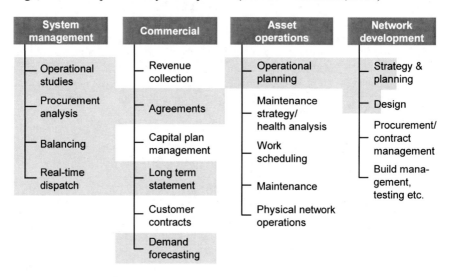

Figure 27.3: Scope of Australian system operator (Frontier Economics, 2007)

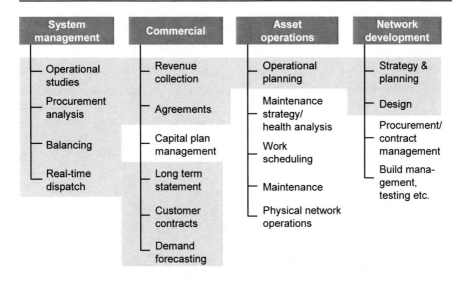

Figure 27.4: Typical scope of US regional system operator (Frontier Economics, 2007)

27.4.2 Geographic Footprints

Within national industry reform programmes, the objectives of unbundling have typically been related to discrimination, with unbundling being seen as a structure remedy for the risk that the natural monopoly network owner might discriminate in favour of affiliated competitive businesses.

However, within the European context there are other issues facing the sector, which arguably should influence considerations around structural changes. Perhaps the two most significant of these are:

- The need for new transmission investment, in the light of the need for new generation sources, particularly given that the efficient locations for renewables generation are unlikely to be the same as those historically chosen for conventional plant;
- The need for cross-border market integration, to improve the competitiveness of European markets and to reduce the impact of horizontal concentration.

Conceptually, ownership unbundling can ensure nondiscrimination and remove disincentives in relation to network investment. However, as a solution it is not well targeted to meet the other requirements; in particular, if the goal is a single European market, further regulatory effort is likely to be required to ensure active promotion of regional investment and regional market integration. There is no reason to assume that nationally unbundled TSOs (operating within national regulatory regimes) will be more likely to deliver international integration.

While this debate is new to Europe, it is not new internationally: indeed, the drive to the formation of Regional Transmission Organizations (RTOs) in the US (see Figure 27.5 and Table 27.2) came, in part, from the recognition that at the wholesale level at least, highly geographically focused solutions may not be the best answer.

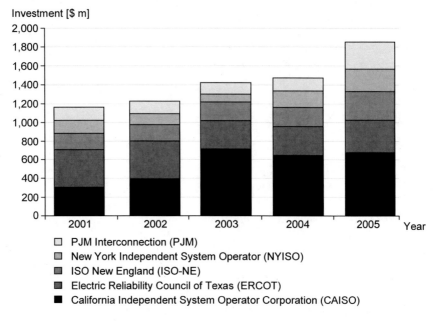

Figure 27.5: RTO investment track record (excluding public utilities and co-ops) (Global Energy Decisions, 2007)

The experience of RTOs in the US demonstrates that the model is not necessarily perfect. There are examples of success, and also examples of RTOs that have been less successful. However, there is evidence to suggest that, at least in terms of delivering transmission investment, RTOs have been successful. They have also – almost by default – been successful at integrating individual state wholesale markets across their defined regions.

Against this background, it is interesting that the EC has pursued policies related solely to national unbundling, rather than attempting to encourage (or require) the development of much stronger horizontal integration.

Table 27.2: Level of wholesale market integration (PJM Interconnection (PJM), New York Independent System Operator (NYISO), Midwest Independent Transmission System Operator (MISO) and ISO New England (ISO-NE) websites; FERC, 2006)

	PJM	NYISO	MISO	ISO-NE
Common approach to price formation?	Yes. Through a day-ahead and real-time market which determines locational marginal prices (LMPs).			
Common approach to determining available transmission capacities?	Yes. Total transfer capability (TTC) and available transfer capability (ATC) calculations consistent with NERC and FERC standards. ATC scheduled through OASIS.			
Common approach to congestion management?	Yes. Consistent with open access transmission tariff (OATT). Congestion determined through LMP levels.	Yes. Zonal congestion determined through LMP levels.	Yes. Consistent with OATT. Uses financial transmission rights (FTRs) to hedge congestion charges.	Yes. Consistent with OATT. Congestion determined through LMP levels.
Common schedule nomination/operational studies/dispatch process?	Yes. Process developed on the basis of the least-cost dispatch.	Yes. Regional process developed on the basis of the least-cost dispatch.	Yes. Process developed on the basis of the least-cost dispatch.	Yes. Process developed on the basis of the least-cost dispatch.
Common ancillary services procurement?	Yes. Procures regulation, synchronised reserve and black start service.	Yes. Procures voltage support, regulation and black start service.	Yes. Proposed ancillary services market.	Yes. Procures operating reserves through a real-time and forward market.
Common contracts for wholesale market?	Yes. Through RTO operating agreement.			

27.4.3   The Road to Mergers and Acquisitions?

The final question, which is on the lips of many industrial players and their financial advisors, is whether the new legislation is likely to lead to a new wave of consolidation in the industry. Particularly in relation to the German and Austrian grid companies, forced ownership unbundling would result in around eight companies being required to divest assets with an embedded value (EV) of more than € 1 billion.

A new wave of mergers and acquisitions (M&A) in the networks segment of the value chain could happen in one of two ways:

- Network assets are unbundled from vertically integrated companies and subsequently acquired by existing and acquisitive network companies, or by infrastructure funds; Gasunie's recent acquisition of BEB's network assets in Germany could mark the start of a period of positioning to acquire central European transmission assets; or
- Network assets are jointly divested from several vertically integrated companies into new 'national transmission champions', which then themselves act as consolidators for remaining grid opportunities.

In the event that unbundling is forced (i.e. if the legislation is passed in a largely unchanged form and countries do not adopt the thick ISO model), then either seems a plausible outcome. While it would not be appropriate for European policy to rely on this as an outcome (as it is beyond the control of policymakers), such a development may go some way towards addressing some of the regional investment and integration problems highlighted above.

However, it would also bring new questions and challenges for regulators:

- How to allocate costs and benefits of co-ordination and investment across countries;
- Loss of comparator data for purposes of tariff regulation, if operations are merged;
- Need for harmonising cross-country regulation approaches, etc.

27.5   Transmission System Operator Revenues and Pricing

TSO management teams are also facing pressure to develop and refine their market-facing activities. This includes a range of things, such as improving the efficiency with which they balance the system and the way in which they organise access to their system. A key issue in relation to this last point is pricing, and the sophistication (or, some may argue, complexity) of approaches taken to network pricing vary significantly across Europe at present. The first step in pricing is to understand TSO revenue requirements. We therefore next explain the revenue streams that accrue to a TSO and how tariffs are set to achieve this revenue.

27.5.1   Revenue Streams

TSOs receive revenue streams from a number of sources:

- *Connections:* They charge for the connection of power stations or lower voltage networks to their grid. Connection charges are often determined on a cost plus basis.

- *Network tariffs:* They charge for the use of their infrastructure. As TSOs exhibit characteristics of natural monopoly, they do not face competition from other network operators but their revenues and tariffs are subjected to regulatory oversight. We explore below what this implies for tariff setting.
- *Congestion revenues:* On cross-border interconnectors that exhibit regular congestions, the capacity has to be auctioned off under EU regulations and the auction revenue typically falls to the TSO. We discuss options for such auctions below (Consentec & Frontier Economics, 2004). Under EU rules congestion revenues have to be used (a) to make operational payments that secure the availability of the interconnector, (b) to fund investments into the extension of interconnector or (c) to reduce domestic use of system charges.
- *Inter-TSO compensation:* The EU has additionally imposed a scheme under which TSOs make each other compensating payments for 'hosting' flows that result from trading or retail transactions in relation to which they do not receive use of system charges because neither the generators nor the respective loads are connected to their system (Consentec & Frontier Economics, 2006; ERGEG, 2006).

27.5.2 Use of System Tariffs

TSOs' regulated tariffs must typically be set to comply with a number of principles:

- *Cost recovery:* They should typically be set at a level that allows a normally efficient operator to recover his operating and capital expenditure (including a fair return on the cost of equity). This cost will include the cost of system control and the procurement of ancillary services. Frequently the level of allowed revenue is determined after netting off additional revenues from congestion rents or Inter-TSO Compensation payments. Tariffs should not be set lower than this, in order to sustain incentives for further investment, and they should not exceed this level, in order to avoid network users being overcharged.
- *Price signals:* Sometimes tariffs must further be set in such a way that they induce an efficient use of the system. Such signals may relate to:
    - *Topology of the system:* For example, the UK TSO, National Grid, applies a tariff scheme where both generators and loads pay use-of-system charges. Both types of charges are regionally differentiated to reflect the long-run incremental cost of expanding the system. Generator charges will tend to be high in regions with a generation surplus and low where there is a deficit. Demand charges will be high in regions with a generation deficit and low in regions with a generation surplus. Many other countries do not put any great weight on such price signals (except for congested interconnectors, where capacity rights are auctioned and a market price for capacity is established) and apply nation-

ally uniform tariffs. Sometimes the use of system tariff is levied only on loads but not on generators.

- *User profile:* TSOs can apply a mix of fixed or load-related charges (per megawatt) and volumetric charges (per megawatt-hour). Given that the largest part of the cost is related to the network infrastructure and this infrastructure is dimensioned to facilitate maximum demand, TSOs tend to recover their costs mainly through load-related (and connection) charges. Some variable charge may be applied, e.g. to cover the cost of losses, which depend mainly on energy throughput rather than peak demand. Such pricing principles imply that a network user with a constant load profile (e.g. a chemical firm) will pay a lower price per megawatt-hour consumed than a customer group such as households with a more varied demand profile.

- *Government influence:* As the transmission grid is technically difficult to bypass, policy makers also sometimes impose additional levies on transmission charges, e.g. to fund subsidies to wind generators or producers that use other sources that are deemed environmentally friendly.

27.5.3 Capacity Auctions

An alternative way of establishing a price for transmission capacity is through auctions of capacity rights. These are frequently applied to transmission interconnectors that link two different transmission systems across national borders. Auctions are the prescribed mode (through Regulation EC 1228/2003) of allocating scarce cross-border capacity in the EU. Different auction approaches are admissible (Frontier Economics et al., 2006; Consentec & Frontier Economics, 2004):

- *Explicit auctions:* Network users explicitly have to buy capacity rights in order to ship power from one country to the next. A cross-border energy transaction would therefore involve a number of market-based transactions: the purchase/generation of power in country A, the transfer of power from country A to country B based on a purchased capacity right, and the sale of power in country B.
- *Implicit auctions:* Implicit capacity auctions are arranged between power exchanges, allowing them to match and clear trades across national borders. All participants in power exchanges implicitly participate in the use of the capacity rights administered through the power exchanges. The congestion rent, which is the energy price differential between the purchase price of power in the low-price country and the sale price of power in the high-price country, will eventually accrue to the network operators involved. TSOs in North-West Europe (Germany, Netherlands, Belgium, France and Luxemburg) are currently preparing for a multicountry coupling of power exchanges through implicit auctions.
- *Hybrid auctions:* In this model, implicit and explicit auction overlay each other. For example, explicit auctions may be used for the allocation of year-

ahead and month-ahead capacity while implicit auctions are used to clear day-ahead or intraday capacities.

27.6   Management Information

The dramatic structural and regulatory changes that have taken place in network industries require updating or redesign of the management information systems and analysis tools used for investment appraisal (Frontier Economics & Consentec, 2002).

27.6.1   New Challenges for Information Systems

For the purpose of operational planning, the traditional approach has been to start by subjecting the existing system and possibly also investment plans to engineering-based simulations and then to check whether reliability could be ensured even in worst-case scenarios. The operator would then decide whether reinforcements of the network were needed and possibly select the investment plan with the lowest apparent cost from among those plans that passed the technical tests. The new planning environment requires an approach that integrates engineering, regulatory and commercial analysis. The framework must be capable of allowing the return on investment to be fully analysed. Four types of performance measure need be brought together in the integrated model:

- *Revenue:* Revenues may change through adjustments of regulated network charges (possibly including charges for the procurement of ancillary services or losses) and revenues from capacity auctions. A detailed analysis of the link between costs and revenue is needed.
- *Cost:* Operating expenditure has to be assessed in a way that takes account of the physical structure of the network and the market environment, leading to projections that account for the expected evolution of demand, electricity wholesale prices, and so forth. Such analysis necessarily requires a link between engineering-based and financial modelling.
- *Risk:* The traditional approach to analysis of rates of return, built around worst-case scenarios, has to give way to analysis based on realistic scenarios with respect to demand (load) and generation developments. Associating a probability with each scenario allows a proper risk analysis to be developed.
- *Service quality:* In addition to (or instead of) quality criteria that the network operator defines from a technical perspective, e.g. the n-1 capacity reserve target, network operators need to approach quality standards from the customer's perspective. Such standards could, for example, be based on the number or average duration of interruptions. The operator then has to establish the relationship between these quality measures, costs and revenue.

27.6.2   A Possible Approach to the Challenge

Integrating engineering-based and financial tools allows the approach we have described to be implemented. Simulations can be built up from three modules, each of which must be calibrated to the particular circumstances of the network operator concerned (see Figure 27.6).

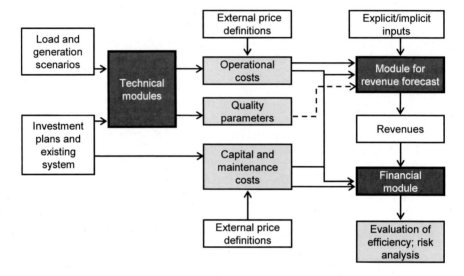

Figure 27.6: Architecture for combining engineering-based and financial analysis for TSOs (Frontier Economics & Consentec, 2002)

- An engineering module simulates trade interaction on the network and the resulting power flows, based on load and generation scenarios. This module also produces an estimate of operating expenditure and network service quality parameters.
- The revenue forecasting module projects the likely revenue stream over time. This revenue stream is based on capital cost calculations, the estimates of operational expenditure derived from the engineering module and revenue adjustments for quality, taking into account the tariff and other rules set by the regulator. This module also serves to analyse the exposure the operator may have to regulatory risk.
- The financial module draws together revenue and cost information, transforms it into cash-flow information, and finally facilitates the financial appraisal of the investment.

27.7 Summary

We can summarise:

- *Challenges:* TSOs today face new operational challenges as they need to integrate new generation technologies into their systems, such as intermittent wind and embedded generation.
- *Constraints:* TSOs need to develop their business strategies subject to a host of constraints uncommon in many other industries. For example they need to optimise operation subject to regulatory and market constraints, to ensure system reliability while improving operating and investment efficiency.
- *Unbundling:* TSOs that are vertically bundled with generation face a further challenge of vertical separation. Their interaction with stakeholders such as generators, traders or retail suppliers has to evolve into a market-based or regulated coordination.
- *Holistic view:* All this implies that TSOs, much more than distribution network operators, need to take a holistic view of their infrastructure and its interaction with wider developments in the generation, trading and retail markets.

References

Anreizregulierungsverordnung (ARegV). 2007. Verordnung über die Anreizregulierung der Energieversorgungsnetze. Bundesgesetzblatt, 1, 55.

Consentec & Frontier Economics. 2004. Analysis of cross-border congestion management methods for the EU internal electricity market. Study commissioned by the European Commission, Directorate-General Energy and Transport. Aachen/London: Consentec/Frontier Economics.

Consentec & Frontier Economics. 2006. Study into further issues relating to the inter-TSO compensation mechanism report prepared for the European Commission, 13 February 2006.

Directive 2003/54/EC. 2003. Directive of the European Parliament and of the Council of 26 June 2003 concerning common rules for the internal market in electricity and repealing Directive 96/92/EC – Statements made with regard to decommissioning and waste management activities.

European Regulators' Group for Electricity and Gas (ERGEG). 2006. ERGEG draft proposal on guidelines on inter-TSO compensation (E06-CBT-09-08). Brussels: Council of European Energy Regulators.

Federal Energy Regulatory Commission (FERC). 2006. RTO-ISO – PJM handbook. Washington: FERC.

Frontier Economics & Consentec. 2002. From engineering to economics – employing simulation tools to appraise network investments. London: Frontier Economics Bulletin.

Frontier Economics, Consentec & Institut für Elektrische Anlagen und Energiewirtschaft der RWTH Aachen (IAEW). 2006. Economic assessment of different congestion management methods. London/Aachen: German Federal Network Agency.

Frontier Economics. 2007. Going their separate ways – next steps for Europe's energy sector. London: Frontier Economics Bulletin.

Regulation (EC) No 1228/2003. 2003. Regulation of the European Parliament and of the Council of 26 June 2003 on conditions for access to the network for cross-border exchanges in electricity. Official Journal of the European Union, 176: 1.

28 The New Entry-exit Model in the EU and Its Consequences for Gas Supply Companies

Christian Hewicker[1]

Stefanie Kesting[2]

Abstract

The entry-exit network access model has become standard in European gas transmission networks. It allows shippers to book capacity rights independently at entry and exit points. Compared to the former common distance or path-dependent point-to-point regimes, this model represents a general improvement towards more flexibility for shippers, system transparency and cost-reflective network tariffs. Nevertheless, efficient capacity management remains crucial to the avoidance of contractual congestion that could minimize the flexibility of the entry-exit system. Furthermore, fair balancing rules are necessary to enable entirely non-discriminatory network access. This chapter explains the characteristics, limitations and implications of the entry-exit model.

Keywords: gas network access, entry-exit, gas network capacities

[1] Christian Hewicker is Managing Consultant and Head of Markets and Regulation at KEMA Consulting GmbH, Bonn, Germany.

[2] Dr. Stefanie Kesting is Senior Consultant at KEMA Consulting GmbH, Bonn, Germany.

A. Bausch and B. Schwenker (eds.), *Handbook Utility Management,*
DOI: 10.1007/978-3-540-79349-6_28, © Springer-Verlag Berlin Heidelberg 2009

28.1   Introduction

The introduction of the entry-exit model for the majority of gas transmission networks in Europe reflects the conviction that this model will best serve the objective to further strengthen the conditions to create a (more) competitive gas market. In this context network access is a precondition to enable competition, which is in turn the major objective of liberalization. Accordingly, the EU Gas Directive 2003/55/EG defines that "for competition to function, network access must be non-discriminatory, transparent and fairly priced".
More specifically, this means that at the same time:

- Access for shippers to network capacities shall be open and unhindered, i.e., provide as much flexibility as is technically feasible;
- Capacity tariffs shall be fair, objective and transparent to the network users, i.e., ideally cost-reflective.

The following Section 28.2 briefly summarizes the main components of a functioning network access regime. Section 28.3 describes the three network access models that are of practical relevance in the gas market, i.e., the point-to-point, entry-exit and postage stamp models. Section 28.4 explains the rationale for choosing the entry-exit as the common standard in Europe. Section 28.5 describes the consequences for gas supply companies, and Section 28.6 summarizes important conclusions.

28.2   Network Access in the Liberalized Gas Market

28.2.1   Structure of the Liberalized Gas Market

The European gas industry is still in the process of being reformed, whereby the move from vertically integrated supply companies covering production, import, trading, transportation (transmission and distribution), storage and sales to the final customer, towards unbundled networks represented a particular paradigm shift. As illustrated by Figure 28.1, transmission and distribution activities are separated from the rest of the value chain in a liberalized gas market, and access to these 'essential facilities'[3] shall be offered to all market participants under equal conditions.

---

[3] The economic concept of 'essential facilities' considers that access to scarce resources or – in the case of network industries – access to a certain infrastructure is a precondition for entering or staying in a market. It is of special relevance in markets where one single incumbent owns (or at least operates) the essential facilities that competitors are dependent on in running their business. Compare examples, e.g., in: Carlton, Perloff (1994): Modern industrial organisation, pp. 831-832 or the so-called 'essential facilities doctrine' that was first established in the U.S. antitrust law.

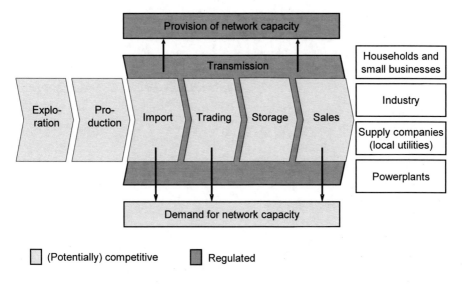

Figure 28.1: Value chain in the liberalized gas market

This implies network access arrangements that are non-discriminatory for new and/or small supply companies in comparison to the (formerly integrated) incumbent supplier. Consequently, the formerly integrated transmission and distribution system operators become providers of network capacity to 'all' current or potential market players whose business depends on access to the transportation infrastructure. These 'shippers' can be importers, wholesale traders or suppliers of final customers and need to have access to the network to ensure transport of their own gas to their customers.

The providers of gas transportation infrastructure usually remain (regional) monopolies even in a liberalized world because the cost structure of gas networks is normally 'sub-additive'. This means that one single company can provide the transportation service more economically than in the case of several different companies, i.e., the network business is a so-called natural monopoly and is thus price-regulated.[4]

28.2.2 Components of a Network Access Regime

The extent to which network access is really non-discriminatory depends on the design choice in three basic areas, i.e., the general model for network access, the

---

[4] The existence of a monopoly implies several problems: because of absent competitors, the monopolist is able to determine the price for capacity and may set this above the actual cost. In addition, the lack of competition leads to missing incentives to cost reduction or efficiency increase. In order to compensate for these disadvantages while keeping the monopoly in networks, network tariffs are regulated. Compare for background on the theory of natural monopolies, e.g., Sharkey (1982), pp. 62-83.

procedures of capacity and congestion management, and the balancing regime. The major determinants and options for these three areas, which are shown in Figure 28.2, are decisive for an entirely fair access regime and are briefly described in the following section.

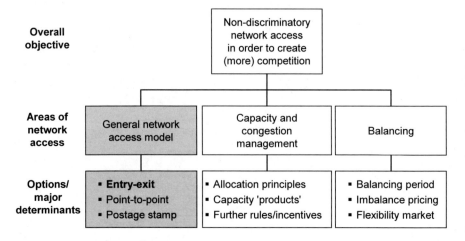

Figure 28.2: Role of entry-exit model for non-discriminatory network access

Firstly, the general network access model determines the basic principles of how capacity is allocated and priced. The three models that are practically relevant for gas markets are the entry-exit, the point-to-point and the postage stamp model. These are explained in Section 28.3.

Secondly, the rules of capacity and congestion management are decisive for an efficient use of limited physical capacities in the network. The choice of corresponding mechanisms may have a significant impact on the (contractual) availability of capacities, and thus the emergence or avoidance of contractual congestion.[5] The availability of capacities can be strongly influenced by the allocation principles, the definition of 'capacity products' and further rules or incentives to ensure an efficient use of the network by supply companies. Capacity allocation can follow different principles, such as first come first served (fcfs), auctions or pro rata, i.e., in proportion to the requested capacity in case of excess capacity demand. Typical capacity products in gas markets are firm versus interruptible capacities, different durations ranging from end-of-day to multi-annual capacities, or specific portfolios, e.g., short haul or back haul capacities that aim at taking into account the impact of a certain portfolio on the overall availability of capacities in the network. Further rules may aim at incentives against hoarding and at reasonable booking practices. As an example, the use-it-or-lose-it principle (UIOLI) defines that shippers lose unused capacities without any financial recovery.

---

[5] Congestion can be contractual or physical. Whereas in the case of physical congestion, the network or point is (almost) fully used over a longer period, a contractual congestion means that the network or point is fully booked, but not actually used 100%.

The balancing regime represents the third fundamental element of a network access regime. Important decisions here are the length of the balancing period (daily or hourly), the application of tolerances, the way in which imbalances are cashed out (single or dual imbalance prices), and the costs and means for procuring balancing gas. The latter is connected to the question to what extent the imbalance prices for shippers can be derived from a market-based mechanism (based upon marginal or average cost of this market) instead of being indexed to other short-term gas prices.

In Figure 28.2 above, we have highlighted the general network access model, or more specifically the entry-exit model, because the choice of the network access model can be seen as the basic decision among the three main components. To clarify why entry-exit has become standard for gas transmission network access in Europe, we will now describe each of the access models in more detail.

28.3   Network Access Models in the Gas Market

28.3.1   Overview

A network access model defines both the basic definition of transport capacity and the main principles of capacity pricing. As previously mentioned, three basic models for network access can be identified: the point-to-point, the entry-exit and the postage stamp model. Although other schemes have been used or proposed over time, these can typically be understood as a special implementation of one of these basic models such that it is sufficient to limit the discussion to the three main approaches.[6]

Table 28.1: Relevant network access models in the EU gas market

Network access model	Capacity allocation	Capacity pricing
Point-to-point	Transportation distance/path	Distance-based
Entry-exit	Separately for entry and exit points	Independent of distance
Postage stamp	At points within a 'postal zone'	Independent of distance/zonal

In the following we therefore focus on the point-to-point, entry-exit and postage stamp models. Table 28.1 summarizes the basic principles of capacity allocation and pricing for each of the three models which are then described in more detail.

---

[6] For instance, Cerbe (2004), pp. 458-459 mentions a pure exit model where shippers need to contract for exit but not for entry capacities; this can be understood as a special case of the entry-exit model. Similarly, several German gas transport companies initially used a so-called 'point model' where tariffs were calculated with the help of a scoring system for different pipeline sections, which obviously corresponds to the definition of point-to-point systems.

28.3.2 Point-to-point Model

In a point-to-point system, shippers do not only have to specify the points where they want to inject and withdraw their gas, but at least in the case of different possible routes, also the transportation path. This is why it is also known as the contract-path model. In the point-to-point logic the tariffs are basically distance-related, i.e., the price for capacity increases with the distance between entry and exit, alongside the contracted transportation path.

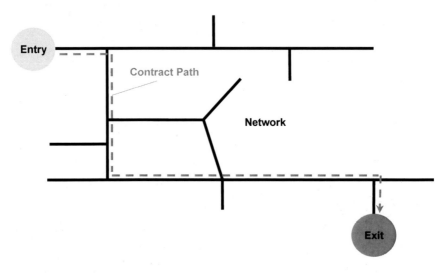

Figure 28.3: Point-to-point model

The example in Figure 28.3 shows that the contracted path is not necessarily the only option to bring the shipper's gas from the defined entry to the defined exit point, i.e., the actual flow can differ from the contracted path. In some cases, the contractual flow may even be in the opposite direction to the actual physical flow, which illustrates that point-to-point models do not necessarily reflect actual costs. The second major disadvantage of the point-to-point model relates to the fact that it is transaction based. This means that entry and exit capacities cannot be separated from each other or from the commodity transaction (gas supply), which represents a major barrier for the development of a liquid market. As a result, this model does not allow for any flexibility. Shippers are obliged to use the predefined entry and exit locations and only in combination with each other, i.e., the contracted transportation path cannot be changed.

28.3.3 Entry-exit Model

Under the entry-exit model, which corresponds to the point-of-connection model in the electricity sector, shippers can book entry and exit capacity independently from each other, without the need to specify the transportation distance or path. The independence of entry and exit capacities is enabled by a virtual trading point, where shippers who booked entry capacity (producers and importers) can sell gas, and shippers who booked exit capacities (suppliers of end customers) can buy it.

In pure entry-exit models, the booked capacities can be flexibly combined within the relevant entry-exit zone,[7] as long as the entry and exit nominations do not exceed the capacities that the shipper has booked at the respective points before.[8] In contrast to the point-to-point system, the entry-exit model is thus largely transaction-independent. After concluding independent contracts for entry and exit capacities, the shipper is usually free to use the booked capacity, independently from other commodity or capacity transactions.

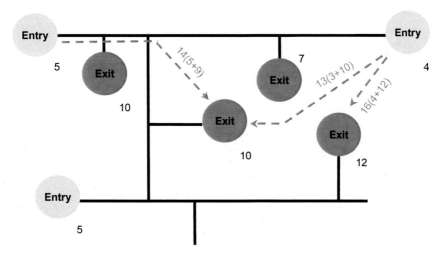

Figure 28.4: Entry-exit model

To enable this flexibility, all possible combinations within the entry-exit zone have to result in technically feasible outcomes and this imposes certain limits on the definition of network zones. This means that persistent congestion should not exist within a network zone. However, where full flexibility is not possible, it may still be more beneficial to allow for certain limitations instead of splitting the area into two or more zones. More specifically, this can be achieved either by finding network users that agree on corresponding restrictions on a voluntary basis (possi-

---

[7] Shippers first book capacities, and then nominate the actual flow for the gas day at short notice, usually 14:00 h on the day before the actual gas flow. Afterwards they can usually still re-nominate (parts of) their nominated capacities up to a defined point of time prior to the gas flow.

[8] The entry-exit zone is also the relevant balancing zone in which the aggregated entry and exit volumes transported are compared to determine the chargeable difference (imbalance) within the relevant balancing period (e.g., daily as in the United Kingdom, France and Germany as of October 2008 or hourly as in Austria or the Netherlands).

bly against payment), or by limiting the flexibility of specific entry and/or exit points, similar to the point-to-point model.

In contrast to distance-dependent point-to-point tariffs, entry and exit tariffs are set individually for each entry and exit point. Once a shipper has concluded an entry or exit point, it is thus principally allowed to transport gas through any number of networks or network levels within the corresponding network zone, without incurring additional costs. For this purpose, all network operators concerned have to cooperate with each other and allocate costs to ensure that tariffs are cost-reflective. Moreover, tariffs should ideally reflect the technical and economic conditions at each specific point and signal the costs of capacity extension that might be required in order to eliminate physical congestion. As a consequence, tariffs will generally be different at different points, as Figure 28.4 depicts.

28.3.4 Postage Stamp Method

This model is the simplest amongst the network access models.[9] It defines the entire network as a zone in which the shippers are free to choose the points where they inject or withdraw gas and where one single tariff, the 'postage stamp', is applied to all exit points and includes all costs of the network: capacity, transportation costs and, possibly, also the costs of other system services. In Figure 28.5 the tariff is equal to 8 monetary units per volume or energy unit per hour per year.

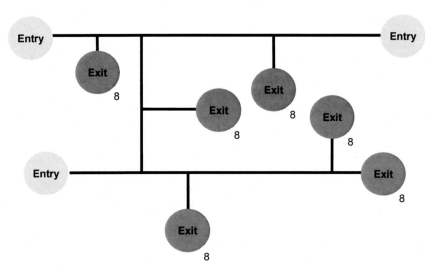

Figure 28.5: Postage stamp model

---

[9] Strictly speaking, the postage stamp method represents a special case of the entry-exit model with an entry tariff of zero and the same tariff applied to all exit points.

Postage stamp tariffs are independent from the transportation distance and transactions. This model is simple and thus highly practicable and allows shippers to shift capacities between different points. In turn, it requires the network to be meshed to a significant degree, so that a frequent relocation of gas flows is possible in order to enable this flexibility. Furthermore, the application of a single tariff assumes that there are no significant differences in the impact of different locations on the costs of the network.[10]

These considerations lead to the conclusion that the postage stamp model is a very appropriate one for the distribution level, but is more difficult to implement for a transmission system with longer distances and a significantly lower degree of intermeshed pipelines. In addition, load can strongly differ at different locations in a transmission network. Consequently, the point-to-point and the entry-exit model are the two remaining network access models that are principally applicable on the transmission level. In Section 28.4 we explain the reasons for the decision to process from the formerly common point-to-point to today's entry-exit standard for gas transmission networks in Europe, while the postage stamp model remains the most practical network access model for distribution networks.

28.4 Decision for the Entry-exit Model

European legal documents, in particular the 2003 Gas Directive and the EU Regulation 1775/2005 on Conditions for Access to the Natural Gas Transmission Networks, are rather general and leave the exact design of the network access arrangements open. They provide criteria for adequate network access conditions rather than defining concrete standards. A specification of gas network access conditions was mainly developed within the context of the Madrid Forum, a European-wide gas regulatory forum consisting of regulators and different interest groups of the gas sector, where the issues addressed in the Directive(s) are discussed in more detail. In particular during the meetings between 2002 and 2004 it was decided that the entry-exit model will best serve the objective of a non-discriminatory network access on the transmission level, as laid down in the 2003 Directive.[11] It was decided that the transmission network operators in Europe had to change their access regimes from point-to-point to entry-exit models. On the

---

[10] In this context, the term 'significance' relates to both the extent and the stability of corresponding differences in costs. For instance in a network with changing flow patterns, it is possible that a given import or export of gas at a certain point will increase the prevailing flow at some times but reduce it at other times. In such cases, it may not be possible to provide for a reasonable representation in network tariffs.

[11] Compare, as an example, a revised version of the Guidelines for Good TPA Practice attached to the conclusions of the 7th meeting of the European Gas Regulatory Forum (Madrid Forum) from 24-25 September 2003, or the 2004 Entry Exit System Guidelines Monitoring Report by ERGEG, or The Brattle Group (2002) at http://ec.europa.eu/energy/gas/madrid.

distribution level, the postage stamp model remains the most practical solution. Table 28.2 summarizes the major arguments.

Table 28.2: Evaluation of network access models

Network access model	Capacity allocation	Capacity pricing	Assumptions/ specific requirements
Non-discrimination criteria	Network user flexibility (open, unhindered access)	Cost-reflective tariffs; fair, objective and transparent tariffs	
Point-to-point	- -	-	Contracted path corresponds to physical flow
Entry-exit	+	+	Entry and exit points are the relevant capacities to the market
Postage stamp	+ +	- -	Network is meshed enough to compensate flexible nominations

The point-to-point model is the least flexible among the three discussed network access models. Its tariffs correspond to the transportation costs only in cases where the contractual path fits with the physical flow of natural gas. This is less likely the more meshed a network is, which is why the point-to-point model is not applicable on the highly meshed distribution level. Here, on the contrary, the postage stamp model best suits the conditions of meshed networks and comparably short distances. The postage stamp is the most flexible model, but therefore also requires a certain flexibility between alternative transportation ways.

The postage stamp tariff system is simple and transparent, but impractical for transmission systems where a uniform tariff may result in distorted prices that are not reflective of transportation costs. Finally, the entry-exit model is slightly less flexible compared to the postage stamp model, but is still much more flexible than a point-to-point regime whilst also applicable on the transmission level. If the tariffs at the entry and exit points vary by location in an economically justified manner, this model can be largely cost-reflective.

It should be noted that, notwithstanding the general decision towards entry-exit, there can be still exemptions, especially where transit is affected. With the repeal of the so-called Transit Directive through the 2003 Gas Directive,[12] transit was principally declared to be treated equally to other transportation in terms of third party access. Thus, most transit system operators enable capacity reservations at (more or less) flexible entry and exit points and introduced independent entry and

---

[12] EU Directive 91/296/EEC from 31 May 1991 and EU Directive 2003/55/EG, Article 32 (1).

exit tariffs.[13] However, the applicability of the network access rules to transit is an issue. For example, the European gas infrastructure association Gas Transmission Europe (GTE) issued a report on transit in 2005 where the specifics of transit are stressed and it is concluded that entry-exit tariffs might lead to cross-subsidization between international transit and domestic transportation. In such a case, tariffs "other than entry-exit tariffs" are recommended which means a continuation of point-to-point tariffs.[14]

Overall, the entry-exit model has become the standard network access model for gas transmission networks in Europe over the recent years. What does that mean for gas supply companies?

28.5   Consequences for Gas Supply Companies

Corresponding to the two spheres of a network access model, capacity allocation and tariffs, the consequences for gas supply companies of introducing the entry-exit model can be divided into capacity and tariff-wise implications. Finally, the extent to which the entry-exit model can ever make gas transmission network access entirely non-discriminatory is discussed.

28.5.1   Capacity

In the point-to-point regime, the contractual definition of the transportation path made capacity planning easier for network operators, but implied a number of problems for shippers. Firstly, a shipper that aimed to use capacities across several networks (for example France and Germany have several market areas) had to conclude a separate transportation contract for each network. As a consequence, capacity reservation was complex and thus caused higher transaction costs. Moreover, a rejection at one network made the entire transportation project infeasible for a shipper. Because of the fixed path, congestion somewhere along the path led to the rejection of a capacity request and furthermore hampered (secondary) trading of capacities, because fixed capacities are more difficult to sell.

The introduction of the entry-exit model makes network access much easier for shippers, because only one entry and one exit contract (plus a balancing contract) are to be concluded instead of the entire contract path. This is a considerable simplification; in particular where several networks are involved between entry and exit point. Also, the (transaction-) independent entry and exit capacities are better tradable on a secondary market, which can help in making commodity markets more liquid, i.e., potentially increase competition. It is worth noting that this fact

---

[13] Compare, for instance, the transportation tariffs and conditions of the transit joint ventures MEGAL or TENP.

[14] GTE (2005), p. 10. For instance, the TAG Trans Austria Gasline offers capacity at distance-dependent tariffs.

will have different impacts on the incumbent suppliers and (potential) new entrants. While liquid markets and increased competition are a threat for the incumbent on the one hand, it opens the market for new entrants on the other.

Balancing also plays an important role in market opening. In an entry-exit regime, shippers can subsume all of their injected and withdrawn volumes within a balancing group. Compared to the point-to-point model, where the entry and exit volume of each single contract determine the chargeable imbalance, the advantage is that differences between entry and exit volumes are netted before they are cashed out as imbalances or penalties. The larger a balancing group, the higher the portfolio effect that minimizes the imbalances at the end of the balancing period.

In spite of these advantages for the creation of a more non-discriminatory network access, the entry-exit model conceptually reduces marketable capacities. Network operators need to make capacities available at entry and exit points in a way that shippers are free to choose independently from each other. The effect of such flexibility is a reduction in free capacities; network operators have to consider all likely scenarios of potential capacity use by shippers when determining available capacities.

28.5.2 Tariffs

In contrast to the point-to-point model, entry-exit capacities are not priced according to the transportation distance or path in between. Total network costs are distributed among all entry and exit points, ideally under consideration of the specific conditions and load at each point. The tariff for transportation is then equal to the sum of the respective entry and exit tariffs.[15]

Because of the inclusion of point-specific conditions, tariffs tend to reflect costs better than the purely distance-related tariffs in the point-to-point model. On the other hand, the allocation of total costs to all points of a network or an entry-exit/balancing zone results from an average calculation and therefore leads to a loss of information or transparency. How closely tariffs reflect costs depends on the complexity of the network and should be weighed against the advantages of a simplified network access on the capacity side.

When using locational pricing, prices at entry and exit points may furthermore be set to reflect the costs of necessary investments into new infrastructure. This may help reducing physical congestion since demand for capacity is exposed to economic signals for network extension.

---

[15] This statement applies irrespective of the network access model, i.e., it is a general principle that total revenues from network tariffs should correspond to the total costs of the network.

28.5.3   Is Entry-exit a Universal Remedy?

As mentioned earlier in Section 28.2.2 (Components of a Network Access Regime), the decision for entry-exit as the underlying network access model is a basic condition rather than a guarantee for non-discriminatory network access.

Firstly, the higher flexibility on the capacity side comes at the expense of a reduction in capacity as long as no further capacity optimization is in place.[16] This means that, particularly in entry-exit regimes, effective procedures and instruments for efficient network use are essential to avoid a situation where additional flexibility can only be gained by reducing capacities at the same time. While physical congestion is considered in the entry-exit tariff regime (through price-inherent signals for the need to extend the network where necessary), contractual congestion is an issue that is not solved by the entry-exit model itself. Contractual congestion emerges when capacity is reserved for more than one shipper even though the actual flow happens only once, or when a single shipper has reserved an amount of capacity which he does not normally use. As a consequence, the flexibility given to all shippers to choose their entry and exit points at short notice often leads to a situation where points are fully booked without being fully utilized. Although this problem is not unique to the entry-exit model, it represents a serious obstacle to the proper functioning of many European natural gas markets, at least at an international level.

To mitigate the problem of contractual congestion, several tools may be applied. These include for example the use of market-based allocation mechanisms, i.e., auctions, which allocate available capacities to those who value it the most, instead of giving certain market participants a priority over others. Other options include the use of instruments against the hoarding of capacities, such as the use-it-or-lose-it principle. Finally, the use of smart capacity products can help making available capacities that are otherwise lost for the market. Besides interruptible capacities, this may include the definition of other non-firm capacities, which can be converted into firm capacities at a certain point in time, i.e., when network operators can be reasonably sure that there will be no physical congestion.

A fair and functioning system for balancing and imbalance settlement represents the third major precondition for non-discriminatory network access. Shippers will inevitably face deviations between the planned and actual volumes of gas injected into and extracted from the network. Although some shippers may be able to manage their portfolio even during the day, not all market participants will have sufficient access to the required sources of flexibility that can be activated at short notice. Moreover, at least a certain amount of imbalances will always have to be compensated by network operators.

An efficient balancing mechanism should provide incentives for proper planning, forecast and actions by shippers, on the one hand, whilst impeding any excessive penalties for deviations that cannot be avoided with reasonable efforts. These partially conflicting objectives require a careful balance. With respect to

---

[16] It should be noted that the effect of reduced capacity is stronger the larger the entry-exit zone is.

efficiency and non-discrimination, it is especially important that imbalance settlement does not create excessive costs for small shippers and new entrants, which could undermine any potential for competition.

The main aspects in this context are the choice of different settlement intervals (ranging between hourly and daily balancing), the potential application of tolerances and the relation between the price to be paid for any imbalances that are finally cashed out and the prevailing market price in the same period. For instance, whilst hourly balancing might seem to reflect the situation of the network in each hour, it ignores the inherent storage capabilities of any transportation network and may penalize especially smaller shippers even if they are able to balance themselves over the course of a few hours. Conversely, daily balancing creates an increasing risk of cross-subsidization and arbitrage with neighboring markets using hourly balancing. Similarly, imbalance charges should ideally reflect the costs of balancing but this requires a functioning mechanism for physical balancing of the system during the day with truly cost-reflective prices.

We therefore emphasize once again that non-discriminatory network access requires an appropriate mix of the right choices for all three elements of network access regime as shown in Figure 28.2 above, i.e., the choice of the general access model, the procedures of capacity and congestion management, and the balancing regime.

28.6   Conclusion

In summary, the entry-exit model increases flexibility, reduces complexity and minimizes risks for gas supply companies. Moreover, its tariffs are principally more cost-reflective and consider capacity demand in locational prices and thus give signals for future network planning. Overall, it therefore creates better preconditions to enable (more) competition on the commodity market compared to point-to-point.

Nonetheless, entry-exit alone is not able to be the universal remedy for the creation of a competitive gas market. In fact, effective capacity and congestion management is essential to compensate for the entry-exit-inherent reduction in available, i.e., marketable capacities.

Furthermore, even the most flexible and cost reflective network access model, combined with efficient capacity and congestion management, might not help in creating fully non-discriminatory network access, as long as further components of network access contain potential for discrimination. For instance, if imbalance charges are high and intransparent in combination with a high risk of overrunning the balancing tolerances within the relevant balancing period, they can act as a market entry barrier to new entrants and can cause severe problems to smaller gas suppliers.

Entry-exit has been a major step towards a more non-discriminatory network access and thus towards enabling better conditions to create a more competitive gas market. Nevertheless, there still seems to be a way to go to give new and smaller gas suppliers genuinely equal chances compared to the incumbents.

References

Carlton, D. W. & Perloff, J. M. 1994. Modern industrial organization (2nd ed.). New York: Harpercollins College Div.

Cerbe, G. 2004. Grundlagen der Gastechnik – Gasbeschaffung, Gasverteilung, Gasverwendung (6th ed.). München [u.a.]: Hanser Verlag.

European Regulators Group for Electricity and Gas (ERGEG). 2004. Entry exit system guidelines – monitoring report. European Regulators Group for Electricity and Gas.

EU Directive. 1991. Council Directive 91/296/EEC of 31 May 1991 on the transit of natural gas through grids. Brussels.

EU Directive. 2003. Council Directive 2003/55/EC of the European Parliament and of the Council of 26 June 2003 concerning common rules for the internal market in natural gas and repealing Directive 98/30/EC. Brussels.

European Commission. 2007. DG competition report on energy sector inquiry. Brussels. 10 January 2007. available at: http://ec.europa.eu/comm/competition /sectors/energy/inquiry.

GTE. 2005. Transit report from 27 June 2005, Gas Transmission Europe. Brussels.

Hewicker, C. & Kesting, S. 2007. Der deutsche Regel- und Ausgleichsenergiemarkt Gas im Rahmen des neuen Energiewirtschaftsgesetzes und des darauf aufbauenden Gasnetzzugangsmodells (The German gas balancing market under the given legal conditions and the new German gas network access model). report on behalf of the German energy regulator. Bonn. November 2007. available at: www.bundesnetzagentur.de.

Kesting, S. 2006. Transmission network access regulation in the European gas market. Intern. Univ. Bremen Diss., Freiburger Studien zur Netzökonomie (edited by Knieps, G.), Baden-Baden: Nomos Verlag.

Madrid Forum. 2003. Guidelines for Good TPA Practice, revised version attached to the conclusions of the 7th meeting of the European Gas Regulatory Forum (Madrid Forum) from 24-25 September 2003.

Sharkey, W. S. 1982. The theory of natural monopoly. Cambridge: Cambridge University Press.

The Brattle Group. 2002. Convergence of non-discriminatory tariff and congestion management systems in the European gas sector. London. September 2002.

29 Implementation of the EU Unbundling Guidelines in Germany – a Legal Perspective

Peter Rosin[1]

Abstract

The unbundling requirements contained in §§ 6-10 German Energy Industry Act [Energiewirtschaftsgesetz (EnWG)] are of great importance within the new EnWG. They have already changed the structures in the German energy industry, which had grown up over decades. In particular, the necessity for many electricity supply companies are required to undergo legal unbundling (§ 7 EnWG) and operational unbundling (§ 8 EnWG), which has led to the establishment of many grid companies. Moreover, the management and staff of these grid companies (or for grid sectors continuing to be legally dependent) have also formed a self-image of their own. This chapter gives a brief overview of the Community Law basis of unbundling and the latest developments in Community Law (and politics), after which the current German requirements of unbundling are specified.

Keywords: legal unbundling, unbundling requirements, grid companies

---

[1] Dr. Peter Rosin is Partner, Head of the German Energy Group and Co-head of the Global Energy & Utilities Industry Group at Clifford Chance, Germany.

A. Bausch and B. Schwenker (eds.), *Handbook Utility Management,*
DOI: 10.1007/978-3-540-79349-6_29, © Springer-Verlag Berlin Heidelberg 2009

29.1 Community Law Bases

The Community Law unbundling requirements are first of all characterised by the fact that the original plans of the European Commission to implement ownership unbundling have still not been realised. The current EU Electricity[2] and Gas[3] Directives refer to this explicitly. However, the various unbundling rules in the directives demand that a system operator "shall be independent at least in terms of its legal form, organisation and decision making from other activities not relating to transmission/distribution" (Directive 2003/54/EC & Directive 2003/55/EC, 2003). In order to ensure such independence in respect of organisation and decision making, Community Law demands the application of so-called minimum criteria.[4] These minimum criteria provide mainly for compliance with the following requirements:

- Those persons responsible for the management of the system operator may not participate in other company structures of the integrated undertaking responsible for the day-to-day operation of the generation of electricity, production of gas and supply of electricity and gas (Directive 2003/54/EC & Directive 2003/55/EC, 2003).
- Those persons responsible for the management of the transmission system operator may not (also) participate in another company structure of the integrated undertaking responsible for the day-to-day operation of the distribution system operator and vice versa (Directive 2003/54/EC & Directive 2003/55/EC, 2003).
- Taking into account the professional interests of the persons responsible for the management of the system operator to ensure that they are capable of acting independently.
- Guaranteeing effective decision-making rights of grid operators with respect to assets necessary to operate, maintain or develop the network.
- Establishment of a compliance programme which sets out measures taken to ensure that discriminatory conduct is excluded and the specific obligations of employees to meet this objective.

---

[2] See recital 8 Electricity Directive (2003/54/EC): "It is important however to distinguish between such legal separation and ownership unbundling. Legal separation does not imply a change of ownership of assets and nothing prevents similar or identical employment conditions applying throughout the whole of the vertically integrated undertakings". See also, for example, Article 10 (1) 2nd sentence Directive 2003/54/EC: "These rules shall not create an obligation to separate the ownership of assets of the transmission system from the vertically integrated undertaking". Compare also Art. 15 (1) 2nd sentence Directive 2003/54/EC for distribution system operators and Art. 17 2nd sentence Directive 2003/54/EC for combined operators.

[3] See recital 10 (3), Art. 9 (1) 2nd sentence, Art. 13 (1) 2nd sentence and Art. 15 2nd sentence Gas Directive (2003/55/EC).

[4] See Art. 10 (2) and Art. 15 (2) 2nd sentence Directive 2003/54/EC and Art. 9 (2) and Art. 13 (2) 2nd sentence Directive 2003/55/EC.

In addition, Art. 15 (2) 3rd sentence Directive 2003/54/EC and Art. 13 (2) 3rd sentence Directive 2003/55/EC explicitly provide for the right of the Member States to exempt integrated electricity and natural gas undertakings supplying fewer than 100,000 customers or small isolated networks from the above obligations for the distribution system area. This means in effect that within the scope of the incorporation of Directives 2003/54/EC and 2003/55/EC into national law the Member States can exempt distribution system operators of a specific size from the obligation with respect to legal form, organisation and decision making independently of other activities not relating to distribution.

The so-called confidentiality for system operators is not regulated in direct connection with the unbundling requirements, but in separate paragraphs (Directive 2003/55/EC, 2003). Here a distinction is made between two obligations for system operators: on the one hand, they have to preserve the confidentiality of commercially sensitive information obtained in the course of carrying out their business; on the other, they must prevent information about their own activities, which may be commercially advantageous, from being disclosed in a discriminatory manner. In Directive 2003/55/EC it is moreover emphasised that system operators shall not, in the context of sales or purchases of natural gas by related undertakings, abuse commercially sensitive information obtained from third parties in the context of providing or negotiating access to the system (Directive 2003/55/EC, 2003).

The above provisions are supplemented by Art. 19 Directive 2003/54/EC or Art. 17 Directive 2003/55/EC, providing for the unbundling of accounts. The following obligations are characteristic for these provisions:

- Obligation of all electricity supply undertakings to draw up, publish and submit to audit their annual accounts in accordance with the rules of national law concerning the annual accounts of companies adopted pursuant to the Fourth Council Directive 78/660/EC of 25 July 1978 based on article 44 (2) (g) of the Treaty on the annual accounts of certain types of companies.[5]
- Keeping of separate accounts for diverse energy industry activities (Directive 2003/54/EC & Directive 2003/55/EC, 2003).

In this context attention is drawn in particular to the fact that the European Commission has laid down its opinion relating to the interpretation of the unbundling provision in a comprehensive note (Generaldirektion Energie und Verkehr, 2004). This so-called Interpreting Note of the Commission comments on many single issues. In many places the statements contained in it are more than a mere interpretation. This shows the actual intention of the Commission, which has used this document to lay down in writing its own ideas, some of which go further than the regulatory content of the directive, and to publish the same. Although it is generally recognised that the Interpreting Note has no legally binding effect, the impact of this document must not be underestimated in practice (Säcker, 2004; Ehricke, 2004). On the one hand, this elaboration will be a decisive basis for the

---

[5] Official Gazette of the EC L 222/11 dated 14 August 1978 amended last by Directive 2001/65/EC of the European Parliament and of the Council (Directive 2001/65/EC, 2001).

Commission in valuation of the national implementation of the unbundling requirements of Community Law. On the other hand, it has to be assumed that the
regulatory authority and the courts will take the views of the Commission into
account, at least in terms of a literature opinion. In connection with the unbundling
regulations this is of particular importance since here – as already set out at the
beginning – the legislator has primarily confined itself to a wholesale adoption of
the Community Law provisions as they were received.

29.2   Current Community Law Development

In summary, the European Commission feels obliged, for various reasons, to en-
dorse a strengthening of the legal standards for the purpose of deconcentrating the
energy sector, to be enacted by the legislature (European Commission, 2007a).
The Commission has stated that, in particular, the survey of the energy sector and
its findings reinforced the Commission's impression that an excessive level of
concentration in the sector distorted competition and impeded the creation of an
internal market (Kroes, 2007). The Commission therefore intends to bring about a
separation at the level of the transmission system operators, at least between system operation and the other levels of the value chain (European Commission,
2007b & 2007c).

The Commission sees ownership unbundling as an appropriate means of
achieving this goal and argues that there was no other way to keep system operators from granting privileges to affiliated producers and distributors, all forming
part of the same vertically integrated structure. The creation of an independent
system operator (ISO) might be an alternative, but is considered by the Commission to be no more than 'second-best' as a solution to the existing issues (Piebalgs,
2007).

In the run-up to the Spring European Council 2007, the European Council initially supported the European Commission's endeavours to implement a factual
separation between system operation and 'competing areas' (General Secretariat of
the Council of the European Union, 2007). Later, when the Spring European
Council was held, the European Council placed more emphasis on the desired
outcome of the deconcentration and requested that the European Commission also
submit suggestions for improving the existing law.

Third-party reactions to the suggestions made by the Commission varied.
Member states who had already implemented ownership unbundling welcomed
the plans (Ofgem, 2006), as did, among others, the Council of European Energy
Regulators. The plans were generally less well received by member states that
have not yet implemented ownership unbundling but have implemented deconcentration provisions from the earlier directives aimed at speeding up the liberalisation of the energy markets. One of the major arguments brought by the latter is
that implementation of the provisions from the earlier directives provided an adequate legal framework, which would, however, take some time to reach its full
potential (Kurth, 2007). Another counterargument is that ownership unbundling

represents such major interference with private property that it raises constitutional concerns.

29.3   Overview of the Systematic of the Unbundling Requirements in Germany

A presentation of the systematic of the unbundling requirements in Germany has to start with the lamentable judgement that such a systematic can hardly be recognised. There are two main reasons for this: on the one hand, §§ 6-10 EnWG, like the entire new law, contains many technical defects. The unbundling rules are characterised by lack of structure, imprecise wording and a lack of regulatory depth. On the other hand, the unbundling requirements are characterised by – one is tempted to say unparalleled – discouragement of the legislator, since the Lower House of the German Parliament [Bundestag] and the Upper House of the German Parliament [Bundesrat] 'waved through' the unbundling requirements of the Community Law instrument, which are very important for the future structure of the German energy industry, with hardly any changes at all. Instead of using the spaces and making the provisions more concrete, the relevant articles of Directive 2003/54/EC and Directive 2003/55/EC were adopted almost to the letter (Directive 2003/54/EC & Directive 2003/55/EC, 2003). Instead of prescribing directions, the legislator was content to adopt the Community Law rules without criticism.[6] This is already doomed to failure, because Community Law has an entirely different structure (Breuer, 2004). It is rather organised functionally and prescribes the target of a regulation. The national legislator, however, must (also) specify the path leading to it and implement the realisation of Community Law requirements in the specific situation of national law. Since in most cases many roads lead to the same target, it is almost thoughtless for the legislator faced with such an important issue as the (new) structuring of the energy industry to act as it did in the case of §§ 6-10 EnWG and adopt the functionally organised Community Law requirements without one-to-one criticism ('copy and paste mentality'), so confronting an entire branch of industry with many problems. In another context, the Federal

---

[6] However, this is what Säcker explicitly welcomes: "In view of the detailed standardisation of the unbundling purpose in the directives the authors of the German ministry draft were well advised not to draft the EC law regulation in accordance with the informal interpreting note on a national level but confine themselves to implementing the rules in the Energy Industry Act both literally and precisely" (Säcker, 2004), Fn. 4. Here Säcker misjudges our intention. We were not dealing with the wording in accordance with the Interpreting Note, which he himself rightly also calls legally nonbinding, but with the prescription of directions in particular in view of the Interpreting Note, since these have evoked considerable discussions in the energy industry in the course of the legislation procedure. Clearer standards would have led to increased legal compliance. In addition, the legislator could have shown responsibility by such a manner of proceeding. However, as things are, he left it to the energy industry to clarify, if necessary by means of legal disputes, how to implement the unbundling requirements and what role the Interpreting Note plays.

Constitutional Court (BVerfG, 2005) and the press have – rightly – heavily censured such adoption of Community Law instruments without criticism.

29.3.1 Scope of Application

If, despite the above-mentioned weaknesses, an attempt is made to show a systematic within the unbundling requirements, it can first of all be said that the general scope of application of the provisions ensues from § 6 (1) EnWG in conjunction with § 3 no. 38 EnWG. According to § 6 (1), 1st and 2nd sentences EnWG, vertically integrated undertakings, and legally independent grid operators which are associated with a vertically integrated undertaking as defined in § 3 no. 38 EnWG, have to ensure the independence of grid operators from other activities relating to energy supply according to §§ 7 to 10 EnWG. Here 'vertically integrated undertaking' is the central term, which is legally defined in § 3 no. 38 EnWG. On account of the contents of this definition the unbundling obligation, on the one hand, affects every single company which, apart from its activity as system operator (transmission and distribution of electrical energy in the electricity area or transmission and distribution in the natural gas area), exercises another economic activity to be assigned to the electricity or natural gas sector (production or supply of electrical energy or generation or supply of natural gas). Thus, only those (natural or) legal personalities are vertically integrated undertakings that, apart from the grid area, are also engaged in any of the so-called competitive areas (Gesetz über die Elektrizitäts- und Gasversorgung, 2005). This must be seen against the background that only in such combination of activities there is a risk of cross-subsidisation and a risk that nondiscriminatory grid access could be refused. On the other hand, certain groups are also subject to the unbundling requirements. In this context those companies are combined in a group in which they are associated with each other as defined in § 3 (2) of Directive 139/2004/EC of the Council of 20 January 2004 concerning the control of concentrations between undertakings (merger regulation) (Directive 139/2004/EC, 2004). If either company in a group, apart from one of the above-mentioned activities with regard to grid operation, is at the same time engaged in another activity relating to the 'competitive areas' the entire group has to observe the statutory unbundling requirements.

If the scope of application of part 2 EnWG includes unbundling of the company, it or the group has to fulfil all requirements set out in §§ 7-10 EnWG as a matter of principle. Each company or the entire group is then, in full, subject to the obligation of legal, operational, informational and accounting unbundling. There are, however, exceptions to this principle: things are different if a company or a group operates liquefied natural gas (LNG) and storage facilities. Inasmuch as these facilities must not be assigned to the natural gas supply systems, according to § 6 (1) 3rd sentence only §§ 9 and 10 EnWG apply, i.e. the operation of LNG and storage facilities is only subject to the requirements of informational and accounting unbundling. On the other hand, in respect of the obligation of legal and operational unbundling a 100,000-customer limit applies: according to § 7 (2) and § 8 (6) EnWG electricity or gas system operators (single companies or groups) with fewer than 100,000 customers are exempted from the legal and operational unbundling. Finally, so-called object networks according to § 110 EnWG are fully exempted from the scope of application of part 2, i.e. from §§ 6 et seq. EnWG. Object networks are different kinds of networks, which are not allowed to serve the general supply as defined in § 3 no. 17 EnWG and, among other things, are each limited to a specific region.

29.3.2   Legal Unbundling

According to § 7 EnWG the obligation of legal unbundling applies first to the company or group covered by the unbundling requirements (the vertically integrated undertaking). According to that provision the grid operator(s) of a company or group shall be independent in terms of their legal form from other activities relating to energy supply (§ 7 (1) EnWG). This means that the network must be operated in a separate company. This is only different – as already set out hereinbefore – in those vertically integrated energy supply companies with fewer than 100,000 customers (see § 7 (2) EnWG). Distribution system operators have been obliged to comply with this obligation since 1 July 2007 (§ 7 (3) EnWG). Therefore, a combination of the transmission and distribution level, for both electricity and natural gas, is admissible in just the same way as a combination of electricity and gas networks in one company (combined operator), as explicitly set out in Art. 17 1st sentence Directive 2003/54/EC and Art. 15 1st sentence Directive 2003/55/EC.

29.3.3   Operational Unbundling

While the legal unbundling is comparatively simple to understand, the structure of the operational unbundling in § 8 EnWG is clearly more complex. § 8 EnWG shows first of all that § 8 EnWG refers to three areas, namely:

- Organisation;
- Decision making;
- Carrying out the network business.

§ 8 (2) EnWG relates to the organisation, i.e. the structure of the company or the group. § 8 (2) no. 1 EnWG demands that the persons relevant to performance of the network business are assigned exclusively to the network operator. Since according to such regulation, persons responsible for the management of the system operator are authorised to make final decisions which are important to guaranteeing a nondiscriminatory network and must participate in an operational facility of the system operator to be able to perform these activities. They are, however, not allowed to be members of operational facilities of the vertically integrated undertakings, which, either directly or indirectly, are responsible for the day-to-day operation of the generation, production and supply of energy to customers. For these 'important' persons working in system operation exclusive assignment to the system operator is demanded ('exclusiveness principle'). Inasmuch as persons in other parts of the company or the group carry out other network operation activities they have to this extent to be placed under the technical instructions of the management of the system operator (§ 8 (2) no. 2 EnWG).

While § 8 (2) EnWG refers to the organisation of the vertically integrated undertaking and regulates what sector of a company specific persons are to be part of and in what cases technical rights to give instructions must be provided for, § 8 (3) EnWG refers to the relationship between the company and the group and those employees responsible for the management of the system operator. The vertically integrated undertaking is obliged to take suitable steps to ensure these persons' capability of acting independently. Without intending to discuss at this point what 'suitable steps' are within the meaning of that provision, it is nevertheless pointed out here that this term includes specific Labour Law measures in particular. The capability of acting independently of the persons responsible for the management of the system operator must, for instance, be ensured by the provision of minimum terms in managing director service contracts. Therefore, § 8 (3) EnWG contains specific Energy Law rules which substantively have to be assigned to Labour Law; that is to say there is a specific Labour Law sector of Energy Law. The issue of remuneration is also referred to: the remuneration of the persons subject to § 8 (3) EnWG must not provide any hidden incentives to orientate to nonsystem operation-specific criteria. This would, for instance, be the case if the performance-related bonus of the network operation management were to depend on the success of the affiliated supply company. This shows that § 8 (3) EnWG even influences the staff policy of the undertakings concerned.

While § 8 (3) EnWG contains specific Labour Law provisions, the central regulation of § 8 (4) EnWG refers to the relationship between Energy and Corporate Law. § 8 (4) EnWG contains provisions referring to guaranteeing the independence in terms of decision making of the related system operators. The essential message of this paragraph is contained in the first sentence. Accordingly, the vertically integrated undertaking has to ensure that the system operators have some degree of actual decision-making power and can also exercise such power independently of the group management. In its scope of application, sentence 1 of § 8 (4) EnWG limits universally valid Company Law principles. Sentences 2 and 3 of § 8 (4) EnWG then again reduce the independence of the system operators: according to these sentences the use of Corporate Law instruments of control for exercise of the commercial powers and the management supervision rights of the parent company in respect of the management of the system operator is admissible in conditions that are defined in detail. In terms of systematic, sentences 2 and 3 of § 8 (4) EnWG thus contain an exception to the basic Energy Law rule in sentence 1, and therefore at the same time a partial return to the general control possibilities under group law of the parent company. Sentence 4 of § 8 (4) EnWG finally concretises the issue of the admissibility of instructions in such a way that specific instructions are declared inadmissible. According to that provision, instructions relating to the day-to-day operation of the system operator and in respect of single decisions on structural measures in energy facilities are always forbidden. Thus, sentence 4 contains an exception to the exceptional rule in § 8 (4) 2nd and 3rd sentences EnWG, as a consequence of which it is returned to the principle of § 8 (4) 1st sentence EnWG.

Just like § 8 (3) EnWG, paragraph 5 contains further Labour Law elements. It obliges the vertically integrated undertaking to establish a compliance programme for the employees involved in the grid operation containing binding measures for the nondiscriminatory performance of the grid business, and to make the employees (and the regulatory authority) familiar with this programme. § 8 (5) EnWG additionally demands the setting up of a 'position' or the provision of a 'person' supervising the observance of the compliance programme; in practice the term of 'person charged with the supervision of compliance' has been adopted. In accordance with § 8 (5) 3rd sentence EnWG the person charged with the supervision of compliance is obliged to provide the regulatory authority annually by 31 March at the latest with a report on the measures implemented in accordance with sentence 1 during the preceding calendar year and to publish such report; in addition, this person has to submit the compliance programme to the regulatory authority in accordance with sentence 1. As far as the preparation of this programme and its publication within the company is concerned, here the relationship between the company or the group and the employees is affected directly. To this extent, § 8 (5) EnWG supplements paragraph 3, and for reasons of systematic it would have been better to put it directly after this paragraph.

29.3.4   Taxation Law Aspects

In § 6 (2) to (4) the Energy Industry Act also contains various special tax provisions to ensure the tax neutrality of reorganisation processes made in close economic context with legal or operational unbundling according to §§ 7 and 8 EnWG. Here, § 6 (4) EnWG provides that these special provisions will also apply if companies perform legal unbundling on a voluntary basis.

29.3.5   Informational Unbundling

The so-called confidentiality requirements for system operators contained in the directives were implemented in the Energy Industry Act within the scope of the unbundling requirements in § 9 EnWG, which bears the heading "Use of information". The requirements contained therein are generally summarised under the heading "Informational unbundling". Here the Community Law requirements were largely adopted to the letter. Paragraph 1 relates to the 'preservation of confidentiality' of commercially sensitive information that system operators have obtained in the course of carrying out their business. Paragraph 2 contains provisions for the case that the vertically integrated energy supply company or the system operator discloses information about its own activities as system operator which may be commercially advantageous. If this happens such disclosure has to be made in a nondiscriminatory way.

29.3.6 Accounting Unbundling

Finally, § 10 EnWG contains the requirements relating to 'accounting unbundling'. This provision relates to both the internal and the external accounting. § 10 (1) and (2) EnWG first of all relate to the preparation of the annual accounts, i.e. the external accounting. Notwithstanding their ownership rights and their legal form, all energy supply undertakings have to draw up and publish their annual accounts and submit them to audit in accordance with the rules of the German Commercial Code (HGB) applying to corporations.

The requirements relating to internal accounting are contained in § 10 (3) EnWG. It provides for the obligation to keep separate accounts for diverse energy industry activities, which are set out in detail in § 10 (3) EnWG. The obligation first of all applies to electricity transmission, electricity distribution, gas transmission, gas distribution, gas storage and the operation of LNG facilities. The obligation of separate accounting applies in this context to any activity within the above sectors, where activity means any commercial use of a property right in electricity or gas supply systems, gas storages or LNG facilities. Accordingly, any leasing or rental of any of the above facilities is an activity as defined in that Act. Consolidated accounts have to be kept in a specific manner for other electricity and nonelectricity and gas and nongas activities.

Apart from the obligation to keep separate accounts, § 10 (3) EnWG also contains an obligation of internal accounting. For any of the activity sectors set out in paragraph 3, internally any of the balance sheets and profit and loss accounts complying with the provisions set out in § 10 (1) EnWG has to be prepared in each individual case. This will cause considerable additional expenses for the companies.

The provisions for accounting unbundling additionally contain single requirements relating to the structuring of the internal accounting and in particular extensions in respect of the auditing obligation of external and internal accounting (see § 10 (1) and (4) EnWG). Apart from the existence of separate accounts within the scope of the audit of the annual accounts it is necessary to examine whether the valuations and the assignment of accounts have been made properly and plausibly and whether the principle of consistency has been observed (see § 10 (4) 2nd sentence EnWG). Finally, the annual accounts have to be submitted to the regulatory authority.

29.4 Unbundling Targets

The targets of a rule are of special importance within the scope of any interpretation in connection with the teleological construction (Canaris & Larenz, 2008). They are of special importance in connection with the interpretation of the unbundling rules of the EnWG. On the one hand, this ensues from the adoption almost to the letter – already mentioned hereinbefore – of the unbundling requirements of Community Law. The latter is however, as also mentioned hereinbefore, functionally oriented, i.e. based on another approach than the national provisions. If the national legislator adopts the wording of a Community Law provision almost to the letter this must be reflected in the interpretation. In other words: in such a case the meaning and object of the corresponding rule are of special importance. On the other hand, the unbundling targets are emphasised within §§ 6-10 EnWG itself. They are mentioned explicitly in the heading of the first paragraph of part 2 EnWG and thus in a highlighted place. This can only mean that special importance is attached to this target.

As already set out hereinbefore, § 6 EnWG among other things bears the heading "Unbundling target". Therefore, the meaning and object of the unbundling requirements will primarily be laid down in this rule. In accordance with § 6 (1) 1st sentence EnWG, vertically integrated undertakings and legally independent operators of electricity and gas grids which are associated with a vertically integrated undertaking are obliged to structure and perform the system operation in a nondiscriminatory way. This obligation is the actual target of part 2 EnWG. In this context we can also mention the primary target of § 6 (1) 1st sentence EnWG. The requirements relating to the nondiscriminatory structuring and performance of the system operation are contained in part 3 of the EnWG, with the heading "Regulation of system operation". § 6 (1) 2nd sentence EnWG then provides that "in order to achieve this target" it must be ensured according to §§ 7-10 EnWG that the system operators are independent. The introduction of this phrase ("in order to achieve this target") shows that the observance of the unbundling requirements is just a means to the projected end of achieving the primary target of nondiscriminatory structuring and performance of the system operation. Thus, the unbundling requirements are not an end in themselves; according to § 6 (1) 1st and 2nd sentences EnWG, they rather have an 'auxiliary function' within the scope of the rules for regulation of the system operation (part 2). They are an additional way of continuing to bring forward the actual target of achieving a nondiscriminatory structuring and performance of the system operation.

This conclusion is confirmed by other passages in the act. §§ 6, 10 (3) 1st and 5th sentences and (1) no. 5 EnWG show that the actual target of unbundling is not the reorganisation of the energy industry as such, but that rather the following aspects are to the fore:

- Ensuring transparency (§ 6 (1) 1st sentence EnWG);
- Ensuring nondiscriminatory structuring and performance of the system operation (§ 6 (1) 1st sentence EnWG);
- Ensuring nondiscriminatory system operation (§ 8 (2) 1st sentence EnWG);
- Avoidance of discrimination (§ 10 (3) 1st sentence EnWG);
- Avoidance of cross-subsidies (§§ 10 (3) 1st and 5th sentence, (1) no. 5 EnWG).

However, obviously all these aspects are closely related to part 3 EnWG (regulation of the system operation). Thus, the above conclusion, according to which the unbundling requirements are just an auxiliary means to implementation of a nondiscriminatory grid access, is explicitly confirmed. This must be particularly taken into account in any interpretation and application of the rules. It is not about reorganising the energy industry as a legal policy value as such, in particular just for the sake of the establishment of grid companies with comprehensive functions. In other words: the target of the unbundling requirements is not to completely detach the grid business as such from the formerly vertically integrated undertakings and to contribute all functions in any way connected with the system operation into this company. The unbundling requirements rather provide for a legal, operational, informational and accounting distinction between the (residual) integrated energy supply undertakings and the system operator for the purpose of a nondiscriminatory exercising and structuring of the system operation and the avoidance of cross-subsidies only. This is a principle of interpretation that is crucial for the construction of the unbundling requirements.

References

Breuer, R. 2004. Umsetzung von EG-Richtlinien im neuen Energiewirtschaftsrecht. NVwZ, 23: 520-529.

Bundesnetzagentur. 2007. Press release: Federal Network Agency publishes guideline on the implementation of information unbundling. http://www.bundesnetzagentur.de/media/archive/10563.pdf.

Bundesverfassungsgericht (BVerfG). 2005. 2 BvR 2236/04 vom 18.7.2005, Absatz-Nr. (1-201). http://www.bverfg.de/entscheidungen/rs20050718_2bvr2236 04.html.

Canaris, C.-W. & Larenz, K. 2008. Methodenlehre der Rechtswissenschaft. 4. Auflage. Berlin.

Council Regulation (EC) No 139/2004. 2004. Council Regulation of 20 January 2004 on the control of concentrations between undertakings (the EC merger regulation). Official Journal – European Communities Legislation, 24: 1-22.

Directive 2001/65/EC. 2001. Directive of the European Parliament and of the Council of 27 September 2001 amending Directives 78/660/EEC, 83/349/EEC and 86/635/EEC as regards the valuation rules for the annual and consolidated accounts of certain types of companies as well as of banks and other financial institutions. Official Journal of the European Communities, L 283: 28-32.

Directive 2003/54/EC. 2003. Directive of the European Parliament and of the Council of 26 June 2003 concerning common rules for the internal market in electricity and repealing Directive 96/92/EC – Statements made with regard to decommissioning and waste management activities. Official Journal – European Communities Legislation, 176: 37-56.

Directive 2003/55/EC. 2003. Directive of the European Parliament and of the Council of 26 June 2003 concerning common rules for the internal market in natural gas and repealing Directive 98/30/EC. Official Journal – European Communities Legislation, 176: 57-78.

Ehricke, U. 2004. Vermerke der Kommission zur Umsetzung von Richtlinien. EuZW 15: 359-364.

European Commission. 2007a. Communication from the Commission: Inquiry pursuant to Article 17 of Regulation (EC) No 1/2003 into the European gas and electricity sectors (Final Report). Brussels: European Commission.

European Commission. 2007b. Proposal for a Directive of the European Parliament and of the Council amending Directive 2003/54/EC concerning common rules for the internal market in electricity (528 final – 2007/0195 [COD]). Brussels: European Commission.

European Commission. 2007c. Proposal for a Directive of the European Parliament and of the Council amending Directive 2003/55/EC concerning common rules for the internal market in natural gas. Brussels: European Commission.

General Secretariat of the Council of the European Union. 2007. Annotation of General Secretariat of Council to delegations relating to: standardised energy policy in Europe.

Contribution of Council (energy) to spring meeting 2007 of European Council – conclusions of the Council (6453/07, 5). Brussels: Council of the European Union.

Generaldirektion Energie und Verkehr. 2004. Note of GD Energie und Verkehr (Directorate-General Energy and Transport) on the Directives 2003/54/EC and 2003/55/EC on the internal market in electricity and natural gas – the unbundling provisions. Brüssel: Generaldirektion Energie und Verkehr.

Gesetz über die Elektrizitäts- und Gasversorgung (EnWG). 2005. Energiewirtschaftsgesetz. EnWG.

Kroes, N. 2007. Improving Europe's energy markets through more competition. Tischgespräch – Industrie-Club e.V. Düsseldorf, Düsseldorf, 23. März 2007. http://europa.eu/rapid/pressReleasesAction.do?referece=SPEECH/07/175&format=HTML&aged=0&language=EN&guiLanguage=en.

Kurth, M. 2007. Eröffnungsrede zum Auftakt des 4. Deutschen Regulierungskongress am 26. September 2007 in Berlin. http://www.regulierungskongress.de/veranstaltung2007/tagungsbericht.asp.

Office of the Gas and Electricity Markets (Ofgem). 2006. Statement – European Commission stands firm on energy liberalisation. http://www.ofgem.gov.uk/Media/PressRel/Documents1/16603-R2.pdf.

Piebalgs, A. 2007. Der Energiebinnenmarkt muss jedem einzelnen EU-Bürger zugute kommen. High-Level-Workshop Energie, Berlin. http://ec.europa.eu/commission_barroso/piebalgs/doc/media/2007_03_29_speech07_210.de.pdf

Säcker, F. J. 2004. Entflechtung von Netzgeschäft und Vertrieb bei den Energieversorgungsunternehmen: Gesellschaftsrechtliche Möglichkeiten zur Umsetzung des sog. Legal Unbundling. Der Betrieb 16: 691-694.

30 The Energy Arteries of a Continent – Natural Gas Networks Secure Europe's Energy Supply

Matthias Warnig[1]

Abstract

Natural gas will become one of the most important raw materials over the next few decades. In Europe alone, the demand for natural gas imports of 314 billion cubic metres in 2005 will increase by approximately 200 billion cubic metres by 2025. Hence, the important question for the future is how the raw material gas is to be transported from the gas fields to the consumers. Faced with their growing import needs, the European countries are required to enlarge their natural gas transport networks and invest in new pipelines to guarantee long-term security of supply. Russia has already proved itself a reliable partner for the European Union.

Keywords: European gas network, pipeline, Nord Stream

---

[1] Matthias Warnig is Managing Director of Nord Stream AG, Switzerland.

A. Bausch and B. Schwenker (eds.), *Handbook Utility Management,*
DOI: 10.1007/978-3-540-79349-6_30, © Springer-Verlag Berlin Heidelberg 2009

30.1   Introduction

Where does energy come from? This is an increasingly critical question – especially in Europe. The EU is the largest importer of energy worldwide, and demand is constantly rising. Natural gas, in particular, will become one of the most important commodities in years to come, for obvious reasons: there are sufficient deposits of natural gas, and gas can be used in diverse ways. In addition, natural gas is clean energy. This natural resource offers not just economic and ecological benefits, but is also very well suited for generating electricity, which explains the ongoing exploration and development of new natural gas fields and extraction sites and the decisive improvements in transportation technology. However, the areas where natural gas deposits are located are limited to a handful of countries worldwide. How to get the natural gas quickly and in large quantities from the distant well-head to the end-consumer will thus be critical in the future. European countries, in particular, will have no choice but to invest in their natural gas networks, storage facilities and pipelines. Europe cannot afford to hesitate, as the example of the United Kingdom illustrates.

For more than 20 years, following the discovery and development of oil and gas reserves in the North Sea on Britain's doorstep, the UK basked in the comfort of being self-sufficient in energy. At its peak, the UK produced more oil than Kuwait or the United Arab Emirates, and for most of that period was a net energy exporter. And for a period in the 1990s, the UK was the world's fourth largest producer of natural gas, producing less than the Soviet Union, the United States and Canada, but still ahead of Norway. Confident of its gas reserves, the government encouraged a progressive switch from coal-fired to gas-powered electricity generation. Many coal mines were closed, and many coal-fired power plants were shut or converted to gas, though coal still accounts for more than 30% of UK electricity generation. Currently, nearly 40% of Britain's electricity supply is generated from gas, and gas has replaced oil as the preferred home-heating fuel. Ample supplies depressed market prices for gas, and consumption nearly doubled during the 1990s.

30.2   Declining Domestic Production in the EU

However, all that is history. In this century, the situation has changed ra-pidly. Gas reserves have proved lower than the optimistic estimates, and production peaked in the years 2000-2004. In 2005, the UK started to import gas once again. Plenty turned into scarcity, which is now being relieved by imports of liquid natural gas (LNG). Further LNG import facilities are under construction.

It is meanwhile understood in the UK that imports possess strategic significance, and it is investing in new transportation routes. The UK gas grid with its 4,500 km of gas pipeline was constructed to accommodate reliable supplies of North Sea gas from the British and Norwegian sectors of the North Sea. Additional work to the gas grid will be needed to take account of new sources of imported gas, and additional underground storage to supplement the 12 days of supply currently available may be needed to ensure supplies to domestic and commercial gas consumers. Spot market prices for gas remain highly volatile and are a source of concern. 'Demand management' can mean allocation of supply by the simple expedient of turning off the tap when short-term demand exceeds supply. One view prevalent in the UK until recently was that it costs less to shut down companies than to maintain large reserve capacities which might never be used. But this approach is unlikely to appeal across Europe as a whole, where many will be alarmed at excessive use of 'interruptible supply contracts' as a response to longer term energy shortage.

For example, the British-Norwegian Langeled natural gas pipeline is an important source of energy for the UK. This gas is sourced in the Norwegian Ormen-Langen deposit and is carried to Easington on the British coast through a 1,200-km-long offshore pipeline under the North Sea. The British-Norwegian joint venture cost a total of € 2.5 billion and will pipe about 25 billion cubic metres a year of North Sea gas to the UK market.

The increasing use of natural gas in Europe should bring environmental and economic benefits, but European reserves and production are in decline, increasing the need for new sources of imported gas. As a result, many countries will be seeking new long-term supply contracts, but will also be confronted with the problems and costs of upgrading and expanding their energy infrastructures.

30.3   The EU Expects Natural Gas Imports to Increase

The European Commission in Brussels expects imports of hydrocarbons to rise and European markets to continue opening up (Commission of the European Communities, 2007a). Even if everything else stays the same, i.e. if neither demand nor need in the EU increases, according to the EU Commission, energy imports will continue to rise from the current 54% of total energy consumption to 68% by 2030. And the EU's calculations predict that imports of natural gas will jump from currently 57% to 81% by 2025.

This means that each and every European country must take the initiative, for global energy resources are under pressure, emerging countries such as China and India are pushing hard to obtain energy from available deposits, and natural gas is concentrated in only a few countries. The International Energy Agency (IEA), for example, expects demand for oil to rise by 41% worldwide by 2030. How supplies might keep pace with this huge demand is anyone's guess. The IEA confirmed in its World Energy Outlook 2006 that it remains completely uncertain whether or not the major producers of oil and natural gas are able and, more especially, willing to make larger investments in order to meet growing global demand (IEA, 2006). The IEA believes importing countries will need to contribute to ensure that the required investment in new capacity is undertaken. Without such measures – the EU Commission is very specific – there will be a growing risk of energy shortages in Europe. In addition, the Commission also found that, "the mechanisms to ensure solidarity between Member States in the event of an energy crisis are not yet in place" (Commission of the European Communities, 2007b).

30.3.1 Insufficient Energy Efficiency

Conservation alone will not close the looming energy gap. The EU Commission calculated in 2006 that investments totalling € 900 billion will be required in the next 25 years purely for electricity generation, even if effective energy efficiency policies are adopted throughout the EU. The Commission argues that huge investments in domestic natural gas and electricity distribution mechanisms will be required to ensure that consumer prices remain competitive.

In fact, the EU is the world's largest importer of energy, and natural gas has accounted for an ever larger share of primary energy use. Just as in the UK, natural gas deposits in the remainder of the EU have been declining overall while consumption has been rising. The projections for both supplies and energy security thus pose new and major challenges for Europe. According to the EU Commission's Green Book, consumption of natural gas will increase from 543 billion cubic metres in 2005 to 630 billion cubic metres a year in 2030 (Commission of the European Communities, 2006).

Figures from 2006 show that European countries obtain their natural gas from seven regions: Norway (24%); Algeria (18%); Russia (42%); Nigeria (5%); Libya (2.7%); Egypt (2.7%); and Qatar (2.1%). The remaining 3.5% is obtained from other, minor sources. Europe will have to accept that it is going to become increasingly dependent on natural gas imports. It is likely that more than one half of all gas will have to be imported by 2010, and approximately 80% by 2030. Unless gas grids are installed and expanded early on, gaps in the energy supply will continue to grow. Major projects, such as the Nord Stream Pipeline, which will pipe about 55 billion cubic metres of natural gas a year into the European network from 2011/2012 onward, are designed to fill the gap.

30.3.2 New Natural Gas Pipelines for Europe

The European natural gas transportation network is considered one of the world's best in terms of performance. However, further investment in new delivery routes will be required to achieve the twin goals of ensuring the security of supplies on the European continent and promoting competition on the European natural gas market. While there are many possible sources of European gas imports, all will require new transport systems. And more investment in Europe's inter-linked natural gas grids will be needed to ensure Europe's long-term energy security.

EU member states have become increasingly aware of the need for closer cooperation in the field of energy, and the Commission has prepared the ground for joint energy policies. In 2006, the EU Commission developed proposals "for a European strategy aimed at competitive and secure energy in the long term" (Commission of the European Communities, 2006). Among other suggestions, one key proposal is to establish a new energy partnership with Russia. The EU itself has been working on a common European energy policy for more than 10 years. Since 1996, it has systematically pushed for the establishment of a pan-European energy infrastructure.

The so-called priority axes and Trans-European Energy Networks (TEN-E) projects are at the core of these efforts. The stated goal is to link the existing European gas transmission to new pipelines bringing gas from outside Europe, especially from Russia. The 'NG1 Axis', as defined by the EU Commission, runs from the UK via the Netherlands and Northern Germany straight across the Baltic Sea to Russia. It includes construction of natural gas pipelines which, according to the EU, are aimed at "linking the most important natural gas deposits in Europe to each other". With North Sea deposits dwindling, such a move should help improve the security of supplies in Europe.

30.4   The Nord Stream Project Is of Interest to Europe

The new focus in European energy policies caught Russia's attention. Several ideas were floated in the mid-1990s, leading to a specific proposal for a new transmission route: a pipeline that would link the as yet undeveloped Shtokman natural gas field in the Barents Sea to Germany's Baltic Sea coast. The route would take in the ice-free harbour of Murmansk in the extreme Northwest of Russia and Russia's Baltic Sea coast, and from there would be laid across the Baltic seabed to end up in north-east Germany. Brussels, too, took up the idea. In 2000, the project was awarded the status of a project of common interest for improving the energy infrastructure in accordance with the 'Trans-European Energy Network Guidelines'. This status was confirmed yet again in 2002 in the context of an energy dialogue between Russia and the EU, and the project was also included in the EU Commission's Second Action Plan for the development of Northern Europe. In 2006, when the TEN-E guidelines were updated, the project – now named Nord Stream – was granted the status of a priority project of interest to Europe and was included among the EU's most important energy infrastructure projects. The pipeline is intended to become one of Europe's key energy arteries.

Importing Russian natural gas will turn Germany into a new hub for European gas supplies and internationalise Germany's natural gas network. According to the experts, bottlenecks in natural gas deliveries are not to be expected, given Russia's proven reserves of 48 trillion cubic metres. The Hamburg-based energy information service, Energie Informationsdienst (EID), even predicts that worldwide natural gas deposits will last for at least another 160 years.

However, gas deposits must be brought to the consumer, which requires, above all, investments in the infrastructure of natural gas grids and storage facilities. Three criteria should govern all planning in connection with new projects in this area, specifically, each project's: (1) Technical feasibility; (2) Ecological compatibility; (3) Economic profitability.

A major pipeline project can proceed only if it can be shown to have a reasonable environmental impact, if the technology is demonstrably feasible, and if there is security of demand for the gas it carries, i.e. if that gas will attract buyers at prices that allow an economic return on investment.

Additional investments in natural gas networks can help with maintaining, repairing and, if necessary, extending the reach and life of existing pipelines. The better a pipeline's performance, the lower the amount of energy lost in transmission. New compressor technology within an existing pipeline system conserves energy, for example, but also greatly enhances its efficiency. This sort of investment represents a crucial task for the natural gas industry, alongside the exploration for and development of new gas fields.

30.5   Economic Benefits from New Natural Gas Networks

The benefits of investments in new natural gas networks extend far beyond their contribution to the security of energy supplies in Europe. Adapting existing infrastructures to meet future rising demand for gas enhances the technological know-how and export opportunities for European companies. Moreover, investments in natural gas grids are generally counter-cyclical and not dependent on the short-term economic climate. As such, they also contribute indirectly to Europe's economic stability.

Europe is laying the foundation for its future by building new pipeline routes. Several important infrastructure projects are due to come on stream in the next few years. Besides Nord Stream (which will run from Vyborg in Russia to the German Baltic Sea coast at Lubmin), the Nabucco pipeline will connect Azerbaijan to Austria via Turkey, Rumania, Bulgaria and Hungary. The Nabucco pipeline, which will be roughly 3,300 km long, is intended to cover 5% of the natural gas consumption in the EU until 2025. Additional projects provide for pipelines to Europe across the Mediterranean. Examples are Transmed from Algeria to Italy via Tunisia, Galsi from Algeria to Italy across the Mediterranean, and Medgaz, which will carry natural gas from Algeria to Spain and France. Most of these projects are in the start-up phase and will be operational between 2008 and 2013. During this period, they should give Europe the capacity to cope with rising demand in the short to medium term. Given the growing importance of natural gas imports in the next 20-30 years, this approach is in keeping with the EU's stated goal of both securing and diversifying additional sources of natural gas imports.

30.5.1   Russia Is a Reliable Natural Gas Supplier

Russia will make an important contribution to the importation of natural gas. Currently, Russia exports about 200 billion cubic metres of natural gas annually. These figures are set to rise to more than 300 billion cubic metres by 2030. This will make Russia an indispensable energy provider to Europe. And Russia sees itself as a close partner to the EU in the long term.

Gas holds the key to the future. Nobody will be able to ignore it. Natural gas will be one of the most important energy sources, if not the most important, of the coming decades. It is already impossible to imagine generating heat and electricity without natural gas. Not only is natural gas in demand, but there is the prospect of even more ample supplies for the long term. In contrast to oil, the production capacity of which appears to have peaked in a number of places, countries with natural gas deposits are reporting large reserves and potential for greatly increased output. Industry estimates suggest that only 18% of the probable worldwide reserves are currently being exploited. Of the world's total natural gas reserves, some 73 trillion cubic metres are thought to be located in the Middle East, with a further 15 trillion cubic metres in Asia. A total of 64 trillion cubic metres of natural gas deposits are attributed to the states of the former Soviet Union, above all Russia. As far as we know, total natural gas reserves worldwide will last far into the next century. Russia, Iran, and Qatar, the world's three leading producers of natural gas, are thought to be home to 56% of the world reserves.

30.5.2 Natural Gas Fulfils Climate Requirements

Many specialists believe that natural gas could conceivably become the world's most important source of energy in the near future. According to the IEA, worldwide demand could increase by 66% by 2030, especially as natural gas clearly has the edge in reducing greenhouse gas emissions. Given the seriousness now accorded to climate protection in Europe, gas is seen as the best candidate of all fossil fuels for combining reduction of CO_2 emissions with future energy supply security.

The well-known Hamburg Institute of International Economics (HWWI) forecasts in a 2007 study entitled Wirtschaftsfaktor Erdgasbranche [The Natural Gas Industry – An Economic Factor] that "natural gas possesses properties that make it a 'bridge technology', even in regards to climate change". And, according to the HWWI, natural gas will be needed in the future not just for generating heat or electricity but also as a transport fuel. This would require further large-scale investment in roadside fuel facilities to encourage consumers to buy gas-powered vehicles. According to the EU Commission, vehicular traffic is responsible for 84% of all traffic-related CO_2 emissions. In 2001, the EU estimated that in the absence of countermeasures CO_2 emissions from road traffic would rise by 50% to 1.1 trillion tonnes between 1990 and 2010. As a result, the EU concludes that more alternative fuels are needed, along with moves to increase the fuel efficiency of vehicles, to reduce our dependence on oil.

In spring 2007, the European Commission set out a target for 2020 of replacing one-fifth of the consumption of traditional gasoline and diesel with alternative fuels, with natural gas supplying 10% of the market. While alternative energies such as wind, the sun, or biomass cannot by any means yield sufficiently secure supplies of energy, natural gas offers high levels of secure supplies in the long term and at substantially lower costs. This is all the more important given the need for technical innovations in connection with regenerative energies.

30.5.3   Producing and Transporting Natural Gas Is Capital Intensive

While natural gas is available in sufficient quantities, it is not easy to obtain. In contrast to coal or crude oil, natural gas cannot be imported at relatively short notice. Natural gas is extracted in extreme climatic conditions, for instance, at temperatures as low as minus 60 °C and from permanently frozen soil in Siberia, or from the depths of the Norwegian North Sea. The costs of developing and transporting natural gas are therefore very high. No single producer and no single importer could pay these costs by themselves. Transporting natural gas across great distances – in Nord Stream's case, from Murmansk via Vyborg (both in Russia) across the Baltic Sea to Lubmin, Germany – requires an extensive and costly infrastructure. Because such expenditures would impose very large risks on any producer of natural gas, producers and importers work closely together in both technical and financial terms based on long-term delivery contracts with terms of up to 30 years. This gives importers security of supply and equally importantly, provides producers and investors engaged in large-scale gas development with security of offtake. It ensures that there will be a secure market for their gas and a predictable rate of return on capital, all of which secures the interests of both parties. Importing countries guarantee their purchases, and the producing countries, in turn, commit themselves not to seek out alternative buyers.

The price of natural gas comprises the costs for the commodity itself, the cost of transporting and distributing it, and taxes and fees. Natural gas thus offers lower energy costs with higher levels of supply security. And energy costs are a substantial factor in the competitiveness of companies located in the EU. Germany, for example, currently consumes approximately 900 million kWh of natural gas per year. As natural gas is used primarily for heating purposes, in 2004 it accounted for 77% of natural gas consumption in households, while also accounting for about 12% of all electricity generated in Germany. A mere 15% of the natural gas used in Germany is derived from domestic sources; the rest is imported. And this requires investment.

Investment in Nord Stream is an example; this project is aimed at securing Western Europe's energy supply from 2011 onward. Since 1997, the energy industry has been investigating the feasibility of laying a pipeline across the Baltic Sea to provide a direct connection between consumers in Western Europe and the enormous gas deposits in Russia. Nord Stream AG is planning and will build the two separate sub-sea Baltic pipelines that make up the system, which it will also operate on its completion.

30.6 Pipeline Across the Baltic Sea – Europe's Energy Artery

30.6.1 Planning of the Pipeline Across the Baltic Sea

Construction of the first Nord Stream Pipeline across the Baltic Sea will begin in 2010. The system will consist of two pipelines, each about 1,220 km long, laid on the seafloor. Initial deliveries to Western Europe of some 27 billion cubic metres a year of Russian natural gas will double to 55 billion a year on completion of the second pipeline. According to the European Commission's Directorate-General Energy and Transport, Europe will need to boost gas imports by almost 200 billion cubic metres a year by 2025 (Commission of the European Communities/DG-TREN, 2007). Nord Stream will be able to cover about one quarter of the additional needs.

Why a pipeline across the Baltic Sea? First, a pipeline of up to 4,500 km is considered the most economic way of transporting natural gas from the production site to the end-consumer. In addition, the oil and natural gas industry consider offshore pipelines, i.e. pipelines that traverse bodies of water and are installed on the seafloor, to be the safest and most secure method of transporting fuel. The improved quality of the materials now used for the pipes, new construction processes and comprehensive inspection and quality assurance plans prior to construction are among the main strengths of Nord Stream. The pipeline through the Baltic Sea also fulfils the aforementioned criteria for an investment: it is technically feasible; it will provide a strong return on investment and be profitable, given high levels of demand in the buyer countries; This is not all, however: the total costs of Nord Stream, including operating costs over 25 years, should be approximately 15% lower than the costs for an onshore pipeline with the same transport capacity. The operating costs of an overland route are relatively high, mainly due to the need for a series of en route compressor stations. One compressor station every 200 km is needed for an onshore pipeline to compensate for pressure losses. This requirement and these costs are minimised when an offshore pipeline is laid.

Finally, Nord Stream is ecologically sound because the pipeline will cross the sea and therefore will not endanger the onshore environment. It will not have any damaging impact on rivers, forests and agricultural areas. Moreover, the displacement of soil is minimal for the installation of an offshore compared with an onshore line. Nord Stream AG will set standards for secure and efficient energy supplies in Europe.

30.6.2 Offshore Pipelines Are Secure

Natural gas is more than just heat. The availability of energy is one of the primary factors when companies with energy-intensive production decide where to locate. Both the price of energy and the security of supplies are critical to a company's competitiveness. Nord Stream has conducted comprehensive studies in order to minimise environmental risks and enhance the operational safety of its pipeline. For instance, munitions dumping sites were excluded from the pipeline route from the outset. Extensive tests that have been conducted in several stages using state-of-the art sensors and echo sounders were used to help Nord Stream to locate potential individual obstacles when the route was fixed. The construction of the pipeline was preceded by extensive studies on risks and the precise determination of a secure route on the seafloor. Careful selection of construction materials is as important to the construction of a pipeline as the use of state-of-the-art technology.

Nord Stream AG is a prime example of a successful investment in the natural gas industry – an investment from which both the consumers and the producers of the gas will benefit. Nord Stream AG is an international joint venture that was established for the purpose of planning, building and operating the pipeline. The world's largest natural gas producer, the Russian firm Gazprom, has a stake of 51% in the project. The balance is made up by two German energy companies, BASF/Wintershall and E.ON Ruhrgas, each with a stake of 20%, and the Dutch natural gas infrastructure company, N.V. Gasunie, which has a 9% stake in the venture. Gazprom and Wintershall (a subsidiary of BASF) joined forces more than 16 years ago to market natural gas. Their aim was to sell natural gas at competitive prices and to secure supplies in the long term. The natural gas that has been piped to Europe in recent years has derived mainly from Russian sources and is delivered by Gazprom via a variety of independent transportation routes.

30.7   Investments Are Profitable

Transporting natural gas through an offshore pipeline is the less expensive option, not just relative to the onshore option, but also against transporting the same amount of LNG, which is much more expensive. This has given rise to gas markets worldwide with substantially different price structures depending on the distance to the well-head. In 2005, for example, natural gas cost 40% more in the United States than in Europe. Russia's large natural gas reserves are particularly important to Europe and Germany, given their relative geographical proximity – especially those in the Caspian region, which account for just under 75% of all European and Eurasian reserves and can be accessed efficiently by means of pipelines.

These investments will necessitate the construction of additional pipelines. Two gas pipelines must be built in order to channel the natural gas that has arrived in Germany via Nord Stream to consumers: OPAL (Ostsee-Pipeline-Anbindungs-Leitung) is scheduled to carry natural gas from Lubmin to Olbernhau in the south, on the German-Czech border. The NEL pipeline (Norddeutsche Erdgasleitung) is to connect Lubmin with Achim near Bremen, Germany, in the west.

The example of WINGAS, a joint venture of Gazprom and Wintershall, also shows how investments in a natural gas grid improve the infrastructure. The transport system of WINGAS links the German and European natural gas market with gas pipelines that run 5,000 km from Russian natural gas sources in Siberia to the

German border and serve the Western European market from there. The 'new' pipeline through the Baltic Sea will be linked to the pipeline systems of both WINGAS and E.ON Ruhrgas in Germany once it is operational. WINGAS is also planning to build new natural gas storage facilities in Europe in order to secure energy supplies. In addition to Western Europe's largest natural gas storage facility in Rehden, Germany, the company is also establishing a new natural gas storage facility in Austria. The STEGAL pipeline (Sachsen-Thüringen-Erdgasleitung) has also been upgraded and expanded. WINGAS expanded this East-West line, a critical gas transmission link, at a cost of about € 200 million, boosting the pipeline's transport capacity by more than 50%. Yet another project, again in collaboration with E.ON Ruhrgas AG, entails the construction of the SEL line, the Southern German natural gas pipeline that is to connect the German states of Bavaria, Baden-Württemberg and Hessen to the major East-West pipelines.

WINGAS and E.ON Ruhrgas are setting a good example, and other companies are following suit. The German natural gas industry has invested a total of € 12 billion since 2000 to secure supplies, i.e. roughly € 2 billion per year. According to HWWI, natural gas not only fuels the German economy but also fills the national coffers. In 2006 alone, the German government earned revenues of € 3 billion from a natural gas tax.

30.8   No Growth without Secure Energy Supplies

Germany is a good example for the future of Europe's energy supply. In Germany, natural gas currently accounts for 23% of the country's primary energy needs, making it the second most important fossil fuel. The natural gas industry is central to supplying energy to both businesses and households, but also fulfils an important wider economic function, as HWWI confirms in its study. "While the gross value added per employee paying social security contributions in Germany was roughly € 75,000 in 2004, the value added per employee in the natural gas industry was three times as high at € 235,000".

For an industrial and export-oriented country such as Germany, investments in the natural gas industry also are necessary to ensure continuous supplies of natural gas to other areas of the economy. Natural gas accounts for 31% of all energy consumed by the industrial sector and for 28% of all energy consumed by commerce, trade and services. According to the HWWI study, "A primary aim of investments in the natural gas industry is the security of supplies". Both the cost of energy and the security of supplies are decisive criteria in companies' decisions on where to locate their operations. Energy-intensive industries, in particular, are affected by decisions resulting from energy policy made at national and European levels.

Investments of this nature are diverse. They serve to expand natural gas storage capacities and upgrade the natural gas pipeline network. And by investing in the natural gas network, local gas companies also fulfil an important structural responsibility. An extensive grid of pipelines fosters the establishment of new companies and the expansion of residential areas with only minor additional development costs. This opens up comparable opportunities all over Europe.

In Germany, the chemical and metal industry, along with energy and water utility companies, account for most of total energy consumption, as well as natural gas consumption. Without secure and timely deliveries of natural gas and other commodities, there is a potential risk of energy and production bottlenecks, which in the medium term could ultimately force companies to relocate. This sends an adverse signal to other firms thinking of setting up in the same region.

In addition to the pipeline network, which absorbs investments of roughly € 1.5 billion each year, 44 subterranean natural gas storage facilities with a capacity of 19.1 billion cubic metres of working gas provide the reserves to ensure stable supplies. By the end of 2005, only the United States, Russia, and the Ukraine had greater storage capacities. Germany, just like the EU as a whole, is aiming to diversify its energy sourcing in terms of both the countries and the suppliers from which it purchases energy. Even so, fixed delivery contracts, most of which are concluded for long terms, are seen as a way of keeping the investment risks as low as possible while also ensuring the security of the national energy supply for the benefit of domestic industries.

The fact is that any energy shortage – whatever its cause – would substantially limit the ability of European countries to act, and indeed to survive. Some might consider the uneven distribution of natural resources and gas deposits a disadvantage, but that is not necessarily the case. Long-term cooperation and partnerships in the energy sector promote international collaboration and reduce the potential for conflicts. The Cold War provides the best example of this. The Soviet Union did not interrupt its deliveries of energy to Western Europe for even one second, in spite of the political and military differences between the two blocks. The liberalisation of the European markets is also increasing consumers' willingness to work with new competitive providers. We expect material parameters to be further optimised in this respect: consistent liberalisation of the European markets, effective reduction of bureaucracy and elimination of artificial trade barriers, and harmonisation of economic parameters in individual EU member states are foreseen. The investments the natural gas industry is making in the expansion and modernisation of the natural gas network provide for the security of supplies and rising efficiency. This is why investments in natural gas grids are necessary, so that we no longer need to ask where energy is coming from, but rather how imported energy is being used in meaningful ways to enable economic growth.

References

Commission of the European Communities. 2006. Annex to the green paper a European strategy for sustainable, competitive and secure energy. Brussels.

Commission of the European Communities. 2007a. An energy policy for Europe. Brussels.

Commission of the European Communities. 2007b. The former Yugoslav Republic of Macedonia 2007 – progress report. Brussels.

Commission of the European Communities/DG-TREN. 2007: European energy and transport. Trends to 2030 – update 2007. Luxembourg: Office for Official Publications of the European Communities.

International Energy Agency (IEA). 2006. World energy outlook 2006. Paris: IEA.

31 Dispatching in Unbundled Electricity Markets

Yong-Hua Song[1]

Jing Sun[2]

Abstract

Throughout the world, unprecedented reform and restructuring of the electric power industry has imposed tremendous challenges on the operation of power systems under this new environment. Regardless of the market structures that may emerge in various parts of the world, system security, reliability, and quality of supply must be maintained. Faced by an increasingly complicated co-existence of technical and economical considerations, new computational tools and software systems are in great demand by generators, system operators, retailers, and other market participants to help them to meet operating, scheduling, planning, and financial requirements. This chapter covers all the major operational issues, such as scheduling and dispatch, congestion management, available transfer capability calculation, price forecasting and optimal bidding strategies.

Keywords: unbundled electricity markets, dispatch, operation

[1] Prof. Dr. Yong-Hua Song is Professor of Electrical Engineering at the University of Liverpool, United Kingdom.

[2] Jing Sun is a Lecturer at the Beihang University, China.

A. Bausch and B. Schwenker (eds.), *Handbook Utility Management,*
DOI: 10.1007/978-3-540-79349-6_31, © Springer-Verlag Berlin Heidelberg 2009

31.1   Operation of Restructured Power Systems

There has been a worldwide trend towards restructuring and deregulation of the power industry over the last decades. The competition in the wholesale generation market and the retail market together with open access to the transmission network can bring many benefits to end-consumers, such as lower electricity prices and better services. However, this competition also brings many new technical issues and challenges to the operation of restructured power systems (Schweppe et al., 1988; Ilic et al., 1998; Einhorn & Siddiqui, 1996; Stoft, 2002).

31.1.1   System Operation in a Competitive Environment

Regardless of the market structures that may emerge in various parts of the world, one fact that seems always to be true is that transmission and generation services will be unbundled from one another. The generation market will become fully competitive, with many market participants who will be able to sell their energy services (or demand side management). On the other hand, the operation of a transmission system is expected to remain a regulated monopoly whose function is to allow open, nondiscriminatory and comparable access to all suppliers and consumers of electrical energy. This function can be implemented by an entity called an Independent System Operator (ISO) (Bhattacharya et al., 2001; Shahidiehpouret et al., 2002; Song, 1999; Overbye, 2000; Hunt & Shuttleworth, 1996; Harris, 2000; Secretary of Energy Advisory Board, 1998; Rahimi & Vojdani, 1999).

Although electricity markets may have many different ISO designs and approaches all over the world, there are nonetheless elements that are necessary to all types of ISOs to allow them to meet their common basic requirements. Basically, the ISO has responsibility for the reliability functions in its region of operation and for ensuring that all participants have open and nondiscriminatory access to transmission services through its planning and operation of the power transmission system. The ISO should conduct all of its functions in an impartial manner so that all participants are treated equitably. The main functions of the ISO can be categorised into reliability-related functions and market-related functions.

31.1.1.1 Reliability-related Functions

The reliability-related functions include two aspects:

- *System operation and coordination:* The ISO should perform system security monitoring functions and redispatch generation as necessary to eliminate real-time transmission congestion and to maintain system reliability; this includes taking all necessary emergency actions to maintain the security of the system in both normal and abnormal operating conditions.
- *Transmission planning and construction:* The ISO should carry out reliability studies and planning activities in coordination with the transmission own-

ers and other market participants to ensure the adequacy of the transmission system. The ISO should publish data, studies and plans relating to the adequacy of the transmission system. Data might include locational congestion prices and planning studies that identify options for actions that might be taken to remedy reliability problems on the grid and cost data for some of these actions.

31.1.1.2 Market-related Functions

First of all, an ISO must be a market enabler with no commercial interest in the competitive generation market. The market-related functions of an ISO must be carried out according to transparent, understandable rules and protocols. The following operational functions are necessary to enable a competitive generation market:

- Determine available transmission capability (ATC) for all paths of interest within the ISO region.
- Receive and process all requests for transmission service within and through the ISO region from all participants, including transmission owners.
- Schedule all transactions it has approved.
- Operate or participate in an open-access same-time information system (OASIS) for information publishing.
- Establish a clear ranking of transmission rights of all the participants on the ISO transmission system. Facilitate trading of transmission rights on its grid among participants.
- Manage transmission congestion in accordance with established rules and procedures for generation redispatch and its cost allocation.
- Ensure the provision of ancillary services required to support all scheduled delivery transactions.
- Market settlement and billing functions.

The minimum functions of the ISO should include the operation and coordination of the power system to ensure security. In this case, a separate market operator (for example, the Power Exchange in California) is needed to perform the market-related functions. On the other hand, the maximum functions of the ISO will include all the reliability-related and market-related functions mentioned above, and in addition the ISO is the transmission owner (e.g. the National Grid Company in the UK). The functions of the ISO at various sizes and time scales are shown in Figure 31.1.

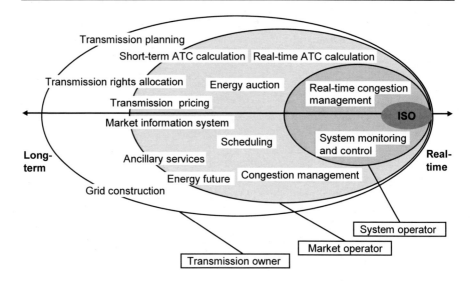

Figure 31.1: Functions of the ISO at various sizes and time scales

31.1.2   Effects of Restructuring the Industry on System Reliability

Maintaining reliability involves two sets of operations: normal and emergency operations. Markets can do much to maintain reliability and prevent outages (by preparing resources for use in emergencies) during normal operations. Markets alone may be much less effective during actual emergencies (Secretary of Energy Advisory Board, 1998).

Response time is the key factor that will determine whether the independent actions of participants in competitive markets can perform some reliability functions or whether technical standards and direct control will be required. Roughly speaking, competition is likely to work well for actions expected to occur half an hour or more in the future. Given this lead time, buyers and sellers can find the price level for each service that will balance supply and demand. For shorter time periods, however, system control is still likely to be required. Technical standards may be needed to specify the amount of each service that is required and to establish metrics for judging the adequacy of service delivery; markets can then determine the least-cost ways to deliver the required services. Disturbance response and generation planning provide useful examples of the two ends of the temporal spectrum.

The system operator must have the ultimate authority to compel actions needed to maintain reliability in real time and to restore the system quickly and safely after an outage occurs, although after-the-fact disputes may occur over who pays for what.

In the future, in a market-based model for providing adequate generation resources, decisions on retirement or repowering of existing generators and the construction of new units are likely to be made by investors with much less regulatory involvement. Of course, governments will still oversee the environmental consequences of these decisions. Nonetheless, with retail choice of generation suppliers, markets (investors and consumers) rather than economic regulators will decide which supplies are needed and financially good value.

These decisions will be made on the basis of trends in market prices and projected revenues from the sale of electricity relative to the construction and operating costs of the unit in question. Generators will be built when projected market prices of electricity are high enough to yield a profit. Spot prices will stop rising only when constrained demand is brought down, or supply is increased, or both. Although these spot prices are likely to be quite low for most hours, they may be very high for a few hours each year. It is the level, frequency, and duration of these high prices that will be the signal for markets to build more generating capacity, rather than the decisions of planners in vertically integrated utilities. This price volatility will also be the signal warning customers about the benefits of managing their loads in real time.

In electricity markets, customer response to real-time pricing signals could also help to improve reliability. The challenge of restructuring the electricity industry is to find an appropriate mix of economic incentives and performance standards that maintain reliability at the lowest reasonable cost.

31.1.3   New Requirement for Computation Tools and Software Systems in Electricity Markets

New computational tools and software systems are needed for generators, retailers, the ISO, and other market participants to meet the operating, scheduling, planning, and financial requirements in the emerging competitive market environment.

The most complex requirement on software systems will come from the ISO, which is responsible for secure operation of the power system and may even run a few markets for energy auction, ancillary services procurement, and transmission rights auction, etc. Historically, the main software system in the control centre of the power system is the well-known Energy Management System (EMS), which consists of four major elements (Harris, 2000; Secretary of Energy Advisory Board, 1998; Rahimi & Vojdani, 1999):

- Supervisory Control and Data Acquisition (SCADA), including data acquisition, control, alarm processing, online topology processor.
- Generation scheduling and control applications, including Automatic Generation Control (AGC), Economic Dispatch (ED), Unit Commitment (UC), hydrothermal coordination, short-term load forecast, interchange scheduling, etc.
- Network analysis application, including topology processor, state estimator, power flow, contingency analysis, Optimal Power Flow (OPF), security enhancement, voltage and reactive power optimisation, stability analysis, etc.

- Dispatch Training Simulator (DTS), including all the three above components but in a separate off-line environment.

The EMS is still needed by the ISO in the electricity market, but some of its functions will change to meet the new requirement. For example, some generation scheduling applications might be removed or redesigned to be something like energy market trading applications, while some other network analysis application, such as OPF, should be extended to be able to perform new functions. DTS is also facing significant changes. It must include all the market applications and power system applications. These new systems may include:

- Market long-term planning subsystem, including such applications as a plan for future transmission expansion, long-term ATC determination and maintenance of transmission facilities. This subsystem needs coordination between the ISO and transmission owners.
- Market trading subsystem, including all the possible functions associated with market administration roles of the ISO or a separate market operator. These functions could be a day-ahead energy auction to match supply offers and demand bids (a spot market), electricity futures trading, ancillary services procurement, transmission rights auction, etc.
- Market operation planning subsystem, including power system scheduling function, short-term ATC determination, short-run transmission-related services pricing, and congestion management, etc.
- Market real-time dispatching subsystem, including power system dispatch function, system balancing, real-time ATC determination, and real-time congestion management, etc.
- Market settlement and billing subsystem, determining deviations from the schedules and bilateral contracts, determining payments to suppliers and ancillary services providers, determining payments to financial instrument holders.
- Market information subsystem. All ISOs are expected to provide a system of open communication for information related to power system operations. In the US, some of this information will be published on the Federal Energy Regulatory Commission (FERC)-mandated OASIS. The information that would assist with the efficiency and security of system operation should include: system information on transmission congestion, locational market clearing prices, need and bid for ancillary services and their prices, and all applicable ATCs.

These new software subsystems are linked tightly with each other and must coordinate with the existing systems in the control room to support the implementation of electricity marketing. Therefore, besides the development of new applications, there is still an enormous amount of work to be done on software system integration. An overview of possible software systems in the competitive market environment and the relationships between them are given in Figure 31.2.

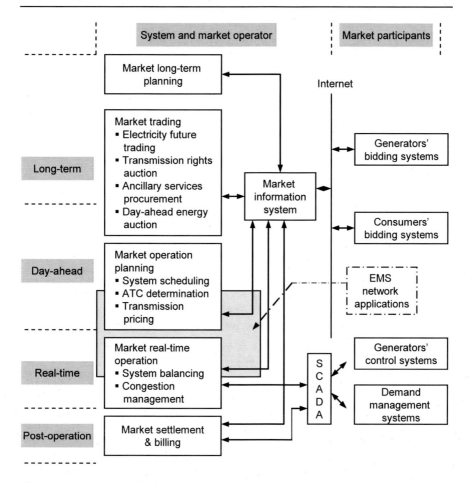

Figure 31.2: Overview of software systems in the competitive electricity market (Energy Management System (EMS), Supervisory Control and Data Acquisition (SCADA))

31.2 Coordinated Real-time Dispatch of Unbundled Electricity Markets

It is well known that the generation and consumption of electricity must occur essentially at the same time. Therefore, real-time operations and the associated markets and pricing approaches are crucial to the design and implementation of a successful competitive wholesale electricity market.

The basic tasks of the ISO during real-time operation should at least include:

- Meeting the imbalance between the real-time and scheduled load and generation;
- Relieving real-time network congestion due to unexpected contingencies.

One possible solution to the problem of real-time dispatch of electricity markets is to establish a real-time balancing market and to encourage all market participants to take part in the competition in this balancing market. The FERC of the United States recognised the importance of these markets in its Order 2000 on regional transmission organisations (RTOs) (FERC, 1999).

31.2.1 Power System Operation

31.2.1.1 Operation in Vertically Integrated Utilities

Traditionally, the three main objectives of power system operation are: power balance, system security/reliability and economy. Generally speaking, the power system operation can be categorised into two basic stages (Wood & Wollenberg, 1996; Hirst, 2001):

- *Scheduling, which takes place a day, week, or year in advance:* Scheduling includes several functions, such as hydro scheduling, maintenance scheduling, interchange scheduling between companies and unit commitment (UC).
- *Dispatch, which is done in real time:* Dispatch includes two main functions: (1) Economic Dispatch (ED), and (2) Automatic Generation Control (AGC).

The output levels of individual units obtained from ED are passed to AGC as the base points of these units during operation.

31.2.1.2 Operation in Competitive Electricity Markets

Power system operation becomes much more complex when generation, transmission and system control are owned and operated by different entities. The primary difference between the operation of a deregulated electricity market and of a vertically integrated power system is that the ISO owns no generation resources. In this case, who should make unit commitment decisions in an electricity energy market, generators or the ISO? The answer to this question decides whether generators should bid into energy markets with simple energy-only bids or with multi-part bids having separate prices for start-up, no-load, and energy costs.

The design of power system operation, particularly if a centralised UC is still required, is determined mainly by the market architecture. Basically, the possible architectures of electricity energy markets can be categorised into three elementary models: (1) pure centralised spot market; (2) spot market with pre-signed bilateral energy transactions; (3) bilateral energy market with centralised real-time balancing market.

In a pure centralised spot market, UC performed by the ISO is indispensable for scheduling. Here, all generations in the market must trade with the ISO and no physical bilateral contracts are allowed. The old England & Wales Pool is a typical example of this type of market. In a spot market built on top of bilateral contracts, suppliers can select whether they want to self-commit or they want the ISO to commit their units. PJM, NYISO, and ISONE can be classed in this category. In bilateral energy markets with a centralised real-time balancing mechanism, such as ERCOT in the USA and the new UK market, UC is no longer one of the scheduling tasks of the ISO. All generators in the energy market must be responsible for committing their own units and reporting the commitment results to the ISO. Although the scheduling process is very different between these three different types of energy market, the common part of the market designs is a centralised real-time balancing mechanism.

As summarised by Angelidis and Papalexopoulos (2001), there are two different structures that can be used to design a mechanism to manage the real-time energy imbalances and real-time transmission congestion. With the first structure, the ISO dispatches resources according to their bids and rolls the costs incurred into an uplift that is allocated pro rata to all market participants. This structure seeks to minimise the uplift costs by imposing penalties on resources that have uninstructed deviations from their schedules established in the forward market, rather than to make use of any real-time price signals. This is the structure that can be found in the electricity market of England and Wales.

With the second structure, the ISO operates a real-time market with transparent market clearing prices. These prices are intended to provide incentives for market participants to operate consistently with the goal of reducing energy imbalances to zero. The regulating markets in Norway and Sweden and the real-time market in California are examples of this structure. PJM adopts a similar dispatch structure. In addition, PJM provides a locational marginal price (LMP) for every node in its system.

31.2.2   Coordinated Real-time Dispatch Through a Balancing Mechanism

With the deregulation of the power industry, the main services in power systems have been unbundled into several separate markets, such as the pool auction energy market, where the generation schedule can be arranged to meet the system load; the bilateral contract market, where the generators and consumers can sell or buy electricity by themselves; and the ancillary services market, where the ISO can procure the necessary services, such as system reserves and voltage support, to maintain system security.

Some research has been undertaken on the dispatch problem in electricity markets. Singh, Hao, and Papalexopoulos (Singh et al., 1998) make some comparisons between the approaches to transmission congestion management in the pool model and the bilateral model. David and Fang (David, 1998; Fang & David, 1999a, b) provide some useful curtailment strategies based on minimising deviations from transaction requests made by market participants in a structure dominated by bilateral and multilateral contracts. Singh and Papalexopoulos (1999) have introduced the basic idea of auction market for ancillary services in California. The dispatch of ancillary services and the interaction between the various markets have also been briefly discussed. Alvey et al. (1998) and Cheung et al. (1999) propose optimal scheduling methods, in which procurement of the operating reserves needed is combined with procurement of the energy (Joint Dispatch), all with due consideration for network constraints.

However, a problem still waiting to be resolved by an ISO is how to use all the possible resources efficiently and in a coordinated way to ensure system security during the real-time execution of various electricity commodity contracts. The main difficulties occurring during real-time coordinated dispatch may include:

- How to utilise the signed operating reserve contracts and the supplementary energy bids in the balancing market to obtain the optimal dispatch solution.
- With the trend to more and more bilateral contracts being used to trade electricity, how to eliminate network congestion if the resources in the balancing market are not adequate.
- In view of the need to maintain a certain level of system security, how to obtain replacement operating reserves in time if any of the prearranged operating reserves are called up to provide energy for real-time system balancing or congestion management.

To resolve these difficulties, a new framework for real-time dispatch of unbundled electricity markets is proposed. With this framework, almost all the contracts in the various electricity markets can be dispatched in a coordinated manner; to this end, the adjustment bids can be submitted to the balancing market. In particular, some bilateral contracts can be adjusted by means of balancing mechanisms if transmission congestion is very serious (Wang & Song, 2000, 2002). Demand-side participants are encouraged to take an active role in the competition on the real-time balancing market. A modified P-Q decoupled Optimal Power Flow (OPF) is applied to solve this problem.

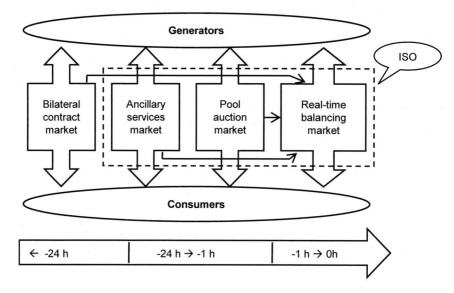

Figure 31.3: Proposed framework of real-time coordinated dispatch

In Figure 31.3, there are four unbundled markets, the Bilateral Contract Market (BCM), the Pool Day-ahead Energy Auction Market (PEAM), the Pool Ancillary Services Auction Market (PAAM) and the Real-time Balancing Market (RBM).

31.3   Several Major Operational Issues in Unbundled Electricity Markets

During the past few years, with funding from both research council and industry, we have been working on different computational models and methods for operation and control of unbundled electricity markets (Bhattacharya et al., 2001; Shahidiehpouret et al., 2002; Song, 1999). It covers all the major operational issues, such as scheduling and dispatch, congestion management, available transfer capability calculation, price forecasting and optimal bidding strategies.

31.3.1   Modelling and Analysis of Electricity Markets

The expectation is that a market-driven structure of the electricity industry will encourage competition in generation and supply, with open transmission and distribution access to enable it, and that this process will finally lead to efficiency, savings and reduced prices (Federal Energy Regulatory Commission, 1996; European Commission, 1997; Bier, 1999; Vojdani & Rahimi, 1998; Murray, 1998; Gans et al., 1998).

There are several restructuring schemes that have been adopted for the electricity industry in different countries of the world, such as (1) a vertically or fully integrated utility (often a state utility); (2) the mixed generation scheme; and (3) the single buyer (SB) model.

When considered as a commodity, electric energy can be traded in a free market, regulated only by consumer demand and supply bids. In particular, a commercial market and an operational market are usually identified (Holmes & Plaskett, 1991; Tabors, 1996). In the commercial market the electricity is traded in a financial framework. In the operational market actual generation schedules are produced, which are re-optimised at regular intervals during the system operation (Christie & Wangensteen, 1998; Fismen, 1996; Kuusela & Viheriävaara, 1997). It is assumed that there are five markets commonly operating: cash market, futures market, option market, swap market and planning market.

31.3.2   Pricing of Electricity

In the emerging electricity market, which relies on price-based competition, an unambiguous, transparent and predictable pricing framework of electricity for both active and reactive power is one of the major issues. Also, with the growing interest in determining the costs of supplying the ancillary services needed to maintain quality and reliability of any electricity service, the spot price should be decomposed and distributed to different ancillary services.

From the economic point of view, spot pricing based on SRMC (short run marginal cost) has the potential to provide economic signals for system operation. Various models and approaches (Einhorn & Siddiqui, 1996; Schweppe et al., 1988; Caramanis et al., 1989; Rivier & Perez-Ariaga, 1991; Ray & Alvarado, 1988; Baughman & Siddiqi, 1993; Dandachi et al., 1996; EL-Keib & Ma, 1997; Li & David, 1993; Siddiqi & Baughman, 1995; Zobian & Ilic, 1997; Caramanis et al., 1987; Kaye & Wu, 1995; Alvarado et al, 1991; Baughman et al., 1997; Finney et al., 1997; Willis et al., 1996) have been proposed for determining spot pricing.

31.3.3   Evaluation of Available Transfer Capability

Open access to transmission systems places a new emphasis on more intensive shared use of interconnected networks being reliably practised by utilities and independent power producers (IPPs) to improve economy and security. In these circumstances, it is very important to obtain a clear understanding of how much unused capacity is available on a transmission interface. Therefore, for better transmission services support and full utilisation of transmission assets, one of the major challenges is accurate gauging of the transfer capability remaining in the system for further transactions, which is termed the available transfer capability (ATC) (FERC, 1995).

In order to foster generation competition and customer choice, and to facilitate wide-area coordination throughout the whole transmission network, the FERC mandates that the ATC information of some specific interfaces must be accessed by electricity market participants and system operators hourly through an Open-Access Same-Time Information System (OASIS) (NERC, 1996). Calculated by ISOs, ATC information usually includes the quantities of ATC, TTC, nonrecallable and recallable ATC and so on.

In recent years, various approaches have been proposed for modelling and calculation of ATC: Sensitivity Analysis, Continuation Power Flow, Optimal Power Flow, and so on. Owing to the commercial and technical significance of ATC in the new electricity market, more and more institutes and utilities (such as Electric Power Research Institute, 1997; East Central Area Reliability Council, 2002; PJM Interconnection, 2001; NYISO manual for transmission services, 1999) have shown increased interest in, and are undertaking studies of evaluation and enhancement of, ATC and related terms.

31.3.4   Transmission Congestion Management

Transmission congestion can be defined as the condition that occurs when there is insufficient transmission capability to simultaneously implement all preferred transactions in electricity markets. Unlike many other commodities, electricity cannot easily be stored, and the delivery of electricity is constrained by physical transmission limits, which have to be satisfied at all times to keep the power system operating in a secure fashion. Without transmission limits, deregulation of the power industry would be much simpler. Therefore, transmission congestion management is a major function of any type of ISO in any type of electricity market. It is important to note that if not managed properly, congestion can impose a significant barrier to trading electricity.

Different market structures and market rules lead to different methods of congestion management (Singh et al., 1998; Fang & David, 1999a, b). Basically, a proper approach to resolving transmission congestion in competitive electricity markets should at least be fair and nondiscriminatory, economically efficient, transparent and nonambiguous and feasible. There are many approaches to congestion management, which are dependent on the market model, the policy, the technical development and many other factors. Generally speaking, they can be classified into three fundamental categories: transaction curtailment, transmission capacity reservation and system redispatch. However, the best solution might actually be a combination of several of the basic methods for different time scales.

31.3.5 Financial Instruments and Their Role in Market Dispatch and Congestion Management

Traditional approaches to transmission access and pricing focus on 'contract path' and cost recovery-based transmission tariffs, which ignore the economic and physical realities of the power grid. Locational marginal pricing (LMP), developed by Schweppe in 1988 (Schweppe et al., 1988), provides a more economic method of transmission pricing and congestion management.

Despite the advantages of LMP, in a spot market both the seller and the buyer of a bilateral trade face two types of price uncertainties: temporal uncertainty and locational uncertainty. Although the two parties are forced to trade directly with the grid at fluctuating spot prices, they can completely insulate themselves from these fluctuations by the use of a contract for difference (CfD) provided that they face the same spot price. If spot prices differ locationally owing to transmission congestion, new price risk arises. This locational price risk can be eliminated by an financial transmission right (FTR). Bushnell and Stoft explain how this works in a long-run electric grid investment (Bushnell & Stoft, 1995).

A fully open electricity market should encourage more bilateral contracts and give market participants more freedom to arrange their own transactions. On the other hand, owing to the special characteristics of the power energy commodity, a bid-based spot market is still needed to balance the system and eliminate potential transmission congestion. How to redispatch bilateral contracts when required has always been one of the main problems facing the ISO that runs the spot market. Some of the physical approaches to redispatch of bilateral contracts have been presented by Fang and David (1999a, b), and Wang and Song (2000, 2002).

31.3.6   Ancillary Services

In the electricity industry, ancillary services are complementary services that interact with the production of energy. Specifically, ancillary services are those functions performed by power systems with regard to generation, control, transmission and distribution of electric power to facilitate technical and commercial electricity transactions. These services are provided by the same equipments as generate and transmit electricity in support of the main services of electric energy and power delivery, which are collectively called ancillary services. Despite the considerable costs of ancillary services, which are roughly 10% of the costs of the energy commodity, these services are important both for bulk-power reliability and for the support of commercial transactions. In power markets, the availability of sufficient ancillary services makes power systems reliable and transactions deliverable.

Generally, ancillary services include, but are not limited to, frequency control, automatic generation control (AGC), spinning reserve, nonspinning reserve (dispatchable load and generation) and black-start capability, which are generation-based ancillary services. Reactive power support and voltage control is another type of ancillary service, which relies on generators and requirements and installation of compensation devices and may probably be better provided by contributions from generating units and from transmission providers. In addition, any problem in one market may cause problems in other markets. A real-time market can provide a balance of energy and ancillary services between generation and consumption (balancing mechanism). Contingency reserves (CR) are the ancillary services that maintain this balance when a major generation or transmission line unexpectedly fails. It can be clearly seen that different power systems have different requirements for ancillary services.

Two important issues with regard to ancillary services are the cost of providing these services and their value to the power system.

31.3.7   Load and Price Forecasting

Short-term load forecasting (STLF) has an important role in the operational planning and the security functions of an energy management system. The STLF is aimed at predicting electric loads for a period of minutes, hours, days or weeks, for the purpose of providing fundamental load profiles to the system. Over the years, considerable research effort has been devoted to STLF and various forecasting techniques have been proposed and applied to power systems. Conventional methods based on time series analysis exploit the inherent relationship between the present hour load, weather variables and the past hour load. Autoregressive (AR), moving average (MA) and mixed autoregressive and moving average (ARMA) models are prominent in the time series approach. The main disadvantage is that these models require complex modelling techniques and heavy computational effort to produce reasonably accurate results (Moghram & Rahman, 1989). The emergence of artificial intelligence (AI) techniques in recent years, effective utilisation of AI in the context of ill-defined processes have led to their application in STLF as expert-system type models (Chow & Leung, 1996).

On the other hand, the electricity supply industry is undergoing unprecedented restructuring worldwide and there is a growing interest in the prediction of system marginal price (SMP) under the competitive market structure of deregulated power systems (Bastian & Zhu, 1999). SMP forecasting, on both a long-term and a short-term basis, is becoming more and more important. Recently, an energy price forecasting method and a neural network-based technique for the prediction of SMP have been proposed by Bastian and Zhu (1999), and Wang and Ramsay (1997), respectively. The wavelet-transform-based model has also been presented (Yu et al., 2002).

31.3.8 Analysis of Generating Companies' Strategic Behaviour

Electricity producers are assumed to bid in a pool-based electricity market (Mendes & Kirschen, 2000). Every day, generators submit prices for each generating set for the following day and the transmission system operator calculates the operating schedules that will meet the forecast levels of demand at minimum cost, based upon the bid prices. Then, for each time interval, typically each half-hour, all generating sets in the schedule are paid the market-clearing price, which varies with demand and is based on the bid of the most expensive set in normal operation during that time interval.

In this context, not every firm sharing the market bids at marginal cost, as would be the case in a perfect competitive market, but profit-maximising strategies are carried out (Post et al., 1995; Losi & Russo, 2000; Li et al., 1999; Geerli et al., 2000; Kumar & Sheble, 1998; Otero-Novas et al., 1999; Lamont & Rajan, 1997; David, 1998). In order to simulate the strategic competition among producers in the electricity market, the bidding process is expressed using linear supply functions. Another important aspect to be taken into account when analysing the electricity market is the presence of private contracts between generating companies and customers. These private agreements may be implemented using financial derivatives such as forward contracts and futures and options contracts (Gans et al., 1998; Powell, 1993; Von Der Fher & Harbord, 1993; Post et al., 1995).

He & Song (2003) propose a methodology to simulate the strategic behaviour of generating companies with the impacts of potential coalitions.

31.3.9 Bidding Problems in Electricity Generation Markets – Decision-Making in Electricity Markets

31.3.9.1 Generation Auction Markets in Electricity Markets

McAfee says that an auction is a market institution with an explicit set of rules determining resource allocation and prices on the basis of bids from market participants (McAfee & McMillan, 1987). From this point of view, auctioning is an ideal pricing mechanism for electricity markets, since the price of electricity depends on the supply-and-demand conditions at a specific moment. There are three auction mechanisms: standard auction formats, single-round bidding and multi-round bidding, and simple bids and multi-part bids.

31.3.9.2 Decision Making in Electricity Markets

Apart from the traditional risks encountered with vertically integrated regulation, many factors (privatisation of generation, transmission network and distribution, open access to electricity network, competitive bidding in electricity markets, demand-side participation, etc.) have arisen since deregulation. The market participants (such as GENCOs, TRANCOs, DISCOs, consumers, system operator and market operator) have to consider these risks seriously.

In electricity markets, each market participant faces its own decision-making problems. Sometimes the ISO might also play the role of market regulator, where it needs to decide transactions in futures markets and forward markets. These transactions may range from real-time power, through operating reserve and reactive power to transmission rights and other ancillary services.

To date, research work shows that the following approaches have been attempted in the generator bidding strategies problem: game theory-based methods (Yeung et al., 1999; Krishna & Ramesh, 1998), optimisation-based methods (Gross & Finlay, 1996; Zhangn et al., 2000; Song et al., 2000; Xievet et al., 2000; Arroyo & Conejo, 2000) and other heuristic methods, such as GA, ANN, ES, probabilistic or statistical methods, and control theory-based methods (Eldukair, 1990).

31.3.10 Improvement of Transmission Services by FACTS Control

To satisfy the open access to transmission networks requirement, and to meet the demand for a substantial increase in power transfers among utilities as a major consequence of electricity market, much more intensive utilisation of existing transmission resources is needed. Obviously, these aspects have motivated the development of strategies and methodologies to improve transmission services. On the other hand, the advent of flexible AC transmission systems (FACTS) technology has coincided with the major restructuring of the electric power industry. By the use of power electronics-based controllable components to control line impedance, magnitude and phase angle of nodal voltage individually and simultaneously, FACTS can provide benefits in increasing system transmission capacity and power flow control flexibility and rapidity. As deregulation picks up speed, meeting the demand for sufficient and improved transmission services is becoming more critical and it is imperative to investigate the capabilities and potential applications of FACTS on power networks (EPRI, 1997; CEC, 1999; Xiao et al., 2002; Wang et al., 2002; Taranto et al., 1992; Ge & Chung, 1999).

31.4 Conclusions

There has been a worldwide trend towards restructuring and deregulation of the power industry over the last two decades. The competition in the wholesale generation market and the retail market together with the open access to the transmission network can bring many benefits to the end-consumers, such as lower electricity prices and better services. And this competition also brings many new technical issues and challenges to the operation of restructured power systems. This chapter has therefore focused mainly on the operation of restructured power systems and new characteristics, coordinated real-time dispatch of unbundled electricity markets and several major operational issues in competitive markets.

References

Alvarado, F., Hu, Y., Ray, D., Stevenson, R. & Cashman, E. 1991. Engineering foundations for determination of security costs. IEEE Transactions on Power Systems, 6: 1175-1182.

Alvey, T., Goodwin, D., Ma, X., Streiffert, D. & Sun, D. 1998. A security-constrained bid-clearing system for the New Zealand wholesale electricity market. IEEE Transactions on Power Systems, 13: 340-346.

Angelidis, G. A. & Papalexopoulos, A. D. 2001. Challenge in real-time electricity market design. Paper presented at the Sixth IASTED International Conference on Power and Energy Systems (Euro-PES 2001), Rhodes.

Arroyo, J. M. & Conejo, A. J. 2000. Optimal response of a thermal unit to an electricity spot market. IEEE Transactions on Power Systems, 15: 1098-1104.

Bastian, J. & Zhu, J. 1999. Forecasting energy prices in a competitive market. IEEE Magazine – Computer Application in Power, 7: 41-45.

Baughman, M. L. & Siddiqi, S. N. 1993. Real time pricing of reactive power: theory and case study results. IEEE Transactions on Power Systems, 6: 23-29.

Baughman, M. L., Siddiqi, S. N. & Zarnikau, J. W. 1997. Advanced pricing in electricity systems. IEEE Transactions on Power Systems, 12: 489-495.

Bhattacharya, K., Bollen, M. H. J. & Daalder, J. E. 2001. Operation of restructured power systems. Boston: Kluwer Academic Publishers.

Bier, C. 1999. Network access in the deregulated European electricity market: negotiated third-party access vs. single buyer. Unpublished CSLE Discussion paper 9906, University of Saarland, Saarbrücken.

Bushnell, J. & Stoft, S. 1995. Electric grid investment under a contract network regime. Unpublished Power Working Paper PWP-034, University of California Energy Institute, Berkeley.

California Energy Commission (CEC). 1999. Flexible AC transmission systems benefits study. Sacramento: California Energy Commission.

Caramanis, M. C., Bohn, R. E. & Schweppe, F. C. 1987. System security control and optimal pricing of electricity. International Journal of Electrical Power & Energy Systems, 9: 217-224.

Caramanis, M. C., Bohn, R. E. & Schweppe, F. C. 1989. WRATES: A tool for evaluating the marginal cost of wheeling. IEEE Transactions on Power Systems, 4: 594-605.

Cheung, K. W., Shamsollahi, P. & Sun, D. 1999. Energy and ancillary service dispatch for the interim ISO New England electricity market. Paper presented at the 21st International Conference on Power Industry Computer Applications, Santa Clara, California.

Chow, T. W. S. & Leung, C. T. 1996. Neural network based short-term load forecasting using weather compensation. IEEE Transactions on Power Systems, 11: 1736-1742.

Christie, R. D. & Wangensteen, I. 1998. The energy market in Norway and Sweden: the spot and future markets. IEEE Power Engineering Review.

Dandachi, N., Rawlins, M., Alsac, O., Prais, M. & Stott, B. 1996. OPF for reactive pricing studies on the NGC system. IEEE Transactions on Power Systems, 11: 226-232.

David, A. K. 1998. Dispatch methodologies for open access transmission systems. IEEE Transactions on Power Systems, 13: 46-53.

Directive 96/92/EC. 1996. Directive of the European parliament and the Council concerning common rules for the internal market in electricity. Official Journal of the European Commission, L27 (30/1/97): 20-29.

East Central Area Reliability Council. 2002. East central area reliability coordination agreement, ATC Calculation/Coordination Procedural Manual, 02-ATCP-60. Canton, Ohio: ECAR.

Einhorn, M. & Siddiqui, R. 1996. Electricity transmission pricing and technology. Boston: Kluwer Academic Publishers.

EL-Keib, A. A. & Ma, X. 1997. Calculating of short-run marginal costs of active and reactive power production. IEEE Transactions on Power Systems, 12: 559-565.

Eldukair, Z. A. 1990. Fuzzy decision in bidding strategies. In First International Symposium on Uncertainty Modeling and Analysis (Ed.): 591-594. Los Alamitos: IEEE Computer Society Press.

Electric Power Research Institute (EPRI). 1997a. Solving the transfer capability puzzle. Grid Operations & Planning News. Palo Alto: EPRI.

Electric Power Research Institute (EPRI). 1997b. FACTS assessment study to increase the Arizona-California transfer capability (Report TR-107934). Palo Alto: EPRI.

Fang, R. S. & David, A. K. 1999a. Optimal dispatch under transmission contracts. IEEE Transactions on Power Systems, 14: 732-737.

Fang, R. S. & David, A. K. 1999b. Transmission congestion management in an electricity market. IEEE Transactions on Power Systems, 14: 877-883.

Federal Energy Regulatory Commission (FERC). 1995. Section III-E4f. Notice of Proposed Rulemaking (NOPR). Docket RM95-8-000.

Federal Energy Regulatory Commission (FERC). 1996. Final Order 888: Promoting wholesale competition through open access non-discriminatory transmission services by public utilities. Docket Nos. RM95-8-000 and RM94-7-001.

Federal Energy Regulatory Commission (FERC). 1999. Order No. 2000, Regional transmission organization (RTO)-final rule. http://www.ferc.fed.us/news1/rules/pages/rulemake.htm.

Finney, J. D., Othman, H. A. & Rutz, W. L. 1997. Evaluating transmission congestion constraints in system planning. IEEE Transactions on Power Systems, 12.

Fismen, S. A. 1996. Experience: Norway. Colloquium digest - IEE, 164: 4/1-4/6.

Gans, J. S., Price, D. & Woods, K. 1998. Contracts and electricity pool prices. Australian Journal of Management, 23: 83-96.

Ge, S. Y. & Chung, T. S. 1999. Optimal active power flow incorporating power flow control needs in flexible AC transmission systems. IEEE Transactions on Power Systems, 14: 738-744.

Geerli, Yokoyama, R. & Chen, L. 2000. Negotiation for electricity pricing in a partially deregulated electricity market. IEEE-PES 2000 Summer Meeting, Seattle: 2223-2228.

Gross, G. & Finlay, D. J. 1996. Optimal bidding strategies in competitive electricity markets. Proceedings of 12th Power Systems Computation Conference: 815–823.

Hakvoort, R. 2000. Technology and restructuring the electricity market. Proceedings of the International Conference on Electric Utility Deregulation: 390-395.

Harris, P. G. 2000. Impacts of deregulation on the electric power industry. IEEE Power Engineering Review, 20: 4-6.

He, Y. & Song, Y. H. 2003. The study of the impacts of potential coalitions on bidding strategies of GENCOs. IEEE Transactions on Power Systems, 18: 1086-1093.

Hirst, E. 2001. Real-time balancing operations and markets: key to competitive wholesale electricity markets. Washington / Alexandria: Edison Electric Institute / Project for Sustainable FERC Energy Policy.

Holmes, A. & Plaskett, L. 1991. The new British electricity system. Financial Times B.I.S.: 6/91.

Hunt, S. & Shuttleworth, G. 1996. Unlocking the grid. IEEE Spectrum: 20-25.

Ilic, M., Galiana, F. & Fink, L. 1998. Power system restructuring: engineering and economics. Norwell: Kluwer Academic Publishers.

Kaye, R. & Wu, F. F. 1995. Security pricing of electricity. IEEE Transactions on Power Systems, 4: 659-667.

Krishna, V. & Ramesh, V. 1998a. Intelligent agents for negotiations in market games, Part 1: Model. IEEE Transactions on Power Systems, 13: 1103-1108.

Krishna, V. & Ramesh, V. 1998b. Intelligent agents for negotiations in market games, Part 2: Application. IEEE Transactions on Power Systems, 13: 1109-1114.

Kumar, J. & Sheble, G. 1998. Auction market simulator for price based operation. IEEE Transactions on Power Systems, 13: 250-255.

Kuusela, A. & Viheriävaara, H. 1997. The role of the Finnish system operator and the interactions of commercial mechanism. Tours: CIGREE Symposium.

Lamont, J. W. & Rajan, S. 1997. Strategic bidding in an energy brokerage. IEEE Transactions on Power Systems, 12: 1729-1733.

Li, C., Svoboda, A. J., Guan, X. & Singh, H. 1999. Revenue bidding strategies in competitive electricity markets. IEEE Transactions on Power Systems, 14: 492-497.

Li, Y. Z. & David, A. K. 1994. Wheeling rates of reactive flow under marginal cost theory. IEEE Transactions on Power Systems, 9: 1263-1269.

Losi, A. & Russo, M. 2000. A simulation tool for evaluating technical and economical issues in the deregulated electric power industry. IEEE-PES 2000 Summer Meeting, Seattle, 4: 2242-2247.

McAfee, R. P. & McMillan, J. 1987. Auctions and bidding. Journals of Economic Literature, 25: 699-738.

Mendes, D. P. & Kirschen, D. S. 2000. Assessing pool-based mechanism in competitive electricity markets. IEEE-PES 2000 Summer Meeting, Seattle, 4: 2195-2200.

Moghram, I. & Rahman, S. 1989. Analysis and evaluation of five short-term load forecasting techniques. IEEE Transactions on Power Systems, 5: 1484-1491.

Murray, B. 1998. Electricity markets. New York: John Wiley & Sons.

North American Electric Reliability Council (NERC). 1996. Available transfer capability definition and determination. Princeton: NERC.

NYISO manual for transmission services. 1999. The New York power pool/New York independent system operator. www.nyiso.com/public/webdocs/docu ments/.

Otero-Novas, I., Meseguer, C. & Alba, J. J. 1999. An iterative procedure for modelling strategic behaviour in competitive generation markets. Paper presented at the 13th PSCC, Trondheim, Norway.

Overbye, T. J. 2000. Reengineering the electric grid. American Scientist, 88: 220-229.

PJM Interconnection. 2001. PJM manual for transmission service request. Manual M-02. Norristown: PJM Interconnection.

Post, D. L., Coppinger, S. S. & Sheble, G. B. 1995. Application of auctions as a pricing mechanism for the interchange of electricity. IEEE Transactions on Power Systems, 10: 1580-1584.

Powell, A. 1993. Trading forward in an imperfect market: the case of electricity in Britain. The Economic Journal, 103: 444-453.

Rahimi, F. A. & Vojdani, A. 1999. Meet the emerging transmission market segments. IEEE Computer Application in Power, 12: 26-32.

Ray, D. & Alvarado, F. 1988. Use of an engineering model for economic analysis in the electric utility industry. Paper presented at the Advanced Workshop on Regulation and Public Utility Economics, Rutgers University.

Rivier, M. & Perez-Ariaga, I. 1993. Computation and decomposition of location based price for transmission pricing. Paper presented at the 11th PSC Conference, Avignon.

Schweppe, F. C., Caramanis, M. C., Tabors, R. D. & Bohn, R. E. 1988a. Spot pricing of electricity. Norwell: Kluwer Academic Publishers.

Schweppe, F. C., Caramanis, M. C., Tabors, R. D. & Bohn, R. E. 1988b. Location based pricing of electricity. Boston: Kluwer Academic Publishers.

Secretary of Energy Advisory Board. 1998. Maintain reliability in a competitive U.S. electricity industry. Washington: U.S. Department of Energy.

Shahidiehpour, M., Yamin, H. & Li, Z. 2002. Market operations in electric power systems: forecasting, scheduling, and risk management. New York: Institute of Electrical and Electronics Engineers, Wiley-Interscience.

Siddiqi, S. N. & Baughman, M. L. 1995. Reliability differentiated pricing of spinning reserve. IEEE Transactions on Power Systems: 1211-1218.

Singh, H., Hao, S. & Papalexopoulos, A. 1998. Transmission congestion management in competitive electricity markets. IEEE Transactions on Power Systems, 13: 672-679.

Singh, H. & Papalexopoulos, A. 1999. Competitive procurement of ancillary services by an independent system operator. IEEE Transactions on Power Systems, 14: 498-504.

Song, H., Liu, C. C., Lawarree, J. & Dahlgren, R. W. 2000. Optimal electricity supply bidding by Markov decision process. IEEE Transactions on Power Systems, 15, 618-624.

Song, Y. H. & Wang, X.F. (Eds.) 2003. Operation of market-oriented power systems. London: Springer Verlag.

Song, Y. H. 1999. Modern optimisation techniques in power systems. Dordrecht: Kluwer Academic Publishers.

Stoft, S. 2002. Power systems economics: designing markets for electricity. New York: Wiley-IEEE Press.

Tabors, R. D. 1996. Lessons from the UK and Norway. IEEE Spectrum, 33: 45-49.

Taranto, G. N., Pinto, L. M. V. G. & Pereira, M. V. F. 1992. Representation of FACTS devices in power systems economic dispatch. IEEE Transactions on Power Systems, 7: 572-576.

Vojdani, A. & Rahimi, F. A. 1998. Electricity market structures. Paper presented at the EPSCOM, Zurich.

Von Der Fher, N.-H. M. & Harbord, D. 1993. Spot market competition in UK electricity industry. Economic Journal, 103: 531-546.

Wang, A. & Ramsay, B. 1997. Prediction of system marginal price in the UK power pool using neural networks. Paper presented at the International Conference on Neural Networks, Houston.

Wang, X. & Song, Y. H. 2000. Advanced real-time congestion management through both pool balancing market and bilateral market. IEEE Power Engineering Review, 20: 47-49.

Wang, X. & Song, Y. H. 2002. A coordinated real-time optimal dispatch method for unbundled electricity markets. IEEE Transactions on Power Systems, 17: 482-490.

Wang, X., Song, Y. H., Lu, Q. & Sun, Y. Z. 2002. Optimal allocation of transmission rights in a network with FACTS Devices. IEE Proceedings on Generation, Transmission and Distribution, 149: 359-366.

Willis, L., Finney, J. & Ramon, G. 1996. Computing the cost of unbundled services. Computer Applications in Power, 9: 16-21.

Wood, A. J. & Wollenberg, B. F. 1996. Power generation, operation, and control (2nd ed.). New York: John Wiley & Sons.

Xiao, Y., Song, Y. H. & Sun, Y. Z. 2003. Available transfer capability enhancement using FACTS devices. IEEE Transactions on Power Systems, 18: 305-312.

Xie, K., Song, Y. H., Stonham, J., Yu, E. & Liu, G. 2000. Decomposition model and interior point methods for optimal spot pricing of electricity in deregulated environments. IEEE Transactions on Power Systems, 15: 39-50.

Yeung, C. S. K., Poon, A. S. Y. & Wu, F. F. 1999. Game theoretical multi-agent modelling of coalition formation for multilateral trades. IEEE Transactions on Power Systems, 14: 929-934.

Yu, I. K., Kim, C. I. & Song, Y. H. 2002. Prediction of system marginal price of electricity using wavelet transform analysis. International Journal of Energy Conversion and Management, 43: 1839-1851.

Zhang, D. Y., Wang, Y. J. & Luh, P. B. 2000. Optimization based bidding strategies in the deregulated market. IEEE Transactions on Power System, 15: 981-986.

Zobian, A. & Ilic, M. D. 1997. Unbundling of transmission and ancillary services: part I and part II. IEEE Transactions on Power Systems, 12: 539-558.

Part VI:
Retail

32 The Retail Electricity Service Business in a Competitive Environment

Clark W. Gellings[1]

Abstract

Retail electricity markets continue to change. These changes are driven by restructuring, the advent of competition, and increasing needs to influence the pattern and/or amount of energy use. Branding, attitude and image measurement, and understanding customer preference and behavior are paramount to electric service providers in this new world.

Keywords: retail electricity sales, competition, branding

[1] Clark W. Gellings is Vice President of Technology at the Electric Power Research Institute in Palo Alto, California, United States of America.

A. Bausch and B. Schwenker (eds.), *Handbook Utility Management,*
DOI: 10.1007/978-3-540-79349-6_32, © Springer-Verlag Berlin Heidelberg 2009

32.1   Enter Competition

Whether retail electric competition is inevitable within a given country or region or not – all electric service providers, whether incumbent distribution utilities or new market entrants, are facing a new competitive future.

As they do, a few key issues emerge. First, as a result of having other market entrants in their traditional market, they immediately turn to branding. Then, in order to establish what brand image they are and how to change it, they turn to attitude and image measurement. Finally, as the realization of marketing in a competitive environment takes root, they begin to analyze their customers' preferences and behavior. These subjects are addressed in this chapter.

32.2   Branding

With the advent of retail electric competition, a host of threats and opportunities confront electric energy service managers. With the loss of market share as the primary concern, competitive threats for one company can be another company's opportunity. For some companies, retention will be their primary business strategy. Other companies will have a strategy of expansion regionally, nationally, or internationally. In either case, much has been discussed regarding the value of keeping the utility's name, either to retain loyal customers or to attract new customers outside of traditional franchise territories. As retail markets open, not all utility executives are convinced that the historical name of the utility has any value at all outside of the existing franchise area. In areas where the electricity market is restructured, a plethora of name changes follows.

When retail markets open up, branding becomes a topic for frequent discussion. Why? Because new entrants to the electricity market are looking to achieve market share quickly and without sacrificing profitability. Some view branding, or more precisely building brand equity, as 'the solution'. However, the vast majority of marketers view branding simply as a name game. In most cases, utilities should stick with their existing name.

Electricity is tasteless, odorless, and invisible. While the production, transmission, and distribution of electricity can vary in cost, reliability, and quality, the actual energy delivered to customers does not. Consumers do not consider their electricity usage as a purchase-based decision. Electricity consumers do not buy electricity per se; they buy heating, cooking, refrigeration and air conditioning. Most consumers do not even know how much electricity they use, although they may be aware of its cost when the next bill arrives.

Where electricity supply markets open for competition, the functions that will usually be subject to competition are wholesale energy production, retail marketing and, possibly, competitive billing and metering services. However, there may be few ways for the service provider to differentiate competitive offerings of electricity besides price.

How will competitors differentiate a basic commodity such as electricity? Consumers will look for the best value, not just in terms of price, but also with due consideration for convenience and service. New entrants into this new competitive industry can demonstrate value in other ways than by offering discounts. Product and service bundling, innovative pricing schemes, alliance cross-selling, and branding are just some of the other approaches that can be pursued.

Branding or brand equity building is an important marketing tool to produce product differentiation. Advertising, promotional giveaways, and price discounts are temporal in nature and subject to response by competitors. Such marketing techniques are costly and diminish earnings. Some consumers will identify customer service, product quality, and competitive price above all other hype. Those consumers will act rationally and buy the product or service providing the greatest value based on their individual needs.

Service, quality, and price do sell products. In an immature market, where advertising, telemarketing, and e-commerce flood consumers with promises and messages, consumers have neither the right information nor the time to do sufficient research to allow them to make rational decisions. Buyers typically buy products based upon an intrinsic trust or bond they have with the manufacturer of the product itself. This relationship, this intangible bond between buyer and seller, is called brand equity. Brand equity supplants the need for the decision-making process by providing the consumer with a name symbolic with service, quality, or price.

Some refer to branding as a 'name game'. Names may help the consumer's memory retention, but the name by itself does not necessarily compel the consumer to buy a product.

Developing brand equity takes time, often years. While market research can help identify a name that communicates who or what you are, brand equity evolves and grows out of past experiences. For regions newly opened to competition for customers for electricity supply, the incumbent utility will inherit substantial brand name equity. The incumbent utility has had decades to establish a solid relationship with energy consumers.

Research consistently indicates that fair electricity prices and high levels of reliability are the two principle values the consumers want from their electricity providers. In countries where reliability is reasonably assured, the remaining product differentiations fall in the following categories:

- Price discounts and innovative pricing;
- Enhanced customer service;
- Value-based service bundling.

32.2.1 Price Discounts and Innovative Pricing

Some electric restructuring schemes have resulted in transitioning of a number of customer services away from the incumbent utility. Such services include meter reading, billing, handling customer complaints, being the provider of last resort, and energy management and energy efficiency.

All restructuring schemes segregate the cost of electric generation that was embedded in the incumbent's fully bundled rates and offer it as a discretely separate item. The price for the generation portion of the bill is basically the price that marketers must beat in order for the consumer to realize cost savings. With stranded costs assigned to the regulated distribution charges, the generation portion of the bill represents the utility's marginal production costs and is a target that offers marketers little margin, assuming they can beat the price at all. Furthermore, generation costs represent only about 30% of the total cost of electricity. Therefore, a 20% discount offered by a competitive marketer translates into an overall discount of just 6%. Experience has demonstrated a customer's reluctance to change providers if the overall savings are less than 10%. Discounts can only be viewed as a short-term strategy to build market share.

Instead, innovative pricing can be used to build market share. Most utilities have offered very basic tariffs. While some utilities offer time-of-use rates to reflect the differences in production costs during peak and nonpeak periods, there has been little progress in introducing real-time pricing, day-ahead pricing, remote monitoring, and control of customer demand and usage to minimize overall electricity costs.

32.2.2   Enhanced Customer Service

Customer service is wide open for innovation and value-added propositions. Traditional electric utilities have invested relatively little in customer service. From billing or service inquiries to complaints, the regulated utility met its basic obligations. Traditionally, utilities' direct contact with the customer has been limited. New market entrants have many opportunities to add value to the energy purchasing experience. Energy information can be collected and presented in a number of graphical and tabular formats that will help business to manage energy purchases better. Direct billing and payment, real-time pricing, energy management, power factor control, and enhanced reliability are just some of the enhancements that can be added to the product offering portfolio.

32.2.3   Value-based Service Bundling

Another means of differentiating one electrical energy service provider from another is to bundle a set of products and services into a value-based offering. Bundling combines a package of products and services for a single price. When this is done, a number of benefits can occur:

- The ability of consumers to make direct comparisons of electric-only prices is diminished, since these prices are obscured.

- Combining energy efficiency offerings with electricity sales can produce greater customer savings than are achieved via electric generation discounts alone.
- Combining energy information systems with load aggregation can produce volume discounts and improved load factor savings.
- Combining energy sales with other popular products and services provides the customer with a one-stop energy shopping experience, one that has the potential to build brand value.

32.3   Attitude and Image Research

Market planners in energy service companies and electricity distribution utilities (electricity service providers) must be concerned with understanding, evaluating, and reacting to both the brand equity the provider has and the overall relationship between customers and the company. In a fundamental sense, both of these types of companies are in a sales and service business, where 'knowing the customer' is a primary corporate value and daily operating exigency.

Compared with many other businesses, these electricity service providers have obvious and unique capabilities for determining 'facts' about the customer–company relationship. There exists, at a minimum, a monthly sale recorded for each customer, a monthly bill sent to each customer, a record of specific contacts with a customer, rate codes, and arrears codes.

In essence, analyzing customer attitudes can play an important part in the decision process for the service provider. Understanding customer attitudes about the company, and the company image in the minds of its customers, becomes a necessary task for managers. Attitudes may refer either to the positive or negative feeling a customer has about some object, or to combinations of knowledge, feelings, and behavioral intentions customers hold about particular issues, policies, and programs that are the components of the relationship between customers and supplier.

'Image' generally refers to combinations of attitudes held by customers, which define a profile, from the customer's perspective, of 'the electricity company'. The image of a company held by a customer can be dominated by one or two attitudes, or can be composed of a variety of attitudinal dimensions which comprise the total customer–company relationship. Attitude research can be used to do the following:

- *The design and evaluation of a communications program:* Many companies communicate with their customers via direct mail, bill inserts, and/or mass media advertising. While customer communications programs may address a variety of topics, there are typically some fundamental objectives the company is attempting to accomplish in the communications program, and these relate to creating or modifying particular attitudes held by customers.

- *The evaluation of customer service contacts with the company:* One of the basic customer–company relationships involves the responsibility of the company to answer customer questions or resolve customer problems.
- *The 'marketing' of electricity service contacts and customer programs:* Customer attitudes to the company as a whole and to the specific products, programs or services available from the company or to the business of the company can play a major part in the success or failure of the company's activities.
- *The management of long-range issues affecting the company's ability to do business:* Because of the high visibility of electricity service companies, and the regulated nature of portions of the business, companies often engage in long-range legislative, regulatory, and governmental affairs strategies to position the companies with regard to broad societal issues such as global warming. Managers have a need to know where 'the public' stands on these issues.

32.4 Customer Preference and Behavior

32.4.1 Are all Customers Alike?

Planners in competitive markets have the task of designing programs that will help their company increase market shares. If, for example, the utility's demand is rising, planners may want to develop a strategy that will reduce the demand for electricity.

The planner decides to use a tactical marketing approach. He identifies a group of people who exhibit a strong sense of social responsibility and express concerns about the ability to preserve the environment in the face of a growing population and expanding technology. The promotion materials designed to appeal to this segment show how, by lowering peak demand through time-of-use rates, the utility can forgo the building of another power plant, and thus reduce pollution. The utility or energy service provider can motivate customers in such a manner as to implement the measures it wants to promote.

32.4.2 The Challenge

If utility managers understand the real drivers that clinch the decisions made by customers, it is much easier to select, design, and promote utility programs that are consistent with those drivers and are, therefore, more attractive to customers. In fact, the same program can sometimes be attractive to customers with very different needs.

In order to develop products, programs, and marketing strategies that are effective, it is critical to understand the energy needs of customers and the benefits they seek from this category. Managers must understand the patterns of needs that tend to be linked together, and the number of people in the perspective market that exhibit those patterns. Armed with this knowledge, products and programs can be developed that are designed to appeal to targeted market segments.

32.4.3   Using a Segmentation System

In many ways, the goal of efficiently promoting utility products and services to customers is best achieved through a commitment to being customer focused and market driven. Customer-focused companies listen to their customers to determine what they want and need. Firms with this approach then determine how they can best meet their customers' requirements in a manner consistent with their corporate capabilities and goals.

Researchers have developed a variety of segmentation or classification systems to give utilities and energy service providers the tools they need to understand the needs and attitudes that drive their customers, so that they can be more responsive to them.

32.5   Understanding Residential Customer Needs

Today, electric utilities face a business and regulatory environment which increasingly demands more efficient use of resources. Making that use a reality, in turn, often requires changing the way utilities do business and assisting customers to use electricity more efficiently. The second half of this equation – changing customer use – is a high-profile goal in many utilities. Programs to accomplish this objective range from offering time-of-use (TOU) rates designed to shift demand away from daytime peak hours to providing rebates on energy-efficient lighting and appliances.

It should be clear that by understanding the strong needs that drive customer decision-making you not only have directions as to how you should position products when talking to potential buyers, but also for the development of new products and services.

In order to accomplish these ends you require some information about your customers, and the first set of information you will want to have is the overall needs profile for the customers in question (for these purposes, residential). The issues here are in defining the key energy-related needs of residential customers and in identifying how important each of those basic needs is to customers taken as a whole. With this information in hand you could:

- Select the products, programs, and services that are most likely to be attractive to customers as a whole because they meet needs that are the most strongly felt by your customers.
- Define the features (pricing or otherwise) of new programs, products, or services that will make them most attractive to customers.

- Specify the messages to use when communicating with customers about why they should purchase your product or service.

32.5.1 Defining Residential Customer Needs

If energy needs and related concerns represent the key factors that residential customers respond to when they make energy decisions, then the first thing you should know about residential customers is what those needs are. Research has identified a total of 11 different US residential needs that appear to be most responsible for driving the kinds of energy-related preferences in which utilities are most interested.

32.5.2 Today's Residential Energy Needs

This section outlines the 11 basic needs that drive residential energy decision-making.

- *Low energy bills:* Customers with this need are concerned about controlling their energy operating costs.
- *Increased comfort:* Some customers indicated a strong need to maintain a comfortable home through the use of heating, cooling, and dehumidification appliances.
- *Surge protection:* This need reflects some customers' concerns about power surges.
- *Time-saving appliances:* The convenience need reflects an interest in using time-saving appliances, such as dishwashers and microwaves, to make more time available to spend on other activities.
- *Resource conservation:* The driving force behind this need is to decrease the environmental impact of electricity usage and protect our natural resources.
- *Enhanced security:* Customers with this need are concerned about their own personal security and that of their home and property.
- *Safe appliances:* A high score on this need reflects concerns about the safety of electrical and gas energy, both inside and outside the home.
- *Personal control:* Customers with this need like to control their own appliances, using them to accommodate their needs for comfort and convenience.
- *Attractive appliances:* When purchasing an appliance, customers who feel this need strongly care more about its aesthetics than its performance.
- *Hassle-free purchases:* Customers who feel this need strongly do not want to devote much time to researching or shopping for appliances, nor are they interested in specials or rebates.
- *High-tech appliances:* Customers with this need are interested in having the latest technology, with lots of features and options.

Not all of the 11 needs described in the current residential customer needs model are equally important to people. While individuals obviously vary in the importance they place on each need when making decisions about appliance purchases or energy usage, there are also clear patterns that emerge in needs importance when you look across all residential customers (see Figure 32.2).

32.5.3   Customer Needs Segmentation

Two people shopping for a product may be seeking to satisfy very different needs or wants. One person wants a car with high-performance characteristics, while another person is primarily concerned about the image his car will convey to others. These two people will probably buy different cars. People with different patterns of needs with respect to a particular product category can be expected to exhibit different purchasing behavior in an effort to satisfy those needs.

If a company wants to influence the behavior of its customers and potential customers, it needs to understand the needs that motivate the customers' behavior in the marketplace. That understanding can then be used to target product development and marketing programs against those segments of the population that are most likely to respond favorably to them. Customer needs segmentation offers a framework for organizing our knowledge about customer needs in a way that will facilitate the development and marketing of new products and the positioning of existing ones. It also offers a set of tools that can be used to gather and analyze the data that are required from consumers to use that framework. How can such a framework apply to your residential customers?

People are likely to differ in their energy needs and concerns for a number of reasons, including their lifestyles and values, the kinds of appliances they use, and their product selection processes. A customer who has invested heavily in computers, fax machines and wide-screen TVs is more likely to be worried about power quality than a customer using electricity primarily for lighting and 'basic' appliances.

A needs-based segmentation recognizes that the way residential customers view their energy needs is likely to be reflected in their behavior toward energy-related products and programs. Customers who place a high value on comfort, even in the face of increased energy costs, may not be the best candidates for direct load control programs. A customer who is deeply concerned about environmental issues may be open to energy efficiency programs.

Clearly, needs-based segmentation goes beyond traditional approaches to market segmentation in our industry, including socioeconomic status, level of usage, and age of residence, and goes more deeply into how customers think about energy.

32.5.4   Using Customer Needs Segmentation

If this approach meant that you had to separately familiarize yourself with all of the needs of every individual customer in your market in order to implement a new program product or service effectively, you would obviously face an impossible task. Luckily, the energy needs and concerns of residential customers tend to fall into patterns. The Electric Power Research Institute (EPRI) research has identified eight such patterns of needs in the US, which can be used as the basis for targeting and for matching energy efficiency options and other utility-sponsored program to your customer's needs. These segments may vary by country or regions, but the basic process can be applied.

While each residential customer is unique in some ways, it is also possible to group them together into categories or types, called segments, based on the patterns of energy-related needs they express. These segments are depicted in Figure 32.1.

Some of these groups will be attractive product or service targets, while others will be of little interest to you. The value of the segment structure is that it enables you to focus your product and program development efforts and your marketing activities on segments targeted for their high potential to yield the results you want.

Each of the eight segments shown in Figure 32.1 is defined by a unique pattern of scores on the eleven basic needs that distinguishes it from the other seven segments.

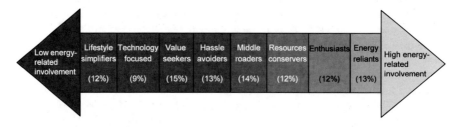

Figure 32.1: Residential customer needs and segments (EPRI, 1994)

In a comparison of the needs of one residential segment and those of customers taken as a whole, these segmentation frameworks (EPRI's CLASSIFY framework was used here) look at the relative intensity of the needs expressed by each group. For example, while the need for enhanced security may be strong for many customers, the relative strength of that need may still vary considerably across segments (i.e., some customers will be higher than average on this need, while others will be lower).

32.5.5   Commercial and Industrial Customer Needs

Because energy needs and general business concerns are key factors that commercial and industrial customers respond to when they make energy decisions, just as with residential customers, the first thing you should know about your customer is what those needs are. EPRI research has identified 22 distinct needs that appear to be most responsible for driving the preferences of commercial and industrial firms in choosing electric utilities' products and services.

The business strategy needs reflect the needs of the executive officer or owner, whose main goal is to achieve strategic objectives. The business operations needs represent the needs of the operating or financial officer, who manages the day-to-day administration of the company. The energy operations needs embody the needs of the functional manager responsible for energy purchase and use. Table 32.1 relates the 22 needs to each of these three areas.

Table 32.1: Three areas of commercial & industrial customer needs (EPRI, 1995)

Business strategy needs	Business operations needs	Energy operations needs
▪ Provide superior service	▪ Departmental cost control	▪ Clean power
▪ Compete on price	▪ Long-range management	▪ Continuous power
▪ Market new products/services	▪ Centralized decisions	▪ Improved equipment efficiency
▪ Lead through technological innovation	▪ Improve business operations	▪ Supportive equipment efficiency
▪ Take risks to grow	▪ Lease equipment	▪ Lower rates
▪ Deliver high-quality products/services	▪ Improve cost position	▪ Efficient technologies and control
		▪ Back-up generation
		▪ Customer services
		▪ Managed energy use
		▪ Flexible billing

32.5.6   CLASSIFY Needs Profiles

Figure 32.2 presents the residential and commercial and industrial CLASSIFY Profiles. It shows the comparative importance of each of the needs to customers.

The most important residential needs are: low energy bills and increased comfort. The five most important commercial and industrial needs belong to the business strategy and business operations sets. These important needs are: provide superior service, compete on price, market new products/services, control departmental costs, and make long-range management decisions.

The remaining 15 commercial and industrial needs are of intermediate importance. In the profile in Figure 32.2, these needs fall between the most important (furthest to the right) and the less important needs (furthest to the left). Energy needs as a group have the least importance; they are clustered toward the bottom of the figure. Three exceptions – the need for clean power, continuous power, and improved equipment efficiency – appear about one-third of the way down the list.

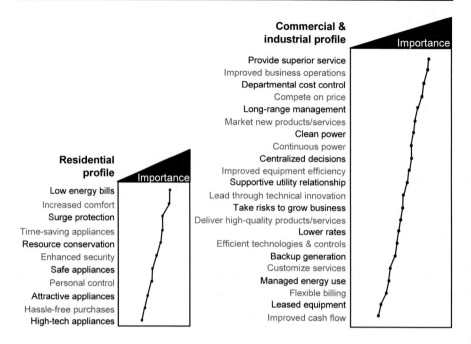

Figure 32.2: CLASSIFY Profiles (EPRI, 1995)

32.6   Commercial and Industrial Needs-based Customer Segments

A look at how commercial and industrial customers as a whole rate the 22 primary needs provides insights into what needs your customers are trying to satisfy when they buy your products and services or participate in your programs. However, examining the needs of particular customer segments can tell you even more. Now that your customers' most important needs have been identified, you can begin to consider how your customers differ from each other – specifically, how they differ in the relative importance of their needs.

How can you learn to anticipate these differences between customers? CLAS-SIFY Profiles have identified nine basic customer types, which are illustrated in Figure 32.3 and differ in the importance the customers in each type ascribe to the 22 needs.

Some customers are on the leading edge of change. They are often early adopters of new technologies, and they are continually seeking to improve their products, market share, and operations.

Other customers have a solid business base. They are economically healthy and readily adopt proven technologies. But they are not innovators. They stick with the proven products, customer base, and operations.

Other customers are slow to change. They may be more marginally profitable and are typically risk averse. They are late to adopt new technologies or to change their product line or markets.

Finally, there is the group of customers who are so far from the leading edge that they are 'falling off the edge' – the edge of survival! These firms are troubled and have difficulty maintaining `profitability year after year. They are the firms that go out of business sooner or later, or about whom you wonder, "How the heck are they still in business?"

Within these four broad groups, CLASSIFY identifies nine different customer types, or segments. Three of the four groups just discussed each comprise two segments, while the 'slow-changing' group encompasses three. Figure 32.3 shows how the nine segments fit into the four broad groups of customers.

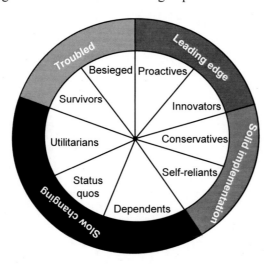

Figure 32.3: The nine CLASSIFY commercial and industrial segments (EPRI, 1995)

32.7   Conclusion

As the retail provider embraces competition, these tools will enable managers to understand and manage brand equity, to measure the attitudes of their customers and the images they have of the provider, and to segment customers so as to enable the delivery of effective and competitive products and services.

References

Electric Power Research Institute (EPRI). 1987. Attitude and image measurement, electric utility market research monograph series. Palo Alto: EPRI.

Electric Power Research Institute (EPRI). 1994. EPRI report TR-104567-V1: CLASSIFY-Profiles, Volume 1: residential customer needs and energy decision making. Palo Alto: EPRI.

Electric Power Research Institute (EPRI). 1995. EPRI report TR-104567-V2 CLASSIFY-Profiles, Volume 2: commercial and industrial customer needs and energy decision making. Palo Alto: EPRI.

Electric Power Research Institute (EPRI). 2000. EPRI technical progress report: brand management, a primer on branding (TP-114844). Palo Alto: EPRI.

33 Customer Segmentation in the Utility Industry

Michiel Boersma[1]

Maaike Vos – van Gool[2]

Abstract

Segmentation has never been an important subject for European energy companies. However, the current liberalisation process forces energy companies to work in a more customer- and market-focused way and, simultaneously, to improve their financial performance. This calls for new, more commercial, competences. Significant examples of this are segmentation and customer value management. Customer value management is the link between customer needs and companies' financial result and is therefore crucial to the success of the company.

Keywords: customer segmentation, customer lifetime value management

---

[1] Dr. Michiel Boersma is Chairman of the Executive Board of Essent N.V., The Netherlands.

[2] Maaike Vos – van Gool is Marketing Manager at Essent N.V., The Netherlands.

A. Bausch and B. Schwenker (eds.), *Handbook Utility Management*,
DOI: 10.1007/978-3-540-79349-6_33, © Springer-Verlag Berlin Heidelberg 2009

33.1   Introduction

Segmentation only became a topical subject in the European energy market in the run-up to liberalisation. The explicit decision to move towards an internal European energy market was taken in 1992 by the European Commission and laid down in various directives, such as the Energy Transit Directive (1986-1992) and the Directive on the Internal Market for Energy (1991-1999). European countries were liberalised over the period 1996-2007: first England and the Scandinavian countries and France last. For each country, a choice was made concerning the phasing of the liberalisation. In all cases, technical and/or consumption limits were taken into account.

The Electricity and Gas Law also necessitated division of the Dutch energy market in the 1990s, into 'Grootverbruik' (industrial) and 'Kleinverbruik' (retail) segments, based on technical and consumption limits: 'Grootverbruik' represents a load of more than 3x80 Ampere (electricity) or an annual consumption of more than 170,000 m³ (gas). The energy market was opened up to the 'Grootverbruik' segment on 1 January 1999 (>2 MW) and 1 January 2002 (>3x80 A). It was not until 1 July 2004 that the retail segment, made up of small and medium-sized companies and households with lower load and consumption, had total freedom in the choice of energy supplier.

Besides consumption or load, the Netherlands has additional provisions in the VAT legislation and Energy Tax legislation. Furthermore, there are criteria concerning the meter market and definitions in Electricity and Gas Law for consumers, business customers and multi-sites. On top of that, there are consumption limit outlines that are observed by the Office of Energy Regulation (DTe) for consumer protection. As a result, customer contracts have to be segmented not only by technical or consumption criteria, but also on the basis of financial legislation. It is a daunting task for energy companies to adapt their systems and operational management to the (still) continuously changing legislation and, with that, continuously changing segmentation.

In the discussions held about this with various stakeholders within the sector, it is notable that one important aspect is still hardly considered: the needs of the customer. As a result of the technical segmentation, many customers with multiple contracts are, therefore, divided over various administrative systems and sections of the business. Internally, these customers are often referred to, not without reason, as 'split customers'. Not by choice but out of necessity, they have to accept being supplied by more than one section of the business, with different service models. Technical, legal, or financial types of segmentation hardly ever address, and sometimes even conflict with, the already more complex and more heterogeneous needs of our customers.

Notwithstanding the fact that segmentation has enjoyed many years of sufficient attention within the science of business economics and the marketing literature, it is a relatively young phenomenon within the energy market. It would be valuable to review the required segmentation criteria for the energy market for private consumers at some point in the light of a European, liberalised market environment and scientific findings within the field of segmentation.

33.2   Conceptual and Contextual Background

33.2.1   Segmentation

Segmentation is defined as the subdivision of a market into segments or submarkets (Verhage & Cunningham 1984). Arndt (1974) and Kotler (2000) describe customer segmentation as identifying and profiling distinct customer groups based on needs (value for the customer). Segmentation stems from the heterogeneity of markets. Customers differ, for example, in their needs or purchasing behaviour. Companies with a single value proposition[3] will reach only a limited section of the market. The more competition there is on the supply side and the more these competitors offer a differentiated supply (or target-specific market segments) the greater the impact. It is a challenge for every company to embed segmentation into the business strategy. This not only offers benefits to the customer (value for the customer), but certainly also benefits to the company itself (value from the customer).

There are four types of segmentation bases (Frank et al., 1972; Gankema & Wedel, 1992). These four types differ in type of customer characteristic and the way these are measured (see Table 33.1).

Table 33.1: Classification of segmentation bases

| | | Customer characteristics | |
		General	Product specific
Method of measuring	Directly observable	▪ Cultural variables ▪ Geographical variables ▪ Demographic variables ▪ Sociographic variables	▪ Frequency of use ▪ Brand loyal ▪ Shop loyal ▪ Situation of use
	Derived	▪ Psychographics ▪ Personality traits ▪ Lifestyle ▪ Values	▪ Psychographics ▪ Perceptions ▪ Attitudes & intentions ▪ Preferences

Every segmentation base has its own specific advantages and disadvantages. Every company that is involved in segmentation issues should weigh the choices against each other. The advantage of segmentation by the directly observable and product-specific characteristic 'consumption' or 'connection value' is that these can

---

[3] Value proposition is defined as: "the perceived worth in monetary terms of the economic, technical, service and social benefits received by a customer firm in exchange for the price paid for an offering, taking into consideration competing suppliers' offering and prices".

be easily identified in the database. However, this characteristic says nothing about the degree to which these segments will react homogeneously to an offer made to them. But on the other hand we have segmentation by inferred psychographic characteristics, such as 'environmental awareness', which is an excellent way of denoting similar needs and behavioural patterns. However, it is much more difficult to determine where the customers in these segments are to be reached.

In attempts to achieve a maximum return on investment (ROI), a balance has to be found between the investments that contribute to several objectives, such as reduction of the cost to serve, improvement of customer satisfaction and keeping up market share. However, there is no one method of segmentation that meets all objectives simultaneously. Companies therefore also often combine several methods.

During the past decade, interest in segmentation based on customer value has increased. Customer value or 'customer lifetime value' is the total value of all current and future profit resulting from the relationship with a customer during the period that the relationship between the customer and the organisation exists (Gupta & Lehman, 2005).

Customer value as an indicator closes the gap between Financial Management on the one hand and Marketing Management on the other. Both disciplines recognise the value of 'intangibles', such as customer loyalty and innovation, for future growth of the company, for example. In the past they did not have a common way of expressing this value in monetary terms (Gupta & Lehman, 2005).

Customer value as a method of segmentation contributes to optimal resource allocation. It supports the formation of effective customer-focused strategies because it takes into account both the value for customers and the value from customers.

33.2.2   The European Energy Market

A liberalised energy market is part of the European train of thought on the free traffic of capital, goods, services and people. Some years ago, a start was made with liberalisation of the European energy markets. This was the green light for a number of major changes, the object of which was to increase efficiency within the energy sector and to give the consumer a freedom of choice among energy suppliers.

Although the initial opening up of the energy markets has so far been largely successful, with electricity prices that are now lower in real terms than in 1997 despite recent price increases for oil, gas and coal, for example, the principal conclusion of the regulators in the field of energy is that more has to be done to ensure that industry and citizens can benefit fully from the opening up of the market. The most tenacious problem is the lack of integration of the national markets, mainly as a result of the lack of convergence in price at EU level and the limited capacity for cross-border trade. A common view is that, on the way to a more integrated European energy market, the regional markets have to be restructured first.

The regional markets have already changed since liberalisation. New companies have entered the market and positioned themselves principally on price. This has led to further commoditisation of such products as gas, power and even green energy. The traditional energy companies focus on expansion through mergers and acquisitions in attempts to become independent and powerful players on the European market. The value from the customer, from the customer base, has a meaningful role in these M&A processes in the energy market. An energy company with a more profitable customer base has a better starting point. A stronger player in the energy market can combine strengths in sustainable innovation and can also source products (commodities) at lower prices. The value for the customer can certainly increase because of this, as long as the takeover is not limited solely to consolidation, which leads to no added value for the customer.

The number of customers that switch suppliers is a natural indicator of the effectiveness of competition. Whilst throughout Europe larger consumers increasingly transfer to other suppliers, smaller entrepreneurs and households remain hesitant to exploit this freedom of choice. As an illustration, this chapter presents the Dutch consumers' market and the question of what contribution segmentation makes to the development of this market.

33.2.3 The Dutch Energy Market for Retail Customers

The Dutch energy market for retail customers can be typified as an oligopoly. In total, 23 independent players are currently active within the electricity market and 19 within the gas market; however, the market has a high concentration. The three major energy suppliers (Essent, Nuon, Eneco) control 82% of the electricity market and 79% of the gas market.

Over the past few years, almost every regional energy company has been taken over by an international player: Obragas by RWE, Intergas by Dong, NRE by E.ON, Rendo and Cogas by Electrabel. Meanwhile, newcomer Oxxio also has a foreign parent company: Centrica. The expectation is that this takeover tendency will continue over future years until a Northwest European energy market has emerged. It is possible that this will lead to switch rates comparable to those seen in the past in the UK and New Zealand.

In the Netherlands, switch percentages are currently modest. In the view of the customer, differentiation is still limited. In terms of both positioning or image and service provisioning and tariffs, customers feel that suppliers barely differ from one another. In 2007, this was still pushing down the actual switch rates considerably. Since the liberalisation, approximately 14% of private consumers have switched for electricity and 11%, for gas.

33.3   Segmentation and Strategy Formation within Essent

33.3.1   Introduction

In 2007, the Electricity Companies Unbundling Act was passed in the Netherlands. This Act implies that energy companies separate network management
tasks from the production, trading and supply of electricity and gas. By means of
this Act, the Dutch government envisages safeguarding reliable network management and encouraging free international production and trading of energy. For
Essent, the adoption of the Electricity Companies Unbundling Act means that internally a decision has to be made about how and how soon the network section of
the company will be separated from the rest of the company, before it is possible
to develop initiatives for growth through increase in scale. In anticipation of
growth by way of an increase in scale, Essent is doing everything in its power to
ensure that the starting position of each part of the unbundled company is as
healthy as possible.

Over recent years, Essent's strategy has been directed at 'Operational Excellence', which means: reliable, affordable and flawless processes and good company return. In a market where millions of customers have to be satisfactorily
cared for and where margins are under massive pressure, Operational Excellence
is a logical point of departure for all our strategic choices. The question for every
investment is whether the costs balance out against the revenues that the client is
prepared to allocate to us.

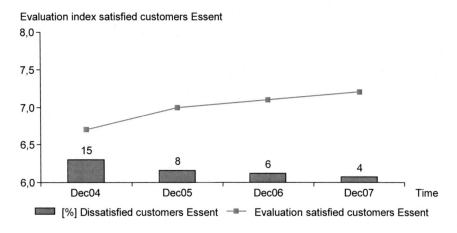

Figure 33.1: Development of customer satisfaction Essent

Essent has designed and implemented the value strategy of Operational Excellence for the consumer market with great care through a limited number of product variations. We only sell three products (gas, heat and electricity), and these in
a limited number of variations, for example, based on the source of production
(green or grey) or contract terms (fixed or variable). In addition to these products,

we deliver high-quality but standardised service. Within the consumers' market, a lot of effort is invested in improving the basic service provisioning. Our detailing of the value strategy has had tremendous consequences for the value from the customer (less rework, lower cost to serve) and also for the value for the customer. This applies to all customer processes; satisfaction has risen substantially. Perhaps even more importantly: dissatisfaction has declined (service provision is often a dissatisfier). The number of customers who indicated that they were dissatisfied with the service provision dropped dramatically to a historically low level of 4% in December 2007 (see Figure 33.1).

Now that the quality of the basic service provision has been guaranteed for processes and channels, Essent has the opportunity to reap the benefits from this and to expand on this success further by differentiating on the basis of customer value. For the Business Unit Essent Service & Sales, whose tasks include serving the consumers, value maximisation will continue to occupy centre stage during future years. In order for this aspect to be able to carry sufficient weight in all strategic decisions, segmentation based on customer value was chosen within this Business Unit. In the paragraphs below, we will examine this type of segmentation on the consumer market.

33.3.2   Customer Value Management

The concept of customer value defines the economic value of the relationship between the company and the customer. Customer value management is the process in which this economic value is developed by the company. Within customer value management (see Figure 33.2), there are three ways to increase the value of the total customer base: allowing the value of customers to grow; extending the lifetime of the relationship with customers; and acquiring new customers.

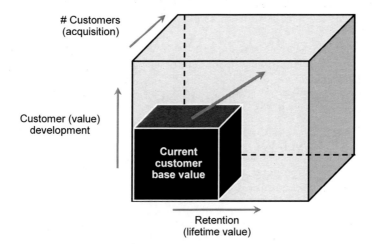

Figure 33.2: Customer value management

In order to be able to start with customer value management, we first of all have to find an answer to the questions of how we can increase the value of customers, how we can extend the lifetime of the company's relationship with them, and what customers we wish to acquire. The next section describes how Essent identifies valuable (customer) segments and explores the opportunities for increasing value.

33.3.3   Customer Value

Within Essent, the customer value is established based on three dimensions: current customer value, retention value and potential customer value. Before we examine each of these dimensions separately, it is worth looking at an important precondition in order to get an insight into customer value.

For the past 6 years, Essent has been investing in the formation of a Marketing Data Warehouse, in which all data from the operational systems is available, plus network details that are publicly available, socio-demographic details and, increasingly, aggregated data obtained from market research. This Marketing Data Warehouse is particularly suitable for the analysis of historical and current contractual, contact and profile data for each customer. This wealth of source knowledge, combined with strongly developed competencies within the field of marketing intelligence, means that within Essent we have been able to develop a single customer view, including an insight into the value and needs of these customers.

33.3.3.1 Current Customer Value

At Essent, we define the current customer value as the gross margin that is added by every individual customer for a certain period of time (12 months), minus the costs that are incurred for service, payment and other (operational) parameters. These costs are allocated, as far as possible, to direct and indirect costs per customer.

The current customer value can differ widely, depending on the payment and communication behaviour of the customer and energy consumption (partly through characteristics of the home in which the customer lives and partly through customer behaviour), but also through the price policy deployed by Essent and the way costs and margins are allocated internally.

33.3.3.2 Retention Value

We define retention value as an index figure that indicates the degree to which customers will continue the relationship with Essent:

Retention value = 100% – chance of switch (expressed as %)

Because we have such a vast and rich database at our disposal, we can perform extensive analyses of the differences between switching and nonswitching customers. We use advanced data-mining techniques, such as decision trees, logistic regressions and neural network algorithms in order to be able to establish the likelihood of switching. First of all, we categorise the most relevant variables, and then we determine which of these have the most predictive value. It has become evident to us that the variables obtained from the internal operational systems have the highest predictive value.

33.3.3.3 Potential Customer Value

The current customer value and the retention value are excellent indicators to support our decisions on what costs and investments are justifiable for which customer. However, they provide only limited footings or bases of methods of deploying this information effectively. Potential customer value does give such footings, as it provides insights into the opportunities for increasing the turnover of a customer on the one hand and reducing the costs for each customer, on the other.

In terms of increase in turnover, in most companies the potential customer value is an important dimension for cross-selling and up-selling. Strictly speaking, within Essent there are only limited possibilities for this. Essent is an energy company, and when we look at our market from this perspective we could quickly come to the conclusion that the maximum potential customer value to be reached is limited. Such a conclusion, however, disregards the opportunities that exist for proposition development and reduction of costs for each customer, and the fact that these opportunities will differ greatly from customer to customer.

In terms of reducing costs, we look at the differences in customer needs. Not all customers are interested in communication or contact with Essent in the same way or to the same degree, and absolutely not at the same moment. Channel preferences also differ from customer to customer. When calculating potential customer value, we calculate the expected profit based on cross-selling and up-selling opportunities, but also the potential for cost reduction.

Having established the value of customers along these three different dimensions and pictured these in a three-dimensional space, we can recognise a distribution of customers in which the first outlines of clusters or segments become clear.

The observant reader will note that in Figure 33.3, on the Current Customer Value and Retention Value dimensions, the Potential Customer Value dimension has been added and not the Acquisition dimension as in Figure 33.2.

Figure 33.3 illustrates our customer value calculation. This relates exclusively to our existing customer base. The core of customer value management lies in interpretation of the profitability of current customers and retention of the most valuable customers. However, Essent also wishes to retain potentially valuable customers. By explicitly adding the Potential Value dimension, we identify these customers and also the opportunities for value development within the existing customer base.

For value development outside of the existing customer base, in Figure 33.2 the dimension Acquisition is used. The profile of current and potential valuable customers from our customer value calculation (see Figure 33.3) is extremely useful for acquisition of new customers.

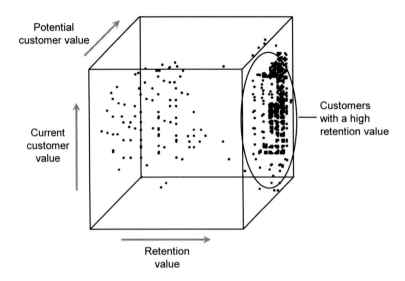

Figure 33.3: Result of customer value calculation (illustrative)

33.3.4   Customer Value Segmentation

Customer value calculations alone are not enough to give a company the ability to decide on a strategy that can be operationalised. In this section, we will examine the process of segmentation. In our search for drivers of customer value, we first analysed the characteristics of customers who move along the three separate dimensions of customer value. Based on this analysis, we arrived at conclusions on segmentation. We can show how this process translates into a practical and workable business strategy.

33.3.4.1 Characteristics of Customers along the Current Customer Value Axis

We do not see an 'average customer' along the current customer value axis. Customers are divided around an average customer value as normal, but the maximum value assigned to an individual customer in our database amounts to eight times the average value. The minimum (negative) value falls to about nine times the average value. Most customers with a higher current customer value are in the higher income classes, are in possession of quite large houses and are relatively more often parents of older children. Customers with a lower current customer value are mainly customers with payment problems, 'newcomers' to the market, such as students, or persons living in smaller (rented) accommodation.

33.3.4.2 Characteristics of Customers along the Retention Axis

On the retention axis, we see a clear clustering of customers with a high retention value. Market research confirms that the vast majority of our customers are loyal to Essent. Since the end of the 'no-free-choice' situation, almost all our customers have become acquainted with the situation of the service provisioning model of just one energy supplier: Essent. They have no experience of the performance of other suppliers, and the media and other customers report "barely none" to "no" differences between the various energy companies. Because customers are not (yet) accustomed to switching for a product such as energy, it is not yet the norm for them to actively go and search for a price or quality advantage. A significant portion of the customers even expect that switching will lead to problems and, therefore, expense (time and energy). Former monopolists therefore find themselves ostensibly in a comfortable position; however, a relationship in which the loyalty is based on a lack of better alternatives is an extremely vulnerable relationship.

It is difficult to prevent customers from switching. Essent's continuous market research shows that even the most satisfied customers may decide to switch under increased pressure from our competition. Increasing customer satisfaction is evidently not the strongest determining factor when we are aiming for retention. The same research reveals that particularly negative publicity and/or negative experience in communication with our company affects the likelihood that customers are open to the alternatives offered by the competition. For Essent it is therefore best to prevent dissatisfaction in all possible ways.

Switching behaviour can fortunately be predicted. On the basis of prediction models in our customer base, segments can be identified that have up to a 100% higher chance of switching than an average customer. These prediction models currently reveal that about 20% of our customer base is in danger of switching and that these 20% are not a statistical group, the composition changing continuously. An example: as soon as the competition targets our base, Essent can interpret which target groups in which region are under fire and which customers will be the first to be approached. Families are currently a popular target group. In countries that liberalised earlier, we saw that, after the families, the segment of the higher income 'empty nesters' (families with grown up children not living at home) were skimmed off. Another example: as soon as customers had to pay Essent three times the amount of their monthly advance payment or more at the year-end invoice, the risk that they would switch increased exponentially. The same applies to customers with complaints. In summary, although it is difficult to prevent customers from switching, we are able to earmark the customers in the database who seem most likely to consider it, and they can be approached before it is too late.

33.3.4.3 Characteristics of Customers along the Potential Customer Value Axis

On the potential customer value dimension, customers differ in the maximum turnover or gross margin to be achieved. There is a considerable group of customers who have energy contracts with more energy suppliers than Essent alone. Although socio-demographic characteristics are generally poor predictors of customer behaviour and, in the energy market, also of switching behaviour, they are evidently extremely useful when we are concerned to predict a part of the potential customer value. Characteristics such as education, wealth and stage of life are dominant for (future higher) energy consumption and, through this, the financial side of customer value.

Both the need for service and the time at which we may, and sometimes have to, contact the customer, are evidently strongly related to the stage of life the customer has reached and the events that occur within that stage, such as expansion or reduction in size of a household, moving house or alterations to a house. With this knowledge, costs can be saved on outbound contacts because these no longer have to be started 'en masse' and with the same terms for all. Moreover, an enormous improvement on the return from inbound contacts is possible. We try, as far as possible, to be a step ahead of the problems that play a part in these events, and the times at which the customers themselves will contact us are often the times at which we can link into the need for service provision that fits in with both the general profile of the individual customer and their current situation.

33.3.5   Strategy Formation

Now that we have explored all three dimensions separately, the secret is to interpret the relevant segments in this three-dimensional space that has occurred and in the spread of customers within this space. These are segments that can be processed in such a way that marketeers deliver a direct contribution to the strategic objectives.

Nine customer programmes grouped by customer value (see Figure 33.4) have been derived from the customer value segmentation within Essent, all of which are directly related to the strategic objectives stated.

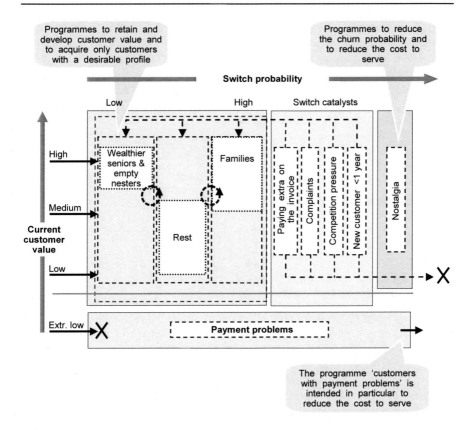

Figure 33.4: Result of customer value segmentation

33.3.5.1 Customer Programmes to Retain and Develop Customer Value

Families and higher income 'empty nesters' and 'seniors' are designated target segments for customer retention. Both segments bring in a higher margin and are popular target groups for the competition. Whereas all other customers can depend on good service provision given as a standard by Essent, the strategy differs when our main concern is to retain and acquire these (potentially) valuable customers per segment.

In order to be able to retain families, for example, we pay extra attention to the lifecycle stage in which a family can find itself liable for unexpected extra energy costs. We offer extra services around the provision of meter readings and the adjustment of monthly advance payments when a family expands or immediately after a house move or a home extension. All of these efforts nurture the customers' trust in Essent, and specifically their confidence that we will not suddenly send an annual invoice containing unpleasant surprises. This is a great basis for cross-selling and up-selling activities, which encourages customers to purchase all energy products from Essent.

As well as developing market share, we now put much more emphasis on the desired value development of the customer base. Based on the knowledge developed in the current customer base, when acquiring new customers it is now good practice to make a distinction between the profiles of interesting and less interesting prospects, as well as the times at which these would be open for approach. The same applies to winning back customers who have already left. 'Nostalgia offers' are not just made at any price. The customers who switch also include the real 'price seekers' and the 'incentive hoppers'. Based on analysis, the profile of customers within this segment is clear and Essent can save itself the effort and the cost of winning back these particular customers. For this segment, Essent has created a separate brand: Energy:Direct. Under this brand, Essent leads the fight for the customers who are seeking the lowest price and are not prepared to pay for the service that Essent offers.

33.3.5.2 Customer Programme to Prevent Switching and Reduce Costs

In the analysis phase, we saw that a number of events led to a sharp increase in the likelihood of switching. These are 'having to pay considerably more money at the annual invoice', 'being under pressure from the competition', 'complaints' and 'being a new customer' events. Because these events can be spotted in our data warehouse, we design customer programmes that are activated the moment such an event occurs for any customer. All customers who, at any time, find themselves in one of these situations can be sure of extra attention from Essent. Depending on the value profile in normal circumstances, sophisticated service recovery or retention actions are carried out that prevent that switch. In addition, the earlier Essent takes such actions, the lower Essent's costs will be and the less annoyance the customer will experience.

33.3.5.3 Customer Programmes to Reduce Costs

For Essent, it absolutely does not go without saying that customers with a low current value do not deserve any attention. In fact, low-current-value customers may even need additional attention, albeit with a different perspective. As an example, customers with payment problems disproportionately increase the cost to serve. A special customer programme is put in force to avoid or manage such events before our most valuable customers experience problems by sorting out any possible issues involving payment at an early stage. Long before the costs for this segment explode to unmanageable proportions, there are various (financial) aid measures that we can take, both in the interests of the customer and in the interests of Essent.

33.4 Conclusion and Outlook

Since liberalisation, the sector has had a different view on segmentation. According to statutory provisions the emphasis for many energy companies was initially to divide their market into segments to be served separately; nowadays not a single energy company is able to avoid segmentation. Segmentation is not worthwhile unless a further economic, but most importantly mutual, foundation is provided for the relationship between the company and the customer.

The value strategy Operational Excellence that is employed by many energy companies is not so compatible with 'differentiation'. Therefore, differentiation within Essent does not mean extensive variations of the product or the services offered. Differentiation concerns segmentation: the right offer at the right moment through the right channel to the right customer. It has become evident that not only the ROI but also the valuation of the customer improves massively when Essent differentiates these costs and investments according to the customer (group), based on customer value.

The European energy market is approaching a challenging period. We firmly believe that, in a period of further concentrations of power, the real winners in this market are the customers of those energy companies that have established the competence to develop segmentation of value from several perspectives: value for itself and, at the same time, for the customer. Ultimately, in this way, segmentation can benefit the whole sector.

References

Arndt, J. 1974. Market segmentation: theoretical and empirical dimensions. Bergen: Universitets-forlaget.

Essent. 2004-2007. Quality Monitor. Metingen.

Frank, R. E., Massy, W. F. & Wind, Y. 1972. Market segmentation. New Jersey: Prentice-Hall.

Gankema, H. G. J. & Wedel, M. 1992. Marktsegmentatie in theorie en praktijk, Jaarboek NVvM 92/93.

Gupta, S. & Lehman, D. R. 2005. Managing customers as investments: the strategic value of customers in the long run. Upper Saddle River: Wharton School Publishing.

Kotler, P. 2000. Marketing Management: Millenium Edition. New Jersey: Prentice Hall.

Kumar, V., Venkatesan, R. & Reinartz, W. 2006. Knowing what to sell, when, and to whom. Harvard Business Review: 131-137.

Marktmonitor. 2007. Ontwikkeling van de Nederlandse kleinverbruikermarkt voor Elektriciteit en Gas. NMa/DTe.

Verhage, B. & Cunningham, W. H. 1984. Grondslagen van het Marketing Management. Leiden: Stenfert Kroese.

34 Current Trends in Serving Industrial Customers

Andreas Radmacher[1]

Abstract

This chapter reviews best practices of energy utilities serving industrial customers. The chapter first addresses 'macro-trends' that are giving rise to direction and momentum in energy market evolution: supply chain management, security of supply and the search for ways of achieving energy efficiency. Secondly, the 'micro-trends', including level of market competition, industrial energy consumer and utility capabilities and the evolution of financial engineering of industrial services contracts, are examined. Finally, with special emphasis on highly developed energy markets, specific best practice examples applied by RWE are reviewed. The conclusion reached is that the new energy service environment is defined by service innovation and a cooperative partnership attitude between energy utilities and customers, allowing the design of tailored products.

Keywords: industrial energy customers, utility and industrial customer cooperation, best practices RWE

---

[1] Dr. Andreas Radmacher is a Member of the Executive Board of RWE Energy AG, Germany.

A. Bausch and B. Schwenker (eds.), *Handbook Utility Management,*
DOI: 10.1007/978-3-540-79349-6_34, © Springer-Verlag Berlin Heidelberg 2009

34.1 Macro- and Micro-trends in Serving Industrial Customers

German energy utilities have been contending with various forms of market liberalisation for most of the last 15 years. Utilities in the United Kingdom have been similarly engaged for a longer period, and the Nordic power markets for even longer. Energy utilities have traditionally tended to be very large companies, which were nonetheless nationally or regionally focused and thus often rather provincial in the scope of their view of global industry trends outside of the various local energy markets. This has occasionally caused energy utilities to be surprised by market liberalisation movements arising predominantly from industrial customers and policy makers concerned about the economic attractiveness for industry of their regions.

The purpose of this chapter is to review the current 'best practices' and trends concerning energy utilities serving industrial customers. By way of context, we shall first address the 'macro-trends' in the competitive space of industrial customers that give rise to direction and momentum in energy market evolution. In addition, the 'micro-trends', or factors driving industrial energy consumer market competition and service innovation will be surveyed. Finally, with special emphasis on the German and other markets in which network regulation and unbundling have created a fair and transparent market access environment, the chapter will explore specific examples of best practices by energy utilities serving industrial customers. These examples will illustrate the energy product innovation that has been the direct result of competitive market forces.

34.1.1 Macro-trends Framing Industrial Customers' Attitudes to Energy Supply

Industrial customers' attitudes to energy supply are framed substantially by their experiences in other (nonenergy) competitive global markets. In this regard, it is worth noting that these trends are applicable to nearly all industrial enterprises, regardless of size. Three trends, in particular, that are experienced by virtually all international industrial customers give rise to their attitudes to energy supply:

Internationally engaged industrial enterprises are almost universally focused on supply chain management. In parallel with creating the most efficient and flexible global supply chains, these same enterprises are focused on the security of supply of raw materials, intermediate manufacturing capacity and the like. With increasing intensity these industrial companies have become very focused on their 'energy efficiency' and supply chain carbon footprint. These three macro-trends give rise to enterprise-wide organisational behaviours that increasingly find expression in the relationship between the industrial enterprises and their energy suppliers.

34.1.1.1 Supply Chain Management

Most industrial enterprises are part of the supply chains of several, and sometimes many other industries. In addition, they manage their own supply chains. Nearly all industrial enterprises face constant pressure to deliver more output, more dependably, faster and at a lower margin. Nearly every industrial company is faced with persistent pressure on its margins. In return, its own suppliers are constantly faced with pressure to increase efficiency and lower costs. No longer is this a periodic cycle reappearing every few years along with contract renewals. Even moderate-sized industrial customers maintain multinational networks of suppliers that they play off against each other to drive costs continuously downward. As a result of this supply chain pressure driving efficiency and cost, industrial enterprises have developed a core competence of supply chain management vis-à-vis their own suppliers. An entire industry of supply chain management, complete with software designers, consultants, auditors and academicians, has grown up.

The intellectual insights gained through managing and participating in a supply chain do not go away, nor do they remain in separate compartments. Gone are the days when industrial companies viewed energy (power and gas, not oil) as something different and of a local nature, not subject to the same methods and approaches as the suppliers of other inputs. Industrial customers and their industry associations have been, and continue to be, among the strongest voices lobbying for increased energy liberalisation. It should hence be no surprise that every tool in industrial enterprises' supply chain management toolkit is now also being used to manage the supply of energy. And, lest there be any mistake about it, that is as it should be.

In the old 'cost plus'-regulated energy pricing era, utilities and their energy prices often served as important tools in national and regional industrial policies. Many countries employed energy price regulatory policy to force some energy market segments to subsidise other market segments through regulated systems of artificially inflated or reduced industry-specific energy-pricing policies. In practice, such nontransparent pricing systems rewarded industries with powerful political connections and effective lobbying associations. Meanwhile, nondiscriminatory network access regulation and unbundling have created a market-based energy commodity price environment that reflects costs only at the margin – at least in the short run. Energy commodity prices reflect constantly changing market supply and demand. Liberalisation is about how prices arise and not about the level of prices. Liberalisation does not guarantee any utility that it will be successful or profitable. Nor does liberalisation guarantee any industrial customer that market prices will favour its industry. Industrial customers are accustomed to these transparent market mechanisms and institutions elsewhere in their value chains and today deploy the same approaches in obtaining competitive energy services and supplies as they use in managing the remainder of their supply chain.

34.1.1.2 Security of Supply

Global supply chain management necessitates a constant focus on security of supply. For many industrial customers, this requires consideration of shipping and harbour capacity, the timely and secure availability of raw materials (including energy), and also the political security of an essential supply region. For essential supplies, many industrial enterprises use multiple vendors subject to different weather, geopolitical and other supply interruption risks. Efficiency gains associated with eliminating 'reserves' or 'inventory' or 'stand-by capacity' from the supply chain (along with the associated costs) can only be safely accomplished by very competent suppliers and near real-time communication between the industrial manufacturer and all elements of its supply chain. In such carefully balanced supply chains, a supplier whose deliveries are interrupted is likely to pay dearly for having become an unreliable supplier.

The California energy crises of nearly a decade ago reminded politicians, utilities and energy consumers of the importance of supply security. Owing to a variety of simultaneously arising circumstances involving energy demand, supply and possible market manipulation, California began to experience frequent interruptions in its electricity supply, which were also of significant duration. For software companies, information technology (IT) and telecommunications companies, and for manufacturers of every sort, the insecurity of energy supply became a geographic risk factor. This perceived risk resulted in some companies relocating, or diverting planned expansions to regions offering more secure energy supply.

The emphasis on energy supply security favours financially strong companies such as energy utilities and large investment banks. Hedge funds, energy traders and brokers can often supply attractive prices; but will they still be there when the lights start flickering? Many large energy utilities – such as RWE – are not only financially strong but can also provide greater supply security owing to their extensive physical presence in energy markets. Furthermore, industrial customers accustomed to balancing price, efficiency and supply security in other segments of the value chain expect to be given a menu of meaningful choices by their energy suppliers.

34.1.1.3 Energy Efficiency

Many energy utilities were surprised at the speed with which industrial enterprises became advocates for the reduction of carbon footprint. While some energy producers and suppliers were still debating whether or not global warming and climate change were actually supported by the science and whether carbon footprint reduction was economically feasible, many industrial enterprises of all sizes became serious advocates of sustainability and carbon footprint reduction. This somewhat surprising trend arises from several motivations.

Many industrial enterprises have found that being able to demonstrate a shrinking carbon footprint and serious dedication to sustainability throughout their supply chain is an attractive marketing lever for their products and their brand. Moreover, industrial enterprises have understood that, regardless of the impact on the climate, efficiency saves money and boosts the bottom line – a great way to do 'good works', to be seen to be doing good works and to make money at the same time.

Further, both investor financial analysts and purchasing representatives of customer companies understand that reducing the carbon footprint can only be accomplished by sustained, forward-looking, active leadership and management. A dedication to sustainability is, therefore, an excellent signalling mechanism both to the purchasing market and to financial capital markets.

Additionally, it is worth noting that many firms have found that their 'green' or 'sustainability' image gives them an edge in attracting and retaining top-quality intellectual capital. Excellent employees want to be associated with an excellent company of which they can be proud.

34.1.2 Micro-drivers of Industrial Energy Consumer Market Competition and Service Innovation

The macro-trends giving rise to customer and political pressure in the direction of liberalised markets only find economic fulfilment in environments where both the legal and regulatory framework and the intellectual and organisational capital have reached a level of advancement and maturity that embraces competition and marshals intellectual energy for product innovation rather than regulatory and legal fights about the necessity, shape, speed and breadth of market liberalisation efforts. The presence of a robust, dynamic, innovative and competitive market for energy supply and services depends on several drivers, including the following:

34.1.2.1 Level of Market Competition

The level of competition in energy supply markets for industrial customers depends simultaneously on the competitive landscape of the energy markets and the competitive environment of the relevant industrial energy consumers themselves. In other words, are real 'choices' available among energy suppliers and energy supply offerings? And, secondly, are the choices 'appreciated' or 'in demand' on the part of the relevant industrial energy consumers? The former is determined primarily by the degree and effectiveness of energy liberalisation measures in the relevant market, especially as concerns unbundling and nondiscriminatory network access. The second is determined primarily by the nature of the industrial energy consumers actually in the geographic space concerned.

A liquid and transparent wholesale energy commodity market with many and diverse participants is the sine qua non for any discussion of competition in or liberalisation of energy markets. In such liquid wholesale markets, buying and selling gas or power is neither mystery nor 'rocket science'. Commodity contracts are standardised, and the markets in which they are traded and their prices are discovered are transparent. In these markets, supplier differentiation leading to a long-term customer relationship or the 'switching' of long-term relationships is based on value-added services and innovative client-tailored products. Some significant European market areas are lacking this essential liquid wholesale market, which depends above all on unbundling and nondiscriminatory network access. Without it, there is little motivation for an energy supplier to innovate or to develop new products or customer-tailored services.

In the case of Germany, especially in the electric power markets, virtually every industrial energy consumer in the country has a variety of supply alternatives, ranging from multiple energy utilities of varying sizes and nationalities to energy brokers and exchanges, in addition to banks and other energy traders. It comes as no surprise, then, that in the German market more than one in every two industrial customers have switched energy suppliers at least twice. In Germany, the combination of multiple to numerous potential suppliers and globally exposed and experienced industrial customers has led to a robustly competitive and innovative energy supply market.

34.1.2.2 Capabilities of Industrial Energy Consumers

Not much more than a decade ago, prior to liberalisation, the principal mechanisms employed in the pursuit of more 'competitive energy commodity prices and terms' throughout Europe by most industrial energy consumers included political lobbying, trade associations (also for lobbying), the ability to develop 'stalking horse' power plant projects and, when necessary, the ability to fight legal battles in court. In spite of these efforts, the legal and regulatory infrastructure was inadequate to ensure a truly competitive market for energy supply and services.

Almost simultaneously with the first meaningful liberalisation laws, energy exchanges arose. At the onset of electricity liberalisation in Germany, the European Energy Exchange (EEX) in Frankfurt and the Leipzig Power Exchange (LPX) in Leipzig were founded. Gradually, an increasing number of large industrial energy consumers began to hedge their energy positions directly on one or more of the meanwhile merged exchanges. Others bought hedging products from banks, energy traders or the trading desks of large utilities. For the last half dozen or so years, the ability to 'trade' either directly on an exchange or via over-the-counter (OTC) brokers or directly with bank or utility trading desks has been the most important skill for an industrial company trying to take maximum advantage of the opportunities arising from energy market liberalisation. Several very large industrial energy consumers have built their own trading divisions (e.g. Deutsche Bahn). However, building up a trading division is expensive and requires especially skilled oversight all the way up to the board level of a company. There are industrial energy consumers which have developed significant skills in trading and hedging, but there are none that have developed substantial 'best in breed' class trading teams. Energy trading is not the 'core competence' of any industrial company other than an energy utility or producer. In regions such as Germany, where both energy competition and service innovation have become quite advanced, it makes no more sense for an industrial energy consumer to maintain a substantial trading capability than for it to maintain a power generation department.

The 'make vs buy' decision is in the process of evolving again. Prior to energy liberalisation, most industrial energy consumers bought in their full energy requirements, more often than not directly from an energy utility. Occasionally, they would 'make' some of their own electricity with an on-site power generation facility. In the first phase of liberalisation, as soon as third-party network access became practically possible, many industrial energy consumers began to make their energy supply by analytically disaggregating their demand into standard products which they could then purchase through brokers or an exchange. This 'trading-dominated' supply strategy is now being eclipsed by more innovative approaches.

Increasingly, industrial energy consumers are beginning to explore the outsourcing of some or all of the energy services they require. Instead of buying a fully aggregated commodity-product all-inclusive contract from a utility or actively and directly participating in traded energy markets, industrial energy consumers are beginning to apply the same supply chain management and 'focus on core competencies' approaches to energy as they have long applied to other important inputs. In the extreme case, this can mean that everything to do with energy is outsourced in its entirety to an energy service provider. This can include light bulbs (and their maintenance), space heating and air-conditioning equipment, energy commodity supply, etc. A combination of robust contracts between large credit-worthy counterparties, transparent market benchmarks, and price triggers makes it possible for an increasingly large number of industrial energy consumers to get out of the energy business completely. This is the ultimate 'buy' scenario along the 'make-vs-buy' continuum. It leverages the full relationship and contract management skills of the industrial company, which have long been honed for managing the outsourcing of other essential elements of their supply and value chain. It is becoming possible to purchase 'heat' and 'cooling' and 'light' delivered at a specific time and place and in accordance with certain standards, while leaving the 'how to do it' up to an energy expert such as an energy utility.

34.1.2.3 Capabilities of Energy Suppliers/Producers

With the introduction of the first effective liberalisation laws and regulations, energy trading groups from markets such as the Nordic Region, the United Kingdom and the US – which have had experience in liberalised markets – began to work vigorously with municipal and industrial customers to move the market in the direction of an actively traded market. Energy utilities were among the last to realise the importance of developing robust trading teams. Today, by any standard of measurement, the finest energy trading teams in Europe include several European energy utility trading groups (e.g. RWE Trading, EDF Trading) and also trading teams from energy producers (e.g. Shell, BP and Gazprom). Often the best prices and terms in the market are to be found with utility or producer trading desks, and not on exchanges or with bank trading teams. To the degree that the current energy market is characterised by energy commodity trading, utilities have become at least the equals of the best participants in traded energy markets.

With the growing diversity of traded products, their liquidity and their transparency, traditional utility energy sales teams have struggled to reinvent themselves. A variety of 'shaped curves' can be purchased competitively from brokers, in some cases already tailored to specific industries or types of customers. In a market environment in which a commodity is easy to buy and prices are relatively transparent, it has become necessary for energy utilities to return to the original concept of being a service company. It is no longer enough to deploy an excellent trading team. Now the energy utility wanting to distinguish itself in the market place must become a comprehensive service provider: helping the customer to reduce overall energy consumption and increase its energy efficiency while helping the customer select, implement and maintain appropriate technology in support of sustainability and emissions goals (e.g. replacing thousands of 'old-fashioned' incandescent light bulbs with the most up-to-date energy-efficient bulbs).

34.1.2.4 Pervasiveness of the Insights of Modern Finance Including Securitisation

A final driver of innovation in energy services for industrial enterprises arises from the pervasive familiarity of globally competitive companies with the financial engineering associated especially with asset-backed securitisations. The financial engineering associated with asset-backed securitisation often enables credit-worthy counterparties to securitise and 'sell' a substantial portion of the cash flows associated with complex long-term service and supply contracts. For instance, a large-scale energy commodity, infrastructure and services outsourcing arrangement between a large industrial manufacturer and a large energy utility is likely to have a substantial component of highly predictable revenues and expenses, some of which may vary as a function of a transparent, tradable, liquid (and thus often hedgeable) price index. Financial tools make it possible to 'package' and 'remarket' (i.e. securitise) this substantially predictable or hedgeable portion of an energy outsourcing arrangement. When both counterparties are excellently rated credit-worthy companies, it is likely that the remaining 'value' to be found in the predictable portion of the services and commodity arrangement will have an effective financial return lower than the cost of capital or return targets of either the energy utility or its industrial customer. This creates an excellent opportunity to monetise the value of the contract to the benefit of both partners. Financial engineering is an extreme and quantitative application of the principle of 'letting each party do what it does best' – another way of saying: "Focus on your core competencies".

34.1.3   Conclusions

We are only at the start of radical innovations in the supply of energy commodities and services to industrial customers. In Germany, the market institutions and legal frameworks are now in place. In addition, both the energy utilities and their industrial customers have extensive experience not only with liberalised energy markets but also with competitive markets globally and with the various methods available to rationalise supply and value chains. What is possible today was not even conceivable a decade or even 5 years ago: the knowledge was not there, the market institutions were not there and the motivation of all parties was not there. The product and service innovation process has only just begun!

34.2   Cases and Trends in 'Best Practice'

In competitive energy markets such as Germany, the best practice in energy commodity supply and services is changing overall, but especially with regard to industrial energy-consuming customers. The pace and direction of this change is moving simultaneously along multiple axes driven by the forces implied by and associated with the macro- and micro-trends described above. Although best practice is constantly evolving, a few examples will illustrate the texture and current state of this evolution.

34.2.1   From Trading to Structured Portfolio Management

34.2.1.1 Trading

For some time now the best practice from the perspective of the industrial customer has been direct energy procurement on wholesale markets, including trading and price hedging. Often the procurement of normal planned power supplies has been performance benchmarked against exchange (e.g. EEX) prices plus or minus an increment. Unexpected changes in demand would be settled in the relevant intra-month market (e.g. day-ahead). Substantial energy consumers have often developed their own in-house energy-trading teams to buy and sell energy on exchanges or through execution brokers. Other industrial customers have often resorted to hedging contracts with either investment banks or other energy trading groups, including the top utility-trading teams, such as RWE Trading. Either practice, but especially exchange trading, demands rigorous senior management oversight including risk management, controlling and appropriate accounting. Many customers have found that the full cost of running their own trading shop, even when any perceived 'savings' in energy cost are factored in, are simply not justified.

34.2.1.2 Structured Portfolio Management

The RWE Key Account organisation was one of the first energy utilities to react to this situation by offering structured procurement contracts as a retail product. Modern energy supply contracts combine transparent and flexible pricing mechanisms based on a detailed portfolio analysis on the one hand, and minimal administrative costs for the industrial customer on the other, so that the customer avoids the expense of building up its own trading capacities.

These structured portfolio management contracts are built up on a detailed analysis of the customer's demand, various procurement options ranging from wholesale trading to fixed-price products with a duration of several years, and sophisticated IT tools for position monitoring and portfolio valuation. Last but not least, owing to the complexity of energy markets, consulting is an essential part of any contract of this type. Once the consulting process is started, it is only a small additional step to analyse the financial effects of possible measures designed to increase energy efficiency and reduce the client's carbon footprint.

In the past, both parties tended to develop their own models as a tool for negotiation. Increasingly, the best practice is for joint utility-customer teams to develop a jointly maintained model as a tool for the joint discovery of ways to reduce energy consumption, increase the efficiency of energy consumption and/or reduce the environmental impact of energy consumption. Both parties realise that the components discovered will be priced or indexed to mutually agreed market prices. The price negotiation then tends to centre around which public index should be chosen and how much is to be added to or subtracted from the index.

Figure 34.1 illustrates the breadth of the Portfolio Management tools shared by RWE Key Account with its industrial customers as they jointly understand and manage the customer's specific portfolio. The market itself provides the remaining necessary tools. Energy brokers and exchanges compete with each other to develop standardised products and associated indices whenever a significant demand exists. Today, shaped curves can be bought competitively through brokers, whereas only a few years ago significant trading skill was required to replicate a specific supply–demand curve with many standardised trading products.

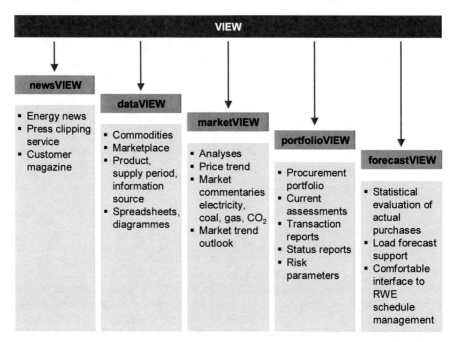

Figure 34.1: Contents of the portfolio management tool VIEW, used by RWE Key Account in cooperation with its industrial customers

34.2.1.3 Structured Pricing

Derivative instruments are now used to design individual price dynamics custom-ised to individual requirements. Well-informed and skilled energy consumers pre-pared to take risks may choose a price structure based on options that retain 'up-side potential' if their market expectations are correct. RWE's product 'Multipe-riod', for example, offers a price discount if market prices remain stable. Indexed pricing allows other energy consumers to buy energy at a price indexed to the product they produce. An aluminium-price-indexed power supply contract, for example, reduces the risk position of an aluminium producer if market prices for power and aluminium should diverge.

34.2.1.4 Division of Labour

Having arrived at a common and detailed understanding of market-mechanisms and the market value of the energy required, increasingly best practice leads to a new phenomenon among industrial energy consumers and their energy utility sup-pliers: detailed negotiations concerning the question of which part of the portfolio management and optimisation – scheduling, energy trading, hedging, etc. – should be provided by the utility, the industrial customer or some third party. Market lib-eralisation and competition are concerned not only with the choice of energy pro-vider, but also with the choice of the provider for many energy-related services.

34.2.2   Consumer-owned Power Generation Revisited

Another aspect of energy supply chain management is the use of consumer-owned power generation facilities as an alternative to buying power in the market.

34.2.2.1 Power Pricing Alternatives

Plant-specific power pricing can be offered using so-called cost-based products that are market-traded: power supply contracts that offer a price following the de-velopment of the costs of power production applicable to a specific power plant and its fuel options instead of the EEX or some other broad-based exchange or market price. Figure 34.2 illustrates the potential advantages of such a relatively stable cost-based pricing regime.

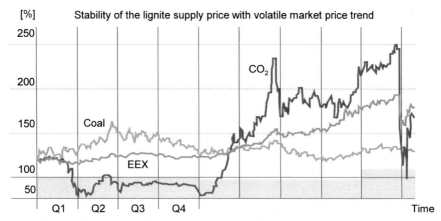

The supply price (area in grey) is more favourable than the corresponding EEX price because two indices cushion the price volatility and smooth the curve overall.

Figure 34.2: Comparison of cost-based lignite supply price to volatile exchange-traded product prices

34.2.2.2 Web-based Dispatching

RWE pioneered what is rapidly becoming acknowledged as best practice for dispatching an industrial customer's own power plant via the internet. An RWE-designed website is prepared for the customer that fixes prenegotiated margins vis-à-vis exchange or other published prices and makes it possible for industrial energy consumers that operate their own power generation capacity to sell excess power into the grid (via RWE) or to buy power rather than generate it. The RWE platform recreates all the options that a company normally has with its own power plant. Everything is online. The industrial customer's energy management function has been made much simpler and more transparent, and RWE maintains the ongoing relationship with the customer. The customer knows that they will always have fair buying and selling prices without having to maintain a trading team to shop for them.

Other industrial customers think they want to build their own power plant. A joint effort can help analytically define what the portfolio of 'real options' would look like in building and owning such a power plant. RWE can provide, via the internet, a 'virtual power plant' that allows the industrial energy consumer to gain all of the flexibility and price benefits of ownership without having to actually build and operate their own power plant. Given that RWE is one of the largest power generators in Europe, it is not surprising that its costs of generation are normally much lower than those of an industrial power generator. Furthermore, the industrial customer does not have to dedicate plant space for the facility nor does it have to maintain a department of experts in power generation. Both the utility and the customer benefit from the installation of a virtual power plant rather than construction of a needless real one.

34.2.2.3 Customer Tailored Service Levels

Customer and energy utility rethinks of energy security of supply have led to innovative contractual relationships that have become best practice for the market. Traditionally, security of supply was the single top priority of energy utilities. The security of energy supply is still important for most energy users, but it comes at the cost of substantial and expensive back-up capacity. A 'proxy' for these costs can be observed in the market, particularly in the form of sudden peak power prices.

Many industrial customers, in the metal and paper industry, for instance, are willing to accept occasional and short interruptions of power supply if they receive an adequate discount on their delivered power price. From the perspective of the energy utility, this right to interrupt the delivery has the same function as a back-up power plant. Modern energy supply contracts – such as RWE Key Account's 'Power Casher' – exploit this trade-off between security of supply and energy price. Some industrial consumers have agreed to accept a limited number of supply interruptions and thus significantly reduced their overall energy costs. Others realise similar effects by considering day-ahead or intraday energy prices for their production plans.

This trend of selling flexibility in energy consumption to the market has just started. With the growing share of wind and solar energy production in Europe, the value of flexibility will increase. Full exploitation of this opportunity requires close cooperation between industrial customers and energy utilities.

34.2.2.4 Emissions 'Cap and Trade' Cooperation

The tendency towards greater focus on energy efficiency and reduced carbon footprint together with the growing intensity of information-sharing and cooperation between energy utilities and their industrial customers is manifesting itself particularly with respect to CO_2 emission trading. In Europe, energy utilities and their major industrial customers are subject to the European emission trading system (EU-ETS). They have developed their own management tools to deal with the regulatory requirements and the additional price risks from volatile markets for emission rights. In competitive energy markets, current market prices for emission rights are reflected in the power prices. The trend is therefore in the direction of an integrated approach so as to manage both commodities simultaneously: the industry's proprietary CO_2-position and its power position.

The initial steps in this direction have already been taken during the first emission trading period from 2005 to 2007: several energy supply contracts for 'decarbonised power' implying a separation of the power price into one part with only the implied CO_2 costs and another part for plain power production costs. These contracts have two main advantages for the industrial customer: first, full transparency concerning the impact of CO_2 prices on its energy costs, and thus the opportunity to manage risk better; and, secondly, a way to use excess CO_2 emission rights in order to reduce the net power price.

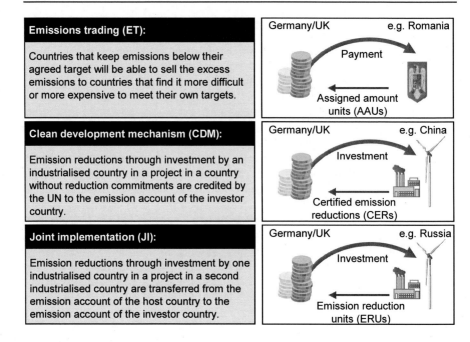

Figure 34.3: Opportunities within the European emission trading system

During the second allocation period, 2008-2012, additional opportunities will arise from the combination of several new factors in the European emission trading system:

- For projects that lead to emission reductions in a country such as Russia or China, a company may receive emission rights (CERs, or ERUs) from so called flexible mechanisms (see Figure 34.3).
- Companies in Europe can substitute allocated European emission rights by CERs or ERUs at their national emission register.
- Energy utilities such as RWE have already built up expertise in emission-reduction projects, including cooperation with local and international regulatory bodies. They are interested in developing additional projects and purchasing additional certificates.
- Many industrial customers have production sites in multiple countries throughout the world and thus access to many emission-reduction-projects.

Collectively, these factors open up a new field for cooperation between energy utilities and their industrial customers: RWE Key Account has already started active trading in CERs and has entered negotiations with industrial customers concerning the joint development of emission-reduction projects.

34.2.3 Intensive Energy Utility and Industrial Customer Cooperation

The intimate level of information sharing and analysis associated with the above-mentioned trends (e.g. division of labour, structured pricing, customer-tailored service levels, emissions cap and trade cooperation) is new to many energy utility–energy industrial consumer relationships. However, it is not new to industrial customers. WalMart, Tesco and many other consumer-products companies share daily cash register feeds directly with their suppliers identifying precisely what has been sold and where, allowing the supplier to immediately replace the sold products, thereby minimising or eliminating inventory and its associated costs throughout the supply chain. Buy a computer from Dell through the internet and it is likely to be 'manufactured' at a site provided by its shipping/logistics service provider, at or near an airport and designed by the customer on line, with on-site components suppliers of such elements as hard disks, central processing unit (CPU) chips, motherboards, memory chips, etc. not delivering until the moment of assembly. Automobile manufacturers now design new cars in collaboration with the manufacturers of the various subassemblies.

There is no reason now why an entire portfolio of energy supply for a credit-worthy counterparty (a large automobile manufacturing plant, say) cannot be securitised and the associated cash flows sold to the financial markets. That would mean that the energy utility and the energy consumer would carefully define the supply-and-demand relationship (for at least a significant part of the energy demand), set all of the pricing to be a function of a tradable benchmark (such as an exchange product closing price), define or hedge out the heating or cooling risk attributable to weather and then calculate the expected cash flow over a period of multiple years. The value monetised through the securitisation of such an energy supply portfolio asset-backed security would benefit both utility and energy-consuming customer – each of which would no doubt have much higher cost of capital and return expectations than the purchaser of the securitised energy supply portfolio. Only stable, credit-worthy and highly sophisticated counterparties could create such a transaction. But such complex transactions are not new for many global industrial enterprises. Energy utilities are just now catching up intellectually to the point where they, together with their industrial customers, can create and release such embedded value.

In such a framework, the macro-trend energy efficiency would develop its full impact on the relationship between energy utilities and industrial consumers. In principle, an industrial energy consumer could package up all of its energy related infrastructure (e.g. light bulbs and wires, heaters and air conditioners) and then lease them to an energy utility, which would then have the opportunity of maintaining the infrastructure and supplying the energy. Were the entire energy services outsourcing contract a multi-year fixed (or fixed index) price deal, the energy utility would be motivated to replace existing infrastructure with more efficient infrastructure so as to capture (and perhaps share) the associated efficiency gains. This is precisely how industrial customers outsource IT, accounting, or call centre management. It is precisely how they outsource the manufacturing of a specialised computer chip or automobile assembly. There is no reason why the same approach should not be applied to energy services. Indeed, in some markets, such true 'full-requirements' energy services sourcing has already begun.

34.2.4 Conclusions

The impact of these trends in best practice for supplying energy services and commodity has already begun to be felt throughout the energy industry. The 'sales teams' of energy utilities now require quantitatively and analytically gifted intellectual capital with finance and engineering education and experience; but they also require experts in different industries being served (or 'targeted for service') by the utility. Rolls Royce does not accept Airbus engine specifications as a given. Rather, it participates in designing the entire air frame and associated systems. Rolls Royce understands the composite materials of which modern planes are made just as it understands jet engine dynamics. Similarly, energy utilities are increasingly becoming specialists in the energy-related processes of their industrial customers. Often, the best solution for industrial customers is to help them spend less on energy by consuming less of it. The savings created can be shared by both the utility and its customer. In the past, a utility's sole objective was to sell more power (by volume) at a higher price. In a liberalised market where utilities are competing on services and prices are transparent, this old way of thinking is a way to go out of business rather than to expand. The change in the intellectual capital requirements of energy utilities is not limited to education and experience, however. A cooperative attitude focused on partnerships rather than on 'us-and-them' relationships is equally important. It is in this new environment that product and service innovation will thrive – fulfilling the myriad opportunities created by energy market liberalisation.

35   The Energy Retail Market from a Customer Perspective

Werner Marnette[1]

Abstract

The general conditions for energy-intensive industrial enterprises have changed significantly since the liberalisation of the energy markets. This applies, in particular, to the German electricity market. Although formally there is competition on the market, this is obstructed by the considerable market power, strong vertical integration and persisting lack of transparency. Against this background, Norddeutsche Affinerie AG, as the largest copper producer in Europe and an energy-intensive enterprise, started in good time to concentrate on securing a long-term electricity supply as well as the continuous reduction of energy consumption and identification of energy-saving potential. This alone, however, was not enough to absorb the dramatically rising energy prices. On the contrary, politicians have the responsibility for ensuring a reliable and economical energy supply and for correcting existing misguided developments.

Keywords: energy policy, in-house production, energy efficiency

---

[1] Dr. Werner Marnette is former Minister for Economic Affairs in Schleswig-Holstein. During 1994-2007 he was Chief Executive Officer of Norddeutsche Affinerie AG, Germany.

A. Bausch and B. Schwenker (eds.), *Handbook Utility Management,*
DOI: 10.1007/978-3-540-79349-6_35, © Springer-Verlag Berlin Heidelberg 2009

35.1   Industrial Energy Consumption – with the Nonferrous Metals Industry as an Example

Energy is a basic input factor in industrial production and has a marked influence on the economic success of industrial enterprises. This applies, above all, to enterprises in primary industries, which have an energy consumption that significantly exceeds their share of gross production value (see Figure 35.1). Despite intensive measures to achieve rational energy utilisation in companies, energy costs have become an increasingly heavy burden for their industrial locations on account of the energy price rises. Germany is one of the countries with the highest electricity and natural gas prices in Europe. A reliable, cost-effective and environmentally friendly energy supply is an elementary precondition for a high-performing and competitive industry. The energy policy must therefore bring short-term cost optimisation in a balanced ratio to medium- and long-term orientation through to high plant efficiency, renewable energy and other low-CO_2 technologies.

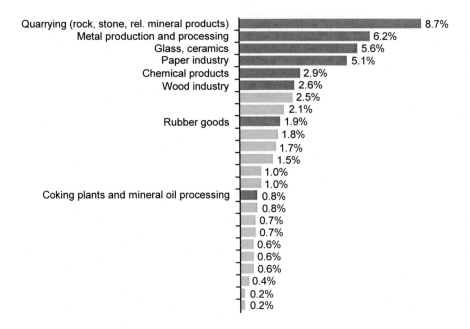

Figure 35.1: Energy cost share of gross production value (Status 2004) (Statistisches Bundesamt, 2007)

The nonferrous metals industry is one of the industries with the highest energy intensity in the processing sector. The production of nonferrous metals requires a great number of different energy-intensive processes that are of both a pyrometallurgical and a hydrometallurgical nature, i.e. include melting processes, tank-houses, leaching and precipitation processes. The raw materials for metal production come in the form of ores and ore concentrates and also as secondary raw materials that are won by metal recycling or originate from the metal scrap of other production branches. These raw materials must, if required, be pretreated, depending on the treatment process. After the crude metal production, further refining steps are generally necessary to separate the by-elements still contained in the metal produced (RWI, 2005). The pyrometallurgical melting processes are mostly performed in a high temperature range of over 1,000 deg C, which is mainly achieved by the use of natural gas. In addition, refining or reduction tankhouses are highly electricity intensive. In 2005 about 31.5 TWh of energy was used in the individual process stages in nonferrous metal production, almost 57% of which was accounted for by electricity and more than 31% by natural gas (WVM, 2007).

Dependence on the energy sources used in the nonferrous metals industry is high. A change in an energy source alone at short notice does not generally achieve its objective and usually involves considerable capital outlay, since the type of energy used is largely linked to the production technology. For this reason, any significant structural change in energy input causes high capital expenditure and thus new dependences. The nonferrous metals industry has made every endeavour in the past to save energy and reduce energy dependence by implementing process improvements and optimising operations. According to Wirtschafts-Vereinigung Metalle (WVM), the technically possible lower limit for energy input has almost been reached meanwhile. Thus, apart from technical possibilities for savings, the possibilities of metal scrap recycling as an energy-saving potential were already identified and utilised early on, since metal production from secondary materials needs much less energy than primary production. The recycling of metals is thus an important contribution to avoiding climate-damaging gases. The current share of metal production from secondary materials in Germany is the highest for lead, at about 70%; for other important metals, such as copper and aluminium, the recycling quota exceeds the 50% mark.

35.2   Basic Energy Management Conditions for Energy-intensive Industrial Companies in Germany

In the days of the regulated energy market up to the end of the 1990s, conditions in Germany were relatively clear and calculable as regards energy policy. This was naturally also reflected in the individual energy supply agreements of the industrial enterprises. Thus, contract lifetimes for electricity supplies were comparably long, for instance, and 5- to 20-year contracts were not uncommon (GfST, 2003). The type of agreement has changed with the liberalisation of the electricity market from an integrated agreement covering the supply of the customers' full energy needs into disintegrated agreements. While the conventional integrated full supply agreement included an electricity price as an 'all-inclusive package' covering all value-added stages and price components such as energy, grid third-party access, Renewable Energy Sources Act and CHP levies and energy taxes, the procurement of electricity today involves a number of agreements relating to the various value-added stages. Although the disintegrated agreements have theoretically enabled higher transparency and flexibility on the energy markets, they have also caused much greater complexity in the contractual relations for the industrial enterprises. In addition, the contract lifetimes have become considerably shorter owing to the current market trends, which are not calculable to any adequate degree. New markets have emerged, and the product range has greatly increased as a result of the liberalisation of the energy markets. For example, in the case of electricity, apart from the products of full supply and reserve generation that are already part of the monopoly system, there are now spot and futures markets. These result in new possibilities and alternative ways for major customers to optimise energy procurement. With the liberalisation of the energy markets and the connected opening up of the market, German industrial enterprises had hoped that energy costs would be reduced and Germany would consequently become more competitive as a location for business and investment.

For German industry, which is sensitive to electricity costs, cost-effective and calculable electricity prices are very important for international competitiveness. Liberalisation of the energy markets only achieved price reductions for a limited period. Thus, although it was possible to amend earlier cost disadvantages relative to other European regions in 2000 and 2001, the next year again brought a significant rise that re-opened the price gap between Germany and its European competitors, very much to the detriment of German locations. The price for an industrial electricity supply of 24,000 MWh per annum in Germany amounts to 120.13 €/MWh on average, almost 68% of which alone is accounted for by the pure energy price, 32% by taxes, more than 13% by grid third-party access and more than 8% by levies (concession levy, Renewable Energy Sources Act levy, CHP levy) (Bundesnetzagentur, 2007). This is a rise of almost 7% on the previous year (Bundesnetzagentur, 2006). While the grid costs were 9% down on the previous year, this was clearly more than made up for by the 9% rise in the energy price, the more than 12% increase in levies and the 9% higher taxes. With a price level of 120.13 €/MWh, Germany is in third place after Italy and Ireland, with higher prices than any of the other 26 states in the European Union (EU). The EU average is more than 20 €/MWh lower (Eurostat, 2007) for industrial enterprises in this consumer class. Similar, and in some instances even significantly greater, electricity price differences compared with the EU average are also to be found in other industrial electricity consumer classes.

In contrast to the domestic electricity price, the part of the price that covers the actual energy supply is decisive for industrial enterprises. The price on the European Energy Exchange (EEX) in Leipzig is the basic price for energy procurement. The EEX, which is the result of the merger of the European Power Exchange (EEX) and the Leipzig Power Exchange (LPX), has been a spot market since 2000 and has been operating as a futures market for electricity since 2001. There have been huge price rises on both markets since 2001. The average price on the spot market increased by almost 41% from 2001 to 2007.[2] Much more important for energy-intensive enterprises, which need to cover a comparably con-

---

[2] 2007 average is calculated from January to October.

tinuous electricity requirement over the whole year, is the price for the base load supply for the following year (Phelix Base Future Price). This rose by more than 128% to 55.24 €/MWh (EEX, 2007) from 2002 to 2007,[3] and it thus has a decisive influence on the trend in electricity prices of major industrial consumers (see Figure 35.2). The reason for the dramatic rise is the combination of intransparency and market power on the supply side of the EEX and the introduction of greenhouse gas emissions trading throughout Europe.

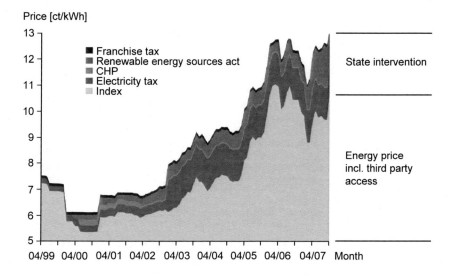

Figure 35.2: VIK energy price index for industry in [cents/kWh] (VIK & Dow Jones)

Both the European Commission and the Federal Cartel Office and the Monopolies Commission regard the competition on the German energy markets as insufficient, on account not only of the market power of the producer capacities but also of the vertical integration, because each of the four major energy producers also owns the transmission network it uses and all have increased their influence on regional suppliers and public utility companies by way of acquisitions over the last few years. The electricity producers can exercise their market power on the exchange by keeping physical capacities back or offering electricity at above their marginal costs. In the period from 1994 to 2004 mergers and takeovers resulted in a clear concentration of supply companies and thus of market power for the production capacities (Pfeiffer, 2005), which enables them to have a decisive impact on the electricity market. In 2006 alone, the three largest electricity producers' share of the entire net electricity consumption amounted to 45.06%. The 48.49% market power (Bundesnetzagentur, 2007) in the segment of electricity consumption above 2 GWh per annum is particularly significant, and the industrial enter-

---

[3] 2007 average is calculated from January to October.

prises are accordingly very concerned. Both the German Federal Cartel Office and the European Antitrust Authority have instituted a procedure to counter this market power. RWE has already had to make allowances for the past practice of inpricing the CO_2 certificates in order to avoid formal proceedings.

The organisation of the electricity trade poses another problem owing to the lack of transparency. This applies especially to the whole of the physical demand, because no information on system loads is published at a price-relevant time for the electricity trade. This is only known to the grid operators. The same applies to information on the transmission network, the cross-border connection points and the production capacities (NERA, 2006). This information is published without relation to the exchange (EEX, 2007) and reflects the lack of harmonisation in data formats, definitions and time periods. Not until identical definitions and information on network loads and production are available will market participants be able to assess the physical supply-and-demand situation. Only the large fully integrated electricity supply companies benefit from the lack of information. In addition, for the producer, the principle of marginal price formation applied at the EEX is almost a guarantee of earning money. This principle enables the last power plant connected to the grid to cover demand to dictate the prices for all quantities produced, with the result that, for instance, electricity from a nuclear power plant that has already been written off, with production costs of less than 2 cents/kWh, can be sold at prices that are three times the production costs.

The deficits in the mode of operation of the electricity market were particularly noticeable in spring 2006. At that time the price for the CO_2 certificates traded on the EEX fell by more than 50%. Although when the prices of the certificates have risen previously the producers have used this as a reason to increase electricity prices, the electricity price declined in the same period by only about 20% and rose again after a few days to its old level. The VIK has described this as 'price formation à la check valve'.

In addition to the existing deficiencies on the electricity market, the EU encouraged a drastic electricity price rise by the implementation of greenhouse gas emissions trading in 2005. After the free-of-charge allocation of emission rights, inter alia to the operators of fossil power plants, these were inpriced in the electricity price. According to the calculations of London Economics (London Economics, 2007), emissions trading was responsible for a load-weighted increase of 13.86 €/MWh in the spot price on the EEX in 2005 and thus a price share of 29%. The prospects for the second trading period 2008-2012 seem poor when we look back on the first trading period of 2005-2007. The main reason for this is the reduced amounts allocated. Compared with the first trading period, in which Germany was still entitled to annual CO_2 emissions in the amount of 499 million tonnes of CO_2, the EU Commission is insisting on a significantly lower quantity of 453 million tonnes of CO_2 (EC, 2006) for the second trading period. This amount is not only significantly less than that in the original draft of the German allocation plan, which was 482 million tonnes of CO_2 (BMU, 2006), but also includes emissions from plants that did not participate in emissions trading in the first trading period. As a result, the volume of emissions has been greatly reduced and further electricity price rises and energy cost burdens for industry are inevitable. In future, more than three-quarters of the global increase in climate-damaging gases will be caused by countries outside today's industrial nations. Exaggeratedly one-sided climate protection targets result in further closures of production facilities in Europe and increase the greenhouse gas emissions in non-European countries. Both nonfulfilment and fulfilment, while we accept that there will be limited economic development, are implausible for climate protection.

In addition to the blatant deficit in competition on the German electricity market and the greenhouse gas emissions trading, the state levies and taxes have taken over an ever increasing share of the electricity price and are expected to burden the electricity customer to the extent of € 12.76 billion in 2007. This is an increase of 84% compared with 2000 (VDEW, 2007a). The additional costs of renewable energy have almost quadrupled from 2000 to 2006 and are expected to reach a level of € 3.4 billion in 2007 (VDEW, 2007b). The forecasts for the next few years assume further increases in the volume subsidised. Not only is the efficiency of the subsidy not guaranteed on account of the current practice of subsidising renewable energy through minimum payment rates with an annual decrease, but there is also no limit to the amount subsidised. This will result in significant electricity price rises for industrial enterprises in future also. The amendment to the Renewable Energy Sources Act, which is currently being processed, is not expected to change this. The amendment just contains further premiums for different technologies and CHP production, which adds significantly to the complexity and conceals the effective payment rates (BMU, 2007). Even now, the effective payment rates are not comprehensible for most plants or are considerably higher than stipulated in the law, since plants with capacity-related payments are reimbursed for not only one, but proportionately for all the capacity classes under the plant capacity (BMU, 2004). The supporters of the Renewable Energy Sources Act subsidy repeatedly state that the spot market price on the EEX is reduced by the power input of renewable energy. Investigations into wind power, for instance, cite the declining effect on the spot market price of 0.55 (Bode & Groscurth, 2006) to 1.9 €/MWh (Neubarth et al., 2006) for additional wind power input of 1,000 MW. Apart from the costs for additional balance energy through the forecasting capability of wind power, which is limited to only a few hours, energy-intensive enterprises do not benefit from spot market price reductions since they cover their electricity needs largely on the futures market. Quite different factors, such as the additional construction of new power plant capacities, the development of the greenhouse gas emissions trading and the phasing out of nuclear power, are decisive for them. The energy policy therefore gains considerably in influence in this respect.

German energy policy does not follow a uniform line and calls the future industrial development of Germany as an industrial location in question. The lack of coordination and uniform strategy is also attributable to the wide spread of responsibilities in energy-political questions. In addition, Germany allows itself the luxury of taking decisions that will result in drastic cuts in the energy supply in the medium to long term. Besides phasing out nuclear power, these include the targets of reducing German greenhouse gas emissions by 40% by 2020 and a 27% expansion of renewable energy by 2020. With the phasing out of nuclear energy, the

German government does not only make it questionable whether there will be a reliable energy supply in the medium to long term, but also makes it inevitable that German emissions will increase when these power plants that worked on an almost CO_2-free production technology are switched off. Currently the German nuclear power plants save CO_2 emissions to the tune of some 130 million tonnes of CO_2 each year. Accordingly, it will be necessary to take other measures to save an equivalent quantity by 2020. In addition, the planning and realisation of new constructions worldwide prove that nuclear power is in no way uneconomic and furthermore makes an important contribution to having a wide energy mix.

Owing to the drastic energy price rises in recent years, energy costs have become an increasingly heavy burden on industrial production. This damages the competitiveness of German industry, because not all competitors on the international markets are affected by a similar cost explosion in the energy sector. Industrial enterprises can only react to increasing energy prices to a limited extent at short notice by improving energy efficiency, and can only pass on the increased energy costs to their customers to a minor degree on account of their international competitors. This, therefore, calls in question the wisdom not only of capital investment in existing and new industrial plant, but also the suitability of Germany as a location for industry. Excessive energy prices result in industry relocation and thus in the slow erosion of Germany as a location for business and investment.

35.3   Adaptability of Energy-intensive Industrial Enterprises – with Norddeutsche Affinerie AG as an Example

Norddeutsche Affinerie AG (NA) is an integrated copper group with 3,288 employees and is positioned along the value-added chain of copper. It produced a total of 570,000 tonnes of copper cathodes in fiscal year 2006/07 and is thus one of the biggest producers of refined copper worldwide. With its current processing capacities, NA is a leader in the processing of copper concentrates. NA is also the market leader worldwide in the copper recycling sector, from the aspects of both throughput and its possibilities for processing an enormous variety of materials.

Copper production is energy-intensive. The production process requires large quantities of energy, in particular for melting down, refining in the copper tankhouse (copper production) and processing of copper intermediates (copper processing). The energy sources for this are electricity, steam and natural gas, plus various auxiliary solid fuels, such as bituminous coal and coke and also heavy and light heating oil. The energy consumption of the NA Group alone amounts to 1 TWh. This is roughly the equivalent of the annual consumption of 350,000 German households. The electricity consumption in the fiscal year 2006/07 caused costs of more than € 48 million. The electricity costs have risen drastically in the last few fiscal years and are now more than 320% higher than the level in fiscal year 1999/00 (see Figure 35.3). To counter this dramatic trend, NA has succeeded in securing a long-term and calculable electricity supply and at the same time in reducing energy consumption by developing savings potential.

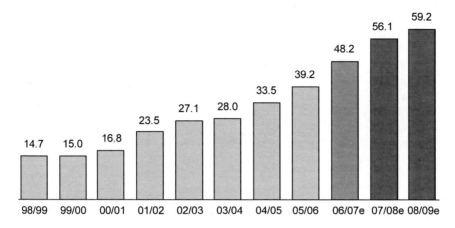

Note: Each cent per kWh of electricity price increase results in additional costs of
€ 10 million p.a. in the NA Group

Figure 35.3: Electricity costs in the NA Group [€ m] (Norddeutsche Affinerie AG, 2007)

To secure a long-term and calculable electricity supply, NA examined the possibility of building its own power plant at an early stage. The decision in 2006 to build a substitute fuel (SF) power plant (100 MW) within the works precincts offered NA the chance of distancing itself long term from the electricity price trend on the EEX. NA found an experienced partner in the Hamburg waste management [Stadtreinigung Hamburg], which would have ensured a reliable supply of SF. The power plant was technically planned in detail, and all preparatory construction measures initiated. Construction was scheduled to start in May this year, with commissioning at the end of 2009. In parallel with NA's SF power plant, Vattenfall also planned to erect a new coal-fired power plant in Hamburg-Moorburg. The applications for planning and building permission for the two power plants were made at the same time. However, the two power plants gradually became competitors during the approval procedure, against a background of increasingly intense discussion on climate protection during the year and political endeavours to make Hamburg a climate capital. The Hamburg Senate only had to give them both a little push in the right direction, and NA and Vattenfall agreed on an optimal solution for both companies. On 4 May 2007 NA signed an agreement with Vattenfall Europe AG, which secured a long-term plannable and cost-based electricity supply for the NA Group. From 2010 onwards, NA will procure its electricity from Vattenfall for a period of 30 years, and it will come from a power plant slice (115 MW) of the planned coal-fired power plant in Hamburg-Moorburg (2 x 860 MW). The environment-technical state-of-the-art power plant to be constructed in Hamburg-Moorburg and fired with imported bituminous coal is expected to be commissioned in 2012. However, regardless of the commissioning of the Moorburg power plant, Vattenfall has taken over the complete supply of electricity to the NA Group as of 1 January 2010 (about 1 billion kWh of electricity p.a.). The delivery conditions of the agreement stipulate that NA will make an upfront payment and the electricity supply will be on a cost basis with completely transparent terms and conditions. Coal, the main cost component, will be charged in US dollars. This reduces the overall currency risk for NA, since treatment and refining charges are also calculated on a US dollar basis. In addition, NA does not have the risks that can arise as a result of the approval procedure, capital expenditure, and operation of and fuel supply to the coal-fired power plant. This agreement is unique in Germany and sets a precedent as a constructive industrial solution between an energy-intensive enterprise and an electricity supplier.

NA strengthens its competitiveness and at the same time makes an important contribution to climate protection through the economical and efficient use of energy. It has been possible to reduce the specific energy consumption as a yardstick for energy-efficient production significantly in recent years. Specific energy consumption at the Hamburg site has decreased by almost 65% since 1990, and in parallel the specific CO_2 emissions have declined by even more than 80% (see Figures 35.4 and 35.5). In 1999, NA firmly institutionalised the continuous increase in energy efficiency by creating the Energy Management Department, which works out the energy-saving programmes and oversees their implementation. The energy-saving programme eNergiA was brought to a successful conclusion in the period 2000-2004. The follow-up eNergiA plus programme is currently in train.

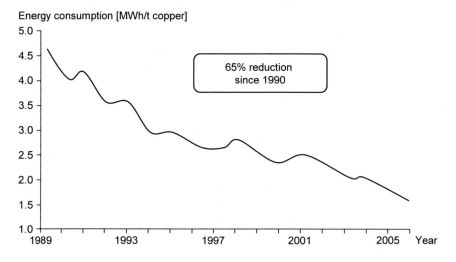

Figure 35.4: Specific energy consumption of NA AG (Hamburg) (Norddeutsche Affinerie AG, 2007)

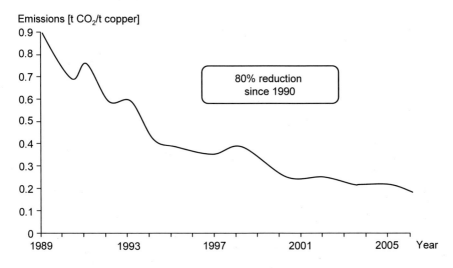

Figure 35.5: Specific CO_2 fuel-related emissions of NA AG (Hamburg) (Norddeutsche Affinerie AG, 2007)

The energy-saving programme eNergiA comprised 400 single projects and involved capital expenditure of some € 16 million. Up to 2004 NA had saved almost 214 million kWh of steam and natural gas through eNergiA each year, more than 37 million kWh of electricity and more than 53 million kWh of coke and oil. The energy volume saved corresponds to the annual electricity consumption of an average four-person household, about 84,000 kWh. The energy savings have resulted in a lasting reduction in emissions from the Hamburg site of more than 80,000 tonnes of CO_2 per annum (see Figure 35.6).

2000-2004	Natural gas/stream:	213,757,971 kWh/a	
	Electricity:	37,711,814 kWh/a	€ 16 million invested from 2000 to 2004 in 400 individual projects to save energy
	Heating oil/coke:	53,484,013 kWh/a	
	Potable water:	350,000 m³/a	
	Total reduction:	**80,000 t CO_2/a**	
Until 2012	Natural gas/stream:	abt. 95,000,000 kWh/a	Future savings require additional capital expenditure of more than € 22 million in more than 200 individual projects
	Electricity:	abt. 25,000,000 kWh/a	
	Planned reduction:	**abt. 40,000 t CO_2/a**	

Figure 35.6: Savings at Hamburg production site (Norddeutsche Affinerie AG, 2007)

The project eNergiA plus consists of about 200 individual measures with a capital expenditure volume of more than € 20 million. Overall, energy savings of around 120 million kWh are expected for natural gas and electricity from 2007 to 2012. This results in a possible reduction in CO_2 emissions at the Hamburg site of more than 40,000 tonnes of CO_2 per annum (Norddeutsche Affinerie AG, 2007). About 48% (19,500 tonnes of CO_2) of the reduction should be achieved by the avoidance of direct CO_2 emissions that arise at NA when fuels are burnt. The remaining 52% (20,500 tonnes of CO_2) is expected to result from the avoidance of indirect CO_2 emissions owing to electricity savings, because each kilowatt-hour of electricity saved at NA reduces the CO_2 discharge from public utility electricity generation.

35.4   Petition for German Energy Policy

The following points are particularly important with the focus on the national and European trends on the energy markets from the viewpoint of industrial enterprises:

(1) The subsidising of new energy sources should not be connected with the abandonment of existing production technologies. The German nuclear power plants must remain a long-term production alternative. The German atomic power plants currently contribute about 27% of the electricity generated and are thus essential to ensure reliable supplies. At the same time, in view of the German energy mix, they avoid about 130 million tonnes of CO_2. The closure of further plants would not only increase the energy dependence on foreign fossil energy sources, but also increase CO_2 emissions and automatically result in a rise in the CO_2 prices.

(2) Germany does not only need new types of energy; above all it needs well-functioning markets. Competition must finally be created on the energy markets. The politicians have allowed the continuing concentration on the electricity and natural gas market without taking any action, and in the case of E.ON and Ruhrgas, for example, have given their support against their better judgement The energy consumers have been left to their own devices for much too long and have had to pay exorbitant prices for electricity and natural gas for many years, while the suppliers' profits grow from year to year. Although the pressure on the energy suppliers is increasing in line with increased control, the complaints procedures initiated by industry at the Federal Cartel Office, the ongoing process at the EU Commission and, last but not least, the GWB amendment, concrete results and the necessary price reductions for the consumers are still outstanding.

(3) The environment-political instruments must be better coordinated to avoid multiple financial burdens. The exemption rulings for energy-intensive enterprises in industry are more than justified and urgently necessary. The environment political instruments of the ecotax, subsidies for Renewable Energy Sources Act, combined heat and power (CHP) and the CO_2 emissions trading

are a burden on energy-intensive production companies and give many companies no alternative but to relocate. Above all, CO_2 certificate trading in combination with the market-controlling position of the four major energy suppliers has resulted in a situation threatening the existence of many companies. This damages not only the electricity consumers, but also emissions trading.

(4) Energy policy is regional economic policy and should therefore be assigned as a whole to one department. The dividing up of the responsibility between the Ministry of Trade and Industry and the Ministry of the Environment leads to disharmony and inconsistent solutions.

References

Behörde für Stadtentwicklung und Umwelt (BSU) der Freien und Hansestadt Hamburg. 2007. Energiebilanz Hamburg 2004. Hamburg: BSU.

Bode, S. & Groscurth, H. 2006. Zur Wirkung des EEG auf den "Strompreis". Unpublished HWWA Discussion Paper 348, Hamburg.

Bundesministerium für Umwelt Naturschutz und Reaktorsicherheit (BMU). 2004. Mindestvergütungssätze nach dem neuen Erneuerbare-Energien-Gesetz (EEG).

Bundesministerium für Umwelt Naturschutz und Reaktorsicherheit (BMU). 2006. Nationaler Allokationsplan 2008-2012 für die Bundesrepublik Deutschland.

Bundesministerium für Umwelt Naturschutz und Reaktorsicherheit (BMU). 2007. Entwurf eines Gesetzes zur Neuregelung des Rechts der Erneuerbaren Energien im Strombereich.

Bundesnetzagentur. 2006. Monitoringbericht 2006 der Bundesnetzagentur für Elektrizität, Gas, Telekommunikation, Post und Eisenbahnen. Bericht gemäß § 63 Abs. 4 EnWG i. V. m. § 35 EnWG.

Bundesnetzagentur. 2007. Monitoringbericht 2007 der Bundesnetzagentur für Elektrizität, Gas, Telekommunikation, Post und Eisenbahnen. Bericht gemäß § 63 Abs. 4 EnWG i. V. m. § 35 EnWG.

European Commission (EC). 2006. Commission Decision of 29 November 2006 concerning the national allocation plan for the allocation of greenhouse gas emission allowances notified by Germany in accordance with Directive 2003/87/EC of the European Parliament and of the Council. Official Journal of the European Union.

European Energy Exchange (EEX). 2007. Marktdaten. http://www.eex.com/de/ Downloads/ Marktdaten, 14th November 2007.

European Energy Exchange (EEX). 2007. Geschäftsbericht 2006. Leipzig: EEX.

Eurostat. 2007. Umwelt und Energie/Elektrizität – Industrieabnehmer – halbjährliche Preise. http://epp.eurostat.ec.europa.eu/pls/portal/url/page/PGP_MISCEL

LANEOUS/PGE_DAT_DETAIL?p_product_code=nrg_pc_205, 15th Novem ber 2007.

Gesellschaft für Stromwirtschaft (GfSt). 2003. 50 Jahre Gesellschaft für Stromwirtschaft m.b.H.: 1953-2003. Mülheim a.d. Ruhr: GfSt.

Neubarth, J., Woll, O., Weber, C. & Gerecht, M. 2006. Beeinflussung der Spotmarktpreise durch Windstromerzeugung. Energiewirtschaftliche Tagesfragen, 56: 42-45.

Norddeutsche Affinerie AG (NA). 2007. Beitrag der Norddeutschen Affinerie AG zum Klimaschutz in Hamburg. Hamburg: Norddeutsche Affinerie AG.

Pfeiffer, J. 2005. Konzentration auf dem deutschen Strommarkt 1994 bis 2004. Unpublished IWE Working Paper Nr. 02 2005, Universität Erlangen-Nürnberg, Erlangen.

Rheinisch-Westfälisches Institut für Wirtschaftsforschung (RWI). 2005. Die Klimavorsorgeverpflichtung der deutschen Wirtschaft, Monitoringbericht 2000–2002. Essen: RWI.

Statistisches Bundesamt. 2007. Kostenstruktur der Unternehmen des Verarbeitenden Gewerbes sowie des Bergbaus und der Gewinnung von Steinen und Erden 2005. Wiesbaden: Statistisches Bundesamt.

Verband der Elektrizitätswirtschaft e.V. (VDEW). 2007a. Anlage zur Pressemeldung. Berlin: VDEW.

Verband der Elektrizitätswirtschaft e.V. (VDEW). 2007b. VDEW-Pressekonferenz: Zahlen und Fakten. Berlin: VDEW.

White & Case LLP & NERA Economic Consulting (NERA). 2006. Gutachten: Verbesserung der Transparenz auf dem Stromgroßhandelsmarkt aus ökonomischer sowie energie- und kapitalmarktrechtlicher Sicht im Auftrag des Sächsischen Staatsministeriums für Wirtschaft und Arbeit. Dresden: Sächsisches Staatsministeriums für Wirtschaft und Arbeit.

WirtschaftsVereinigung Metalle (WVM). 2007. Geschäftsbericht 2006/2007; Perspektiven. Düsseldorf: WVM.

Part VII:
Regional Peculiarities
in the Utility Markets

36 Options for and Regional Peculiarities of Investment Funding in Energy Markets

Dirk Beeuwsaert[1]

Abstract

The energy sector will require huge investments over the next decades. This chapter discusses the barriers to and constraints on attracting private investment in energy projects. The pace of private investment in the power sector is influenced by three key elements. A first crucial parameter is the investment climate. In addition to that, the regulatory framework and predictability of the projects' revenues are the two single most important boundary conditions by far for successful funding of large energy projects. This chapter finally analyzes the most important instruments for attracting investments, including national and international financial institutions, capital markets, and other sources.

Keywords: investment climate, regulatory framework, financing instruments

[1] Dirk Beeuwsaert is Chief Executive Officer at GDF SUEZ Energy International, Belgium.

A. Bausch and B. Schwenker (eds.), *Handbook Utility Management,*
DOI: 10.1007/978-3-540-79349-6_36, © Springer-Verlag Berlin Heidelberg 2009

36.1   Introduction

The energy sector will require huge investments over the coming decades. This chapter discusses the barriers and constraints involved in attracting private investment in energy projects. The pace of private investment in the power sector is influenced by three key elements. A first crucial parameter is the investment climate. In addition to that, the regulatory framework and predictability of the projects' revenues are by far the two single most important boundary conditions for successful funding of large energy projects. At the end of the chapter the most important instruments that can be used to attract investments, including national and international financial institutions, capital markets and other sources, are analyzed.

36.2   Main Characteristics of the Energy Markets

The investment needs in the energy sector are of mind-boggling magnitude. The latest available figures for both renewal of existing assets and addition of new capacity are provided by the International Energy Agency (IEA) in its World Energy Outlook 2006. The IEA projects the cumulative investment needs up to 2030 at a total of $ 20.2 trillion (in real terms). This amount is up by $ 3 trillion on the 2005 IEA forecast because of a sharp capital cost increase, essentially in the oil and gas sectors. The principal contributors to these needs are as follows.

- The power sector, with $ 11.3 trillion splits almost equally between investments in generation and transmission and distribution. On the generation side, building of 5,087 GW is forecast, more than half of this in developing countries (China alone requires 1100 GW), and some 2,000 GW is required in OECD countries.
- The oil industry requires $ 4.3 trillion, approximately three quarters of which is to be devoted to exploration and development and the remainder to refining.
- The gas industry (including upstream facilities, LNG tankers, liquefaction and regasification plants, and transmission pipelines) needs $ 3.9 trillion, almost two thirds of which is destined for investment in exploration, development, and the LNG chain and approximately one third, for transmission and distribution investments.

More than half of this amount is required for investment in developing countries. Major investment needs have been identified in China ($ 3.7 trillion), Europe ($ 2.4 trillion), and North America ($ 4.1 trillion).

Over recent years, we have observed the following main trends with respect to the funding of energy infrastructure needs:

- The energy sector is a capital-intensive industry in which the pay-back period is typically very long (exceeding 10 years).

- As the primary energy demand increases, primary energy will most probably remain expensive and also entail larger investments per unit (because of the use of lower quality fuels, environmental constraints, and so on). With respect to the power sector, capital costs tend to increase when fuel prices are high, as the investors switch to technologies that increase the efficiency of the energy conversion cycle.
- Operational performance inefficiency and financial losses of state utilities, lagging public investment, power outages and poor quality of supply have resulted in a need to attract private capital in the power sector. Moreover, fewer and fewer governments can afford public funding, except for oil- and gas-exporting countries, and then only when these commodity prices are high. States that have limited financial resources tend to exit the energy sector, focusing on other sectors, and tend to invite foreign investors into their energy market. Indeed, the utilization of public debt for energy projects reduces their ability to finance other projects that have even less chance of access to private funds. Under tight budgetary constraints, governments are facing increasing needs in competing infrastructure sectors and also in social sectors, such as health care and education (not to mention military expenses in certain developing countries). On the other hand, if a government has ample funds it will invest itself and may even look beyond its own home market for investment opportunities.
- The public sector will remain an important source of power project investments where country and market risk deter foreign investors. It may also remain the main investor for networks and certain other generation assets that are kept public as a matter of policy.
- There has been a lack of private and global investment in most segments of the energy chain during the period 2000-2004 owing to the lack of perceived predictability (because of deregulation and unbundling) and low electricity (because of overcapacity from the past lower economy growth, etc.) and primary energy prices, particularly in emerging countries. The reasons for declining investment and the difficulty of attracting private funds to the energy sector (or the infrastructure sector in general) are multiple: country risk, weak project structures, regulatory risk, subsovereign rather than governmental risk, currency risk, payment and creditworthiness risk, downgrade of investors' credit ratings, unfavorable conditions on the international capital markets, lack of legal protection of investors and previous bad experiences of investors in emerging power markets, to name a selection. In the electricity sector, returns were historically based on a utility return, which was based in turn on a highly predictable and limited-risk environment. In the actual market circumstances of liberalization, unbundling, and fluctuating primary energy prices, the risk and volatility are quite different, so that there is a need for higher returns or better predictability.
- One might wonder whether the consumers are willing to pay for this additional return, which is necessary in a fragmented market model, and certainly when energy prices are already increasing for other reasons. Do the perceived freedom of choice for the customer and the competition really balance

out the more expensive cost structure? If not, there might be a need for public funding, with subsidies or re-regulated tariffs motivated by short-term political interventions.

- In a world of high oil and gas prices, national oil companies are able to reinvest a substantial portion of their revenues, both domestically and abroad. In this way they immediately impact the level of foreign private investment in the energy sector and thus the level of financial resources required from the private sector. When the energy landscape is dominated by the national oil companies, one can also wonder about the incentives to develop additional production capacities (in order to have an adequate equilibrium between supply and demand): will these be market driven, as is the case in a market dominated by private players, or rather driven by political – often cross-border – considerations? On the other hand, in a context of low primary energy prices, a relatively higher share of the national oil companies' revenues will be draining towards the funding of investments of public interest, which may not necessarily be in the capital-intensive energy sector, thus allowing foreign investors to come in.

- We also observe the emergence of Clean Development Mechanism (CDM)-related revenue schemes. The CDM outlined in the Kyoto Protocol is a mechanism that allows private and public entities to invest in greenhouse gas (GHG)-mitigating activities in developing countries and to earn abatement credits, which can then be applied against their own GHG emissions or sold on the market. As such, CDM is an important tool in the promotion of foreign investment by developed countries in GHG reduction projects in developing countries while at the same time also contributing to the sustainable development of the countries where the projects are built (host country). The CDM projects (typically renewable energy projects, fuel-switching projects, and the introduction of new technologies leading to improvements in energy efficiency) essentially rely on the receipt of Certified Emission Reductions (CER) and the revenue from their sales.

- Whereas the financial sector is beginning to play an important part in the development and promotion of CDM projects, there are still a few challenges. The single most important risk is inherent in the uncertainty with respect to the value and existence of the CERs after 2012. CER purchasers are very reluctant to commit to purchasing CERs beyond 2012. This is aggravated by the fact that most energy projects have lifetimes that extend far beyond the Kyoto Protocol's first commitment period.

36.3   Barriers to Investment

One of the key elements in any investment decision is the cost of capital. This section presents a number of elements that have a direct impact on sustainability of the cost of capital in the energy sector and the ability of the power sector to attract investments compared with other sectors that are competing for the same funds.

A brief reminder of how the cost of capital is determined will allow us to get a better perspective on the impact of the suggestions developed in this chapter.

The cost of capital for an investment – commonly referred to as weighted average cost of capital (WACC) – is made up of the cost of debt and the cost of equity. Three main elements influence this WACC:

(1) On the equity side: the required return for the investor;
(2) On the debt side: the interest rate required by the financing institutions;
(3) The proportion of debt to equity or financial leverage the investment will be able to obtain.

Both the financial institutions and the investor will determine the above elements for each project, depending on their analysis of the investment, the country, the technology, investment horizon, etc. The pace of private investment in the power sector is influenced by three key elements. One crucial parameter is the investment climate. In addition, the regulatory framework and predictability of the projects' revenues are cornerstones in determination of the cost of capital and are the two single most important challenges by far in funding large energy projects.

36.3.1 Investment Climate

In order to attract private investment in the energy sector, a number of business climate conditions should be met in the country. A stable investment framework is clearly essential for foreign direct investment (FDI) inflow into emerging markets. Many developing countries have been (and several continue to be) unable to attract private funds because of flaws in their investment climate. As mentioned above, the investment climate in a country is a direct driver of the cost of capital and debt and is an all-encompassing notion that captures a broad range of concerns, all of which will be considered by an investor or a financial institution:

- Sustainable macro-economic stability, including stable foreign exchange rates, and sustainable economic growth with the ability to overcome economic shocks;
- Risk of deterioration of the political and economic condition of a country, usually resulting in a rating downgrading;
- Political events such as confiscation, (creeping) expropriation, nationalization, war, civil war, revolution, invasion of the country, acts of foreign enemies, mobilization, rebellion, blockade, riots, sabotage, embargoes;
- Stable business regulation and capital flow regulation, such as the ability to repatriate profit and capital, safety of assets, and stable and efficient customs and trade regulations;
- Risk of uncontrollable events that can make the profitability of the project questionable, such as specific laws (e.g., tax) or regulations that are changed or not enacted as anticipated;

- Institutional climate: contract enforcement, protection of property rights, effective judicial and contracting system, corruption;
- Red tape, and particularly delays in regulatory approvals;
- Labor availability, productivity and education;
- Payment discipline of government entities and end consumers;
- Efficient financial system; presence of a domestic capital market or stock market;
- An acceptable level of personnel security in the operating environment;
- The maturity of cross-sector markets such as fuel markets (e.g., coal, natural gas).

These elements directly impact on the return an investor can expect and on country's capacity to attract private foreign investment.

36.3.2   Regulatory Framework

One of the key risks for a power sector investor is the regulatory risk. Regulatory risk is a broad caption that covers several elements:

- The regulator may exercise his powers in such a discretionary way that it undermines previously agreed contracts with other governmental entities.
- Certainty that the tariff and the key parameters, particularly during the initial period, will allow the investor to reach its return objectives. This includes tariff revisions, which may be at the regulator's discretion.
- Quality standards of technical and customer service that may be arbitrarily changed, thus leading to unforeseen investments.
- Absence of any impartial dispute-resolution mechanism, including international arbitration.
- The more subsovereign the regulatory body is, the higher the risks for political short-term intervention. This is often combined with increased difficulty of conflict resolution at sovereign level.
- One new source of regulatory risk is the CO_2 market. It is likely that there will be a CO_2 market after 2012, when the Kyoto ratification period ends, but what will it look like? The impact on the electricity sector, as a major source of CO_2 emissions, will in any case be significant.

With respect to financing, we believe that the area of focus should be the regulatory environment, meaning oversight and definition of the context and framework within which the energy sector could be organized and protecting both investors' and consumers' short-term and long-term interests. A robust regulation is a condition sine qua non for attracting long-term private investments. If well conceived, the regulatory environment is a major mitigant of regulatory risk for investors and financiers.

The regulator needs to be a credible party with the necessary technical and market organization capabilities and empowered with clear objectives. This includes the autonomy to carry out duties, transparency in procedures, and accountability to government and consumers. This agency has to be able to function in a neutral manner, independently of political authorities. It needs an institutional status that gives it wide autonomy unrestricted by political and market influences and the freedom to respond to quickly changing market evolutions, without turning to arbitrary remedies but with a long-term view. Absence of political independence creates a constant threat for short-term focused tariff intervention under political pressure, certainly in a volatile political context.

Further key requirements of a regulatory system and the legal framework embodying it are that it should bring stability and efficiency over the long term. This need for a transparent, predictable and independent regulation exists in all three sectors of generation, transmission, and distribution.

It is important for regulators to design regulatory tools that stimulate investments. One possibility is the introduction of a capacity element in the tariff structure; this will be discussed at length in the next section. Another important element is the licensing system. As one aspect of offering predictability to the investors, it is crucial to have advance regulatory approval for large projects (such as hydro and nuclear power plants, but also for transmission and grid projects), rather than having to wait for a review after the fact. This is even more important in an environment of high investment costs and a growing NIMBY attitude, particularly in developed countries.

Within the whole spectrum ranging from fully centrally regulated business to regulation by contract, it is important to have national regulation rather than local. If regulation is implemented at local level it reduces the predictability, as such regulation is subject to the interest of fewer persons. Local authorities tend to focus on short-term matters and electors' satisfaction. If regulation is placed in a national context, there are generally more players that can put their weight in the balance against discretionary changes in the regulation, which therefore makes regulation more stable.

This regulatory feature has an important impact on the ability to fund the energy system, through both equity and debt. The more a business is deregulated down to the residential consumer, the more the chain disintegrates, becoming focused on the short term and less predictable. The trend of deregulation has been to limit the regulation to the transmission and distribution assets (wires and pipes), while the generators have to bear the full uncertainty of the business. Long-term contracts with regulated distribution companies (pipes, wires, and supply) bring a certain predictability and stability that helps in securing more competitive financing for investments in generation.

The presence of regulated distribution companies is not a sufficient condition per se. This scheme has been unsuccessful in many countries because governments did not allow a pass-through of cost evolutions when needed. Distribution companies globalizing the residential customers are a stabilizing element only when governments and public owners act fairly and respect their contracts.

Therefore, we believe that for emerging markets and as a first step in the deregulation process (even in developed countries), it is important to have a secured collection of revenues through distribution companies that are regulated with medium- and long-term competitive supply contracts and have the incentives to make their consumers pay. This will bring more certainty to the generators and enable investment in time and at the lowest cost over the long term, helped by a lower funding cost and long-term predictability.

Governmental failure to develop such a regulatory framework is often seen to lead to a requirement for credit enhancement mechanisms, such as sovereign guarantees, subsidies, grants, or multilateral agency involvement (such as the World Bank).

The need for new investments, along with discontent with the poor performance of state-owned utilities, have triggered a need for reform of the energy sector in many countries. Several of these reforms have been implemented successfully; many reforms have unfortunately been unsuccessful or only partially successful in terms of the establishment of a regulatory framework and the resulting level of private sector involvement.

36.3.3   Predictability of Revenues

As already indicated in the previous section, predictability of revenues is an equally important requirement for attracting funding at a competitive cost. Whereas investors consider operational risk as part of their day-to-day business, they commonly dislike uncertainty with respect to factors they have no control over.

Over recent years, several developments have been observed that accentuate the lack of predictability. These are normal business elements, but combined with the aforementioned uncertainties they increase the importance of predictability:

- Technological evolution (e.g., CO_2 taxes, renewable energy, nuclear fusion, oil sands) leads to a higher investment cost per unit with longer pay-back periods. If the environment remains volatile and risky investors will be even more reluctant to embrace those new technologies.
- When predictability is low, investors will require a higher return. Thus, the energy prices will be higher, and indirectly this will have a negative effect on the competitiveness of the national economy. This brings with it a risk of political intervention and a danger that policy makers will change the rules.
- The behavior of governments will determine how things develop: interventionism in the electricity market, stability of regulation, and fairness towards industry players will be key to reduce risk perception, the resulting cost of capital and, ultimately, the ability to attract new investments.
- The volatility in commodity prices has impacted both investment costs (steel, for instance, is a major element in the cost of a power plant) and primary energy cost.

In many markets, shortly after liberalization the focus was on such short-term issues as balancing and network access regulation. However, the aspects of long-term development (i.e., how to organize network capacity increases and expansion and how to ensure adequate investment in generating capacity) were and are often not adequately addressed. So the key issue is how to organize electricity markets in such a way that they provide the right investment incentives to generating companies. One of the major questions is indeed whether markets provide sufficient investment incentives for investment in generation. The current high level of reliability in Europe, for instance, can only be maintained if there is some excess generating capacity. Whereas current reserve margins in Europe may still be acceptable, they are decreasing. The security of supply of electricity is clearly at risk, because the right incentives for investment in generation capacity are not present in a liberalized model based on short-term marginal cost competition.

Several approaches are possible for the structuring of an electricity market, all of which have different impacts on the medium- and long-term predictability of revenues. Market design plays a crucial role in the promotion of private participation in the power sector. The three existing key approaches are:

(1)   The energy-only model;
(2)   Capacity-based models: the capacity obligation model and the capacity payment model; and
(3)   The power purchase agreement model.

36.3.3.1 The Energy-only Model

With this model, market competition and the demand–supply balance set the prices. This is obviously the ultimate system of competition.

As in any other market, the energy-only model assumes that electricity prices will encourage investment in generation capacity. The incentive for investments in energy-only markets comes from the price spikes that occur when demand exceeds available capacity.

These sharp price increases are obviously problematic for the consumers, the government, and the regulator, or even for the economy as a whole. On the other hand, they are not a sustainable basis for investment decisions as they may not happen frequently (e.g., be linked to events such as abnormal temperatures and major outages of key generating units, not to mention market manipulation situations in which generators might be tempted to withdraw capacity at times of high demand) and may even be absent for several years, which of course creates problems for the investors who want to recover their investment costs.

Such price shocks are obviously likely to lead to political interventions by the regulator through price caps. Moreover, there is a tendency for regulators to define caps that are too low to encourage new investments. However, these caps may have another adverse effect in that they may make the supply shortage even worse. Obviously neither of these threats will encourage new investments.

Investors have shown interest in such markets only in rare cases when these markets have been operating on a relatively stable basis, without government intervention. Some electricity markets may indeed function on the basis of an energy-only scheme. This is the case in markets that are based predominantly on hydro energy, as these systems, because of their inherent storage capacity, tend to level out price spikes. Two well-known cases are Scandinavia (Nord Pool) and New Zealand.

36.3.3.2 Capacity-based Models

The above illustrates why many would like to introduce some form of capacity mechanism in addition to the spot market in attempts to ensure sufficient investment in generation capacity. Energy-only markets do indeed work best in combination with long-term contracts that have the advantage of stabilizing prices to consumers, regulator, and investors.

This is what capacity-based schemes are intended to remedy, by rewarding investment capital by making capacity available constantly, rather than based on investment decisions when shortages in supply occur. In this case capacity remuneration no longer depends on the occurrence and level of price spikes, and furthermore the likelihood of regulators intervening by price caps is much lower.

The true challenge for the regulators is thus to put such mechanisms in place. Governments need to consider providing these clear incentives, which will encourage private sector funds for their long-term investments.

The feasibility of a capacity-based scheme also depends on the level of integration of markets. In decentralized markets with significant exchanges with neighboring systems it is quite difficult to implement a capacity mechanism that provides incentives for investment in the local market and is also effective during a local shortage.

One of the drawbacks of capacity-based mechanisms is that since they support reliably available generating capacity, wind and solar energy are at a disadvantage. Other measures will be needed to support such technologies.

A wide range of capacity-based schemes exists, and there is no one solution that fits all situations. Two key mechanisms can be discerned within the capacity-based models: one that improves the investment incentive by influencing the price mechanism and one that directly affects the demand for capacity. In this chapter we examine a number of schemes that are designed to support investment in generation assets.

The Capacity Obligation Model

This model – also referred to as the ICAP (installed capacity) model – imposes an obligation on the load-serving entities or retailers to buy their expected peak load capacity in long-term markets. A central entity establishes a quantity of capacity that is needed, and the market determines the price for this. This price can be determined through an auction or tender process.

This is the solution that has been implemented in the PJM market in the northeast of the US.

The Capacity Payment Model

In this model, a regulatory mechanism for the payment of capacity on top of energy payments is established, thereby effectively recognizing the existence of two commodities: energy and capacity. This capacity component relatively stabilizes the volatility of the energy payments. This is the mechanism chosen in Chile and Argentina, for instance.

36.3.3.3 The Power Purchase Agreement Model

Under a power purchase agreement, a single national buyer enters into electricity purchase agreements with generators. A typical example of such a mechanism is today encountered in many countries in the Middle East and in Brazil.

This model is often used as a first step along the way to liberalization and as a means of attracting private sector participation in the energy sector. Competition in such a market remains limited to the selection of the project developer by the local regulator or electricity authority; once the contract is secured there is no market competition. Obviously, the model is incompatible with many countries' requirements for liberalization up to the end-consumer.

The key advantage from the generator/investor point of view is obviously the long-term stream of payments from an entity that in most cases is a creditworthy entity or at least has the benefit of a credit enhancement mechanism. From an off-taker standpoint, this benefit should obviously flow through to competitive low electricity prices, certainly if the contract has been awarded pursuant on an international tender process.

Finally, the PPA model can be an interesting model even in countries with a high perceived investment risk when an appropriate risk allocation is implemented. The PPA model creates problems for some countries, however, as their commitments under these PPAs are regarded as sovereign liabilities, which may impact their credit risk perception by the IMF, credit rating agencies, etc.

In conclusion, one of the cornerstones of efficient and lowest-possible-cost development of the energy sector is increased predictability of revenues achieved through organized competition. In nonrecourse or limited-recourse project finance schemes, which are the most commonly used funding techniques in the energy sector, predictability is even a condition sine qua non for attracting funds under favorable conditions. This predictability is all the more important because the energy sector has high capital needs, combined with a regional or local market where the investors cannot easily geographically transfer out their activities.

Bearing the aforementioned considerations in mind, the following recommendations are made:

- For developed countries: introduce a capacity mechanism (within as large an interconnected area as possible in order to avoid trades outside the system that would reduce the effect of the capacity system) such as exists in the PJM market, which is the most effective solution that has been tried so far. This could for instance be implemented in Europe's decentralized markets in a region that is large enough for trading outside of it to be minimal.
- For emerging markets or developing countries: start the liberalization process through a single-buyer PPA model and gradually move to market segmentation with a competitive market for industrial users and a regulated market with long-term contracts for distribution companies.

Furthermore, the electricity market designers should have the courage to question the principle of retail competition. The introduction of retail competition is an important cause of underinvestment. It breaks the chain of contracts extending from producers through distribution companies to small consumers, which are allowed to switch to another retailer at short notice.

36.3.4 Specificity for Emerging Countries

The need for energy in emerging countries is alarming; few people have access to electricity in these countries. Many emerging markets unfortunately cannot offer the business climate discussed in the previous sections (sufficiently stable framework, predictability of revenues, etc.), which is why substantial private sector participation has failed so far. The distressing needs in emerging countries cannot currently be met without subsidies, donations, or soft loans. Subsidies will also enable developing countries to direct their own funding sources towards other important sectors, such as education and health. To avoid any doubt, this chapter obviously does not question the need for and importance of donations or soft loans to developing countries to allow them to develop their energy infrastructure. We, however, strongly believe that these development aid mechanisms should be closely tied to a commitment from the host government to put in place an adequate institutional climate and framework, so as to enable and facilitate the transition towards commercial funding at some point in the future.

Investment funds, subsidies or donations – whether from private or public sources – will only remedy short-term funding needs and will not be funding sources that are sustainable over the long term when the right framework is not in place in emerging markets. From this perspective, putting grant mechanisms in place, in the absence of the efficient and country-specific market model and political stability referred to above, might turn out to be a chronically subsidiary measure in that it does not solve the problem at its root (i.e., the need for a sound framework), but only tackles the symptoms (i.e., unwillingness to fund).

Investors essentially need governments of emerging markets to commit to predictability in their behavior and to a regulatory context that will be stable and focused on the long term. Support from international sources, which are essentially inspired by political considerations, can be temporarily considered as a catalyst, but for a commercial funding system to develop one should look at predictable legal, political, and business conditions, so as to enable nonsubsidized investments subsequently.

On top of the need for a predictable and stable environment, investors are also concerned about the sovereign and subsovereign risks in emerging markets. Therefore, the issuance to the benefit of the investor of a sovereign guarantee in certain emerging countries – making it possible to take away part of the political risk – is bringing a necessary element of stability. In order to attract the necessary investments in the energy sector, we believe it is important to consider the issue of state guarantees for emerging countries either by the country itself or indirectly by sponsor countries for an intermediate period.

Contracts at subsovereign level create an additional risk layer in an already challenging environment and should be avoided for developing countries. Globally, when investing in a country, political risk insurance can indeed be contracted at the level of the host country, but not easily at the level of the municipalities, for instance. With respect to subsovereign risk, we believe that the key question is how to mitigate this risk at affordable cost, particularly in a context where it is not easily transferable into a sovereign risk. Here again, the key message is to try and have national, impartial, independent regulators as far as possible, rather than regulators on sublevels. This would be better than developing new risk-mitigating products – and increasing costs – intended to address subsovereign risk. Even if today many regulators act at a subsovereign level, they should be aware of the impact this has on whether investors and funds are attracted on competitive terms, certainly in developing countries where the liquidity and interconnections between markets are often limited or nonexistent.

36.4   Financing Considerations

One of the key questions, in the aftermath of the Enron debacle, at the World Energy Conference in Sydney in September 2004 was: "Is there enough money for the power sector? Is someone still willing to invest?" Assuming that the liquidity crisis, which arose in the second half of 2008 and which has a global impact on all infrastructure financings, is a short term event, we do not think that, looking beyond this liquidity crisis, there will be a lack of financial resources to fund the development of energy infrastructure. Fundamentally, there are sufficient available financial resources.

It is, however, important to understand that these funds are competing (i) for the best projects within the energy sector in terms of risk/reward profile and (ii) also with other infrastructure projects offering more predictable revenues and attractive returns with shorter project horizons and a more acceptable risk profile. What is critical is to put in place the conditions discussed in the previous sections, thus creating the right framework to attract these resources on competitive terms.

One commonly used mechanism for funding energy sector investments is project finance. Any project finance definition essentially includes the four following characteristics:

(1) Involvement of a corporate sponsor;
(2) Investment in and ownership of a single-purpose industrial asset, usually with a limited lifetime;
(3) Investment through a legally independent entity or special purpose vehicle (SPV);
(4) Financing with nonrecourse debt.

Both project finance and corporate funding schemes can coexist in a company, as shown in Figure 36.1. The SPV is funded by both equity injected by the project sponsors and debt.

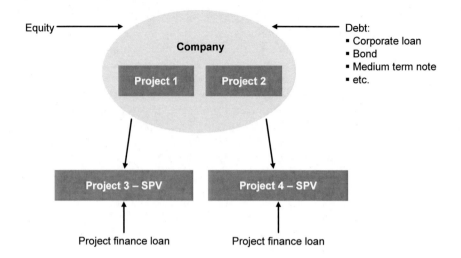

Figure 36.1: Coexisting project finance and corporate funding schemes

Heavy leverages (60-90% of total project funds being provided by debt) are not uncommon.

In typical project financing, the financier looks at the assets/revenues of the project, which has no credit history and no assets outside the project, in order to secure/service the loan, as opposed to the situation with corporate finance, where lenders rely on the overall creditworthiness of the enterprise financing a new project. The debt repayment capacity in project finance is dependent on the cash-flow generation capacity of the project, and not the credit quality of the sponsors.

There is little or no recourse to the nonproject assets of the sponsors in the project, and the debt from this project entity is often completely separate from the sponsors' direct obligations, which is why the term 'limited recourse' financing is often used as a synonym.Typical project finances come with longer maturities and higher interest rate margins and a very detailed loan covenant package, severely limiting the managerial decision flexibility. Investors often revert to project finance mechanisms for asset-rich and capital-intensive projects with predictable and transparent (often hard currency) cash flows. Key reasons for using project financing are:

- The sponsors' equity exposure can be reduced in 'difficult' countries: the maximum loss remains limited to the equity injected. Project finance thus reduces the possibility of risk contamination whereby one failing asset drags a healthy firm into distress. In fact, project finance offers the investors the option to walk away from the project if all recovery mechanisms have failed.
- Leveraging the project through debt increases the sponsors' equity return and optimizes the tax basis.
- Political risks can be mitigated by the presence of government entities such as export credit agencies or multilateral agencies, which deter host nations from taking political steps that would have an adverse impact on the project

(to some degree at least), and which encourage them to respect the legal system and contractual enforcement.

- In the case of joint partnership, financially weak partners may need project finance to participate in the project.

36.4.1 Financing Sources

We believe that there are sufficient and diversified financing instruments available in the commercial market and with multilaterals, bilaterals and export credit agencies to fund the various energy project requirements. In this section, we will focus concisely on the range of instruments, guarantees, loans, etc. that have been developed over the last 10 years by various financing institutions.

The following are the most commonly used sources for the funding of energy projects:

- Export credit agencies;
- Commercial loans;
- Multilateral institutions;
- Bond markets;
- Islamic financing;
- Investment funds;
- CDM-related funding schemes.

36.4.1.1 Export Credit Agencies

An export credit agency (ECA) is a governmental or private entity set up with a view to promoting and supporting exports by its country's manufacturers. Examples are ECGD (UK), Coface (France), Delcredere (Belgium), and the Export-Import Bank of the US.

ECA support essentially comes through:

- Loan insurance or guarantees for banks, lending to the project; or
- Direct loans provided to the project by the ECA.

Both options are visualized in Figure 36.2. Under the loan insurance scheme, a commercial bank lends to the project and an ECA insures the project SPV's obligations under its loan agreement in respect of political risks and commercial risks. Essentially, then, an ECA protects financiers against a payment default by the borrower/SPV and largely transforms a project company risk into a sovereign risk (namely that of the supporting ECA).

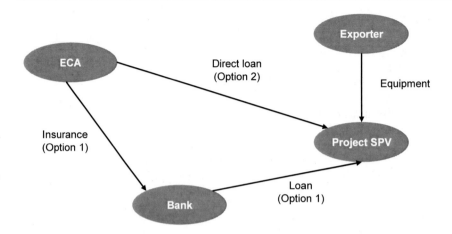

Figure 36.2: First option: loan insurance/guarantee scheme

The risks covered by ECAs are:

(1) Political risk associated with the particular jurisdiction and political envi-
      ronment in which the project operates. These risks are traditionally fourfold:

   ▪ Confiscation, (creeping) nationalization, expropriation;
   ▪ Exchange control: inability to convert local currency into hard currency
      and hard currency transfer restrictions;
   ▪ War, political violence, revolution, civil strife, etc.;
   ▪ Contract frustration.

(2) Commercial risk, i.e., risk associated with the individual project company,
      such as a delay in completion, failure to achieve the projected level of opera-
      tion, commercial insolvency, payment default not related to political risk.

   These risks are largely borne by the ECA. Proportions insured vary across the
different ECAs. Typically the commercial risks are insured 85-95% and political
risks, around 95%. The residual risk is then borne by the commercial banks lending to the project.
   The second option is the direct loan scheme, in which the ECA lends to the project directly. No commercial banks intervene for the funding.
   The main terms and conditions of an ECA-backed funding, which are based on
a 'consensus' between OECD countries in order to create an orderly market and
avoid increasingly unbridled competition between exporting countries, are:

   ▪ Maximum repayment terms (including final repayment within 12-14 years
      from when the credit starts).
   ▪ Minimum interest rate (Commercial Interest Reference Rate (CIRR)).
   ▪ Link between the amount qualifying for ECA support or the so-called eligi-
      ble portion and the exported goods/services and a limited amount of local
      costs and third-country services/goods.

- Payment of an ECA insurance premium, which may be quite high for some of the riskier countries.

The key advantages of ECA support are:

- These funds are available in markets where commercial banks would not be willing to go without ECA support. This is essentially the case in many sub-investment-grade countries.
- Long tenures are possible.
- The direct support of the government behind the ECA creates a political leverage over the host authorities, thereby discouraging undesired intervention by the host country authorities in the project.
- Cheap fixed interest rates can be offered in some cases.

Disadvantages or restrictions of working with an ECA are:

- A relatively lengthy process (especially in multi-sourcing cases) because of the high level of due diligence;
- A high up-front cost (ECA insurance premium);
- Dependence of the availability of the funds also on the export content of the goods and services used for the project, so that the financing schemes offered by these institutions are less well suited for projects with a high local sourcing content, such as hydropower plants;
- Difficulty, if not impossibility, of covering subsovereign risks.

36.4.1.2 Commercial Loans

These are simple loans provided by commercial banks.
The advantages are:

- Fewer financing parties are involved, which leads to a more straightforward implementation process.
- Drawdown and fund utilization can be very flexible (relative to ECA financing, for example).
- In some markets (e.g., Middle East), extremely long tenures (longer than can be offered by multilaterals or ECAs) and low margins are available, making this source a very attractive one.

The disadvantages are:

- No protection is offered for lenders through political and commercial risk insurance, which means that there is usually no or limited appetite for long-term debt in sub-investment-grade countries.
- The availability is volatile.

Even when lenders are prepared to take on the commercial and political risk of a project on an uncovered basis, there are capacity restrictions for large projects (particularly the mega-projects we currently see being developed in the Middle East). This has led to a recent surge in the utilization of ECA and multilateral sources alongside uncovered commercial lending, even for investment-grade countries.

A particular application of commercial loans can be found through local markets' commercial loan funding. This is the case, for instance, in South Africa, Thailand, and Brazil. These local banks can:

- Sometimes offer longer maturities than the international market in their home market; and
- Offer a natural foreign currency hedge (through the local currency funding).

As a drawback, interest rate hedging possibilities are often limited in local markets and the availability of these sources can be volatile. Also, local banks often have less experience in project finance than corporate finance. Local commercial loans need a well-developed and stable local financial sector. One of the roles of multilateral institutions (cf. below) is to stimulate the development of such local markets.

36.4.1.3 Multilateral Institutions

A multilateral institution is a creature of treaties between several governments and/or is sponsored by multi-governmental institutions such as the World Bank or the EU. Their mission is to assist in the development of emerging markets through participation in infrastructure projects. Examples are the International Bank for Reconstruction and Development (IBRD), the Multilateral Investment Guarantee Agency (MIGA), the International Finance Corporation (IFC), the European Bank for Reconstruction and Development (EBRD), the Asian Development Bank (ADB), the European Investment Bank (EIB) and the Inter-American Development Bank (IADB).

These institutions have a different mission than ECAs: an ECA focuses on the development of export and national economy, whereas multilaterals want to benefit the host country's economy. As such, they are not worried about where the equipment is sourced, in contrast to ECAs.

They are of paramount importance when insufficient private or public capital is available on reasonable terms, because of the significant political risks or insufficient export content (and thus ECA support).

Multilateral institutions offer:

- Direct loans;
- Loan insurance, risk guarantees or other credit enhancement systems for various instruments (commercial loan, bond);
- Direct equity (Some of these multilateral institutions take an equity share in the project.).

The advantages of working with multilateral institutions are:

- Their presence can act as a catalyst for bringing in investors, commercial banks, and other lenders, as they promote confidence in the project.

- They can lend large amounts, which are independent of the export content of the goods and services involved in the project.
- They can lend with long periods of tenure that would never be possible without their support.
- They allow for a limited weighting on the country limits for the banks, benefiting from a multilateral credit enhancement instrument.

The disadvantages are:

- In some cases the approval process can be lengthy and highlight many characteristics of large administrations.
- The implementation process tends to be long, given the high standards of due diligence.
- The protection they offer for the lenders may be less explicit than is the case for ECAs, which offer an explicit guarantee to the lenders. In some cases the protection is merely implicit through their simple presence in the project, essentially discouraging the local authorities from misbehaving.
- Some impose very formal international competitive bidding rules (at project or EPC level).
- Some multilaterals benefit from a specifically preferred creditor status, which renders their association with other types of creditors challenging.
- It is difficult, if not impossible, to cover subsovereign risks.

36.4.1.4 Bond Financing

Various types of bond issues are possible:

- A private placement with institutional investors such as insurance companies, pension and mutual funds;
- A public offering.

The advantages of using bonds are:

- Longer tenures are possibly available.
- Traditionally, a fixed rate is offered (no need for hedging).
- Covenant packages are less restrictive than those from the sources described above.
- They offer access to a larger group of lenders that would otherwise not be available through other instruments (e.g., pension funds, insurance companies).

Potential difficulties and disadvantages are:

- Burdensome disclosure requirements are imposed.
- Negative arbitrage because of a single issuance versus staged payments of project costs. This is why a bond is often used to refinance a construction loan.

- The volatility in emerging markets may restrict the timing of the offer; therefore there is often a need for a fallback arrangement in the bank market or a credit enhancement product.
- Rating agencies (such as Standard & Poor's, Moody's, or a local rating agency) need to be involved for assessing the creditworthiness of the bond issuance.

36.4.1.5 Islamic Finance

Islamic finance is starting to enter the mainstream project finance market. The key to understanding Islamic finance is that all dealings are governed by Shari'a law, whereby the payment or receipt of interest is deemed to be usury and on the other hand making profit on the trading of physical goods is encouraged. Its utilization is essentially seen in infrastructure projects in the Middle East and other Islamic countries, the kingdoms of Bahrain and Saudi Arabia being very active promoters.

Based on this principle, various Islamic finance instruments compliant with Shari'a have been developed, which are often based on a lease type of structure and which are often intended to mirror Western financing structures.

Key features of Islamic financing include:

- Typically short tenures (5-7 years);
- The integration of Islamic debt into commercial project financings and the intercreditor issues with 'traditional' lenders tend to be complicated, but solvable.

36.4.1.6 Investment Funds

Investment funds have become an increasingly important source of funds over recent years. These funds have a huge leverage effect, in that they can bring about other investors. Their leverage factor can be as high as 3. The funds they possess and seek to invest over horizons as long as 10 years are important and can sometimes easily be $ 15 billion per fund.

Three types of funds can be distinguished:

(1) *Infrastructure capital funds:* The typical key characteristics of these investors can be summarized as follows:

  - They primarily take majority positions and are an active investor.
  - They invest in assets that generate strong predictable cash flows or in a regulated environment.
  - They seek a moderate return and low risk.
  - They have a long-term investment horizon. They do not necessarily require an exit.
  - Infrastructure funds are particularly keen to invest in the energy sector as:

    - There are long-term predictable cash flows (cf. above).

- The long duration of the asset provides for a good match with their underlying liabilities (e.g., pension funds).
- The projects they invest in often create a natural hedge against inflation or long-term interest rates.
- The underlying assets are less affected by economic cycles than other products and there is a low correlation to equity market volatility.

(2) *Private equity funds:* The main characteristics of private equity funds are:
- They take majority positions and want control. They invest in situations where they can have management control or co-control.
- They have a medium investment horizon (3-5 years) and wish to exit thereafter.

(3) *Hedge funds:* Key features of hedge funds are:

- They take minority positions and generally do not require management involvement.
- These are very sophisticated and focused investors that have a short-term investment horizon and often act as corporate agitators.

36.4.2   Specificity for Funding of Renewable Energy Projects

We may have to temper our confidence that private funds will be easily available for renewable energy projects somewhat. Financiers are concerned about the technology risk and the nature of renewable energy investors, which often tend to be small companies with a limited track record. More importantly, the main issue is undoubtedly the lack of clarity with respect to the post-2012 period (cf. Introduction). In this context, there is a definite need for a clear long-term framework defining the carbon price as a cornerstone for the economic context needed for clean energy developments.

Currently, the World Economic Forum and the World Business Council for Sustainable Development are exploring ways of stimulating greater private sector investment in renewable energy. Their summary findings are that if the private sector is to play a role in channeling greater resources to cleaner energy projects, the following actions need to be taken:

- Improve the predictability of the regulatory framework governing such investments.
- Buy down incremental investment costs of clean energy technologies.
- Improve the financial returns on investment in such projects, so that they can compete with conventional resources.

To that extent, the World Economic Forum and the World Business Council for Sustainable Development propose the creation of a multi-purpose finance facility of $ 20 billion in the form of partial guarantees (to increase the creditworthiness of the future cash flows from carbon credits) and loans (for buying down the incremental investment cost for renewable energy), which should be able to leverage $ 40 billion in private investments.

36.5   Conclusion

As huge investments in energy will be needed in the coming decades, attracting private sector participation is a growing challenge, especially in the present context of increasing capital costs, tight government budgets, and poor state-utility performance.

We are confident that the necessary funds will be available through various funding schemes. Long-term interest from private players can only be secured, however, if a number of preconditions are fulfilled, as these are the kingpins that are essential for the success of private sector involvement. In addition to creating the right investment climate, governments need to focus on putting a robust regulatory framework in place, along with a market design allowing for predictability of revenues.

37 A Comparison of Market Structure and Regulation Between US and European Utility Markets

Wolfgang Pfaffenberger[1]

Fereidoon P. Sioshansi[2]

Abstract

Despite fundamental similarities, the organization, management and regulation of utilities have evolved along different paths in different parts of the world. With the current interest in liberalizing the industry and introducing competition into electricity markets, policymakers in the US and in Europe have similar goals and are following similar strategies and facing similar challenges. This chapter provides an overview of the regulatory structure of the two continents and their approaches to regulations while pursuing functioning integrated electricity markets in large interconnected networks.

Keywords: regulation, competition, electricity markets

---

[1] Prof. Dr. Wolfgang Pfaffenberger is Professor of Economics at Jacobs University Bremen, Germany.

[2] Dr. Fereidoon P. Sioshansi is President of Menlo Energy Economics, United States of America.

A. Bausch and B. Schwenker (eds.), *Handbook Utility Management,*
DOI: 10.1007/978-3-540-79349-6_37, © Springer-Verlag Berlin Heidelberg 2009

37.1   Introduction

Over a century, as the electric power sector grew, vertically integrated monopolies gradually evolved under regulated rate-of-return paradigms in different parts of the world. In some countries, such as France and Britain, these turned into state-owned enterprises, while in other countries they turned into privately-held, regulated monopolies. In many countries, an incongruent combination of state-owned, investor-owned, municipality- and customer-owned utilities emerged, as in Germany and the US. In most cases, however, a few dominant players with exclusive franchise territories emerged whose monopoly powers were checked by a regulator. In the US, for example, roughly 80% of the industry's turnover is concentrated among approximately 100 large investor-owned holding companies. In Germany, four large vertically integrated players control roughly the same market share.

One of the justifications for the emergence of dominant monopolies was the belief that vertical integration results in significant economies of scale while making it easier to regulate. This theory held for decades, as utilities grew in size while offering lower per-unit costs. The generation sector, in particular, exhibited remarkable economies of scale – larger generating plants typically resulted in lower per-unit costs.

Apart from economies of scale, in many countries it was assumed that only the government or vertically integrated monopolies with exclusive service areas and captive customers could finance the capital-intensive industry. The long-term financing necessary to build a vast interconnected generation, transmission, and distribution infrastructure could not, it was thought, be feasible except within a monopolistic framework or through direct government financing.

To prevent monopolies from abusing their power, pervasive regulations evolved. In the US, for example, state-level regulators monitor and control the investor-owned utilities' (IOUs') retail prices and profits through elaborate rate cases. Similarly, until recently, investments in new plants and infrastructure were subject to regulatory review and approval. On some occasions, excessive costs and investments were disallowed, putting the IOUs on notice.

Regulations, while pervasive, were never perfect. The regulators never knew as much as they wanted to and were always at the mercy of those whom they regulated to provide them with the facts and the details. Rate-of-return regulation also led to perverse incentives, for example, the incentive to over-invest in assets, which allowed more revenues to be collected from captive customers, as described in the seminal work of Averch & Johnson (1962). Another chronic problem with rate-of-return regulation was that when utility management made poor investments the risks were borne by the customers and not by the private investors. Until recently in the US, utility stocks were characterized as safe bets for widows and orphans.

There were always lingering suspicions that the industry employed too many people, did not optimize the use of its fixed network, did not have sufficient incentives to optimize the mix of labor, capital, and fuel or select the best generation technology. The industry was not necessarily sensitive to customer needs and had insufficient incentives to engage in product or service innovation. Under rate-of-return regulations, utilities had strong incentives to build more plants and sell more kilowatt-hours, which meant that there was little or no interest in promoting energy conservation or encouraging efficient use of power.

Unintentionally, the regulation resulted in players becoming insular and self-centered, in some cases avoiding trade even when it would have been in the interests of consumers. Many vertically integrated companies, for example, preferred to rely on their own internal resources rather than buy in resources from a neighboring utility even when this latter course would have been cheaper. They had strong incentives to keep their own plants and networks fully loaded regardless of the underlying economics.

Antiquated metering and billing technology meant that the vast majority of customers were buying power at flat rates with no incentives to avoid usage during peak demand periods even though the cost of supplying power varies widely over time. The industry would over-build and over-invest to maintain service reliability and pass on the costs. In the words of one insider, the industry was "dumb and happy".

Beginning in the 1970s, economists began to question the long-held views that vertically integrated regulated monopolies were necessary or efficient. In the US, over-investment in costly nuclear plants was partly responsible for this. In Europe, one of the essential principles of the European Union is open interchange between the member countries on commodities and services. The tension between this principle and the closed systems in the electricity market in most member countries led to the formation of policies progressing in the direction of market opening.

Another significant development was the emergence of highly efficient and clean gas turbine technology, which could deliver low-cost electricity in smallish increments with minimal risk. Overnight, the economies of scale in generation became a myth. Virtually anybody could now finance, build, and operate a small generating plant with modest investment and relatively little risk.

In 1987, Chile became the first country to undertake a major reorganization of its electric power sector, followed by Britain in 1989 (Newbery 2006). Intrigued by the prospects, other countries began to study and ponder the purported benefits of market liberalization and privatization (Sioshansi & Pfaffenberger, 2006).

Among the underlying tenets of market reform was the desirability of breaking up vertically integrated companies into subcomponents, forcing them to compete when appropriate, and removing cross-subsidies that might have flowed from regulated operations to competitive functions. It was generally agreed that generation and retailing functions could be turned into competitive enterprises, with the fixed network infrastructures remaining under regulation as natural monopolies. The dispatching of plants and maintenance of reliability could remain in pseudo-government hands, be given to a non-profit third-party organization, or even be handled by an independent for-profit entity, as with the National Grid Company in Britain. Various markets and exchanges would emerge to facilitate trade, provide fluidity, and offer opportunities for risk-hedging.

Now, two decades after the introduction of market reform in many parts of the world, many previously unbundled companies have rebundled, notably by combining generation with retail business. Moreover, there is empirical evidence to suggest that such combinations are more efficient, can manage risks and price volatility better, and may be preferred by investors. At the same time, there is evidence, not universally convincing, that vertical integration – despite its obvious shortcomings – might have offered economies of scale after all (Michaels, 2006).

Some scholars now argue that the restructuring of the electric power sector is an evolutionary process, which must be allowed to develop along a middle path, somewhere between the two extremes of full vertical integration or full physical unbundling and introduction of competition at both wholesale and retail levels (Chao et al., 2008). There is an ongoing debate on whether the physical nature of the industry necessarily implies one extreme or the other.

The evolving thinking is that neither view is conclusive, as pros and cons can be mustered on either side of the argument without any clear indication that one or the other extreme is better. It is suggested that the most important determinants of the optimal degree of vertical integration is how market risks are allocated and managed (Chao et al., 2008).

On another, more fundamental level, for over two decades policy makers and regulators in a number of countries around the world have been tinkering with market reform initiatives, with vastly mixed results. While a great deal has been achieved – including many useful lessons in what works, what does not, and why – successful design and implementation of market reform still remains partly an art (Sioshansi, 2008a). Even in reasonably successful competitive markets, there is still debate on how best to regulate the players and how intrusive this function should be (Littlechild, 2006).

Moreover, the international experience to date indicates that, in nearly all cases, initial market reform leads to unintended and occasionally unpleasant consequences or introduces new risks, which must be addressed in a subsequent 'reform of the reforms'. Another previously unexpected reality is that many liberalized markets have evolved into hybrids, neither fully competitive nor entirely regulated, further complicating the job of regulators (Sioshansi, 2008b).

Ironically, in many cases, and especially in hybrid markets, the pseudo-competitive industry requires more regulatory oversight today than it did when it was vertically integrated and fully regulated (Correljé & de Vries, 2008). For example, there is an increased need for market monitoring to prevent abuse of market power by dominant generators. Cross-border transmission and trading, always challenging issues, have become even more complicated, as has the management of the transmission network. There are increased concerns about long-term reliability and adequacy of investment in infrastructure.

In Europe the liberalized markets at first inherited a generous infrastructure, so that security of supply did not seem to be a problem. In the meantime, however, owing to the emergence of new sources of energy at different locations (e.g., wind), the significant increase of trade within Europe and the cost-cutting exercises in many companies (partly also caused by regulatory interference), the adequacy of investment in generation and transmission has become an issue for the public and regulators.

In recent years, new concerns about fuel costs, energy security, mergers and acquisitions, private equity ownership of the industry, and global climate change have increased the regulatory and market complexities. These developments pose significant new challenges for the organization and regulation of the industry, which are examined in this chapter.

The chapter is organized into three sections: first, an overview of regulations, followed by a discussion of the US and European developments, and ending with conclusions.

37.2   Why Regulate? A Short Survey

In addition to the general regulation, which applies to all industries, the electricity sector is subject to a number of special regulations owing to its unique fixed-network characteristics. This section explores some of the reasons for sector-specific regulation.

37.2.1   Infrastructure Arguments

This argument is highly relevant in the development phase of the industry but becomes relatively unimportant when most of the population has access to the electricity network. Briefly, the argument runs as follows: Electricity is necessary for a lot of services that are not available without connection to the delivery network. In the development phase there is therefore general consensus that the network should be extended so that access is available to everybody. By the same token, universal access to electricity is important for economic development.

Whereas the primary interest in the phase of development is making electricity available, the conditions of access, and particularly the pricing of electricity, are also of general concern. Thus, price regulation was common in pre-liberalization times and remains important even today. Strictly speaking, economic reasoning would only allow regulating prices in the monopolistic section of the industry, which consists of transport and distribution functions.

The infrastructure argument has lost its relevance not only because general access is now available, but also because there are technical possibilities for producing electricity in small-scale units, such as in distributed generation, where power is produced and delivered near the point of consumption.

37.2.2   Control of Monopolistic Bottlenecks

Sector-specific regulation is justified if there is network-specific market power (Knieps, 2006). Sector-specific market power exists if there is no active substitute or potential substitute available. Table 37.1 shows the result of the analysis regarding monopolistic bottlenecks in the electricity industry. It shows that electricity transmission and distribution, because of their natural monopoly characteristics and because investment costs are irreversible, have to be considered monopolistic bottleneck facilities, necessitating regulatory intervention. This chapter does not go into detail on regulatory approaches, which are covered by Knieps (2006) and Bauknecht and Brunekreeft (2008).

Table 37.1: Electricity networks as monopolistic bottlenecks (Knieps, 2006)

Segment	Natural monopoly	Irreversible cost
Generation	–	X
Transmission	X	X
Distribution	X	X
Retail	–	–

37.2.3 Environmental Concerns

There are significant environmental externalities associated with electricity production. Markets are not able to correct for those externalities without appropriate policies, pricing, and instruments. In recent years, environmental regulation has become one of the most important issues in Europe and elsewhere, with the introduction of a large number of legal and technical standards, compensation payments, preferential treatment for renewable energy, and market-based instruments for reduction of greenhouse gas emissions.

The significant question in this context is how to make the regulatory instruments for competition (e.g., control of monopolistic bottlenecks) and environment compatible. Environmental regulation interferes with many decisions concerning investment and operation of power plants and thus may also have consequences for other parts of the electricity value chain. Also, the question arises of whether sector-specific regulation is adequate or whether it makes more sense to apply general environmental regulation to the electricity sector. In most cases the source of environmental emissions is irrelevant; rather the emission itself is important. Therefore, there is no real case for sector-specific environmental regulation. On the other hand, it is tempting for policy makers to use the electricity industry for certain instruments, such as the feed-in regulation for renewable energy, because the network characteristics of the industry make it easy to interfere with the product portfolio in this sector.

Theoretically, the marginal cost of increasing environmental quality by reducing emissions in the electricity industry should be the same as in all other industries. For this to become effective, environmental control should be the same in all industries, so that low-cost potential contributions to environmental quality will be given priority. This is often not the case, because the electric power sector is highly concentrated and much easier to monitor and control.

37.3   Regulatory Approaches in the US

This section provides an overview of regulatory trends and approaches in the US, starting with a brief description of federal and state regulations and how these have evolved in recent years in response to recent market developments.

37.3.1   Who's Who in the US Power Sector?

There are currently over 3,000 'utilities' in the US (see Table 37.2). Depending on their ownership, they may be regulated by a multitude of regulatory bodies at federal, state, and local levels. At the federal level, the two most important regulatory bodies are the US Congress and the Federal Energy Regulatory Commission (FERC). The former periodically passes energy-related legislation, often to be implemented at state level, by FERC, or through other federal agencies, including the US Department of Energy (DOE), the Environmental Protection Agency (EPA), the Nuclear Regulatory Commission (NRC), the Securities and Exchange Commission (SEC), and others. The latter is in charge of all aspects of intrastate transmission, which affects all states with the possible exception of Texas, which – electrically speaking – operates as an isolated island.

Table 37.2: The makeup of the US power sector (Energy Information Administration, 2006)

Entity	No.	End-use customers	Sales to end-use customers [kWh m]	Revenue [$ m]	Installed capacity [MW]	Average revenue per kWh
Investor-owned utilities	240	92,424,160	2,437,982	169,444,470	484,054	6.95
Publicly owned utilities	2,009	18,604,131	516,681	33,054,956	80,737	6.40
Cooperatives	894	14,967,459	305,792	20,501,791	34,361	6.70
Federal power agencies	9	34,648	49,094	1,242,031	68,758	2.53
Total	**3,152**	**126,030,398**	**3,309,549**	**224,243,248**	**677,810**	**6.78**

At state level, IOUs come under the purview of state regulatory commissions everywhere, including the District of Columbia.[3] For a variety of reasons, including ownership, organization, prevailing regulations, and a number of other factors, average retail prices charged to customers vary considerably among utilities in different regions and states, and within states depending on the local supplier (see

---

[3] The only exception is the state of Nebraska, which does not have any IOUs and hence has no regulatory commission.

Table 37.3). In some cases, two identical customers living across the street from one another may be paying significantly different prices for electricity.

Table 37.3: Average US residential retail prices* (US cents/kWh, 12-month average ending June 2006) (Edison Electric Institute, 2007)

Region/State	Average retail rate	Average residential rate	Region/State	Average retail rate	Average residential rate
New England	13.29	14.93	MD	8.58	8.60
CT	13.20	15.02	NC	7.42	8.94
ME	10.63	13.98	SC	6.89	9.75
MA	14.04	15.44	VA	6.74	8.31
NH	13.65	14.44	WV	5.05	6.22
RI	13.32	14.49	East South Central	6.55	7.82
VT	11.22	13.27	AL	6.85	8.41
Mid-Atlantic	11.20	13.00	KY	5.18	6.74
NJ	11.33	12.11	MI	8.27	9.44
NY	13.81	16.49	TN	6.68	7.35
PA	8.48	10.19	West South Central	9.18	10.82
East North Central	7.23	8.81	AK	6.54	8.29
IL	7.04	8.43	LA	8.61	9.38
IN	6.20	7.89	OK	7.36	8.47
MI	7.92	9.20	TX	9.96	11.88
OH	7.38	8.94	Mountain	7.40	8.84
WI	7.81	10.07	AZ	7.94	9.04
West North Central	6.51	7.83	CO	7.84	9.18
IA	6.88	9.51	ID	5.14	6.35
KS	6.79	8.11	Mont	6.81	8.20
MN	6.81	8.51	NV	9.26	10.57
MO	6.18	7.25	NM	7.64	9.25
ND	5.99	7.12	UT	6.02	7.63
SD	6.66	7.41	WY	5.16	7.52
South Atlantic	7.98	9.25	Pacific	9.93	10.72
DL	8.14	9.68	CA	11.89	13.00
DC	9.57	9.33	OR	6.38	7.37
FL	9.56	10.39	WA	5.90	6.65
GA	7.73	8.96	HA	20.06	22.55
			US average	8.51	9.92

* These are averages for all applicable retail and residential rates, respectively, for each state including IOUs, municipal utilities and co-ops. Average rates are weighted by taking the total revenues and total kWh sales for each company. Non-IOU data is from EIA; no data provided for Alaska, or Nebraska, which has no IOUs.

Ownership is an important determining factor in the sense that there is virtually no regulation on retail rates or rate of return for municipally owned or consumer-owned utilities. These entities are under the control of locally elected or appointed bodies and operate, more or less, as non-profit enterprises. There are a dozen federally owned power generators, which are loosely controlled by the US Congress through appointed administrators.

In addition, all entities engaged in generation, transmission and distribution must abide by many state and local regulations on a host of environmental, labor, safety, and other laws.

37.3.2   Brief Regulatory Overview of US Wholesale Markets

In 1978, following the 1973 Arab oil embargo and the first 'energy crisis', the US Congress passed a seminal piece of legislation that (among other things) for the first time made it possible for new players to enter the power generation business without being a 'utility', without having a franchise service territory, or captive customers, or transmission and distribution networks. The Public Utility Regulatory Policy Act of 1978, better known as PURPA, had many objectives, including promoting fuel diversity and renewable energy, but this aspect of it has turned out to be the most significant.

Among PURPA's least expected outcomes was that it led to the birth of the so-called independent power producers (IPPs), also known as merchant generators, who now account for over a quarter of all power generation in the US. Under PURPA, these unregulated players could build and own power plants and sell their output to regulated utilities – which had to buy it under terms and conditions to be implemented by individual states. The most important distinction between an IPP and a regulated utility is that the former have no captive customers and no exclusive service area. In some cases, an IPP may have secured long-term contracts for a portion of the output of its plants, but IPPs generally finance and build plants without any such assurances, selling what they produce to the highest bidders in competitive wholesale markets, which have evolved over time.

However, as is often the case with regulation, PURPA had many unintended consequences. As the IPP industry grew, frustration grew among the new IPPs that could not – initially – sell electricity directly to end-customers. The right to sell to retail customers was originally reserved for regulated utilities. Large industrial customers, who were IPPs' major clients, also became frustrated, since regulations did not allow them to bypass the incumbent-regulated utilities to buy less expensive power directly from the IPPs. The obstacle was the transmission and distribution network that belonged to private utilities in the US, and these entities were not obliged to 'wheel' the power across their transmission network. Without access to transmission lines there was not much the IPPs could do but to sell their output to IOUs, which would in turn sell it to customers at 'blended' regulated rates. This led to a protracted debate on the need for open transmission access in the 1980s.

Partly in response to pressures emanating from the introduction of PURPA, in 1992 the US Congress passed a second seminal piece of energy legislation, the Energy Policy Act of 1992, also known as EPAct, essentially turning the nation's high-voltage transmission network into an open and nondiscriminatory regime. But the implementation of EPAct was complicated, preoccupying the FERC for

years. For a large integrated system such as the one in the US (see Section 37.4.1)
to become a common carrier, FERC had to encourage the development of independent system operators (ISOs) or regional transmission organizations (RTOs).
These independent entities, with no ties to generators, loads, or transmission owners, were (and are) seen as essential to efficient operation of large regional markets
(Singh, 2008). A second, equally important, requirement was to facilitate transmission trade using standard prices and protocols.

Not surprisingly, following the passage of EPAct, FERC began to push for the
creation of independent and large centrally dispatched ISOs or RTOs, while proposing standardized protocols for handling transactions among market participants. In the mid-1990s, FERC was publicly advocating a 'handful' of large RTOs,
roughly covering the Northeast, the Southeast, the Midwest and the West plus
Texas, which is poorly connected to the rest of the country.

However, state-level initiatives to restructure the electric power sector, which
began in the mid-1990s, pre-empted FERC's grand national design. Newly established ISOs, such as those in New England and New York, for example, could not
agree on how they would merge into a bigger RTO. Other RTOs, including PJM
Interconnection, and later the Midwest Independent System Operator (MISO),
grew exponentially. California, and Texas, each created their own state-level
ISOs, while plans to create RTOs in the Southeast and Northwest stalled owing to
opposition by some utilities, which did not want to relinquish control of their
transmission lines to an independent entity. Other obstacles included disagreements among the parties on how to form an effective alliance or over-pricing and
so-called 'seams issues' (O'Neill et al., 2006).

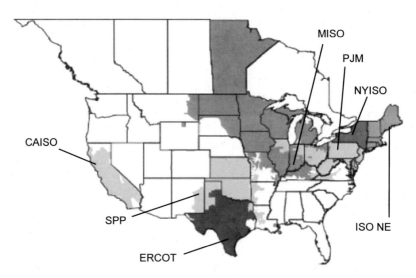

Figure 37.1: Approximate footprint operating ISOs and RTOs in the US (FERC,
2006)

Yet, despite these setbacks, FERC has succeeded in gradually promoting the formation of ISOs and RTOs (see Figure 37.1). Today, more than half of the wholesale market in the US is under the control of large ISOs and RTOs and wholesale competition is taken for granted virtually everywhere in the country (see Table 37.4).

FERC's efforts to introduce standard market design (SMD), including locational marginal pricing (LMP), also known as nodal pricing, however, ran up against strong political opposition and has been largely shelved. But even in this area, FERC's wish has essentially prevailed among the ISOs and RTOs, which have largely adopted LMP as their modus operandi.

Competition at the wholesale level has resulted in significant cost savings that benefit end-consumers. Studies suggest that centrally dispatched markets in the Mid-Atlantic region dominated by PJM resulted in cost savings in the range of 0.50-1.80 $/MWh from 1998 through 2004, net of the costs of RTO operations. The New England ISO claims that it has contributed to an 11% reduction in wholesale power prices – adjusted for cost of fuel – since 2001.

In summary, the US has by all accounts succeeded in fostering competition among generators and in forcing transmission owners to provide nondiscriminatory access to their transmission lines. In a survey article on the state of the US electricity market, Joskow (2006b) concludes that "significant progress has been made on the wholesale competition front", but adds, "The framework for retail competition has been less successful". A study of the wholesale and retail markets by FERC came to similar conclusions (FERC, 2006).

Table 37.4: US wholesale markets under ISO or RTO control, 2005 (Joskow, 2006b)

System operator	Generating capacity [MW]
ISO – New England (TRO)	31,000
New York ISO	37,000
PJM (expanded) (RTO)	164,000
Midwest ISO (MISO)	130,000
California ISO (CAISO)	52,000
ERCOT (Texas)	78,000
Southwest Power Pool (RTO)*	60,000
ISO/RTO Total	552,000
Total US generating capacity	**970,000**

* Organized markets being developed

37.3.3   Brief Regulatory Overview of US Retail Markets

With PURPA and EPAct in place and the growth of the IPPs, large industrial customers became aware of new opportunities to shop around for lower electricity prices, something they had not realized they could do before. The remaining obstacle, in most cases, was lack of direct access, the option to choose their electricity supplier. Nearly everywhere in the US customers were generally bound to buy from a single local provider, who in turn had an obligation to serve them. This so-called regulatory compact meant that customers could not select service from a lower cost provider even if one was available and willing.

For the majority of small commercial and residential customers this was not much of an issue, but for large energy-intensive customers every penny mattered, since they were competing with their peers both domestically and internationally for low-cost power.

Starting in the 1990s, customers in general, and large, energy-intensive customers in particular, began to push state regulators in states with above-average rates to allow direct access, i.e., to give them the right to choose their supplier. In many high-cost states, such as California, where average rates were 50% above the national average, the regulators found themselves in the uncomfortable position of having to explain to irate customers why they could not abandon their expensive regulated incumbent utility in favor of someone else who was offering them lower prices.

The conventional wisdom at the time was to allow customer choice, introduce competition at both wholesale and retail levels and, broadly speaking, let market discipline – as opposed to regulatory fiat – set prices and provide appropriate signals to investors. Electricity market liberalization had already been implemented in Chile and Britain and was in vogue among market-oriented policy makers everywhere on economic and/or ideological grounds.

Combined, these factors led state-level regulators to begin deliberations for 'restructuring', initially in a handful of high-cost states on both coasts, but gradually spreading to other states. These deliberations eventually led to restructuring of the industry in some 20 states and in the District of Columbia by 2002, when Texas opened its market (see Figure 37.3). But experience at the retail level has been mixed, mildly successful in a few states and not so in others. In California, the restructuring led to run-away prices leading to financial hardship for utilities and customers and contributed to the Governor's defeat in mid-term elections (Sweeney, 2006).

Since the collapse of the Californian market in 2000-2001 (Sweeney, 2006) no other state has restructured, with the single exception of Texas, which opened its market in 2002. A 2007 survey of state regulators in the US found virtually no support for retail competition among the states that had not thus far implemented it (RKS, 2007). Even among those who have, many regulators are now considering a return to regulation. Moreover, presently, there is no interest in the US Congress in pushing retail competition at the national level.[4]

Many consumers and consumer advocates are calling for a return to the regulated rate-of-return of yesteryear – admitting that it was not perfect but insisting that it was more predictable and tolerable. The Electricity Consumers Resource Council (ELCON), the association of large industrial users of electricity, which is

---

[4] This lack of interest is evident in the Energy Policy Act of 2005, where the phrase "retail competition" does not even appear in the massive Bill.

normally fond of competition and free markets, has been vocal in its opposition to what it considers to be botched-up markets. In a position paper ELCON states, "Today's organized markets are not competitive, are anti-consumer, and are likely to remain that way". Moreover, it does not believe that the problems are self-correcting. "Staying the course will only extend harm to consumers" (ELCON, 2006).

It is rather ironic that ELCON, whose members were once eagerly pushing for competition and consumer choice, are now advising states that have not yet re-structured not to do so. ELCON's most recent position goes even further, stating, "If today's organized markets cannot be fixed, explore all options including a re-turn to traditional regulation".

The disillusionment with retail markets has effectively stalled any prospects of further progress, including any move towards a national competitive retail market – which was once debated as an option. Not only that, but in a number of states there is now serious discussion about returning to regulation.[5] One state, Virginia, has effectively done so already. The reasons are complex and vary from one state to another, but include the following:

- The failure of the Californian market has left lingering concerns among state-level regulators and legislators about the complexities, serious risks, and lim-ited benefits of competitive markets.
- A number of states which introduced retail competition are now facing 'rate shocks' as the original retail price freezes are lifted, exposing customers to significantly higher prices.[6]
- Lingering problems persist in some competitive wholesale markets, which have not performed as expected.

Despite these setbacks, the competitive US retail markets has gradually grown and now tops 90 GW (see Figure 37.2). According to a 2007 survey, annual en-ergy sales to customers buying power from competitive suppliers are estimated at around 480 TWh, up 41% from 2005, and the number of customers is around 8.3 million, from 3.3 million in 2005 (Kema 2007).

---

[5] The State of Texas, after examining the options, has decided to stay with its competitive market despite experiencing higher wholesale prices (mostly due to higher natural gas prices) and abnormal price volatility.

[6] When retail competition was introduced in the mid-1990s in some states, rates were typi-cally rolled back and frozen, in some cases for as long as 10 years. These rate freezes are about to become unfrozen, resulting in rather significant price increases in some cases. This has resulted in public discontent in a few states, notably Maryland, where the regulatory commission was essentially dismissed following a significant price increase in 2006-2007.

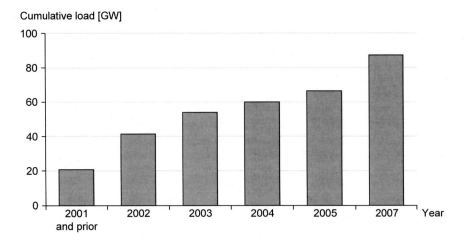

Figure 37.2: Cumulative load served by competitive suppliers in the US, 2001-07 (Tschamler, 2005; Kema, 2007)

Part of the growth may be attributed to reclassification of the Texas market as fully competitive and to significant increases in the numbers of customers switching to competitive suppliers in five states that have reached the end of their restructuring transition periods and retail price freezes (see Table 37.5).

Table 37.5: Status of competitive retail market in the US, 2007 (Kema, 2007)

	Eligible customers* (million)	Switched to competition (million)	[%]	Total sales [TWh]	Sales diverted [TWh]	[%]
Residential	55.7	6.8	12	550	91	17
Non-residential	7.6	1.5	20	1,028	388	38

* The Texas market was fully opened to competition beginning January 2007, with the phase-out of the price to beat regulated tariff for residential and small commercial consumers, resulting in reclassification of these eligible customers as competitively served by KEMA.

Confronting efforts by state officials to derail competitive power markets, 35 former state utility regulators issued an open letter stressing the positive aspects of competitive markets (Platts, 2007). Their position statement claims: "electricity consumers are seizing their own destiny, changing their behavior and taking control to limit the impact of rising prices".[7]

---

[7] The signatories included former Texas regulator and FERC Chairman Pat Wood; former Pennsylvania and FERC member Nora Brownell; Bill Flynn, a former chairman of the New York Public Service Commission, and David Svanda, a former Michigan regulator and past president of the National Association of Regulatory Utility Commissioners (NARUC).

37.3.4   Why the Disillusionment with Markets?

To understand the current US dissatisfaction with markets, we need to return to the mid-1990s, when restructuring was a fad among state regulators (see Figure 37.3). At the time, the motivating factor for many was the desire among large industrial customers for more choice in selecting their power supplier. They did not wish to be restricted to buying from the local monopoly utility, especially if it offered higher prices and/or less flexibility or customized terms and conditions than were desired by energy-intensive users.

In these circumstances, regulators in high-cost states were led to believe that restructuring and customer choice would result in lower prices for consumers and, as an added bonus, less need for regulations and fewer regulators. They were wrong on both counts: prices in high-cost states have not fallen, nor have the regulators' jobs become any easier.

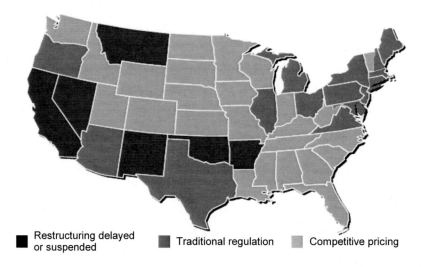

Figure 37.3: Status of retail access in the US (Energy Information Administration, 2006)

An examination of prices between restructured and nonrestructured states suggests that there has been no significant difference in average retail rates between the two categories, mostly reflecting changes in prevailing higher fuel prices (Pfeifenberger et al., 2007). The average rates have increased by roughly 31% over the past decade in the 20 states and the District of Columbia (DC), about the same as in states that did not bother to introduce retail competition.

This suggests that restructuring and the introduction of retail competition, which were intended to reduce prices in high-cost states, have not delivered as expected. It also suggests, however, that the current political uproar in states such as Maryland, Connecticut, Delaware, Virginia, and Illinois is due to the fact that at the outset, retail rates in these states were rolled back and legislatively frozen for a decade. The price shocks being experienced today are merely due to prices adjusting to prolonged rate freeze.[7]

True, restructured states tend to be higher cost states, but that was true before restructuring (see Figure 37.4). "The perception that the average rates in restructured states are significantly higher than the rates in nonrestructured states is correct, but that was already the case in the mid-1990s before these states restructured their electricity markets" (Pfeifenberger et al., 2007).

Retail rates [cents/kWh]

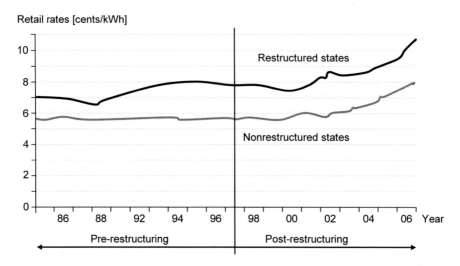

Figure 37.4: Retail rates in restructured and nonrestructured states, cents/kWh, 1985-2006 (Pfeifenberger et al., 2007)

The inescapable conclusion to be drawn from this and similar studies is that restructuring in the US has failed to reduce the rate differentials that existed in the mid-1990s, but neither has it made them worse. "It also means that the available facts do not support a conclusion that the average customer in restructured states would have been better off under traditional cost-of-service regulation, nor that customers would necessarily benefit from re-regulation of the industry" (Pfeifenberger et al., 2007).

There have been a number of other studies, generally reaching similar conclusions (Sioshansi, 2008a). Some authors interpret the results – the fact that the introduction of retail competition has not resulted in significant lowering of costs in high-cost states – as negative, and in some cases have suggested that we might be better off if we returned to regulation. Others are not so sure whether the fact that prices have not fallen can be blamed on retail competition and do not favor a return to the status quo.

Pointing out that the grass was in fact not greener under utility regulation, Lesser observes, "abandoning wholesale electric competition now, just as needed market signals have developed, and re-instituting an outdated, failed central planning approach – even one with a fancy name like integrated portfolio management – is solution looking for a problem" (Lesser, 2007).

Among recent studies on the subject, the Alliance for Retail Choice (ARC) examined the experience of 28 states and 2 Canadian provinces, concluding that retail choice has definitely been successful in Texas and New York because the electricity market has "advanced sufficiently for competition to work effectively". The study found that more than 3.7 million residential customers are served by competitive suppliers in these two states alone.[8] Ten other states, including Massachusetts, Connecticut, Illinois, Maryland, and Pennsylvania, are classified as achieving moderate progress. The situation may be characterized as less successful in the remaining cases.

New York state and Texas are generally regarded as successful retail markets in the US, suggesting that retail competition can work given suitable circumstances. The fact that it has not been so in some states should not be interpreted as a failure of competitive electricity markets per se; nor can it be used as justification to return to regulation.

37.3.5 Expectations vs Reality

The current debate in Illinois exemplifies the disappointment some policy makers and consumers have experienced, resulting in a backlash against so-called deregulated electricity markets. The main idea behind deregulated markets was to create competitive wholesale auctions. This would allow multiple generators to bid to sell, and multiple distributors to bid to buy from the same auction to serve the needs of end-use customers. The transparency of competitive auctions with multiple generators would result in lower prices for consumers. And the evolution of competitive retailers would ensure that lower prices would be passed on to customers.

Things did not, however, go as expected in the US. The price of fuels, notably natural gas, which is the marginal fuel in many markets for most hours, has increased significantly over the past decade. Adequate reserve margins and depressed prices that existed in some markets around the time of restructuring have vanished. Private investors, who now own and operate a significant part of the US generation base, demand higher prices, not merely to recover their fuel and operating costs but also to cover their debts and generate profits. More significantly, the same investors require significantly higher prices to build additional capacity, which is needed in many parts of the country.

A second contributing factor is that, for a variety of reasons, competing retailers have not materialized or play only a marginal part in many markets where retail competition is allowed.

---

[8] Nat Treadway of Distributed Energy Financial Group, who conducted the study, Baseline Assessment of Choice in the US (ABACUS), says that 41% of electricity usage in New York state is currently provided by competitive suppliers including 625,000 or 11% of residential consumers. In one utility service area, residential customers have 37 different offerings, including a variety of fixed, indexed, blended, and green power.

When market reform was introduced in the late 1990s, regulators assumed that a competitive retail market would quickly evolve and a significant percentage of customers would switch to alternative suppliers, which would presumably be offering lower prices and better services.

Since it was assumed that the incumbent retailers would not be serving very many customers after a few years, it was also assumed that they would not need their own generation. Hence, integrated utilities were typically forced to divest their generation assets to independent generators.

By and large, however, consumers did not switch to alternative providers, partly because of the guaranteed rate reductions and the mandated freeze, and partly because in many markets it was very hard, if not impossible, for new entrants to consistently offer lower prices than incumbents and remain profitable. This was certainly true in California, where no more than 1% of residential consumers took advantage of their opportunity to switch at any one point.[9] Residential consumers in California, as in many other states, were automatically given a 10% discount for doing absolutely nothing. In these circumstances, why would anyone switch from the known and dependable incumbent utility to a new supplier that no one had ever even heard of?

The story is identical in other parts of the country. In Maryland, as of October 2007, only 12,000 customers of Baltimore Gas & Electric Company (BGE), a mere 1.1% of residential customers, had switched. The numbers are similar in many other states where retail choice is available, including Massachusetts, where 99% of residential customers in the Boston area have remained with the incumbent distribution company, now called Nstar.

Matters are further complicated in that retail rates were initially rolled back and frozen, sometimes for as long as a decade, but these frozen rates are now expiring, resulting in necessary but unpopular rate shocks in such places as Maryland, Illinois, Virginia, and elsewhere. Consumers who were promised lower prices are now confronted with higher nominal prices – even though in many cases they are only moderately higher than a decade ago when adjusted for inflation.

Fast-forward to 2007, when the frozen retail rates have been unfrozen in states such as Illinois and Maryland, and when companies such as BGE and Commonwealth Edison Co. of Chicago (ComEd) continue to serve the bulk of the market but have lost most or all their generation. The expectation was that by now they would be marginal players in retail, mostly focused on distribution business. But this is not the case. The incumbents must now buy the bulk of their power at competitive auctions and pass on the costs to their customers.

In the case of ComEd, its unregulated parent, Exelon Generation, initially provided power to the distribution company at 38 $/MWh, but in auctions held in 2006, prices rose to 63-90 $/MWh starting in 2007 and had to be passed on to

---

[9] Despite its bad reputation and abusive practices, the now defunct Enron was among the first to realize that there was no way any new entrant could consistently beat the California Power Exchange (PX) price. Even before the California market had opened, Enron announced that it was pulling out of residential market in the state, a decision vindicated by passage of time.

consumers, resulting in rate increases ranging from 22% to 55%. The competitive auction that resulted in the price hikes has been declared fair, transparent, and efficient according to a report by the Illinois Commerce Commission (ICC) staff released in December 2007.

The ICC examined bids from 14 competing generators to supply ComEd with over 18,000 MW of capacity and concluded that, even with a 22% rate increase, ComEd's 2007 rates would still be 3% below what they were in 1997. When adjusted for inflation, overall rates are actually 22% lower. ComEd's chairman and CEO, Frank M. Clark felt vindicated by ICC's findings, stating that, "the ICC staff's report shows that the Illinois auction was competitive, and that electric rates in 2007 will be below what they were in 1997".

ComEd points out that inflation in energy costs has been 67% since 1997, compared with the paltry 22% rate increase following a 9-year rate reduction and freeze that has already saved consumers more than $ 4 billion. The 72% rate increase affecting BGE customers in Maryland is far more worrisome, but the facts are essentially the same as in Illinois.

In the current debate in the US, the facts are sometimes buried in hyperbole or stated wrongly and totally out of context by the media and politicians. Competition is, no doubt, messy and imperfect, but the alternatives are even worse.

There are those who say deregulation has failed and it is time to go back to regulation. Among those advocating this position is Maryland's Office of the Peoples' Counsel, which has proposed scrapping the current scheme, where such companies as BGE buy their power at competitive auctions, and returning to regulatory-approved 10- to 15-year-long term contracts, including allowing distributors to build and operate their own generation.

Others have suggested maintaining parts of the current system but modifying others, resulting in hybrids that are partly market driven and partly regulated. To reduce price shocks, for example, distributors would be forced to secure their long-term needs as a portfolio of contracts, some as long as 10-15 years, some 5-10 years, and the rest in auctions going forward 1-5 years. Free market advocates are aghast at the idea of returning to such an administratively mandated paradigm, fearing that the emerging hybrid markets will retain the worst, not the best, features of competition and regulation.

37.3.6   Are We Better off Now?

In the US context, the relevant question, of course, is whether we are better off – and if not, what can be done about it. The answer to the former is not as easy as one might like. A report published in June 2006 by the Edison Electric Institute, representing the investor-owned utilities in the US, concluded that roughly 40% of all customers in the states that allow customer choice "paid modestly lower prices over the past decade", but adds that most of the accrued savings resulted primarily from mandated price cuts or rate freezes imposed by regulatory fiat and not from competitive market forces.

Most experts who have examined the US retail experiments agree that the disappointing result, "stems in good part from the fact that a genuinely competitive market for electricity production has not developed" (The New York Times, 2006).

There is, of course, a lot of disinformation about the price increases, with some consumer advocates attempting to promote ratepayer revolts by exaggerating the facts. Those who have attempted to ascertain the actual impact of competitive markets on retail rates have had a difficult time determining what is going on and why. A report to Congress prepared by FERC, for example, acknowledges the existence of rate shocks and the fact that they can lead to public pressure to put the regulatory regime back to where it started.

But the FERC report correctly points out that, "it has been difficult to determine whether retail prices (in states that have introduced customer choice) are higher or lower than they otherwise would have been (i.e., in the absence of restructuring)". Harvard University economist Mark Fagan points out that in 12 out of 18 states who offer customer choice, industrial customers have benefited. But even in this case, it is not clear whether small commercial and residential consumers have benefited because of market reform (The New York Times, 2006). Other studies are inconclusive or only apply to a given state or utility service area.

Part of the problem is how savings are defined and measured, over what period, and for which classes of customers. Different studies come to different conclusions based on differences in methodology, definition, and time frame. Are actual rates measured and compared with what they would have been? In this case, how can one tell what the rates would have been had there been no market reform? How can the effect of significant external factors, such as rising fuel prices, be accounted for?

Despite these difficulties, it is safe to assume that industrial customers have benefited as a result of having retail choice. For smaller consumers, the record is mixed. In New York, for example, residential consumers, on average, paid 16% less in 2004 than in 1996 on an inflation-adjusted basis. In the Boston area, which is served by Nstar, on the other hand, average retail rates have gradually risen by 78% since 2002. In Pennsylvania (see Table 37.6), residential prices were down by between 13% and 47% in constant dollars between 1991 and 2006 (PennFuture, 2006).

Richard Blumenthal, Connecticut's Attorney General, says the whole competitive experiment has been "a complete failure and a colossal waste of time and money", a statement reminiscent of former California Governor Gray Davis, who pronounced that state's market experience a "colossal and dangerous failure". Blumenthal has asked FERC to revoke the competitive pricing scheme in CT. Likewise, the Cato Institute, a staunch pro-market think-tank, has concluded that the current market reform movements in the US are hopelessly botched and should be scrapped. In a statement released in 2006, the Cato Institute said, "We recommend total abandonment of restructuring" and a "return to an updated version of the old system".

Table 37.6: Average residential bills in Pennsylvania for 500 kWh, 1991-2007 (PennFuture, 2006)

Utility	Con-stant $ Nomi-nal $	1991	1996	2006	2007	Change 1991-2006	Change 1991-2007
Met Ed	C	$62.94	$57.09	$50.10	–	-20%	–
	N	$42.25	$44.15	$50.10	–	19%	–
Penelec	C	$60.78	$56.25	$47.62	–	-22%	–
	N	$40.80	$43.50	$47.62	–	17%	–
Penn Power	C	$106.87	$78.30	$57.10	$76.46	-47%	-28%
	N	$71.74	$60.55	$57.10	$74.23	-20%	3%
Allegheny Energy	C	$43.50	$43.97	$38.04	–	-13%	–
	N	$29.20	$34.00	$38.04	–	30%	–
PPL	C	$65.15	$61.40	$53.95	–	-17%	–
	N	$43.73	$47.48	$53.95	–	23%	–
Duquesne	C	$93.48	$78.69	$54.30	$63.30	-42%	-32%
	N	$62.75	$60.85	$54.30	$63.30	-13%	1%
PECO	C	$102.92	$90.72	$75.27	$81.59	-27%	-21%
	N	$69.09	$70.15	$75.27	$79.21	9%	15%

37.4   Regulation of the Electricity Industry in Europe

One of the basic principles of the European Union (EU) is to promote a common European market and have unrestricted trade of commodities and services between the member countries (Cornwall 2008). When the internal market started most of the member countries had regulation in the market for electricity, which was not compatible with open exchange. Basically, in most member countries the supply of electricity was based on local or regional, vertically integrated monopolies. On the other hand, the networks of many countries were interconnected and there were rules of cooperation and assistance that had been developed by the industry itself in order to secure quality of supply in continental Europe. The present UCTE[10] system interconnects continental European countries (see Figure 37.5). A number of countries that do not belong to the EU are nonetheless members of the UCTE, however. One prominent country in this context is Switzerland. Swiss companies have been very active in promoting exchange activities. The non-EU-

---

[10] UCTE: Union for the Co-ordination of Transmission of Electricity. For more detail see: www.ucte.org.

member countries are under a certain pressure to restructure their electricity system on lines compatible with EU regulation.

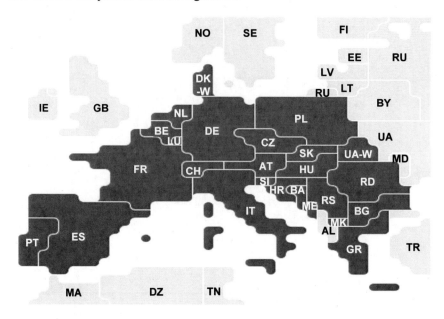

Figure 37.5: The interconnected UCTE system (UCTE, 2006)

The Nordic countries are not interconnected with continental Europe, but have developed a highly interconnected market of their own (Amundsen et al., 2006). Britain was the first country to start an open market model, but is not directly linked to other European regions. The British system of regulation is to some extent much more inward oriented than those in force in other European regions. It is often considered a blueprint for the European market as a whole, but a number of important problems regarding cross-border exchange (e.g., dealing with cross-border congestion issues) and market integration with other countries are not addressed in this model.

The new regulatory regime introduced step by step with the help of a number of European directives theoretically allows customers to buy electricity from whomever they want within their country of residence. Many companies have set up subsidiaries in other countries, so that suppliers may indirectly also market imported power. Explicit import by final customers is not (yet) possible, however. On the other hand, there are often restrictions on trade because of physical bottlenecks in cross-border transmission.

It is interesting to note that European regulation has changed the interior market regimes of all member countries considerably, although strictly speaking the European Commission does not have the competence to interfere with national market rules, but rather with the conditions of exchange between member states. The long-term goal of the Commission was to transform the electricity markets in member countries so as to create a market regime that would also allow increased competition between countries later on.

Table 37.7: Key figures for UCTE system (UCTE, 2006)

33	Transmission system operators (TSO)
23	European countries
450	Million people served by the represented power systems
620	GW installed capacity
2,500	TWh electricity consumption in 2006
295	TWh of electricity exchange in all between member TSOs under rules of UCTE
220,000	km Length of high-voltage transmission lines managed by the TSOs

The Commission had the responsibility to issue directives that obliged the member states to make corresponding changes to their national laws. The most important directives and the present discussion on future development will be explained below.

37.4.1   Electricity Market Directive

This directive (Directive 2003/54/EC, 2003) set out the basic rules for generation, transmission, distribution, network access, and regulation.

The rules referring to transmission, distribution, network access, and regulation are particularly important for market development and competition.

Unbundling

The directive requires that any transmission system operator (TSO), if part of a vertically integrated undertaking, must be "independent at least in terms of its legal form, organization and decision making from other activities not related to transmission. These rules shall not create an obligation to separate the ownership of assets of the transmission system from the vertically integrated undertaking" (Directive 2003/54/EC, 2003). Basically the same conditions also hold for distribution companies. However, unbundling is not required if a company serves fewer than 100,000 customers. In parallel with these rules the accounts also have to be unbundled.

Network access and regulation

Transmission and distribution system operators are required to give access to third parties on a nondiscriminatory basis and at tariffs that have to be submitted to and approved by the authorities before publication.

Member countries had the choice of introducing network access on a step-by-step basis, granting network access to nonhousehold customers first and opening up the market for all customers by July 2007 at the latest.

To ensure that network access is implemented, and in addition to monitor all aspects of market development, member states are required to set up regulatory institutions with a wide range of tasks designed to make sure that the markets function efficiently. Regulatory authorities are specifically required to approve the network fees submitted to them by transmission and distribution operators. To promote the unification of the various national markets the national regulatory bodies also have the duty of cooperating with each other and with the European Commission.

Future Developments

In January 2007 the European Commission made a new proposal[11] to further develop the European markets for electricity and natural gas. Basically, the proposal involves ownership unbundling for TSOs, and possibly also for DSOs. After an extensive sector inquiry[12] into the energy industries the commission concluded that to promote competition within member countries and between member countries complete separation of the transmission system from production and supply is necessary. This has led to intense debate, and it is expected that legislative procedures will come to an end in the year 2009, possibly obliging member countries to implement the new rules.[13] Interference with ownership structures in member countries is, however, restricted by the European Treaty and requires that considerable welfare gains can be achieved by this measure. Discussion has shown that this is rather doubtful.

Table 37.8 provides a short survey of the arguments put forward by the commission and the discussion on these arguments.

Figure 37.6 shows cross-border congestion between various European countries in relation to ownership unbundling. There is no clear-cut result indicating that unbundled network operators experience less congestion than vertically integrated ones. Basically the congestion at cross-border connection points depends largely on the production structure between different countries and the capacity of interconnectors.

---

[11] Memo-07-9, January 10, 2007.

[12] DG Competition, Report on Energy Sector Enquiry (EC, 2007).

[13] As a consequence of the discussion some companies decided voluntarily to sell their transmission network.

Table 37.8: EU Arguments for electricity market liberalization

Argument	Discussion
TSOs discriminate against third parties	Wholesale markets in many European countries work quite well in electricity, regardless of ownership regime. It thus seems that market rules and market regulation are far more important than ownership for the development of competition.
Network access is difficult for new participants in the markets	The physical interdependence between network and the siting of generation activities is quite intensive. Any market regime has to solve the problem of how to coordinate operation and development of transmission system on the one hand and operation and development of power production on the other. Ownership unbundling will not automatically lead to incentives for network operators to support new entrants by investment. In a regulated network the TSO will have an incentive to invest if the regulator accepts the cost of this investment in the rate base. Whatever the ownership structure, regulation will therefore automatically lead to a very strong role of the regulator as far as investment plans are concerned.
Bundled TSOs will decide on the basis of the company interest in production and supply and not in the interest of network operation	Potential discrimination by vertically integrated TSOs is a problem. On the other hand, unbundled TSOs have no economic interest in production and supply, which may create problems in future development of the coordination between those spheres. The answer in both cases is that regulation has to eliminate potential discrimination by vertically integrated TSOs or to create economic incentives in unbundled TSOs in order to make the system work.
Integrated TSOs invest too little and too late	This argument assumes that the main driver for integrated TSOs is a kind of defensive behavior against new entrants. On the other hand, vertically integrated companies may also be interested in expanding their market, which may require strengthening of their network to make it possible to increase electricity trade. The empirical basis for the argument put forward by the commission is very weak. A lot of new projects for transmission lines were developed by companies with a strong interest in production.
Security of supply is at risk without ownership unbundling	It is difficult to see how security of supply, which depends on sufficient resources in production and transmission, will suddenly be dependent on the ownership structure of transmission lines. It is much more likely that the long-term security of supply of the system will depend on state regulation governing future sites for power plants, location of transmission lines, and access to primary energy.
Without ownership unbundling the future of the European internal energy market will be at risk	There are a number of problems concerning the interchange between European countries and the further development of the European market. This will require better coordination between neighboring TSOs, coordinated rule books, and simplified procedures and processes. The European Commission has proposed that neighboring TSOs cooperate in the form of regional system operators, a format similar to the RTO in the US. This approach seems to be much more promising.

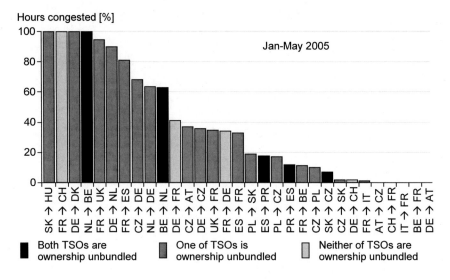

Figure 37.6: Congestion in cross-border trade in electricity (Frontier Economics, 2007)

Table 37.9 shows the capacity of each of these interconnectors as a percentage of its generation capacity. For smaller countries interconnection is much more important than for larger countries, and exchange is much more important for central European countries than for peripheral countries such as Portugal and Spain.

Table 37.9: Capacity of interconnectors between EU countries (European Commission, 2007)

Country	Import capacity: % of generation capacity 2004	Country	Import capacity: % of generation capacity 2004
UK	2%	Czech Republic	23%
Italy	6%	Austria	24%
Spain	6%	Belgium	25%
Ireland	6%	Sweden	29%
Portugal	9%	Hungary	38%
Poland	10%	Slovakia	39%
Greece	12%	Denmark	50%
Finland	14%	Estonia	66%
France	14%	Slovenia	68%
Germany	16%	Luxembourg	90%
Netherlands	17%		

For the development of the European market the need for exchange might change as a result of production decisions depending much less on availability of transmission than on policy on generation. These policies might be quite different between countries, which will create a certain pressure to increase transmission resources. The ban on nuclear energy in Germany, for instance, might lead to additional imports from nuclear power stations in other countries (possibly financed by German utility companies).

Table 37.10 shows the unbundling status of different TSOs in the European countries of EU 15. There is certainly no clear connection between the unbundling status and availability of interconnecting capacities.

Table 37.10: Unbundling* status of TSOs in EU 15 (European Commission, 2007)

Country	Unbundling	Number of TSO	Country	Unbundling	Number of TSO
Austria	L	3	Italy	O	1
Belgium	L	1	Luxembourg	M	2
Denmark	O	1	Netherlands	O	1
Finland	O	1	Portugal	O	1
France	L	1	Spain	O	1
Germany	L	4	Sweden	O	1
Greece	L	1	UK	O	2
Ireland	L/M	1			

* Ownership, Legal, Management Unbundling. L/M means system operator is legally unbundled, system owner management unbundled.

37.4.2   Environmental Regulation

Environmental regulation of power plants and power installations is part of the general regulation of environmental protection, and in addition there are specific rules and regulations for power plant emissions, particularly airborne emissions.

In general, every installation that may interfere with nature has to be subjected to a so-called Environmental Impact Analysis, which is a kind of documentation of expected effects if the installation is realized. In addition, certain interactions with nature have to be analyzed on the basis of the directive on the conservation of natural habitats and of wild fauna and flora (Directive 2003/35/EC, 2003).

Specifically, power plants have to fulfill a number of quality standards regarding emissions of sulfur dioxide, natural oxide, dust and other substances (Directive 2001/80/EC, 2001). The operator has to prove that these standards will be fulfilled during operation. The standards set by European regulation are considered to be minimum standards. National standards may be more ambitious, and within nations regional emission control may set higher standards depending on local conditions.

The emission standard system has been quite successful in reducing the emission of a number of substances such as sulfur dioxide, NO_x, dust, and heavy metals.

On the subject of the emission of greenhouse gases, the European Union has started a scheme of special permits for emission of greenhouse gases, particularly carbon dioxide (Directive 2003/87/EC, 2003). Operators receive a certain amount of permits, and at the end of the year have to prove that the quantity of carbon emitted corresponds to the quantity of permits that the company has available. The system is flexible in that permits can be bought and sold on a market that has meanwhile been established. This system of flexible mechanisms anticipates the procedures that have been envisaged in the Kyoto Protocol for all participating countries. This system will strongly influence decision making on the choice of fuel and plant in the future. In addition to the markets for fuel and plant, the conditions of this additional market influence all strategic and operational decisions. The price in the market for emission certificates will determine decision making in the same way as the price for fuel or the power plant itself.

The carbon certificate scheme is applied to all combustion units above 20 MW. National governments have to set up a so-called National Allocation Plan, which lists the emission certificates granted to operators of energy combustion plants. The bulk of the certificates go to the electricity sector, and mainly to plants fired by coal or lignite. In the beginning the certificates were allocated to operators at no charge. Although there was a surplus of certificates over emissions in the first period the price of the certificates rose considerably owing to a lot of uncertainties when the new system started, and also as a result of some regional imbalances (Britain had to buy in certificates to avoid running high-price natural gas plants). In the present phase of the system the number of certificates allocated has been reduced, so that the environment is becoming a limiting factor for the enterprises. Present regulation in the European Union does not allow auctioning of all certificates to operators. In Germany it was decided that the government should sell a share of certificates to electricity operators rather than allocating them at no charge. The price has presently settled at around 20 €/t CO_2 for the coming allocation period.

For the future, the European Commission now plans to sell all certificates to avoid the negative distributional impacts seen in the first phase (freely allocated certificates were regarded as valuable assets by the enterprises, and they increased their power prices accordingly).

Table 37.11: Effect of carbon prices on generation costs (own calculation based on carbon content of fuel and efficiency of plant)

| Price of CO_2 in €/t | Additional cost in €/MWh | | | |
| | New plant | | Old plant | |
	Coal	Natural gas CCGT	Coal	Gas turbine
5	3,71	1,82	4,51	3,57
10	7,42	3,64	9,03	7,14
20	14,84	7,27	18,05	14,29

The cost of power is strongly influenced by the new certificate system (see Table 37.11). In competition the price of power depends on the marginal cost of the marginal plant at different times of consumption. Figure 37.7 shows as an example that the marginal plants in Germany are either coal or natural gas plants, both of which are subject to a price increase owing to CO_2. The price for power from coal almost doubles while the price for natural gas increases by a lesser amount, but natural gas itself is much more expensive.

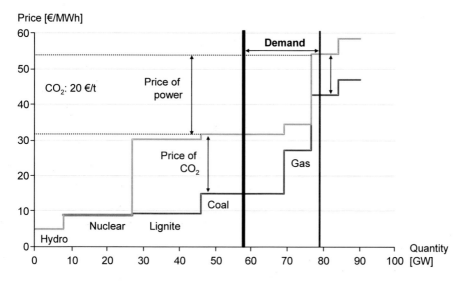

Figure 37.7: Stylized merit order of power plants with a CO_2 price of 20 €/t (authors' own calculation)

One of the very important questions in present decision making on power plants is how the future regime for CO_2 certificates will influence investment behavior. As explained above, the market price for power in the future is uncertain anyway, because in liberalized markets the operator of the plant has to take a market risk. The uncertainty about the future price of CO_2 being responsible for about half of the cost of a coal-fired power plant will be a very important determinant of investment decision in the future.

There is a strong incentive in the carbon certificate system to invest in carbon-free energy or alternatives with low carbon content. Whether the introduction of a CO_2 certificate system will lead to a revival of nuclear energy has led to controversial debates in recent years; there are also discussions on the possibility of extracting carbon from the flue gas and depositing it safely. However, no reliable technological and institutional concepts for this are available as yet.

37.4.3 Promotion of Renewables

The promotion of renewable energy is one of the targets of European countries, and also of the Union as a whole. At present, countries are still free to choose their system of support for the development of renewables in electricity, the heat market, and transport.

Basically, two different systems of support have been established. One is based on fixed prices for renewables set by regulation, leaving the development of quantities to the market ('feed-in' tariff), while the other is based on fixed obligations ('quotas') to buy a certain amount of renewables, leaving the market price free and allowing trade with the help of certificates of origin.

Feed-in tariffs are more widespread in Europe than is the system based on quotas.[14] Most continental European countries use the feed-in tariff system, which was developed as long ago as in the early 1990s in Germany. In this system the government fixes the price and can use technology-specific price differentiation. The market risk is taken away from potential producers by obliging network operators to buy any quantity of renewables offered to them by qualified producers. Producers are guaranteed a fixed price for a period of up to 20 years (in Germany). Thus, investment in renewable technology is practically free of market risk. This explains the boom in the production of renewable energy for the electricity sector that followed the introduction of the law in 2000.

This model of promotion of renewables is very effective in the sense of increasing renewable production. On the other hand, there has been a lot of criticism to the effect that, as in the case of any subsidized production, prices may be higher than necessary and there is no built-in check for economic efficiency. This is the case because subsidies for renewables are not paid out of the government budget but are raised by adding a premium for renewable energy on the price of electricity, so that suppliers of electricity have to collect the money and distribute it to the producers of renewables.

In order to take account of technical progress in the production of equipment for renewable energy, the premium price paid for renewables declines from year to year for new installations, whereas existing installations receive a fixed price for 20 years.

The system is beloved of policy makers, because it allows them to promote different renewable energy technologies by using different prices. Thus, there has recently been a boom in production and electrification of biogas, because special premiums are paid for the use of biomass. The disadvantage of a fixed price system, however, is that in a world of changing energy prices and changing prices for agricultural products the biomass system has recently gone into crisis because of the sharp increase in the price for agricultural products in the world market. The promise of high subsidies has also led to severe inefficiencies in the planning and design of plants and their organization.

One of the main problems of the feed-in system within Europe, however, is that such a system is by its nature national and does not allow any trade in renewable energy between European member countries. Thus, it is in sharp contradiction to the principle of the internal European market.

The quota system introduced in the UK and some other countries basically splits the price for renewables into the market price for electricity plus a quality premium depending on supply of and demand for the renewable quality. Demand for renewables is set through the government by renewable obligation; the supply

---

[14] For a more detailed analysis see Haas et al., 2008.

arises from market-oriented investment by producers. In a network the physical property of different sources of power cannot be distinguished by the consumer. Therefore, the whole system is based on certificates of origin that are given to producers. These certificates can be sold to suppliers for them to fulfill their obligations. The market price for these certificates then induces potential investment for renewable energy.

In this system a certain amount of market risk remains with the producers of renewable energy. They do not know the price for certificates in advance, and the price may also be quite volatile, depending on government decisions on the obligation to buy. It depends very much on the market design whether, and if so how, this system can be effective in the sense of inducing the desired amount of additional investment for renewable energy production.

The feed-in system works well in the electricity industry because all energy produced can be fed into a system and easily measured and monitored. It does not work in the heat market, because in this market there are many sources of energy to be used for heating and there is no easy way to measure and monitor as there is in the case of electricity. In the heat market, therefore, promotion of the obligation to buy or to produce renewable energy is a potential instrument. Thus, in the heat market the system of promoting renewable energy has to be much closer to the quota system as used in the UK.

For both systems we can ask what relevance the promotion of renewables has for climate policy. Theoretically, the marginal cost of avoiding carbon emissions by reducing carbon emissions in carbon-fuelled plants, by substituting carbon with renewable energy or any other carbon-free energy (e.g., nuclear), and by increasing the energy efficiency in energy use should be equivalent to find the least-cost solution to greenhouse gas reduction.

It is well known that the cost of avoiding carbon with renewables is much higher than the present and expected future market price for carbon certificates. It could be argued that the promotion of renewables with the high cost of carbon reduction could be considered a necessary investment in the development of new technologies. On the other hand, we might ask whether the massive promotion of renewables creating subsidized structures ('artificial market') really does lead to the maximum learning effect.

Future Developments

The European Union now plans to introduce general regulation[15] for renewable energies, obliging all countries to reach a certain level of production and introducing the possibility of trade between countries.

---

[15] Memo on the Renewable Energy and Climate Change Package, Memo 08-33, and draft Proposal for a directive of the European Parliament and the Council on the promotion of the use of energy from renewable sources.

This makes sense for two reasons:

- Trade allows more economically efficient solutions because there are considerable comparative cost differences between European countries in the potential of renewable energy production for electricity, heat, and fuels.
- The European market is based on the principle of open exchange within Europe, and in the long run it will not be possible to allow government policies that are not compatible with the open European market.

A lot of problems in transition will have to be solved before an open European market for renewables based on certificates of origin can be installed.

37.5   Conclusions

Clearly, market liberalization and restructuring policies promulgated in Europe and the US in recent years have exerted strong influences on the industry. While the broad intention of the policymakers in both continents is similar – integrating large interconnected systems owned and operated by incongruent players governed at national or state level – the approach pursued and the results achieved to date are strikingly different.

Europeans looking across the Atlantic Ocean are amazed to see that the US, as a federal union of dissimilar states, has followed policies that leave quite a lot of room for different states to follow different models of market design and tolerate a wide variety of approaches and outcomes with little or no national coordination. This is manifested in market restructuring or support of renewable energy technologies, which varies from state to state. For Europeans, it appears odd that the US federal government takes such a back-seat approach on issues of such national significance as global climate change, forcing individual states or regions to adopt their own solutions, to the disappointment of economists, who prefer a more unified approach.

Americans looking the other way feel equally baffled by the relatively strong and pro-active stand of the European Commission (EC) on electricity market liberalization, on global climate change, or renewables, where there is a consistent push – at least in principle – to harmonize and apply the same policies across the entire continent. Granted, this is work in progress.

The reasons for these striking differences are partly historical, cultural, institutional, and political. Europe, historically an amalgamation of separate and often competing states, has gradually moved towards a centralized, federalist model. The US, on the other hand, was founded on the principle of checks-and-balances among state vs federal power–never-ending friction, to put it mildly. This is manifested whenever FERC attempts to over-exert its limited authority, as it did, for example, in trying and failing to implement standard market design a few years ago.

In Europe, the EC has limited competence in energy policy matters and thus has to delegate most energy-related issues to the member countries. On the other hand, the European Treaty clearly gave priority to markets against other forms of coordination, and on this basis the EC has so far quite successfully established a uniform set of market rules, a process that is progressing at a relatively fast pace. This approach is accepted by most players and governments, which see market liberalization as offering potential for future stability and growth.

Much more controversial is the increased emphasis on environmental aspects, which are currently taking center stage in Europe. The many instruments developed so far and planned for the future do not show a clear understanding of an efficient division of tasks between enterprise-oriented markets, on the one hand, and government intervention on the other. The European Carbon Trade System (ECTS) introduced in 2005, for example, is a market-oriented approach. Direct interference in other areas, however, is much more blunt command-and-control intervention. The ECTS could take an important role in delivering longer term signals to the market players for combining GHG abatement with economic efficiency and becoming part of an international market regime. What has emerged so far is a multi-regulation approach with a lot of inconsistencies.

On the environmental issues, it is fair to say that Europe has set itself very ambitious goals and, in doing this, has clearly taken the high moral ground. For the utility sector this involves an enormous task of transformation. It remains to be seen whether the present framework will be adequate for the task at hand.

References

Alliance for Retail Choice. 2007, Washington DC.

Amundsen, E., Von der Fehr, H. & Bergman, L. 2006. The Nordic market: robust by design? In F. P. Sioshansi & W. Pfaffenberger (Eds.), Electricity Market Reform – An International Perspective: 145-170. Amsterdam: Elsevier.

Averch, H. & Johnson, L. L. 1962. Behavior of the firm under regulatory constraint. The American Economic Review, 52: 1052-1069.

Bauknecht, D. & Brunekreeft, G. 2008. Distributed generation and the regulation of electricity networks. In F. P. Sioshansi (Ed.), Competitive Electricity Markets: Design, Implementation and Performance: 469-498. Amsterdam: Elsevier.

Chao, H., Oren, S. & Wilson, R. 2008. Reevaluation of vertical integration and unbundling. In F. P. Sioshansi (Ed.), Competitive Electricity Markets: Design, Implementation and Performance: 27-64. Amsterdam: Elsevier.

Cornwall, N. 2008. Achieving electricity market integration in Europe. In F. P. Sioshansi (Ed.), Competitive Electricity Markets: Design, Implementation and Performance: 95-138. Amsterdam: Elsevier.

Correljé, A. & de Vries, L. 2008. Hybrid electricity markets: explaining different patterns of restructuring. In F. P. Sioshansi (Ed.), Competitive Electricity

Markets: Design, Implementation and Performance: 65-94. Amsterdam: Elsevier.

Directive 2003/35/EC. 2003. Directive of the European Parliament and of the Council of 26 May 2003 providing for public participation in respect of the drawing up of certain plans and programmes relating to the environment and amending with regard to public participation and access to justice Council Directives 85/337/EEC and 96/61/EC. Official Journal of the European Union, L 156: 17-25.

Directive 2001/80/EC. 2001. Directive of the European Parliament and of the council of 23 October 2001 on the limitation of emissions of certain pollutants into the air from large combustion plants. Official Journal of the European Union, L 309: 22-30.

Directive 2003/54/EC. 2003. Directive of the European Parliament and of the council of 26 June 2003 concerning common rules for the internal market in electricity and repealing Directive 96/92/EC. Official Journal of the European Union, L 176: 37-55.

Directive 2003/87/EC. 2003. Directive of the European Parliament and of the council of 13 October 2003 establishing a scheme for greenhouse gas emission allowance trading within the Community and amending Council Directive 96/61/EC. Official Journal of the European Union, 275: 32-46.

Edison Electric Institute. 2006, Washington DC.

Electricity Consumers Resource Council (ELCON). 2006. ELCON paper faults organized markets, calls for "exploring" return to traditional regulation, Press statement of 4th December. Washington.

European Commission (EC). 2007. DG Competition report on energy sector enquiry. Brussels: European Commission.

Federal Energy Regulatory Commission (FERC). 2006. Report to Congress on competition in the wholesale and retail markets for electric energy. Washington: FERC.

Frontier Economics. 2007. Unbundling in den europäischen Energiemärkten. London.

Haas, R., Meyer, N. I., Held, A., Finon, D., Lorenzoni, A., Wiser, R. & Nishio, K. 2008. Promoting electricity from renewable energy source – lessons learned from the EU, United States and Japan. In F. P. Sioshansi (Ed.), Competitive Electricity Markets: Design, Implementation, Performance: 419-468. Amsterdam: Elsevier.

Joskow, P. L. 2005. The difficult transition to competitive electricity markets in the US. In J. M. Griffin & S. L. Puller (Eds.), Electricity Deregulation: Choices and Challenges: 31-97. Chicago: Bush School Series in Economics and Public Policy.

Joskow, P. L. 2006a. Introduction to electricity sector liberalization: lessons learned from cross-country studies. In F. P. Sioshansi & W. Pfaffenberger (Eds.), Electricity Market Reform – An International Perspective: 1-32. Amsterdam: Elsevier.

Joskow, P. L. 2006b. Markets for power in the United States: an interim assessment. The Energy Journal, 27: 1-36.

Kema. 2007. Retail energy markets advisory service. Energy Informer, Sept 07.

Knieps, G. 2006. Sector specific market power regulation vs. general competition law: criteria for judging competitive vs. regulated markets. In F. P. Sioshansi & W. Pfaffenberger (Eds.), Electricity Market Reform – An International Perspective: 49-74. Amsterdam: Elsevier.

Lesser, J. 2007. Déjà vu all over again: the grass was not greener under utility regulation. The Electricity Journal, 20: 35-39.

Littlechild, S. 2006. The market versus regulation. In F. P. Sioshansi & W. Pfaffenberger (Eds.), Electricity Market Reform – An International Perspective. Amsterdam: Elsevier.

Michaels, R. J. 2006. Vertical integration & the restructuring of the US electricity industry, Policy Analysis no. 572: 1-32. Washington: Cato Institute.

Newbery, D. 2006. Electricity liberalization in Britain and the evolution of market design. In F. P. Sioshansi & W. Pfaffenberger (Eds.), Electricity Market Reform – An International Perspective: 109-144. Amsterdam: Elsevier.

O'Neill, R., Helman, U. & Hobbs, B. 2008. The design of US wholesale energy and ancillary service action markets: theory and practice. In F. P. Sioshansi (Ed.), Competitive Electricity Markets: Design, Implementation, Performance: 179-244. Amsterdam: Elsevier.

Pfeifenberger, J. P., Basheda, G. N. & Schumacher, A. C. 2007. Restructuring revisited: what we can learn from retail rate increases in restructured and nonrestructured states. Public Utility Fortnightly, 145.

Platts. 2007, New York, NY.

RKS Research & Consulting. 2007. Changing course: latest RKS survey of state utility regulators documents retreat from deregulation, Press release. New York.

Singh, H. 2008. Transmission markets, congestion management & investment. In F. P. Sioshansi (Ed.), Competitive Electricity Markets: Design, Implementation, Performance: 141-178. Amsterdam: Elsevier.

Sioshansi, F. P. & Pfaffenberger, W. 2006a. Electricity market reform – an international perspective. Amsterdam: Elsevier.

Sioshansi, F. P. & Pfaffenberger, W. 2006b. Why restructure electricity markets? In F. P. Sioshansi & W. Pfaffenberger (Eds.), Electricity Market Reform – An International Perspective: 35-48. Amsterdam: Elsevier.

Sioshansi, F. P. 2008a. Competitive electricity markets: design, implementation, performance. Amsterdam: Elsevier.

Sioshansi, F. P. 2008b. Competitive electricity markets: questions remain about design, implementation, performance. The Electricity Journal, 21: 74-87.

Sweeney, J. 2006. California electricity restructuring, the crisis, and its aftermath. In F. P. Sioshansi & W. Pfaffenberger (Eds.), Electricity Market Reform – An International Perspective: 319-382. Amsterdam: Elsevier.

Tschamler, T. 2006. Competitive retail power markets and default service. In F. P. Sioshansi & W. Pfaffenberger (Eds.), Electricity Market Reform – An International Perspective: 529-562. Amsterdam: Elsevier.

38 Investment Opportunities in South America

Rafael Miranda Robredo[1]

Abstract

During the 1990s, Latin America underwent important privatization steps accounting for 69% of all the electricity assets privatized in the entire world. Nevertheless, the region still offers many investment opportunities, especially in the electricity sector. The major South American countries boast growth rates of around 5% per year, a positive macroeconomic outlook, and a regulatory framework that favors investment. ENDESA began operations there in 1992 and positioned itself as the region's leading private electricity company. ENDESA now faces the future's major challenges of the new investment cycle that will take place in the energy industry with significant projects in the pipeline aimed at maintaining its commitment to the region.

Keywords: South America, ENDESA, utility

[1] Rafael Miranda Robredo is Chief Executive Officer of ENDESA, Spain.

A. Bausch and B. Schwenker (eds.), *Handbook Utility Management,*
DOI: 10.1007/978-3-540-79349-6_38, © Springer-Verlag Berlin Heidelberg 2009

38.1   Investment Wave in the Region: The Privatization Process of the 1990s

The privatization of state-owned companies began in Chile in the 1980s. Companies in key sectors were privatized as governments that had previously believed state-run companies were the best way to allocate resources concluded that privatization was the best way to boost the efficient management of these resources. By the mid-1980s this trend had taken off, reaching a peak by the mid-1990s when Latin America accounted for 60% of the companies privatized worldwide (Inter-American Development Bank, 1996).

Macroeconomic data of some countries showed gross domestic product (GDP) growth rates above those of the US, Europe or Japan, coupled with declining interest rates. The sound economic situation along with a favorable regulatory framework made these countries highly attractive to companies seeking investment opportunities.

For all the above reasons, during the 1990s a large number of utilities and other strategic industries were privatized. According to Comisión Económica para América Latina (CEPAL), the privatization of electricity companies in Argentina, Brazil, Chile, Peru and Colombia (see Box 38.1), where ENDESA had a significant role, amounted to more than $ 43 billion (CEPAL, 2001).

> **Box 38.1: Breakdown of privatizations of electricity companies by country**
>
> *ARGENTINA:* Between 1992 and 1999, Argentina privatized most of its electricity utilities (30 in total), for a total value of $ 4.6 billion. Initially, the government kept 40% of the generation and 49% of the distribution companies, but it then sold them off in successive tenders. The vast majority were acquired by foreign companies, mostly European, such as Electricité de France or ENDESA; but also American, such as AES Corp., CMS Energy, PSEG Global, and Duke Energy, and Chilean companies, such as Chilgener and the current subsidiaries of ENDESA, Chilectra, Enersis and Endesa Chile.
>
> *CHILE:* During the 1990s, much of the foreign investment in Chile came, again, from European companies. In the period 1992-1999, ENDESA, Iberdrola, Powerfin, and Tractebel made direct investments in the electricity sector amounting to $ 5.6 billion. The period 1997-2000 also saw significant privatizations, with 14 Chilean companies acquired for a total value of $ 8.8 billion, a process in which Endesa Chile and Enersis again had a key role.
>
> Endesa Chile and Enersis have been great partners in our investments in Latin America. They have served as platforms to facilitate its integration into the businesses of the country, permitting comprehension of the characteristics of the markets in which they operate. The role of these partners is fundamental, and they provide their know-how to

help taking decisions locally and in the dialogue with the regulatory authorities.

However, we must mention other companies, such as the AES Corporation, PSEG Global, the Sempra Energy Group, and PP&L Global.

BRAZIL: During the second half of the 1990s, Brazil experienced a huge surge in foreign investment owing to the new economic and financial policies and the regulatory changes made during the first half of that decade.

The companies that acquired the approximately 30 electricity companies for $ 27.1 billion were more heterogeneous than in the aforementioned two countries, because of the size of the Brazilian market itself. A consortium formed by Electricité de France, AES Corp., and Houston Energy Services made the most significant purchases, while other companies, such as ENDESA, Duke Energy, Iberdrola, and numerous local companies and pension funds, also had important roles.

COLOMBIA: Colombia also received significant amounts of foreign investment in the 1990s. Fourteen national electricity companies were privatized for a total of $ 4.85 billion. ENDESA and the AES Corp. once more played a key part in this process, acquiring most of the companies sold by the Colombian government.

PERU: Between 1995 and 1999 foreign companies, mostly from Spain, invested an average of $ 2 billion per year, as against the average of $ 29 million per year during the 1980s. This illustrates the shift in the Peruvian legislation to entice foreign investment.

Focusing on the electricity sector, Peru privatized 16 companies, which amounted to approximately $ 1.5 billion. Again, ENDESA had a key role in these transactions. Interestingly, some of these companies were bought by Peruvian investors (which was uncommon in the region), mainly the Rodríguez Banda and Romero Groups.

ENDESA's expansion, which took place in the region during the 1990s, was a natural extension of its electricity business in Spain, which, at the time, was more a mature market. The reasons why ENDESA chose to extend its experience in the electricity business to Latin America can be summarized as follows:

- The cultural or, at least, linguistic affinities were expected to ease the process of business adaptation. In fact, experience has shown that even though speaking the same language (or a very similar language in the case of Brazil) eases the personal acclimation of executives, companies need to be very cautious of cultural, social, and business differences that might not be fully appreciated back in Spain.
- ENDESA would be able to exchange better managerial and operational practices with the acquired companies.
- Numerous investment opportunities were offered by the privatization processes in the region.

- Developments in several countries of regulatory frameworks for the electricity sector were currently at the forefront of liberalization, and there were clear business incentives, with objective and undiscriminating treatment for players and investments.
- Finally, the macroeconomic outlook suggested economic stability and growth perspectives.

ENDESA began operations in South America in 1992 when, in a joint venture with the French company EDF, it bought the Argentinean distribution company Edenor. However, it was not until 1999 (with the takeover of the Chilean holding Enersis) that it finally reached its current status as the leading private electricity company in Latin America. ENDESA holds a leading position in Argentina, Chile, Colombia, and Peru and has a significant presence in Brazil, managing a total generation capacity of more than 14 GW and 12 million clients in the region, which represents 30-35% of ENDESA's total business.

38.2   Future Investment Requirements

South America in general, and those countries where ENDESA operates in particular, will be sure to experience pressure from increasing electricity demand (expected annual growth rates of 5-6%) on the one hand, and supply complicated by rising prices in fossil fuels and delays in highly necessary investments in infrastructure on the other.

One of the reasons behind the need for investment in the region is the high growth potential of electricity consumption. On a per capita basis, the current electricity consumption in South American countries is still much lower than that of developed economies even in such countries as Chile or Venezuela, which consume much more than their neighbors (see Figure 38.1).

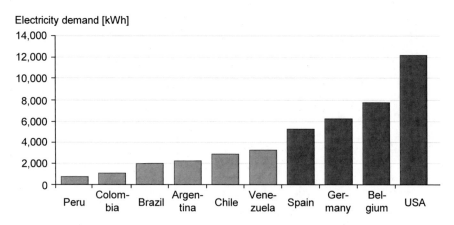

Figure 38.1: Electricity demand per capita 2006 (CIA, 2006)

Nevertheless, in any discussion about South America, we must highlight the differences between its countries. Electricity markets differ both in size and in power generation mix (see chart of each country's electricity sector overview in Figure 38.2). There is a common trend at the moment for demand still to outstrip supply. In some cases, the low investment in the infrastructure and network capacity has led to a wide range of incidents and power restrictions. Investment is not keeping up with the growth in demand, and reserve margins are therefore shrinking at a fast pace and already reaching dangerous levels, particularly under adverse hydrological conditions, in a continent where water is one of the most important sources of electricity generation. The regulatory entities and the electricity companies face the challenge of taking all the necessary steps to avoid future problems.

This view of shrinking reserve margins, and the consequently expected bullish electricity prices, becomes an incentive to develop large projects and, when added to a favorable macroeconomic outlook and a positive regulatory framework, creates the ideal environment for attractive investment opportunities. In the case of relevant players such as ENDESA, it also offers the challenge of maintaining an equilibrium between clients, regulatory agents, and society in general.

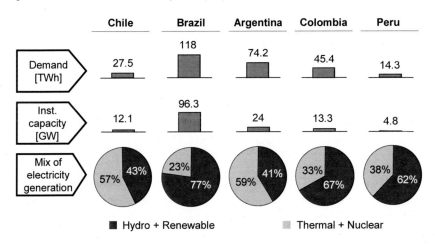

Figure 38.2: Electrical sectors by country (company information)

The investment requirements in Latin America will be noteworthy. The International Energy Agency (IEA) estimates in its World Energy Outlook 2006 report (IEA, 2006) that over the next 25 years the electricity sector in Latin America will need an annual average investment of $ 28 billion, 44% of which will be needed for investment in generation, 38% for investment in distribution, and the remaining 18% for investment in transmission (see Figure 38.3).

The latest estimates indicate, for example, that Brazil alone will need around 4,000 MW per year of new firm capacity over the next 5 years. In addition, Argentina will need 800 MW per year, while Chile, Colombia, and Peru will require 500 MW, 370 MW, and 200 MW, respectively.

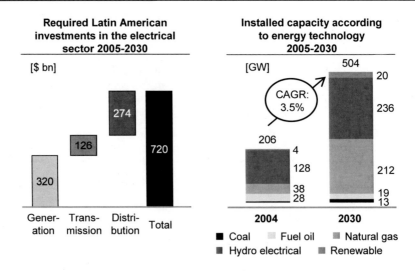

Figure 38.3: Required Latin American investments in the electricity sector 2005-2030 and installed capacity according to energy technology 2005-2030 (IEA, 2006)

38.3   Latin America's Macroeconomic Situation

As previously mentioned, during the 1990s Latin America offered an attractive macroeconomic outlook; there was an economic bonanza, and there seems to be one in train again now, but this time seemingly on sounder foundations.

This has not always been the case. During the 1950s and 1960s, most Latin American economies introduced import substitution industrialization policies, combining them with protectionist measures that allowed the imports needed to develop the domestic market. These measures were a failure and led to the region's increased dependence on other countries while limiting exports of raw materials.

Throughout the 1970s, the previous economic policies combined with a sharp decline in commodity prices and rising oil prices created huge trade deficits. As a result, Latin American economies had to increase their debt.

The 1980s, also known as 'The Lost Decade', were a terrible time for Latin American economies. Countries in the region went into recession when they faced higher interest and debt repayments in a worsening exchange rate scenario. The Central Banks implemented contractive economic measures to contain the deficits, but when they failed to attract new investments the crisis got worse.

During the 1990s, governments tried to attract foreign investment by establishing measures to promote capital transfers (for both loaning and investment). In order to do this, they applied monetary measures to adjust their exchange rates and created new regulatory frameworks in key sectors of their economies (such as the electricity sector) to attract foreign investment. These measures led to the modernization of numerous sectors. However, they could not prevent the public sector from coming under even greater financial pressure.

Latin American economies are now growing rapidly at a rate of around 5% per year. There are countries such as Argentina, Venezuela, Panama, and the Dominican Republic that are growing at 'Asian' rates (7-10%). This is extraordinary, and the future still looks promising. There are various reasons for this positive outlook and, unlike previous growth periods, this one does not just rely on the GDP growth.

There has been a substantial improvement in the balance of payments of most economies in the region derived from higher commodity exports, both in quantity and in price. This can be confirmed by looking at the positive trade balance, the increase in currency reserves, and the reduction of foreign debt (see Figure 38.4). As a result, South American economies are less vulnerable to external shocks. The probability of strong adjustments of their economic indicators (devaluation, inflation, salary and loans restrictions, etc.) is lower.

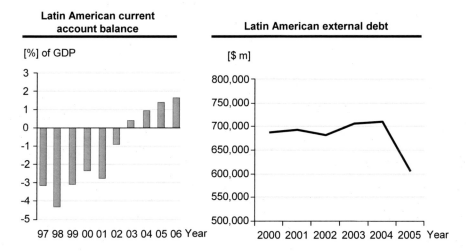

Figure 38.4: Latin American current account balance 1997-2006 and external debt 2000-2005 (International Monetary Fund, 2007; EIU; Analistas Financieros Internacionales, 2006)

South American public accounts have been reorganized owing to an increase in revenues from taxes and higher exports of raw materials (in both quantity and price) and to a more dynamic domestic economy. In countries such as Chile, the extraordinary revenues from exports have allowed the implementation of reserve funds to prevent economic crises arising from economic cycles (see Figure 38.5).

There is also a clear improvement in the access to private loans, as a result of the increasing professionalism of the banking systems of the region's major economies (mainly Brazil, Mexico, Argentina, and Chile). This situation has obvi-

ous effects both on the leverage of the private investors, and on the spending capacity of some society segments. It consolidates domestic demand (with reasonable inflation rates) and economic growth, while taking into consideration that this
domestic demand (consumption plus investment) represents approximately more
that two-thirds of GDP.

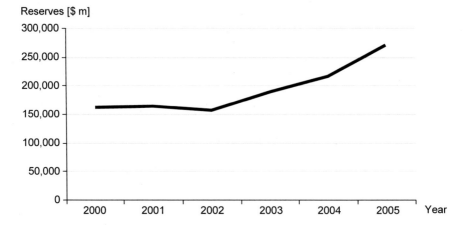

Figure 38.5: Latin American reserves (in million USD) 2000-2005 (EIU, Analistas
Financieros Internacionales, 2006)

Currently, South America could be more resistant to 'foreign' financial crises.
The improved trade deficit, increasingly diversified commerce with other regions,
and the incipient internationalization of some South American companies are new
and strong indicators of the region's new-found development.

South America faces the future in a state of economic health that would have
been unimaginable less than two decades ago. Its economic growth is sustained by
both domestic and foreign demand. Its GDP per capita has reached the $ 10,000
mark, which is higher that of the Asian emerging economies (IMF, 2007).

Despite these advances, South America still has important pockets of poverty
and an unequal income distribution. Therefore, political debate over economic
development vs improvement of social indicators has come to the fore in recent
years.

Macroeconomic and legal stability are both essential to attract new investments.
However, they are not enough. Social stability is also needed to attract investors,
posing a challenge not only to the governments of each country, but also to the
companies, which increasingly give more weight to social responsibility.

ENDESA, for example, is implementing several programs aimed at easing this
issue, which have already benefited more than 12 million people.

38.4   Regulatory Framework

As already mentioned, most of the privatization processes of the 1990s took place in a favorable regulatory framework that was changing into a more liberal system and which became one of the most advanced in force at the time.

Chile is a clear example of the countries that defended the privatization of state-owned companies from the start. In 1982, the government passed an Electricity Act setting out clear and efficient rules of the game. This Act created the Energy Superintendence Commission; a regulatory framework for distribution based on predetermined efficiency standards; and a spot market based on marginal costs and full pass-through to the final consumer.

Other countries, such as Peru, which at the beginning of the privatization processes in 1994-1998 showed several irregularities, have evolved into very stable regulatory frameworks much like Chile's.

Although there are exceptions, most South American economies have regulatory frameworks that favor foreign investment:

- Overall, the energy distribution and transmission business is under the scrutiny of different regulatory agencies that seek to ensure, in theory, a stable revenue level for companies that decide to invest in the business.
- Each country periodically reviews tariffs by estimating the value of the assets of each distribution company, and also their operating and maintenance costs.
- The regulatory bodies recognize that distribution companies have technical and nontechnical energy losses, establishing pre-agreed levels or offering incentives for investments aimed at avoiding higher energy costs. In some countries, they also take account of these investments in the tariff.
- The demand growth allows distribution companies to increase their profits through economies of scale. However, electricity tariffs are periodically reviewed to keep their margins within certain limits.
- In the generation business, the guidelines that set the price paid by the distribution companies specify the regulation criteria and the calculation procedures in great detail, giving generators and distributors the chance to become actively involved in the process.
- There are different types of investment incentives for generation in each country: Brazil, Chile, and Peru offer long-term contracts with distribution companies through public tenders, while Colombia guarantees a capacity payment and Argentina has developed a specific program (FONIMVEMEM) based on the investment of part of the earnings made by the power plants currently in operation in the construction of combined cycle power plants.

Therefore, the main challenge electricity companies face is to at the very least reach, or preferably exceed, the predetermined returns set by the regulatory agencies.

Finally, it is very important to take into account that regulation has to constantly adapt to an ever-changing market. Every agent in the sector, through a close and proactive contact with regulatory authorities, must seek greater transparency and clearer rules, to ensure a stable regulatory framework.

38.5   Generation and Energy Mix

According to research carried out by PricewaterhouseCoopers in 2006 (PWC, 2006), security of supply tops the list of concerns of the electricity sector worldwide, being rated higher in importance than issues such as encouragement of renewable energy, increasing regulation, efficiency improvement on conventional power sources, price volatility, and emissions reduction.

The main South American countries are no exception, and they are not limiting themselves to using their own energy sources but are also actively seeking new ways to diversify their energy mix, presenting investment opportunities in hydroelectric generation, but also in generation with natural gas, coal, nonconventional renewables, etc.

ENDESA is the leading generation company in Argentina, Chile, Colombia, and Peru and one of the main private generation companies in Brazil. With an installed generation capacity of over 14 GW, ENDESA operates diverse generation technologies, including natural gas combined cycles, hydroelectric, fuel oil, and coal power plants, and wind farms. ENDESA has one of the most renewable generation mixes and the lowest marginal cost in the region (60% of its generation output comes from hydroelectric power plants). It also owns a 2,100 MW interconnection line between Brazil and Argentina.

38.5.1   Hydroelectric Power

Latin America's hydroelectric generation potential is one of the strengths it can rely upon when faced with the strong growth in demand expected over the coming years. Besides the obvious advantages associated with this kind of generation (renewable and with limited environmental impact), it is also more reliable than others because it does not depend on external factors such as political or economical issues, which have a very strong influence on fossil fuel-dependent power sources.

Hydroelectric power generation represents 67% of the energy output in Central and South America; comparison with the world average of 17% illustrates how important this power source is for the region (see Figure 38.6).

In addition, countries such as Brazil, Chile, and Colombia, which still have abundant unexploited hydrological resources, offer interesting investment opportunities for the future. This applies in the case of HidroAysén in Chile, a joint ENDESA and Colbún project designed to meet the energy demand in Chile using its hydroelectricity potential (see Box 38.2).

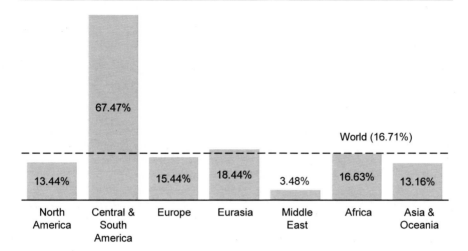

Figure 38.6: Hydroelectricity as share of total electricity consumption 2005 (EIA, 2005)

Box 38.2: HidroAysén

In Chile, the demand for energy is expected to grow at an annual rate of more than 6% in 2008-2010, i.e. it will almost double in a decade and more than triple in 20 years.

HidroAysén, with a capacity of 2,750 MW and an estimated investment of more than $ 2.5 billion, is key to guaranteeing the country's security of supply in the medium and long term. Its future location in the South of Chile (on the Baker and Pascua rivers) will have the biggest flow rates during the periods when the Interconnected Central System (which supplies 90% of Chile's population) may face low hydroelectricity production rates. Therefore, HidroAysén will make a considerable contribution to Chile's independence in terms of power independence and system reliability.

The project will flood a total of 5,910 hectares, 1,900 of which are already flooded by the two rivers' basins. Therefore, only 4,010 hectares will be artificially flooded, resulting in one of the highest energy generation-to-flooded area ratios in the world.

Initial plans contemplated a flooded area of 9,300 hectares. This significant reduction will help to protect an environment of extraordinary ecological value.

HidroAysén and its shareholders (ENDESA owns 51% of the company) are aware that sustainability is essential for any type of economic endeavor if it is to stand the test of time. Consequently, they will develop this project with due consideration for protection of the local flora and fauna, minimizing the number of relocations and prevention of any adverse influence on glaciers. At the same time, they will protect the region's agricultural and tourist industries.

Finally, it is important to point out that this project will also improve the local economy and will create more than 4,000 jobs.

38.5.2 Natural Gas

Natural gas is a much more attractive choice than its most common alternative, diesel fuel. It offers a competitive, stable, and safe fuel supply for combined cycle power plants, while fully respecting the environmental regulations.

One of the most relevant issues in the South American electricity sector is the current natural gas supply crisis. The region's important resources are not being optimized. The reasons include lack of political will, lack of transport infrastructures, and inefficient price-setting mechanisms that reduce the attractiveness of investing in the exploration of reservoirs and production. Therefore, some countries are looking for a liquefied natural gas (LNG) infrastructure even though it involves higher costs.

This leads to opportunities that did not exist even a few years ago. Owing to the uneven distribution of natural gas in the region, South America is undergoing dramatic shifts in the energy market that have led to the development of several natural gas-processing projects. For example, Peru, a country that has recently discovered new reserves of this commodity, is building a liquefying plant for exportation, while Chile, Brazil, Uruguay, and Argentina are doing the opposite: installing regasification facilities (see Box 38.3).

> #### Box 38.3: Liquefied natural gas projects in Chile, Brazil, Uruguay, Argentina, and Peru
>
> The Chilean government has given strong backing for LNG regasification projects, given the precarious situation of the Argentinean gas supply (which prior to 2004 covered 80% of Chile's natural gas needs) and the significant infrastructure developed to generate power with this fuel in recent years. There are now two LNG regasification projects in this country: GNL Quintero, in which our subsidiary Endesa Chile, is involved, and GNL Mejillones.
>
> The regasification plant GNL Quintero, a joint project of Endesa Chile, Metrogas Inc. (main natural gas distribution company in Chile), Enap (Chilean national oil company), and British Gas, will be operational in mid-2009 with an initial capacity of 4.7 million cubic meters per day rising to 9.5 million cubic meters per day by mid 2010. Located at Quintero bay, it will require an estimated investment of $ 950 million and provide natural gas to supply both the electricity industry (combined cycle gas turbines) and gas distribution companies in several metropolitan areas, including Santiago de Chile. In addition, GNL Quintero's natural gas will be used as a power source at oil refineries.

One advantage of using natural gas as the primary energy source in Santiago is that it causes much less pollution than the alternative fossil fuels, which the pollution makes unsustainable in some cases.

The Chilean government's support for generation using this fuel resulted in the Ley Corta II Act of 2005, which allows generation companies to sign contracts with distribution companies at prices that allow them to recover the costs associated with this technology. At the same time, they promote the development of new technologies to diversify energy mix, reducing the risk associated with relying on just a few energy sources.

GNL Mejillones, a joint project of the Chilean copper company Codelco and Suez Energy International in the north of the country, will start construction in March 2008. The plant will require an estimated investment of $ 500 million and will start operation in 2010-2012, when it will be able to process 5.5 million cubic meters per day.

Brazil will start importing LNG by 2009, through two regasification plants that will process a total of 20 million cubic meters per day. Petrobrás, the Brazilian state oil company, is building one in the State of Ceará (northeast of the country) with a capacity of 6 million cubic meters per day and another one close to Río de Janeiro, which will process 14 million cubic meters per day. The total estimated investment for these two projects is $ 1.35 billion.

Argentina and Uruguay are jointly developing a regasification project that will supply Uruguay and Buenos Aires and its surrounding area. The project will start by producing 10 million cubic meters per day, progressively increasing production to 25 million cubic meters per day. The total amount that will be invested in the project is estimated at $ 1.5 billion.

On the other hand, there are interesting opportunities in countries with significant reserves of natural gas. Peru is building a plant to liquefy natural gas in the south of the country. The new plant will be operational by 2009 and will be part of a project named Camisea II, which includes a 408 km gas pipeline, improvements to existing plants, and a marine gas terminal (from where the gas will be loaded onto ships for export). The liquefaction plant will produce almost 18 million cubic meters per day and will require an estimated investment of $ 1.1 billion.

The Camisea gas will enable the country to produce electricity at very competitive prices. ENDESA has already installed the country's first combined cycle gas power plant, and other players are currently building similar power plants to take advantage of this resource.

38.5.3 Coal Power Plants

The need for diversified competitive portfolios is leading to urgent development of coal power plants to meet rising energy demand.

Chile is an example to highlight, given the difficult situation of the Argentinean natural gas supply. In this country, ENDESA is developing a project to build a coal power plant adjacent to its Bocamina plant, which currently has an installed capacity of 128 MW. Bocamina II will be operational by 2010, with an installed capacity of 370 MW and an estimated investment of roughly $ 500 million. It will cover an area of 4 hectares next to the pre-existing facilities that were already owned by Endesa Chile and will use the same infrastructure as Bocamina, minimizing the environmental impact.

38.5.4 Nonconventional Renewable Energy

Notwithstanding Latin America's huge potential for nonconventional renewable resources, the projects currently developed in this area are scarce. The estimated nonconventional renewable energy potential in the region for the year 2010 is around 10,000 MW, only 5% of which was operative in 2004 (CNE, 2007).

The reason why these projects are so limited is lack of incentive, in the form of a fair return on the significant investment levels required to develop them. Also, there are still huge potential operational difficulties, such as the low installed capacity (and therefore production) and problems in transferring the energy to the electricity grid.

Latin American countries present important nonconventional renewable generation regulatory framework differences that will favor those countries that implement rules to promote the development of these technologies, attracting investments from countries that need to comply with the Kyoto Protocol and their companies.

Most South American countries have implemented policies with such a goal, but with limited incentives. For example, Brazil launched the PROINFA program, which offers 20-year-long contracts through public tenders and guaranteed connection to the power grid. Chile is discussing a law to foster the development of nonconventional renewable energies. However, even in these countries, and even more so in the others, there are still issues pending around fostering the development of these technologies.

ENDESA ECO (a company 100% owned by Endesa Chile to develop nonconventional renewable energies) installed the first wind farm supplying the Chilean Interconnected Central System (see Box 38.4).

Box 38.4: Canela wind farm

Inaugurated in December 2007, Canela has an installed capacity of 18.5 MW from 11 wind turbines that produce 1.65 MW each. The total amount invested in this wind farm was $ 44 million.

With this type of project, ENDESA aims to increasingly diversify its energy mix so as to better fulfill its commitment to providing the best electricity service in Latin America.

38.6 The Distribution Business

The distribution business in South America is in dire need of investment owing to the sharp rise in demand and the need to reduce electricity losses and improve the reliability of the network.

As mentioned above, since ENDESA began operating in the region it has transferred its best practices to the companies it has acquired, promoting improvements in energy efficiency and productivity, sale of nonessential assets, financial integration, and cost reduction. This process was complex, as the six distribution companies ENDESA currently controls operate in diverse markets.

To add to the different economic and social realities, from a legal standpoint each country has different political, administrative, labor, and institutional aspects. We have already mentioned the existing regulatory frameworks in the area, and the various degrees of liberalism and stability they have, along with the different forms of remuneration schemes. Other issues that may interfere are, from an economic and financial perspective, the different currencies and tax systems and the almost nonexistent mobility of workers from one country to another.

The above-mentioned diversity provides valuable opportunities for ENDESA that, through a global view of the region, make better use of the possible synergies, giving a clear competitive advantage in an ever changing business.

ENDESA distributes energy in five South American countries: Argentina, Brazil, Colombia, Chile, and Peru. The combined areas of operation in those countries total 202,833 square kilometers, and they were serving 11.6 million clients by the end of 2006. This means 2.2 million more clients than the 9.4 million it had in 2000 (without taking into consideration the 2.2 million clients of Edenor, sold in 2001).

Even though most of the clients of our distribution companies live in large cities (Buenos Aires, Río de Janeiro, Fortaleza, Bogotá, Santiago de Chile, and Lima), many live in highly populated neighborhoods on the outskirts of these cities and in the adjacent shantytowns. It is important to point out that many of these clients did not have electricity until ENDESA took over responsibility for the concession areas.

That is why, along with the improvements to infrastructures (power grids, converters, substations), a large part of the on average $ 430 million ENDESA invested annually in distribution in the region between 2000 and 2006 was spent on expanding the distribution network to new areas. Therefore, ENDESA made services available to a large number of people who were then able to enjoy a better quality of life than before thanks to the arrival of electricity in their homes, contributing to economic development of those areas.

ENDESA has also improved the quality of the service provided, reducing both the average duration and the number of service interruptions (from 18.7 hours in 2000 to 9.9 hours in 2006 and from 18.6 interruptions of service per megawatt on average in 2000 to 7.9 in 2006, respectively).

Our clients have also changed over the last few years: they are no longer passive individuals, but are the center point of the commercial process. ENDESA's distribution companies have focused their efforts on improving customer service in their areas of operation, reducing the time to when potential clients start receiving the service requested, the waiting time at call centers or our commercial offices and, finally, the time taken to deal with incidents.

At the same time, ENDESA has made a huge effort to ensure that its operations are carried out to comply with guidelines specifying the highest possible standards of quality and safety. As a result, by the end of 2006 all the South American distribution companies had obtained ISO 14.001 environmental management certification, and 67% of them (measured on distributed energy basis) were also awarded certification according to the strict occupational, health, and safety management system OHSAS 18.001. To put this in perspective, we should point out that in 2004 52% of the companies held an ISO 14.001 certification, while only 33% were awarded the OHSAS 18.001 certification, a clear demonstration of the efforts made in the area.

Some of the measures adopted by ENDESA's distribution companies involve implementing additional services (other than the supply of electricity) that give its clients access to new products, goods or services that they would not be able to access in any other way. Therefore, some of the distribution companies offer financial services (loans for the acquisition of home appliances); home, life, and funeral insurances, and the opportunity to pay for other products (journals, magazines, cell phones) on the electricity bill.

The future growth of the distribution business will be based on four main aspects. First, making the distribution grids profitable, building new power lines, and improving the existing ones to ensure customers are offered a good quality of service. Second, optimizing the management of these companies by reducing costs and controlling electricity losses, which in some cases are still alarmingly high. Third, traditional growth is not enough and possible alternatives need to be explored, such as the sale of electricity-related products and services or attracting clients in areas operated by competitors but where clients are free to choose their supplier. Finally, assuming a leadership role in the regulatory changes and the critical aspects of the business.

38.7   Sustainability – an Unavoidable Choice

There is no doubt that concern about environmental issues is growing in the world (in the widest sense this includes nature and society). This concern has a direct impact on the electricity industry, given its significance in the social and industrial fields.

According to most experts, Latin America's most critical sustainability issue in the near future is the need to reduce its poverty and social inequality levels. In some countries, more than half the population lives below the poverty level and GDP distribution is highly uneven. Economic improvement in these countries must have an effect on the whole of society; it is essential that living conditions improve, as otherwise economic and social tension will lead to great turmoil, which may threaten the sustainability of the political and economic advances already achieved.

ENDESA has incorporated the principles of sustainable development into its strategic goals via the development of a Strategy of Corporate Sustainability, focusing on its three aspects: environmental, social, and economic.

To illustrate this Strategy, we will use two examples focusing on its social aspects (see Box 38.5).

Box 38.5: Codensa Hogar and Luz Para Todos

'Luz Para Todos' means Light for Everybody. It is a social program promoted by the Brazilian government and aimed at reducing the energy distribution deficit among the rural population and contributing to its economic and social development, therefore improving the country's economy. To do this, it must first cover basic electricity demand in a safe and continuous manner.

ENDESA's distribution companies in Brazil have already contributed important resources to this program. Ampla, which operates in Rio de Janeiro, had invested almost $ 19 million from the start of the program in 2004-2006, resulting in more than 8,700 consumer units. The goal set for 2007 is to reach 2,500 clients in the rural areas plus an extra 1,000 in isolated villages.

In the case of Coelce, which operates in the State of Ceará, Luz Para Todos will benefit some 112,000 consumer units in 2004-2008. In 2006 some 25,000 families profited from the program, which is financed with an investment of $ 42 million, $ 36 million of this a government subsidy.

The other program that will serve as an illustration is 'Codensa Hogar', which was developed by ENDESA's distribution company Codensa, in Colombia. The aim of this program is to improve the living conditions of Codensa's low-income customers, offering solutions for their homes with favorable financing. At the same time, Codensa has designed an array of home insurances intended to protect these families. It has also developed 'Crédito Fácil', a credit program designed to facilitate the acquisition of home appliances and other basic goods.

From the start of the insurance program in 2002 up to the end of 2006, more than 170,000 clients had obtained accident, life, and home insurance. The Crédito Fácil program, which began in November 2001, had met the financing needs of over 450,000 clients, all of them from low-income families, up to 2006.

Turning now to the environmental aspect of sustainability, Latin America is still in an advantageous position to face some of the current global threats. According to the World Energy Outlook 2006, the emissions produced by the electricity sector in Latin America relative to the total emissions of the sector worldwide will rise from 1.6% at present to 2.1% in 2030. Electricity will have a significant role in this. Of the total Latin American emissions, the electricity sector will account for 19-24% in the same time period (World Energy Agency, 2006).

The estimated annual average growth rate of electricity production for Latin America between 2005 and 2030 is 3.2%. However, estimates by technology show significant differences, with a clear commitment to natural gas and renewables. The International Energy Agency estimates that energy production with coal will grow by an average of 3.6% per year; with natural gas, by 6.4%; with hydroelectric power, by 2.4%; and with renewable power, by 5.7%; while the energy output coming from the use of oil fuels will decline by an average of 2.4%.

In conclusion, this unavoidable commitment to sustainability is one of the main challenges facing the electricity companies in the region.

References

Comisión Económica para América Latina (CEPAL) & Rozas, P. 2001. European investment in South American energy companies.

Central Intelligence Agency (CIA). 2006. The world fact book. Washington: Central Intelligence Agency Publications.

CNE & Task Force MDL ARIAE. 2007. II jornada internacional sobre el sector eléctrico en el ámbito euroamericano. Madrid: Asociación Española de la Industria Eléctrica (UNESA).

Endesa. 1996. Endesa annual report 1996. Madrid: Endesa.

Endesa. 1997. Endesa annual report 1997. Madrid: Endesa.

Endesa. 1998. Endesa annual report 1998. Madrid: Endesa.

Endesa. 1999. Endesa annual report 1999. Madrid: Endesa.

Endesa. 2000. Endesa annual report 2000. Madrid: Endesa.

Endesa. 2001. Endesa annual report 2001. Madrid: Endesa.

Endesa. 2002. Endesa annual report 2002. Madrid: Endesa.

Endesa. 2003. Endesa annual report 2003. Madrid: Endesa.

Endesa. 2004. Endesa annual report 2004. Madrid: Endesa.

Endesa. 2005. Endesa annual report 2005. Madrid: Endesa.

Endesa. 2006. Endesa annual report 2006. Madrid: Endesa.

Energy Information Administration (EIA). 2005. International energy annual: 2005. Washington: EIA.

Inter-American Development Bank. 1996. Economic and social progress in Latin America. Washington: Inter-American Development Bank.

International Energy Agency (IEA). 2006. World energy outlook 2006. Paris: OECD/IEA.

International Monetary Fund (IMF). 2007. World economic outlook. Washington: IMF.

PricewaterhouseCoopers (PWC). 2006. The big leap: utilities global survey 2006. Frankfurt am Main: PWC.

39 Final Stages in the Reform of RAO UES of Russia – Future Developments in the Russian Energy Market

Anatoly Chubais[1]

Abstract

Reform of Russia's RAO UES is in its final phase. The initial basis for it was the policy of shareholders' receiving assets pro rata. Changes to Russian law then also required full ownership unbundling by 1 July 2008 and specified that from 1 January 2011 the government would no longer regulate electricity tariffs (this does not yet apply to domestic tariffs). The way management of the power industry in Russia will be configured after the reorganization is thus enshrined in law; the structural changes and market creation measures required for implementation of the reform are discussed.

Keywords: liberalization, financing, market creation

---

[1] Anatoly Chubais is Chief Executive Officer at RAO UES of Russia, Russia.

A. Bausch and B. Schwenker (eds.), *Handbook Utility Management,*
DOI: 10.1007/978-3-540-79349-6_39, © Springer-Verlag Berlin Heidelberg 2009

39.1 Introduction

Today RAO UES of Russia, which is one of the world's largest energy holding companies, accounting for 70% of the energy production and one-third of the heat supply in Russia, is in the final phase of reform.

The reform concept was developed in 1998, and the practical implementation phase was launched in 2003, when six federal laws governing transformations in Russia's electric power industry came into force. The essence of the reform is the unbundling of Russia's electric power sector into monopolistic and competitive businesses and the creation of a liberalized electricity market.

In 2007, two critical final decisions were adopted (see Figure 39.1). One of these was the extraordinary meeting of shareholders that approved the final reorganization of RAO UES: it provides for the shareholders to receive assets on a pro rata basis as a result of the reorganization. This very principle was the initial basis of the reform.

The second event was the adoption of amendments to the Russian laws on the electric power industry that set a number of fundamental standards. The first standard was that the final date of RAO UES's existence was to be 1 July 2008. From that day onward, full ownership unbundling of competitive and monopolistic sectors has been ensured.

The second standard is that as from 1 January 2011, the government will no longer regulate electricity tariffs; so far, this does not apply to household tariffs. This crucial standard is coordinated with the government's decision on step-by-step market liberalization, which started on 1 September 2006 and will be complete by the beginning of 2011. Market liberalization is now guaranteed not only by government resolution but also by the statutory provision signed by the President of Russia.

Another standard lays down the principles for managing the power industry when RAO UES ceases to function. It is based on two branches. One branch is governmental, and the other is self regulated and market based.

39.2 Progress

The task of creating a new governmental model for managing the reformed power industry in a new environment will be accomplished by the Russian Energy Agency. The self-governing branch is represented by the Non-profit Organization Market Council. The Non-profit Partnership Trading System Administrator (ATS), the existing trading site of the electricity market, will become its subsidiary. The Market Council will be made up of suppliers' and customers' agents.

Consequently, the entire configuration of the power industry management after the reorganization of RAO UES has been laid down and is enshrined in the law.

In the implementation of these decisions, RAO UES of Russia specifies two ways in which the company's transformations will be completed: the first is through structural changes and the second is through market creation.

Figure 39.1: Two final chords of the reform

As far as structural transformations and the basic idea of unbundling of monopolistic and competitive sectors are concerned, the work can be considered complete. Six thermal wholesale generation companies (OGKs) and 14 territorial generation companies (TGKs), a hydro generation wholesale company (HydroOGK) and INTER RAO UES were established in the competitive sector. These generation assets will enter the competitive market in strict conformity with the original reform plan (see Figure 39.2).

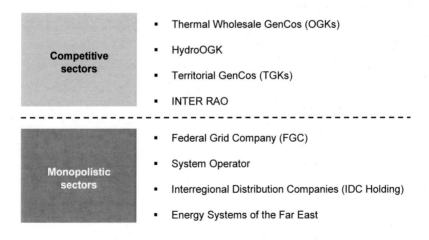

Figure 39.2: Competitive and monopolistic sectors: target structure companies

The following monopolistic businesses have been established: the Federal Grid Company (FGC), which is responsible for the reliability of the Unified National Power Grid; the System Operator, responsible for dispatch; and the IDC Holding Company and Energy Systems of the East, an entity that consolidates the assets of the power systems of the Far East of Russia.

For a long time after we started the reform of RAO UES, we were involved in the same discussions as our EU colleagues are having now. These concern the most reasonable model for unbundling of the monopolistic and competitive sectors. The phases of this unbundling are well known and include functional, legal, and ownership unbundling. If the whole process is depicted as a toaster making hot bread (see Figure 39.3), the electricity industry of Europe in general is in the second phase.

This is accompanied by a discussion on whether ownership unbundling down to the deepest level is acceptable. RAO UES has already left this discussion behind. We took the way of full ownership unbundling, including unbundling into transmission and distribution networks and a system operator. Anything else is impossible in the Russian environment if there is a true intention to ensure competition in generation and to provide equal access to grids.

It should be noted that Russia and Europe take different approaches to the process of unbundling. Europe is discussing various alternative solutions under EU directives. If a decision on full ownership unbundling is adopted, the time will come when the next step has to be taken: each EU member state will have to ensure that its national laws comply with this decision. RAO UES of Russia took a different approach: the company conducted full de facto unbundling and it was only then enshrined in the law.

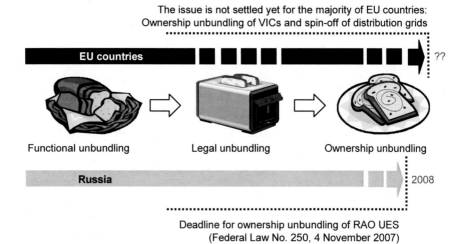

Figure 39.3: Power sector: functional, legal and ownership unbundling

Time will show which of the two approaches is more effective. It is my firm conviction that no other approach would have worked in Russia, although realistically weighted estimates will not be possible until some 10 years from now.

39.3   Finance

Simultaneously with the structural transformations, RAO UES of Russia has launched the process of attracting large-scale private investment (see Figure 39.4). In 2007, RAO UES of Russia raised € 17.5 billion as a result of share placement and the sale of shares in generation companies in the tendering process. These funds obtained from both Russian and foreign private investments have already been deposited in the accounts of generating companies.

The sale process will continue in 2008. During this year, the company intends to raise another € 9.3 billion.

For RAO UES of Russia, whether sales are made certainly depends on the real situation in the global financial markets. We do not intend to sell assets at a price lower than their real value if the market situation is unfavorable.

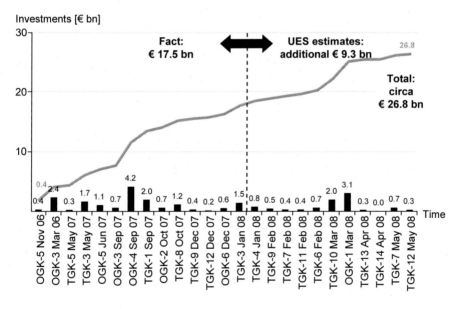

Figure 39.4: From competitive share placements and sales to strategic investors

It should be noted that despite all evident difficulties in the global financial markets, the sector of sales to strategic investors looks fairly optimistic. Constant negotiations with potential investors convince me that this is true. Competition among strategic investors for the Russian power industry remains permanently high.

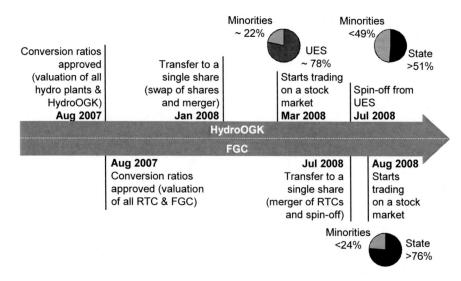

Figure 39.5: HydroOGK and FGC – consolidation timeline

At the same time, the consolidation of assets of the companies over which the government will retain control continues. These include HydroOGK and FGC. On July 1, 2008, FGC will become fully consolidated, convert to a single share, and then enter the stock market. HydroOGK will undergo consolidation and enters the stock market in February (see Figure 39.5).

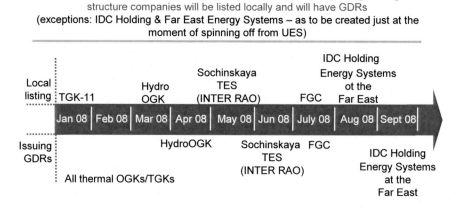

Figure 39.6: Liquidity guarantees

It is extremely important to ensure the liquidity of shares in special purpose companies (see Figure 39.6). All companies have liquidity support programs. By the date of allocation of shares in special purpose companies among the shareholders of RAO UES of Russia, the shares in all special purpose companies will be trading on the Russian stock markets and have global deposit receipt (GDR) programs. The only exceptions will be IDC Holding Company and Energy Systems of the East. They will enter the market and launch their GDR program in July/August 2008.

39.4   Market Creation

An equally important direction of the reform, apart from the structural reorganization of RAO UES of Russia, is market creation. Six months of operation of the Russian competitive wholesale market met our expectations. The Russian wholesale electricity market is one of the world's most advanced, state-of-the-art, and efficient electricity markets. It responds flexibly to supply and demand fluctuations, which is easy to show. Figure 39.7a displays intra-day market parameters: in any 24-hour period it demonstrates night decline in demand and morning and evening demand peaks, as described in all classic textbooks. Figure 39.7b shows a monthly market chart, in which weekdays, with a relatively high price, alternate with weekends, with a relatively low price. These are classic charts.

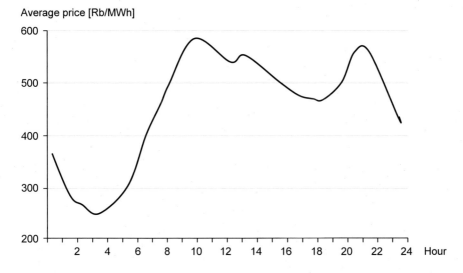

Figure 39.7a: Average prices (Europe, Urals, and Siberia), [Rb/MWh] per day (Administrator of Trade System)

Figure 39.7c does not show a classic chart. This is because the 2006/07 winter was very warm. Accordingly, winter peak prices were also 'canceled'. Instead, from July to September 2007 prices in the market unexpectedly peaked. Having analyzed the situation, we understood why. July, August and September are the period of the most intense repair operations in the power system; in an environment of excessive electricity demand the suspension of any transmission line and any power unit for repair inevitably leads to price rises in the market. It should be noted that prices were lower in September than in August; while in October they were lower than in September. We were thus convinced that the market had responded to the situation in a well-thought-out way, and even wisely, so to speak.

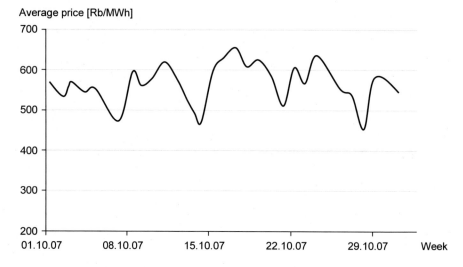

Figure 39.7b: Average prices (Europe, Urals, and Siberia), [Rb/MWh] per week and month (Administrator of Trade System)

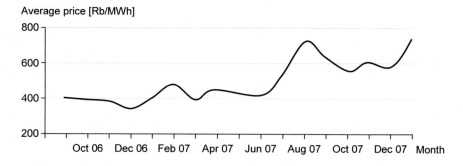

Figure 39.7c: Average prices (Europe, Urals, and Siberia), [Rb/MWh] per year (Administrator of Trade System)

Therefore, to date, the electricity market has demonstrated its absolute efficiency, and future plans are widely known. Figure 39.8 shows the chart of both mandatory (rate was approved by the government) and voluntary market liberalization. Notably, as we can see, the actual liberalization rates are higher than the planned rates: real liberalization has already reached 20% of the total market size and the share is still growing.

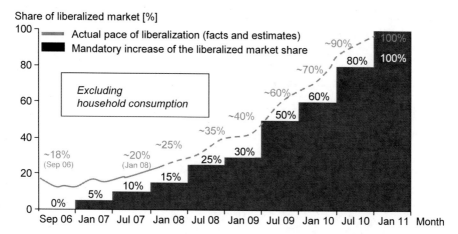

Note: All new capacity and consumption commissioned after 2007 go to the free market

Figure 39.8: Pace of liberalization: government's plan and actual progress

In addition, Russia is launching a capacity market (see Figure 39.9). This is a very important task, which ensures the necessary capacity commissioning rates. In parallel, a competitive ancillary service market is being created.

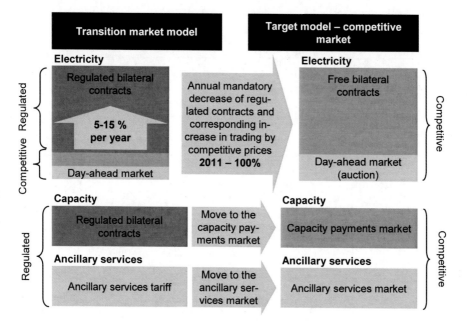

Figure 39.9: Power market model electricity, capacity and ancillary services markets

All market-related tasks are aimed at accomplishing one super-task called "attracting investments in the electric power industry". It is common knowledge that the electricity demand situation is very challenging (see Figure 39.10). In a certain sense, the whole power industry reform was implemented to ensure investment inflow and meet growing electricity demand.

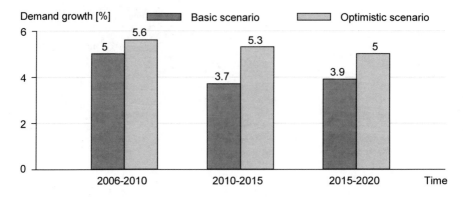

Figure 39.10: Electricity demand growth outlook: mid-term and long-term view (Ministry of Industry and Energy; UES estimates)

39.5 Commissioning Energy

	2006	2007	2008	2009	2010	2006-2010
Thermal generation OGKs, TGKs, RAO UES [MW]	1,186	1,545	2,050	5,788	14,364	24,934
Hydro OGK [MW]	67	690	420	1,224	1,612	4,013
Total commissioning [MW]	1,253	2,235	2,470	7,089	15,919	28,947

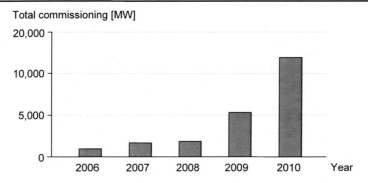

Figure 39.11: 2006-2010 RAO UES capacity commissioning program

Figure 39.11 shows that in 2010 we will have to commission about 16,000 MW of generating capacity. It is clear that we shall not be able to commission 16,000 MW in 2010 without having a feasibility study, completed engineering documentation, engineer, procure and construct (EPC) contracts with appropriate financial guarantees, etc. available today.

Most of our projects are now in this very stage. Construction under most large projects of 100 MW or higher is under way in these very days.

This amount of capacity to be commissioned needs to be ensured by the investment program, which is estimated from 2006 to 2010 at approximately $ 92.3 billion (see Figure 39.12).

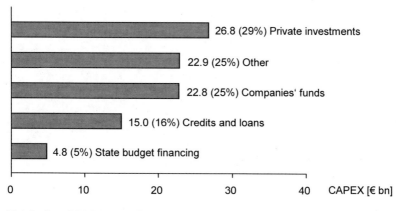

Total: circa € 92.3 bn (private investments: circa € 26.8 bn)

Figure 39.12: CAPEX 2006-2010 – over 92 bn Euro – sources of financing

Direct private investments are the basic source within the program. It is private investment that guarantees the success of the reforms being implemented. The total amount of direct private investments it is hoped to attract by 2010 is $ 26.8 billion. More than half this amount has already been deposited in the accounts of energy companies. The remaining funds will be raised in the next 6 months. Other sources of finance are the equity of companies, credits and loans, budget investments, etc.

All these transformations mean that Russia is currently building a new market-based energy sector with new opportunities and new investors.

Part VIII:
Special Issues in Utility Management

40 Creating Competitive Advantages Through Co-operations Between Municipal Utility Companies

Oliver Runte[1]

Abstract

This chapter deals with the options available for increasing the competitiveness of municipal utility companies by means of co-operation at various stages of the value chain. In the course of this, the fields of electricity generation and exploration and trading of gas, electricity and gas supply network systems in particular are examined, as are distribution matters, as they offer municipal utility companies chances to optimise their cost structure and to develop new profit potentials. For the future, the co-operation between municipal utility companies seems inevitable if they are to continue to exist as independent players on the German energy market as its general conditions change.

Keywords: municipal utility companies, competitiveness, co-operation

[1] Dr. Oliver Runte is Executive Director of citiworks AG, Germany.

A. Bausch and B. Schwenker (eds.), *Handbook Utility Management,*
DOI: 10.1007/978-3-540-79349-6_40, © Springer-Verlag Berlin Heidelberg 2009

40.1   Introduction

In the course of the past 3 years, the energy environment has changed dramatically for municipal utility companies. At the beginning of the electricity market's liberalisation, municipal utility companies actually managed to strengthen their competitive position by taking advantage of more favourable conditions in electricity procurement and stable earnings from the supply network system sector. Meanwhile, however, we have to say that price development on the wholesale markets and increasing competition in the key account segment, but most of all in the standard customer segment, have combined to challenge the competitive capacity of small and medium-sized municipal utility companies. In addition, the results of regulatory interventions in the field of power grids and gas distribution systems are causing drastic reductions of profits from the grid system.

Margins predominantly generated in the supply system sector have increasingly shifted into the fields of electricity generation and exploration and/or importation of gas, which are stages in the value added process that are not as yet accessible to municipal utility companies.

This chapter examines to what extent the profitability, and thus the independence, of municipal utility companies can be maintained in the changing general conditions by means of co-operation with other municipal utility companies and regional suppliers at various stages of the value chain. To this end, the options and chances of co-operation for municipal utility companies in the fields of electricity generation, exploration and trading with gas, power grids, and gas distribution systems and distribution to key accounts and standard customers are examined.

40.2   Development of New Profit Potentials
by Entering the Market of Electricity Generation, and
Importation, Production and Trading of Gas

40.2.1   Electricity Generation

As the liberalisation of the German electricity market began, municipal utility companies concentrated above all on optimising their electricity procurement through improved portfolio management by exploiting the chances offered by the price developments on wholesale markets. During this period, a number of co-operations in electricity trading were established, which in addition to providing access to the over-the-counter (OTC) market and to European Energy Exchange (EEX) took over significant parts of the portfolio management services for the participating municipal utility companies.

During the past years, the creation of oligopolies and a shortage of production capacities have led to significant price increases on the wholesale electricity markets (see Figure 40.1).

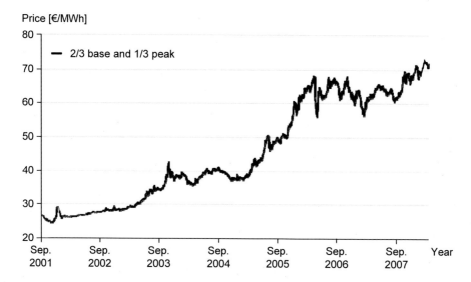

Figure 40.1: Development of wholesale prices Germany (EEX settlement)

A lasting improvement in procurement costs, which are a basic key factor in securing competitiveness, can only be guaranteed through long-term portfolio diversification.

Investments in Thermal Generating Plants

Greater investment in the development of companies' physical own power plant output capacities is a significant alternative to long-term contracts for portfolio optimisation. Here, in addition to the development of renewable energies, investment in thermal generating plants is especially to the fore. These generating plants, which are usually run on fossil fuels (lignite, anthracite, gas), typically reach an output of 800-1100 MW at overall investment costs in the range of € 400 million to € 1.2 billion. Mainly as a consequence of its capital intensity, this field has been restricted so far to the four affiliated companies that control the market in Germany.

To allow their market entry at this stage of the value added process and to allocate the risks arising out of the high investment costs in a better manner, various German municipal utility companies have joined together in generating co-operations. As examples, we can name Trianel, Südweststrom and the Gekko[2] task group, with their generating plant projects in Hürth, Lünen, Krefeld (Trianel) and Brunsbüttel (Südweststrom). There are now more than 50 municipalities in Germany that are involved in power plant projects with installed capacity in excess of 400 MW.

---

[2] Gekko is the name of a joint venture by 26 municipal utility companies with RWE Power to build a new hard coal power plant.

As the specific know-how required for the planning and building of generating plant projects will often not be available within a co-operation itself, some projects are also accomplished in co-operation with a major domestic affiliated company or an affiliated company from abroad. In such a case, the part of the municipal utility companies' co-operation is limited to the financing and representation of interests to the generating plant companies developing the project respectively.

Once the plant is in operation, such services as allocating the physical supply to the partners (schedule management), balancing of planned cancellations or unplanned breakdowns of the generating plant and optimising the marketing of the generating plant's volume on wholesale markets and stock markets are performed by the joint co-operation company.

Risks of Generating Plant Construction

However, it must be borne in mind that investing in conventional generating plants, besides offering a chance to optimise procurement costs, also involves significant risks for the participating municipal utility companies. Nowadays, price developments on the wholesale electricity markets both for carbon dioxide certificates and for primary energies (e.g. coal or natural gas) are difficult to predict. Moreover, the risks of generation plant breakdowns over the economic life-time have to be considered. Therefore, it cannot be ruled out that, in future times, conventional generating plants might not yield their variable and capital costs in the course of their entire life-time. Thus, it is of significant importance for generating plant co-operations, among other matters, to minimise the risks as far as possible by diversifying the generating portfolio according to primary energy sources and by a long-term hedging strategy for the generating capacity.

40.2.2   Importation, Production and Trading of Gas

Although the EU Gas Directive that became effective in 1998, like the corresponding EU Directive on Electricity, had provided the basics necessary for the gas market's liberalisation in good time, until recently the gas market in Germany was characterised by complicated network access regulations, lacking regulations on access to storage facilities, fragmentation into numerous market areas and inadequate access to liquid hubs or trading spots.

However, new tendencies are developing that will exert a significant influence on the German gas market in the future.

Price Fixing on a Liberalised Gas Market

The price fixing at relevant trading spots such as the Title Transfer Facility (TTF) in the Netherlands may be increasingly trend setting for gas supply contracts in Germany. Should the situation develop in a similar way to that in Great Britain, where gas prices are geared to the quotations on spot markets and derivatives markets, this might result, in the medium term, in the uncoupling of gas prices from the relevant oil quotations.

Especially in the municipal gas sector, the linking of prices to the price of heating oil has led to significant price increases over the past 2 years.

Whether and to what extent these gas price increases can be passed on to end customers (distributors, industrial customers, etc.) in future times is not predictable at the moment, as these price adjustment mechanisms might become increasingly obsolete in the course of the gas market's further opening.

Restructuring of Gas Procurement

Another developing tendency is that in addition to the re-orientation in price-fixing, there will be a general reduction of contract periods, resulting in the necessity for short-term gas procurement. Turning away from today's full service supply contracts, however, will also mean that, as in the electricity market, structuring the gas portfolio and active gas trading for portfolio optimisation will be necessary.

Optimisation of the Gas Portfolio by Means of Access to Gas Importation

Alongside the simplifications of access to the grid system (reduction in the numbers of market areas, two-contracts model and suchlike), development on the gas market is accelerated by two main factors:

(1) The voluntary agreement of E.ON Ruhrgas – though forced by German Federal Cartel Office – to terminate its long-term supply contracts as of 1 October 2008; and
(2) The market entry of newcomers who target the German market partly from foreign countries (e.g. the UK, France, the Netherlands), from other markets (e.g. banks) or other subsegments (e.g. electricity, oil).

Therefore, municipal utility companies are already being offered new options for gas procurement and for optimising their delivery costs. In addition to structuring their own gas portfolio and to the option of procurement at a virtual trading spot, as against the city- and regio-gate contracts prevailing in the past, municipal utility companies now also enjoy the possibility of direct gas procurement from importers or producers of gas, thus avoiding the classic gas supply chain of the grid gas companies presently controlling the market in Germany. In order to obtain effective access to gas upstream stages in the value chain, municipal utility companies need to co-operate and to bundle their gas volumes for procurement.

Foundation of Gas Purchase Co-operations

In addition to the established communal procurement co-operations such as Bayerngas or Gasunion, new co-operations of municipal utility companies in the form of gas purchase co-operations are now being set up in Germany. These gas purchase co-operations aim at the development of a diversified gas procurement portfolio consisting of short-term, medium-term and long-term supply contracts in the course of a transitional period of 2-3 years. The long-term objective is to perform an own portfolio structuring, depending on the development of the market or on market liquidity. The co-operation are also intended to offer services related to the gas industry. Among these, especially gas trading at liquid spots, structured procurement, portfolio management, risk management, and accounting grid management aimed at minimising the balancing energy required are planned and need to be mentioned.

Quality of the Gas Forecast as a Significant Criterion of Success

A decisive factor in the success of future gas procurement is accurate knowledge of the demand for gas for the forecast period. This does not mean only the volumes concerned, but also detailed knowledge of the hourly output value throughout a complete year of gas supply.

As this gas industry-related service, in addition to the necessary IT infrastructure, requires specialised know-how, it may be expected that it will be covered by gas purchase co-operations or external service providers in the future. This would mean the development of structures within the gas industry that are similar to those already in place in the electricity segment. This makes it seem more than likely that these two branches will combine at some later point.

40.3   Co-operation in the Field of Supply Network Systems as an Answer to Cost Pressure and Unbundling

Since 2005, developments in the field of supply network systems within the German energy industry have been influenced above all by regulatory interventions. The legal framework was provided by the Energy Economy Law (EnWG), which became effective in 2005. This law deals with informational, accounting, legal and ownership unbundling of the electricity and gas supply network systems from the other activities of the integrated energy supplier. In addition, the Federal Network Agency (former Regulatory Authority for Telecommunications and Posts) is named as the competent authority for the control of access and for determination of the fees payable for the use of power grids and gas distribution systems.

Legal Unbundling

The legal separation of the supply network systems from distribution and procurement, the so-called legal unbundling, was provided for by the EnWG of 2005. The operators of distribution systems for electricity and gas were obligated to outsource their operation of such systems into a legally independent company by 1 July 2007. Excluded from this obligation were municipal utility companies with fewer than 100,000 electricity and gas customers (de minimis rule). A legal spin-off from the (electricity) transmission grid was achieved by 1 July 2006.

Pursuant to the law, the legally independent company has to comply with minimum requirements, the main one of these being the responsibility for operation of the supply system.

Incentive-based Regulation

The central element of the new EnWG is the mandate to the Federal Network Agency to develop a draft incentive-based regulation for the Federal Government. It is meant to offer the operators of supply network systems additional incentives to lower their costs and to increase their systems' efficiency.

In the course of the first and second regulation periods, discrepancies in efficiency between the various supply system operators are to be eliminated. Subsequently, the transfer to yardstick competition is to allow a situation as close as possible to actual competition in regulating the fees payable for use of the supply network systems.

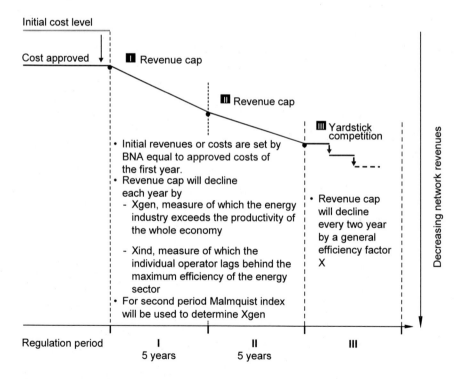

Figure 40.2: Impact of incentive regulation for German energy network operators

As a consequence, authorisation for the operators of supply network systems to charge fees will be based on the validated costs. During the first regulation period, approved fees were generally 10-30% lower than the fees applied before, resulting in a significant reduction of the profit made from the supply network systems (see Figure 40.2).

Municipal utility companies now fear for their competitive capacity, as a stand-alone collapse of profit is difficult to realise by means of supply system-related cost cutting.

Municipal Utility Companies' Co-operations in the Field of Supply Network Systems

Owing to the cost pressure resulting from the incentive-based regulation and to the legal requirements, municipal utility companies feel the need to redirect their supply network systems in a strategic manner. Municipal utility companies under such obligations transferred their distribution systems to legally independent companies before 1 July 2007. Generally, the structure of these companies will allow the participation of further, mostly regional, partners from the power or water industries or of further supply system companies. This also, and especially, applies to those municipal utility companies that are not under any obligation to transfer their supply system operation to a legally independent company.

As the legislator merely arranged for minimum functional requirements of the distribution system operator, different forms of distribution system operators have developed. A significant distinctive feature of so-called larger versus smaller distribution system companies is the offering of additional service functions, such as service and maintenance of the distribution systems, which are contributed to the companies in addition. Moreover, the owners of the systems are allowed to choose from the options of contributing their supply network systems to the new company directly by means of a transfer or making the systems available to the company by way of leasing (see Figure 40.3).

Co-operations of municipal utility companies in the field of distribution systems will often, besides mere service relationships, be constituted as joint distribution system companies. The joint company's objective is to increase the system's cost efficiency. Often, the co-operation will encompass:

- Joint regulation management, equal opportunity;
- Company for operating the distribution system as a platform for increasing efficiency (bundling of operational premises within the region, control room, etc.);
- Standardisation of maintenance resources (technical purchase, provision of spare parts, etc.);
- Joint planning for system development.

Co-operation is especially important both in functional system operation and in technical purchase. The latter often allows municipal utility companies to achieve savings of up to 30% through bundling their procurement volumes, but requires standardisation of maintenance resources as far as possible. Savings in functional system operation especially will lead to reduced personnel costs, e.g. through the combination of individual premises. Moreover, there are numerous savings opportunities on a case-to-case basis, such as the joint use of special vehicles and joint operation of the system control room.

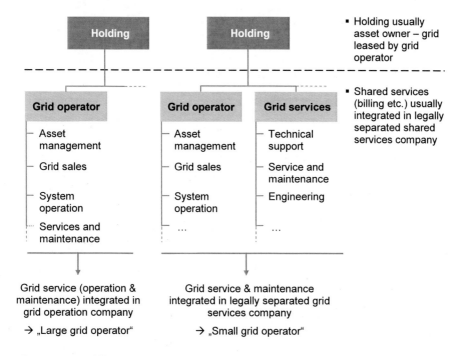

Figure 40.3: Different organisational forms of grid operators

In spite of numerous existing examples, co-operation in the field of distribution systems is still in its infancy today. For one thing, efficiencies have been only incompletely realised so far, and for another, talks between regional power suppliers and system operators on further co-operation have partly failed for now. In addition, discussion on the strategic importance of distribution systems for municipal utility companies has only just started, so that the coming years can be expected to bring far-reaching modifications in the distribution system field of municipal utility companies; these modifications will range from wider co-operation to the sale of distribution systems.

40.4 Nationwide Distribution to Standard Customers to Compensate for Customer Losses and Development of further Market Potential

Right from the beginning of liberalisation, municipal utility companies' co-operation focused on the distribution to industrial and batch customers. The necessity to professionalise the interface between procurement and distribution, the in-

creased requirements for distribution products (especially those close to trade) and
the nationwide handling of batch customers were only a few motivations for the
founding of co-operation; examples are Enetko, an affiliated company of Trianel,
and citiworks AG, an affiliated company of the Stadtwerke München, HEAG Süd-
hessische Energie AG and Stadtwerke Mainz.

Nationwide Competition in the Standard Customer Segment

In contrast to the industrial customer or batch customer segment, the standard customer segment, all in all, showed only a small number of customers switching to
another energy supplier throughout the years from 1998 to 2005. The market was
dominated by regional brands, which often held far more than 90% of the market
share in the region in question. The market entry of the Yello brand, which belongs to the EnBW group and has offered electricity to private customers since
1999, did not change this.

Upon the Federal Network Agency's implementation, but also as a result of political discussions about prices for electricity and gas, an increasing readiness to
switch supplier can now be noted within the standard customer segment. This development was assisted by the introduction of brands like "E wie einfach" [E how
simple] for the nationwide distribution of electricity and gas. With this brand,
E.ON, the leader in the field, gave a clear signal of a nationwide distribution offensive targeted at the standard customer segment, thus turning away from the
former strategy of the regional brands; other power suppliers, such as RWE
("eprimo"), were to follow.

This development means for municipal utility companies that for the first time
since the opening of the market in 1998, there is serious competition for the end-
customers in their own traditional distribution areas. In the long run, the measures
applied so far for maintaining and developing customer relationships will not be
able to prevent the loss of customers in the traditionally supplied region.

Compensation for customer losses within the region of their own supply system
through growth in new regions is one of the challenges municipal utility companies currently have to face.

Co-operations for Nationwide Distribution of Electricity and Gas in the Standard Customer Segment

The need to compensate for customer losses in their traditional distribution regions has forced municipal utility companies for the first time to organise their
entry into supra-regional distribution. This also implies a supra-regional brand
appearance, as well as increased requirements for supply management, energy
data management and customer accounting. In order to keep a low complexity at
the beginning, customers are sought through offers on the internet, which often are
restricted to certain regions of the markets. So far, there are no plans for direct
marketing such as is already practised in areas of high population density by large
power suppliers.

All in all, we can say that supra-regional distribution in the standard customer segment is currently being specifically tested or has already been implemented by large municipal utility companies, including Enercity in Hanover and N-Ergie in Nuremberg with their joint distribution affiliate Clevergy. Further co-operations of municipal utility companies, especially from the 8KU-circle (co-operation of 8 German utility companies), are likely.

So far, the complexity and costs of a nationwide concerted distribution are dealt with by focusing on selected regions, approach customers via the internet, bundling handling-related services in a joint shared-service company (accounting, accounts receivable, management, etc.) and bundling distribution activities (marketing, product design, etc.) in a separate unit. In most cases, nationwide market coverage is planned for a later point in time.

40.5   Successful Change Management

The topic of successful management of change processes appearing in the course of implementing co-operations between municipal utility companies has received little attention so far. As frequently noted, it will not be sufficient for partners to determine the key points of their co-operation within the scope of a syndicate agreement. In fact, the existence of a concept that has been agreed on by all partners and also includes an implementation concept is required; this concept has to set out the key points of the partners' co-operation in detail.

Co-operation Strategy

The key points of the co-operation to be agreed on between the partners include, especially, the significant key points concerning strategy, which embrace the objectives and the criteria of their achievement. In addition to the strategy, the concept also has to contain clear definitions of the extent of individual tasks and the operational and organisational structure, and also to take account of the organisational adjustments required in the mother companies, which have to be performed in parallel with the implementation of the co-operation. For this purpose, suitable management systems need to be implemented within the scope of the co-operation to assist with the implementation process.

Once the strategy has been implemented, the organisation set up and the operational day-to-day business taken up, it is still important that the partners check their original objectives on a regular basis. Only those co-operations that are capable of reacting at short notice to changes in the market and are able to adjust their objectives in due time will have a long life on the market.

Internal, External Communication

The process has to be accompanied by intensive external, but most of all internal, communication. Executives need to be involved in the process of change at an early stage to safeguard the workforce's support for the co-operation's objectives right from the start. This need is not limited to the co-operation itself. As there will be frequent interfaces to the mother companies, a parallel communication is as important here as it is within the co-operation.

Personnel Recruitment

The selection of suitable personnel on a co-operation's foundation is essential to its success, but this has received little attention so far. The mother companies will often provide the permanent staff for the structural organisation. However, a systematic selection procedure is as necessary in this case as is the option of drawing on external know-how to complement expertise already within the organisation.

40.6   Summary

The changes in both the legal framework and the competitive environment in Germany have put municipal utility companies under a new pressure to act. In the past, the electricity and gas supply network systems in municipal hands especially created adequate margins for the municipal utility companies, which could compensate or even more than compensate for losses, if any, incurred by the operation of local traffic systems or swimming baths; in the course of incentive-based regulation, however, municipal utility companies have to anticipate severe loss of profits. Moreover, the increasing supra-regional competition in the standard customer segment forces the companies to think beyond the borders of their former distribution areas. All of this presents a general challenge to the economic independence of, in particular, small or medium-sized municipal utility companies in Germany and forces them into strategic redirection.

Many municipal utility companies will lack the critical size necessary to enter the upstream stages of the value added process and thus obtaining access to new profit potentials, such as electricity generation or importation and exploration of gas, but also increased efficiency in the electricity or gas supply system. In order to compensate for this disadvantage and to keep up their competitive capacity, municipal utility companies will have to increase the frequency of their co-operation with other municipal utility companies or with regional suppliers in the future. This development, which has already started in electricity trading resulting from the liberalisation of the German electricity market, will continue in other stages of the value added process. The creation of larger units by shifting services und tasks to the co-operation companies is accompanied by a part-loss of independence for the municipal utility companies. At the same time, municipal utility companies and their co-operation companies have to be ready to react to changes on the market within shorter reaction times. For this, the process of change management, cultural integration and flexibility, and also readiness to embrace change are of decisive importance.

41   Growth Options for Regional Utilities

Christoph Helle[1]

Abstract

By implementing a new strategy based on costs and price leadership in the traditional business segments, and by expanding the municipal utility network and investing in selected growth segments, MVV Energie AG has set the cornerstones to remain a successful player despite the saturated, challenging markets and the ongoing consolidation. The adaptation of the company structure and the realization of internal implementation programs as well as the tightrope walk between the various interests of different shareholders, employees and – last but not least – the customers are the biggest challenges that decision makers in regional and municipal utilities have to overcome.

Keywords: courage, change, success

---

[1] Dr. Christoph Helle is Managing Director of MVV Energie AG, Germany.

A. Bausch and B. Schwenker (eds.), *Handbook Utility Management,*
DOI: 10.1007/978-3-540-79349-6_41, © Springer-Verlag Berlin Heidelberg 2009

41.1   What Is Growth?

There is a multitude of definitions for growth. The Encyclopædia Britannica, for example, defines growth as: "the increases in cell size and number that take place during the life history of an organism" and economic growth as: "the process by which a nation's wealth increases over time".

If put into a business context, growth can be defined, as on the homepage of the MIT Sloan School of Management, as: "an approach that has enabled the company to grow substantially in size or profits or market penetration".

In most definitions we find the common denominator 'increase in' or 'increase of', which is then followed by a word such as size, number, value, or strength.

If applied to regional/municipal utilities, there are basically two possibilities: internal growth and external growth. In both cases company growth is measured in figures such as revenues and earnings, and growth is usually the objective to which managers are aspiring. Internal growth, also called organic growth, is achieved by the company's own development of projects, technology, and capital, while in most cases external growth is the result of acquisitions, joint ventures, strategic alliances, and mergers, as it is for MVV Energie AG.

Organic growth is a strategy that takes time to yield results, but it is a strategy that builds on the strengths, processes, knowledge, and experience of a company. An internal growth strategy is considered a less risky strategy, because it allows some control over the pace of growth and therefore allows for enough time to optimize the use of financial and human resources, improve processes, and replicate a functioning business model. This intense nurturing and knowledge of developing projects, the in-house creativity, and the ability to control investment costs allows for projects to be stopped, if necessary, before they reach a point of no return, which can save a significant amount of resources. A company that has a significant and successful organic growth is more likely to engage successfully in external growth, simply because it has more choices available.

External growth is generally limited by capital availability, risk aversion, and the availability of opportunities. In the case of regional and municipal utilities, municipal, regional, and sometimes also national politics can put an additional damper on external growth, and therefore regional utilities should primarily be looking to cooperate or enter on joint ventures with other regional or municipal utilities, or other wise to acquire or merge with them. One of the advantages of external growth is that joint ventures or acquisitions provide immediate cash flows. However, these strategies are generally more expensive than the others. This is not the place to enter into a lengthy discussion on the pros and cons of internal and external growth, but it is worth pointing out two factors affecting the external growth strategy: (1) the lack of available potential targets, and (2) the major challenge of external growth: the integration of acquisitions. Depending on the management's or the shareholders' willingness to take risks, then, a company can be taken down the internal or external growth strategy path. More risk-averse companies will favor the internal growth approach, while others, such as MVV Energie AG, may opt for a combination of both internal and external growth.

41.2   German Municipal and Regional Utility Sector Structure

In 1997 the Internal Electricity Market Directive came into force in the European Union. This was followed by a string of national legislation that has started a fundamental change of the European utility sector in general and the municipal utility sector in particular.

Competition only arose in the generation and the wholesale markets. Existing overcapacities meant reduced investment opportunities for new players wishing to enter the playing field and led to the dominance of the existing market participants.

In Germany these changes have led to the market dominance of E.ON (created from the merger of VIAG and VEBA in 2000) and RWE (created from the merger of RWE and VEW in 2001), two large, vertically integrated (from generation to end-customers) electric and gas utilities that also have a dominant market position in the municipal utility sector. As a by-product of the market liberalization, additional foreign players have entered the German municipal utility landscape.

Through its ownership of EnBW, EDF is one of the major municipal players, with a near-monopoly in Southwest Germany and with the drive to expand into other German regions. EnBW has been successful outside its historical service territory and has purchased a major participation in the Stadtwerke Düsseldorf. Recent activities show that EnBW's goal is to continue adding municipal utilities to its shareholdings.

Vattenfall has benefited from the German authorities' objective of adding new strong players in the utility market (acquisition of the Hamburg utility HEW in 1999) and from external circumstances, such as the exit in 2001 of the US utility Southern Energy, shareholder of the Berlin utility Bewag. In 2002, Vattenfall announced the merger of the utilities Bewag, HEW, and VEAG and the lignite company Laubag, to form Vattenfall Europe. Previously RWE and E.ON were forced to give up their assets in the former East Germany to prevent them from further dominating the German power market.

Today E.ON, RWE, Vattenfall, and EnBW generate 90% and distribute 71% of the German electricity production. This situation has become possible as a result of the vertical integration of the municipal utilities by the big players. By taking majority or minority stakes (usually with a presence on the utility's supervisory board) these companies have been able to exercise a significant influence on the utility's decision making.

In the gas sector, the concentration is not as pronounced as in the electricity sector; however, the top three gas distributors, E.ON, RWE, and EWE, control about 65% of the sales to secondary distributors and nearly 40% of the sales to end-customers.

Like the electricity industry, the German gas industry is marked by a high degree of horizontal concentration, particularly at the long-distance transportation level, along with pronounced vertical integration across various stages of the value chain. The integrative tendency within parts of the gas industry is expected to continue and even intensify, bringing about greater competitive pressure as the deregulation of the German gas market progresses.

Recent decisions by the Federal Cartel Office [Bundeskartellamt] and higher regional courts have confirmed the Bundeskartellamt's aim "to put a stop to increasing vertical concentration in the electricity sector" (Bundeskartellamt, 2007). This applies especially to E.ON and RWE. "The confirmation of its prohibitive stance by the Higher Court Decision, against which E.ON can still appeal, reinforces the Bundeskartellamt in its strategy in other merger control and abuse proceedings in which the electricity duopoly E.ON and RWE are involved" (Bundeskartellamt, 2007).

Because of the significant amount of cross-ownership of municipal utilities and regional sales companies, further vertical or horizontal expansion by E.ON and RWE into the municipal and regional utility market is seriously compromised. Because of their more regional focus, Vattenfall and EnBW, the two other major players in Germany, have not yet experienced any major limitation in their expansion as a result of decisions made by federal or regional authorities.

Today there are over 700 municipal utilities [Stadtwerke], with about 100 mainly small- to medium-sized companies estimated to be still in 100% municipal ownership. This means that most of the municipal utilities have handed the sector's liberalization by engaging in a strategic partnership and have then been vertically integrated into the four utilities, E.ON, RWE, Vattenfall, and EnBW, or by entering into other strategic alliances.

As one of the first movers among the municipally owned utilities, MVV Energie AG was taken public in 1999 by its shareholder, the city of Mannheim. Since then, MVV Energie AG has grown to be Germany's largest network of municipal utility companies. First, in 2000 MVV Energie AG acquired Energieversorgung Offenbach and Energie Köthen and took up a participation in Stadtwerke Buchen, followed in 2001 by participations in Stadtwerke Solingen and Stadtwerke Ingolstadt. The last acquisitions of municipal assets were these of Stadtwerke Kiel in 2004 and a participation in the Stadtwerke Schwetzingen in 2006. Today MVV Energie AG is a major player in the municipal market and is considered to be a natural strategic partner, especially given the growth limitations imposed on the dominant market players.

However, new players, especially foreign entities, are also benefiting from the ongoing municipal sector consolidation. These entities include, but are not limited to, the French groups Suez, Veolia, and Gaz de France, the Dutch companies Essent and Nuon, and the Danish utility Dong Energy. The French companies have to be considered especially potent, since their activities (including water supply and waste water treatment, energy services, public transport and waste management) and their financial resources are formidable.

Financial investors, especially infrastructure specialists, have found it difficult to score any major successes in the municipal utility sector. The main reasons for these difficulties are the lack of successful municipal references and experience in dealing with municipal entities and their shareholders and also the predatory image of financial investors.

Given the expected continuation of the consolidation of the German municipal utility sector, it would not be surprising to see additional players entering this market.

The classic activities of the municipal utilities in Germany include the distribution and sale of electricity, gas, district heating, water, waste management and energy services to end-customers. The profits from the municipal utilities have hitherto been used to finance other municipal activities, such as the operation of public transport, public swimming pools, and the construction of a social and educational infrastructure. Because of the liberalization of the energy sector, the pressure on municipal utilities to become more efficient has been increasing and will continue to increase, thus threatening the classic municipal utilities business model. This will put extra pressure on the managers of municipal utilities, but also on their shareholders, i.e., politically elected officials who could find it more and more difficult to balance aspects such as company profits and dividends, the drive for more efficient operations and job security, moderate service costs, and happy customers/constituents.

It is expected that the German municipal utility sector will be going through further changes in the near future. As a result of grid regulation, numerous municipal utility companies in Germany will be exposed to increasing pressure on earnings. Any resultant consolidation could provide the MVV Energie AG Group with the possibility of acquiring further shareholdings in the medium term, especially since antitrust restrictions on large vertical players mean that the MVV Energie AG Group is the first choice for companies interested in cooperating in the sector.

41.3   Market Changes and Competition Despite Saturated Markets

41.3.1   Energy Sector in Constant Change

The changes in the utility sector are remarkable, as can be seen especially in the electricity sector. In the 1990s about 15 electricity generators were responsible for producing electricity in Germany. Today electricity generation is dominated by four companies, i.e. E.ON, RWE, EnBW, and Vattenfall Europe.

Since mid-1995, the federal and state authorities have mostly withdrawn from or significantly reduced their shareholdings in E.ON, RWE, EnBW, and Vattenfall. Examples of this are the Federal Republic of Germany and the State of Bavaria exiting E.ON, the States of Berlin and Hamburg exiting Vattenfall Europe, the State of Baden-Württemberg exiting EnBW and GVS, and municipal authorities reducing their shareholdings in RWE.

Another sign of a cultural revolution is the fact that in the 1990s and up to 2007 the CEOs of these entities came from outside the energy sector. This was the case for Mr. Bernotat (E.ON) formerly with Royal Dutch/Shell, Mr. Großmann (RWE) owner of the steel company Georgsmarienhütte Holding, Mr. Claassen (EnBW), who came from Sartorius, an internationally leading laboratory and process technology company, and Mr. Rauscher (Vattenfall Europe), who came from the Bavarian State Bank.

E.ON, RWE, EnBW, and Vattenfall Europe had very similar and successful strategies based on their focus on the core business and cost leadership. In a market that is not growing and is currently tending rather to shrink, and in addition is characterized by homogeneous products – and the grid-bound energy supply market is such a market – the classic company strategy is cost leadership. That is why these companies have put so much emphasis on consistent cost management and controlling. Intensifying competition will show that for the customer the only real distinguishing feature between electricity from 'company A' and from 'company B' will be the price. The quality of supply is often emphasized, but this is taken as a given and is therefore only a marginal competitive advantage.

After 1998, because of the drop in wholesale electricity prices, the municipal utilities were the winners in the liberalization, but with the amendment to the Energy Law 2005 this has been changing. The German Federal Network Agency [Bundesnetzagentur] has since clearly indicated that it will no longer tolerate the current cost levels of the utilities, and this applies especially in the case of network infrastructure costs.

41.3.2 Regulation of Natural Monopolies

It is especially tricky to find a balance between the regulation of municipal utilities, liberalization of the energy sector and the development of management models that are new to the municipal sector. This new situation, which is characterized by a significant shift away from the attitude of monopolists and a certain 'business as usual' mentality in the direction of a competitive entity forced to generate growth and profits while maintaining its municipal root, is a challenge that municipal utilities, their shareholders and their supervisory boards must master und understand.

In addition to new management models, municipal utilities in particular may be expected by their customers/inhabitants living in their service territories to have new attitudes about their roles as energy suppliers. Inhabitants are also voters, and voters elect public officials (e.g., mayors, city councils) that are supervising the utilities. A certain public welfare role is thus out of step with the search for profitability.

Management of municipal utilities has to stimulate the companies' competitiveness while keeping the overall municipal development strategy and municipal politics in mind. A delicate balance needs to be maintained between the public sector interests, the private sector conditions in which municipal utilities are operating, and the framework provided by regulatory authorities.

41.3.3 Energy Policy Decisions

Given their role in society as energy suppliers and significant elements in economies, utilities have been, are, and will be under intense scrutiny from politicians
(at all levels: European, national, regional, and local). This is also true for municipal utilities, even if their role is less dominant than those of the larger utilities.
This scrutiny has manifested itself in rules and regulations issued by local governments, states, and federal entities, and last but not least, in European directives.

To illustrate the complexity of the legal environment I would like to highlight,
without going into further detail, a few classic municipal utility issues that are
subject to different regulations: grid access, unbundling, public utilities services,
price controls, road use and license, promotion of renewable sources of energy,
combined heat and power (CHP), emissions trading, taxes, and industrial plant
law.

The business activity of municipal utilities is subject to legal frameworks that
can result from German federal and state laws, regulations promulgated under
them and also from requirements of European Community Law (in particular
regulations and directives).

The German Federal Networks Agency and the regulatory authorities of the
Länder are proposing regulation of networks coupled with the unbundling of network operation from the other activities of energy supply enterprises and far-
reaching control of grid access fees. Grid operators must therefore generally obtain advance approval from the regulatory authorities for the cost basis of their
grid utilization fees.

Electricity and gas prices for end-customers are subject to general antitrust supervision. This also applies to end-customer prices for district heating and water,
so that here too, unrestricted price setting by the suppliers does not apply. There
may also be additional restrictions in price setting in the electricity and gas sectors
as a result of the Draft Bill for Combating Price Abuse in the Area of Energy Supply and Food Trade (Amendment of the Law against Restraint of Competition),
adopted on 25 April 2007 by the German Federal Cabinet and approved by the
German Federal Council. The cabinet draft, in addition, provides both for intervention rights for the antitrust authorities with respect to electricity and gas suppliers in the event of abuse of a dominant market position and for cost-based price
controls.

As a result, the action of municipal utilities is subject to extensive control by
the regulatory and antitrust authorities at federal and state levels, and it finds itself
exposed to intense regulation.

The time for self-regulation by the energy industry itself, a typical characteristic of the German energy market, has shown its limitations according to officials
of the European Commission and some German officials, and according to these
same officials and institutions no longer suffices to ensure sound competition.

In order to allow for more competition at all levels of the energy sector, but especially at the energy distribution level, German and European regulatory bodies
have put pressure on the costs of transmission and distribution. Efforts have been
made by municipal utilities to reduce these costs, and their efforts have not been

limited to transmission and distribution but have also been applied to other areas of the municipal utilities, such as striving for more efficient company structures.

The EU Commission is convinced that the German energy market lacks competition and efficiency and is therefore making a strong case for an ownership-related unbundling, [2] increased competencies for regulation authorities and the creation of an EU Regulation Authority.

41.4   Challenges and Options for Regional Utilities

Regional and municipal utilities are facing a number of challenges arising from the ongoing liberalization of the energy market. These challenges include: cost and financial management, necessary structural changes, customer and shareholder expectations, regulatory measures and social responsibility and employees' expectations.

Increasing competition in the municipal utility sector poses new challenges for management and their supervisory authorities. Two of the most topical questions that are looming concern the reaction of customers to rising energy costs and how the intervention of regulatory authorities and politics is expected to interfere with management activities.

For municipal and regional utilities it is not easy to find the necessary growth strategy to evolve in a significantly changing market environment. This is especially true given the limited organic growth rate or even shrinking market of the sector. Add an intense industry consolidation resulting from the cut-throat competition exercised by a few dominant companies and new market entries willing to pay market entry prices, both groups with very deep pockets.

For independent municipal utilities and utilities that have third-party minority shareholders 'independence vs dependence' is a major question.

Municipal utilities that have not yet implemented efficiency programs designed to offset the regulatory demands are characterized by important fixed costs and inefficiencies of processes. This is especially the case for smaller municipal utilities, which sometimes simply do not have the resources necessary to fulfill the latest regulatory conditions. For utilities that are unprepared for competition and the smaller municipal utilities, it is often simply not possible to use economies of scale and scope to reduce their fixed costs, restructure, and improve their processes. As mentioned above, the most successful utilities have all focused on cost leadership, and the reduction of fixed costs is paramount to a more efficient business, so that finding and implementing ways to reduce fixed costs has to have a crucial role in the growth strategy of any utility.

Addressing some of the challenges that municipal utilities are facing is a daunting and sometimes unappreciated task. Options that management can take up include the implementation of efficiency measures and restructuring organizations in order to render them able to respond to the changing market environment. One

---

[2] Unbundling here is defined as the separation of grid operations from other activities.

major decision, which can put a company on a path of no return, is the search for a strategic or financial partner, or alternative financial engineering. This is an option, especially if the company is not able to implement the necessary changes quickly enough or if the shareholder is in dire need of financial resources.

At a very early stage of the energy market liberalization in Germany, MVV Energie AG went public in March 1999 as the first municipal and regional utility in Germany to do so. At the time, that decision was driven by the intention to remain an independent company and to use the capital markets for financing growth (creation and expansion of a premier municipal utility network).

The horizontal integration and networking of multi-utility companies means that MVV Energie AG's strategy differs from that pursued by the four large German energy generators, which focus on vertical integration in the German energy market. They integrate companies from generation through to distribution, while MVV Energie AG seeks the horizontal integration of multi-utility companies in our network of municipal utility companies in order to reap the following benefits:

- Multiplication of successful business models and processes as examples of best practice in economically interesting regional markets;
- Expansion of the customer base and access to new customers;
- New locations as a platform for marketing energy services and innovative product ideas that have proved successful;
- Exploitation of synergies in technology and procurement as well as in the group's share services companies dealing with energy trading, IT, networks, insurance, metering, and billing.

The business model of horizontal integration and interconnection of municipal utility companies with multiple lines of business and the value-oriented controlling of our shareholdings in municipal utilities has led to greater efficiency and earning power for the individual companies, and thus will also increase the aggregate value of the group.

In addition to expanding its network of utilities, MVV Energie AG has undertaken measures to address and prepare itself for the challenges mentioned above. In addition to cost-cutting programs, reorganization of the company, and adjustment of the strategy, MVV Energie AG has created shared-services companies to pool its internal services divisions with those of the shareholdings within its municipal utility network so as to be better able to tap into the full potential of optimal scale advantage, outsourcing, and exploiting market opportunities by acquiring new customers.

The small- and medium-sized companies that have not yet prepared themselves for the changing market conditions are expected to suffer most from the market liberalization and are expected to seek cooperation with regionally close companies, ideally with neighboring service territories, and/or to look for strategic or financial investors that will help them navigate to the expected rough waters that lie ahead.

The difficulty experienced by many decision makers is that cooperations, alliances or mergers, if set up correctly, do address the necessity to become more competitive, but they also mean giving up power and control over one's own assets.

41.5   Strategy of MVV Energy

41.5.1   Costs and Price Leadership in the Traditional Business Segments Power, Gas, Water, and District Heating

In our traditional business we move within saturated markets, because each household has an electricity and water connection and only relatively few have no gas or district heating connection. Because of savings measures it is expected that the traditional business will even be declining. The same can be said for commercial and industrial customers. The entity that wants to grow has to take away market shares from other entities, and that is mainly possible through pricing, ecological differentiation, sales partnerships with established brands, and combining products ('dual-fuel', i.e., electricity and gas, approach). Until recently, there was no really serious competition in Germany, but over recent months we have seen that this situation is changing. One thing is clear: only the entity that will be able to compete on prices and therefore on costs will be able to survive. The big challenge for managers in our industry is that for decades we have lived in a monopoly and that many employees are only slowly realizing and accepting that the world has changed significantly around them. Similar difficulties have been and are being experienced by management and staff of former monopolies, such as Deutsche Telekom and Deutsche Bahn. Managing traditional businesses or business segments is more of a challenge than managing growth businesses, because we do not start from scratch and we have to manage existing resources and deal with old structures and patterns of thought. Especially in our public sector companies, management needs a lot of patience and perseverance, and a high level of tolerance for dealing with frustrations.

41.5.2   Adapting the Company Structure

The implementation of a strategy can only be successful if the necessary structures have been or are being created. The appropriate structure for a growing group is without a doubt based on a holding configuration with the task of managing growth and the necessary resources.

After exhaustive discussions, in 2004 we decided to opt for a parent company organization in which we have distinguished between head office and corporate functions. At the time, the main reason for this decision was that we did not want to overburden the organization with too many changes too fast.

The creation of a holding organization poses a string of legal, fiscal, financial and managerial questions that management and the supervisory entities will have to deal with in the next phase of MVV Energie AG's restructuring process. A holding structure is, however, the logical consequence of our growth strategy of wanting to develop continuously.

41.5.3 Internal Implementation Program

In order to execute our strategy in 2004 we decided to implement a program that has been put into action step by step.

41.5.3.1 Step 1: Portfolio Reassessment

Three years ago, the reassessment of our business portfolio was our highest priority. By reducing and eliminating risk positions and loss-making activities we have significantly reduced the financial burden on the company.

The portfolio reassessment is complete; we have become more profitable, and this step is reflected in the financial community's assessment of MVV Energie AG and in the price of our company shares.

41.5.3.2 Step 2: Reorganization of Headquarters

In 2003 the corporate organization was not suited to the management of a group of over 6,000 employees. By reorganizing MVV Energie AG's headquarters we have taken an important first step towards becoming a holding organization.

Important principles in this organization are decentralization of responsibility and management by clearly defined goals. Both principles have to be continuously applied and supported by the establishment of sovereign and impulse functions that need to be further developed.

An important organizational change for MVV Energie AG was the clear separation of the executive responsibilities between different supervisory and management entities of MVV Energie AG and MVV GmbH and of the MVV GmbH's public transport subsidiaries MVV Verkehr AG and MVV OEG AG. This has also allowed us to set up transparent rules for internal service charges and cost allocation.

41.5.3.3 Step 3: Strengthening the Economic Controls and Financial Stability

In order to implement our strategy effectively, we needed actual and meaningful data and information. In 2004 we therefore created a new controlling structure and introduced new instruments.

An effective risk-controlling management was established, the planning process was changed significantly, and a new portfolio controlling and reporting structure was introduced. In addition to the value-based management, we have also established investment controlling and considerably changed and strengthened both the internal service charge and the cost controlling process.

41.5.3.4 Step 4: Cost Reduction

In the last 2 years, MVV Energie AG has been able to reduce its costs significantly, especially the costs for materials. The programs already implemented and those newly initiated will take full effect in terms of personnel costs in the coming years. Programs pushing an optimization of technical processes, efficiency enhancement intended to reduce administration expenses, administrative issues, and the professionalization of the procurement department have been remarkably successful.

By reducing costs we are strengthening our position and our independence in this very competitive market. It should be understood that cost reductions belong to the everyday responsibilities and duties of every management and result from constant technical progress and constant improvement of processes.

41.5.3.5 Step 5: Development of the Synergy Potentials in the Group

Once we had addressed and set up the basis for cost reduction and process improvement at our company's headquarters, we turned to similar activities at group level. The professionalization and expansion of our procurement network, coupled with process improvements and the exploitation of further synergies in cooperation with our municipal utility shareholdings, also enabled us to achieve considerable cost savings. The current cost-saving programs are also being consistently implemented at our other locations.

To use identified synergies optimally, MVV Energie AG has pooled some internal services divisions together with those of the shareholdings within its municipal utility network. These shared-services companies have been established for grid operations, information technology, invoicing, metering, energy trading, and insurance services.

MVV Energie AG expects the pooling of tasks to enable the group of companies to achieve two important objectives in the coming years. On the one hand we will thus meet the new legal requirements governing grid operations, and on the other we will realize significant synergy potential, thus enhancing the competitiveness of the entire group of companies.

Our ability to maintain our economic success in spite of increasingly intense price competition is dependent on our achieving efficiency enhancements and cost savings in all our core business processes. We will therefore maintain our efforts and continue to focus on enhancing the competitiveness of our group of companies in coming years.

41.5.3.6 Step 6: Corporate Culture

The path or the transformation from a municipal utility to a competitive company is long and rocky. An open dialogue between management and the workforce is of paramount importance to achieve the necessary corporate cultural changes and openness for more individual responsibility and initiative, especially from managers. In times of major structural company changes, uncertainty and frustrations are a common factor. Time often heals a lot of situations; nevertheless, one thing is absolutely necessary: openness and the willingness to discuss things at all levels of the organization. In order to foster cultural changes that will improve MVV Energie AG's competitiveness, we have started a cultural change program called MOVE. MOVE stands for courage [Mut], openness [Offenheit], change [Veränderung] and success [Erfolg].

41.5.3.7 Step 7: Group Reorganization/Holding

The next logical step is to create a corporate group structure (holding) such as other companies of similar size have already established. As in every major structural change, because of personal interests, uncertainty and speculations will be part of the transformation process. Nevertheless, with appropriate guidance from the supervisory board, uncertainties and a certain unrest should disappear once the final target organization has been decided. There is an agreement that the corporate group structure is the correct organizational form for a company such as MVV Energie AG.

41.5.4 Expansion of the Municipal Utility Network Despite Market Consolidation

In Germany a significant number of municipalities do not have any financial margin, and budget deficits are more often the rule than the exception. Holding on to municipal shareholdings becomes significantly difficult, especially if they bear increasing entrepreneurial risks. Value-based management of companies does not belong to the traditional competencies of a municipality. Municipal utilities have for decades been used as cash cows to finance public transport and other public sector tasks while benefiting from fiscal advantages. As long as the monopoly functioned, the intact world was kept alive.

Should profits of municipal utilities collapse – and current events confirm that this is not an unreasonable expectation – most municipalities will be taken unprepared. These municipalities will ask themselves whether the sale of their municipal utility is a viable option. Should the value of the utility to the buyer be higher than the value to the municipality – for example because the buyer can realize synergies, additional efficiency measures or better strategies, for managing the regulator, sales, and trading, perhaps – a sale of the asset makes economic sense for both parties. This is true especially in the case of municipal utilities that are now not working at a high level of efficiency.

With the recently implemented capital increase, MVV Energie AG has increased its financial means and can therefore offer municipalities the opportunity of becoming strategic municipal investors. However, because of the shareholdings by third parties, we are expected to perform well and at least deliver the profits that are expected by the capital markets.

The development of our network of municipal utilities together with our municipal partners has confirmed and strengthened our independence of the four large German players and will continue to do so in the future.

41.5.5 Expansion of the Growth Segments

In the business segments 'Environment' and 'Energy Services' MVV Energie AG is dealing with similar clients, competitors, technologies, and market mechanisms to those in our traditional core business, the grid-bound energy and water supply. To work into both markets is therefore a sensible approach.

In both cases we have growing markets. In the business segment Environment, which includes waste-to-energy and biomass-fired facilities, regulatory frameworks and the search for alternative fuels because of high oil and gas prices have led to a real boom. MVV Energie AG's strategy is to grow faster than the market and to achieve market leadership. We are already among the top three companies in this segment, and we intend to invest additional resources. The business segment Environment is one of the most important pillars of our earnings, making us less dependent on our core business, which will be increasingly under cost pressure.

The business segment Energy services is also a growing market in Germany, both with municipal and with industrial customers. Experts expect double-digit growth in the next few years, especially as Germany still has a lot of catching up to do. However, the market is characterized by a high level of fragmentation and by strong competition. There is no market shake-out in sight. Here our strategy is to use our market position (among the top three in Germany) and to continuously generate competitive advantages by using standardized products and processes. Since this market is characterized by continuous change, constant strategy assessment and readjustment are necessary.

The strategy of both growth segments is based on the overall trend of the importance of climate protection, increasing energy efficiency and the use of renewable energy.

41.6 Conclusion and Outlook

On the basis of our new strategy, MVV Energie AG has begun to prepare the group to face the future challenges of the energy market which are in particular coping with liberalisation and environmental issues. The present results reassure us that continuing on this path is the right thing to do. Certainly, we could have some discussion on whether the changes have been quick and radical enough; however, we have consciously decided to opt for cautious step-by-step, and therefore also socially responsible, changes. This tightrope walk between economic pressure and the interest of the employees – as well as the managers – is not simple.

Our strategy and our company targets serve to increase the value of the company in the long term. We assess all our strategic decisions and actions in terms of their short-term and long-term impact on our earnings and company value. MVV Energie AG's economic success and profitability have improved significantly, but we can still do better.

The strategic progress and improvement in operating earnings figures achieved by our group of companies has also been honored by the capital market. This is reflected in the performance of the share of MVV Energie AG as well as in the recently successful capital increase.

In coming years we expect to see a further intensification of the competition in our sector and increasing pressure on costs resulting from the regulation of grid utilization fees as well as increasing ecologically-related challenges; however, we are well prepared to face the challenges that our industry will have to deal with.

References

Bundeskartellamt. 2007, Press release of June 6th. http://www.bundeskartellamt. de/wEnglisch/News/Archiv/ArchivNews2007/2007_06_06.php.
MIT Sloan. 2008. Keywords & Definitions for IO. http://ccs.mit.edu/21c/iokey. html, 26th May 2008.

42 Climate Protection Requirements – the Economic Impact of Climate Change

Claudia Kemfert[1]

Abstract

In order to avoid severe climate change, it is necessary to stabilize global green-house gas concentrations at about today's level. Significant emission reduction would require the countries that are primarily responsible to implement emis-sions-reducing measures immediately. The sooner a policy of climate protection is implemented, the less climate change damage humankind will face in future decades. The impacts of climate change are highly uncertain. However, the recent UN climate report confirms that more severe extreme climate impacts will cause economic damage. Future climate policy needs ideally to be global and long term.

Keywords: climate protection, climate change, economic impacts

---

[1] Prof. Dr. Claudia Kemfert is Director of the 'Energy, Transportation, and Environment' Department at the German Institute of Economic Research and Professor of Environmental and Energy Economics at Humboldt University Berlin, Germany. Claudia Kemfert is an Adviser to the German Government and to EU President Barroso in the High Level Group on Energy and Climate Change.

A. Bausch and B. Schwenker (eds.), *Handbook Utility Management,*
DOI: 10.1007/978-3-540-79349-6_42, © Springer-Verlag Berlin Heidelberg 2009

42.1   Climate Change – Why Do We Bother?

The global earth surface temperature will increase sharply in the future as a consequence of a rise in climate-damaging greenhouse gas emissions, in particular carbon dioxide (CO_2) emissions. The Intergovernmental Panel on Climate Change (IPCC) has reported that an increase in global concentrations of CO_2 to between over 450 ppm and 1,000 ppm in 2100 would lead to an increase in global surface temperature of between 2 °C (Celsius) and 5.8 °C. The consequence of exceeding these limits would be both more frequent and more violent extreme climate events. A higher surface temperature will lead to a rise in the sea level. The anthropogenic (caused by human activity) concentration of greenhouse gases [mainly CO_2, methane (CH_4), and nitrous oxide (N_2O)] has increased exponentially in the twentieth century. The concentration of CO_2 alone in the atmosphere has risen by 31% (± 4%) since weather records began.[2] CO_2 emissions result mainly from burning fossil fuels.

If the combustion of fossil energy sources is not curbed, then global concentrations of emissions will greatly exceed the critical level of 450 ppm of carbon dioxide concentration as early as the second half of this century, thereby generating a temperature increase of up to 5 °C over the next three centuries. The number of hot days has increased, and the number of cold days has decreased. The consequences will be severe climate fluctuations and extreme weather events, such as storms, floods caused by heavy rains, and cold and heat waves. Such extreme climate events could become both more frequent and more intense. Depending on assumptions on future developments, temperature increases of between 1 °C and 3.5 °C are to be expected in 2100. As the emission of greenhouse gases increases and temperatures rise, the global sea level will also continue to rise. Again depending on the assumptions and scenarios on which the prognosis is based, the amount the sea level will rise by is put at between 10 cm and 90 cm by the year 2100.

In the twentieth century the global surface temperature rose by 0.2 (±0.6) °C. The rise in the surface temperature in the northern hemisphere was greater during that period than in the previous 1000 years; 2007 was the warmest year globally in the twentieth century; and 2005 was the warmest year since weather records began (WMO, 2007). The year 2007 was the year of extremes: it was the second warmest year in the Northern Hemisphere since weather observation started, while in the Southern Hemisphere it was the ninth warmest. The January of 2007, with an average temperature of 12.7 °C, was the warmest January ever recorded. From 1961 to 1990 the average January temperature was 12.1 °C. In some parts of Europe the spring and winter of 2007 were the warmest ever recorded. The April of 2007 in England was the warmest for 348 years, and the wettest since 1766, with heavy rainfall causing serious flooding. In June and July of 2007, the extremely hot summer in South East Europe and very high temperatures in the West-

---

[2] Today there are 150 gigatonnes (Gt) more of carbon dioxide emissions in the atmosphere than before industrialisation. The quantity is growing by 3% a year and in 2050 it will have reached 300 Gt if this growth rate continues unchanged.

ern USA caused droughts and forest fires. Extreme droughts have led to water scarcity in China. In addition, so much of the Artic ice melted that the North-West Passage was passable in 2007.[3]

42.2   Economic Impacts of Climate Change

A temperature rise to more than 2 °C above preindustrial levels will result in significant climate change and major economic costs (IPCC, 2007). Estimates of future climate change damage are highly uncertain. One of the reasons the uncertainties and margins of fluctuation regarding potential consequences are so great is that the effects are subject to temporal and spatial disparities. The positive effects of a climate protection policy pursued in Europe today, for example, will not necessarily also be felt in Europe. They could equally manifest in Southeast Asia, where exposed island nations might perhaps be spared a flood that would otherwise be produced by a rise in the sea level. Moreover, as a result of the time delay and the long life-span of greenhouse gases in the atmosphere, these potential effects can emerge in the distant future. Such uncertainties render the formulation and implementation of a constructive and determined global political strategy both complicated and arduous.

The number and severity of natural catastrophes, such as floods caused by extremely heavy rainfall, will continue to grow and accelerate, as will those of heat waves and storms. Table 42.1 shows the extreme weather events that are possible, how likely they are to occur, and their possible impacts. Many regions in the world are already more intensely affected by climate change than others, and this will also be the case in future. In North America worse storms and tornadoes are to be expected, while floods are more likely in Asia. In Europe, as well as extreme heat waves and flooding, such storms as tornadoes and hurricanes are also likely in future.

Extreme heat phenomena and rainfall have been striking features in Europe in recent years, especially in Germany. In 2002 Middle and Eastern Europe suffered catastrophic floods. In the east and south of Germany, the southwest of the Czech Republic, and Austria and Hungary, the rivers Danube, Elbe, Moldau, Inn, and Salzach burst their banks. The millennium flood hit Germany hard, causing damage amounting to about € 9.2 billion (Münchner Rück, 2007).

---

[3] Because of the drastic melting of arctic ice all abutting countries – Russia, Norway, Canada, USA – claim tenure. Russia has raised a symbolic flag at the floor of the ocean in order to demonstrate their serious demand – especially for oil and gas reserves. The US Energy Information Administration (EIA) estimates 25% of global oil and gas reserves to be under the Artic, see US Energy Information Administration (EIA) 2007 http://www.eia.doe.gov/emeu/international/reserves.html. Russia will now try to prove that Russia is connected with the Artic with the so-called Lomonossow Headland.

Table 42.1: Examples of extreme climate events and potential impacts (positive/negative) (IPCC, 2007)

Extreme climate event	Probability	Impacts
Higher maximal temperatures. More hot days and heat waves	Very high	• Increase in no. of deaths and incidence of serious diseases among elderly people, especially in poor regions • Increase in heat stress to animals • Shift of tourist areas • Increased risk of crop losses • Reduction of energy security • Increase in energy demand for cooling
Fewer colder days and reduced frequency of cold waves	Very high	• Reduced probability of deaths because of fewer cold days • Reduced risk of crop losses • Increased prevalence of 'tropical' diseases • Greater spread of pests • Reduced energy demand for heating
More extreme rainfall	Very high	• Increased damage from floods, landslides and avalanches • More soil erosion • Higher state expenditures on compensation payments • Higher risks for insurance companies
Rise in summer dry periods and risk of drought	High	• Lower harvest yields • Increased damage to buildings from changes in ground conditions and contraction • Reduced water resources and poorer quality of water • Greater risk of forest fires
Rise in violence of hurricanes; increase of medium and heavy rainfall (in some regions)	High	• Greater risk to human life • Greater risk of disease and epidemics • Increased coastal erosion and more damage to buildings and infrastructure near to coasts • Increase of damage to the ecosystem on coasts
More floods and drought from the El Nino effect	High	• Lower agricultural productivity in areas liable to drought and flooding • Increased damage in Central Asia • Fewer water resources in drought regions
Greater fluctuation in monsoon rainfalls in Asia	High	• More flooding and droughts
Greater severity of storms in equatorial regions	Low	• Greater risk to life and health • Greater loss of welfare and more damage to infrastructure • More damage in coastal areas

In 2003 the whole of Europe suffered an extreme heat wave. The economic damage caused by such catastrophes includes those who died of heat stroke (particularly in France), increased ill-health from the greater risk of disease, harvest losses, disruptions to energy provision and more forest fires.[4] Altogether it is estimated that the heat wave in 2003 caused between € 10 and 17 billions' worth of damage in Europe.[5]

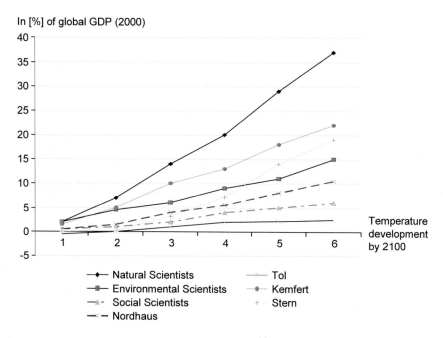

Figure 42.1: Economic impacts of climate change with rising temperature change of different authors

The economic damage resulting from extreme weather events has increased by a factor of 15 in the last three decades (Münchner Rück, 2007). The impacts of anthropogenic climate change are smaller than they will be in the future, as a major factor in the damage increase noted by insurance companies is the fact that the wealth of society is increasing as well as its vulnerability. Because of increasing wealth and insurance density, the wealthy also tend to move to especially vulnerable regions, e.g. Florida. The assessment of economic impacts of climate change vary widely (see Figure 42.1). The reasons for the variation are manifold. The

---

[4] High river water temperatures also bring the risk that nuclear reactors will not be adequately cooled. In 2003 this caused nuclear reactors in Germany and France to be closed.

[5] In a speech, the British Prime Minister, Tony Blair, actually spoke of 26,000 dead and put the damage at $ 13.5 billion: speech given to mark the tenth anniversary of the Prince of Wales' Business & the Environment Programme (abbreviated), London, 14 September 2004 (www.britischebotschaft.de/de/news/items/04091.4.htm, 4 October 2004).

major reasons, though, are how the estimation model is constructed, whether or not trade is covered and what parameters are chosen (Edenhofer et al., 2006).

Different sectors are affected by climate change (Tol, 2002a & 2002b; Tol et al., 2004; Nordhaus & Boyer, 2000; Fankhauser, 1994; Hope, 2005 Pittini & Rahman, 2004; Stern, 2006; Kemfert, 2002a & 2007; Schellnhuber et al., 2004). The agriculture and forestry sector suffers when there are extremely hot days during the summer, as forest fires then increase in frequency. Water scarcity could bring negative growth effects. Forest cultivation needs to be changed, as mixed forests are more resistant than monocultures to climate change; agriculture and forestry in particular have to increase expenditures for adaptation. Because of more intense rainfall some regions are more vulnerable to flooding, which can cause damage to buildings and to the infrastructure. Together with the increased number of extremely hot summer days, less cold winter temperatures are causing a reduction in the volume of ice in glaciers, especially in the region of the Alps (OECD, 2007). This causes adaptation costs to tourist branches in the Alps and also economic losses owing to declining tourism. Extremely hot summer days will also shift tourist areas to less hot regions. A higher number of hot days in the year will also reduce labor productivity and increase the energy demand for cooling. Furthermore, less availability of cooling water for energy production increases energy costs. Extreme weather events such as storms and hurricanes can destroy energy exploitation fields.[6] Energy costs will rise because conventional energy production may be reduced or substituted if not enough cooling water is available in high-temperature periods. In addition, indirect energy costs will increase because of supply disruptions. An increase of energy costs by 20% will harm the economy by negative growth impacts of up to 0.5% of gross domestic product (GDP). The financial sector can suffer from different impacts. On the one hand, insurance companies face additional losses because of higher direct damages resulting from climate change. On the other, firms listed on the stock exchange can be evaluated negatively if they contribute to climate change or cannot demonstrate a clear strategy for sustainable development.

42.3   Climate Protection Requirements

Greenhouse gas emissions, and consequently greenhouse gas concentrations, have been rising constantly over the last few decades. CO_2 concentrations now already amount to close to 400 ppm. The main producers of greenhouse gas emissions are industrialized countries with high per capita energy consumption and high levels of emissions, such as the USA, Europe, and Japan (see Figure 42.2).

Meanwhile, China's energy-intensive growth has already led to this country moving into second place amongst worldwide emitters of CO_2 (see Figure 42.3).

---

[6] In summer 2006, hurricane Katrina destroyed oil platforms in the Golf of Mexico. The Gulf region is especially vulnerable to climate change. The oil price increased because of supply disruption of up to 80 $/barrel.

If climate change is to be reduced or prevented altogether, emissions of greenhouse gases must be lowered drastically. Climate experts assume that a reduction of greenhouse gases by 60-80% will be needed by the year 2100 (IPCC, 2007).[7]

In view of the length of time greenhouse gases remain in the atmosphere the states responsible should start on these drastic reductions as soon as possible. The main responsibility lies with the United States, which is the chief emitter of all greenhouse gases worldwide; it is followed by China, Europe, Russia, and Japan (UNFCCC, 2006). To be effective a climate protection policy must require binding levels of reduction, especially from countries with high levels of greenhouse gas emission. Currently, significant effort is still required at global level even just to achieve the moderate goals laid out in the Kyoto Protocol. At the same time, targets and policies must be formulated for the years to follow the first commitment period (2008-2012) so as to avoid long-term climate damages in a cost-effective manner.

Carbon dioxide emissions [tons] per capita

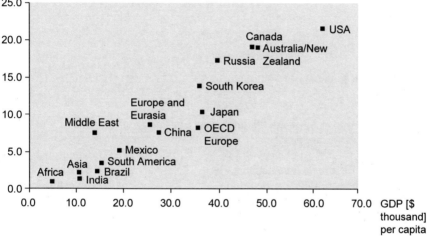

Figure 42.2: GDP and CO_2 emissions per capita of different nations (EIA, 2007)

The coming into force of the Kyoto Protocol means that most industrialized countries have now committed themselves to reducing their greenhouse gas emissions (very moderately overall) over the period 2008-2012. However, progress in efforts to obtain international agreement on effective climate protection measures remains sluggish, and it appears doubtful whether definite and binding emissions targets for the period following the Kyoto Protocol's first commitment period, which expires in 2012, will be implemented globally. While Germany and the European Union are pushing for binding commitments on climate protection and

---

[7] The IPCC puts the costs of so great a reduction in emissions at up to $ 150 billion worldwide.

have themselves already adopted numerous measures, other countries reject these demands. And yet it is vital that the USA join an international climate protection agreement so as to persuade countries such as China and India by way of good example also to take action.

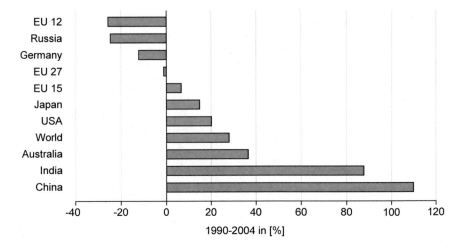

Figure 42.3: Change in CO_2 emissions of different regions, 1990-2004 in [%] (EIA, 2007)

In the discussion on when climate protection measures should be adopted, the following elements are particularly important:

Some critics do not believe sufficient proof has yet been provided that climate change is a consequence of human activity. They advocate first carrying out further climate research and observation of climate trends before investing in costly measures. The response of those in favor of climate protection is that the well-founded suspicion of anthropogenic climate change is sufficient to justify measures, almost as a kind of insurance against potential damage. In particular, they argue, the risk of irreversible damage necessitates early action (Lomborg, 2005).

Another argument in favor of postponing the implementation of climate protection measures is that technical progress will make such measures cheaper in the future. At present, it would therefore be better, the argument goes, to invest in appropriate research measures. The response to this argument is that technical progress and cost reductions might be achieved most effectively if the technology is not developed in the research laboratory but in practice via 'learning by doing'. Moreover, measures adopted at a later date would have to be much more drastic and implemented over a much shorter period time in order to achieve the necessary level of atmospheric greenhouse gas concentrations (Nordhaus, 2002).

Advocates of early measures point out that the climate system does not react perceptibly to human intervention until after enormous time delays. It is therefore necessary, they argue, that we start with climate protection measures today if we are ever to succeed in even stabilizing the concentration of greenhouse gases at today's levels. Immediate action could substantially mitigate the foreseeable climate change damage (Rahmstorf, 2003).

However, without clear-cut allocation of the costs of climate change and specification of the advantages of climate protection, it will be very difficult in political terms at the international level to push through explicit emission reduction measures that apply to the years after expiry of the Kyoto Protocol's first commitment period in 2012. In particular, it will not be easy to win over those countries that refuse point blank to implement active climate protection policies. Many of these countries argue that climate protection measures are currently too expensive and that postponement would open up the possibility of more economical options for reducing greenhouse gas emissions. Apart from the need to begin implementing climate protection measures today, it is also necessary to make targeted investment in research and development so as to develop more economical ways of reducing greenhouse gas emissions in the future (Kemfert, 2005). If, for example, investment were made today in research into the possibility of a 'CO$_2$-free power plant', this technology could be used at low cost in the long term.

42.4   Climate Protection: What Next?

The Kyoto Protocol came into force in 2005, after ratification by Russia in November 2004, and it expires in 2012. The aim of the Protocol is a 5.2% reduction in the 1990 level of greenhouse gas emissions by the end of the commitment period 2008-12. The main overall intention of the Kyoto Protocol is to reduce emissions by concrete and binding emissions reduction limits on more than 55 countries, covering more than 55% of total world emissions. High-income countries such as the EU, Japan, and Canada have committed themselves to reducing emissions by binding emissions cuts; upper-middle economies such as Russia and Ukraine have to stabilize on 1990 emissions; and lower-middle and low-income economies, such as China and India, have no emissions reduction target. The USA has never ratified the Kyoto Protocol. The Kyoto Protocol allows for flexible mechanisms such as an emissions trading system between the industrialized countries, the Clean Development Mechanism (CDM), and Joint Implementation (JI). Both CDM and JI allow for project transfers between industrialized and developing nations to reduce greenhouse gases.

Europe allocated national emissions reduction targets by a burden-sharing rule (see Figure 42.4). At the beginning of 2005, the European Union launched an emissions trading scheme (the 'EU ETS'), under which firms operating in the energy and industry sectors of all EU countries are free to buy and sell CO$_2$ emissions allowances. Initial experiences with this new instrument indicate that incomplete information and imperfect competition – and consequent strategic behaviour – have led to an over-allocation of emissions allowances in almost all European countries (see Figure 42.5). The emissions trading market almost collapsed as a result, with the price of allowances dropping to almost zero in 2007.

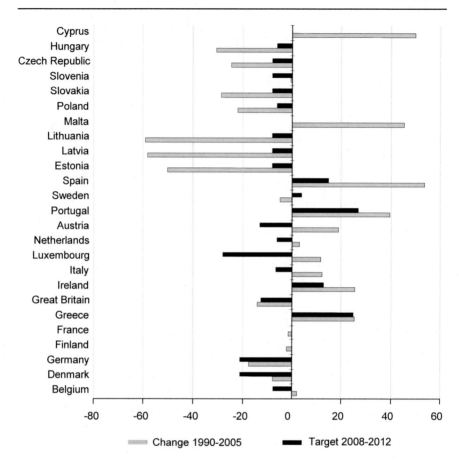

Figure 42.4: Greenhouse gas emissions of different European countries (change 1990-2005 and Kyoto target)

Overallocations of this kind are unlikely to be repeated in the future, however, because the member states' national allocation plans (NAPs) for emissions allowances now require the approval of the European Commission. The future market price of emissions allowances for 2008 currently stands at 20 €/tonne of CO_2. Some EU countries have decided to auction a small share of their emissions permits (EU member states may auction no more than 10% of their allocated emissions); for example, Germany plans to auction 9% (i.e. 40 million tonnes of CO_2 emissions) of its annual emissions allowances, which still leaves 91% of its allowances to be freely allocated. Given the existence of market imperfections and strategic behavior, an open auction would probably drive up the price of allowances so that the remaining, freely allocated share of emissions allowances would be valued as highly as possible. Thus, with a view to avoiding distortions of this nature, a book-building or fixed-price system is recommended as the most appropriate auction format.

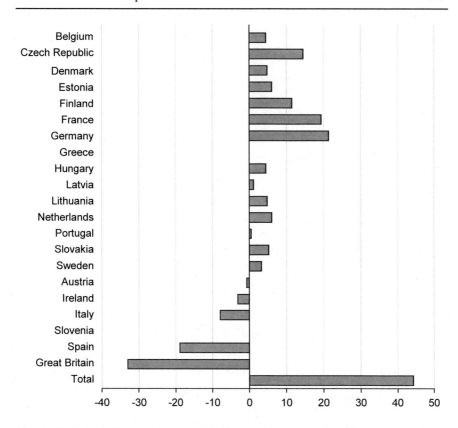

Figure 42.5: Emission surpluses and deficits under NAP I in million tonnes of CO_2 (BMU, 2006)

All in all, it can be said that the instrument of emissions trading is basically an effective and cost-efficient tool for diminishing greenhouse gas emissions. However, its success will depend on inclusion of the maximum possible number of countries, sectors, and greenhouse gases in the scheme and on the freedom of member states to auction 100% of their emissions allowances. Full auctioning of emissions allowances would increase transparency; partial auctioning would neither resolve the problems of optimal free allocation nor reflect the real situation on the market. Recent moves in the USA towards joining the EU ETS at the county level could be a step in the right direction. The revenue from auctions could be used to promote low-emission technologies, and possibly to compensate those sectors that are subject to evident competitive disadvantages on international markets. In the long term, an effort must be made to make emissions trading a global instrument for climate protection.

Although the emissions reduction target of the Kyoto Protocol will not be enough to eradicate climate change, it is essential that the nations responsible agree on a joint proposal for shrinking emissions: an effective climate policy needs to be global. Both the USA and Australia should have committed to some kind of climate policy. One advantage of the Kyoto Protocol is the flexibility of the instruments involved: emissions trading allows for cost-effective emissions cuts, while CDM and JI bring innovative low-carbon technologies to middle- and low-income countries. The flexibility of the instruments yields a double dividend of climate improvement and economic benefits. The main disadvantage of the Kyoto Protocol is that it does not allow for flexible emissions reduction targets. Flexible targets such as index-linked targets cannot guarantee concrete emissions reductions, but they do allow for the necessary economic flexibility. The APEC declaration illustrates that economic concerns are substantial, as the nations agreed on index-linked targets that take account of dynamic growth. An intelligent climate policy should combine economic growth and emissions cuts, and a decoupling of economic growth and greenhouse gas emissions would be indispensable. Promoting innovative CO_2-free technologies not only brings more energy security, reducing vulnerability to energy supply disruptions and fossil-fuel price shocks as it does, but can also strengthen economic growth and competitiveness.

The Kyoto Protocol is an important first step in the direction of an international climate agreement in which the nations responsible take the lead in reducing emissions. There was a long negotiation process between the first joint signing of the Protocol in December 1997 in Kyoto and ratification by the last required nation, Russia, in November 2004. The current negotiations cannot take so long; agreement is needed very soon. The main concern of high-emissions countries such as the USA was that concrete emissions reduction measures could harm economic development. The USA feared economic decline and disadvantages in the competitiveness of US firms and therefore never ratified the Kyoto Protocol. In addition, Russia has never made any secret of its skepticism of the Protocol. Russia is a nation with one of the largest shares of oil and gas reserves in the world and therefore has a great interest in selling fossil fuels to the world, thus improving its economic performance and becoming a world market leader. The ratification of the Kyoto Protocol in 2004 by Russia was motivated not by climate policy, but basically by economic reasons: both emissions trading and JI projects can have positive impacts on the Russian economy. More importantly, Russia has a strong interest in joining the World Trade Organization (WTO). It is very likely that Russia's position on climate and energy policy will change in the future and it will become a real opponent of any kind of emissions reduction. China and India, on the other hand, want to see concrete steps towards emissions reduction by such responsible nations as the USA and Europe before they are willing to commit to any kind of emissions reduction target.

42.5   Final Remarks

Today's society is facing two main challenges that no previous generation has been confronted with: first, how to guarantee secure and affordable energy supply; and second, how to reduce and abolish environmental and climate harm caused by energy consumption. Over 80% of today's primary energy consumption comes from nonrenewable fossil fuels, such as coal, oil, and gas. If we do not change our behavior, the share of fossil-fuel resources in the future will remain as high as it is today. As the major oil and gas reserves are located in few areas of the world, importing countries would become more vulnerable to supply disruptions and energy price shocks. Furthermore, fossil-fuel consumption causes CO_2 and greenhouse gas emissions, and therefore climate change. The future energy mix should not be underfunded, vulnerable, and dirty, but clean, clever, and competitive. Secure, reliable, and affordable energy resources are fundamental to sustained economic development. The threat of disruptive climate change, the erosion of energy security, and the world's growing demand for energy all pose major challenges for decision makers. Meeting these challenges and transforming our energy system will require better use of existing technologies, along with significant scientific innovation to spur on the adoption of new energy technologies. Therefore, urgent action is needed to allow rapid advancement of available energy efficiency and low-carbon technologies and practices. Basic science and energy research funding has been declining in the public and private sectors for several years. Additional funding is critically needed to develop a sustainable energy future. Research priorities encompass (inter alia) photovoltaics, carbon capture and sequestration (CCS), biofuels, and hydrogen generation, storage, and use. The largest share of CO_2 emissions is caused by fossil-fuel combustion for energy production and transportation. Methane is also produced by the energy (gas exploration) sector as well as by agriculture. In order to reduce emissions, fossil fuels need to be replaced by CO_2-free energy technologies; energy efficiency needs to be improved considerably; and more sustainable energy and agricultural production procedures need to become standard. As energy security, competitiveness, and the effect on the climate cannot and should not be separated, future policy options should combine all aspects. Europe, as the first nation in the world, has taken the lead in combining concrete targets for energy and climate policy (European Commission, 2007). Future climate policy negotiations should take account of joint initiatives and national activities. The Kyoto Protocol comprises concrete and binding emissions reduction targets. However, it only covers a few nations and specifies only very small emissions reduction targets.

Europe intends to cut emissions by 20% (compared with the 1990 level) by 2020 and to increase the share of renewable energy by 20% in the same time period. However, Europe is ready to reduce its emissions by as much as 30% if other nations are willing to accept climate policy commitments. It is important that Europe demonstrates the willingness and ability to cut emissions drastically. The Kyoto protocol needs to be fulfilled, the emissions trading scheme needs to be improved, and fair burden-sharing needs to be implemented. Europe cannot convince other nations to agree to any kind of climate commitments without being willing to reduce emissions by 30% by 2020.

References

Bundesministerium für Umwelt, Naturschutz und Reaktorsicherheit (BMU). 2006. Nationaler Allokationsplan 2008-2012 für die Bundesrepublik Deutschland. Berlin: BMU.

Edenhofer, O., Lessmann, K., Kemfert, C., Grubb, M. & Koehler, J. 2006. Induced technological change: exploring its implications for the Economics of atmospheric stabilization. The Energy Journal, Endogenous Technological Change (Special Issue): 57-107.

Energy Information Administration (EIA). 2007. World proved reserves of oil and natural gas, most recent estimates. Washington: EIA.

Fankhauser, S. 1994. The social costs of greenhouse gas emissions: an expected value approach. The Energy Journal, 15: 157-184.

Hope, C. (2005): Integrated assessment models. In D. Helm (Ed.), Climate-change Policy: 77-98. Oxford: Oxford University Press.

Intergovernmental Panel of Climate Change (IPCC). 2007. Climate change 2007, fourth assessment report, scientific basis. Cambridge: Cambridge University Press.

Kemfert, C. 2002a. An integrated assessment model of economy-energy-climate – the model WIAGEM. Integrated Assessment, 3: 281-299.

Kemfert, C. 2002b. Global economic implications of alternative climate policy strategies. Environmental Science and Policy, 5: 367-384.

Kemfert, C. 2005. Induced technological change in a multi-regional, multi-sectoral, integrated assessment model (WIAGEM): Impact Assessment of Climate Policy Strategies. Ecological Economics, 54: 293-305.

Kemfert, C. 2007. Economic costs of climate change Die Kosten des Klimawandels: Der Mensch heizt die Erde auf – was muss er dafür bezahlen? Internationale Politik, Februar: 38-45.

Lomborg, B. 2005. Global crisis, global solutions. www.copenhagenconsensus.com, 26th May 2008.

Münchner Rück. 2007. Jahresrückblick Naturkatastrophen 2006. Munich: Münchner Rück.

Nordhaus, W. & Boyer, J. 2000. Roll the dice again: economic modeling of climate change. Cambridge: MIT Press.

Nordhaus, W. 2002. Modelling induced innovation in climate change policy. In A. Grübler, N. Nakicenovic & W. Nordhaus (Eds.), Technological Change and the Environment: Resources for the Future: 97-127. Washington: RFF Press.

Organisation for Economic Co-operation and Development (OECD). 2007. Climate change in the European Alps: adapting winter tourism and natural hazards management. Paris: OECD.

Pittini, M. & Rahman, M. 2004. The social cost of carbon: key issues arising from a UK review. The benefits of climate change policies. Paris: OECD.

Rahmstorf, S. 2003. Rote Karte für die Leugner. Bild der Wissenschaft, 1: 56-61.

Schnellnhuber, J., Warren, R., Haxeltine, A. & Naylor, L. 2004. Integrated assessment of benefits of climate policy. The benefits of climate change policies. Paris: OECD.

Stern, N. 2006. The Stern review on the economics of climate change. Cambridge: Cambridge University Press.

Tol, R., Downing, T., Kuik, O. & Smith, J. 2004. Distributional aspects of climate change impacts. Global Environmental Change (Special Edition on the Benefits of Climate Policy Part A): 259-272.

Tol, R. S. J. 2002a. New estimates of the damage costs of climate change, part I: benchmark estimates. Environmental and Resource Economics, 21: 47-73.

Tol, R. S. J. 2002b. Estimates of the damage costs of climate change, part II: dynamic estimates. Environmental and Resource Economics, 21: 135-160.

United Nations Framework on Climate Change Convention (UNFCCC). 2006. Greenhouse gas emissions data for 1990-2005. Bonn: UNFCCC.

World Meteorological Organization (WMO). 2007. The global climate in 2007. Geneva: MeteoWorld Editor.

43 European Energy Policy on the Basis of the New Provisions in the Treaty of Lisbon

Ulrich Ehricke[1]

Daniel Hackländer[2]

Abstract

The Lisbon Treaty is intended to introduce a significant number of changes to the European Union's primary law, including the creation of a legal basis for an autonomous energy policy. Article 194 of the Treaty on the Functioning of the European Union (TFEU) provides the facility for a broad range of measures in the energy sector. In view of the most recent progress of Union activities in this sector, it is expected that the new competence will be exercised on a large scale even if the Lisbon Treaty does not come into force. This chapter outlines substance and scope of the prospective European Energy Policy by examining the objectives and guiding principles of Art. 194 TFEU.

Keywords: European Union, energy policy, legislative power

---

[1] Prof. Dr. Ulrich Ehricke, LL.M. (London), M.A., is a Judge at the Court of Appeals (OLG) Düsseldorf and Director of the Institute for European Law at the University of Cologne and the Institute for Energy Law at the University of Cologne, Germany.

[2] Daniel Hackländer is an Associate at the Institute for Energy Law at the University of Cologne, Germany.

A. Bausch and B. Schwenker (eds.), *Handbook Utility Management,*
DOI: 10.1007/978-3-540-79349-6_43, © Springer-Verlag Berlin Heidelberg 2009

43.1 Introduction

43.1.1 Basis for Current European Energy Policy

In recent times, European energy policy has experienced a considerable growth in significance, which should not be underestimated. It represents the benchmark for harmonization of national interests in the energy sector and forms the basis for balancing national and European interests and international commitments. According to the principle of limited authority, in accordance with Art. 5(1) of the EC Treaty (EC) the institutions of the EU may only act within the limits of the powers conferred upon them and of the objectives assigned to them in the Treaty. However, a comprehensive assignment of powers with respect to energy policy is lacking in the EC Treaty. The goals specified in Art. 3(1)(u) EC, energy, civil protection, and tourism, are the only ones in Art. 3 EC for which, according to current law, no competence provisions are laid down. The goals specify only that the Community should be active in the areas mentioned, and not what manner form this activity is to take.[3] In order to fulfill the assignment in Art. 3(1)(u), the Community institutions have so far had to rely on their own competence provisions, authorizations to act that are directed toward other goals. In particular, the harmonization competence with respect to the internal market in Art. 95 EC and the catch-all provision of 308 EC also serve as the legal basis for the enactment of energy policy measures, which in light of the principles of proportionality and subsidiarity represents a questionable practice. The absence of a legal basis for a comprehensive EU energy law is at odds with the need for a common approach to the regulation of further aspects of the relevant energy policy issues. In addition to the creation of a European internal energy market, it is the challenges of foreign energy and environmental policy that are best resolved at the EU level. Current law allows a loophole that Art. 194 Treaty on the Functioning of the Union (TFU) is intended to close (Fischer, 2008).

43.1.2 Development of the Energy Competence Provision

Even during the negotiations about the Maastricht Treaty in 1992, efforts were made to establish the energy sector as an independent policy area within the primary law of the EC (Maichel, 2005). In fact, in Art. 3(1)(t) EEC [now Art. 3(1)(u) EC] 'energy' is mentioned with respect to primary law for the very first time. By no means, however, do the measures in the area of energy represent an independent competence provision; rather, they just represent the setting of goals (Streinz, 2003, Art. 3 margin number 5 EG; Ruffert, 2007, Art. 3 margin number 2 EG; von Bogdandy, 2008, Art. 3 margin number 3 EG). In addition, Title XII (now Title XV), on trans-European networks, Art. 129(b-d) EEC (now Art. 154-156 EC), was inserted into the treaty; however, it does not authorize measures beyond the devel-

---

[3] Basedow (1995) therefore refers to the goals of Art. 3(u) EEC as 'area goals' to differentiate them from those that commit policy to a situation or a direction.

opment of the energy infrastructure. It was not until the deliberations at the European Convention were in progress that the energy sector made an appearance in the treaty language of the European Constitution.[4] Among the numerous changes foreseen by the Lisbon Treaty for the institutional framework of the European Union is a chapter on 'Energy', under Title XXI, Art. 194, of the Treaty on the Functioning of the Union (TFEU).[5] A norm was thus established that grants the Union extensive general energy policy authority while at the same time being intended to provide a legal basis for the energy policy that was already being applied. Art. 194 TFEU was based on the text of the Constitution and incorporated the language of Art. III-256 of the Treaty Establishing a Constitution for Europe (TCE) with editorial changes with respect to the legislative process in par. 2, 3 and substantial amendments to par. 1. A reference to energy solidarity and objective (d), i.e., promotion of the interconnection of networks, were added.

43.1.3   Reorganization of the European Competence Provisions

The creation of the competence provision for energy must be viewed in the context of the development of a better allocation and definition of the Union's powers. The implementation of this agenda was one of the major tasks of the European Convention. Questions of competence also play an important part in the Lisbon Treaty, since for the most part the corresponding provisions of the TCE were incorporated into the TEU and the TFEU.[6] In contrast to the current legal situation, the Treaty of Lisbon will fundamentally alter the allocation of the Union's competences. In accordance with Art. 3 and 4 TFEU, a distinction will be made between exclusive and shared competences. At the same time, in Art. 6 TFEU, a coordinating, supporting, and supplementing function has been proposed. In accordance with Art. 4(2)(i) TFEU, the area of 'energy' falls within the shared competence that will be regulated by Art. 2(2) TFEU. In the case of a competence shared by member states and the EU, European legal provisions on a matter are conclusive and binding if the Union has chosen to exercise its competence. A member state accordingly has regulatory authority only when the Union has issued no regulations or has retracted a previously existing regulation. Furthermore, the 2007 Intergovernmental Conference issued a "Declaration in relation to the delimitation of com-

---

[4] The preliminary draft of the constitution did not yet contain the energy competence provision. The first mention of the energy sector occurs in the article on the competences divided between Union and the member states. At the same time, it was pointed out that the incorporation of the energy sector in the list of areas of divided responsibility would necessitate the establishment of a special legal basis in the area of policies (European Convention, 2003).

[5] In the treaty language the energy chapter is labeled, "Title XX, Art. 176a." According to Art. 5 of the Treaty of Lisbon, however, the numbering will be revised in accordance with the printed table of equivalences in the Treaty annex; hereinafter, the new numbering method will be followed.

[6] For an overview see Weber (2008).

petences" (cf. OJ 2007 C 306, 256f.). This declaration specifies the conditions in which an EU institution may repeal legislation, specifically, "to ensure constant respect for the principles of subsidiarity and proportionality." The principles of conferral and subsidiarity, as well as the principle of proportionality, are stipulated in Art. 5 TEU – which largely corresponds to the provisions of Art. 5 EC.

43.1.4   The Future of European Energy Policy

Against the backdrop of the – currently still uncertain – fate of the Treaty of Lisbon, it is not possible to say with any certainty whether or in what form Art. 194 TFEU will actually come into effect. There are presently three conceivable options for the future of the Union treaties:

- The Treaty of Lisbon, either in its present form or in a modified and possibly renamed variant, will be presented to the Irish people once again.
- The reform process will be suspended and integration resumed at some time in the future, with the treaties in the Nice version.
- A new 'European core', consisting of those states agreeing to integration in accordance with Art. 43ff. TEU, will be established.

Regardless of further political developments and the question of whether provisions for a European energy policy in the context of a specific provision of competence will be included in the text, it is safe to say that the goals for a European energy policy that were formulated in the Treaty of Lisbon will remain valid in the future. Even though defeat of the Lisbon Treaty is possible, they thus definitely have a significant relevance, and it is fully to be expected that in future treaty revisions the legal basis already formulated for a European energy policy will be taken into account.

43.2   The Elements of Art. 194(1) TFEU

43.2.1   The Energy Policy of the Union

To address the substance of the individual energy policy targets, it is necessary to define the term 'energy policy of the Union'.

The lack of restrictions in the conceptual version leads to the conclusion that all activities directed at influencing the production, distribution, or consumption of energy will be addressed by the Union. Already, on the basis of the previous understanding of the EU institutions, all raw energy resources and sources of energy would also be included in European energy policy. Thus, the energy policy of the (joint) Commission addressed the supply of oil, gas, and electricity in general, but equally the production of electricity by nuclear energy in particular (cf. European Commission, 2007a, b). It is questionable, however, whether Art. 194 TFEU also covers measures in the area of nuclear power, or whether in that case only the Euratom treaty is relevant.

According to prevailing law, the specialized Euratom treaty, in accordance with Art. 305(2) EC, has priority over the general regulations of the EC (Petersmann & Spennemann, 2004, Art. 305 EG margin number 14; Kokott, 2003, Art. 305 margin number 9f. EG; Schmalenbach, 2007, Art. 305 margin number 3 EG). On the other hand, neither TFEU nor TEU contains any provision for priority of Euratom. The Treaty of Lisbon, however, does specify crucial changes in the Euratom agreement and introduces Art. 106a (OJ 2007 C 306, 199ff.). Art. 106a(1) lists the provisions of the TFEU that are to be applied to Euratom; however, no reference to the policies of the Union – particularly Art. 194 and/or 176a TFEU – is found there. The referenced regulations of TEU and TFEU deal first and foremost with procedural and institutional provisions, such as institutional stipulations, general procedural principles, judicial protection before the European Court of Justice, and financial regulations. Deviating provisions of Euratom, particularly those with respect to the institutional bodies of the European Atomic Energy Community (EAEC), are abrogated. Accordingly, Art. 106(3) Euratom states that the new provisions in TFEU and TEU: "shall not derogate from the provisions of this treaty." This, however, still does not answer the question of whether, after deletion of Art. 305(2) EC, Euratom will retain its special position with respect to TFEU.[7] But even if basically a special case is assumed for the Euratom regulations, a subsidiary application of Art. 194 TFEU cannot automatically be ruled out. Whether the EAEC competences represent definitive special provisions was already contentious in the context of the application of EC subsidies for state support of the establishment and operation of nuclear power plants according to Art. 87ff. EC (cf. Pechstein, 2001). Under the new law, it is thus worth examining the pre-emptive effect of the Euratom regulations in the context of the particular individual cases, as nuclear energy policy measures could also come under the provisions of Art. 194 TFEU.

43.2.2   The Regulatory Mechanism of Art. 194(1) TFEU

The enumeration of the goals in Art. 194(1)(a-d) TFEU is preceded by 'a spirit of solidarity', 'the establishment and functioning of the internal market', and 'the need to preserve and improve the environment', three principles that are to be taken heed of, and within whose framework the Union's energy policy must unfold. The linking of the objectives with these three different standards raises questions about the sense and purpose of this method of regulation. The term 'guiding principles' is used hereinafter as the generic heading for the concepts to follow and their differentiation by legal nature and significance. The placement of the guiding principles sets them apart from the energy policy goals. The guiding principles have been 'bumped up', so to speak, and are thus applicable to all goals named in

---

[7] Schmidt-Preuß (2003); for other views: Jasper (2003); each with respect to Art. III-157 of the Draft Constitutional Treaty (=III-256 TEC).

Art. 194(1)(a-d). Because of these differing approaches, the goals and the guiding principles must be examined separately.

43.2.3   The Goals Defined in Art. 194(1)(a-d) TFEU

In accordance with Art. 194(2) TFEU, the Union is authorized to enact the measures necessary for the attainment of its energy policy goals and goals. Art. 194 TFEU thus represents both an allocation of tasks and the provision of competence. The content and meaning of the goals named in Art. 194(1) TFEU, "the functioning of the energy market" (a), "security of energy supply" (b), "energy efficiency and [...] renewable forms of energy" (c), and the "interconnection of energy networks" (d), are thus crucial in the provision of competence for the enactment of legal instruments. To answer questions about the legal aspects and the binding nature of the goals set down in Art. 194(1) TFEU, we can look at comparable regulations in the EC. On the basis of similar regulatory methods and the closeness of the content to the area of energy policy, we can draw on the standards for industrial and environmental policy, Art. 157 and 174 EC. Both the goals of the joint industrial policy in accordance with Art. 157(1) EC and those of the environmental policy Art. 174(1) EC are generally held to be legal obligations, rather than nonbinding policy guidelines (Kallmayer, 2007, Art. 157 EG margin number 5 / Calliess, 2007, Art. 174 EG margin number 42; Kahl, 2003, Art. 174 EG margin number 41). Thus, it is reasonable to conclude that the standards in Art. 194(1) TFEU likewise represent specific directives for action. If a need for regulation thus exists (and ascertainment of this admittedly leaves a great deal of room for interpretation), the Union is therefore not only authorized, but also obligated, to take action.

43.2.3.1 Functioning of the Energy Market

According to Art. 194(1)(a) TFEU, functioning of the 'energy market' is to be ensured. Initially this might appear to refer to the internal energy market as a subset of the general internal market concept of the Union. Should this be the case, it is then necessary to explain what is meant by the formulation: efforts "to ensure the functioning of the energy market" will be pursued "in the context of the establishment [...] of the internal market." It is possible that this repeated reference to the internal market is merely a superfluous repetition, but the emphasis on the significance of a functioning internal market for the energy sector could equally be intentional.

The appellation 'energy market', as opposed to 'internal energy market', however, has led us to conclude that a distinction must be drawn between the goal of Art. 194(1)(a) TFEU and that of creating an internal market. In the interests of comprehensibility of the legal text, the differing designation can only be justified if the two concepts also differ in substance.[8] While the energy market represents the market for the commodity 'energy', use of the term 'internal energy market' presupposes dissociation from the corresponding national markets. The internal energy market is thus concerned with internal cross-border issues within the Union. Unlike the internal energy market, which conceptually is concerned with the realm of the member states, it is not possible to "ensure the functioning of the energy market" without reference to the international aspects. Inasmuch as most of the member states of the Union are to a large degree dependent on imports,[9] securing a sufficient offering of energy necessitates reliable delivery of the same. The functioning of the energy market in its current form would be unthinkable today without a 'foreign energy policy' based on good relations with the supplier countries (Schmidt-Preuß, 2007; Müller, 2006). If the lack of a topographic reference is accentuated, the goal of Art. 194(1)(a) TFEU could possibly justify corresponding diplomatic activities by the Union.

Unlike the internal market (Art. 14(2) EC; Art. 26 TFEU), which, as a central goal and fundamental tenet of the Union, is first and foremost a concept of law, 'market' refers to a place where supply and demand meet, and is thus an economic term. It is questionable whether all aspects of supply and demand in all 'energy markets' that can be distinguished – which on the basis of the products being bought and sold (fuel or electricity), for example, might involve the temporal dimension (balancing power and forward markets) or trade volume and type of participants (power wholesale trade and retail suppliers) – would fall under the regulatory authority of the Union or whether the term must be understood in a narrower sense. In addition to the relationship to the internal market concept, the extent to which a functioning energy market embraces lowest possible energy prices is also questionable. European primary law does not specifically name favorable pricing of the supply as an energy policy goal. Nor does the European energy policy use such terms. Rather – with the pursuit of the internal energy market in mind – the talk is instead of 'competitiveness'. At the same time, there are no signs of a positive effect of competition on energy prices. European energy policy assumes that the liberalization of the energy markets will simultaneously ensure low energy prices, contribute to energy savings, and promote investment (European Commission, 2007a, c). As a result, the fundamental question on the relationship between low prices for the supply of energy and notions of competitiveness remains unanswered. The particular emphasis on ideas about the market and about competition is certainly logical, in light of the fact that to date the Community has based the vast majority of its energy policy measures on the internal market authority invested in Art. 95 EC.[10] This legislative practice, characterized by instrumental use

---

[8] For other views see Maichel (2005), who views the goal and scope of Art. III-256 TEC as identical.

[9] In 2005, the average EU-27 dependence on imported fuel was 52.5%, and Germany was 61.6% dependent (European Commission, 2007d).

[10] Important examples would be the directives concerning the internal market in electricity and natural gas, 96/92/EC and 98/30/EC respectively, as well as the so-called acceleration directives 2003/54/EC and 2003/55/EC.

of the competition competence, must, however, be seen against the backdrop of the lack of an overall energy policy authority. The Commission points out the absence of the needed coherence in existing EU energy policy strategy, which derives from both environmental and internal market measures (European Commission, 2007a). It is thus all the more remarkable that even after the modifications to the Treaty of Lisbon, the influencing of energy prices is apparently linked to the de lege lata available instrument of market influence.

43.2.3.2 Security of Energy Supply in the Union

Security of energy supply is generally understood to mean the sufficient and reliable fulfillment of the demand for energy. To ensure the security of energy supply, first of all the procurement or production of energy is required, and secondly the provision and maintenance of the technical infrastructure necessary to meet the needs of the end-user. Ensuring a secure supply of energy is one of the fundamental goals of the energy policy. In this context, the problematic relationship between Euratom and TFEU could be relevant. After notifying the Council and Parliament, the Commission proposed a directive providing for a uniform framework for the disposal of used fuel rods and radioactive waste and also uniform standards to ensure nuclear safety (European Commission, 2003). The measures were to be based on the Euratom competence for the protection of health in accordance with Art. 30 ff. Euratom. Prevailing opinion was that a corresponding legal basis could be derived neither from the provisions mentioned nor from the unwritten legal powers of the Community (von Danwitz, 2003; Heller, 2002; Maichel, 2003; drawing a distinction: Hermes, 2004). Thus, in the end, the proposed draft directive, the so-called nuclear package, was not implemented. With the passage of the TFEU, however, the legal framework with respect to the competence in the field of radiation protection and the monitoring of nuclear materials must be newly assessed;[11] it may be that the measures proposed by the Commission can now be based on the competence to ensure security of the energy supply.[12]

43.2.3.3 Energy Efficiency, Energy Saving, New and Renewable Forms of Energy

A further goal concerns the promotion of energy efficiency and savings, and the development of new and renewable sources of energy. All four aspects of the objectives of Art. 194(1)(c) TFEU serve the protection of the environment and supply in one way or another. With these various approaches and effects as the starting point, it is necessary to differentiate systematically between the promotion of

---

[11] The question of the Union's regulatory authority is not only of theoretical interest. That the Commission is still striving for the establishment of a uniform legal framework can be seen in the recommendation of "the management of financial resources for the decommissioning of nuclear installations, spent fuel and radioactive waste" (2006/851/Euratom).

[12] The competence to ensure the functioning of the energy market could also be relevant; see also Jasper (2003).

energy efficiency and savings on the one hand and the promotion of new and renewable energy resources on the other. The first two aspects aid in the more effective use of already existing resources. 'Energy savings' means avoidance of the unnecessary use of energy, and 'energy efficiency' refers to a higher yield in the unavoidable expenditure of energy. Thus, both involve contributions of a quantitative nature. The end-goal of both energy efficiency and energy savings is to reduce the total demand for energy. Consequently there is increasing leeway for the implementation of politically preferable (new and renewable) energy sources for energy production. Art. 2(a) in Directive 2001/77/EC, on the promotion of electricity produced from renewable energy sources in the internal electricity market, begins with a negative definition of renewable energy sources by first classifying fossil fuels as conventional, nonrenewable energy sources. A listing of what are seen as renewable energy sources follows, which, as the parentheses make clear, cannot be viewed as conclusive.[13] No basis for an alternative meaning of the term 'renewable energies' is evident in Art. 194(1)(c) TFEU. It may well be decisive that renewable energy overcomes the disadvantages of the use of coal, oil, and gas – the foremost of which are the production of greenhouse gases and the threat to a secure supply posed by dependence on imports.

43.2.3.4 Promotion of the Interconnection of Energy Networks

The essence of the goal of interconnection of energy networks can only be ascertained in the context of the other goals, and particularly the internal energy market. The connection between the energy networks of the member states is the necessary precondition for transnational trading of grid-bound energy supplies. Thus the development of the Trans-European Energy Networks (TEN-E) initially serves the import and export of electricity and gas and thus the implementation of the internal market concept. At the same time, TEN-E makes a contribution to security of supply, the extent depending on the relative import dependence of the various member states. The Commission also emphasizes the importance of the networks for an "internal energy market that ensures the secure supply." (European Commission, 2006). Network security, meaning safeguarding against power failures by means of technical safety and reliability standards, is to be accompanied by the establishment of a "formal grouping of transmission system operators," which, it is suggested, could develop into a "European Centre for Energy Networks." However, it is questionable whether such measures can actually be supported by Art. 194 TFEU, or whether Art. 171-172 TFEU (Art. 154-155 EC) are more probably relevant. Owing to the lack of a legal basis for energy issues, such issues have not yet arisen. The (few) Community measures in this area, in accordance with the standards in Art. 155 EC, are based on the guidelines instrument.[14] EU guidelines are, of course, binding, legal planning instruments (according to

---

[13] Listed as renewable energy resources: wind, solar, geothermal, wave, tidal, hydropower, biomass, landfill gas, sewage treatment plant gas, and biogases.

[14] Cf. Decision No 1364/2006/EC of the European Parliament and of the Council, which rescinds the two previous TEN-E directives 1229/2003/EC and 96/391/EC.

current opinion: Calliess, 2007, Art. 155 EG margin number 4; Schäfer, 2003, Art. 154 EG margin number 24, Art. 155 margin number 4; Erdmenger, 2003, Art. 155 EG margin numbers 16ff. Lecheler, 2008, Art. 155 EG margin number 3). Even so, the actual development of TEN-E is plodding along slowly, as there are no standards in place with respect to the form and duration of the frequently prolonged national ratification procedures.[15] Thus, directives based on Art. 194(1)(c) TFEU, which obligates the member states to expedite projects in the European interest in the area of energy, could provide a remedy.[16]

43.2.4 The Guiding Principles of the Energy Policy

The designation of the internal market concept as the 'context' ['Rahmen' in the German text] for the energy policy suggests a certain delimitation of the energy competence. The same goes for the 'regard' for environmental issues. The pursuit of the energy policy 'in a spirit of solidarity', in contrast, initially seems to represent more of a stand-alone goal than a delimitation. It is possible that the principle of solidarity is intended to serve as a corrective to the internal market concept. The legal character of the guiding principles is consequently not as easy to ascertain as that of the goals and calls for a more finely differentiated approach.

43.2.4.1 The General Framework of the Internal Market

Art. 194(1) TFEU says that the goals of the energy policy shall be pursued "in the context of the establishment and functioning of the internal market." The essence of the internal market that Art. 194(1) TFEU makes reference to is defined in Art. 26 TFEU (previously Art. 14 EC) and specifically comprises – unchanged from the current law – the four fundamental freedoms of free movement of persons, services, goods, and capital, in addition to protection from distortion of competition. Nevertheless, the general goals of the internal market will need to be reassessed in future EU treaties. "The internal market" was the first title in the third section of TFEU and this thus automatically becomes an autonomous policy area. It is furthermore cited as a consideration in the preamble to the TEU and is legally sanctioned and enshrined ("The Union shall establish an internal market") in Art. 3(3) TEU, which means it is still an important goal and instrument of Union policy. In German linguistic usage, the word 'Rahmen' establishes the outermost scope or framework of a matter, thus embodying a spatial delimitation. The French, Spanish, and Italian versions, too, use terms ('cadre', 'marco', and 'quadro', respectively) whose meaning corresponds to the German 'Rahmen' and calls up the same association. The English version uses "in the context of", a more open-ended formulation that does not necessarily lead to the conclusion that the internal market concept represents a barrier to the energy policy goals. Logically, the inwardly oriented concept of the internal market could represent a spatial limitation with

---

[15] For details of the problems see Meier-Weigt (2007).

[16] Meier-Weigt (2007), which proposes Art. 14, 154 EC as a legal basis.

respect to ensuring the functioning of the energy market, a limitation with numerous cross-border aspects. The same is true for the goals of Art. 194(1)(b) and (c) TFEU. The teleological interpretation of the term, on the other hand, makes this interpretation doubtful. The internal market was always a means to attainment of the greater goals of the Community and Union. As already mentioned, the numerous energy policy measures of the EU generally drew on the legal grounds for harmonization of the internal market. If the internal market concept did indeed represent the outermost limit of the Union's energy policy measures, it would suggest that the new legal authorizations do not extend beyond the measures that the internal market competence already permits. The introduction of a general competence provision for energy would bring with it no additional competences and thus would be largely of a declaratory nature.[17] Such an interpretation, however, conflicts not only with the long-standing controversy about the introduction of an energy competence into European primary law, but also with the carefully worked out standardization of goals, boundaries, and procedures of the EU energy legislation in Art. 194 TFEU.

43.2.4.2 Regard for Environmental Protection

A further guiding principle of the energy policy is the 'regard for the need to preserve and improve the environment'. As with the internal market, environmental protection here involves an independent policy area of the Union, to which the energy competence makes reference. Art. 191-193 TFEU, which replace Art. 174 ff. EC, regulate the Union task of environmental protection. The term 'environment' is not defined any more specifically, which leads to the general conclusion that neither material nor geographic limitations apply and that the meaning was intentionally left open (Calliess, 2007, Art. 174 EG margin number 8; Kahl, 2003, Art. 174 EG margin numbers 35ff.; Krämer, 2003, Art. 174 EG margin number 3). Art. 191 ff. TFEU are to be decisively reformed with respect to the regulations in the EC: the goal of, "deal[ing] with [...] worldwide environmental problems" [Art. 191(1)(indent 4) TFEU] is amended to include a reference to 'combating climate change'; however, the Community has pursued a comprehensive environmental protection policy since the introduction of its environmental competence with the Single European Act (SEA) in 1987.[18] Thus, the effect of the reference to climate change is most likely above all declaratory. The change does make it clear that environmental protection also encompasses protection of the climate and thus underscores an aspect of environmental protection that has a decisive influence on European and national energy law. Issues of environmental protection, however,

---

[17] For this approach see Schmidt-Preuß (2003) on Art. III-157 of the Draft Constitutional Treaty (=Art. III-257 TEC).

[18] Ex Art. 130r–130t EC. The first legal instruments making reference to the environment were issued in the late 1970s. Since 1972 the EC has pursued its own environmental action programs, the legal instruments being based on the harmonization competence and on the competence for closing gaps according to Art. 100, 295 EEC (cf. Kahl, 2003, Art. 174 EG margin numbers 1ff).

influence not only energy law but also the various other areas of nonenvironmental law, such as chemicals, planning and building, and local law. Climate protection law thus cannot be viewed as merely a subset of environmental protection law. It is very much a classic cross-sectional field of law. Consideration of environmental and climate protection in the energy competence provision must also be gauged against the backdrop of the so-called integration principle. Art. 194 TFEU reveals the increasing intertwining of energy and environmental concerns, not only through the explicit reference in par. 1, but also through its categorical placement directly after the environment title. The significance of 'regard for the need to preserve and improve the environment' must thus be assessed especially in light of the EU environment competence.

43.2.4.3 Energy Solidarity

The explicit anchoring of the solidarity principle in the area of energy represents a change with respect to the wording of the energy competence in the TCE. It already differs from the other two guiding principles in that no corresponding policy area exists in primary law [cf. Art. 4(2)(a, e) TFEU]. The principle of solidarity is mentioned not only in Art. 194 TFEU: Overall, the frequency of references to the concept of solidarity – a term in need of expansion – in the EU treaties has increased significantly in the language of the Treaty of Lisbon. Art. 2 EC (as amended by the Treaty of Nice) contains a single positive legal reference to the principle of solidarity as a structural principle of the Union. In contrast, in the TFEU, with the multiple mentions of the term in various areas of the internal policies as well as the 'solidarity clause' in the section on Union foreign trade, the term is used not only more frequently, but also more specifically.[19] Solidarity among the member states and 'between their peoples' was already established as a fundamental goal in the TEU [cf. Preamble and Art. 1(3)(2nd sentence) TEU]. The ECJ paraphrases the 'duty of solidarity' as the balance between the advantages and encumbrances associated with membership in the Community.[20] Solidarity in energy matters will most likely be relevant with regard to measures to ensure supply security, but it may also have an influence on the goal of interconnection of networks. The Commission policy confirms this assessment; it also criticizes the lack of mechanisms to ensure solidarity in the form of mutual assistance among member states in the event of an energy crisis (European Commission, 2007a).[21] Finally, a "European Energy Supply Observatory [...] to monitor the demand and supply" is to be established in order to monitor the energy markets, identify shortfalls, and continue the work of the International Energy Agency at EU level (European

---

[19] In addition to Art. 194 TFU, see also Art. 67, 80 TFU (border control, immigration, asylum), Art. 122 TFU (economic policy), Art. 222 TFU (terrorist attacks, natural and manmade disasters).

[20] ECJ, Case 39/72, Court of Justice Reports 1973, 101, margin number 24 f (Commission/Italy).

[21] Whether such support refers to technical assistance to rebuild destroyed infrastructure or to the delivery of substitute energy to fulfill demand is left open in this opinion.

Commission, 2006). As long ago as in 2002 the Commission had already proposed a directive including measures to ensure the secure supply of natural gas, and also the alignment of measures regarding the secure supply of petroleum products (European Commission, 2002). The comprehensive proposal for a directive called not only for stockholding obligations for crude oil and gas, but also for the creation or harmonization of a crisis intervention mechanism. The legal instrument was to be based on Art. 95 EC. In the end the proposal was rejected by the Council for various political reasons (Council of the European Union, 2003). The questionable choice of the internal market competence for regulation of the area was not criticized. The question of the extent and the choice of the appropriate legal basis for such measures is likely to return in the future. In the withdrawal of their legislative proposal, the Commission emphasized their intention of adjusting the current legal framework to suit the geopolitical requirements and reserved the right to put forward further proposals for directives (European Commission, 2004). The proposals in the Energy Green Paper of 2006, in which reference was once again made to the necessity for monitoring of the energy markets and identification of supply shortfalls as well as taking up the tasks of the IEA, demonstrate that the establishment of crisis intervention mechanisms continues to be on the Commission's political agenda (European Commission, 2006).

Finally, there remains the question of how the principle of solidarity relates to the internal market. A common point of reference with respect to the principle of solidarity and the principle of competition as represented by the market and the internal market is common welfare. The approaches of these two principles, however, could not be more different. According to the classic lessons of economics, the individualistic pursuit of gain in a free market, through its positive effect on price levels, also leads to an increase in common welfare (Stavenhagen, 1998). The principle of self-interest thus drives economic events to the benefit of all. According to these classic liberal notions of competition, which are still accepted as valid today, it is thus the egotistic striving of the individual that is the foremost priority. The principle of solidarity, on the other hand, typifies common interest, shared identity, and mutual support.

Just as the market must be protected from events that are harmful to competition, legally binding energy solidarity requires the enactment of regulations by the Union and/or the member states, as discussed above with reference to the example of crisis intervention mechanisms. The implementation of such regulations has the potential to impede the free flow of economic and social processes. Institutionalized solidarity and EU competition law exist side by side in an uneasy relationship that needs to be critically examined. In this context, introduction of the energy solidarity principle could suggest a weakening of the competitively organized energy economy model (Basedow, 2008). On the other hand, the competition policy of the European institutions has proved in the past to be one of the most effective instruments of integration by far (Basedow, 2008). In this sense, the principle of competition also serves to promote solidarity.

43.2.5   Goal Conflicts and Hierarchies

EU energy policy has so far had to get along without primary law objectives. It has oriented itself on the general consideration that the supply of energy should proceed in a manner that is as secure, economical, and environmentally responsible as possible (cf. European Commission, 1995, 2006, 2007a). The ongoing supply of energy to consumers at manageable prices forms the common point of departure of the entire energy policy. Along with this comes the goal of environmental protection, pursuit of which is intended to ensure the secure and economical supply of sustainable energy. Under these premises, the goals and guiding principles mentioned in Art. 194(1) TFEU are not – for the most part – an end in themselves. In any case, the goals of interconnecting networks and promoting energy efficiency and renewable energy are not identical with the three end-goals of energy policy and therefore represent at most only a means to the attainment of these and/or subordinated goals. In the light of the differences with respect to the goal of low energy supply prices, the same applies to the goal of a functioning energy market. It does not apply to the goal of a secure energy supply, which is easily defined as one of the three end-goals of energy policy. Low price, secure supply, and environmental sustainability retain their validity as overriding goals, so that Art. 194(1) TFEU can only be understood as a clarification of what are viewed as intermediate goals of expediency on the way to attainment of the ultimate goals. The significance of the codification of certain aspects of energy policy by means of the goals and guiding principles in Art. 194(1) TFEU lies in what they reveal about the emphasis being given to the overriding objectives.

43.3   Legislative Procedures, Art. 194(2) TFEU

In accordance with Art. 194(2) TFEU, legal instruments for the implementation of energy policy goals are to be enacted through the ordinary legislative procedure (Art. 289(1), 294 TFEU). Compared with the codecision procedure in Art. 251 EC, there is new language in Art. 294 TFEU, but it essentially conforms to the EC procedure (Fischer, 2008). It is thus to be expected that the still dominant legal form of the directive will continue to shape the secondary energy legislation of the Union.

43.4   The Limits of the EU's Energy Competence

The limits of the Union's authority in the area of energy can be derived, on the one hand, as Art. 194(2)(1) makes clear, from the general principles of law and, on the other, from the powers of the member states mentioned in Art. 194(1)(2).

43.4.1 Subsidiarity and Proportionality

According to the principle of subsidiarity, which is set down in Art. 5(3) TEU with only minimal modifications from Art. 5 EC, the member states have priority over the Union in matters in accordance with their capabilities (Calliess, 2007, Art. 5 EG margin number 2 EG; Zuleeg, 2003, Art. 5 EG margin number 27). A new development, drawn from the TEC, is the explicit reference to the "Protocol on the application of the principles of subsidiarity and proportionality" (OJ 2007, C 306, 150).[22] Compared with the subsidiarity protocol of the Amsterdam Treaty (OJ 1997, C 340, 105), certainly the Protocol contains no substantial innovations with respect to interpretation of the material substance of the subsidiarity principle, but there are two procedural developments that should be mentioned. First, the proposals of the Commission will no longer be considered only at Union level, but will also be sent on to the national legislatures. Secondly, there will be the possibility to bring an action for nullity before the ECJ in the case of a violation of the subsidiarity principle. With the expansion of the competences in the energy sector, there will thus also be new instruments for assertion of the subsidiarity principle by the member states – control ex ante by means of the national parliaments and ex post before the ECJ. A further legal restraint on the exercise of competences is created by the competence principle of proportionality in accordance with Art. 5(4) TEU. In this connection, we must also observe the protocol regulations on the application of the principles of subsidiarity and proportionality.

43.4.2 The Restrictions in Art. 194(2)(2) TFEU

Further restrictions on the energy competence of the Union crop up in the special barriers laid out in Art. 194(2)(2) TFEU. The paragraph enumerates three 'rights' of the member states that energy measures legislated by the Union 'shall not affect'. Art. 194(2)(2) TFEU defines the legal rights that the member states are entitled to regardless of the competing energy competence of the Union in accordance with Art. 194(1) TFEU. The interpretation of these material restrictions may become quite significant in light of the overlap between the rights of the member states and the measures to be implemented on the basis of the energy policy goals. As an example, the provision of a solidarity mechanism between the member states enacted on the basis of the competence to ensure a secure energy supply would be very likely also to touch on their right to stipulate the conditions for utilization of their energy resources (e.g., the decision to release oil reserves).

The rights of the member state remain valid, but only insofar as this does not involve any prejudice to Art. 192(2)(c) TFEU. Accordingly, measures that significantly affect a member state's choice of energy sources and the general structure of its energy supply will not be enacted in ordinary legislative proceedings, but rather by unanimous decision of the Council. In both the above-mentioned aspects, the wording is exactly the same for two of the three member state rights in

---

[22] On the legal nature of protocols, see Kokott, 2003, Art. 311 EG margin numbers 3ff.

Art. 194(2)(2) TFEU. Interpretation of the implications of this reference is not unproblematic, since a standard that materially restricts a competence contains a reference to a procedural provision. Various conclusions can be drawn from the reference, one being that (only) the consensus requirement of the environmental measures would be conveyed to the energy competence. Such a conveyance would ensure that environmental and energy law procedure were compatible, thus ensuring that the national right of veto provided for in accordance with Art. 192(2)(c) TFEU in the event of measures 'significantly affecting' the concerns mentioned could not be gotten around; so understood, the reference is a matter of a procedural restriction (Maichel, 2005). This interpretation, however, is undermined by the development of the energy competence provision. In accordance with Art. 194(3) TFEU, the requirement of unanimity is also to be applied to measures in the field of energy when these are of a predominantly tax-related nature. Paragraph 3 deals with an exception to the regulation of the ordinary legislative proceedings according to paragraph 2; however, the second paragraph also precisely encompasses the second subparagraph, and thus the reference to Art. 192(2)(c) TFEU. Aside from the methodological irregularity of the appearance of the requirement for unanimity in both paragraphs, the unambiguous wording "by way of derogation from paragraph 2" also argues against understanding it as a procedure.

According to Art. 192(2)(c) TFEU, only those measures that 'significantly' affect a member state's choice between various energy sources and the general structure of its energy supply are to be unanimously enacted by the Council. Art. 194(2)(2) TFEU, on the other hand, contains no reference to the extent of the legal intervention. On the contrary, the open-ended formulation leads to the inference that all measures of legal relevance, regardless of their gravity, come under this provision. In this case, Art. 194(2)(2) TFEU would have to be classified as a strict prohibition on intervention. Such an interpretation would mean that measures that come up against the legal basis of the environmental competence could justify extensive interventions in the energy sector that would not be covered by the genuine energy competence.

References

Basedow, J. 2008. Das Sozialmodell von Lissabon: Solidarität statt Wettbewerb? EuZW, 19: 225.

Basedow, J. 1995. Zielkonflikte und Zielhierarchien im Vertrag über die Europäische Gemeinschaft. In O. Due, M. Lutter & J. Schwarze (Eds.), Festschrift für Ulrich Everling, vol I: 49-68. Baden-Baden: Nomos.

Calliess, C. 2007. C. Callies & M. Ruffert (Eds.), EUV/EGV: Das Verfassungsrecht der Europäischen Union mit Europäischer Grundrechtecharta. Munich: C. H. Beck.

Council of the European Union. 2003. Draft Minutes: 2507th meeting of the Council (Transport/Communications/Energy) held in Brussels on 14 May 2003. 9317/03. Brussels.

Erdmenger, J. 2003. H. von der Groeben & J. Schwarze (Eds.), Kommentar zum Vertrag über die Europäische Union und zur Gründung der Europäischen Gemeinschaft, vol 3, Baden-Baden: Nomos.

European Commission. 1995. White Paper – an energy policy for the European Union, COM(1995) 682 final. Brussels.

European Commission. 2002. Proposal for a Council Decision repealing Council Decision 68/416/EEC on the conclusion and implementation of individual agreements between governments relating to the obligation of Member States to maintain minimum stocks of crude oil and/or petroleum products and Council Decision 77/706/EEC on the setting of a Community target for a reduction in the consumption of primary sources of energy in the event of difficulties in the supply of crude oil and petroleum products, COM(2002) 488 final. Brussels.

European Commission. 2003. Proposal for a Council Directive (Euratom) on the management of spent nuclear fuel and radioactive waste, COM(2003) 32 final. Brussels.

European Commission. 2004. Withdrawal of legislative proposals on oil stocks: the Commission will prepare fresh initiatives, Press Release IP/04/1274. Brussels.

European Commission. 2006. A European strategy for sustainable, competitive and secure energy, COM(2006) 105 final. Brussels.

European Commission. 2007a. An energy policy for Europe, COM(2007) 1 final. Brussels.

European Commission. 2007b. Nuclear illustrative programme, COM(2007) 565 final. Brussels.

European Commission. 2007c. Commission staff working document – accompanying the legislative package on the internal market for electricity and gas – Impact Assessment Summary. SEC(2007) 1180. Brussels.

European Commission. 2007d. Statistical pocket book energy 2007, Part 2: Energy.

European Convention. 2003. Draft of Articles 1 to 16 of the Constitutional Treaty, CONV 528/03. Brussels.

Fischer, K. H. 2008. Der Vertrag von Lissabon. Baden-Baden [u.a.]: Nomos.

Heller, W. 2002. "Nuclear package" – ante portas – zur Regelungskompetenz der EU, atw 47: 788.

Hermes, G. 2004. Auf dem Weg zu einem europäischen Atomrecht? Zur Kompetenz der Europäischen Atomgemeinschaft für das „Nuklearpaket" vor dem Hintergrund der jüngsten Rechtsprechung des EuGH, ZUR 15: 12-25.

Jasper, M. 2003. Der Verfassungsentwurf des europäischen Konvents und mögliche Konsequenzen für das Energie- bzw. Atomrecht. ZNER, 7: 210-213.

Kahl, W. 2003. Streinz, R. (Ed.), EUV/EGV, Vertrag über die Europäische Union und Vertrag zur Gründung der Europäischen Gemeinschaft. Munich: C. H. Beck.

Kallmayer, A. 2007. C. Callies & M. Ruffert (Eds.), EUV/EGV: das Verfassungsrecht der Europäischen Union mit Europäischer Grundrechtecharta. Munich: C. H. Beck.

Kokott, J. 2003. R. Streinz (Ed.), EUV/EGV, Vertrag über die Europäische Union und Vertrag zur Gründung der Europäischen Gemeinschaft. Munich: C. H. Beck.

Krämer, L. 2003. H. von der Groeben & J. Schwarze (Eds.), Kommentar zum Vertrag über die Europäische Union und zur Gründung der Europäischen Gemeinschaft, vol 3. Baden-Baden: Nomos.

Lecheler, H. 2008. E. Grabitz & M. Hilf (Eds.), Das Recht der Europäischen Union, vol III. Munich: C. H. Beck.

Maichel, G. 2003. Energiepolitik in Europa, Perspektiven für den Standort Deutschland, atw 48: 156-160.

Maichel, G. 2005. Das Energiekapitel in der Europäischen Verfassung – mehr Integration oder mehr Zentralismus für die leitungsgebundene Energiewirtschaft Europas? In R. Hendler, M. Ibler & J. M. Soria (Eds.), Für Sicherheit, für Europa: Festschrift für Volkmar Götz zum 70. Geburtstag: 55-70. Göttingen: Vandenhoeck & Ruprecht.

Meier-Weigt, B. 2007. Die Vorhaben von europäischem Interesse nach den Transeuropäischen Energienetze – TEN-E – Leitlinien und ihre Umsetzung in den europäischen Mitgliedsstaaten. IR, 4: 7-8.

Müller, F. 2006. Energie-Außenpolitik – Anforderungen veränderter Weltmarktkonstellationen an die internationale Politik. Berlin: Stiftung Wissenschaft und Politik.

Pechstein, M. 2001. Elektrizitätsbinnenmarkt und Beihilfenkontrolle im Anwendungsbereich des Euratom-Vertrags. EuZW, 12: 307-311.

Petersmann, E.-U, Spennemann, C. 2004. H. von der Groeben & J. Schwarze (Eds.), Kommentar zum Vertrag über die Europäische Union und zur Gründung der Europäischen Gemeinschaft, vol 4. Baden-Baden: Nomos.

Ruffert, M. 2007. C. Callies & M. Ruffert (Eds.), EUV/EGV: das Verfassungsrecht der Europäischen Union mit Europäischer Grundrechtecharta. Munich: C. H. Beck.

Schäfer, P. 2003. R. Streinz (Ed.), EUV/EGV, Vertrag über die Europäische Union und Vertrag zur Gründung der Europäischen Gemeinschaft. Munich: C. H. Beck.

Schmalenbach, K. 2007. C. Callies & M. Ruffert (Eds.), EUV/EGV: das Verfassungsrecht der Europäischen Union mit Europäischer Grundrechtecharta. Munich: C. H. Beck.

Schmidt-Preuß, M. 2003. Energiepolitik – jetzt in Brüsseler Hand? et, 53: 776.

Schmidt-Preuß, M. 2007. Energieversorgung als Aufgabe der Außenpolitik? – Rechtliche Aspekte. RdE, 16: 281-287.

Stavenhagen, G. 1998. Geschichte der Wirtschaftstheorie (4th ed.). Göttingen: Vandenhoeck & Ruprecht.

Streinz, R. 2003. EUV/EGV, Vertrag über die Europäische Union und Vertrag zur Gründung der Europäischen Gemeinschaft. Munich: C. H. Beck.

von Bogdandy, A. 2008. E. Grabitz & M. Hilf (Eds.), Das Recht der Europäischen Union. Munich: C. H. Beck.

von Danwitz, T. 2003. Fragen vertikaler Kompetenzabgrenzung nach dem EU-RATOM-Vertrag, Bochumer Beiträge zum Berg- und Energierecht, Band 39, Stuttgart [u.a.]: Boorberg.

Weber, A. 2008. Vom Verfassungsvertrag zum Vertrag von Lissabon. EuZW, 19: 7-14.

Zuleeg, M. 2003. H. von der Groeben & J. Schwarze (Eds.), Kommentar zum Vertrag über die Europäische Union und zur Gründung der Europäischen Gemeinschaft, vol 1, Baden-Baden: Nomos.

44 The Role of Energy Efficiency in Electric Power Systems: Lessons from Experiments in the US

Michal C. Moore[1]

Abstract

Electricity systems are dynamic, reflecting a complex and continuous interaction of generation supply, and load or customer demand. Demand intensity, from magnitude to timing, can be influenced in strategic and significant ways by employing techniques of energy efficiency. It can include changes in processes, behavior modification, pricing, and the inclusion of energy-saving technologies, all in the interests of changing the load profile and making it either more responsive or more efficient in the face of resource scarcity. Efficiency programs in the United States provide an historical overview of initiatives with corresponding success and failure over the past two decades.

Keywords: energy efficiency, demand management, energy market

[1] Dr. Michal C. Moore is Senior Fellow at the Institute for Sustainable Energy, Environment and Economy, the University of Calgary, Canada. He is a former regulatory commissioner for the State of California, United States of America.

A. Bausch and B. Schwenker (eds.), *Handbook Utility Management,*
DOI: 10.1007/978-3-540-79349-6_44, © Springer-Verlag Berlin Heidelberg 2009

44.1 Introduction

Energy efficiency can be characterized as the twinned opposite of energy supply, the negative to that positive. Just as any electric system depends on VARs (Voltage Amps Reactive Power) to stay in dynamic balance, future energy systems must also intelligently incorporate opportunities and incentives for consumers to behave rationally in the face of real or relative shortages and of volatile prices for energy. This chapter explores the role of energy efficiency in those power systems, specifically in electricity generation. It differentiates between energy efficiency and conservation, where energy efficiency implies a more intensive or cost-effective use of resources or technology over some period of time and conservation is taken to mean forestalling or eliminating consumption. In terms of electric systems, it deals with both supply and demand, and excludes the transportation-related conservation and fuel efficiency.

The chapter begins by defining energy efficiency and briefly discusses the growth of energy efficiency policies, exploring the issue of why regulators, policy-makers, utilities, and finally consumers have come to see the value of energy efficiency. We then move on to a description of the range of applications of energy efficiency tools, from economic incentives and disincentives to inclusion of new technologies and behavioral modifications brought on by both. Finally, the effectiveness of including energy efficiency in long-range planning and the cost implications of these decisions are discussed. The chapter concludes with a discussion of the value to date of energy efficiency in overall grid operations, investment, and consumer behavior.

Most energy efficiency gains have been driven by a combination of cost saving from industry and commercial enterprises (which can afford the investment in technology that minimizes an important cost of operation) and incentives initiated in the public policy arena. Until the 1980s the structure of large-scale electricity systems was dominated by monopoly-regulated and vertically integrated utility systems. Here, since the returns were set by the regulator and generally reflected cost of service provisions and regulated returns for the companies, the logical location for demand management, including rewards and incentives, was with the utilities themselves. Access to customer load data was self-contained, and communication via the billing system was routine. Losses that were reflected in load destruction or shifting were buffered by the regulated rate structure. Customer education programs, although mandated through public policy initiatives, were run by the utilities, with wide variance in themes, timing, and ultimately effectiveness, as revealed by a regional comparison (Levine, 2006).

On this same scale, the public policy initiatives also reflected the growing interest in the expanding base of new electricity demand in the building sector, prompting the creation of such diverse programs as time of sale energy checkups, new building codes and standards, and incentives to promote more innovative building designs.

As consumer interest in energy efficiency grew, a broader interest in energy generation and overall environmental quality began to emerge. The creation of both NYSERDA and the California Energy Commission, with their mandates of encouraging more efficient energy use and the promotion of alternative energy resources, provided incentives for further innovation in information available to them. A colorful example of this trend was the creation of an energy 'content' label in California, which told the consumer the blend of power sources that was being provided to them from their utility or energy service provider (ESP).

44.2   Background

The concept of energy efficiency can be applied to virtually any sector of the electricity generation, transformation, distribution, and consumption system. For our purposes an electricity system is presumed to consist of a fuel supply such as natural gas, coal or petroleum byproducts, or nuclear fissionable materials (also including renewable 'fuels' such as wind, hydro power, and solar light). The fuel is used to generate electricity, at which point it is delivered as a bulk or wholesale commodity at extremely high voltages on a transmission system to distribution points where the voltage is lowered and it becomes a retail commodity. It is then delivered to and consumed in industry, commercial establishments, and residences. It is worth mentioning these broad categories, because each embodies distinct styles, load profiles and, ultimately, incentives to consume or engage in more efficient behavior.

Basically, energy efficiency is important simply by inspection. Like the fuels that produce it and the system that generates it, electricity, is not available in infinite cost-free quantities. Given the long time periods involved in siting new generation facilities, not to mention the cost of capital, efficient use of energy provides a buffer for investment demands and ultimately conserves scarce or reserve fuels, offering time for substitutes to appear or for alternative and more efficient generation to be developed.

The impetus for energy efficiency tools and technology, however, did not appear until there were hints of shortages ahead, and consumer reaction to environmental quality issues manifests itself in political policy designed to encourage or reward savings achieved through shifts or diminished patterns of consumption.

In a seeming paradox, however, whatever the future gains may be the historical evidence is clear: higher efficiency of energy conversions leads eventually to higher, rather than lower, energy use, and eventually we will have to accept some limits on the global consumption of fuels and electricity (Smil, 2005). The rewards, however, can extend far beyond simple fuel savings. Casten (1998) points out the correlation between reduced power generation and the ultimate production of CO_2, suggesting that if we double the efficiency of the use of electricity we simultaneously reduce prices by about 30% and cut CO_2 emissions in half.

When managed properly, and used consistently in operation of the overall electricity system, the role and importance of energy efficiency becomes magnified, changing not only the shape of the load curve, but ultimately the type of technology dispatched to meet it.

44.3   Demand-side Management – a Brief History

Demand-side management (DSM) programs in the US were initially used in the 1970s during growing public debates over dependence on oil imports and public concerns over the perceived externalities of electricity generation, in large measure focused on nuclear facilities. During the 1980s state utility regulators provided a broad panoply of incentives for regulated utilities to pursue least-cost, or integrated-resource, planning to manage future supplies (Eto, 1996). The peak of utility-based DSM programs in the US was reached in 1993, accounting for approximately 1% of total US utility revenues.

In its purest form, DSM is designed to change the level or timing of customer electricity demand. Most DSM programs originate with state and regional regulators and span several different but consistent elements:

- Information on energy saving – typically included in customers' regular billing;
- Availability of energy audits, which can identify areas of either vulnerability (such as heat loss from walls and windows) or savings (new efficient appliances);
- Low-interest loans or utility-sponsored upgrade programs;
- Contracting at reduced rates for installation of new energy efficiency technologies;
- Direct control of high-intensity appliances, such as air conditioners and water heaters, by the affected dispatch agency or utility;
- New tariffs, including time-of-day and real-time pricing (Wilson et al., 2002), designed to change the shape of or shift the load profile faced by utilities.

The US government instituted a far-reaching law known as the Public Utilities Regulatory Policy Act of 1978 (PURPA), which required utilities to purchase their power from nonutility generators (typically renewable generation), so as to avoid generation of power that would otherwise have been needed. A parallel law, known as the National Energy Conservation Policy Act of 1978 (NECPA), required utilities to offer their customers on-site utility use audits. This was the first acknowledgment that saving energy was cheaper than generating and using it.

The concept of least-cost planning followed. The idea of least-cost planning now included the concept of meeting energy demands at lower cost or by deferring investment (Lovins, 1976).[2] This technique thus ran counter to the prevailing pattern of rewarding utilities for capital investment used to create surplus capacity.

A range of technical analyses were conducted, leading to the conclusion that the ratio of energy saving to cost of new plant construction was clearly net posi-

---

[2] Lovins (1976) described a dire situation involving choices of business as usual, which would lead to nuclear and fossil generation, which would contaminate society, his so-called First Path, and a softer Second Path, which made the most effective use of energy efficiency to forestall or eliminate a majority of the traditional and less environmentally friendly electric generation technologies.

tive (Messenger, 2003; Brown & Koomey 2003). However, this was not adopted as widely as it could have been, owing to market barriers such as some regulatory practices that priced electricity at less than marginal cost and the limited availability of information on the implementation and integration of energy-saving technologies.

44.4   Energy Efficiency vs Energy Conservation

Most definitions of energy efficiency actually describe energy intensity. The Energy Information Administration (EIA) defines energy intensity as the ratio of energy consumption to some measure of demand for energy services, or the ability to do work. The reverse is input divided by output, the 'specific energy consumption' (Blok, 2005), which is simply the physical energy consumption involved. According to Blok (2005), in the long term, declines of approximately 1% per year can be expected in specific energy consumption, with exceptions for periods in which pressure on energy use is experienced. In the years 1973 to 1985, for instance, which saw high prices and corresponding interest in new energy policies, consumption fell between 1.5% and 2.2% annually (IEA, 1997).[3]

In this chapter a distinction is made between energy efficiency and conservation, where energy efficiency implies a more intensive or cost-effective use of resources or technology over some period of time and conservation is taken to mean forestalling or eliminating consumption.

When the EIA (1997) asked participants in energy-efficiency workshops to define 'energy efficiency', participants' definitions reflected two different perspectives: either (1) a service perspective or (2) a mechanistic, strict intensity, perspective.

Some participants believed that energy-efficiency indicators could measure some kind of economic well-being, and suggested that a wide range of indicators would offer insight into the 'ordinary business of life' and the relationships, causes, and opportunities in observed trends. Another suggested concept of efficiency is a strict technological (equipment-based) concept. However, according to the EIA, energy-intensity measures are at best a rough surrogate for energy efficiency. This is because energy intensity may mask structural and behavioral changes that do not represent 'true' efficiency improvements, such as a shift away from energy-intensive industries. The choice of a measure of demand for energy services (a 'demand indicator') in efficiency analysis is critical not only as a datum for performance measures over time, but also as a cross-platform analytic and comparative statistic As examples, in the building sector intensity measures could include BTUs per square foot of heating required per annum or energy lost by reliance on a given level of technology, such as single-glazed windows or minimally insulated walls.

---

[3] A distinction is worth noting here. Most consumers do not care about directly consuming energy. Rather, they care about the ability to do work as a result of energy consumption.

Most energy-efficiency programs are built up on the idea that consumers at every level will respond to implied price changes, which in turn reflect conditions of surplus or shortage. That is to say, most consumers respond well to price signals and adapt their behavior to reflect their understanding of costs or trends.

However, the electricity consumption, whether in North America or in Europe, does not provide a price bridge to consumers either in terms of use intensity in real time or in relative response to changing costs of energy. To put it simply, there is typically little price information that can be easily correlated with use.

Consumption meters are typically aggregate data logs, spanning a period such as a billing cycle month and made available to the consumer after some processing lag. Tying consumption patterns to periods of high price, network congestion or shortages, and times of day or even week is impossible. This aggregate information leads to behavior that can at best be generalized in application.

This highlights the importance of embedding efficient practices or devices in the economy at points where they will perform without intervention or can be programmed to respond to special signals regarding use or price.

Turnover of stock is an accepted way of introducing new technology to the marketplace. The range is considerable, from months (light bulbs) to years (appliances, automobiles) to decades (heavy appliances, electric motors). Therefore, the incentive system must be matched to the system elements we hope to influence. There may be transitional technologies as well, such as adding sophisticated thermostats to existing heating systems to increase overall efficiency.

Not all expected efficiencies are realized. As Smil (2005) points out, the scope of potential savings is large, but realistically, so is the gap between what is technically possible and perfectly optimized and what is likely to be achieved in real applications.

Lighting quality and efficiency has improved rapidly, especially in the last two decades. As more jurisdictions preferentially support the inclusion of alternatives to incandescent light in planning and permissions, industry responds with greater cost reductions on a per-unit basis and wider retail and wholesale access. The transition from magnetic to electronic ballasts has not only improved the performance of fluorescent lamp alternatives, but also extended their lifespan. The result is higher performance and a range of new values for consumers, including improved color rendition with matching to daylight frequencies and a greater range of color temperatures from 2,500 to 7,500 K. And alternatives derived from LED photons used to excite phosphorus are now beginning to appear, offering choices beyond just green or red wavelengths. We now have higher power and efficacy sulfur and sodium vapor lamps that can increase luminosity and improve cost efficiency in public applications.

Roofs can make a large difference in surface albedo: high-absorption dark roofs that will get up to 50 °C warmer than ambient air temperature and, for hotter climates, 'cool' roofs that will only get up to 10 °C warmer than ambient temperature will reduce the demand for air conditioning by up to 50% (CEC, 2005).

We know the value of auctions and incentives as well as that of arming the consumer with informed 'choice'. The Energy Star competition resulted in an energy-efficient refrigerator design that reduced per-unit energy demands by more than 50% in some cases (CEC, 2005).

44.5   The Energy Efficiency Paradox

Some economists have predicted a perverse outcome of employing energy efficiency tools. Rubin (2007) points to the Khazzoom-Brookes postulate (see Saunders, 1992), which is based on standard theories of substitution and income effects, where a reduction in energy costs that could follow the implementation of energy-saving techniques would lead to an increase, and not a decline, in overall energy demand. This is analogous to the case of increased efficiency in automobile engines: progress in terms of declining overall demand has been eroded as vehicle miles traveled (VMT) have increased. Added to overall population growth, the intensity of total demand for energy has increased, in part as a function of additional tools for consumption acquired by consumers at every level. And in a further slight to objectives that are linked to social goals, such as CO_2 reduction from reduced energy demand, additions of new alternative generation sources are outpaced by more traditional forms. The consequence is that growth continues to boost the demand for energy, the majority of which is derived from fossil energy resources.

As summarized by Rubin (2007), most public programs to date have been targeted at transportation and residential sectors. In the case of residential use overall the improvements have been impressive, with energy efficiency gains here occurring more than 50% faster than elsewhere in the economy (EIA, 2006). The paradox is that within this sector total use of energy has increased faster than in the rest of the economy. As an example, the energy efficiency of air conditioners has risen by 17% since 1990, but the number of air conditioners sold has increased by over 35%. Homes have been increasing in total average square footage during this same period, causing consumers to seek out larger units capable of servicing larger and larger areas. Design characteristics of large commercial buildings have addressed this issue by building energy efficiency and management into the building characteristics, but strict adherence and tight management controls for the entire life of the building are essential to maintain the theoretical vs practical energy savings balance (Borenstein et al., 2002).

44.6   The Nature and Value of Energy-efficiency Techniques

The generation and dispatch of electricity are tied to demand, and they change from minute to minute, hour to hour, and season to season. Electric grids operate in precise balance, meeting not only load but voltage and frequency characteristics within a narrow range. Excursions of demand beyond expected boundaries are met by calling in reserve power supplies, typically at a higher price or with less desirable characteristics than the power used to meet baseload or normal load-following demands.

The use of energy-efficiency tools or changes in behavior, especially in critical or peak demand periods, can dramatically influence utility and dispatch capacity to meet demands. Implementation or integration of energy efficiency in the electricity system over time can change the shape of the load curve itself, enabling more predictable purchasing of energy in longer term contracts, which effectively act as a hedge against volatility from weather or other unforeseen events. Wilson et al. (2002) have suggested that a small change in thermostat settings in 2000 during the Energy Crisis in California would have eliminated the 'needle peak' on critical days and consequently prevented or dramatically reduced the need for rolling brown- and blackouts.

Ultimately, the role of dispatch and load curves will reflect the contribution and timing of energy-efficiency implementation. Since energy efficiency is a relative concept, it can be used to measure service levels or, especially in the industrial sense, mechanical performance. The agency or utility specifying performance will assign a standard or datum, but these may vary from jurisdiction to jurisdiction. What all programs have in common is the desire or aim to change consumer behavior, alter time-sensitive patterns of consumption, and promote more predictable load characteristics beyond extrapolation from previous-year or seasonal aggregation.

44.7 Elasticity of Demand

In general, economists suggest that energy consumption has a limited degree of elasticity. Studies suggest (EIA, 2007) that in all end-use sectors increases in energy prices initiate only a limited amount of change. Most intensive energy consumption involves the use of relatively long-life capital goods, such as refrigerators, heaters, or air conditioners. The opportunities to switch to more efficient units are infrequent, involve large one-time expenditures, and can be difficult to justify when based on ambiguous estimates of cost of use. Price increases tend to have short-lived spikes, which become absorbed into the background of overall energy payments.

The manufacturing sector provides an exception. Here, in spite of an ability to pass costs on to the ultimate consumer, the competitive nature of products forces companies to seek out efficiency whenever possible, often taking the form of direct measurement of energy use vs time-of-use energy prices, changes in manufacturing hours, and investment in new energy-efficient capital equipment chosen for its performance and energy payback period.

The short-run elasticity of energy demand reflects the limited existence or nonexistence of any substitute and the cost of changing behavior, justifying the inelastic characterization. Long-term energy demand, in part because price signals are inconsistent or not visible, is only marginally less inelastic, providing little direct incentive for consumers to invest in new behavior or technology. In urban areas where demand is intensive, the issue may be complicated further by owner–tenant relationships, disrupting the connection between energy-efficient design, operation, and investment.

44.8   The Relationship of Power Systems and Use Sectors

Every sector of the economy has an interdependent need for electricity, which to some degree has an important role in budgets, comfort, and productivity. Beyond manufacturing and its intensive demand for machinery (e.g., the extreme electricity dependence of the cement and aluminum industries), most electricity consumption is associated with buildings. This association varies with design, including the amount of daylighting and the consequent need for lighting, insulation, window design, lighting characteristics, HVAC characteristics and, ultimately, the standard of control over building and construction adherence to standards. In 1999 for instance, the California Energy Commission found that savings that had been forecast in energy use were not occurring in residential dwellings because the heating/cooling ductwork was not secure, and this in turn reflected a lack of consistent building inspection before occupancy.

In the buildings sector, which includes residential and commercial end-uses, building structures are long-lived capital assets that reflect energy consumption through the standards that were imposed at the time of construction and normal maintenance and operation. A typical objective of building design will maximize daylighting while minimizing heat gain or loss over the life of the structure, which on average will exceed the life of the original mortgage by approximately double, which could be in excess of 70 years. The energy-consuming equipment will be replaced slightly more than twice during that period. The result is that the demand characteristics that are embedded in the building itself will persist for long periods of time, with limited adjustment potential in the face of energy shortages or extreme price changes. More effective changes will occur in operating equipment, but in either case adjustments will typically take years rather than months to implement even if energy prices do change radically. By contrast, the manufacturing sector tends to respond to higher factor input prices, including energy prices, even when energy expenditures do not constitute a significant portion of operating costs. In this sector, however, average energy intensity has tended to decline over time in the face of higher energy prices.

According to the California Energy Commission, "during 2001 the state provided almost $ 1 billion for energy efficiency and demand response programs. Of these funds, about $ 50 million was spent on creating demand response capability in buildings, and $ 35 million was spent to install about 23,300 real-time meters for all customers with over 200 kW maximum demand. By the end of 2001, the demand response capability attributable to energy-efficiency programs was about 250 MW.

In addition, customers with real-time meters, representing about one-fourth (12,000 MW) of the statewide demand, will have meters and communication that will enable their participation in demand response programs" (Wilson et al., 2002). The goal of the Commission was "[...] to obtain about 2,000 MW of demand response (or 17 percent of the air-conditioning and lighting load) from non-residential customers at the specific times when reliability of the system was threatened" (Wilson et al., 2002).

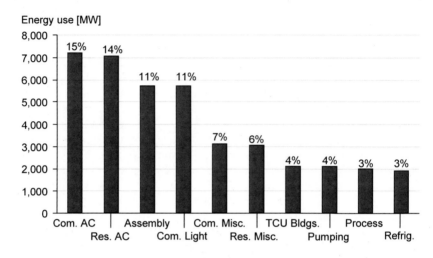

Figure 44.1: Percentage energy use per category (Wilson et al., 2002)

The categories of use shown in Figure 44.1 highlight the concentration of demand in just a few large categories, making their optimization a clear objective.

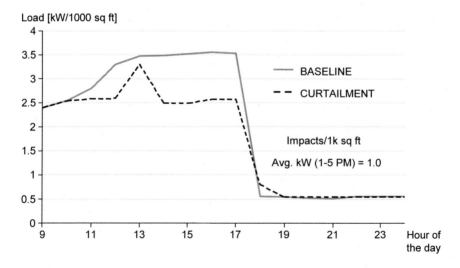

Figure 44.2: Load impacts/1000 sq. ft. (Hamzawi, 2001 contained in Wilson et al., 2002)

Two examples show the impact of concentrating on curtailment of use in a primary category such as air conditioners, as shown in Figure 44.2, with approximately 30% of use curtailed (without performance loss).

When shown scaled to a region in the context of total demand, as in Figure 44.3, which illustrates the example of a northern Californian city, the impacts are even more dramatic.

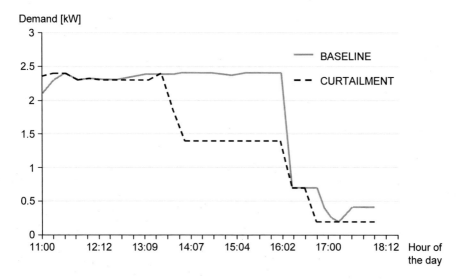

Figure 44.3: Baseline vs curtailment day (Hamzawi, 2001; CEC, 2002b)

44.9 Demand-side Management in Practice

The use of DSM and energy-efficiency policies draws on a wide range of overlapping, but not always coordinated, strategies. These can be divided into two categories, which are relatively distinct but certainly not mutually exclusive:

(1) Technology incentives; and
(2) Market transformation, which includes subsidies or price change initiatives.

Neither of these is solely confined to states or regions, as shown by the national programs such as Energy Star appliances (which have a standardized level of performance and citation available only to appliances that meet at least a minimum threshold). On the other hand, the majority of them are initiated and managed at state and regional levels, where the most effective connection with the consumer is available.

44.9.1   Technology Behavior

In addition, advances in technology have always been associated with efforts to achieve higher levels of energy efficiency. A key objective of public energy laboratories, such as the Lawrence Berkeley National Laboratory, the National Renewable Energy Laboratory, and the Oak Ridge National Laboratory, is to test and advance new technology into the marketplace. The result has been dramatic, ranging from improvements in lighting (fluorescent ballasts, white light LEDs, compact fluorescent bulbs) through new appliances (Energy Star refrigerators, new oven and microwave designs) to building insulation, vapor barriers, low e-window coatings, and double- and triple-glazed window panels (Brown, 2007).

44.9.2   Market Transformation

A great deal of interest and effort has been expended in the public policy sector to develop a range of economic and fiscal tools that will promote and ultimately embed more efficient and predictable use patterns in the electricity generation system. These include the positive reinforcement of tax incentives, which are applied most often for large-scale capital investments, or rebates (effective instant subsidy) for the purchase of appliances or energy management systems that meet a specified threshold of performance. These programs are often administered by the utility or local service agency, but the capital goods are ultimately owned by the consumer and generally assumed to stay with the structure over time.

In some regions, pooled funds are made available either in the form of no- or low-interest loans or of loan-guaranteed programs to encourage consumer participation in either replacement or acquisition of energy-saving technologies. These funds, typically a redirection of some percentage of ratepayer billing (Public Benefit Funds), might be effectively termed emerging incentives and cross over several policy and funding boundaries. Examples include:

- Green building tax credits;
- State tax deductions for energy-efficiency investment;
- Sales tax exemptions for efficient products;
- Residential and business tax credits;
- Differing LEED levels for government or public buildings.

44.10   Effectiveness

One of the most aggressive and symbolic programs designed to support demand management and promote energy efficiency is arguably that managed by the California Energy Commission and the California Public Utilities Commission. Their goals are organized around three different but related targets, including the need to forestall or eliminate new power plants in state, diminishing the State's CO_2 footprint, and meeting a high percentage of new 'incremental' energy needs, especially during peak periods. During the period 2006-2008 they met their goals, estimating that they eliminated the need for three new power plants (averaging 2.5 GW per plant), avoided approximately 3.4 million tonnes of CO_2 emissions, and fully kept pace with the incremental demands associated with new population growth.

Actual expenditures on energy efficiency have come in waves, in California's case in 1984 (peak $ 140 million), 1994 (peak $ 270 million) and 2001 (peak $ 370 million). Each peak was followed by a decline in investment and savings, but without erasing net gains from the previous peak (CEC, 2005). By 2003 the result was impressive, with sustained estimates of savings relative to total demand at approximately 15%. In terms of planning for forward-load accommodation, every electricity region in the US now includes energy efficiency as a factor in both reducing and managing overall load projections.

In terms of relative effectiveness, the experience of the California Energy Commission illustrates the potential to be realized from this suite of techniques and technologies. The greatest gains were realized through a combination of new (enforced) building standards and consumer conservation- and efficiency-directed programs, which together accounted for more than 80% of the savings achieved. Of the balance, the imposition of new appliance standards resulted in approximately 15% of the savings, a gain that becomes embedded in future performance. The balance was a combination of load management, fuel substitution and public agency programs.

44.11 Going Forward

Energy efficiency as a tool to moderate or shift demand and load profiles has demonstrated its range of potential benefits in myriad jurisdictions. When applied consistently, benefits approaching 20% of total load seem possible, which when combined with peak usage or high fuel cost periods can dramatically increase the impact of use.

The issue of forestalling, curtailing, or diminishing energy use in the context of new and expanding supplies of generation systems is attractive on the face of it, but ultimately must depend on an unpredictable combination of new market structures (e.g., partially deregulated industries now prevail in many formerly monopoly-regulated arenas), constraints, and opportunities represented by new environmental policies (carbon trading, CO_2 management) and, more importantly, the public perception of the availability and efficacy of energy-efficiency programs offered within energy service markets.

Diffusion of new technologies and acceptance of behavioral changes is a measure of the ultimate effectiveness of any energy-efficiency program. Here, turnover of stock is an accepted way of introducing new technology to the marketplace. The range, however, is considerable, from months (light bulbs) to years (appliances, automobiles) to decades (heavy appliances, electric motors). Therefore the incentive system must be matched to the system elements we hope to influence.

There may also be transitional technologies, such as adding sophisticated thermostats to existing heating systems to increase overall efficiency.

In the end, not all expected efficiencies are realized. As Smil (2005) points out, the scope of potential savings is wide, but so, realistically, is the gap between what is technically possible and perfectly optimized and what is likely to be achieved in real applications.

As an example, both the quality and the efficiency of lighting have been improving at rapid rates, especially in the last two decades. As more jurisdictions preferentially support the inclusion of alternatives to incandescent light in planning and permissions, industry responds with greater cost reductions on a per-unit basis and wider retail and wholesale access. The transition from magnetic to electronic ballasts has not only improved performance for fluorescent lamp alternatives but also extended their life-span. The result is higher performance and a range of new values for consumers, including improved color rendition with matching to daylight frequencies, and a greater range of color temperatures from 2,500 to 7,500 K. Alternatives derived from LED photons used to excite phosphorus are currently beginning to appear, offering choices beyond just green or red wavelengths. We now have higher power and efficacy sulfur and sodium vapor lamps that can increase luminosity and improve cost efficiency in public applications.

In the building construction sector, simple and durable features such as roofs can make a large difference in surface albedo, with high-absorption dark roofs that will reach temperatures up to 50 °C higher than ambient air temperature and, for hotter climates 'cool' roofs that will not get more than 10 °C warmer than ambient temperature, these will reduce the demand for air conditioning by up to 50% (CEC, 2005).

We can combine good economic precepts with technological advances. For instance, we know the value of auctions and incentives as well as of arming the consumer with informed 'choice'. The Energy Star competition resulted in an energy-efficient refrigerator design that reduced per-unit energy demands by more than 50% in some cases (CEC, 2005).

Blok (2005) forecast that a combination of technologies such as the use of new insulation materials, the reduction of heat loss through window design, plus the application of heat pumps (perhaps powered from solar energy sources) combined with passive compact energy storage systems would result in optimized building designs. He forecast that it would "[...] make it possible to realize dwellings with zero-energy use at affordable cost".

While this is an optimistic and desirable goal, more realistic is the idea that if energy-efficiency programs are used consistently, with support and continual refinement they can take on an important role in defining the shape of the utility load curve, deferring investment until needed, and providing a buffer for unanticipated shortfalls.

44.12 Conclusion

Energy efficiency works, and in terms of overall energy consumption is the 'low-hanging fruit' of balancing the demands for new supplies and the changing nature of demand. Returns on investments are estimated as clear multiples with benefits that extend for years, a compelling reason to include them in energy planning. Thus, in terms of the standard of success, cost effectiveness, ease of integration, and acceptance, energy efficiency is clearly net positive.

The fact that major jurisdictions have had inconsistent programs, some have discontinued programs, and others are simply waiting for some future period to introduce energy-efficiency programs suggests either a shortfall in confidence and/or information, or disbelief in the escalation of costs of supply and generation technologies. This is a troubling outcome, and underlines the fragile nature of the balance of continuously meeting demand and supplying needs in a dynamic system which must be continuously renewed and managed, all while maintaining an affordable rate structure in three major sectors. Since the pattern typically looks cyclic, in terms of both investment and returns on investment, a sound public policy could easily be justified in using energy-efficiency programs as a counter-hedge during periods of increasing demand, forecast shortfalls in supply, or increases in fuel costs, to buy time. Thus, the true value of energy efficiency may lie in the ability of its potential to buffer trends and allow more effective long-term utility and energy systems management.

References

Battles, S. J. 1997. Developing energy indicators in the US: the EIA experience. Paper presented at the 18th Annual North American Conference, Washington.

Blok, K. 2005. Improving energy efficiency by five percent and more per year. Journal of Industrial Ecology, 8: 87-100.

Borenstein, S., Jaske, M. & Rosenfeld, A. 2002. Dynamic pricing, advanced metering and demand response in electricity markets. Unpublished Working Paper (CSEMWP-105), UC Berkeley, Berkeley.

Brown, M. 2007. Energy independence for North America: an alternative future. Paper presented at the Bishop's Lodge, Santa Fe.

Brown, R. E. & Koomey, J. G. 2003. Electricity use in California: past trends and present use patterns. Energy Policy, 31: 849-864.

California Energy Commission (CEC). 2001a. Petition (to the CPUC) of the CEC for modification of Decision 01-04-006 by proposing a real-time pricing tariff. Sacramento: CEC.

California Energy Commission (CEC). 2001b. CEC Proposal: new UDC-administered demand response program. Sacramento: CEC.

California Energy Commission (CEC). 2002a. 2002-2012 electricity outlook report. http://www.energy.ca.gov/reports/2002-02-14_700-01-004F.PDF, 30th May 2008.

California Energy Commission (CEC). 2002b. Summer 2001 conservation report. http://www.energy.ca.gov/papers/2002-08-18_aceee_presentations/PANEL05 _WILSON.PDF, 29th July 2008.

California Energy Commission (CEC). 2005. Extreme efficiency: lessons from California. Presentation by Commission Art Rosenfeld to the AAAS, February 21, 2005, Washington, D.C.

Casten, T. R. 1998. Turning off the heat. Why America must double energy efficiency to save money and reduce global warming. Washington: American Council for an Energy-Efficient Economy.

Emshwiller, J. 2001. White roofs, digital meters – Dr. Rosenfeld tests solutions he says won't require state to sacrifice comfort. http://www.energy.ca.gov/ commissioners/rosenfeld_docs/2001-02-22_rosenfeld_wsj.html, 29th July 2008.

Energy Information Administration (EIA). 1997. Developing energy indicators in the US: the EIA experience, 18th Annual North American Conference, US Association for Energy Economics.

Energy Information Administration (EIA). 2006. Annual energy outlook. Washington: EIA.

Energy Information Administration (EIA). 2007. Annual energy outlook. Washington: US Govt Printing Office.

Eto, J. 1996. The past, present and future of U.S. utility demand-side management programs. Unpublished Working Paper (LBNL-39931), University of California, Berkeley.

Grueneich, D. M. 2005. California's energy efficiency programs (Powerpoint Presentation).

Hamzawi, E. 2001. Personal communication, Sacramento Municipal Utilities District.

International Energy Agency (IEA). 1997. Indicators of energy use and energy efficiency. Paris: IEA/OEDC.

Levine, M. D. (Ed.). 2006. Electricity efficiency in California's future, Lawrence Berkeley National Laboratory (Powerpoint Presentation). Berkeley: University of California.

Lovins, A. B. 1977. Energy strategy: the road not taken? Foreign affairs. Carlton: Friends of the Earth Australia.

Messenger, M. 2003. Discussion of proposed energy savings goals for energy efficiency programs in California. Unpublished California Energy Commission Staff Paper, CEC, Sacramento.

Rubin, J. 2007. The efficiency paradox, CIBC World Markets Report. StrategEcon, November: 1-12.

Saunders, H. D. 1992. The Khazzoom-Brookes postulate and neoclassical growth. The Energy Journal, 13: 131-148.

Smil, V. 2003. Energy at the crossroads. Cambridge: MIT Press.

Wilson, J., Rosenfeld, A. & Jaske, M. 2002. www.energy.ca.gov/papers/2002-08 -18_aceee_presentations/PANEL-05_WILSON.PDF, 29th July 2008.

45 Private Water and Economic Regulation in the United States

Janice A. Beecher[1]

Abstract

The water industry in the United States exhibits complex structural features. Compared with other public utilities, and despite substantial capital investment needs, the water industry in the US continues to be dominated by public ownership – as it does in most corners of the world. The reality of 'privatization' in the form of expanded ownership or operation of water supply assets does not seem to match the rhetoric. Effective economic regulation is a necessary but insufficient condition for private involvement in the water sector because of water's monopolistic character, reinforced by other market imperfections. Expansion of the private role may depend on the industry's ability to demonstrate clear economic advantages, regulatory and other policy reforms, and political and public acceptance.

Keywords: water, privatization, regulation

[1] Dr. Janice A. Beecher is Director of the Institute of Public Utilities at Michigan State University, the United States of America.

A. Bausch and B. Schwenker (eds.), *Handbook Utility Management,*
DOI: 10.1007/978-3-540-79349-6_45, © Springer-Verlag Berlin Heidelberg 2009

45.1   Introduction

The US water industry can be characterized as persistently fragmented, bifurcated, and pluralistic. The water industry is fragmented in terms of the large number of geopolitically based systems in operation, which is due mainly to a history of prolific and serendipitous growth and development, unchecked and unrestrained for the most part by local planning or coordinated regulation. As of 2007, the US Environmental Protection Agency tallied about 52,000 community water systems serving more than 286 million people, excluding many thousands of additional noncommunity systems serving transient and nontransient populations (US EPA, 2007).[2] The total is close to the 1986 count, although in the interim the number grew by a few thousand more systems, peaked in the mid-1990s, and then declined steadily (US EPA, 1986). Water 'utilities' may operate multiple water 'systems' that may or may not be physically interconnected.[3] About 15% of the systems primarily purchase their water from another system on a wholesale basis (US EPA, 2000). The cultural preference for local control of water utilities comes at a price in terms of lost scale economies especially in water treatment but also in management. Despite the potential for interconnection or common management, growing interest in watershed-based resource management, some federal and state policy incentives designed to encourage consolidation,[4] regionalization of the US water industry has been largely underachieved.[5]

The water industry is bifurcated because so few systems serve so many people, and vice versa. Systems serving fewer than 3,300 people or about 1,000 connections account for more than 80% of the systems but serve under 10% of the population served by community water systems. Conversely, more than 80% of the population is served by fewer than 10% of the systems serving populations of 10,000 or more. At the top of the scale are very large, publicly owned metropolitan water systems, including those serving New York, Philadelphia, Detroit, Chicago, Dallas, Los Angeles, Phoenix, and Seattle. Although the US also sees large numbers of small private systems, the private side of the water business is concentrated on one end with an oligopoly of holding companies. For policymakers, bifurcation presents dilemmas with regard to regulatory compliance, financial viability, and service affordability, all of which are more challenging for smaller

---

[2] The community/noncommunity and transient/nontransient distinctions are pertinent to the development of federal drinking water standards because of degrees of exposure and potential health risks (US EPA, 2007).

[3] A distinction exists between a system (an operating characteristic used by drinking water regulators) and utilities (an ownership characteristic).

[4] The 1996 Safe Drinking Water Act (SDWA), for example, gently promotes restructuring in the form of capacity assurance for new and existing systems (§1420), a consolidation option to in the enforcement context (§1455), variances and exemptions (§1415 and §1416), funding support (§1452), and research (§1420).

[5] See AWWARF study. By contrast, UK water systems were structured regionally around watersheds prior to privatization. See Daniel Okun, Regionalization of Water Management (Okun, 1977).

water systems that lack scale, as well as associated technical, financial, and managerial capacity (SDWA, 1996, §1420).

The water industry is pluralistic in terms of the multiple interests involved in the sector and the potential for conflict among them. The many stakeholders in the water industry include public and private water utilities and their customers; water utility operators and other private vendors; various governmental agencies at the federal, state, and local levels; users of water for different purposes (public supply, fire protection and other governmental purposes, commercial enterprises, industrial processes, energy production, irrigation and agriculture, and aesthetics and recreation); and advocates for the environment, public health, and human rights. The industry is also pluralistic with regard to the ownership, operation, and regulatory oversight of drinking water systems and systems providing wastewater collection and treatment.

45.2   Market Structure of the US Water Industry

Distinctions of ownership and operation, as well as of size, are integral to the water industry's complex structure. Community water systems may be publicly or privately owned, and federal and state environmental regulation is largely indifferent to ownership. Throughout the 1800s, publicly and privately owned water utilities shared the market and grew at a relatively comparable pace (Baker, 1899). Today's US water utility sector, unlike its energy and telecommunications counterparts, is dominated by public ownership, with most large urban areas served by city-owned systems. Municipal ownership is prevalent, but public ownership also extends to water districts and authorities, as well as county and state governments on a very limited basis. Some municipal water systems operate with a high degree of financial and operational autonomy and independent oversight (for example, Denver, Colorado). Hybrid forms include at least one wholly owned municipal water company (in Louisville, Kentucky), as well as various forms of privatization arrangements. Nonprofit water utilities include homeowners' associations, cooperatives, and organizations or corporations organized accordingly.

At about $ 7.4 billion in annual revenues, privately owned utilities account for less than 10% of water sold (US EPA, 2000) but about 15% of revenues from water sales (US Census Bureau, 2008a and 2008b). A few of the larger water systems operating in the US, but many of the smaller systems, are privately owned and operated. Private operations include utility companies, but also very small systems and ancillary systems that provide drinking water in conjunction with another primary commercial or institutional function.

Much of the investor-owned water industry is concentrated in the Eastern region and on the West Coast, with some presence in the Midwest, Southeast, and Southwest but a limited presence in the Upper Midwest and mountainous Central states. Some of the larger private water companies evolved from family-owned enterprises to conglomerates with holding company structures and multistate operations (for example, American Water, Aqua America, and United Water). Others operate as stand-alone and solely owned utilities in a defined geographic area. Some provide wastewater services in addition to water services, and a few energy companies also operate water systems.

Once a relatively quiet and stable industry, the private water industry has come to experience both corporate consolidation ownership turnover. Today, only about one dozen of the investor-owned water utilities are publicly traded; consolidation halved the number within a decade (see Table 45.1). Founded in 1886 as the American Water Works and Guarantee Company, and with properties in 16 states, American Water dominates as the nation's largest investor-owned water company, followed by Aqua America (13 states) and United Water (8 states). The major utilities also extend their reach by providing operational services to a number of communities across the country.

Table 45.1: Prominent water and wastewater privatization agreements (National Council for Public Private Partnerships, 2008)

Year	Public entity	Private entity
1972	Burlingame, CA	Veolia Water (USFilter, EOS)
1977	Great Falls, MT	Veolia Water (EOS)
1978	Vancouver	Veolia Water (Wheelabrator EOS)
1982	Sioux City, IA	Veolia Water (EOS)
1984	Oklahoma City, OK	Veolia Water (EOS)
1987	Edwardsville, IL	Veolia Water (EOS)
1990	Atlanta-Fulton County, GA	Veolia Water (EOS)
1990	Corning, CA	ECO Resources (SouthWest)
1993	Monmouth, IL	Environmental Mgmt. Corp.
1994	El Paso County Water Auth., TX	ECO Resources (SouthWest)
1997	Buffalo, NY	American Water
1998	Jersey City Mun. Util. Auth., NJ	United Water
1998	Long Beach, MS	OpTech (SouthWest)
1999	Gulport, MS	OpTech (SouthWest)
1999	Keystone, SD	ECO Resources (SouthWest)
1999	Camden, NJ	United Water
1999	Milwaukee Met. Sew. Dist., WI	United Water
2000	Corning, CA	ECO Resources (SouthWest)
2000	Oklahoma City, OK	Veolia Water North America
2000	Springfield, MA	United Water
2000	Coatsville, PA	PA American Water (asset sale)
2002	Hinesville, GA	OMI, Inc.
2002	City of Indianapolis, IN	Veolia Water North America
2002	Sugar Land, TX	ECO Resources (Southwest)
2002	Lake City Comm. College, FL	OMI, Inc.
2003	Tampa Bay Water, FL	Veolia Water North America
2003	Seattle Public Utilities	CH2M HILL – OMI

Foreign investors have taken, and in some cases have withdrawn, major stakes in most of the major US water companies. United Water is owned by a unit of the French utilities conglomerate Suez Environnement. Another French giant,

Vivendi, divested its substantial share of Aqua America in 2002. Utilities Inc. was acquired by Dutch company Nuon in 2002, but sold to AIG High Capital, a private equity firm, in 2006. At about the same time, the UK-based parent company, the Kelda Group, agreed to sell Aquarion, located in Connecticut, to Australia's Macquarie Bank. American Water was purchased by the UK's Thames Water in 2001, just as Thames was acquired by Germany's RWE. Six years later, RWE announced plans to divest its ownership through an initial public stock offering, which took place in 2008. The industry's major contractors and vendors are multinational, with the French prominent. More recently, domestic and international private equity players (such as Highstar and Macquarie) have shown expanded interest in the US and global water business, although their involvement has been met with mixed opinions (DeBenedictis, 2006; Stewart, 2007; Maxwell, 2008).

Foreign ownership of water utilities is not without positive potential in terms of participation in global markets, access to the knowledge and experience of large companies, promotion of technological innovation, professionalization of the labor force, and exploration of new models and tools for operation, management, and regulation. However, foreign ownership also evokes negative perceptions and sensitivities that seem particularly acute for the water industry, which manages vital natural resources, maintains critical infrastructure, and produces a product that consumers physically ingest. Uncertainty about foreign ownership and associated instability may play a hand in the resistance to or even the reversal of privatization.

Some of the 'fear of foreign' may be based on nationalism, but it may also reflect doubts about exporting profits, tilting the balance of trade, and undermining the competitive position of domestic firms. For economic regulators, foreign ownership raises issues that all holding company structures raise, including risk assessment and allocation, protection of assets needed to serve customers, and access to and accountability of ultimate owners. Many local communities are reluctant to consider transferring ownership of water assets to any and all 'outsiders', including regional public entities and private companies of any type. Worries about foreign ownership of infrastructure and implications for security have obviously heightened in the post-9-11 era.[6]

Foreign interest in the US water industry has been guided by investor expectations of profit, driven by perceptions of comparatively better opportunities for returns on capital and achievement of scale economies in an industry that to many has appeared 'ripe for consolidation'.[7] Some foreign investors may have mis-

---

[6] Like drinking water standards, rules, regulations, and practices related to infrastructure security apply regardless of ownership.

[7] The phrase has been become a well-worn selling point. In 2001: "The large number of systems, most of which serve fewer than 5,000 customers, makes the water utility industry ripe for consolidation [...]. The proposed acquisition of American Water by RWE is the next logical step in our company's focus on consolidation" (American Water Works, 2001). As RWE moved to sell its interests, the ripeness remained: "The industry is ripe for consolidation and there is strong investor appetite for water distribution assets", said Joseph Sorce, Director, Fitch Ratings. "The water business is low-risk with stable and predictable

gauged the structural, regulatory, political, and cultural character of the US water industry, where market conditions and opportunities for profit are rather constrained.

As water utilities in the United States embark on their most ambitious cycle of infrastructure investment, strive to meet stringent quality standards, expand to meet the growth requirements, manage resource scarcity, navigate the water-energy nexus, and impose rising prices to meet higher costs, alternative structural models for the industry may emerge. Consolidation and privatization constitute two important structural dimensions of the water industry, although neither has clearly materialized in the US experience. Consolidation is aimed primarily at achieving scale economies and privatization is aimed primarily at capital investment; both offer the possibility of performance improvement, but neither can promise profitability. In any case, the regulatory framework provides the context in which structural change occurs.

45.3   Privatization

The reasons for privatization can be ideological (less government), populist (better society), pragmatic (greater efficiency), or commercial (more business) (Savas, 1987). Much attention is paid to ideology in the general literature. For infrastructure industries, including the water sector, all four reasons apply, although the commercial underpinnings may be especially relevant. Privatization is attractive because it comports with the theories of competition and contestability. It can also provide for the influx of private-sector capital at a time when needs are great and when raising capital in the public sector is constrained for economic, fiscal, or political reasons. In terms of performance, privatization introduces the profit motive, which in turn should promote efficiency in operations with regard to the deployment of capital and inputs (labor, energy, and chemicals) and professionalism and innovation in management. The profit motive can be harnessed to achieve social and environmental goals, although skeptics are concerned that corners may be cut as well.

'Privatization' is used loosely to describe any level of private-sector involvement in the provision of goods and services that play a significant role in maintaining the health, safety, or well-being of the public. The chief rationale for privatization is economic, while the chief criticism is political. Privatization promises efficiency and innovation, but also raises a spectrum of concerns about control, delegation, and responsibility. In the water industry, privatization takes many forms, from outsourcing of basic tasks or functions; to the use of developer financ-

cash flows." "Fitch: Escalating Capital Costs May Lead to Consolidation for US Water Utilities" (Reuters, 2008).

ing and private activity bonds; to various contracts for design, construction, and/or operation; to full asset acquisition and ownership by private-sector investors.[8]

Table 45.2: Comparison of investor ownership and contract management

	Investor ownership	Contract management
Key features	▪ Characterized by investor ownership; most larger utility companies are publicly traded and operate multiple water systems ▪ Infrastructure projects are funded with private capital. ▪ Assets are owned and managed by the same entity. ▪ Competition is limited but includes some contestability (public v. private). ▪ Utilities are subject to economic regulation by state public utility commissions, including relatively standardized rules for accounting and ratemaking.	▪ Characterized by public ownership with 'delegated' management. ▪ Use of private capital for infrastructure projects may be limited. ▪ Competition for contracts can be intense but oligopolistic. ▪ Contracts are often long in term and can be highly complex. ▪ Public ownership 'substitutes' for regulation; state oversight is non-existent, limited, or indirect; accounting and ratemaking practices vary.
Potential advantages	▪ Brings private capital investment, long-term commitment to ownership, and expert management. ▪ Can promote cost-effective regionalization. ▪ Provides broad incentives for performance efficiency and managerial innovation. ▪ Encourages proper valuation and cost-based ratemaking. ▪ Ensures accountability through independent regulatory oversight.	▪ Brings expertise, efficiency, and innovation to utility systems. ▪ Relies on a mobile, professional workforce. ▪ Maintains public-sector financing and tax advantages. ▪ Publicly owned systems retain local control over water and land assets. ▪ Presents less formidable barriers to market entry.
Potential disadvantages	▪ Raises concerns about lack of local control and responsiveness to local needs. ▪ Introduces the potential for ownership complexity and instability. ▪ Forgoes financing and tax advantages. ▪ Entrusts vital land and water assets to the private sector. ▪ Depends on a responsive and effective system of economic regulation.	▪ Decouples ownership and operations, with possible tensions and suboptimality. ▪ Relies on a form of competition that is oligopolistic at best and monopolistic once a contract is signed. ▪ Allows for subsidies and transfers, and does not ensure cost-base rates. ▪ Raises potential for conflicts of interest, values, and ethics. ▪ May blur responsibility and ultimate accountability.

---

[8] For definitions, see the National Council for Public–Private Partnerships, http://ncppp.org/ howpart/ppptypes.shtml. See also National Association of Water Companies "Common Public–Private Partnership Arrangements" (undated handout).

One survey revealed that 165 water-sector privatization projects valued at $ 14.6 billion were planned in the US between 1985 and mid-2007; 114 of these, valued at $ 10.1 billion, were actually funded (PWF, 2007). Although privatization is often represented as a continuum, a distinct dichotomy is found in the contrast between the two principal options for privatization, investor ownership and contract operations (see Table 45.2).

Contracts between public-sector entities (usually cities) and private contractors are sometimes described and marketed as 'public–private partnerships'. The relationship is more accurately described as one of principal and agent, with the public entity as principal delegating to the private contractor as agent. Care must be taken to avoid impropriety and all parties must understand that ultimate responsibility rests with the principal, that is, the public sector. The field of providers is oligopolistic, particularly for larger operational agreements, because certain qualifications (such as financial assurances and certified personnel) limit eligibility (see Table 45.3). Contract terms are often several years (even decades), barriers to exit are substantial, and incumbents tend to prevail in renewals and often by negotiation versus robust competition (PWF, 2008). When cities enter into privatization arrangements, the loss of in-house technical capacity must be compensated by an increase in oversight capacity, which may include economic regulation (as discussed below.)

Table 45.3: Prominent private water contractors and estimated revenues and market share for US operations in 2007 (Public Works Financing, 2008)

Company	Revenues [$ m]	Est. market share
Veolia Water North America	438	34%
United Water	216	17%
CH2M HIll - OMI	193	15%
American Water	175	14%
Severn Trent	135	10%
SouthWest Water Services	120	9%
Alliance Water	20	1%

Note: includes water and wastewater operation and maintenance agreements and design-build contracts.

Investor ownership is institutionally distinct from other forms of privatization because it involves comprehensive private ownership and operation, as well as economic regulation. Investor ownership is prevalent in the UK, with national-level regulation by the Water Services Regulation Authority (Ofwat). Despite a relative small market share overall, many US communities are served by privately owned water companies (see Table 45.4). Investor ownership brings private capital to infrastructure investment needs, along with advantages of efficiency and innovation. As noted, investor-owned utilities range from many very small private systems to a select number of large, multisystem and multistate operations. The larger systems offer advantages in terms of operational scale and regionalization, but also of technical capability (such as advanced analytics and methods for water testing and treatment, resource planning, and asset management).

Table 45.4: Major US investor-owned utilities (Hoovers, 2008)

Company	Stock ticker	Sales revenues 2007 [$ m]
American Water	AWK	2,214
Aqua America, Inc.	WTR	603
United Water (Suez)	–	Na
California Water Service Group	CWT	367
American States Water Company	AWR	301
SouthWest Water Company	SWWC	217
San Jose Water Company	SJW	207
Aquarion (Macquarie)	–	Na
Middlesex Water Company	MSEX	86
Utilities, Inc. (AIG)	–	63
Connecticut Water Service Inc.	CTWS	59
Artesian Resources Corporation	ARTNA	53
Baton Rouge Water	–	40
The York Water Company	YORW	31
Pennichuck Corporation	PNNW	30

In contrast to contract operations, investor ownership places all responsibilities for asset ownership and operation in the same hands, which avoids conflict between principals and agents and may facilitate optimization. Investor ownership also relies on regulatory incentives to ensure performance instead of highly detailed contracts, oversight, and enforcement, or redundant management systems.

Expansion of the private sector's market share in the US beyond about 10% has been elusive. The recent experience of private involvement in the water business has been punctuated by failures and reversals. Enron at one time hoped to leverage its acquisition of the UK's Wessex Water and the formation of Azurix to transform North American and global water markets along the lines of its energy-trading model, both of which of course ended catastrophically. Some investor-owned systems have been lost or nearly lost to 'reverse privatization', in many cases via the exercise of eminent domain by local governments. Prominent is the case of the venerable Indianapolis Water Company; following municipalization in 2002, responsibility for operations was soon assumed by Suez under a contractual agreement. An ambitious contract agreement between United Water and the city of Atlanta collapsed when conflicts could not be resolved. The bottled water industry also has found itself in the center of the US privatization debate, notably with respect to Nestlé's tapping into Great Lakes water. Water privatization has been linked to unwelcome globalization, environmental injustice, and civil conflict; maligned by vocal interest groups (such as Public Citizen and Sierra Club); and even vilified in documentary films (such as "Thirst" in 2004 and "The Big Sellout" in 2007). Politics and emotions run high when it comes to corporate involvement in water management, perhaps more so than other services.

The barriers to transferring assets from the public to the private sector are formidable and include concerns about rate differentials, but also a preference for government and local control (Beecher et al., 1995). Economic regulation is a central feature of the investor ownership model and one of its chief advantages in terms of blending the performance incentives associated with the private sector with the accountability imposed by the public sector. Regulation may also be perceived as an obstacle, particularly if it is not regarded as sufficiently protective of local interests. For cities, transferring assets means surrendering control over property and operations to a private company and control over rates to a state agency. Privatization in the form of contract operations retains local control and also effectively circumvents economic regulation by the state in most cases, which may be perceived by some market participants as advantageous.

45.3.1   Ownership and Rates

Perceptions of the public and private sectors have much to do with perceptions about their prevailing ethic (Beecher, 2001). Neither sector is inherently superior in theory or practice; rather, each brings potential strengths and weaknesses. Any change in institutional form should be motivated by clear expectations of improvement over the status quo. Indeed, the interest in changing ownership often seems associated with a perception that the 'grass looks greener' (or perhaps the 'water seems purer') on the 'other' side rather than a comprehensive analysis.

Comparatively, advocates of privatization have hypothesized that public water systems: experience more construction-cost overruns; postpone needed improvements; overcapitalize (even more than private companies); over-utilize debt; incur higher capital and operating costs; are less efficient in procurement and scheduling; innovate slowly, if at all; provide longer tenure to personnel; have greater debt capacity; are more risky and realize lower returns; subsidize or receive subsidies from other local government activities; favor voters, businesses, and organized groups; and set rates farther from economic costs (Beecher et al., 1995; NAWC Water, 1989).

Costs and rates clearly are at the center of the privatization issue. While advocates believe that privately owned enterprises are more cost efficient, critics are quick to point out that services provided by the private sector are often costlier to customers (see SERC, 2004). Although a highly variable and very imperfect benchmark, rates of publicly owned utilities often compare favorably with rates for comparable service supplied by privately owned utilities. Several factors may contribute to the rate disparity. An obvious one is profit. Private investors, whether individuals or groups of shareholders, expect a 'return of' and a 'return on' their chosen investment in the water system; US constitutional and regulatory law provides for a nonconfiscatory and reasonable rate of return. Another big factor for privately owned utilities is payment of federal corporate income taxes, along with a variety of state and local property and other taxes; publicly owned utilities may or may not be obligated to provide payments in lieu of taxes to local governments. Private utilities may have less access to subsidies in the form of federal and state grants and loans to water systems. Publicly owned water systems may also fund improvements with revenues from assessments or debt instruments supported by taxpayers versus ratepayers.

Ratemaking practices can also vary by ownership. Publicly owned water systems may be more likely to charge system-development charges to new customers that help cover the cost of capital expansion associated with new capacity needs; privately owned systems often charge basic connection or hook-up charges only. For investor-owned utilities, recovery of capital investment is accomplished through a depreciation expense; publicly owned systems will generally account for depreciation in some manner, but not necessarily reflect this expense in rates. Metropolitan water systems may differentiate rates for customers within and outside geopolitical boundaries. Higher 'outside' rates may be justified by differences in costs and risks, but they can also be somewhat arbitrary or used to help suppress the 'inside' rates charged to municipal customers.

Privately provided water may come at a higher price in part because privately owned utilities have strong incentives to invest, while cities (certainly not all) might defer investment for fiscal or political reasons, particularly if bond issuances or rate increases are required but resisted. Service cost differences might also apply. In some cases, especially for some smaller utilities, private companies emerged in unincorporated and underserved territories that faced higher costs because of remote or challenging physical terrain or lesser access to water resources. Their smaller size also means foregone scale economies, regardless of their ownership.

Privately owned utilities must be financially viable and sustainable within their particular sphere of business. Publicly owned systems are often part of a larger governmental entity, such as a municipality, that may benefit from subsidies in the form of tax revenues, bonds and other forms of public-sector financing, intergovernmental transfers, federal or state grants and loans, and access to large-scale public water projects.[9] Some subsidies are less obvious or hidden, such as access to shared resources (personnel, equipment, etc.). As a counterpoint, however, some publicly owned water systems are considered 'revenue-producing' utilities that channel subsidies back to the public entity (sometimes to the detriment of water system investment). A final reason for the rate disparity is that economic regulation may force prices to more accurately reflect costs (that is, higher rates may be more efficient rates). Virtually all privately owned water utilities are subject to state economic regulation,[10] which provides institutional accountability for their need and ability to charge customers for the cost of service. In contrast, not all publicly owned water systems express a comparable 'willingness to charge' for the true cost of providing water services.

---

[9] Subsidies are controversial because they weaken or undermine price signals, leading to inefficient behavior on the part of consumers and producers. Subsidizing water systems (via loans and grants), rather than households in need, is not uncommon in the US and the subject of some debate.

[10] Under special circumstances, when the state defers, local regulation may apply.

The private sector's advantages in terms of capital, scale, efficiency, and innovation are countered substantially by profits and taxes. Some privatization proponents rationalize that income and property taxes, which constitute a significant share of the utility revenue dollar, also constitute positive returns to governments. The rate shock that might come with the transfer from public to private ownership, regardless of whether the increase is justified by remediation needs or the reconciliation of rates and costs, presents a particularly significant challenge to the private water sector.

45.3.2   Ownership and Performance

The operational performance of the many water systems in the US is also variable and not easily generalizable. In reality, 'good' and 'bad' systems can be found in every shape, size, and ownership form. A good public-sector water system follows good business practices and is reasonably efficient and innovative. A good private-sector water system acts as a responsible 'public steward' and is relatively transparent. The two will share much in common; indeed, their commonalities may be greater than their differences. Certainly, neither model is a proven panacea for the water sector, and the ideal institutional form for meeting the water sector's multiple challenges may yet be discovered.

In the larger scheme of things, other factors may prove more important than ownership in influencing utility performance. The motivations provided by profits in the private sector may well be matched by the motivations provided by sound public administration. What may be more important than ownership for performance is competition or contestability, or their substitute in the form of economic regulation, in terms of providing incentives, as well as accountability. With regard to costs, economies of scale and the adoption of efficiency practices may overwhelm institutional factors altogether. The implication of these educated hypotheses is ownership may be relevant to water utility performance, but mainly in the context of broader structural and regulatory considerations.

45.4   Regulatory Structure

Like the industry itself, the regulation of the US water industry is somewhat fragmented. Federalism for the water sector encompasses discrete and also shared responsibilities across the federal, state, and local levels. All water utilities, regardless of ownership structure, are subject to three principal areas of jurisdiction.

First, water-quality regulation (in terms of biological, chemical, and other forms of contamination) is dictated by federal policy pursuant to the Safe Drinking Water Act and the rules and regulations of the US Environmental Protection Agency; states have 'primacy' in terms of implementation and enforcement through state environmental quality or protection departments. Second, in most states, the same or a separate agency (such as a natural resource department) is also responsible for water quantity regulation. Rules governing quantity may include watershed delineation and monitoring, the administration of water rights, and the registration or permitting of water withdrawals, which in turn affects market entry and exchange. Third, the applicability of economic regulation, including but not limited to, the approval of prices, varies by state and according to utility ownership. Private or investor-owned water utilities are regulated by the state public utility or public service commissions (PUCs or PSCs) that also regulate other investor-owned utility companies (that is, electricity and natural gas providers). Despite relative consistency in principles and practices, the particulars of regulatory jurisdiction, authority, and methods also differ from state to state. The rates and finances of publicly owned utilities are typically approved through local governing processes, although some states (such as Wisconsin) extend regulatory oversight to municipal utilities. Regional water districts or authorities, as well as nonprofit systems, may or may not be subject to state economic regulation. Unlike the US energy and telecommunications sectors, there is no federal economic regulatory presence for water utilities. Private water companies are, however, subject to securities and other financial regulations that apply to US corporations.

45.4.1 The Role of Economic Regulation

Economic regulation is the public policy response to market failure. The market fails when the conditions for competition cannot be met or when competition does not achieve social goals (such as when distributional consequences of markets are not acceptable). Commission regulation focuses primarily on market failure in the form of monopoly (sometimes called 'natural monopoly') and the potential abuse of market power. According to traditional regulatory theory, a utility monopoly has a variety of distinct technical, economic, and institutional features. In particular, utility monopolies are highly capital intensive, demonstrate significant scale economies, and provide services 'on demand' to core or 'captive' customers; these services also are considered very essential, difficult or impossible to supplant, and relatively price inelastic. Monopolies are enfranchised by the state and in the absence of competition their prices, profits, and performance are regulated. When it works well, regulation balances the interests of utility investors and ratepayers in accordance with an institutionally grounded and well understood 'social compact'.

For traditional monopolies, regulation provides a necessary proxy for competition. The chief rationale for regulation is that monopolists have the potential to exploit their position by taking advantage of customers by restricting production output, degrading service quality, charging exorbitant or discriminatory prices, and earning excessive profits. Regulation 'in the public interest' refers to the responsibility of regulators to the greater good, the long-term interests of society at large as compared to the immediate interests of the individual parties appearing before them. Economic regulation provides an essential system of accountability and incentives for private-sector and sometimes public-sector monopolies. Regulation typically involves restrictions on market entry, governed by a regulator-issued certificate of public convenience and necessity, in return for which incumbent providers accept an obligation to serve on a nondiscriminatory basis, while meeting standards for adequacy, safety, and reliability.

Regulated services often are considered essential for maintaining an acceptable quality of life for people and communities. Regulation can be used to promote desirable activities and advance social objectives, including public health and welfare, economic development, environmental sustainability, consumer protection, affordability, and universal service. In many respects, water and wastewater utilities are particularly essential and the quintessential monopolies, that is, not amenable to competition in its ideal form.

45.4.2 Regulatory Jurisdiction

Public utility commissions in forty-five states regulate investor-owned water utilities. Georgia, Michigan, Minnesota, North Dakota, South Dakota, and the District of Columbia do not impose economic regulation, mainly because of the very limited operation of private water companies in these jurisdictions.

Fewer than half of the states extend economic regulation to nonprivate systems; about one dozen have some jurisdiction for municipally owned systems. Several states also regulate investor-owned wastewater utilities (which are much fewer in number than investor-owned water utilities); in some states, jurisdiction extends to municipalities, districts, authorities, and other publicly owned wastewater systems. Changes in ownership form and changes in commission authority can affect whether or not a water or wastewater system is regarded as a jurisdictional utility, as well as which particular types of regulatory authority apply. In the absence of economic regulation by the states, control over pricing is left to the scrutiny of local governing bodies (often city councils, but sometimes independent boards). State laws or commission policies provide for applying simplified regulation to smaller systems and for exempting some systems from regulation based on their size or rate levels. In a few states, regulation of municipal utilities may be triggered by the extension of service outside of city boundaries when rates for service are differentiated. Also rarely, customer complaints may trigger authority for otherwise unregulated systems.

Based on survey data for 2000, the total number of commission-regulated water utilities is approximately 7,700. These utilities include about 3,300 privately owned utilities and 1,800 municipal utilities; the rest are owned by other units of local government or nonprofit organizations. Although drinking water regulators recognize 'systems' as the regulated unit, many water companies operate multiple water systems; some are combination utilities that provide both water and wastewater services. In effect, commission jurisdiction extends to approximately 20% of the nation's community water systems; many of the regulated systems are very small. As also noted, the commission role in regulating the wastewater industry is more limited than that for the water industry. As of 2000, regulated wastewater utilities totaled about 3,000; about 1,300 were investor-owned utilities and many of these are part of combination water and wastewater systems.

Despite the relatively limited jurisdiction of the commissions with respect to the water industry, the extended influence of regulation in terms of recognized accounting, financing, and ratemaking standards should not be understated. Moreover, commission policies and practices directly influence the industry's structure, particularly with regard to privatization. Given the many challenges of the water industry and the ongoing interest in alternative structural configurations, the protections and accountability afforded by economic regulation are more vital then ever.

45.4.3 Regulatory Authority

Regulatory authority may vary by the type of water utility under a commission's jurisdiction. For investor-owned water utilities, all of the state commissions with jurisdiction regulate rates and returns, and require financial reports that comport with accepted accounting systems. The commissions also may have authority and discretion to: conduct financial and management audits; approve asset sales or transfers; authorize financial issuances; confer certificates of need; sanction service territories; establish performance standards; specify terms of service; resolve customer complaints; and mandate forecasting and resource planning.

Commission authority is broadest in scope for the investor-owned utilities; for publicly owned and nonprofit utilities, the scope of authority may be much narrower. Specific areas of authority also may be limited. For example, the commissions may be able to review certain kinds of data (such as asset valuations, capital structures, and forecasts for supply and demand) primarily in the context of a rate case. In many states, the commissions are not considered the central state agency with regard to water resource management, deferring to their sister agencies with authority for water quantity concerns. Economic regulators also generally defer to public-health regulators on issues of quality. However, the commissions are concerned with non-health-related aspects of water quality, such as water pressure, aesthetics (taste, odor, and color), service reliability, and general responsiveness to customers. The regulatory agency provides a forum for hearing and resolving consumer complaints about rates, as well as service quality, metering and billing, and disconnection practices.

Regulatory commissions in many, but not all, jurisdictions control market entry by requiring providers to secure a certificate of need or 'public convenience and necessity', a process often used to establish an enfranchised service territory, review the utility's financial viability, and set initial service conditions and rates. Facility construction or expansion may also require certification before construction begins, as well as a prudence review afterwards, to ensure that projects are in the public interest. Commission approval may be required for issuing financial instruments used for infrastructure financing (that is, debt, bonds, and stocks). Some of the commissions also have authority to approve and place conditions on changes in ownership (mergers and acquisitions) or transfers of assets involving regulated utilities (as sellers or purchasers).

Most of the commissions impose a uniform system of accounts for water utilities prescribed by the National Association of Regulatory Utility Commissioners (NARUC), or a variant thereof. Many unregulated water utilities in the US also use the NARUC accounting system, or a variant thereof. In addition, utility accounting and reporting is governed federally by the Securities and Exchange Commission (SEC) and the Financial Accounting Standards Board (FASB); publicly owned systems are subject to the requirements of the Governmental Accounting Standards Board (GASB). Regulated utilities typically file annual financial reports to the commissions; the rigor and detail of the accounting requirements depend on the size of the water system as measured by revenues. On occasion, regulators conduct financial or management audits, often in conjunction with ratemaking or prudence reviews.

Rate regulation is a core function of the state commissions and rate review provides an opportunity to consider a wide range of issues. This quasi-judicial process is normally initiated by a formally filed request by a utility to change its rates; customers, other stakeholders, and regulatory staff can weigh in during evidentiary proceedings. The ratemaking process involves the determination of the utility's revenue requirements based on operating and maintenance expenses, depreciation expense, income and other taxes, capital investment or 'ratebase', and an overall rate of return that compensates debt holders and shareholders. Private utilities are motivated to invest by the opportunity for profit. Regulators assess both expenditures and investments in terms of whether they are 'prudent', as well as 'used and useful' to ratepayers. The regulated rate of return is authorized but not guaranteed; utilities must perform efficiently between rate-case adjustments in order to actually realize their returns. Profits that result from rates must reflect a rate of return deemed reasonable by the regulator. Regulators approve not only rate levels but tariff design (that is, the fair assignment of costs to particular customer classes and water uses in the form of fixed and variable charges).[11] Cost-of-service studies and demand forecasts are used to design rates that will recover approved revenue requirements. Rates are evaluated in terms of how well they reflect and allocate the cost of service, promote economic efficiency, and satisfy the standard of 'just and reasonable'. Modern regulation continues to adhere to traditional core standards, but some innovations in ratemaking have allowed for adaptive practices and refined performance incentives in the context of emerging needs and goals (Beecher, 2006).

45.5   Regulation and Utility Ownership

Economic regulation and private utility monopolies share a symbiotic co-existence. Regulation substitutes for public ownership on the one hand and com-

---

[11] More varieties of rate design are used by unregulated water utilities, although regulated utilities are increasingly drawn to new rate forms, particularly for conservation and other policy purposes.

petitive markets on the other; an unregulated, profit-seeking monopoly is not a socially acceptable option. By overseeing the private role, regulation makes that role possible. Like markets, regulation is imperfect, but it must be fair to competing interests, sufficiently rigorous, and cautiously adaptive to changing conditions. When regulation is perceived as 'too strong' utility owners lose faith and they may be unwilling to invest. But when regulation is perceived as 'too weak' utility customers lose faith, and they may turn to institutional alternatives in the form of public or nonprofit ownership. In these regards, regulatory climate is intrinsically related to long-term structural trends. Good regulation in its historic and modern forms provides a system of standards, accountability, and incentives within which utilities can prosper while customers are well served and protected.

As discussed, economic regulation by the state does not apply to most publicly owned and nonprofit systems in the US. One of regulation's core purposes, to curb excessive profits, is generally a nonissue. Another guiding assumption is that cities, other governmental units, and nonprofit groups can self-regulate. Indeed, many municipal governing boards act independently and effectively to oversee well-performing water systems. Regulation also exacts its own price in the form of administrative fees paid to the state and the effort and time required for compliance (including regulatory filing requirements, processes and time lag). Regulation will not and should not be supported politically if it does not provide sufficient social benefits relative to administrative costs, as might be the case if regulation is regarded as unresponsive, ineffective or, even worse, if regulators are perceived as overly influenced by regulated interests (Beecher, 2008b).

45.5.1 Expanding Regulatory Oversight

Several arguments favor some degree of legislative expansion of economic regulation to the public sector. Regardless of ownership, water and wastewater utilities are highly monopolistic, providing an essential public service intrinsically related to public health, environmental protection, and economic prosperity. Economic regulation would level the playing field among the different types of water service purveyors by imposing common standards and expectations. In particular, regulation would ensure that all water systems follow established and uniform systems of accounting and reporting, and accepted methods of ratemaking (including full-cost pricing). Clear economic regulatory standards might also facilitate some limited forms of structured competition (for example, wholesale marketing and competitive bidding).

Regulation confers the authority of the state and is institutionally superior to oversight by legislative or judicial means. Regulation provides a high degree of accountability and transparency, along with due process for affected stakeholders and opportunities for public input. While often disagreeing over specific regulatory findings, parties and the public generally accept the validity and legitimacy of outcomes; if they do not, appeal mechanisms are available. States generally have greater capacity for regulation than local governments. In some instances, state regulation might free up local resources used for utility oversight. State agencies build expertise, achieve economies, and develop complementary skills by regulating multiple utilities and multiple industries. Coordination at the state level with public health and environmental regulators, and harmonization of policies, would help ensure the effective and efficient achievement of social goals. Resource constraints and global climate change bolster the case for consistent policies, standards, and incentives.

Regulation also provides an effective forum for resolving disputes between utilities and their customers. In theory, of course, citizens can vote their displeasure with publicly provided utility services, but this is a very indirect, less immediate, and often impractical form of accountability. Exacting accountability from public officials requires an informed, engaged, and mobilized public, with political acumen, resources, and clout. For customers with specific issues related to utility prices or services, regulation generally provides a better means of remedy than can be found in political processes, the courts, or other venues. Regulation can also ensure equity in customer assistance and other programs.

Regulation has always provided a significant degree of stability for investors in utility infrastructure industries, and the expansion of utility services throughout the US in the twentieth century is owed in part to the federal and state regulatory frameworks. Water utilities remain highly capital intensive, with long-life assets that present unique challenges, regardless of ownership. As systems age and infrastructure needs mount, regulatory review can help ensure that expenditures and investments by all systems will be sufficient, as well as appropriate. Regulation can help ensure adequate outlays by publicly owned utilities, which unlike their profit-motivated counterparts may be prone to underinvestment.

Regulation helps ensure that prices are cost based to encourage efficient investment, resource allocation, and usage. Outside of economic regulation, prices may or may not reflect costs in the short or long term. Some water systems may want to impose rates higher than the cost of service in order to generate revenues for other purposes. Publicly owned monopolies that seek a 'return' on their investment should be regulated. For many water systems, however, rates may be lower than the cost of service. Regulation can also help redress ratemaking politics and the 'willingness-to-charge' problem on the part of some communities and their leaders. Regulation can also help expose subsidies to daylight so that the choice to subsidize and compromise efficiency will be informed by public discourse. Regulatory oversight of rates can be especially important when water prices are escalating, as they are in the US. The combination of relatively flat demand and rising costs associated with infrastructure replacement and variable inputs is placing pressure on US water prices, which are increasing faster than the overall rate of inflation (Beecher, 2008a). Diminished availability of federal funding for capital projects, other fiscal constraints, and population growth (in some areas) add to the cost and price pressures.

The need to build public confidence in costs and rates may be one of the strongest rationales for economic regulation. Regulation can directly address cost allocation and rate equity within and across service classes, customer generations, and geographic areas (including rates for wholesale or retail service outside of a system's service territory). Ratemaking is always political to the extent that it requires choices among competing interests, but ratemaking outside of economic regulation may be especially vulnerable to politicization in the form of rate suppression or the allocation of costs away from the politically influential. In the extreme, though rarely, the process may become coercive or corrupt. Regulation may afford a particular political advantage, in that local officials can lay the blame for unpopular but necessary decisions about rates at the door of state officials who might be better positioned to support and defend them. Certainly, regulation by the state may not be needed for publicly owned systems with proven capacity for self-regulation, evident regulatory compliance, and demonstrable financial sustainability. For many unregulated utilities, however, some form of economic oversight may offer appreciable benefits that also extend to their customers and society.

45.5.2 Regulation and Privatization

In the context of privatization, regulation offers additional specific benefits. Privatization cannot be equated with competition for any industry, and certainly not for water and wastewater utilities given the barriers to competition that persist regardless of ownership or operational arrangements. Competitive contracts and other market-like mechanisms do not alter the water industry's basic monopolistic tendencies.

In any political or developmental context, the public interest argues for establishing regulatory capacity as a precondition for any substantial involvement of the private sector in the provision of water services.[12] Regulation is relatively certain in the case of asset sales to the private sector, where the system becomes part of an investor-owned water company and traditional regulatory jurisdiction applies. Other forms of privatization, where assets are not owned but operated by the private sector, also suggest the need for regulation in order to protect utilities and their customers. Expanded regulation would bring some of the advantages of the investor ownership model to other forms of privatization. Regulation would provide not only accountability, but continuity and assurance in the context of an evolving industry.

Although economic regulation typically targets the private sector, the object of regulation arguably should be the monopoly that owns the infrastructure assets and has ultimate responsibility for decision making, including pricing. In the case of contract operations or other agreements, jurisdiction should apply to the monopolist, that is the principal (the contractee) and not the agent (the contractor). Privatization agreements themselves might be subject to regulatory review and

---

[12] "Lack of government oversight and public scrutiny has been one of the strongest criticisms of water privatization. Without proper government supervision, privatization will not address issues related to conservation, water quality, or fair access to water regardless of income. To ensure public-private water agreements are carefully designed and implemented to protect public interests concerning these issues, strong public regulatory oversight should be a fundamental requirement before a public agency shifts its responsibility for water utilities to a private entity" (SERC, 2004).

approval. In the US, the New Jersey Board of Public Utilities has this review authority and it can be recommended for wider adoption.

Though not the direct target of oversight, private contractors doing business with jurisdictional utilities could potentially find themselves within reach of the regulator. Regulators could exercise powers of fact finding, discovery, and investigation to look into the workings of privatization agreements. Books and accounts could be scrutinized to ensure that expenditures, investments, and rates for service are consistent with regulatory standards for prudence and reasonableness. The regulator's job is not to micromanage performance under contracts, but rather to provide a framework of accountability. On one hand, regulation could help overcome the differing interests and incentives of asset owners and asset managers. Regulation could protect utility customers from risks by segregating activities and ring fencing assets. Regulation could also help ensure that costs prudently incurred under contractual arrangements will be recovered through cost-based and appropriately designed rates. On the other, regulation might also have the potential to beget conflicts. An example would be a disallowance (from rate recovery) by the regulator of an expense incurred by the contractor with the approval of the contracting utility. Regulation could provide a means of resolving these and other disputes that might arise between principals and their agents pursuant to their contractual agreements. Regulation could also place conditions on contracts, oversee renegotiations, and ensure a smooth transition in cases of transfer or termination.

Regulatory jurisdiction, capacity, and efficacy may not be the only preconditions for private involvement in the water sector. Other public policy reforms may be needed as well. In particular, the contribution of taxes to the price of private water presents a significant comparative disadvantage, but given the complexity and controversy of tax policy the prospect of major tax reforms conducive to privatization seems unlikely. Exemptions might also appear to afford preferential status to the private sector and raise the ire of privatization opponents. Perhaps the most formidable challenge to expanding the private role is public acceptance, which in turn depends on public confidence and trust. Despite the dominant presence of private companies in the energy and telecommunications sectors, the predominant ownership form and cultural character of the US water sector is public. In the eyes of the general public and many policymakers, the potential benefits of private involvement in the provision of water services may not be perceived as clear or convincing enough to justify a fundamental institutional shift from public to private.

45.6   Conclusion

Water utilities exhibit persistent characteristics of monopoly, along with other limits to competition. Water bears an intimate relationship to public health, the environment, and the economy. Water service is interdependent with sanitation services, and also with fire protection. Water is a product of nature, renewable but transient and finite. The essential nature and monopolistic character of water service sets it apart not only from other goods and services, but also from other infrastructure-intensive and network-based utility services.

Privatization can and does play a part in the water sector in the form of investor ownership and contract operations. Privatization does not, however, equate with competition. Privately owned utilities face very limited competition from other utilities, except on occasion for additions to service territory, system acquisitions, wholesale customers, and some ancillary services. Institutional contestability between privately and publicly owned utilities provides some discipline, but is an insufficient substitute for genuine competition. Private contractors may compete for contracts, but oligopoly and incumbency, barriers to market entry and exit, and long contractual terms make for competition that is less than robust. To some extent, bottled water competes with tap water in terms of service-quality image, but it is a very impractical substitute for most purposes. For the most part, the water sector does not lend itself to sustainable and effective competitive forces.

Institutional change requires policymakers to give explicit consideration to the appropriate roles of the public, nonprofit, and private sectors in achieving long-term social goals and the tradeoffs involved in alternative models for owning and operating water utilities. When markets fail, government must decide how to delineate its core roles, responsibilities, and functions with respect to ownership, regulation, or both. Regulation can establish and maintain standards, accountability, and incentives for performance. Regulatory jurisdiction can be expanded, regulatory authority can be modified, and regulatory capacity can be enhanced to accommodate utilities that embody alternative structural forms.

The private role in the water sector may always be regarded with a somewhat skeptical eye, in part because profiting from essential but monopolistic water services tends to invite political, ideological, and even moral conflict. Concern about the private role, in the US and elsewhere, is well justified in the absence of regulatory safeguards to guard against abuse of monopoly power, instill public confidence, and promote the public interest. In sum, effectual privatization may well depend on effectual economic regulation.

References

American Water Works. 2001. Position paper on significance of consolidation and the proposed RWE acquisition (DEFA14A). http://www.secinfo.com/dr8Pp .4f8N5.htm.

Baker, M. N. 1899. Water works. In E. W. Bemis (Ed.), Municipal Monopolies. New York: Thomas Crowell & Company.

Beecher, J. A., Dreese, R. D. & Stanford, J. D. 1995. Regulatory implications of water and wastewater utility privatization. Columbus, OH: The National Regulatory Research Institute.

Beecher, J. A. 2001. The ethics of water privatization. In C. K. Davis & R. E. McGinn (Eds.), Navigating Rough Waters: Ethical Issues in the Water Industry. Denver: American Water Works Association.

Beecher, J. A. 2006. Sourcebook of regulatory techniques for water utilities. Washington, DC: National Association of Water Companies.

Beecher, J. A. 2008a. Trends in Consumer Prices for Public Utilities. Institute of Public Utilities Research Note. Available at http://ipu.msu.edu.

Beecher, J. A. 2008b. The prudent regulator: politics, independence, ethics, and the public interest. Energy Law Journal, 29: 577-613.

DeBenedictis, N. 2006. Speech to the 29th Annual National Conference of Regulatory Attorneys, 11-14 June 11-4 2006.

Hoovers. Data rerived in November 2008 at http://hoovers.com.

Maxwell, S. 2008. Private equity interest in water filtration continues to grow. Filtration Industry Analyst. Volume 2008, Issue 4, April 2008.

National Association of Water Companies (NAWC). 1989 (unpublished paper). Comparing the efficiency of private and public production – Twenty-Nine Case Studies.

National Council for Public Private Partnerships. 2008. "Case studies" accessed at http://www.ncppp.org/cases/index.shtml.

National Council for Public Private Partnerships 2008. "Types of public-private partnerships" accessed at http://ncppp.org/howpart/ppptypes.shtml.

Okun, D. 1977. Regionalization of water management. London: Elsevier.

Public Works Financing (PWF). 2007. 2007 International survey of public-private partnerships. Volume 209, October. http://www.pwfinance.net/pwf_major_projects.pdf.

Public Works Financing (PWF). 2008. 12th Annual water outsourcing report. Volume 225, March. http://www.pwfinance.net/2008_conops_survey.pdf.

Reuters. 2008. Fitch: escalating capital costs may lead to consolidation for US water utilities. http://www.reuters.com/article/pressRelease/idUS219530+23-Jan-2008+BW2008 0123.

Savas, E. S. 1987. Privatization: the key to better government. London: Chatham House.

State Environmental Resource Center (SERC). 2004. Water privatization. http://www.serconline.org/waterPrivatization/index.html.

Stuart, A. 2007. Water for profit. CFO Magazine, 1 February 2007.

US Environmental Protection Agency (EPA). 1986. Community water system survey. Washington: EPA.

US Environmental Protection Agency (EPA). 2000. Community water system survey 2000. http://www.epa.gov/safewater/consumer/pdf/cwss_2000_volume_i.pdf.

US Environmental Protection Agency (EPA). 2007. Factoids: drinking water and ground water statistics for 2007. http://www.epa.gov/ogwdw/data/pdfs/data_factoids_2007.pdf.

US Census Bureau. 2008a. Statistical abstract of the United States (Table 887). Available at http://www.census.gov/compendia/statab/index.html.

US Census Bureau. 2008b. State and local government finances (Table 1). Available at http://www.census.gov/govs/www/estimate06.html.

Index